Auditing: Integrated Concepts and Procedures

To the Student: This text will be an important reference source in your future professional career. You should retain it for your personal library.

A Study Guide for this textbook is available through your college bookstore under the title **Study Guide to Accompany Auditing: Integrated Concepts and Procedures,** Fourth Edition, by **Donald H. Taylor** and **G. William Glezen.** The Study Guide can help you with course material by acting as a tutorial, review, and study aid. If the Study Guide is not in stock, ask the bookstore manager to order one for you.

ACCOUNTING TEXTBOOKS FROM WILEY

Auditing: Integrated Concepts and Procedures

Fourth Edition

Donald H. Taylor, Ph.D., C.P.A.
University of Arkansas, Fayetteville

G. William Glezen, Ph.D., C.P.A.
Former partner of Arthur Andersen & Co.
University of Arkansas, Fayetteville

John Wiley & Sons
New York   Chichester   Brisbane   Toronto   Singapore

ISBN 0-471-85651-7

Printed in the United States of America

10 9 8 7 6 5 4 3 2 1

*To Rosetta, Michael, Timothy, George, and Ethel
and to Sylvia, Paul and John, and Addie Belle*

About the Authors

Donald H. Taylor teaches accounting at the University of Arkansas. He received a B.S. in accounting from Louisiana Tech University and an M.B.A. and Ph.D. from Louisiana State University. He is a CPA.

Professor Taylor has had several years of public accounting experience with national and local CPA firms. During his academic career, he has taught basic and graduate auditing courses. Much of his practical and academic experience is reflected in this text. Professor Taylor is the author of a number of textbooks including *Principles of Accounting,* which was coauthored by John Cerepak and published by Prentice-Hall, Inc. in 1987. He also coauthored the case study in auditing that is available with this book.

G. William Glezen is a Professor of Accounting at the University of Arkansas. A native of Texas, he received a B.B.A. in accounting from Texas A & M University and an M.B.A. and Ph.D. from the University of Arkansas. He is a CPA and a member of a number of professional accounting organizations. He has published articles on auditing topics in several academic and professional journals.

Many of the concepts, examples, and illustrations in this book are the result of Professor Glezen's 17 years of experience in public accounting with Arthur Andersen & Co. During this period, which included seven years as a partner, he participated at all levels in, and supervised, audit engagements of both large and small enterprises in a broad range of industries. Professor Glezen also coauthored the case study in auditing that is available with this book.

Preface

An important characteristic of any textbook is its ability to adapt to significant changes in the subject matter that it addresses, explains, and illustrates. In addition to the traditional strengths of our first three editions (readability, balanced approach, comprehensive end-of-chapter material, and versatility), we now have a state-of-the-art fourth edition that contains some of the most comprehensive changes in auditing standards and guidelines that have occurred in the last 50 years.

Here are some of the many changes that we have made in this edition.

1. The changes in the auditing standards and in the standard audit report (from two to three paragraphs) have been reflected in every appropriate chapter.

2. Chapter 1 contains coverage of the new attestation standards.

3. Chapter 3 has been rewritten to reflect the new *AICPA Code of Professional Ethics* proposed in 1987 and passed by the AICPA membership in early 1988.

4. The positions of Chapters 5 and 6 have been reversed, and Chapter 5 now has a comprehensive coverage of materiality and audit risk serving as a "cornerstone" to the rest of the text.

5. Chapters 7 and 8 have been rewritten and now contain the most up-to-date material on the new auditing standards that cover the internal control structure, assessment of control risk, tests of controls, and the auditor's responsibilities for the detection of errors and irregularities.

6. Chapters 9, 10, and 11 now incorporate the new terminology of the recently issued auditing standards on the internal control structure and tests of controls.

7. Chapters 19, 20, and 21 have been appropriately revised to reflect the new auditing standards on reporting and the new three-paragraph standard audit report.

In response to your reviews and helpful comments, we have also made a number of changes to the text to make it even more readable and useable.

1. Chapter 1 clearly distinguishes among financial statement auditing, compliance auditing, and operational auditing.

2. Chapter 2 has a new section on compliance auditing and an introduction to the Single Audit Act.

3. Chapter 4 begins with a section on legal liability terminology and sharply distinguishes (1) common and statutory law, (2) ordinary negligence, gross negligence, and fraud, and (3) privity relationships, primary beneficiaries, foreseen parties, and foreseeable parties. Discussion of additional cases also clarifies some of the concepts of auditors' legal liability.

4. Chapter 6 (Chapter 5 in the third edition) illustrates the use of the audit risk model in audit planning.

5. The statistical sampling tables in Chapter 9 on tests of controls have been simplified for easier use by the students.

6. Chapters 17 and 18 in the third edition, covering sampling for substantive tests and use of computers in substantive testing, have been moved forward to the new Chapters 13 and 14. This was done to enhance the background material for Chapters 15 to 18 on audit procedures and working papers.

In keeping with the tradition of most textbook prefaces, we now briefly explain the general content of our 21 chapters. Rather than repeat what is shown in our table of contents, we will identify new and/or unusual features of these chapters and any flexibility in the sequence in which they may be used.

Chapter 1 is an overview of the audit process and contains discussions of the rationale for auditing as well as descriptions of the various types of audits. Chapter 1 also has an example of the new three-paragraph standard audit report.

Chapter 2 covers operational auditing and compliance auditing, increasingly important subjects. This material can be covered at a later point in the course, although we place it here to emphasize its importance.

Chapter 3, of course, contains the new *AICPA Code of Professional Ethics*. We retained discussions of the parts of the old code that are still applicable. Some instructors prefer to delay coverage of this chapter to near the end of the course, and this can be easily accomplished.

Chapter 4 covers the legal environment in which auditors operate, including its history and landmark cases that have changed this environment. We think you will like the new section on terminology at the beginning of the chapter. Like Chapter 3, some instructors wish to defer coverage of this chapter to near the end of the course.

Chapter 5 reflects the increasing emphasis on materiality and audit risk as two key factors in the audit process. In keeping with this emphasis, we have placed it here so that the material can serve as a type of "foundation" for the rest of the text. We suggest that Chapter 5 be covered before any subsequent chapters are assigned.

Chapter 6 establishes the framework of an audit and discusses audit planning, execution, and documentation. It also serves as an introduction to Chapters 7 through 11 on the internal control structure, Chapters 12 through 18 on substantive testing, and Chapters 19 through 21 on audit reports.

As indicated above, Chapters 7 through 11 cover the internal control structure. Chapters 7 and 8 explain the general concepts of understanding the internal control structure, assessing control risk, and tests of controls. Chapter 9 illustrates nonstatistical and statistical sampling techniques that are applicable to tests of controls. The statistical sampling section of this chapter can be omitted if you wish. Chapters 10 and 11 take the general concepts of Chapters 7 and 8 and apply them to the study and evaluation of computer controls. Chapters 10 and 11 can be assigned as a unit, and many instructors prefer to do this.

Chapters 12 through 18 cover substantive testing. Chapter 12 discusses the general nature of evidence gathering and demonstrates the derivation of audit procedures from audit objectives. Chapter 13 illustrates nonstatistical and statistical sampling techniques that are applicable to substantive tests. Like Chapter 9, the statistical sampling material in this chapter can be "lifted" if a concentration only on nonstatistical sampling techniques is preferred. Chapters 15 through 18 have extensive discussions of audit procedures for substantive tests, many of which are illustrated with microcomputer-generated working papers. Some instructors may wish to condense the coverage of Chapters 15 through 18 if they place the major emphasis in the course on auditing theory. We suggest some coverage of these chapters that contain very practical material on audit techniques.

Chapters 19 through 21 are in the same sequence as they were in the preceding three editions. Extensive updating has been done to reflect the current reporting standards issued by the Auditing Standards Board, including illustrations and extensive discussions of the new three-paragraph standard audit report.

The end-of-chapter material contains the same three sections as the first three editions. Review questions enable the user to determine how well he or she has learned the chapter material. Objective questions adapted from CPA and CIA examinations require the user to relate the chapter material to subject matter covered in technical tests. Discussion/case questions allow the user to see the highly subjective nature of the audit process. If time permits, we strongly suggest use of all three types of questions; each type has a special and distinct purpose. We have revised end-of-chapter material to accommodate revisions in the chapter discussions and illustrations. New and provocative discussion/case questions have been added to each chapter.

The fourth edition retains the versatility of the previous editions in that it can be used in either a one- or two-semester course. If the book is used for one semester, the course can be conducted as an overview of auditing by covering all 21 chapters. Alternatively, certain chapters can be omitted and the remaining chapters can be covered in more depth. If the book is used for two semesters, all 21 chapters could be covered briefly in the first semester, with selected chapters covered in-depth in the second semester. Or, cover Chapters 1 through 8, 12, and 19 through 21 in the first semester, and Chapters 9 through 11 and 13 through 18 in the second. The latter option could be chosen if the user wishes to concentrate on concepts in the first course and techniques in the second.

To assist the instructor and the student in using our text, a number of supplements are available. The *Solutions Manual* contains a guide and outline for covering each chapter, answers to all of the end-of-chapter materials, and a set of transparency masters. The *Test Bank* contains a number of test questions for each chapter. The *Study Guide* includes chapter highlights and objective, true-false, and completion questions as well as the answers to all questions to reinforce the student's study of the text.

Taylor, Glezen, and Ehrenreich's *Case Study in Auditing, Fourth Edition* is a comprehensive practice case on the internal control structure and substantive testing. It is accompanied by an Instructor's Manual.

Guy Owings' *Interactive Audit Sampling System for the IBM-PC* provides the capability of practicing some of the most efficient sampling methods formerly unavailable because of the computer requirement.

DONALD H. TAYLOR
G. WILLIAM GLEZEN

Acknowledgments

We thank the American Institute of Certified Public Accountants for permission to quote or reproduce material from [1] Statements on Auditing Standards, [2] the AICPA Code of Professional Ethics, [3] Statements on Standards for Accounting and Review Services, [4] Statements on Quality Control Standards, [5] questions from uniform CPA examinations, [6] tables from the AICPA statistical sampling volumes, and [7] procedural flowcharts from AICPA booklets on internal control.

We are grateful to The Institute of Internal Auditors for permission to reproduce and quote from [1] Standards for the Professional Practice of Internal Auditing, [2] The Institute of Internal Auditors, Inc. Code of Ethics, [3] *The Internal Auditor,* and [4] questions from CIA examinations.

We thank Ernst & Whinney for permission to use several of their case studies as discussion and problem material. Special thanks go to Arthur Andersen & Co. for allowing us to reproduce and adapt portions of their Transaction Flow Analysis material.

Our reviewers were very helpful in making suggestions to improve the manuscript. We appreciate the helpful comments of Professor Robert R. Davis of Canisius College, Professor Ann Marie Hearn of California State University, San Bernardino, Professor Duane M. Ponko of Indiana University of Pennsylvania, and Professor Alan Reinstein of Wayne State University.

Finally, we express appreciation to our editors, Lucille Sutton, Katharine Rubin, Deborah Herbert, and Pam Landau, for valuable aid in the writing and production of the book.

D.H.T.
G.W.G.

Contents

4. The Auditor's Responsibility—Legal Environment   113

14. The Use of Computers to Gather and Document Audit Evidence for Substantive Testing   539

The Audit Function

Learning Objectives *After reading and studying the material in this chapter, the student should*

Know the broad definition of auditing and be able to distinguish among the various audit classifications discussed in the chapter.

Be able to relate selected important auditing postulates to the modern auditing function.

Know why there is a demand for audits in our society and understand the benefits derived from an audit.

Know the general organizational structure of and the types of services offered by public accounting firms.

Understand how auditors communicate with users of their work.

Know what standards auditors use in performing an audit.

Know the professional and standard-setting organizations that directly influence the audit function.

Know the reasons for the issuance of the attestation standards and be able to paraphrase these standards.

Of all the subjects taught in the various accounting curricula, auditing is one that can be regarded as truly interdisciplinary. During a semester's study, business law, ethics, accounting theory, statistical sampling, and computer processing are all referred to and, in one form or another, integrated into the course material.

This interdisciplinary approach to auditing is not followed merely to pull together material taught at earlier points in the business administration curriculum (although there is some justification for performing this synthesis). The integrated teaching techniques are an expression of the fact that practicing auditors, whether public, industrial, or governmental, actually are called on to use the entire range of business knowledge. Whether individuals are engaged in auditing functions *or* are the preparers of audited data, they need to understand the purposes, techniques, and limitations of this subject matter.

In addition, the work of auditors is in the public spotlight. The financial statements on which public accountants express opinions serve as a basis for securities trading and credit extensions. The reports issued by governmental auditors contribute to various forms of legislative scrutiny. In modern-day society, it is imperative that many types of organizations be subjected to an audit. Management, stockholders, credit institutions, regulatory agencies, and legislative and executive branches of federal, state, and local governments require such audits.

The modern auditor must be a talented individual who has the ability to make vital decisions on many important issues, and the courage and depth of character to stand by personal convictions. The auditing function offers individuals an opportunity that is rare in other fields of endeavor; that is, the opportunity, on almost a daily basis, to be responsible for making decisions and judgments as to what is right and what is wrong, and to stand by those decisions and judgments regardless of the pressures that may be brought to bear. This opportunity has attracted many outstanding individuals to the field of auditing and has helped to retain them.

Broad Definition of Auditing

Auditing has been defined broadly as "a systematic process of objectively obtaining and evaluating evidence regarding assertions about economic actions and events to ascertain the degree of correspondence between these assertions and established criteria and communicating the results to interested users."[1]

As an example, an organization could make the following *assertions* (sometimes called representations):

1. The financial statements represent fair measurements of the economic events and business transactions that affected the organization during a certain period of time.

2. The computerized accounting system used by the organization is efficient and reliable.

[1]Committee on Basic Auditing Concepts, *A Statement of Basic Auditing Concepts* (Sarasota, Fla.: American Accounting Association, 1973), p. 2.

Each of these assertions is made by the organization through its accounting process, which collects, summarizes, classifies, and reports business data. Auditing obtains and evaluates the evidence necessary to determine whether the organization's assertions are in accordance with whatever appropriate criteria are established.

In the case of the assertions made through the financial statements, the established criterion is whether these statements are fair in conformity with generally accepted accounting principles. On the other hand, the criteria for the assertions made through the computerized accounting system are judgments on what constitutes an efficient and reliable system. Auditors could assess the degree to which these system assertions meet any criteria of efficiency and reliability deemed appropriate.

Financial Statement, Compliance, and Operational Auditing

In a narrower sense, auditing can be classified according to the objective of the function performed.

Financial Statement Audit

A *financial statement audit* is the gathering of evidence on the financial statement assertions of an entity and using such evidence to ascertain adherence to generally accepted accounting principles or other comprehensive basis of accounting. This is the type of audit that is discussed throughout most of the text and makes use of a process called attestation. As used in financial statement auditing, *attestation* refers to an independent, competent, and authoritative person communicating an opinion or judgment as to whether an entity's financial statement assertions correspond in all significant respects with the established criterion (usually generally accepted accounting principles). The opinion or judgment should be based on sufficient competent evidence. Attestation could also be referred to as "witnessing" the degree to which financial statement assertions correspond to generally accepted accounting principles. Throughout the book, we will assume that financial statement auditing uses the function of attestation.

Compliance Audit

The purpose of a *compliance audit* is to determine whether a person or entity has adhered to policies or stated regulations. The criteria against which the person's or entity's actions are compared could be a management directive (such as a policy concerning employee overtime) or a code and accompanying set of regulations (such as the Internal Revenue code and regulations). In fact, the audit of an income tax return is a prime example of a compliance audit in which the IRS is determining a person's or entity's adherence to tax regulations.

Operational Audit

Operational auditing falls within the broad definition of an audit. However, the criteria against which management's assertions are measured differ from the type of audit emphasized in the text. The American Institute of Certified Public Accountants (AICPA) Special Committee on Operational and Management Auditing describes *operational auditing* as "a systematic review of an organization's activities (or a stipulated segment of them) in relation to specified objectives for the purposes of assessing performance, identifying opportunities for improvement, and developing recommendations for improvement or further action." A review of a company's computerized accounting system, assessment of its efficiency and reliability, and recommendations for improvement of the system could constitute an operational audit.

Comparative Illustration

The following diagram shows the relationship between financial statement, compliance, and operational auditing.

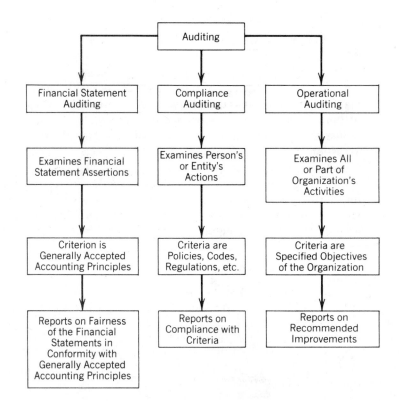

External, Internal, and Governmental Auditing

Auditing can also be classified according to the affiliation of the individual or group that performs the audit. This classification cuts across those discussed in the previous section.

External Auditing

Public accountants are not employees of the organizations whose assertions or representations they audit. They offer their independent audit services on a contractual basis. Although these services consist of a variety of audits, the majority of audits performed by public accountants are financial statement audits, that is, an examination of financial statements to form an opinion of their fairness in conformity with generally accepted accounting principles.

Internal Auditing

Conversely, *internal auditing* is described as "an independent appraisal function established within an organization to examine and evaluate its activities as a service to the organization."[2] Internal auditors are employees of the organizations whose activities they appraise. However, measures can be taken to give these auditors a certain degree of independence. In many organizations, for example, internal auditors report directly to a financial vice-president, or in some cases to the audit committee of the board of directors.

Both compliance and operational audits may be performed by a company's internal auditors. Internal auditors measure the degree to which various functions of their organization adhere to stated managerial policies or requirements. Many internal auditors also perform operational auditing functions for their company. An appraisal of their firm's computerized accounting system and recommendations for improvement is an example. Unlike the outside or external auditors, however, the internal auditors may become involved in the day-to-day implementation of their recommendations.

Governmental Auditing

Members of local, state, and federal governmental units audit various organizational functions for a variety of reasons, such as the following:

1. Local and state governmental units audit businesses to determine whether sales taxes have been collected and remitted according to stipulated laws or regulations (a type of compliance audit).

[2] *Standards for the Professional Practice of Internal Auditing* (Altamonte Springs, Fla.: The Institute of Internal Auditors, Inc., 1978), p. 1.

2. The Internal Revenue Service audits corporate and individual income tax returns to determine whether income taxes have been calculated according to the applicable laws or interpretations of these laws (another type of compliance audit).

3. The General Accounting Office (GAO), which reports to the U.S. Congress, audits various programs, functions, activities, and organizations of the federal executive branch. Such audits include[3]

A. Examinations of financial transactions, accounts, and reports to determine compliance with applicable laws and regulations (a type of compliance audit).

B. Reviews of efficiency and economy in the use of resources, such as government equipment (a type of operational audit).

The following diagram shows the relationship among external, internal, and governmental auditing.

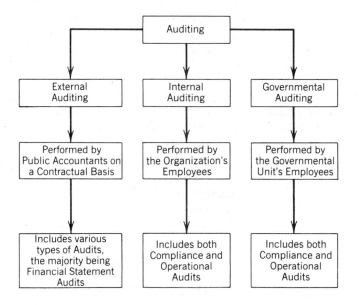

Theoretical Framework of Auditing

The auditing function, whether classified by objective (financial statement, compliance, or operational) or by affiliation of auditors (external, internal, or govern-

[3] *Standards for Audit of Governmental Organizations, Programs, Activities, and Functions* (Washington, D.C.: General Accounting Office, 1981).

mental) operates within a theoretical framework.[4] In this section, we have adapted and related some selected postulates to modern-day auditing to provide a theoretical foundation for many of the auditing ideas discussed throughout the text.

1. The auditing function operates on the assumption that financial statements and financial data are verifiable.

The degree of verifiability depends on the type of audit undertaken and the particular account, department, or program being examined. The existence of cash is easier to verify, for instance, than the quality of operation in a purchasing and distribution system.

2. There is no necessary long-term conflict between auditors and managers of organizations being audited. A potential short-term conflict, however, may exist.

Both auditors and managers should be interested in fair presentation of financial statements because in the long run society benefits from informed investment decisions and efficient allocation of resources. Audits are conducted to provide relative assurance that the financial statements are fairly presented. However, short-term conflicts between auditors and managers might appear for several reasons.

A. Managers may need high earnings or other favorable measurements to satisfy the reward system (e.g., bonus plan) under which they operate.

B. Auditing examines and appraises assertions made by managers. Some attempt may be made to "hide" assertions that would prove potentially embarrassing to managers.

In collecting evidence, auditors should maintain a skeptical attitude about management's assertions. Neither honest nor dishonest assertions are necessarily assumed by the auditor.

3. Effective control structures lower the probability of fraud or irregularities in an organization.

Without proper controls, it is easier for errors to occur in the financial statements and for assets to be misappropriated, making it more difficult to produce verifiable financial statements and financial data. For this reason, it is standard practice in financial statement audits for company controls to be reviewed and evaluated.

---

[4]Adapted from R. K. Mautz and Hussein A. Sharaf, *The Philosophy of Auditing*. American Accounting Association, Monograph No. 6, 1961.

4. Application of generally accepted accounting principles results in fair presentation of financial statements.[5]

A current interpretation of this postulate is that generally accepted accounting principles are the major factor in an auditor's opinion as to whether financial statements are fairly presented. These accounting principles are assumed to be appropriate standards or guidelines. Without such a standard, it would be difficult for auditors to form judgments on financial statement fairness.

5. Except for evidence to the contrary, what was true in the past will hold true for the future.

For example, assume that auditors in the past encountered management bias in the financial statements or a poor control structure. Unless the auditors acquire evidence to the contrary, they generally assume that these same conditions will exist in the current audit, and appropriate planning is made for them. In addition, management's financial statement assertions assume that certain courses of action will be taken. A case in point is the projection of past experience in estimating bad debts to the future.

6. The financial statements are free from collusive and other unusual irregularities.

The auditing profession has traditionally taken the position that a search for unusual irregularities (e.g., defalcations) in financial statements would require audit procedures far beyond those normally employed. Some auditors question whether enough audit procedures could be performed to provide absolute assurance that no unusual irregularities exist.

A recent auditing pronouncement helps to relate this postulate to responsibilities of modern-day auditors—that is, an audit conducted in accordance with generally accepted auditing standards should be designed to detect material misstatements, including errors and irregularities, that affect the financial statements.[6]

The same pronouncement, however, says that the auditor is not an insurer or guarantor; the auditor's responsibility is to exercise due care with the proper degree of professional skepticism.

---

[5] This postulate, as stated here, is applicable to most financial statement audits.

[6] Errors are unintentional mistakes in financial statements; irregularities are intentional distortions of financial statements.

7. When examining financial data for the purpose of expressing an independent opinion thereon, the auditor acts exclusively in the capacity of an auditor.

This postulate does not preclude auditors from using their accounting knowledge to provide their audit clients with other forms of service and aid. Auditors, for example, often suggest ways in which their client's records can be kept more accurately or control over assets can be improved. The postulate does imply that other services rendered during the course of an audit engagement must be regarded as of secondary importance and could be harmful if such services interfere with duties as an auditor. The postulate also implies that auditors must not have conflicts of interest that prevent them from being independent of their clients during audits.

8. The professional status of the independent auditor imposes commensurate professional obligations.

The meaning of this postulate is almost self-evident. The status enjoyed by any professional carries with it the obligation to conduct oneself in a manner worthy of this status. We will emphasize the importance of this postulate throughout this text.

Taken together, these postulates, written many years ago but still largely valid, form a theoretical foundation for a discussion of audits, particularly financial statement audits. Financial statements contain data that can be audited. Because of society's needs for audits, there should be no long-term conflict between auditors and those whose representations are being audited. Good company controls and application of generally accepted accounting principles provide suitable benchmarks for auditors to judge the fairness of their clients' financial statement representations. Unless evidence suggests otherwise, events that occurred in the past can be expected to occur in the future. Auditors do not approach an audit engagement with a biased view that their clients' financial statements contain significant irregularities, but do exercise professional skepticism. Auditors must be independent and conduct themselves in a professional manner.

As we discuss auditing standards and procedures in subsequent chapters, the student should reference these postulates. In many cases they will provide a good theoretical rationale for the audit approaches and audit procedures suggested.

Reasons for and Benefits Derived from Financial Statement Audits

With discussions of auditing classifications and auditing postulates as a background, we will now describe the reasons financial statement audits are conducted and the benefits derived therefrom. Such audits would not exist, of course, if there were no demand for them in our society.

The American Accounting Association has issued *A Statement of Basic Auditing Concepts*. The publication describes the four following conditions that create a demand for auditing.

1. Conflict between an information preparer (managers) and a user (owners, creditors, or other third-party groups that do not manage the company) can result in biased information.

2. Information can have substantial economic consequences to a decision maker.

3. Expertise is often required for information preparation and verification.

4. Users are frequently prevented from directly assessing the quality of information.

Together, these conditions essentially say that, if there is conflict between owners, creditors, and other groups using financial statements and the company managers who prepare them, such financial statements could be biased. In addition, because financial statement information is used to help make financial decisions and users either lack the expertise or are prevented from directly verifying the quality of the information they use, the need for an independent audit is obvious.

The Needs of the Present or Potential Investor

Assume that you are considering an investment in the securities of a company. You are able to make a reasonably intelligent analysis of financial statements, but you do not have sufficient assurance that the statements are fair representations because you were not privy to the accounting system that produced them. One potential problem is that you cannot be certain of what may have been omitted, such as an important contingent liability. How can you tell whether the published information is fair and not misleading?

It is the duty of the independent auditors to provide the potential investor with an unbiased expert *opinion* as to whether the statements are fairly presented. They are an appropriate group to perform this function because (1) they have the knowledge and training, (2) they are allowed to examine the necessary records and gather sufficient evidence, and (3) they are independent of management.

In the latter part of the nineteenth century and the early part of the twentieth century, the owners and managers of a company knew each other. In many cases they were the same people. Today, widely dispersed ownership of business has created a class of absentee stockholders that have little, if any, contact with management's operations. Some person or organization must perform the audit function for them. To the extent that their decisions are dependent on management's financial statements, present and potential investors must place a certain amount of trust in the auditors. They tend to regard public accountants as guardians of the integrity of financial statements. Indeed the U.S. Supreme Court has stated, "By certifying the public reports that collectively depict a corporation's financial status, the independent auditor assumes a *public* responsibility transcending any employment relationship with the client. The independent public accountant performing this special function owes ultimate allegiance to the corporation's creditors and stockholders, as well as to the investing public . . ."

Stewardship or Agency Theory

In addition to the needs of the present or potential investor, *stewardship* or *agency theory* also explains the demand for audits.[7] This theory implies that the manager, as well as the owners, of a company wants the credibility an audit adds to the financial statement representations. The owners' needs are reasonably obvious and have been discussed previously.

The company manager's desire for an audit arises from the fact that the manager is the agent or steward of the owner. Thus, there is a real or perceived conflict between the goals or objectives of each party. Owners may attempt to compensate for the effects of this perceived conflict by reducing the manager's reward. The manager may lessen this perception of conflict by having his or her representations audited by an independent party. Owners would therefore have less incentive to reduce a manager's reward. By obtaining audited financial statements, the manager's own position in the company is improved and mistrust of the manager's stewardship is lessened.

The Motivational Theory

There is also a belief among some that an audit, in addition to providing credibility to the financial statements, adds value to the information contained in the financial statements because of motivational considerations. According to this belief, the preparers of financial statements are motivated to do a better job because they know that their representations will be subjected to an audit. Thus financial statement representations will be brought more in line with the needs of financial statement users.

Although the motivational benefits of an audit are difficult to prove conclusively, there is an instinctive belief by some that the knowledge of an audit prevents or discourages improper financial statement preparation.

---

[7]For an excellent summary of agency theory, see Wanda Wallace, *The Economic Role of the Audit in Free and Regulated Markets* in *Auditing Monographs* (New York: Macmillan, 1985).

Commentary

Audits are needed in our society for a variety of reasons. The need is well documented. In the remainder of this chapter, we will discuss the structure of organizations that provide these needed audit services, the standards used to perform the audits, and the structure of other accounting organizations that affect and are affected by the audit function.

The Roles of CPAs and Public Accounting Firms

Certified Public Accountants (CPAs) are individuals who have been licensed by various states to provide public accounting services. The requirements for obtaining a CPA license or certificate are discussed later in this chapter.

Although auditing is performed by a number of organizations and for a variety of purposes, the focus here is on the organizational structure of CPA *firms* because most of the text is devoted to financial statement auditing.

CPA firms are professional organizations that may take the form of proprietorships, partnerships (the most common) or, in some states, professional corporations. These firms render a variety of services to the public, among them auditing, tax, management consulting, and accounting services. The extent to which each of these services is rendered within a given firm depends on its clients' needs.

The Types of Services

1. *Auditing*—In many CPA firms this is the dominant service in terms of both time and revenue. In some cases the audit services are performed for a purpose other than reporting on the fairness of financial statements. For example, the CPA may be asked to audit the records of institutions that receive Medicare funds from the federal government. Political candidates may request an audit of their campaign finances. The CPA is a logical choice to perform all these tasks. In general, however, most audits are conducted by CPAs for the purpose of attesting to the fairness of financial statements, and the audit is made because management, investors, creditors, or governmental units ask for one.

2. *Tax Services*—Most accounting students are well aware of the demand for tax return preparation services because of the large body of tax laws passed by federal, state, and local governments. This service appears to be a "natural" one for public accountants because many of the methods for determining financial statement net income are basically the same as those for arriving at taxable net income. In addition, many CPAs engage in tax planning and assist their clients in matters of tax litigation. Because the latter

services often require legal training, it is not unusual for an individual to acquire both a CPA certificate and a law degree.

3. *Management Consulting Services*—This area is known by several names, such as management advisory services, management information consulting, or administrative services. They all refer to the newest, and in some cases the fastest growing, function performed by public accountants. Management consulting services might be referred to as practically everything done by public accounting firms other than auditing, tax, and accounting services. Some examples are a computer systems study, a revision of the management accounting system, a marketing study, executive recruiting, personal financial planning, or the installation of budgeting techniques. Management consulting services may be rendered in addition to the auditing service or as the only function. If the CPA firm renders management consulting services *and* conducts audits, an obvious question arises. How can a CPA firm conduct an independent audit for a company for which it performs other services, such as helping to set up parts of the accounting system? This question is by no means settled. At present, most practicing CPAs believe that management consulting services are compatible if advice is given and no decisions are made for the client. This matter is discussed further in Chapter 3.

4. *Accounting Services*—Many CPA firms, particularly smaller ones, perform a variety of accounting services for their clients. Smaller clients who lack qualified accounting personnel often require basic bookkeeping assistance. Other clients maintain their basic accounting records but need assistance in preparation of financial statements. CPAs perform a service referred to as compilation, which involves the preparation of financial statements without expressing any assurance on those statements. Another service performed by CPAs that falls between a compilation (no assurance by the CPA) and an audit (expression of a positive opinion by the CPA) is a review. A review involves inquiry of the client and certain analytical procedures to serve as a basis for giving limited assurance that the CPA knows of no material modifications that should be made to the financial statements. Compilations and reviews are discussed in Chapter 21.

The Sizes of CPA Firms

Small firms normally have one office and conduct their business within the immediate area of a town or city. The ownership is held by one or a few CPAs, and generally the clients require substantial accounting and tax return preparation services. These small firms also render management consulting services, although this type of service may not be structured in a formal way. Their audit clientele is sometimes limited because most companies that offer securities to the public are audited by large firms. However, local banks sometimes require audited financial statements and much of this work is performed by the local CPAs.

Firms that have offices and clients in several cities are referred to as regional. Tax return preparation and accounting services represent a smaller percentage of the total business than do the same services in a local firm. Auditing constitutes a larger share of the work, and usually formalized management consulting services are provided.

Firms that have offices in the major cities are called national firms; many operate in several countries. The eight largest public accounting firms in the country, all of which have international operations, commonly are referred to as the "Big Eight." These firms are (in alphabetical order) Arthur Andersen & Co., Arthur Young & Company, Coopers & Lybrand, Deloitte Haskins & Sells, Ernst & Whinney, Peat, Marwick, Main & Co., Price Waterhouse, and Touche Ross & Co. These firms have annual revenues in the hundreds of millions or billions of dollars. National firms have a considerably larger number of owners than do local or regional firms.

The hierarchy of a public accounting firm is not significantly different from that of other organizations. General staff personnel (called staff accountants) serve under the direct guidance of experienced members (seniors) and have little or no supervisory responsibility. Seniors generally direct one engagement at a time, such as the audit of a particular client. Supervisors and managers have responsibility for several engagements that run concurrently. Sometimes their duties extend to an entire activity, such as all company audits. Partners (or stockholders if the firm is a corporation) are at the top of the hierarchy and represent the ownership. They sign the audit reports, tax returns, and other documents. In many large organizations one individual has primary responsibility for an office. This person generally is referred to as a managing partner. The entire firm also has a managing partner who acts as the major representative or spokesperson.

The Modern-Day Audit of Business Enterprises

As indicated earlier, the most common type of audit performed by CPAs is a financial statement audit. Its purpose is to provide an *opinion* of the *fairness* of the financial statements, in conformity with generally accepted accounting *principles*.[8] An audit of this type includes three phases or steps.

1. The planning step of acquiring an understanding of the business and the control structure used to process the data that ultimately result in financial statements.

---

[8] *AICPA Professional Standards* (Chicago: Commerce Clearing House, Inc., 1987), AU Section 110.01 (*SAS No. 1*).

2. The step of gathering and evaluating evidence used to assess the fairness of the financial statements.

3. The step of reporting the audit results.

The following is an example of the audit report issued when the auditors have followed all auditing standards and accept the financial statement assertions as fair in the aggregate. The first paragraph describes the financial statements examined. The second paragraph reports "what was done" or the scope of the audit. The third paragraph reports the auditors' opinion formed as a result of the audit.

Independent Auditor's Report

To the Shareholders and Board of Directors of X Company:

We have audited the accompanying balance sheet of X Company as of December 31, 19X8, and the related statements of income, retained earnings, and cash flows for the year then ended. These financial statements are the responsibility of the Company's management. Our responsibility is to express an opinion on these financial statements based on our audit.

We conducted our audit in accordance with generally accepted auditing standards. Those standards require that we plan and perform the audit to obtain reasonable assurance about whether the financial statements are free of material misstatement. An audit includes examining, on a test basis, evidence supporting the amounts and disclosures in the financial statements. An audit also includes assessing the accounting principles used and significant estimates made by management, as well as evaluating the overall financial statement presentation. We believe that our audit provides a reasonable basis for our opinion.

In our opinion, the financial statements referred to above present fairly, in all material respects, the financial position of X Company as of December 31, 19X8, and the results of its operations and its cash flows for the year then ended in conformity with generally accepted accounting principles.

Jones & Jones, CPAs

March 4, 19X9

Each part of this standard report is important and needs a short explanation.

1. The report is addressed to the shareholders and board of directors of the audited company. These groups rely upon the auditor to audit the financial statement representations or assertions of management and report the results to them.

2. The first paragraph specifically names the financial statements that were audited. It is important for the recipients of the report to know exactly which management representations or assertions were examined.

3. The first sentence of the scope paragraph indicates that generally accepted auditing standards were followed. The remainder of the paragraph describes how the audit provides reasonable assurance against materially misstated financial statements.

4. The opinion paragraph consists of one sentence and has the following key words and phrases:

- Opinion

- Present fairly, in all material respects

- Generally accepted accounting principles

"Opinion" means exactly that. The auditors have made no guarantee but have rendered an expert opinion that adds credibility to the financial statements compiled by management.

"Present fairly, in all material respects" does not mean that the financial statements are completely accurate or without minor errors, but rather that the financial statements are, in the aggregate, unbiased and are "what they are purported to be."

"Generally accepted accounting principles" are the broad concepts, assumptions, and conventions used to formulate financial statements. They are the criteria against which management's assertions are compared to determine whether such assertions are fair.

It should be pointed out that responsibility for preparation of the financial statements rests with management. This process typically is referred to as the accounting function. It is in part a process of *compiling* figures by using the system designed and supervised by company personnel. Normally, the accountants who perform this function work for the company that publishes the statements.

In contrast, an audit is a process of performing certain analytical and judgmental procedures on the data that are summarized in the financial statements. Included are such steps as observation, inspection, confirmation, comparison, analysis, computation, and inquiry. On the basis of the evidence gathered by applying these audit procedures, a report is issued on the financial statements.

External Auditing Standards and Procedures

The *Auditing Standards Board* promulgates auditing standards and procedures that are to be observed by members of the AICPA in accordance with the AICPA's *Code of Professional Ethics*. The basic pronouncements of the board are the Statements on Auditing Standards. *Auditing standards* differ from *auditing procedures* in that the former are guidelines and the latter are acts to be performed. The board also issues interpretations and other forms of guidelines.

The Auditing Standards Board consists of people from the academic community and from large, medium, and small CPA firms. In addition, the board is supported by a staff, including a vice-president, auditing, and a director of auditing research.

Pronouncements of the Auditing Standards Board generally go through a multistage process.

1. A need for a pronouncement is identified. This identification can come in a variety of ways, such as requests from practicing CPAs or other members of the business community, the result of litigation, or pressure from government regulatory agencies.

2. Research of various forms is conducted on the identified problem.

3. A proposed pronouncement is considered and discussed by the board.

4. An exposure draft of the proposed pronouncement is issued to CPA firms with AICPA members and to other interested and relevant parties. Comments are usually received from some of these parties.

5. If the comments from the exposure draft do not uncover a serious omission or problem, the pronouncement is issued and becomes an official interpretation of generally accepted auditing standards.

The auditing standards adopted by the AICPA are summarized briefly in the diagram on page 18 and listed on this page and on pages 18–20.[9] Many of them are self-evident, even to nonaccountants. Some, however, need considerable explanations, which are given in the following chapters.

General Standards

1. The examination is to be performed by a person or persons having adequate technical training and proficiency as an auditor.

[9] AU Section 150.02 (*SAS No. 1*).

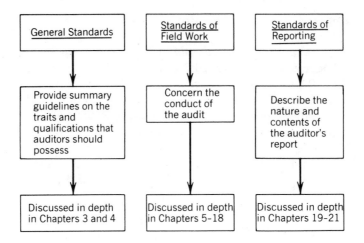

2. *In all matters relating to the assignment, an independence in mental attitude is to be maintained by the auditor or auditors.*

3. *Due professional care is to be exercised in the performance of the examination and the preparation of the report.*

Qualifications of the Auditor

Most independent audits are performed by a person or a group of people with the designation of certified public accountant or CPA. It is not necessary to hold this title to perform bookkeeping services or to prepare income tax returns. However, CPAs enjoy the highest reputation for competence of any of the various groups that engage in these activities. In an attempt to ensure a high quality of service, many states require that accountants be CPAs before they perform independent audits.

CPA is a designation granted by the states, which have their own rules as to what criteria must be satisfied. For this reason there is no way for an accountant to acquire a national CPA certificate. Generally, the states' rules have three common components.

1. *An Educational Requirement*—Most states require a college degree with the equivalent of a major in accounting, and other states are moving in this direction. Some states even require education beyond the first college degree and an increasing number of states are moving toward mandatory continuing education in order to maintain the right to practice public accountancy.

2. *An Experience Requirement*—The type and length of experience required depend on the state's requirements. Some states allow industrial work or teaching as substitutes for experience in public accounting.

3. *A Testing Requirement*—On this point there is unanimity among the states. A licensed CPA must have passed a written examination that tests his or her ability in several accounting areas. A uniform examination is prepared and graded by the AICPA, and the results are furnished to the respective states.

Historically, the granting of a CPA certificate within a state gave the recipient the right to practice public accounting. In recent years, however, some states have moved toward a "two-tier" registration process for CPAs. Although the provisions of each state law differ, here are some generally common features of the two-tier registration process.

1. Individuals can become CPAs by passing the Uniform CPA Examination and meeting other requirements of the individual states. Annual renewal is necessary to remain a CPA.

2. Individuals can practice public accounting only if they obtain a license or a permit to practice. This license or permit generally requires recent accounting experience or mandatory continuing education on a fairly continuous basis, or both, in addition to passing the CPA examination.

Standards of Field Work

1. The work is to be adequately planned, and assistants, if any, are to be properly supervised.

2. There is to be a proper study and evaluation of the existing internal control as a basis for reliance thereon and for the determination of the resultant extent of the tests to which auditing procedures are to be restricted.

3. Sufficient competent evidential matter is to be obtained through inspection, observation, inquiries, and confirmations to afford a reasonable basis for an opinion regarding the financial statements under examination.

The standards of field work are more specific than the general standards. They provide guidance to auditors in gathering evidence to support an opinion. Basically, this support comes from the evidence obtained from testing the financial statement balances and the transactions that underlie these balances. The extent to which auditors gather evidence depends on the reliance they place on the client's internal control structure. This is why the second standard of field work specifies that the auditor's study and evaluation of internal controls determine the extent of audit tests.

The third standard of field work underlines the importance of evidence-gathering to support the auditor's opinion on the financial statements. Without proper evidence, auditors would have no basis to decide on the proper opinion to render and would be committing a dishonest act if they gave one. To provide additional guidance in this regard, the third standard specifies the *general* evidence-gathering techniques an auditor should follow, such as confirmation and observation.

Standards of Reporting

1. The report shall state whether the financial statements are presented in accordance with generally accepted accounting principles.

2. The report shall identify these circumstances in which such principles have not been consistently observed in the current period in relation to the preceding period.

3. Informative disclosures in the financial statements are to be regarded as reasonably adequate unless otherwise stated in the report.

4. The report shall either contain an expression of opinion regarding the financial statements, taken as a whole, or an assertion to the effect that an opinion cannot be expressed. When an overall opinion cannot be expressed, the reasons therefore should be stated. In all cases where an auditor's name is associated with financial statements, the report should contain a clear-cut indication of the character of the auditor's examination, if any, and the degree of responsibility he is taking.

Unqualified Opinions

The three-paragraph report shown earlier in the chapter contains an unqualified opinion. The auditors stated that they followed generally accepted auditing standards in the conduct of the audit and that in their opinion the financial statements are fairly stated in accordance with generally accepted accounting principles.

However, conditions may prevent the auditors from completely following generally accepted auditing standards or the auditors may find something during the course of the audit that prevents them from reporting that the financial statements are fair in all respects. In such a case, one of three types of reports other than unqualified is issued: (1) a qualified opinion, (2) a disclaimer, or (3) an adverse opinion.

Qualified Opinions

Basically, there are two reasons auditors might issue a qualified opinion. First, circumstances might prevent them from performing all the audit procedures necessary to follow generally accepted auditing standards. For example, the auditors may not be on hand to observe the count of inventory quantities conducted by the client. If inventory represents a significant portion of total assets (as it often does), the auditors may have to issue a qualified opinion because of the inadequate scope of their audit.

Second, during the course of the audit, the auditors may conclude that certain accounting techniques followed by the client are not in accordance with generally accepted accounting principles or that all proper informative disclosures have not been made in the financial statements. In other words, the auditors have conducted the examination in accordance with generally accepted auditing standards and have *found* omissions or discrepancies that require a qualified opinion.

Disclaimers

In some cases the scope of an audit might be so inadequate that auditors will not render any opinion on the financial statements. In other situations an uncertainty might have such a serious potential impact on the financial statements that auditors could refuse to give an opinion. The applicable report in these circumstances is one that *disclaims* an opinion on the financial statements and gives the reasons for so doing. A disclaimer in an auditor's report can have a serious impact on readers' views of the accompanying financial statements. This type of report is therefore rendered only if the auditors are convinced that the inadequate scope or the uncertainty is too serious to warrant a qualified opinion.

Adverse Opinions

If, as the result of audit evidence, the auditor concludes that the financial statements taken as a whole are not fairly stated in accordance with generally accepted accounting principles, an *adverse* opinion is appropriate. For example, such a conclusion might be formed because the client records a significant amount of its fixed assets at appraisal value rather than cost.

An adverse opinion, like a disclaimer of opinion, can have a serious effect on the views of readers of the accompanying financial statements. Such an opinion would be issued by the auditors only if they believe that the deviation from generally accepted accounting principles is too serious to warrant a qualified opinion. The following diagram summarizes these four types of opinions.

A Flowchart of Auditors' Opinions

1. If the scope of the audit is adequate,

2. If no significant uncertainty exists,

3. If generally accepted accounting principles have been followed and there is adequate disclosure.

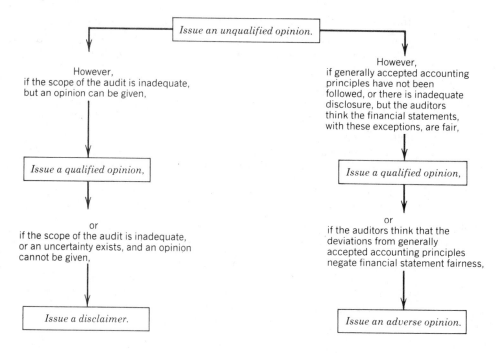

Organizations of the Accounting Profession

The State-Level Regulatory Board

Because each state grants its own CPA certificate, the public agency that regulates accounting practice within a state generally is called a *State Board of Public Accountancy* (or a similar title). Although its functions differ from state to state, its typical duties and responsibilities include (1) granting certificates and registering certified public accountants, (2) administering examinations, and (3) suspending or revoking certificates.

In addition, many state boards have issued a *code of ethics* specifying the behavioral patterns to which holders of a CPA certificate should adhere. If a serious enough breach of the code occurs, the CPA could be denied the right to practice public accountancy in that particular state. Although in the past state boards have relied on complaints from the public to identify violations, some have now instituted positive enforcement programs whereby CPAs or CPA firms must submit examples of their reports, which are reviewed for possible violations.

The State-Level Voluntary Organizations

In addition to a regulatory agency, there are voluntary organizations of CPAs within each state, generally called *state societies*. Their major purpose is to enhance the reputation of professional accounting within the state.

State societies also issue codes of ethics that are enforceable only against members. Because membership is voluntary, this code is not as effective as that of a state board. An individual is not required to belong to a state society in order to practice as a CPA.

The National-Level AICPA

One of the most influential accounting organizations in the United States is the *American Institute of Certified Public Accountants* (AICPA). Its voluntary membership includes CPAs from all of the states and the various territories. On a national level, the AICPA performs many of the functions that the state societies perform on a local level. In addition, various committees have issued authoritative pronouncements on accounting principles and auditing standards. Over the years these pronouncements have formed the basis of "generally accepted accounting principles" and "generally accepted auditing standards."

The AICPA has evolved a code of ethics over the years. Because association with the AICPA is voluntary, a person may practice as a CPA without adhering to this code. Many of its major provisions, however, have been adopted by state societies and state boards. As a result, practicing CPAs operate under one or more of the codes of ethics of a state board, a state society, or the AICPA. Chapter 3 contains extensive discussion of auditors' ethical considerations.

The Financial Accounting Standards Board

The *Financial Accounting Standards Board* sets accounting standards in the private sector of the profession and has the status of an independent organization. Its members consist of *former* members of CPA firms as well as other business and professional people. To avoid conflicts of interest, all of the members are required to divest themselves of any affiliation with their former organizations and to devote full-time effort to the FASB. The board is not affiliated with the AICPA.

The business and political climates in which the FASB operates are different from those that existed in previous years. Today, investor discontent with the credibility of financial statements has spawned a record number of lawsuits directed at companies (and their auditors) for alleged faulty reporting in their published financial statements. This situation has caused governmental authorities and courts to influence the formulation and application of accounting principles.

The organization's pronouncements, entitled *FASB Statements,* supersede (where applicable) pronouncements of the Committee on Accounting Research and the Accounting Principles Board.

The Securities and Exchange Commission

One of the organizations that is taking an active role in influencing the formulation and application of accounting principles is the *Securities and Exchange Commission* (SEC). In 1934, shortly after the stock market crash of 1929, Congress created this federal agency to regulate the distribution of securities to the public and the trading of securities on open exchanges.

One concern of the SEC is that investors have adequate financial information about firms that sell securities to the public. Therefore, regulations have been written requiring such firms to file reports with the agency. Most of these reports are public information and can be secured by anyone. Many companies now include this information in the published financial statements issued to stockholders.

The SEC has statutory authority to determine accounting principles for use in published financial statements of companies that sell securities to the public. Its pronouncements on accounting principles are distributed in documents to the public at large. Until a few years ago, the SEC generally did not exercise this authority, because its traditional position was that the private sector of the profession should set standards for itself. However, with public pressure growing and creditor-investor lawsuits increasing, the SEC has taken a more active role in matters of full disclosure and fair representation in financial statements. It stated that accounting principles issued by the FASB would be considered as having substantial authoritative support, whereas those contrary to FASB promulgations would be considered to have no such support. The SEC activity has led to a certain amount of conflict on accounting principles with the private sector of the profession; for instance, several accounting firms and the AICPA formally objected to a provision requiring the approval of any accounting change by a company's independent public accountant. They maintained there was no basis for choosing between equally acceptable alternative methods. Some accountants believe that the SEC eventually may take a dominant role in pronouncements on accounting principles. More is said about the SEC's role in Chapter 4. Pronouncements of the SEC are discussed in several subsequent chapters.

Internal Auditing and The Institute of Internal Auditors

Most audits performed by CPA firms are for the purpose of attesting to the fairness of financial statements. However, another important type of auditing is carried out by employees within an entity. This type is referred to as internal auditing. *The Institute of Internal Auditors,* in its *Statement of Responsibilities of the Internal Auditor,* previously described this function in the following way.

> Internal auditing is an independent appraisal activity within an organization for the review of operations as a service to management. It is a managerial control, which functions by measuring and evaluating the effectiveness of other controls.

This prior definition implied a broad scope of activities. The current objective and scope of internal auditing, taken from *Standards for the Professional Practice of Internal Auditing,* provide additional evidence of the broadness of the function.

> Internal auditing is an independent appraisal function established within an organization to examine and evaluate its activities as a service to the organization. The

objective of internal auditing is to assist members of the organization in the effective discharge of their responsibilities. To this end, internal auditing furnishes them with analyses, appraisals, recommendations, counsel, and information concerning the activities reviewed.

This current definition represents a significant change of emphasis from the prior definition by the Institute of Internal Auditors, which referred to internal auditing as a "service to management." The present definition reflects the concept of internal auditing as accountable to the organization as a whole, including the board of directors as well as management. Internal auditing and operational auditing are discussed further in Chapter 2.

A necessary condition for the independent auditor to make an objective appraisal of financial statement fairness is that he or she not be an employee of the entity that prepares the statements. Although the same amount of overt independence cannot be provided the internal auditor, steps can be and are taken by management to allow these auditors to operate with objectivity to ensure that their reports and recommendations will be received by the proper level of authority. The proper level of authority has increasingly become an audit committee of the board of directors.

In addition to providing a valuable service to management, internal auditors can aid the independent auditors by improving the financial operations of their company. More is said in Chapter 7 about the relationships between the functions of the independent and internal auditors.

The General Accounting Office

The *General Accounting Office* (GAO) is under the administrative supervision of Congress and has broad responsibility for auditing various executive branches of the government. The GAO has had this responsibility since 1921, when it was established as a result of an administrative change transferring the federal government audit function from the executive to the legislative branch. Since that time, the scope of GAO audits has expanded from examination of financial transactions to a range of activities covering many areas of executive department programs. Two significant duties are (1) ascertaining that executive department spending programs are carried out in accord with the intent of Congress and (2) determining that contract payments to commercial companies are made in accordance with federal regulations.

Audits of government programs may be much more extensive than audits of commercial companies. The GAO's *Standards for Audit of Governmental Organizations, Programs, Activities and Functions* defines a governmental audit as having the three distinct elements of a financial compliance audit, an economy and efficiency audit, and a program results audit.

It is easy to see that the audit responsibilities of the GAO differ from those of independent CPAs or internal auditors. Nevertheless, all the aforementioned audit functions in the chapter have several things in common. These are (1) adequate technical training, (2) proper planning and supervision, (3) a certain measure of independence, (4) sound judgment in conducting the audit, and (5) the ability to provide an adequate and understandable report to the appropriate parties.

Developments in the Auditing Profession

Auditing is a dynamic profession in constant search of ways to meet the growing public demand for quality services. The following developments vividly exemplify this trend.

The Commission on Auditors' Responsibilities

In the early 1970s a gap became apparent between the public's and auditors' perceptions of audit functions and responsibilities. A need developed to investigate the reality of such a gap and to suggest ways to close it if it did indeed exist. To accomplish this task, the Board of Directors of the AICPA appointed an independent group in 1974 to examine the problems and issues facing CPAs in the role of independent auditors. This group was called the Commission on Auditors' Responsibilities (also known as the Cohen Commission).

After three years of study, the commission issued a set of recommendations covering a wide variety of auditing issues. These recommendations were designed to clarify auditors' responsibilities in several critical areas and to restore any perceived or actual loss of confidence by the public in auditing services.

Investigations by the U.S. Congress

The public's "expectation gap," which caused the auditing profession to suggest changes in its perception of auditors' responsibilities, also resulted in investigations by congressional committees in the late 1970s. These investigations were directed at accounting practices *and* auditing services and were conducted by committees of both houses of Congress. The findings contained in the *Report of the Subcommittee on Reports, Accounting and Management of the Committee on Governmental Affairs of the U.S. Senate* (also known as the Metcalf Report) are the basis for this subcommittee's suggestions on the improvement of auditing services offered to the public.

More recently, Congressman Dingell began a series of investigations that covers both auditors of publicly owned companies and the SEC. The purpose of these hearings was to determine how well each of these groups was serving the public and meeting their responsibilities as auditors and regulators, respectively. Congressman Dingell was particularly critical of the profession's failures to (1) detect fraud, (2) alert the public to potential business failures, and (3) discipline its members for ethics violations. Another committee chaired by Congressman

Brooks cited a report by the GAO that contained numerous examples of substandard auditing of government entities by CPAs. These criticisms have prompted actions to deal with these problems by the AICPA (issuing new auditing standards) and state boards of accountancy (implementing new ethics enforcement programs).

A Comprehensive Set of Attestation Standards

To provide comprehensive standards for an increasing variety of attest services performed by certified public accountants, the AICPA issued in 1986 a pronouncement called *Statement on Standards for Attestation Engagements*. The purpose of this statement is to provide a definitive set of standards for all types of attest engagements. As described in the statement:

> An attest engagement is one in which a practitioner is engaged to issue or does issue a written communication that expresses a conclusion about the reliability of a written assertion that is the responsibility of another party.

Some examples of attest services, other than opinions on historical financial statements, are

1. Reports on descriptions of internal control structures.

2. Reports on descriptions of computer software.

3. Reports on compliance with statutory, regulatory, and contractual agreements.

These new attestation standards do not supersede the generally accepted auditing standards discussed previously in this chapter and referred to consistently throughout the text. Rather, they provide a broad overview under which generally accepted auditing standards as well as standards for other specific types of attest engagements can develop. Recently standards for an attest engagement, other than an audit of historical financial statements, were proposed that give a CPA guidance when examining and expressing an opinion on management's discussion and analysis of information contained in the annual report of a company subject to SEC regulation. The opinion is directed toward whether the discussion and analysis conforms with SEC requirements.

Listed next are the attestation standards adopted by the AICPA. Note that, like generally accepted auditing standards, they are divided into general, field work, and reporting. Note, also, that the attestation standards are broader, signifying that certified public accountants are increasing the scope of their attest services.

ATTESTATION STANDARDS

General Standards

1. The engagement shall be performed by a practitioner or practitioners having adequate technical training and proficiency in the attest function.

2. The engagement shall be performed by a practitioner or practitioners having adequate knowledge in the subject matter of the assertion.

3. The practitioner shall perform an engagement only if he or she has reason to believe that the following two conditions exist:

- The assertion is capable of evaluation against reasonable criteria that either have been established by a recognized body or are stated in the presentation of the assertion in a sufficiently clear and comprehensive manner for a knowledgeable reader to be able to understand them.

- The assertion is capable of reasonably consistent estimation or measurement using such criteria.

4. In all matters relating to the engagement, an independence in mental attitude shall be maintained by the practitioner or practitioners.

5. Due professional care shall be exercised in the performance of the engagement.

Standards of Field Work

1. The work shall be adequately planned and assistants, if any, shall be properly supervised.

2. Sufficient evidence shall be obtained to provide a reasonable basis for the conclusion that is expressed in the report.

Standards of Reporting

1. The report shall identify the assertion being reported on and state the character of the engagement.

2. The report shall state the practitioner's conclusion about whether the assertion is presented in conformity with the established or stated criteria against which it was measured.

3. The report shall state all of the practitioner's significant reservations about the engagement and the presentation of the assertion.

4. The report on an engagement to evaluate an assertion that has been prepared in conformity with agreed-upon criteria or on an engagement to apply agreed-upon procedures should contain a statement limiting its use to the parties who have agreed upon such criteria or procedures.

Commentary

Auditing is not a sterile subject. Its value to the functioning of the economy in the United States has been firmly established, and the demand for auditing services continues to increase. At the same time, its objectives and techniques are being challenged by various groups that have a financial interest in the quality of this service. Accounting students need to understand (1) the ethical and legal environment in which auditors function, (2) the responsibilities that an auditor assumes when engagements are undertaken, (3) the techniques that are used to satisfy the audit objectives, and (4) the nature and limitations of the auditor's output.

It is the purpose of the succeeding chapters to satisfy these needs.

Chapter 1
Glossary of Terms

(listed in the order of appearance in the chapter, with accompanying page references where the term is discussed)

Term	Page in Chapter
Assertions representations by management that are embodied in financial statement components, records, or systems.	2
Auditing a systematic process of objectively obtaining and evaluating evidence regarding assertions about economic actions and events to ascertain the degree of correspondence between these assertions and established criteria and communicating the results to interested users.	2
Financial statement audit the gathering of evidence on the financial statement assertions of an entity and using such evidence to ascertain adherence to generally accepted accounting principles or other comprehensive basis of accounting.	3
Attestation an independent, competent, and authoritative person communicating an opinion or judgment as to whether an entity's financial statement	3

	Page in
Term	*Chapter*

Attestation standards   a comprehensive set of standards issued by the AICPA   27
that covers the variety of attest services performed by certified public
accountants.

Attest engagement   one in which a practitioner is engaged to issue or does issue   27
a written communication that expresses a conclusion about the reliability
of a written assertion that is the responsibility of another party.

Chapter 1
References

American Institute of Certified Public Accountants. *Professional Standards*:

AU Section 110 [*SAS No. 1*]—Responsibilities and Functions of the Independent Auditor.

AU Section 150 [*SAS No. 1*]—Generally Accepted Auditing Standards.

AU Section 230—Due Care in the Performance of Work.

Chow, Chee W. "The Demand for External Auditing: Size, Debt and Ownership Influences," *The Accounting Review* (April 1982), pp. 272–291.

Committee on Basic Auditing Concepts. *A Statement of Basic Auditing Concepts*. Sarasota, Fla.: American Accounting Association, 1973.

Connor, Joseph E. "Enhancing Public Confidence in the Accounting Profession," *Journal of Accountancy* (July 1986), pp. 76–83.

Mautz, R. K., and Sharaf, Hussein A. *The Philosophy of Auditing*. Monograph No. 6. Sarasota, Fla.: American Accounting Association, 1961.

Mednick, Robert. "The Auditor's Role in Society: A New Approach to Solving the Perception Gap," *Journal of Accountancy* (February 1986), pp. 70–74.

Standards for Audit of Governmental Organizations, Programs, Activities, and Functions. Washington, D.C.: General Accounting Office, 1981.

Standards for the Professional Practice of Internal Auditing. Altamonte Springs, Fla.: The Institute of Internal Auditors, Inc., 1978.

Stilwell, Martin C., and Elliott, Robert K. "A Model for Expanding the Attest Function," *Journal of Accountancy* (May 1985), pp. 66–78.

Wallace, Wanda A. "The Economic Role of the Audit in Free and Regulated Markets," *Auditing Monographs*. New York: Macmillan, 1985.

Chapter 1
Review Questions

1-1.   Give the broad definition of auditing.

1-2.   Explain the differences among the following (use the comparative illustration in the chapter):
a. Financial statement auditing.
b. Compliance auditing.
c. Operational auditing.

1-3.   Explain the differences among the following (use the comparative illustration in the chapter):
a. External auditing.
b. Internal auditing.
c. Governmental auditing.

1-4.   Describe the eight auditing postulates discussed in this chapter.

1-5.   According to the Committee on Basic Auditing Concepts, what are the four conditions that create a demand for auditing?

1-6.   Describe how stewardship or agency theory helps to explain the demand for audits.

1-7.   Explain how motivational theory describes the effect of an audit.

1-8.   Describe the four types of services performed by CPA firms.

1-9.   Distinguish among the characteristics of local, regional, and national CPA firms.

1-10.   Describe the three general phases or steps of a financial statement audit.

1-11.   Answer the following questions about the standard audit report:
  a. To whom is the report addressed?
  b. What is specifically named in the first paragraph?
  c. What is contained in the first sentence of the scope paragraph?
  d. What four important phrases are contained in the opinion paragraph?

1-12.   What is the difference between auditing standards and auditing procedures?

1-13.   Describe the five-stage process of issuing Auditing Standards Board pronouncements.

1-14.   Briefly explain the difference between the general standards, the standards of field work, and the standards of reporting (refer to the illustration in the chapter).

1-15.   What are the three common components of the states' rules on becoming a CPA?

1-16.   Describe the differences between the four types of auditors' opinions.

1-17.   Describe the differences between a state board of public accountancy, a state society of certified public accountants, and the American Institute of Certified Public Accountants.

1-18.   What is the purpose of the Financial Accounting Standards Board?

1-19.   What is the purpose of the Securities and Exchange Commission?

1-20.   What is the current definition of internal auditing?

1-21.   To whom does the General Accounting Office report and what is its broad responsibility?

1-22.   What was the purpose of the Commission on Auditor's Responsibilities?

1-23.   What is the purpose of Statement on Standards for Attestation Engagements?

1-24.   What is an attest engagement?

Chapter 1
Objective Questions Taken from CPA Examinations

1-25.   The essence of financial statement auditing is to
   a. Detect fraud.
   b. Examine individual transactions so that the auditor may certify as to their validity.
   c. Determine whether the client's financial statements are fairly stated in accordance with generally accepted accounting principles.
   d. Assure the consistent application of correct accounting procedures.

1-26.   Governmental auditing often includes audits of efficiency, effectiveness, and
   a. Thoroughness.
   b. Evaluation.
   c. Accuracy.
   d. Compliance.

1-27.   The independent auditor lends credibility to client financial statements by
   a. Stating that the financial statements are stated in accordance with generally accepted auditing standards.
   b. Maintaining a clear-cut distinction between management's representations and the auditor's opinion.
   c. Attaching an auditor's opinion to the client's financial statements.
   d. Testifying under oath about client financial statements.

1-28.   Which of the following best describes the reason why an independent auditor reports on financial statements?
   a. A management fraud will be detected by independent auditors.
   b. Different interests may exist between the company preparing the statements and the persons using the statements.
   c. A misstatement of account balances is corrected as the result of the independent auditor's work.
   d. A poorly designed internal control system may exist.

1-29.   The independent audit is important to readers of financial statements because it
   a. Determines how management will operate the company whose financial statements are audited.
   b. Measures and communicates financial and business data included in financial statements.
   c. Involves the objective examination of and reporting on management-prepared statements.
   d. Reports on the accuracy of all information in the financial statements.

1-30.   Auditing standards differ from audit procedures in that procedures relate to
a. Measures of performance.
b. Audit principles.
c. Acts to be performed.
d. Audit judgments.

1-31.   What is the general character of the three generally accepted auditing standards classified as general standards?
a. Criteria for competence, independence, and professional care of individuals performing the audit.
b. Criteria for the content of the financial statements and related footnote disclosures.
c. Criteria for the content of the auditor's report on financial statements and related footnote disclosures.
d. The requirements for the planning of the audit and supervision of assistants, if any.

1-32.   A CPA is most likely to refer to one or more of the three general auditing standards in determining
a. The nature of the CPA's report qualification.
b. The scope of the CPA's auditing procedures.
c. Requirements for the review of the internal control structure.
d. Whether the CPA should undertake an audit engagement.

1-33.   Competence as a certified public accountant includes all of the following except
a. Having the technical qualifications to perform an engagement.
b. Possessing the ability to supervise and evaluate the quality of staff work.
c. Warranting the infallibility of the work performed.
d. Consulting others if additional technical information is needed.

1-34.   An investor is reading the financial statements of Sundby Corporation and observes that the statements are accompanied by an unqualified auditor's report. From this, the investor may conclude that
a. Any disputes over significant accounting issues have been settled to the auditor's satisfaction.
b. The auditor is satisfied that Sundby is operationally efficient.
c. The auditor has ascertained that Sundby's financial statements have been prepared accurately.
d. Informative disclosures in the financial statements but not necessarily in the footnotes are to be regarded as reasonably adequate.

1-35. With respect to errors and irregularities, the auditor should plan to
   a. Detect errors or irregularities that would have a material effect on the financial statements.
   b. Detect errors or irregularities that have either material or immaterial effect on the financial statements.
   c. Detect errors that would have a material effect and irregularities that would have either material or immaterial effect on the financial statements.
   d. Detect irregularities that would have material effect and errors that would have either material or immaterial effect on the financial statements.

1-36. A primary purpose of an operational audit is to provide
   a. The results of internal examinations of financial and accounting matters to a company's top-level management.
   b. A measure of management performance in meeting organizational goals.
   c. A means of assurance that internal accounting controls are functioning as planned.
   d. Aid to the independent auditor, who is conducting the examination of the financial statements.

Chapter 1
Discussion/Case Questions

1-37. Reread the broad definition of auditing in the chapter and discuss the meaning of each of the following key words and phrases as they relate to the definition.
   a. Systematic process.
   b. Objectively obtaining and evaluating evidence.
   c. Assertions about economic actions and events.
   d. Degree of correspondence between these assertions and established criteria.
   e. Communicating the results to interested users.

1-38. Reread the definition of operational auditing in the chapter. Select the key words and/or phrases that distinguish this definition from that of financial statement auditing. Discuss the meaning of each of these key words and/or phrases as they relate to the definition of operational auditing.

1-39. For purposes of this discussion, assume that auditing postulates form a theoretical foundation for the audit function. From postulates come auditing standards.

   Required:
   Take the eight auditing postulates discussed in the chapter and indicate which auditing standards, in your opinion, emerged from which auditing postulates. For each of the auditing standards, discuss why that particular standard emerged from a particular postulate.

For your convenience, here is a paraphrased list of both the auditing postulates and auditing standards.

Postulates:

1. Financial statements are verifiable.

2. There is no necessary long-term but a potential short-term conflict between auditors and managers.

3. Effective control structures lower the probability of fraud or irregularities.

4. Generally accepted accounting principles result in fair presentation of financial statements.

5. Unless there is evidence to the contrary, what was true in the past will hold true for the future.

6. Financial statements are free from collusive and other unusual irregularities.

7. When examining financial data to express an independent opinion thereon, the auditor acts exclusively in the capacity of an auditor.

8. The professional status of the independent auditor imposes commensurate professional obligations.

Standards:

1. Adequate technical training and proficiency as an auditor.

2. Independence in mental attitude.

3. Due professional care.

4. Adequate planning and proper supervision.

5. Proper study and evaluation of the control structure.

6. Sufficient competent evidential matter.

7. Presentation of financial statements in accordance with generally accepted accounting principles.

8. Informative disclosures in the financial statements.

9. A clear-cut indication of the character of the auditor's examination, if any, and the degree of responsibility taken.

For each of the eight auditing postulates, describe what you would consider to be the effect on the modern-day audit function if the postulate has no validity. Indicate the reasons for your opinions.

1-40.   Odom Co. is a medium-sized producer of fishing rods with approximately $5 million of annual sales. The company is wholly owned by Mike Odom, who serves as its president and is active in its daily operations. There is no long-term debt and no current plans to incur any. Mr. Odom has no interest in expanding his company's operations in the future, because to do so would reduce the amount of time he is able to devote to his favorite pastime, fishing. Some of Mr. Odom's friends who operate businesses of the same size have annual audits of their financial statements.

Required:
a. Give reasons why Mr. Odom should have a financial audit performed by an independent CPA.
b. Give reasons why Mr. Odom should not have a financial audit performed.

1-41.   Ms. Wilson is president of Wilson Co., which operates hamburger restaurants in Houston, New Orleans, Memphis, and Dallas. She believes that her company may be large enough to need an operational audit of its activities. Profits have been good but not as good as expected. Certain accounting records are maintained at each restaurant, and others are maintained centrally. She has estimated the cost of an operational audit and would like to compare the cost with the potential benefits to be gained from such an audit. Ms. Wilson has a sales background.

Required:
a. Describe the general differences between a financial and an operational audit.
b. Describe some general benefits Ms. Wilson may derive from an operational audit of her business.

1-42.   Timmon's Bakery completed its first year of operations and must select the generally accepted accounting principles it will use in the preparation of its financial statements. Depending on the following alternative accounting principles selected, either of the two net income figures could result.

	A	*B*
Net Income (Loss)	$250,000	($100,000)
Accounting principles		
Inventories	First-in, first-out method	Last-in, first-out method
Depreciation	Straight-line method	Declining-balance method
Pension cost	Prior service cost	Prior service cost
	amortized over 40 years	amortized over 10 years

Required:

a. Which financial statement fairly reflects the results of operations for the year?

b. Can an auditor express an opinion as to the fairness of financial statements with such varying net incomes? If so, justify the reasons. If not, indicate why an opinion cannot be expressed.

1-43.   Feiler, the sole owner of a small hardware business, has been told that the business should have financial statements reported on by an independent CPA. Feiler, having some bookkeeping experience, has personally prepared the company's financial statements and does not understand why such statements should be audited by a CPA. Feiler discussed the matter with Farber, a CPA, and asked Farber to explain why an audit is considered important.

Required:

a. Describe the objectives of an independent audit.

b. Identify ten ways in which an independent audit may be beneficial to Feiler.

(*AICPA Adapted*)

1-44.   Read the descriptions and indicate why you consider each to be (1) accounting or (2) auditing.

a. Balancing the accounts receivable control account with the accounts receivable subsidiary ledger.

b. Sending letters to customers asking them to reply as to whether the amount on the company's records is correct or not.

c. Inquiring about the status of doubtful accounts.

d. Preparing a schedule showing the amount of time each accounts receivable account has been owed.

e. Preparing footnotes for the financial statements.

f. Reviewing the adequacy of footnotes for the financial statements.

g. Tracing data from the voucher register to purchase invoices.

h. Preparing purchase invoices.

1-45.   A business associate makes the following statements.

1. The auditing standards for your profession are general and provide no real guidelines. In fact, it would be very difficult to tell whether an audit is substandard or not.

2. The standard audit has too many vague terms and phrases. In particular, "generally accepted auditing standards," "opinion," "fairly," and "generally accepted accounting principles" are terms that are hard to understand.

3. A qualified opinion in an audit report is hard to understand. If the financial statements are accurate, why not say so? If they are not accurate, why not indicate the reasons?

Required:

Reply to the business associate's comments. In your replies, indicate

a. What specific acts or omissions in an audit engagement could result in violations of which specific auditing standards.

b. The meaning of each term in the second statement.

c. The meaning of a qualified opinion.

1-46.   Read the following audit report for a financial audit. Indicate where it appears that generally accepted auditing standards were violated either in the conduct of the audit or the style of the audit report.

> As a stockholder of ABC Corporation, I was asked to briefly review the records of that company and render an opinion as to whether the financial statements are in accord with the accounting policies set forth in the company's manual.
>
> In my opinion, the financial statements are fair and reflect the system of accounting traditional for this company.

CHAPTER 2

Operational and Compliance Auditing

Learning Objectives *After reading and studying the material in this chapter, the student should*

Understand the concept of an operational audit.

Know the general functions performed in an operational audit.

Understand how individuals accomplish the general functions in an operational audit.

Comprehend the benefits that may be derived from an operational audit.

Understand the nature of a compliance audit.

Operational and compliance audits are sometimes associated primarily with audits of government entities. Although operational and compliance audits are often prescribed for governmental audits, they may be applicable in a broad range of settings.

Operational Audits

Because operational auditing is not as common as financial auditing, it has not been as well defined. Operational auditing is often used interchangeably with "management auditing," "performance auditing," "program results auditing," and "management review." Internal auditors and government auditors are often associated with operational auditing although they may perform many financial auditing functions as well.

Most definitions of operational auditing include some reference to efficiency, effectiveness, economy, or performance of an entity. Operational auditors ask such questions as: Have specific policies and objectives been defined? Are established policies being followed and are established objectives being met? Are desired results being obtained? Although operational auditing has been defined in various ways, we will use the following simple, straightforward definition:

> An operational audit is an organized search for ways of improving efficiency and effectiveness. It can be considered a form of constructive criticism.[1]

An important question in an operational audit is what unit of measure to use. Most financial audits concentrate on attesting to the fairness of the financial statements in accordance with generally accepted accounting principles as defined by authoritative bodies and accepted practice. Thus, the criteria for evaluating the amounts and disclosures contained in financial statements are fairly well defined. On the other hand, the measurement or evaluation of effectiveness, efficiency, economy, or performance in an operational audit is more difficult. Obviously, some surrogates for effectiveness, efficiency, and economy must be used. Some examples will be provided later in the chapter.

Other differences between financial and operational auditing include the following: (1) financial audit results are often reported to parties outside of the entity (e.g., stockholders, regulatory agencies, and the general public) whereas operational audit results are usually reported to management; and (2) operational audits may be directed toward many nonfinancial areas such as personnel and engineering.

A properly conducted operational audit should provide management with a number of benefits, including (1) increased profitability, (2) more efficient allocation of resources, (3) identification of problems at an early stage, and (4) improved communications. Management is responsible for all of these functions. In a small enterprise, management can perform them by direct personal supervision and there may be little need for an operational audit. As enterprises grow and add levels of authority between management and the operating functions, the needs for operational audits increase and we see the development of internal audit departments.

Although internal, external, and government auditors may perform operational auditing, the emphasis in this chapter will be on operational auditing performed by internal auditors.

---

[1] Dale L. Flesher and Stewart Siewert, *Independent Auditor's Guide to Operational Auditing* (New York: John Wiley & Sons, 1982).

Internal Auditors

Like external auditing, internal auditing has evolved from a simple clerical function into a highly professional operation. At one time, internal auditing consisted primarily of the audit of compliance with internal financial procedures; now it extends to the appraisal of efficiency and effectiveness in nonfinancial as well as financial matters. The importance of the internal audit function increases as organizations grow larger and more geographically disbursed. Today it is not unusual to find internal auditors reporting directly to the audit committee of the board of directors and using the latest electronic data processing and statistical techniques in their work. In fact, The Institute of Internal Auditors (IIA) changed its standards to emphasize that internal auditing serves the organization as a whole and not merely the management of the organization. This change recognizes a joint responsibility to the board of directors and management. IIA was formed in 1941 as an international association dedicated to the continuing professional development of the individual internal auditor and the internal auditing profession. Over the years it has adopted a *Code of Ethics,* approved a *Standards for the Professional Practice of Internal Auditing,* established a program of continuing education, developed a *Common Body of Knowledge,* and instituted a certification program leading to an individual's designation as a certified internal auditor (CIA). The *Code of Ethics* (see Appendix to Chapter 3) emphasizes honesty and objectivity. The *Standards for the Professional Practice of Internal Auditing* are to internal auditors what generally accepted auditing standards are to external auditors. They establish general levels of performance against which internal audit departments may be evaluated and cover such areas as independence, professional proficiency, scope and performance of work, and management of the internal audit department. The CIA examination lasts two days and covers (1) theory and practice of internal auditing, (2) management, quantitative methods, and information systems, and (3) accounting, finance, and economics. With this background and a generous portion of business sense, the internal auditor should be well qualified to perform an operational audit.

It is an oversimplification to say that external auditors are independent and internal auditors are not. Independence is a continuous rather than a discrete concept. The fact that the external auditor is selected and paid by management affects his or her independence, but this situation is not considered so serious that it invalidates the audit function. Since independence is a matter of degree, internal auditors should increase the degree of their independence to the maximum practical extent. One method used in some companies is to have the internal auditor report to the Board of Directors or its audit committee. This assures that the internal audit findings will be considered at the highest corporate level and reduces the influence of management on the work of the internal auditor.

The internal auditor usually has opportunities to (1) see many aspects of the company very quickly, (2) get broad exposure to management, and (3) apply a variety of accounting, auditing, and personal skills. Because of the broad understanding of company operations obtained, internal auditors are often promoted to key management positions.

An Approach to an Operational Audit

Because of the many areas of coverage, no single approach can be taken to operational audits. However, some general functions are usually applicable to most operational audits:

1. Plan the work to be performed, including the establishment of standards by which the audited operation is to be evaluated.

2. Gather evidence with which to measure the performance of the operation.

3. Analyze and investigate deviations from the standards.

4. Determine corrective action, where needed.

5. Report the results to the appropriate level of management.

Each of these general functions is discussed further in the following sections.

Planning the Operational Audit

Often the subject area and objectives of an operational audit are designated by top management. The internal auditor must then plan the work to accomplish the designated objectives. The evidence of this planning should be documented.

A preliminary survey is a common procedure for the auditor to use to become familiar with the operation to be audited. The auditor may use questionnaires, flowcharts, inquiries, management reports, and observation in the performance of the preliminary survey.

The questionnaire contains questions regarding matters affecting effectiveness, efficiency, and performance of the operation. The auditor will then evaluate the answers obtained. Later he or she will gather evidence to substantiate the answers received. Some examples of the types of questions that might be included are as follows:

1. How is the performance of this operation evaluated by top management?

2. What authority has been delegated to meet the performance criteria?

3. Has performance of this operation been satisfactory?

4. What areas need the most managerial attention?

5. What methods are used to safeguard assets?

6. Are sufficient but not excessive personnel assigned to the operation?

7. Is there a program to control excessive or duplicate paperwork?

To aid in understanding the flow of goods, services, and transactions to, from, and within the operation, the auditor may review or prepare flowcharts, which are pictorial diagrams of operations. When studying a flowchart, the auditor will be looking for inefficiencies and lack of controls, such as duplicate operations, unnecessary forms and operations, and lack of approvals.

While an auditor will make inquiries throughout the audit, many inquiries will be made at a preliminary meeting with the supervisors of the operation being audited. At this meeting the auditor should attempt to establish rapport and promote a cooperative attitude with the personnel of the operation being audited. Their cooperation is important to the efficient completion of the operational audit. At this meeting the auditor may ask such questions as the following:

1. What reports and other information do you need to manage the operation?

2. What use do you make of each report?

3. What operating problems are you experiencing?

4. Describe your training programs.

5. How do you set priorities for the operation?

The auditor will also review such management reports as interim financial statements, budgets, and sales and production reports. Of particular interest to the auditor are such things as budget variances, cost increases, inventory shortages, and production spoilage. All of these may indicate lack of efficiency. While performing other parts of the preliminary survey, the auditor should observe his or her surroundings. Idle personnel or equipment, unsafe operations, unsecured assets such as cash or inventory, or inefficient plant or office layout may suggest areas for potential increases in efficiency and effectiveness.

Based on the information obtained from these sources, the auditor may establish some objective criteria to evaluate the operation. Data from internal company records or from statistics of the industry in which the company operates may also be useful. Usually there are no perfect criteria, and the auditor must develop the best he or she can under the circumstances. What criteria, for example, would be used to evaluate the effectiveness of a purchasing department?

One could look at the dollar volume of purchases compared to the number of personnel in the department, but this does not take into account whether or not the purchases were made at the lowest price. To take this into account, one might determine the percentage of purchases subjected to competitive bidding, but this does not take into account the timeliness of the delivery of the purchased product or the quality of the product. As this example illustrates, multiple criteria often will be required.

With this information the auditor will design an audit program to use as a guide to gathering the evidence for a final evaluation of the operation.

Gathering Evidence of Performance

The purpose of gathering evidence is to obtain a factual basis for evaluating the performance criteria previously identified. Examples of evidence that might be examined to evaluate performance follow.

Performance Criteria	*Evidence of Performance*
1. Employees receive 40 hours of training per year.	1. Examine personnel files or training records to verify 40 hours of training per year.
2. Budget reports are received by the tenth of the subsequent month.	2. Interview department head to determine time of receipt of budget reports.
3. Budget variances are investigated and corrective action taken where necessary.	3. Review budget reports for variances and examine documentation of corrective action taken (e.g., reallocation of personnel, equipment adjustments, changes in production scheduling).
4. EDP equipment is not used by the operator for personal purposes.	4. Review console log of computer operations.
5. Excess funds are invested in interest-bearing obligations.	5. Review cash flow budget and minimum daily cash balances.

The interview is an important means of obtaining evidence during an operational audit. The better the interviewer, the more evidence that will be obtained. A good interview involves more than merely asking questions. The interview should be planned and as much information obtained in advance as possible. The interviewee should be made to feel as comfortable as possible. The interviewer should be tactful and avoid implying an expected answer to a question. For example, the question, "You do use this report, don't you?" will usually result in a positive response. A better question would be, "What use do you make of this report?" After the interview is completed, a memorandum should be prepared of the important points covered in the interview. This memorandum will constitute the evidence of information obtained in the interview.

The auditor will accumulate the evidence obtained in a file. The evidence may take the form of schedules listing information examined (e.g., a list of employees and the number of hours of training received per year), memoranda of discussions held (e.g., interview with department head to determine time of receipt of budget reports), and copies of documents (e.g., budget reports and console logs). Regardless of the form it takes, the auditor must have some documentary evidence to support his or her findings.

This documentary evidence, referred to as working papers, is compiled primarily from sources internal to the company. Operational audits seldom include external verification of internal data, although external information such as industry statistics may be useful in evaluating the efficiency of some operations. Working papers may be organized by the subunit of the entity being audited (e.g., by branch, department), the sequence in which audit procedures are performed (e.g., preliminary survey, evidence), or any other logical system that enhances the auditor's understanding of the work performed.

Analysis and Investigation of Deviations

While gathering evidence, the auditor should be alert for deviations from company policy and ineffective or inefficient performance. He or she should learn to distinguish between insignificant deviations (one minor supply order slightly in excess of the economic order quantity) and significant ones (numerous large supply orders for which competitive bids were not requested). Past deviations may or may not be correctable, but the auditor's main concern is with the potential effect on the company if the deviations continue in the future.

For example, in the operational audit of a research and development division, the auditor may note that security is lax because the area is not separately locked during nonbusiness hours and research results are not protected. Investigation might lead him or her to the following conclusions:

1. This is a significant deviation because of the possible loss of potential new or improved products to competitors or others.

2. These were not isolated deviations but regular occurrences.

3. The deviation is caused by the need for employees of this division to check and monitor experiments during nonbusiness hours.

4. There are no formal security controls for this division.

The analyses and investigations of deviations should be documented in the auditor's file because they are the basis for determining corrective action.

Determining Corrective Action

After analyzing and investigating a deviation the auditor must answer two questions: What corrective actions can be taken? Are the corrective actions practicable? The second question is often the most difficult to answer because the auditor is required to consider such factors as cost/benefit relationships, effect on employee morale, and consistency with other company policies.

In the example of lax security in the research and development division, one possible corrective action would be to allow no admittance to the area during nonbusiness hours, but this would be self-defeating since admittance is required to monitor experiments. Another possible corrective action would be to hire 24-hour guards for the area. This would be a costly action, but it might be considered in some cases. A third possible corrective action would be to lock the area and provide selected employees with keys and identification badges that would allow them admittance.

All proposed corrective actions should be discussed with the personnel involved to obtain their ideas and cooperation.

Reporting the Results of an Operational Audit

Although formal reporting may be considered the final step in the operational audit, informal reports should be made throughout the audit. For example, if the auditor notes a serious inefficiency during the preliminary survey, it should be investigated, evaluated, and reported immediately rather than waiting for the entire audit to be completed.

Formal reporting may include (1) a conference with department or division supervisors at the completion of the audit, (2) a written audit report to the department or division that includes detailed audit findings and recommendations, and (3) a written audit report to top management or the audit committee of the board of directors that summarizes only the more significant audit findings and recommendations.

Because economy and efficiency are relative terms, an auditor does not express an opinion as to whether an operation was performed at maximum levels of economy or efficiency. Instead, the auditor should report specific findings and conclusions. There is no standard form for reporting on an operational audit, but several matters would be covered in most such reports. An opening or scope paragraph should describe the operation that was audited, the time period covered, and so forth. Any limitations placed on the scope of the auditor's work should also be noted. Another paragraph should give an overall evaluation of the operation and an assessment of its performance. This may be followed by a section presenting detailed findings on individual issues. Here it is important to report both favorable and unfavorable findings. Giving proper credit for good performance promotes an objective image of the auditor and encourages cooperation with the auditor in future audits. Unfavorable findings should include a description of the deviation, suggested corrective action, and comments by department or division personnel. A final paragraph may express the auditor's appreciation for the cooperation and assistance received during the audit.

Determinations of the actual corrective actions to be taken on the findings included in the report are management responsibilities and are normally beyond the scope of the operational auditor.

A partial illustration of a report on an operational audit is shown in Figure 2.1.

Auditors must keep in mind that although their reports are not intended for use outside their companies, there is no assurance that they will not be seen by outsiders. The Internal Revenue Service, for example, has obtained copies of reports of internal auditors by court action. The reports should not contain speculations or assumptions that could be misconstrued by adverse parties.

Operational Audits of Specific Activities

Although it is beyond the scope of this chapter to present detailed programs for the audit of specific departments, the following partial examples were taken from *Modern Internal Auditing—An Operational Approach* to illustrate the types of matters that might be investigated.

Production

1. To what extent does the production department study new manufacturing approaches for current products?

2. How much waste or spoilage occurs in the processing of materials?

3. How much idle time or overtime is incurred? What are the causes?

4. What is the program for preventive maintenance?

5. Describe the safety program. Is it based on existing hazards and past experience?

Marketing

1. What provision is made for periodic reappraisal of major product market strategy?

2. What is the procedure for the formal presentation of new product proposals and the overall product planning and development program?

Mr. D. Z. Williams
General Manager
California Products, Inc.
Pearson, California 98641

Dear Mr. Williams:

As you requested, we have reviewed the operations of the company's data processing department. Our review was conducted during the period from April 16, 19X3 to June 3, 19X3, and consisted of (1) interviews with key personnel in the department, (2) review of operational guidelines including organizational charts, job descriptions, procedures, forms, and system and program documentation, (3) observation of activities within the department, and (4) review of productivity reports including equipment utilization reports and budgets. The data processing department utilizes 20 employees and has a budget for the current year of $5,100,000.

We are pleased to report to you our findings and recommendations.

General Evaluation

We found the overall operation of the department to be efficient and effective. Employees exhibited good technical expertise and expressed a desire to be of service to other departments of the company. Some additional coordination with user departments would be useful in meeting future hardware demands at the lowest cost.

Summary of Major Findings

1. Lack of a long-range plan for data processing.

2. Lack of periodic review of data processing reports that might be discontinued.

Discussion of Major Findings

1. Lack of a long-range plan for data processing.

Findings

The utilization rate of the present data processing equipment will approach the maximum sustainable rate within a year. Additionally, certain user departments are considering the acquisition of minicomputers to process special information needs. While data processing department personnel have discussed their future needs with various computer equipment manufacturers, no long-range plan that considers the total company data processing needs for future years has been developed.

Recommendation

We recommend that the data processing department, in consultation with the user departments, prepare a detailed projection of data processing needs for the next five years. This projection should include estimates of increases in the data presently processed as well as expected new applications. Top management also should be consulted for information that might affect future data processing needs such as mergers, acquisitions, dispositions, etc. Based on this projection, plans may be made to obtain both the equipment and personnel to supply the company's data processing needs at the lowest cost.

We appreciate the cooperation and many courtesies extended to us during our review. We will be pleased to answer any questions you may have regarding this report.

Sincerely,

Susan Davis
Chief Internal Auditor

Figure 2.1   Illustrative operational audit report.

3. How are sales promotion budgets developed, approved, and used as a basis of project control?

4. Are advertising agency billings supported as to company authorization, actual rendering of services, and best available rates?

5. Are customers being adequately serviced in terms of available stock?

Personnel

1. Does each manager evaluate the personnel for whom he or she is directly responsible?

2. What records and files relating to recruitment are maintained?

3. Are personnel being trained satisfied with their training? If not, why not?

4. How are specifications developed for individual jobs?

5. Are individual personnel files kept up to date and available for current reference?

Computer Operations

1. Has a long-range plan for company computer utilization been prepared and, if so, is it adequate?

2. How adequate is the computer department staff in terms of numbers, types of expertise, and personal qualifications?

3. Are computer processing activities consolidated adequately as a basis for reasonable achievement of potential operational economies, such as (a) purchase of equipment of more efficient size and with most advanced operational features, (b) best possible equipment utilization, and (c) uniform programming and operational practices?

4. Is proper provision made for controlling access to operational areas?

5. Are priority policies clearly stated and periodically reviewed?

Examples of Efficiencies Resulting from Operational Audits

Each issue of *The Internal Auditor* publishes examples of audit findings reported by its members. The following cases are examples of the results of actual operational audits that were reported.[2]

> For numerous years, the internal auditors found that the company's insurance department was not inviting competitive bids for fire, boiler, and machinery insurance. Management's responses to the auditors' recommendations for competitive bidding were always the same: "The present carrier . . . provides excellent service . . . has an outstanding relationship with us . . . provides numerous intangible services . . . et al." Management was also aware of what other carriers were quoting on similar coverage. As a result of the auditors' continued perseverance on the subject, the

[2]The examples from *The Internal Auditor,* copyright © by The Institute of Internal Auditors, Inc., are reprinted with permission.

insurance department finally solicited competitive bids for the insurance coverage. The leverage obtained from the competitive bidding caused the current carrier to restructure premium deposit requirements and premium amounts which reduced the company's insurance costs by more than $500,000 a year.

Productivity for workers on an incentive plan was recorded as more than double the output of day-rate workers. With this in mind, the internal auditor asked why only 75 percent of the applicable jobs had been converted to the incentive plan after many years of plant operation. "The union won't stand for it," was the plant manager's response. The auditor studied the union contract and found a clause that allowed management to install temporary estimated incentive standards pending the introduction of new engineering standards. After the auditor informed the plant manager of this clause, an industrial engineer was added to expedite the necessary time studies in order to devise temporary performance standards for the 25 percent of the jobs not converted to incentive plans. An annual increase in productivity was projected at more than $150,000.

A consumer goods company used to require each of its manufacturing plants to submit monthly samples of raw materials and finished product to a company-owned laboratory for quality control testing. The internal auditor found that management, due to quality improvements, had phased out the testing over a period of years. However, the plants were still faithfully sending the samples month after month. Why was this, wondered the auditor—who found it was because no one had told the plants to stop sending the samples. Management had only told the lab to stop making the tests. When informed of the auditor's findings, management notified the plants to stop sending the samples for an estimated savings of about $60,000 a year.

During an operational audit of the advertising department, the internal auditor was compiling costs for the printing of advertising inserts which are distributed inside newspapers. The auditor found that a high percentage of the cost was for the ink alone and questioned its validity. Research determined that the higher the density of the ink, the more costly the insert. Samples of inserts printed with ink that had a lesser density convinced management that using a less costly ink would change the appearance of the insert so insignificantly that customers would not notice. About $2.5 million a year will be saved.

The internal auditor, while reviewing accounts payable, found that most invoices were paid immediately upon receipt even though the majority had terms of "Net 30." Using the current cost of money, the auditor calculated that not taking advantage of the vendors' terms was costing the company approximately $46,000 a year. Management agreed to the auditor's recommendation to take full advantage of vendors' terms and time the mailing of checks so that they would reach the vendors on the due dates.

An Example of Operational Auditing by an Independent Public Accounting Firm

Although not a predominant part of their practice, some independent public accountants provide various services that would be the equivalent of "operational audits." Arthur Young & Company's Management Services department has entered into numerous engagements to perform "energy audits," also referred to as energy management studies. Such an audit is conducted by specially trained individuals normally with an industrial engineering background.

The energy audit process involves on-site surveys of the energy sources and uses at several of the company's offices, warehouses, plants, and other facilities. The typical energy audit preliminary survey may involve investigating the energy consumption associated with lighting, heating, ventilation, and air conditioning as well as that consumed in the production and transportation processes. The objective of such a survey is the identification of opportunities for energy consumption and cost savings. Such opportunities may include reduced lighting in remote warehouse areas, consideration of replacing lighting, heating, ventilation, and air-conditioning equipment with more energy-efficient equipment (assuming it is economically wise), cycling heating and air conditioning, and simply eliminating energy waste (turning equipment off during employee breaks; reducing heating and air conditioning during holidays, weekends, and other off hours). The survey also typically involves investigating energy source rate schedules. Frequently the public and private utility companies have reduced rate scales for energy used during certain hours. Some of a company's energy consumption may be conveniently cycled to those reduced rate hours.

This survey is followed with an analysis of the entity's energy consumption, both in units of energy and dollars and the potential measured savings opportunities that were identified in the survey. The energy audit also normally includes a mechanism for future energy management control (monitoring accomplishment toward the energy savings recommended).

Summary of Operational Auditing

The benefits top management may receive from an operational audit may easily be seen from the foregoing illustrations. If problems are identified at an early stage, profitability should be enhanced. Department and division personnel should also benefit by having their good performance recognized and by receiving suggestions for further improvement. Finally, the nonroutine nature of the work should provide internal (and other) auditors with challenging engagements and increasing recognition.

Compliance Audits

All audits are, in a sense, a form of compliance auditing. In financial audits a determination is made of whether financial statements comply with generally accepted accounting principles. In operational audits a determination is made of whether an entity's performance complies with standards of efficiency developed by management or the operational auditor. In the auditing literature, however, compliance auditing has a narrower definition. It refers to the determination of whether transactions and events conform with laws and regulations. Compliance auditing has added significance in audits of governmental entities because generally there are more compliance requirements than in audits of nongovernmental entities.

Compliance audits of governmental entities may be performed by government auditors at federal, state, and local levels or by independent public accountants. Regardless of the type of auditor performing the engagement, all are required to conduct their examinations in accordance with *Standards for Audit of Governmental Organizations, Programs, Activities, and Functions* (often referred to as the "Yellow Book") if the audited entity receives financial assistance from the federal government. If the audit is performed by independent public accountants, the requirements contained in the Yellow Book are *in addition* to those imposed by generally accepted auditing standards.

GAO Report on the Quality of Governmental Audits

In 1986 the U.S. General Accounting Office released a report entitled "CPA Audit Quality—Many Governmental Audits Do Not Comply with Professional Standards." The report, which was based upon reviews of 120 randomly selected governmental audits, included findings that (1) CPAs did not satisfactorily comply with standards on 34 percent of the governmental audits they performed; (2) more than half of the unsatisfactory audits had severe standards violations; and (3) CPAs' two predominant problems in performing governmental audits were insufficient audit work in (a) testing compliance with governmental laws and regulations and (b) evaluating controls, including those over federal expenditures.

This problem has been studied by an AICPA task force and others. An important contributing factor to the deficiencies was the failure of CPAs to recognize the *additional responsibilities* imposed on them by the Yellow Book in governmental audits. Even though some of the CPAs may have conducted their audits in accordance with generally accepted auditing standards, failure to perform the additional required procedures such as testing and reporting on compliance with laws and regulations may have resulted in their reports being classified as unsatisfactory. Others may have had more serious problems.

Assessing Compliance in a Governmental Audit

One of the first steps in assessing compliance in a governmental audit is the identification of the applicable laws and regulations, which may be classified as general requirements and specific requirements. General requirements are prescribed by statute and deal with such matters as political activity, construction contracts, civil rights, and cash management. Specific requirements are often included in the terms or provisions of an individual grant program and include such matters as types of expenditures allowed and unallowed, eligibility for the grant, requirements for matching funds, and reporting requirements.

After identifying the applicable laws and regulations the auditor may select a sample of transactions (e.g., expenditures under a particular grant) and test them for compliance. This may involve determining that they were for a purpose allowed under the grant, were properly authorized, and were properly reported.

An auditor may question an expenditure because it is

1. *Unallowable*—not for a purpose allowed by the provisions of the grant.

2. *Undocumented*—not supported by the required documentation such as a vendor's invoice.

3. *Unapproved*—not approved for payment by an authorized person.

4. *Unreasonable*—not of a type or amount normally expected for a particular type of grant.

Compliance auditing can involve the exercise of a considerable amount of judgment in evaluating a particular type of transaction.

Reporting on Compliance in a Governmental Audit

In addition to the standard audit report on the financial statements of a governmental entity, the Yellow Book requires the auditor to report whether items that were tested were in compliance with applicable laws and regulations. Material instances of noncompliance and all instances or apparent indications of fraud, abuse, or illegal acts found during the audit should be reported.

The Single Audit Act

Because of a diversity of federal government funding sources, state and local governments often receive funds from several programs administered by various federal agencies, each of which has its own audit requirements. For example, a city might receive funds from different federal agencies for its transportation needs, poverty programs, educational assistance, and health care facilities. The same payroll system may be used to pay the personnel costs for all four programs. If the four programs are audited by four different auditors, portions of the same payroll system may be audited four separate times, but no auditor may audit the entire system.

Rather than continue the inefficient, and often ineffective, audits of each of the federal programs, the government decided to replace the audits of individual programs with a single entity-wide audit. The emphasis has shifted from individual programs to the entity's overall financial management policies and practices. The requirements for performing and reporting under the Single Audit Act have been incorporated in the Yellow Book and generally include a determination of whether

1. The financial statements of the organization present fairly its financial position and the results of its financial operations in accordance with appropriate accounting principles.

2. The organization has accounting and other control systems to provide reasonable assurance that it is managing federal funds in compliance with applicable laws and regulations.

3. The organization has complied with laws and regulations that may have a material effect on its financial statements and on each major federal assistance program.

Auditors involved in audits of state and local governments receiving federal assistance should be aware of the special provisions of the Single Audit Act.

Chapter 2
Glossary of Terms

(listed in order of appearance in the chapter, with accompanying page reference where the term is discussed)

	Page in
Term	*Chapter*
Operational auditing an organized search for ways of improving efficiency and effectiveness. It can be considered a form of constructive criticism.	44
Institute of Internal Auditors (IIA) an international association of internal auditors dedicated to the continuing professional development of the individual internal auditor and the internal auditing profession.	45
Preliminary survey a process in an operational audit for gaining familiarity with the operation to be audited.	46
Compliance auditing a determination of whether transactions and events conform with laws and regulations.	56
Yellow Book common name for *Standards for Audit of Governmental Organizations, Programs, Activities, and Functions,* the guide to governmental auditing.	57

Chapter 2
References

Brown, Clifford D., and Burnaby, Priscilla. "A Study on the Evolving Single Audit," *The Government Accountants Journal* (Winter 1985–86), pp. 30–36.

Brown, Douglas S. "A Commonsense Approach to Operational Auditing," *The Internal Auditor* (August 1987), pp. 45–49.

Deck, Glenn E., and Thompson, Raymond. "Auditing and Management of Consultants," *The Internal Auditor* (February 1986), pp. 41–45.

Flesher, Dale L. "Writing the Operational Audit Report," *The Internal Auditor* (February 1984), pp. 41–43.

Goldstein, Ira, O'Connor, Thomas F., and Raaum, Ronell B. "Summarizing Audit Results to Satisfy an Internal Auditor's Many Customers," *The Government Accountants Journal* (Winter 1985–86), pp. 24–28.

Gordon, William D. "Auditing the Legal Department," *The Internal Auditor* (April 1986), pp. 24–27.

Gray, O. Ronald. "Audit Project Evaluation Methodology," *The Internal Auditor* (June 1983), pp. 31–34.

Gruber, Thomas J. "The Operational Audit—An Integrated Approach," *The Internal Auditor* (August 1983), pp. 39–42.

McGhee, Archie. "Auditing for Innovation," *The Internal Auditor* (April 1983), pp. 12–15.

Ried, Glenda E. "Legal Compliance Audits for Municipalities," *The CPA Journal* (June 1986), pp. 46–54.

Welsch, Joseph P. "Auditing for Project Cost Containment," *The Internal Auditor* (April 1986), pp. 57–60.

Wilder, Michael C. "Good Internal Audits Don't Just Happen," *The Government Accountants Journal* (Summer 1987), pp. 31–34.

Chapter 2
Review Questions

2-1.   Describe operational auditing.

2-2.   Why may the unit of measure be difficult to establish in an operational audit?

2-3.   Differentiate between financial and operational auditing.

2-4.   List four potential benefits of an operational audit.

2-5.   Discuss the activities of The Institute of Internal Auditors.

2-6.   What are the principal parts of the CIA examination?

2-7.   What general functions are usually applicable in an operational audit?

2-8.   What is the purpose of a preliminary survey and how is it performed?

2-9.   Why does the auditor gather evidence of performance?

2-10.   What are some attributes of a good interview?

2-11.   What forms may the auditor's evidence take?

2-12.   What investigation does an auditor make of deviations?

2-13.   What questions must an auditor consider in determining what corrective action to propose?

2-14.   List three forms of formal reporting of an operational audit's results.

2-15.   Discuss the sections or paragraphs that might be found in a formal written report.

2-16.   What is the purpose of a compliance audit?

2-17.   What publication provides guidance to auditors who perform compliance audits of government entities?

2-18.   For what reasons may an auditor question an expenditure in a compliance audit?

2-19.   What is the effect of the Single Audit Act?

Chapter 2
Objective Questions Taken from CIA Examinations[3]

2-20.   The primary difference between operational auditing and financial auditing is that in operational auditing
a. The auditor is not concerned with whether the audited activity is generating information in compliance with financial accounting standards.
b. The auditor is seeking to help management use resources in the most effective manner possible.
c. The auditor starts with the financial statements of an activity being audited and works backward to the basic processes involved in producing them.
d. The auditor can use analytical skills and tools that are not necessary in financial auditing.

2-21.   In conducting an appraisal of the economy and efficiency with which resources are employed, an internal auditor is responsible for
a. Determining whether operating standards have been established.
b. Verifying the existence of assets.
c. Reviewing the reliability of operating information.
d. Resolving disputes over operating standards.

2-22.   Which of the following objectives is most auditable?
a. To improve supervisory morale and leadership.
b. To reduce substantially the production scrap rate.
c. To improve community relations by 20 percent.
d. To improve the production rate by 5 percent.

2-23.   The first step in an operational audit is for the auditor to
a. Define problem areas.
b. Identify objectives of the company and the function being audited.

    c. Evaluate financial statements.

    d. Determine pertinent facts and conditions.

2-24.   Governmental effectiveness auditing seeks to determine whether the desired results are being achieved and objectives are being met. The first step in performing such an audit would be to

    a. Evaluate the system used to measure results.

    b. Determine the sampling frame to use in studying the system.

    c. Collect and analyze quantifiable data.

    d. Identify the legislative intent of the program being audited.

2-25.   You are preparing for an operational audit and discover that the operating standards used by the auditee are vague. In this situation, due professional care requires that you

    a. Modify the standards.

    b. Establish new standards.

    c. Seek authoritative interpretations of the standards.

    d. Report the activity as unauditable at this time.

2-26.   During an audit of the personnel function, an auditor notes that there were several employee benefit programs and that participation in some of the programs is optional. Which of the following would be the best evidence in assessing the attractiveness of various benefit programs to employees?

    a. Discuss satisfaction levels with program participants.

    b. Evaluate program participation ratios and their trends.

    c. Discuss satisfaction levels with the director of personnel.

    d. Evaluate methods used to make employees aware of available program options.

2-27.   The internal auditor is performing an operational audit of data processing's budgeting procedures. Which of the following procedures is least likely to be performed?

    a. Review the extent to which the budget identifies controllable expenditures.

    b. Review the total monetary budget and compare it with that of prior periods.

    c. Compare billing rates charged to users with those approved for the specified level of service.

    d. Reconcile depreciation on computer equipment to the property ledger.

2-28.   As part of the operational audit of the treasury function, which of the following factors should be given most consideration by the internal auditor in evaluating strategic plans for issuance of long-term debt?

    a. Review of the company's current requirements for working capital.

b. The company's planned dividend rate.

c. The advantages and disadvantages of including debt securities in the planned capital structure of the company.

d. The current market interest/dividend rate on comparable long-term debt and equity securities.

2-29.   The internal auditor in a consumer products company plans to review marketing activities. Which of the following would contribute the most to determining whether the product planning and development group has executed its responsibilities effectively?

a. Evaluation of the organizational status of the group and its organizational structure.

b. Evaluation of coordination between the group and other interested parties, such as sales, finance, market research, and production.

c. Evaluation of the qualification of personnel working in the group in relation to their specific assignments.

d. Evaluation of the acceptance of the company's products in the market by comparison with those of competitors.

2-30.   In an operational audit of the transportation function, which of the following tests is most appropriate to determine whether there is favoritism to individual carriers?

a. Investigate selected demurrage charges to determine whether they were appropriate.

b. Determine whether the selection of carriers is reviewed and approved by a higher-ranking member of the traffic department.

c. Determine whether freight bills have received a post-audit by the transportation department or an outside specialized freight auditor.

d. Determine that the amount of freight billed to the customer on the sales invoice is equal to the amount actually charged your company by the carrier.

2-31.   Which one of the following is the best objective performance criterion for an electrical engineer?

a. Exhibition of creative talents on company projects.

b. Project completion within budget constraints.

c. Ability to work well with fellow engineers on projects.

d. Cooperativeness with superiors and upper-level management.

2-32.   The numerical process that would be most helpful to an auditor in evaluating projected general and administrative expense rates for a division under review is

a. Game theory.

b. Linear programming.

    c. Probability theory.

    d. Regression analysis.

2-33.   If the objective of the audit is to determine that adequate environmental protection and alarm devices are installed and operating, the auditor should

    a. Review the architect's alarm specification documents.

    b. Examine invoices for alarm devices.

    c. Observe and test the operation of the units.

    d. Interview the plant safety officer and plant management.

2-34.   When the auditor and the auditee reviewed the draft audit report, they found they had different interpretations of the facts. The auditor should

    a. Eliminate the item from the audit report.

    b. State only the auditor's position in the report.

    c. Refer the matter to the auditee's supervisor for review and resolution.

    d. Report both interpretations.

2-35.   Which of the following is a necessary requirement for inclusion of a deficiency finding in an operational audit report?

    a. The associated recommendation must have been agreed to by the auditee.

    b. The finding must not have been reported previously.

    c. The deficiency relates to excessive operating costs.

    d. The supporting evidence must be competent and relevant.

2-36.   In an audit of the tax department you found that certain officers were abusing some of their executive perquisites and that this abuse may have a tax effect for the company. The tax department manager took strong exception to this finding, stating that these matters were of minor importance and their inclusion in an audit report would be embarrassing to the officers. Which of the following reporting practices would be unacceptable?

    a. State the findings and include comments by the tax department manager.

    b. State the findings without the comments by the tax department manager.

    c. Do not report the findings.

    d. Omit the findings but report the details in a confidential communication to the company president.

*2-37.   In a compliance audit, an auditor is concerned with whether an entity's transactions are in conformance with

    a. Management objectives.

    *Not a CIA examination question.

    b. Laws and regulations.

    c. Board of director directives.

    d. Accepted business practices.

*2-38.   In the audit of a government entity that receives federal funds, an auditor should seek guidance from

    a. Generally accepted auditing standards.

    b. Provisions of the Yellow Book.

    c. Both generally accepted auditing standards and provisions of the Yellow Book.

    d. Generally accepted standards for auditing federal funds.

*2-39.   In auditing expenditures for compliance under a federal grant program, an auditor would be least likely to question an expenditure for supplies that is not

    a. Supported by a receiving report.

    b. Paid within the discount period.

    c. Initialed as approved for payment by an authorized official.

    d. Used in connection with the program.

Chapter 2
Discussion/Case Questions

2-40.   The audit committee of Jones, Inc., has asked the director of internal auditing about the concept of "systems development auditing." They are specifically interested in

1. An operational audit of the system development process.

2. An audit of the accuracy of the internal controls in the new system.

Required:
a. Define the phrase "operational audit of the systems development process."
b. Identify the major audit objectives associated with an operational audit of the systems development process.
c. State and briefly describe the more important auditing procedures the auditor would perform while conducting an operational audit of the systems development process.
(*IIA Adapted*)

*Not a CIA examination question.

2-41.   The director of internal auditing of a city has been requested to audit the operations of the highway department for possible waste and inefficiency. The department is responsible for maintenance of city roads and highways and for minor road improvement projects. Major road improvement projects are let to outside contractors. The scope of the audit includes

1. Personnel utilization.

2. Inventories.

3. Quality control.

4. Planning.

Required:
a. For each of the four areas, list the activities for which the auditor would expect to find standards.
b. Describe the specific issues that should be addressed by the designated standards.

(IIA Adapted)

2-42.   List five opportunities provided by the preliminary internal audit conference for establishing good auditor/auditee relationships.

(IIA Adapted)

2-43.   You are asked to plan and prepare for an operational audit of customer service and inventory levels of a wholesaling division that handles various types of small electric motors and parts.

Required:
a. Specify in detail the type of information the auditor should gather in the preliminary survey and identify the source of the information.
b. The division operates in a dynamic environment. Your primary audit thrust will be to determine the effectiveness of the division to (1) meet customer delivery demand so that 95 percent of all orders are delivered on time and 99 percent are delivered on time or within two weeks of specified delivery, and (2) determine that inventory levels are not excessive. Write a general audit program to accomplish the two objectives.

(IIA Adapted)

2-44.   The internal auditor recently conducted a preliminary survey of the purchasing activities of a manufacturing plant. Three general management objectives for the purchasing activity related to obtaining goods and services were identified:

1. Right time.

2. Right quantity.

3. Right quality.

Each of these objectives has been determined to be appropriate for the audit.

Required:
For each of these objectives, identify audit procedures that would be likely to produce evidence relative to the organization's success in meeting these objectives.
(IIA Adapted)

2-45.   As a senior internal auditor for a large industrial organization, you have been assigned to perform an audit of the personnel function. Your preliminary survey disclosed the following information:

1. The personnel department is responsible for establishing company-wide procedures to carry out management's personnel policies. These procedures are administered by local management in the various plants.

2. A year ago the company adopted an affirmative action program for recruiting new employees and evaluating personnel for possible promotion.

3. The personnel department has established a detailed system of job classification analysis with corresponding compensation grades.

Required:
Develop a series of questions to organize your major concerns in preparing a detailed audit program, particularly in regard to the following areas:
a. Coordination of company-wide personnel policies and procedures with management at regional plants and offices.
b. Elements of a system to provide adequate control over the affirmative action program.
c. Assurance that minority employees hired under the affirmative action program will be able to meet standard job classification requirements.
d. Effectiveness of the job classification and related compensation program in meeting market competition.
(IIA Adapted)

2-46.   Risk assessment can be useful to an internal audit director in setting audit priorities.

Required:

Explain how the audit director should employ risk assessment in developing audit work priorities. Be specific and identify the risk indicators that would be included in the analysis.

(IIA Adapted)

2-47.   Heretofore, senior executives have not read your internal audit reports. You believe that these executives should be interested in receiving copies of your reports, particularly because you have expanded your audit program to cover operations throughout the entire organization.

Required:

Identify *three* qualities—in terms of form, content, or both—of internal audit reports that you believe will help capture and hold the interest of senior executives.

(IIA Adapted)

2-48.   The following sentences appear in an internal auditor's notes concerning an accounts payable activity. The sentences, which are in no logical order or grouping, are to be used in the audit report.

1. Generally, we were concerned with evaluating the system of control.

2. We did not seek to determine whether discounts were being taken.

3. The review of discounts was covered in a separate draft.

4. The Accounts Payable Department is staffed by 15 employees.

5. Specifically, we set out to verify the sufficiency of the approvals and/or documentary support for the receipt of goods.

6. We found that written procedures were current and complete.

7. We were also concerned with the adequacy of distribution of charges to accounts.

8. We believe that the system of internal control is adequate.

9. The 15 Accounts Payable employees process 10,000 invoices each month.

10. Our test of 200 invoices requiring management approval showed that 35 were not approved.

11. In addition, the Accounts Payable employees process invoices for payment amounting to $30 million annually.

12. We believe the approval and support activities were not carried out satisfactorily.

13. Of 500 paid invoices we examined, 25 percent showed incorrect distributions to accounts.

14. We also believe that the function of distributing charges to accounts was not carried out satisfactorily.

Required:
Construct a report outline, using the following section headings and putting the *numbers* of the sentences under the appropriate headings in a logical, consistent order.
a. Foreword.
b. Purpose.
c. Scope.
d. Opinions.
e. Statements of condition.
(*IIA Adapted*)

2-49.   You have just received the following draft audit report that was prepared by one of your staff auditors.

1 Audit of the Purchasing Department

2   Introduction

3 The purchasing department is responsible for
4 all procurements except those involving
5 executive approval. During the past months,
6 purchasing issued 19,736 purchase orders for
7 a variety of products. Our audit covered
8 only 4 of the 12 separate product classifi-
    cations for which purchasing is done.

9   Purpose and Scope

10 We made our audit to determine whether
11 a. Competitive bidding was employed.
12 b. Purchase orders were being approved at
13   an appropriate level.
14 c. Buyers were following up appropriately.

15   Findings and Opinion

16 a. New procurement procedures prescribe an
17   adequate control system which is designed to
18   require supervisory review of all bidders'
19   lists to see that all qualified suppliers
20   are permitted to bid.
21 b. We found that 43 purchase orders for
22   more than $25,000 had been approved only by
23   the buyer. We reported this to the
         purchasing agent.
24 c. Follow-up action on late shipments has
25   been ineffective because shipments continue
26   to be received late.
27 d. Based on a random sample of 200 items,
28   there shouldn't be more than a 2% error rate
29   in the purchase orders issued.

30   _____

                            (Signed)   Auditor

Required:
Evaluate the quality of the report and recommend improvements therein.
Please use the following format.

Line Number	Weakness in Report	Improvement Suggested

(IIA Adapted)

2-50.   You have been assigned to perform an operational audit of the vehicle mainte-
        nance department of a large university. What factors will you consider in deter-
        mining if the department is operating efficiently and effectively?

2-51.   Your audit of a United Fund agency that received a grant of federal funds included
        tests of transactions for compliance with applicable laws and regulations. Indicate
        whether or not and why you would question the following grant expenditures.
        a. Cost of newspaper ad for secretarial assistance.
        b. Cost of medical insurance for employees.
        c. A $500 contribution to the governor's campaign fund.
        d. Cost of having lunch with the auditors.
        e. Cost of a first class airfare to attend a meeting that was necessary for the proper
        administration of the grant.
        f. Cost of a monthly retainer paid to an attorney.
        g. Cost of penalty for late filing of a payroll tax return.

The Auditor's Ethical Environment

Learning Objectives   *After reading and studying the material in this chapter, the student should*

Understand the current ethical environment in which the CPA operates.

Understand how the *AICPA Code of Professional Ethics* is structured and implemented.

Know the Standards of Professional Conduct.

Know the Rules of Performance and Behavior.

Most groups that refer to themselves as *professionals* have a code of ethics. Although the individual provisions may differ, all codes generally have one thing in common—a requirement that the members maintain a higher standard of conduct than that called for by the law. The code of ethics of the accounting profession is no exception.

Certified public accountants cannot truly call themselves *professional* unless they accept certain responsibilities to the public. Since members of the public cannot individually assess the quality of services rendered by CPAs, it is imperative that the public accept their competence and integrity. CPAs should project an image to the public that they

1. Possess independence, integrity, and objectivity.

2. Possess the technical expertise of their profession.

3. Serve their clients with professional concern and in a manner consistent with their responsibilities to the public.

4. Have appropriate professional relationships with their colleagues.

The Changing Ethical Environment

Changes in Recent Years

In the last 20 years there has been a dramatic change in the auditor's ethical environment. During most of the 1960s this environment was somewhat "restrictive," as evidenced by the following prohibitions.

1. CPAs were not allowed to advertise in a commercial manner. For example, newspaper advertising of a firm's services was generally forbidden. "Word of mouth" was considered the most proper form of advertising.

2. CPAs were not allowed to solicit the clients of other CPAs.

3. Competitive bidding for clients was forbidden.

4. CPAs were not allowed to practice in corporate form. It was considered improper to "hide" behind the corporate shield of limited liability.

By the end of the 1970s virtually all of the preceding prohibitions had disappeared. What emerged in the late 1970s and early 1980s was a more openly competitive environment that had these characteristics.

1. Virtually any form of advertising and solicitation was permitted as long as it was not "false, deceptive, or misleading." Thus, CPAs joined the ranks of commercial advertisers. Today, it is not uncommon to see large newspaper advertisements by CPA firms.

2. CPAs became openly competitive in soliciting clients.

3. Competitive bidding not only became acceptable but in many cases necessary to maintain client business. Coupled with this was an expansion of services that CPAs offered their clients.

4. Practice in corporate form was acceptable.

What caused such massive changes during the late 1960s and 1970s, and what has been the effect of such changes on the current ethical environment in which CPAs now operate? In general these changes were brought about by pressure from the U. S. Department of Justice for a more competitive environment.

The effect has been to cause (or perhaps force) CPAs to operate in a manner that is often referred to as commercial, that is, aggressive bidding for clients by offering low prices and openly soliciting other CPAs' clients. In addition, there has been a significant increase in the variety of services offered by CPAs, another indication of the increasingly competitive environment.

The Positive and Negative Aspects of These Changes

It is difficult, at best, to generalize on whether the previously mentioned changes in the CPA's ethical environment have been beneficial or detrimental. On the positive side increased competition may have forced CPAs to be more efficient and "public relations minded" and may have resulted in an enhanced public awareness of the CPA's role in our society.

On the negative side there is a belief by some that CPA firms have become too commercial, that is, overly concerned about the business aspects of their operations at the expense of the professional and public interest aspects. Remember from our discussions in Chapter 1 that CPAs have a dual responsibility to clients and third-party groups and are viewed by the public as a "watchdog" of the integrity of financial reporting.

This concern about *commercialism* was voiced strongly in an article in the October 1985 issue of the *Journal of Accountancy* in which the following statement was made.

> The threat of commercialism within the profession is an equally serious concern and, because it is more subtle, it is perhaps more dangerous. Because it is a relatively new phenomenon, it has the potential to cut a costly swath before remedies can be brought to bear to bring it under control. Because commercialism is the antithesis of a public-first attitude, it has the potential to undermine seriously the accounting profession's hard-won gains—and thereby endanger the capital system.[1]

Why the Code of Professional Ethics Needed to Be Changed

There were additional factors that encouraged the accounting profession to reconsider the existing *AICPA Code of Professional Ethics* and suggest a complete revamping of it.

1. During the 1980s there has been a dramatic rise in the number of lawsuits levied against CPAs. Some would call it an explosive rise. We will discuss the CPA's litigation issue in more detail in Chapter 4.

2. The business community and the public at large have higher expectations of the performance of CPAs than they did in previous years. Although many in the accounting profession may look upon it as a flawed perception, there

---

[1]Robert J. Sack, "Commercialism in the Profession: A Threat to Be Managed," *Journal of Accountancy* (October 1985), p. 126.

is, nevertheless, an image of the CPA as a "public watchdog" of the financial reporting process. In other words, much of the public thinks that it is the job of the CPA to prevent and/or detect business fraud.

As a result, there was a gap between what the public expected CPAs to do and what the CPAs expected of themselves, given the ethical code under which the CPA operated.

Some of this gap will never be closed. But it was the belief of the accounting profession in the late 1980s that some of this "public perception" problem could be eased by substituting a new code of professional ethics for the one that then existed. In addition, many members of the accounting profession simply believed that it was time for a code with a more positive tone.

The Anderson Report—A Proposal for a New Code

In 1986 a special AICPA committee issued its recommendations in a report entitled *Restructuring Professional Standards to Achieve Professional Excellence in a Changing Environment,* otherwise known simply as the *Anderson Report.* The report's major recommendation was to restructure the *AICPA Code of Professional Ethics.*

To understand the scope of this restructuring, we will briefly examine the structure of the old code in Figure 3.1.

The *Concepts of Professional Ethics* consisted of nonenforceable guidelines for proper behavior. They were very philosophical in nature and contained "suggestions" on proper behavior by CPAs. For example, the section of the code covering concepts of independence contained a statement that independence is the ability to act with integrity and objectivity.

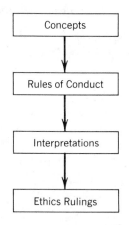

Figure 3.1   The basic structure of the old code of professional ethics.

The *Rules of Conduct* contained enforceable prohibitions and tended to be more definitive than the concepts. The rules of conduct covering independence stated emphatically that

> independence will be considered to be impaired if, during the period of his professional engagement, or at the time of expressing his opinion, a member of the AICPA or his firm had or was committed to acquire any direct or material indirect financial interest in the enterprise.

The *Interpretations* were necessary to provide guidelines as to the scope and limitations of the Rules of Conduct. For example, it was necessary to more sharply define the term "he or his firm" in the Rule of Conduct covering independence. An interpretation was issued stating that "he or his firm" included (among others)

> proprietors, partners, or shareholders in the firm, including certain of their close relatives.

It was also necessary for *Ethics Rulings* to be issued that were even more specific than Interpretations. Using the same example of independence referred to previously, an Ethics Ruling was issued that defined as a close family relationship

> a brother of a CPA who was a stockholder and vice-president in a closely held corporation that was a potential audit client of the CPA.

Summarizing our example, then, we had the following hierarchy in the old code.

> An example of the concept of independence.
>> Independence is the ability to act with integrity and objectivity.
> An example of a rule of conduct covering independence.
>> The CPA or his firm cannot have a direct or material indirect financial interest in an audit client.
> An example of the CPA or his firm.
>> Proprietors, partners, or shareholders in a firm and certain close relatives.
> An example of an unacceptable family relationship.
>> A brother of a CPA who is a stockholder and vice-president of a closely held corporation that is a potential audit client of the CPA.

The old code was replaced by a new one with a more positive tone and also a new structure as shown in Figure 3.2.

Another significant change was made in the way the code was enforced. Under the old code, the major quality control measures were actions of the AICPA Committee on Professional Ethics, which handled individual complaints against members. Under the new code, the major quality control measures will be

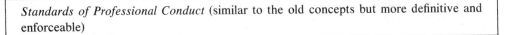

Standards of Professional Conduct (similar to the old concepts but more definitive and enforceable)

↓

Rules of Performance and Behavior (enforceable applications of the standards)

↓

Interpretation of Rules by the Senior Technical Committees that deal with the areas covered by a rule (e.g., the senior technical committee on auditing will interpret rules covering auditing, the senior technical committee on tax will interpret rules covering tax, etc.)

Figure 3.2   The basic structure of the new code of professional ethics.

self discipline and the monitoring of the practice of CPAs through quality or peer review programs (although mechanisms for handling complaints still exist).

In the remainder of this chapter we will discuss the standards of professional conduct and the rules of performance and behavior that apply these standards.

The Structure of the AICPA Code of Professional Ethics

Although the *AICPA Code of Professional Ethics* adopted in 1988 has a more positive tone than the one that preceded it, the new code, nevertheless, has rules of performance and behavior that are enforceable applications of the standards of professional conduct. These rules identify both acceptable and unacceptable behavior and members of the AICPA are required to observe them in their professional activities.

Under the old code, interpretations and ethics rulings were made by a committee on professional ethics of the AICPA. However, interpretation of the rules of this code is assigned to the senior technical committees of the AICPA that have responsibility for areas covered by a particular rule. These committees consist of the following:

1. Ethics

2. Accounting and auditing

3. Accounting and review services

4. Taxes

5. Management advisory services

Interpretations and ethics rulings that were made under the old code will continue in effect until the groups listed previously change them with their own interpretations. In fact, many provisions of the old rules of conduct will remain interpretations of the new rules unless and until changed by the action of one of these groups.

The Standards of Professional Conduct

As indicated earlier in the chapter, the Standards of Professional Conduct are similar in tone to the Concepts of Professional Ethics that were a part of the old code. Both sets of pronouncements contain admonitions about proper behavior of CPAs and the special role of CPAs in our society. However, the Standards of Professional Conduct are enforceable through the Rules of Performance and Behavior and through interpretations of the various senior level committees of the AICPA mentioned earlier.

We will divide our discussion of the standards into these areas.

1. Purpose

2. Applicability

3. Responsibilities

4. Public interest

5. Integrity

6. Objectivity and independence

7. Due care

8. Scope and nature of services

9. Performance standards

10. Compliance

Purpose of the Standards   A key element of the *AICPA Code of Professional Ethics* is that many of its provisions could be violated without also violating a law or some set of federal or state regulations. A major reason for a code of ethics is to encourage members to exercise self-discipline above and beyond laws and regulations.

For example, it would not be a violation of the law for a CPA to charge a fee to an audit client that is based on the amount of net income shown in that client's audited financial statements. But if the CPA is conducting an independent audit, such fees are improper because of the potential effect on objectivity. The CPA might be tempted to "overlook" needed adjustments to the financial statements that would decrease audited net income and lower the CPA's fee. In later parts of this chapter we will discuss other examples of acts that are lawful but unethical.

Applicability of the Standards   The standards apply to all members of the AICPA, including those in public practice, industry, government, and education. Also, the standards cover all professional responsibilities of each of these categories of members.

Responsibilities of Members   Once again, we are reminded that CPAs have responsibilities to their clients (e.g., the independent auditor/client relationship), their employers (e.g., the internal auditor/employer relationship), and to the general public. As we pointed out in Chapter 1, there will be inevitable conflicts when CPAs attempt to serve all of these parties.

This section contains an interesting comment about these relationships, however. When members observe their responsibility to the public, the interests of clients and employers are also best served. Remember this theme because it will be emphasized many times throughout the book.

Public Interest   As indicated in the earlier part of this chapter, the CPAs' current environment is highly competitive, has few restrictions on advertising, and allows competitive bidding for engagements. In addition, CPAs are offering a wider range of services than in past years.

In the context of this environment the section on public interest contains a statement that best summarizes the CPAs' obligation to the public.

> The public expects members to provide quality services, conduct promotional activities, enter into fee arrangements, and offer a range of services all in a manner that demonstrates a level of professionalism consistent with these Standards of Professional Conduct.

An unanswered question is how is such a general statement enforced.

Integrity   This section merely admonishes members to discharge their responsibilities with a sense of integrity. It is interesting to note that the need for confidentiality of client information is separately mentioned. CPAs consistently have access to information about clients' activities. Tax return information is a prime example. As professionals, it is the CPAs' obligation to keep such information private unless the need for disclosure is clearly overriding. Again, we will discuss this issue at more length when we cover the Rules of Performance and Behavior.

Objectivity and Independence   Of all the standards in the code of professional ethics, perhaps no other is more important than *independence,* which is often defined as the ability to act with integrity and objectivity. In fact, independence is such an integral aspect of auditing and other attest services that without it no real attest service can be performed.

To take it a step further, the section on objectivity and independence states that independence precludes certain relationships that may appear to impair objectivity in rendering attestation services. For example, a CPA's ownership of a small percentage of an audit client's stock may do nothing to impair the CPA's *independence in fact*, but it would impair the CPA's *independence in appearance*. As a result (and as we will discuss later) no direct ownership of stock of an audit client is allowed.

This section contains this type of guidance about objectivity and independence.

1. A member who provides auditing and other attestation services should be independent in fact (mental attitude) and in appearance (the image projected to the public).

2. In providing nonattest services, a member should be objective and avoid conflicts of interest.

The question of independence and its potential impairment when attest services are performed is interesting. Consider these four situations.

1. A CPA expresses an unqualified opinion on financial statements that are prepared in such a way as to deliberately cover up his or her client's poor business decision. For example, the client made a poor investment that is obviously worth less than its cost. Yet, the auditor does not qualify his or her opinion when the investment is stated at cost on the financial statements.

2. The CPA performing what is supposed to be an independent audit is actually an employee of the audit client.

3. The CPA owns a small percentage of the audit client's stock.

4. The CPA's income is derived solely from attest services performed for clients.

Which of these four situations is an impairment of independence? Clearly, the first situation is unacceptable. The second situation, although not as apparent, is also considered an impairment of independence. The third situation may be less damaging than the first two. Still, the AICPA believes that any direct stock ownership in an audit client might appear to impair independence. What about the fourth situation? The auditor/client relationship is considered acceptable and would not impair independence.

The point is that the general public, when asked about each of the previously listed situations, would probably give a variety of opinions as to which situations are proper and improper. Thus, we can easily see that the defining of independence, although necessary, may also be difficult.

Due Care   This section emphasizes that CPAs should be competent and diligent in carrying out their responsibilities. In addition, CPAs should know the limitations of their competence and should seek consultation or referral when necessary.

This last admonition is especially important because of the vast array of services now offered by CPAs. For example, a CPA who is performing an audit may be called upon to assist the client in deciding on the proper computer software to use in some accounting applications. If the CPA is qualified to give such advice, he or she should feel free to do so. Lacking that qualification, however, the CPA should consult with someone else or refer the client to a more knowledgeable person.

Scope and Nature of Services   The rendering of nonaudit services to audit clients is a controversial subject. In earlier years this was less of a problem because the practice of many CPAs consisted, for the most part, of audit and tax services. Today, the variety of services rendered by CPAs has increased at a seemingly geometric rate.

A classic example is the rendering of management consulting services to audit clients. Some of these services are natural extensions of audit services because the business community looks to CPAs for a variety of financial advice. Advice on budgeting and cost accounting systems are cases in point. Other types of management consulting services may raise questions about conflicts of interest.

Assume that a CPA is asked to install or help install a complete accounting system that will later be audited by the same CPA. Is it possible to perform both services without losing independence in the audit engagement? The code does not attempt to provide answers to these specific questions. Rather it suggests that members use the following guidelines.

1. Practice in firms that have good internal quality-control procedures.

2. Give serious consideration as to whether nonaudit services provided to audit clients might eventually create or appear to create conflicts of interest.

3. Think about whether each nonaudit service is consistent with the CPA's role as a professional and is a reasonable extension of existing services offered by the profession.

Performance Standards   This section is simply a reminder that the Council of the AICPA has delegated to senior technical committees the responsibility for applying the standards of professional conduct to situations in practice.

Compliance   This section reminds members of the AICPA that compliance with the standards is expected and that the standards provide guidelines to members.

Rules of Performance and Behavior

Rule 101. Independence   This rule is much shorter than the equivalent rule on independence in the old code. In fact this rule contains a single sentence.

> A member shall be independent in the performance of professional services as required by standards promulgated by bodies designated by Council.

This general rule is applied to situations in practice through standards published by the appropriate bodies of the AICPA. These standards indicate whether independence is required when a particular service is performed. For example, the Auditing Standards Board would issue independence standards for the performance of audits. Members that are not in public practice are not subject to this rule.

Even though the present code of professional ethics is more positive in tone than the previous one, there are, nevertheless, certain relationships between auditors and clients that the AICPA believes will impair independence and therefore are prohibited. Generally they include:

1. Certain financial relationships.

2. Relationships that the public might view as making auditors a part of their client's management or an employee of their client.

Direct financial interest   The rule on independence prohibits CPAs from having any direct or material indirect financial interest in their audit clients. *Direct financial interest* simply means owning an investment in a client. The SEC also prohibits any direct financial interest in audit clients.

In fact, the AICPA feels so strongly about this issue that it prohibits CPAs from having financial interests in nonclients who, in turn, have certain investor or investee relationships with an audit client. For example, independence is impaired if a CPA holds a direct financial interest in a partnership that invests in an audit client. This relationship is held to be equivalent to holding a direct financial interest in the audit client.

However, exceptions to the rule on direct financial interest are sometimes allowed. A case in point is the ownership of stock in a country club that is an audit client. This type of ownership is essentially a social matter and, therefore, falls outside the rule on direct financial interest.

Conversely, the AICPA takes the opposite view when a CPA owns bonds of a municipal authority that is an audit client. The CPA has a direct financial interest in the authority. It is interesting to note that the amount of the bondholdings is not important. The materiality of the holdings to the CPA's wealth or to the total amount of bonds outstanding is not an issue.

Indirect financial interest   The rule on independence also prohibits CPAs from having a material *indirect financial interest* in an audit client. The term *material* refers to significance or importance. If the indirect financial interest is significant in relation to either the CPA's wealth or the audit client, independence is impaired. The test of materiality is, of course, a matter that must be determined in each individual audit engagement.

Indirect financial interest is also a subjective concept. For example, would CPAs' independence be impaired if they invested in a bank that loaned money to an audit client? Such stock ownership is an indirect financial interest in the bank's customers; thus, the ownership is an indirect financial interest in the audit client. If the ownership is material, independence is impaired.

Another example of an indirect financial interest is the ownership of a mutual fund which, in turn, owns the audit client's stock as part of its investment portfolio. Such holdings are indirect because the CPA who owns mutual funds has no influence over investment decisions.

Loans from audit clients   The rule on independence prohibits loans from audit clients; however, loans from financial institution clients are acceptable in certain circumstances if made under "normal lending procedures."

Assume, for example, that a CPA has a savings and loan association as an audit client. Would independence be impaired if the CPA is indebted to the savings and loan association through a home mortgage loan? This relationship is acceptable if the loan is made under "normal lending procedures." Exceptionally liberal repayment terms or a very low interest rate on such a loan might bring the auditor's independence into question, however.

Positions with clients   The AICPA permits its members to be associated with the financial statements of charitable, religious, or civic organizations if they are directors or trustees of such organizations. These directorships or trustee positions must be purely honorary, must include only the use of the members' names, and must not involve participation in management functions.

Accounting services for audit clients   Under certain conditions, CPAs can perform auditing and bookkeeping services for the same client. In light of the stringent rules on financial, managerial, and employee relationships, one might wonder why the AICPA considers auditing and bookkeeping for the same client to be compatible. Would auditors not lose their independence if they create the representations they audit? How can a person be objective in auditing his or her own work?

The rationale for allowing such a relationship may lie in the fact that auditors judge the fairness of presentation of the results of management's operating decisions, not the wisdom of the decisions.

The conditions that must be met before CPAs can audit representations created by their own bookkeeping are as follows:

1. The CPA must not have any conflict of interest that would impair his or her objectivity.

2. Management must know enough about the operations and financial condition to be able to accept responsibility for the financial statements.

3. The CPA must not assume the role of employee or manager, that is, have custody of assets or exercise authority on behalf of the client.

4. The CPA must still make sufficient tests and conduct the audit in accordance with generally accepted auditing standards.

The SEC does not allow this auditor/bookkeeping relationship. According to SEC regulations, auditors lose their independence if they maintain the accounting records of clients.

Auditors' independence and management consulting services Another issue related to independence must be explored—the question of whether CPAs lose their independence when they perform management consulting services for their audit clients. As pointed out in Chapter 1, management consulting services are a special type of service in which the CPA furnishes aid and advice on some aspect of a company's operations. Examples are design of a computer system, installation of budgeting techniques, and implementation of inventory control procedures. Unlike an audit, management consulting services do not include an opinion on the fairness of financial statements.

Management consulting services range from functions that have some financial base or relationship, such as the installation of a responsibility accounting system or a computerized billing system to services further removed from the accounting records, such as merger assistance, actuarial services, executive recruiting, office layout, and personal financial planning.

Of the foregoing examples, executive recruiting seems to be the most potentially damaging to independence in appearance, and perhaps independence in fact. The public might not believe an accounting firm could recommend an individual as a client's controller and later be completely objective in its review of the controller's work. The public might believe that the accounting firm would rather overlook certain errors during an audit than suffer the embarrassment of having recommended a less than competent individual.

The AICPA takes the position that no impairment of independence occurs when management consulting services are confined to advice rather than management decisions. Some members of the accounting profession do not believe that the AICPA position fully answers the difficult questions. How can CPAs truly conduct an independent audit of a computer system, for example, when they have helped the client design that system? At the present time, the general consensus is that it can be done if a CPA insists on a proper arrangement of roles.[2]

Client litigation   Under certain conditions, independence may be impaired if an audit client starts or indicates an intention to start litigation against the CPA conducting the audit. To understand why the AICPA takes this position, consider two essential features of an audit:

1. Audit clients must be willing to disclose all aspects of their business operations to auditors.

2. Auditors, in turn, must be objective in their appraisal of clients' financial reporting decisions.

Actual or threatened litigation against the auditor could make it difficult for these two essential features to exist. The same potential impairment to independence could exist if there is actual or threatened litigation by the auditor.

All actual or threatened litigation does not impair independence, however. Disputes over the proper amount of a bill for services does not impair independence if the amounts are immaterial to the CPA's firm and to the client's financial statements.

Rule 102. Integrity and Objectivity   This rule is very general and consists of the following short paragraph.

> In the performance of any professional service, a member shall maintain objectivity and integrity and shall not knowingly misrepresent facts or subordinate his or her judgment to others. In tax practice, a member may resolve doubt in favor of the client as long as the position taken has reasonable support.

The rule applies to all members of the AICPA who perform professional services.

Tax practitioners often face a difficult task of deciding whether to accept all of the tax data presented to them by a client or to reject some of the data (e.g., refuse to classify an expenditure as deductible). The last sentence in this rule is intended to provide some guidance and to caution the tax practitioner that reasonable support must exist for questions to be resolved in favor of the tax client.

Rule 201. General Standards   The following rule established general standards as a part of the code of professional ethics.

---

[2] A contrary position is expressed by Mautz and Sharaf in *The Philosophy of Auditing*. In this publication, the authors state, "Management wants the advice and intends to use it; advice is sought and paid for to be followed, not to be ignored. It seems folly indeed to separate advising and judgment making."

A member and a member's firm shall comply with the following standards and with any interpretations thereof by bodies designated by Council.

- A. Professional Competence.   Undertake only those professional services that the member or the firm can reasonably expect to complete with professional competence.
- B. Due Professional Care.   Exercise due professional care in the performance of professional services.
- C. Planning and Supervision.   Adequately plan and supervise the performance of professional services.
- D. Sufficient Relevant Data.   Obtain sufficient relevant data to afford a reasonable basis for conclusions or recommendations in relation to any professional services performed.

The similarity between these standards and some of the auditing standards discussed in Chapter 1 should be evident. All of the above standards, however, are applicable to all AICPA members.

If CPAs do not believe they possess the knowledge to do a competent and complete job on an engagement, they need not immediately refer the engagement to someone else. The CPA may first attempt to acquire this competence with additional research and consultation. If the necessary competence cannot be gained in this way, the CPA should refer the engagement to or work with someone else who has the necessary competence. The other general standards are self-evident.

Rule 202. Compliance with Standards   To broaden members' responsibilities for upholding the standards beyond that associated with auditing services, the following rule was adopted.

A member who performs auditing, review, compilation, management advisory, tax, or other professional services for which standards have been promulgated by bodies designated by Council shall comply with such standards.

Under this rule, all members of the AICPA must adhere to the standards in all the areas of services mentioned above.

Rule 203. Accounting Principles   Here is another rule that applies to all AICPA members who perform audits and certain other services (such as review services discussed in Chapter 21).

A member shall not (1) express an opinion or state affirmatively that the financial statements or other financial data of any entity are presented in conformity with generally accepted accounting principles or (2) state that he or she is not aware of any material modifications that should be made to such statements or data in order for them to be in conformity with generally accepted accounting principles, if such statements or data contain any departure from an accounting principle promulgated by bodies designated by Council to establish such principles that has a material effect on the statements or data taken as a whole. If, however, the statements or data contain such a departure and the member can demonstrate that due to unusual circumstances the financial statements or data would otherwise have been misleading, the member can comply with the rule by describing the departure, its approximate effects, if practicable, and the reasons why compliance with the principle would result in a misleading statement.

The bodies designated to establish accounting principles are the Financial Accounting Standards Board (FASB) and the Governmental Accounting Standards Board (GASB). Before the establishment of these boards, certain committees of the AICPA issued pronouncements on generally accepted accounting principles. These pronouncements are Accounting Research Bulletins and Accounting Principles Board Opinions; they are authoritative until superseded.

Under limited circumstances, members can express unqualified opinions on financial statements that utilize accounting principles other than those described above. Here are some exceptional circumstances that may necessitate the use of nonauthoritative accounting principles by an audit client:

1. New legislation.

2. The evolution of a new form of business transaction.

However, the following are not exceptional circumstances:

1. An unusual degree of materiality.

2. The existence of conflicting industry practices.

The essence of Rule 203 that applies to audits is this: Audit clients must present financial statements in accordance with standards of designated bodies before CPAs can express an opinion that such statements are in conformity with generally accepted accounting principles. Some exceptions are allowed, however, if the auditor believes they are necessary to keep the financial statements from being misleading. Such exceptions are presumed to be rare, and the burden of proof is on the auditor to show that the exceptions are justified.

Rule 301. Confidential Client Information   CPAs have a dual responsibility to their clients and to the public. They must have professional concern for their clients' best interests and at the same time serve the public by maintaining their independence, integrity, and objectivity.

A good example of this dual responsibility is the CPA's obligation of *confidentiality*. Information about the client's affairs that is acquired during an engagement should be held in confidence. But the CPA should not use this obligation of confidentiality as a reason to accept a client's inadequate disclosures in financial statements. A CPA who can satisfactorily balance these two obligations is successfully serving both the client and the public.

The concept of confidentiality is well illustrated with this rule.

> A member shall not disclose any confidential client information without the specific consent of the client.

> This rule shall not be construed (1) to relieve a member of the member's professional obligations under Rules 202 and 203, (2) to affect in any way the member's obligation to comply with a validly issued and enforceable subpoena or summons, (3) to prohibit review of a member's professional practice under AICPA or state CPA society authorization, or (4) to preclude a member from initiating a complaint with or responding to any inquiry made by a recognized investigative or disciplinary body.

> Members of a recognized investigative or disciplinary body and professional practice reviewers shall not use to their own advantage or disclose any member's confidential client information that comes to their attention in carrying out their official responsibilities. However, this prohibition shall not restrict the exchange of information with a recognized investigative or disciplinary body or affect, in any way, compliance with a validly issued and enforceable subpoena or summons.

Though the concept of independence is unique to a CPA's services, the notion of confidentiality is not. Members of all professions are expected to use discretion in disclosing information that they acquire from clients. Lawyers should not reveal the results of their confidential conversations with civil or criminal clients. Medical doctors are obligated to keep secret any sensitive facts gathered from their patients. Also, certain members of the clergy are sworn to secrecy about facts learned during the course of their duties.

A CPA, like members of these other professions, acquires confidential information during the course of audits, tax return preparations, and management consulting engagements. If this confidence were to be broken, the CPA's credibility would drop and clients would no longer be willing to allow him or her access to the records that are necessary to carry out engagements. Consider, for example, the damage that could result if a CPA revealed details of a firm's payroll or a plan to acquire property for plant expansion.

The CPA's obligation of confidentiality does not extend to incomplete or improper disclosure in the financial statements, however. If auditors discover that a lawsuit levied against the client is unsettled at the report date and that its possible consequences are material to the financial statements under examination, they should reveal this finding in their report.

A major problem arises when a CPA learns, during the course of an engagement, that a client apparently has broken a law. Assume, for instance, that a CPA discovers, while preparing a tax return, that the client has failed to file returns for previous years. What should the CPA do? Is there a "higher" duty to breach the rule of confidentiality and inform the Internal Revenue Service of the omission? According to official guidelines of the AICPA, the answer is ''no'' unless the client grants permission. As a practical matter, CPAs would be well advised to withdraw from an engagement if they advise their client to go voluntarily to the IRS and the client refuses to do so.

Generally, CPAs do not enjoy the same protection on confidentiality as that possessed by members of certain other professions (legal, medical, etc.). CPAs can and have been required to disclose confidential client information in court proceedings. On the other hand, professions enjoying *privileged communications* cannot be required to reveal information received from a client, even in a court of law.

Rule 302. Contingent Fees CPAs are expected to provide services in a competent manner and are expected to charge fees that are appropriate to these services. Unlike some other professionals, however, CPAs are not allowed to make their fees contingent on their findings or on the result of their services when the engagement is one that requires independence (an audit being a classic example).

Thus, the code of professional ethics contains this rule.

A member in public practice who performs engagements for a *contingent fee* would be considered to have lost independence with regard to that client because a common financial interest has been established.

Fees are not regarded as being contingent if fixed by courts or other public authorities.

A wide variety of net income figures can be produced in financial statements, depending on which accounting methods are followed. Even though the statements belong to the client, auditors are in a position to influence the financial results. For example, auditors will ask the client to record adjusting entries if they believe the amounts or classifications of items in the financial statements are improper and are material. If the audit fee were based on financial statement results (net income), one can easily imagine the temptation for an auditor to ''overlook'' an adjustment that would lower profit.

Such a rule is unique to the accounting profession because of the requirement of auditor independence. Lawyers are allowed to collect a percentage of the amounts gained for their clients in civil suits. This practice is permissible because lawyers act as advocates for their clients and are expected to place the clients' interests above the interests of other parties. In contrast, auditors are expected to report on the fairness of financial statements read by third-party groups that have an economic interest in such statements.

Rule 501. Acts Discreditable   This rule is self-explanatory as shown below.

> A member shall not commit an act discreditable to the profession.

Rule 502. Advertising and Other Forms of Solicitation   A rule that has been historically controversial and that has been radically changed in recent years is the one on advertising and other forms of solicitation. Here is the rule in its current form.

> A member shall not seek to obtain clients by advertising or other forms of solicitation in a manner that is false, misleading, or deceptive. Solicitation by the use of coercion, overreaching, or harassing conduct is prohibited.

Until 1978, the AICPA had a rule that prohibited most forms of advertising and solicitation commonly practiced by commercial organizations. Certain forms of newspaper advertising by individual CPA firms were considered improper. Generally, the accounting profession believed that open advertising and solicitation did not create a professional public image. Clients were to be obtained through professional contacts and a sound reputation for quality services.

In the 1970s the possibility of antitrust action by the U.S. Department of Justice persuaded the AICPA to amend the rule that had been in effect for almost 60 years. The rule stated that advertising and solicitation were not in the public interest and were prohibited. The new rule, as shown above, permits normal types of advertising and solicitation.

As a result of this significant rule change, any type of advertising media can be used to show the following:

1. Information about the CPA and the CPA's firm, such as names and addresses of partners, services offered by the firm, and educational and professional attainments by the firm's members.

2. Policy or position statements related to public accounting or matters of public interest (a CPA firm's position on a pending congressional bill, for example).

However, there are some activities that CPAs might consider to be false, misleading, or deceptive such as those that:

1. Create false or unjustified expectations of favorable results.

2. Imply the ability to influence any court, tribunal, regulatory agency, or similar body or official.

3. Consist of self-laudatory statements that are not based on verifiable facts.

4. Make comparisons with other CPAs that are not based on verifiable facts.

5. Imply that certain fees or fee ranges will be charged when it is likely that such fees would be substantially increased and the prospective client was not told of that likelihood.

6. Contain any other representations that would be likely to cause a reasonable person to misunderstand or be deceived.

The pre-1978 rule on advertising and solicitation contained specific prohibitions and tended to be general about what actions were permitted. The current rule is general about those acts that are prohibited. The following acts are likely to be considered false, misleading, or deceptive by many CPAs.

1. A CPA firm advertises that it can obtain a reduced tax liability for tax clients because some of its members are former employees of the Internal Revenue Service.

2. A CPA firm advertises that it has larger clients than its in-town competition and this assertion is not verifiable. (Presumably, a verifiable advertisement that a CPA firm has more public clients than in-town competition is acceptable.)

3. A CPA firm advertises cheaper fees than its competition. Prospective clients have not been told that the CPA firm cannot make a profit on the engagement using the proposed fees. The fees almost certainly will be increased before the engagement is completed.

As can be seen, the current rule on advertising and other forms of solicitation is liberal, however, good judgment and a belief in the reputation of the profession as a whole is encouraged both by the AICPA and state CPA organizations.

To underscore this belief, the AICPA board of directors published the following statement on direct, uninvited solicitation.

The relaxation of ethics pertaining to solicitation, including advertising, has resulted in increasing competition in the profession. Excesses in those competitive practices could jeopardize adherence to technical and ethical standards. Adherence to those standards in combination with the assumption of personal responsibility, independence and self-restraint is the foundation upon which the profession rests.

The Board believes that members should exercise appropriate restraint if they elect to engage in the commercial practices of advertising and solicitation. Such self-restraint can be exercised through the application of common sense, good taste, moderation, and individual responsibility. This exercise of self-restraint contributes to adherence to technical and ethical standards and, as a result, serves the public interest.

This statement is not intended to enlarge upon the prohibition against false, misleading, or deceptive solicitation set forth by Rule 502. Accordingly, conduct which does not violate that rule will not be deemed unprofessional, nor will it subject the member to disciplinary action.

Rule 503. Commissions   In a further attempt to discourage potential conflicts of interest in rendering services to clients, the code of professional ethics contains this rule.

The acceptance of a payment for referral of products or services of others by a member in public practice is considered to create a conflict of interest that results in a loss of objectivity and independence except under those circumstances where bodies designated by Council have determined that such conflicts of interest do not arise.

A member shall not make a payment to obtain a client. This rule shall not prohibit payments for the purchase of an accounting practice or retirement payments to individuals formerly engaged in the practice of public accounting or payments to their heirs or estates.

For example, assume that a CPA arranged for a client to purchase an interest in a tax shelter. If the organizer of the tax shelter was also a client, would it be acceptable for the CPA to accept a commission to compensate for this referral? Many CPAs believe that the acceptance of a *commission* would violate Rule 503 because the CPA may base his or her recommendation on the size of the commission rather than the best interests of the client.

Rule 505. Form of Practice and Name   The last listed rule of performance and behavior is intended to assure that the form of practice and the names of CPA firms remain professional and are in keeping with the spirit of the code of ethics. Here is the rule.

A member may practice public accounting only in the form of a proprietorship, a partnership, or a professional corporation whose characteristics conform to resolutions of Council.

A member shall not practice public accounting under a firm name that is misleading. Names of one or more past partners or shareholders may be included in the firm name of a successor partnership or corporation. Also, a partner or shareholder surviving the death or withdrawal of all other partners or shareholders may continue to practice under such name which includes the name of past partners or shareholders for up to two years after becoming a sole practitioner.

A firm may not designate itself as "Members of the American Institute of Certified Public Accountants" unless all of its partners or shareholders are members of the Institute.

Practice in corporate form is allowed if certain stipulations of the Council of the AICPA are met. Some of the more important stipulations are that all shareholders must be CPAs, transfer of shares can be made only to a CPA, and non-CPA directors or officers cannot exercise any professional authority. One purpose of this rule is to ensure that CPAs who offer one or more types of services rendered by public accountants obey the code of ethics. This adherence to the code is necessary even if the CPA engages in public accounting and participates in the operation of a separate business with non-CPAs. The CPA cannot avoid an obligation to obey the code simply because the separate business does not refer to itself as a public accounting practice. If the separate business offers public accounting–type services, the CPA must adhere to the provisions of the code and is also responsible for adherence by non-CPA members of the same business.

There is no list of public accounting–type services. Certainly, auditing, tax, management consulting services, and accounting services fall into this category. Members in public practice are well advised to inquire with the AICPA and state associations before forming an affiliation that may or may not fall under the definition of public accounting.

Summary

1. CPAs, as well as members of other professions, operate in a special environment; the personal nature of their services makes them subject to special rules.

2. It is not enough for CPAs merely to act "within the law," for many actions that are considered unethical are legal. Contingent fees are an example.

3. In many cases, the guidelines by which CPAs are expected to conduct themselves are not simple and clear-cut, and judgment must be exercised. To illustrate, consider the decision auditors should make in disclosing certain sensitive information in their report. The rule on confidentiality must be balanced against the full disclosure requirement of generally accepted accounting principles.

One impression that should not be given (which is difficult to avoid in this type of discussion) is that CPAs are frequently subjected to disciplinary measures. This is not the case. CPAs can and do avoid most ethical problems simply by using good professional judgment in their relations with clients, colleagues, and others.

If CPAs have any doubt as to the propriety of their actions, they can consult the AICPA, their state society, or their state board and usually receive an answer. If their past actions are discovered to have been improper, immediate corrective measures may be sufficient.

The purpose of this chapter (and Chapters 1 and 4) is to provide background for the technical material that follows by discussing the environment in which auditors operate. In succeeding chapters, these concepts are drawn on to place the function of auditing in its proper perspective.

Appendix to Chapter 3

The Institute of Internal Auditors, Inc. Code of Ethics*

To provide a basis of comparison with the *AICPA Code of Professional Ethics,* we are reprinting *The Institute of Internal Auditors, Inc. Code of Ethics.* The provisions of this Code of Ethics cover basic principles in the various disciplines of internal auditing practice. Members shall realize that individual judgment is required in the application of these principles. They have a responsibility to conduct themselves so that their good faith and integrity should not be open to question. While having due regard for the limit of their technical skills, they will promote the highest possible internal auditing standards to the end of advancing the interest of their company or organization.

Articles

I. Members shall have an obligation to exercise honesty, objectivity, and diligence in the performance of their duties and responsibilities.

II. Members, in holding the trust of their employers, shall exhibit loyalty in all matters pertaining to the affairs of the employer or to whomever they may be rendering a service. However, members shall not knowingly be a part of any illegal or improper activity.

III. Members shall refrain from entering into any activity which may be in conflict with the interest of their employers or which would prejudice their ability to carry out objectively their duties and responsibilities.

IV. Members shall not accept a fee or a gift from an employee, a client, a customer, or a business associate of their employer without the knowledge and consent of their senior management.

*Reprinted by permission of The Institute of Internal Auditors, Inc., 249 Maitland Avenue, Altamonte Springs, Fla. 32701.

V. Members shall be prudent in the use of information acquired in the course of their duties. They shall not use confidential information for any personal gain nor in a manner which would be detrimental to the welfare of their employer.

VI. Members, in expressing an opinion, shall use all reasonable care to obtain sufficient factual evidence to warrant such expression. In their reporting, members shall reveal such material facts known to them, which, if not revealed, could either distort the report of the results of operations under review or conceal unlawful practice.

VII. Members shall continually strive for improvement in the proficiency and effectiveness of their service.

VIII. Members shall abide by the bylaws and uphold the objectives of *The Institute of Internal Auditors, Inc.* In the practice of their profession, they shall be ever mindful of their obligation to maintain the high standard of competence, morality, and dignity which *The Institute of Internal Auditors, Inc.,* and its members have established.

Chapter 3
Glossary of Terms

(listed in the order of appearance in the chapter, with accompanying page references where the term is discussed)

Term	*Page in Chapter*
Commercialism as used in this chapter, an excessive concern about the business aspects of a CPA firm's operations at the expense of the professional and public interest aspects.	75
Anderson Report a report of the Special Committee on Standards of Professional Conduct for Certified Public Accountants. The report contains a proposed new code of professional ethics.	76
Concepts of Professional Ethics the part of the old AICPA Code of Professional Ethics that consisted of nonenforceable suggestions on proper behavior for members.	76

Term	*Page in Chapter*
Commission an amount paid to obtain a client or the acceptance of an amount for a referral to a client of products or services of others.	93

Chapter 3
References

Anderson, George D. "A Fresh Look at Standards of Professional Conduct," *Journal of Accountancy* (September 1985), pp. 91–106.

Anderson, George D. "Restructuring Professional Standards: The Anderson Report," *Journal of Accountancy* (September 1986), pp. 92–104.

Burton, John C. "A Critical Look at Professionalism and Scope of Services," *Journal of Accountancy* (April 1980), pp. 48–56.

Burton, John C., and Fairfield, Patricia. "Auditing Evolution in a Changing Environment," *Auditing: A Journal of Practice & Theory* (Winter 1982), pp. 1–22.

Elliott, Merle S., and Kuttner, Monroe S. "MAS:Coming of Age," *Journal of Accountancy* (December 1982), pp. 66–74.

Firth, Michael. "Perceptions of Auditor Independence and Official Ethical Guidelines," *The Accounting Review* (July 1980), pp. 451–466.

Olson, Wallace E. "What Is Auditor Independence?" *Journal of Accountancy* (April 1980), pp. 80–82.

Pany, Kurt, and Reckers, Philip M. J. "The Effect of Gifts, Discounts, and Client Size on Perceived Auditor Independence," *The Accounting Review* (January 1980), pp. 50–61.

Reckers, Philip M. J., and Stagliano, A. J. "Non-Audit Services and Perceived Independence: Some New Evidence," *Auditing: A Journal of Practice & Theory* (Summer 1981), pp. 23–37.

Report of the Special Committee on Standards of Professional Conduct for Certified Public Accountants—Restructuring Professional Standards to Achieve Professional Excellence in a Changing Environment. New York: American Institute of Certified Public Accountants, 1986.

Sack, Robert J. "Commercialism in the Profession: A Threat to Be Managed," *Journal of Accountancy* (October 1985), pp. 125–134.

Chapter 3
Review Questions

3-1. In what four ways was the auditor's ethical environment "restrictive" during most of the 1960s?

3-2. What were the positive and negative aspects of the changes that occurred in the auditor's ethical environment during the 1970s and 1980s?

3-3. Give two reasons why the accounting profession believed that the Code of Professional Ethics needed to be changed.

3-4. Name and briefly explain the four parts of the old code of professional ethics.

3-5. What is the basic structure of the new code of professional ethics? (*Hint:* Refer to Figure 3.2.)

3-6. Name and briefly describe the purpose of each of the ten sections of the Standards of Professional Conduct.

3-7. Describe two relationships between auditors and clients that are prohibited by the AICPA because independence will be impaired.

3-8. What is a direct financial interest?

3-9. What four conditions must be met before CPAs can audit representations created by their own bookkeeping?

3-10. Under what conditions will there be no impairment of independence when CPAs offer management consulting services to audit clients?

3-11. Why may litigation with a client impair independence?

3-12.   Under what conditions may a member in tax practice resolve doubt in favor of the client?

3-13.   What four areas are covered by the rule on general standards?

3-14.   Under what conditions may members express unqualified opinions on financial statements that utilize accounting principles other than those issued by authoritative bodies?

3-15.   What dual responsibility does a CPA have in relation to the concept of confidentiality?

3-16.   State the rule on confidentiality.

3-17.   State the rule on contingent fees.

3-18.   State the rule on advertising and other forms of solicitation.

3-19.   State the rule on commissions.

3-20.   What is the AICPA trying to discourage with the rule on commissions?

3-21.   What is the purpose of the rule on the form of practice and name?

Chapter 3
Objective Questions Taken from CPA Examinations

---

*3-22.   During the 1970s and 1980s, all of the rules of ethical behavior listed below were either substantially modified or eliminated except
a. Advertising and solicitation.
b. Independence.
c. Competitive bidding.
d. Practice in corporate form.

*Not a CPA examination question.

*3-23.   All of the following were part of the structure of the old code of professional ethics except
   a. Concepts.
   b. Rules of Conduct.
   c. Rules of Performance and Behavior.
   d. Interpretations.

*3-24.   All of the following are part of the structure of the new code of professional ethics except
   a. Standards of Professional Conduct.
   b. Rules of Conduct.
   c. Rules of Performance and Behavior.
   d. Interpretations of rules by senior technical committees of the AICPA.

*3-25.   The Standards of Professional Conduct bear the greatest resemblance to
   a. The Concepts of Professional Ethics.
   b. The Rules of Conduct.
   c. Interpretations.
   d. Ethics Rulings.

3-26.   Fenn & Co., CPAs, has time available on a computer, which it uses primarily for its own internal record keeping. Aware that the computer facilities of Delta Equipment Co., one of Fenn's audit clients, are inadequate for the company needs, Fenn offers to maintain on its computer certain routine accounting records for Delta. If Delta were to accept the offer and Fenn were to continue to function as independent auditor for Delta, then Fenn would be in violation of
   a. SEC, but not AICPA, provisions pertaining to auditors' independence.
   b. Both SEC and AICPA provisions pertaining to auditors' independence.
   c. AICPA, but not SEC, provisions pertaining to auditors' independence.
   d. Neither AICPA nor SEC provisions pertaining to auditors' independence.

3-27.   A CPA, while performing an audit, strives to achieve independence in appearance in order to
   a. Reduce risk and liability.
   b. Maintain public confidence in the profession.
   c. Become independent in fact.
   d. Comply with the generally accepted standards of field work.

*Not a CPA examination question.

3-28.   In which of the following instances would the independence of the CPA not be considered to be impaired? The CPA has been retained as the auditor of a brokerage firm

a. Which owes the CPA audit fees for more than one year.

b. In which the CPA has a large active margin account.

c. In which the CPA's brother is the controller.

d. Which owes the CPA audit fees for current-year services and has just filed a petition for bankruptcy.

3-29.   In which of the following instances would the independence of the CPA not be considered to be impaired? The CPA has been retained as the auditor of a

a. Charitable organization in which an employee of the CPA serves as treasurer.

b. Municipality in which the CPA owns $25,000 of the $2,500,000 indebtedness of the municipality.

c. Cooperative apartment house in which the CPA owns an apartment and is not part of the management.

d. Company in which the CPA's-investment club owns a one-tenth interest.

3-30.   An audit independence issue might be raised by the auditor's participation in management consulting services engagements. Which of the following statements is most consistent with the profession's attitude toward this issue?

a. Information obtained as a result of a management consulting services engagement is confidential to that specific engagement and should not influence performance of the attest function.

b. The decision as to loss of independence must be made by the client based on the facts of the particular case.

c. The auditor should not make management decisions for an audit client.

d. The auditor who is asked to review management decisions is also competent to make these decisions and can do so without loss of independence.

3-31.   In determining independence with respect to any audit engagement, the ultimate decision as to whether or not the auditor is independent must be made by the

a. Auditor.

b. Client.

c. Audit committee.

d. Public.

3-32.   Inclusion of which of the following in a promotional brochure published by a CPA firm would be most likely to be considered by many CPAs to be a violation of the AICPA Rules of Performance and Behavior?

a. Reprints of newspaper articles that are laudatory with respect to the firm's expertise.

    b. Services offered and fees for such services, including hourly rates and fixed fees.

    c. Educational and professional attainments of partners.

    d. Comparison of the firm's quality with another firm's quality.

3-33.   According to the AICPA Code of Professional Ethics, a CPA who has a financial interest in a partnership that invests in a potential client is considered to have

    a. An indirect financial interest in the client.

    b. A direct financial interest in the client.

    c. No financial interest in the client.

    d. A partial financial interest in the client.

3-34.   In which of the following circumstances would a CPA who audits XM Corporation lack independence?

    a. The CPA and XM's president are both on the board of directors of COD Corporation.

    b. The CPA and XM's president each own 25 percent of FOB Corporation, a closely held company.

    c. The CPA has a home mortgage from XM, which is a savings and loan organization.

    d. The CPA reduced XM's usual audit fee by 40 percent because XM's financial condition was unfavorable.

3-35.   A CPA purchased stock in a client corporation and placed it in a trust as an educational fund for the CPA's minor child. The trust securities were not material to the CPA but were material to the child's personal net worth. Would the independence of the CPA be considered to be impaired with respect to the client?

    a. Yes, because the stock would be considered a direct financial interest and, consequently, materiality is not a factor.

    b. Yes, because the stock would be considered an indirect financial interest that is material to the CPA's child.

    c. No, because the CPA would not be considered to have a direct financial interest in the client.

    d. No, because the CPA would not be considered to have a material indirect financial interest in the client.

3-36.   Clark, CPA, wishes to express an opinion that the financial statements of Smith Co. are presented in conformity with generally accepted accounting principles; however, the financial statements contain a departure from APB Opinion No. 5.

    a. Under any circumstances, Clark would be in violation of the Code of Professional Ethics if he were to issue such an opinion.

    b. Clark should disclaim an opinion.

c. Clark may issue the opinion he desires if he can demonstrate that because of unusual circumstances the financial statements of Smith Co. would otherwise have been misleading.

d. This specific situation is not covered by the rules established by the Code of Professional Ethics.

3-37.   The AICPA Code of Professional Ethics states that a CPA shall not disclose any confidential information obtained in the course of a professional engagement except with the specific consent of his or her client. In which one of the situations given below would disclosure by a CPA be in violation of the code?

a. Disclosing confidential information in order to properly discharge the CPA's responsibilities in accordance with professional standards.

b. Disclosing confidential information in compliance with a subpoena issued by a court.

c. Disclosing confidential information to another accountant interested in purchasing the CPA's practice.

d. Disclosing confidential information in a review of the CPA's professional practice by the AICPA Quality Review Committee.

3-38.   The AICPA Code of Professional Ethics states that a CPA shall not disclose any confidential information obtained in the course of a professional engagement except with the consent of the client. This rule should be understood to preclude a CPA from responding to an inquiry made by

a. The trial board of the AICPA.

b. An investigative body of a state CPA society.

c. A CPA-shareholder of the client corporation.

d. An AICPA voluntary quality review body.

3-39.   The CPA should not undertake an engagement that requires independence if his fee is to be based on

a. The findings of a tax authority.

b. A percentage of audited net income.

c. Per diem rates plus expenses.

d. Rates set by a city ordinance.

3-40.   A CPA's report on a client's balance sheet, income statement, and statement of cash flows was sent to the stockholders. The client now wishes to present only the balance sheet along with an appropriately modified auditor's report in a newspaper advertisement. The auditor may

a. Permit the publication as requested.

b. Permit only the publication of the originally issued auditor's report and accompanying financial statements.

c. Not permit publication of a modified auditor's report.

d. Not permit publication of any auditor's report in connection with a newspaper advertisement.

3-41. Many CPAs believe that the *AICPA Code of Professional Ethics* has been violated when the CPA represents that specific consulting services will be performed for a stated fee and it is apparent at the time of the representation that the
   a. Actual fee would be substantially higher.
   b. Actual fee would be substantially lower than the fees charged by other CPAs for comparable services.
   c. Fee was a competitive bid.
   d. CPA would not be independent.

3-42. Which of the following is required for a firm to designate itself "Member of the American Institute of Certified Public Accountants" on its letterhead?
   a. At least one of the partners must be a member.
   b. The partners whose names appear in the firm name must be members.
   c. All partners must be members.
   d. The firm must be a dues-paying member.

Chapter 3
Discussion/Case Questions

3-43. As a CPA, you are encountering some difficult questions from professional associates about the concept of independence. Here are some examples.
   a. Why does the accounting profession prohibit CPAs from owning any stock in audit clients? It seems highly improbable that owning 1 percent of the client's stock would actually cause auditors to lose their independence.
   b. Why are AICPA members restricted from owning any stock of audit clients, but allowed to keep books for audit clients and to become involved, to a certain extent, in providing management advice?
   c. Isn't the biggest impairment to auditors' independence the fees they receive from clients? How can auditors maintain that they are independent from companies that supply their major source of revenue?
   d. How can a CPA firm maintain independence when it audits systems that were designed by its members during the course of a management consulting engagement?
   e. Why do CPAs insist on "remaining quiet" when they observe that a client has filed improper tax returns in recent years or paid some employees less than the minimum wage? Doesn't the CPA owe a duty to society to report such events?
   f. Why is it wrong in certain circumstances for CPAs to charge fees to audit clients based on the audit findings? Wouldn't the CPA perform a better service if he or she knew that there was a chance of earning a better fee?

g. Why does the AICPA have any rule at all on advertising? Doesn't advertising promote competition and ultimately reduce fees charged to the CPAs' clients? Also, isn't advertising a good way to let the public know the types of accounting services being offered by CPAs?

h. Why does the taking of a commission for a referral of services create a potential conflict of interest?

Reply to each of these questions.

3-44.   In each of the following cases, indicate whether in your opinion there is a violation of the rule on independence of the *AICPA Code of Professional Ethics*. Support your answer.

a. A CPA is a director of a charitable organization that serves some audit clients. Part of the directors' responsibilities is to decide who will receive benefits from the charitable organization.

b. A CPA provides bookkeeping services for some small audit clients. These services include the preparation of financial statements. Some of these clients have asked the CPA to "circle the net income figure" so that this amount will be apparent to them.

c. A CPA recommends controller position descriptions for audit clients, including screening and recommending candidates to the client. All the clients have indicated that they will follow these recommendations. All CPA recommendations have been followed.

d. During an audit, the client indicates an intent to start litigation against the CPA for deficiencies in the prior year's work. The auditor decides to finish the current year's engagement.

e. A CPA owns a small percentage of stock in a company audited by another office of the CPA firm for whom he is employed. He performs audit and tax work for his firm. He has never participated in the audit of the company in which he has this small stock investment.

f. A CPA has an investment in a bank that has loaned money to an audit client. The investment is about 5 percent of the CPA's wealth.

g. A CPA is interested in serving the community. She asked the vice-president of her client to help her get an appointment to the board of directors of the United Fund. The CPA received the appointment and has devoted many hours to this activity.

h. A CPA attends a formal dinner party given by a client officer at the local country club.

i. The treasurer of a client pays for two of a CPA's lunches. Only the client's business was discussed at one lunch; no business was discussed at the other lunch.

3-45.   Savage, CPA, has been requested by an audit client to perform a nonrecurring engagement involving the implementation of an EDP information and control system. The client requests that in setting up the new system and during the period prior to conversion to the new system, Savage do the following:

1. Counsel on potential expansion of business activity plans.

2. Search for and interview new personnel.

3. Hire new personnel.

4. Train personnel.

In addition, the client requests that during the three months subsequent to the conversion, Savage do the following:

1. Supervise the operation of the new system.

2. Monitor client-prepared source documents and make changes in basic EDP-generated data as Savage may deem necessary without concurrence of the client.

Required:
Which of these services may Savage perform and which may Savage not perform and retain independence? Give reasons for your answers according to your understanding of the Code. Without regard to the Code, indicate your opinion as to whether each of these activities would affect independence.
(*AICPA Adapted*)

3-46.   For a number of years, Mr. Alserv, a CPA, has performed bookkeeping services for a corporate client, including the recording of the journal entries and the posting of the accounts. Mr. Alserv also prepared the tax returns. In partial payment for these services, the client often gave the CPA shares of stock in the company in lieu of cash.

In March 19X5, Mr. Alserv sold his accounting practice to Ms. Partserv, another CPA. Mr. Alserv agreed to stay on as a part-time employee. He also agreed to continue handling certain accounts, including the client for whom he kept books.

In April 19X5, a local bank notified this client that an audit was required in order to continue loans. Ms. Partserv asked Mr. Alserv to perform the audit, subject to the resolution of two problems:

1. The question of Mr. Alserv's stock holdings in the client company.

2. The matter of the bookkeeping that Mr. Alserv did for the client.

Mr. Alserv suggested a solution to both problems.

1. Ms. Partserv would sign the audit report as owner and Mr. Alserv would keep his stock as an employee.

2. The client could hire a part-time bookkeeper to record and post the entries. Mr. Alserv's functions would be confined to such things as making adjusting journal entries, writing up the quarterly payroll reports, and reconciling the bank accounts.

Required:
Answer the following questions.
a. What do you think of Mr. Alserv's arrangement with his client to receive stock in lieu of cash?
b. What do you think of Mr. Alserv's first suggestion? If you have any objections, suggest alternatives.
c. What do you think of Mr. Alserv's second suggestion? If you have any objections, suggest alternatives.
d. How, if at all, would your answers to Questions b and c change if the client planned to offer securities to the public?

3-47.   The president of Shambra Products has consulted you in regard to an audit. Shambra, which has never been audited, has been developing a process to convert swamp gas into natural gas. Although developments to date have been encouraging, numerous problems remain to be resolved.

The company has expended substantially all of the funds it has been able to raise to date, and an audit is needed in connection with further attempts to raise money from a stock or debt offering. The company does not have sufficient funds to pay for an audit now, but it will be able to pay if additional financing is acquired. Although the company is small at the present time, it has the potential for becoming one of the largest companies in the nation if it is successful in developing its process.

Should you accept the audit of Shambra Products? If so, why? If not, why not?

3-48.   Judy Hanlon, CPA, prepared the federal income tax return for the Guild Corporation for the year ended December 31, 19X5. This was Ms. Hanlon's first engagement for this client.

Ms. Hanlon found a significant error on the 19X4 return. She reported this error to Guild's controller, the officer responsible for tax returns. The controller stated "Let the revenue agent find the error." The controller offered to furnish Ms. Hanlon with a letter assuming full responsibility for the error and his refusal to change it.

Required:
Answer the following questions, giving reasons for your answers.
a. Would Ms. Hanlon have acted properly to accept the letter and take no further action?

b. Would Ms. Hanlon have acted properly to take this information to the IRS?

c. What course of action should Ms. Hanlon have taken?

3-49.   Mr. Meek discovers that an audit client has a pending lawsuit against it for a significant sum of money. If the lawsuit is lost, the client's assets will be reduced by a substantial amount. Mr. Meek suggests to the client that a contingent liability should be disclosed in the audited financial statements. The client objects for two reasons.

1. The subject of the lawsuit is highly sensitive. Revealing its contents would be a breach of the auditor's rule on confidential client information.

2. Disclosure of the liability in the financial statements would provide the plaintiff with evidence of admission of a liability. Disclosure of the liability could damage the client's case in the lawsuit.

Required:
Reply to both of the client's points.

3-50.   During the course of an audit, Fred Curious, the senior assigned to the job, noticed that several employees were paid at a rate less than that required by the federal minimum wage law. He checked into this matter and found that the company was engaged in interstate commerce, which means that all employees are subject to the federal minimum wage law.

He decided to tell the company controller, feeling that the violation was probably an oversight and could be corrected easily. However, the controller was irritated when told of this situation by the senior. She informed Mr. Curious that this matter had nothing to do with the audit and that it should be dropped.

Mr. Curious took his information to the CPA firm's partner in charge of the audit. The partner showed concern for the senior's feelings, but was reluctant to do anything about it. He suggested that Mr. Curious make a notation of the underpayment in his working papers and assured Mr. Curious that, as partner, he would take full responsibility.

Required:
a. If you were Mr. Curious, what position would you take about the partner's suggestions?
b. What position should the partner have taken when he learned of this situation? What action should he have taken?
c. Answer this question without regard for the *Code of Professional Ethics.* Do you think that Mr. Curious or the audit partner, or both, should take this matter directly to the applicable federal authorities?

3-51.   During the audit of Park Co., a bottler and distributor of "Marshwater" soft drink, your discussion with the financial vice-president reveals that the company is paying rebates to certain of its larger customers for carrying Marshwater. The financial vice-president is reluctant to discuss the rebates and tells you that information regarding them is confidential and cannot be discussed further. He points out that your Code of Ethics requires you to respect confidentiality.

Discuss what, if any, further action you would take on this matter.

3-52. During the course of his audit, Mr. Atest discovered that the clerical work in the Accounting Department was very slow and inefficient. It occurred to him that a computer system might increase the efficiency of operations. Therefore, he orally recommended such a system.

Mr. Atest's knowledge of computers was very limited, so he referred the client to Mr. Consult, a fellow CPA, who had a good reputation in this area. Arrangements were made and the consulting engagement was started.

The client seemed to be quite pleased with Mr. Consult's work, and when she learned that Mr. Consult also conducted audits, she suggested that Mr. Consult take over both the audit and any future consulting engagement. Mr. Consult hesitated to do this, but after considerable urging from the client, he accepted the offer.

During the course of the computer study, Mr. Consult virtually supervised the installation of new equipment and wrote all of the system documentation. Whenever he spoke to the client controller about his recommendations, the controller would reply that the matter was strictly up to Mr. Consult because no one else in the firm knew anything about computers.

Required:
Did Mr. Consult violate the code of ethics in any manner?

3-53. You are a member of a quality control committee of your local state society. You are reviewing the work of a CPA who practices in your state. In recent years numerous oral complaints have been made against him by other CPAs in the same locality.

During the course of your investigation, you learn the following about Mr. Quest, the CPA against whom complaints have been made.

a. Mr. Quest started his business by soliciting interviews with clients of other CPAs in the same city. During the course of the interviews, he indicated that he could perform the same services as his competitors at a lower fee and with the same quality. He was factual about his own background and qualifications.

b. Mr. Quest managed to find out how much his competitors were charging for audit fees and consistently bid a lower price. He was successful in obtaining some of the audits.

c. During the audits Mr. Quest continued to keep the books and prepare the financial statements of the new clients. In many cases the clients had never kept books or prepared financial statements.

d. Mr. Quest recommended that the controllers of some new audit clients be discharged and replaced by people that he knew and considered to be better qualified.

e. Mr. Quest learned that some of his new audit clients had not filed tax returns for several years. He took this information to the board of directors.

f. Mr. Quest paid a referral commission to obtain some of his audit clients. However, his fee schedule was based on the number of hours spent on the audit and did not include any part of the commission.

g. Mr. Quest's tax fees were based on the amount of reduction in tax liability he could obtain for his clients; that is, he charged a larger fee if he reduced the taxes of his clients below what he believed the amount would have been if another CPA had prepared the tax return.

h. Mr. Quest advertised all of his audit, tax, and management consulting services specialities in the local newspaper.

i. The name of Mr. Quest's firm is "Quest for the Best, CPA."

Required:

a. Write a report indicating which of these actions you consider to be acceptable and which ones you consider to be violations of the *Rules of Performance and Behavior* of the *AICPA Code of Professional Ethics*.

b. Without regard to the code of professional ethics, write a narrative indicating which actions you consider to be acceptable and unacceptable.

CHAPTER

The Auditor's Responsibility— Legal Environment

Learning Objectives   *After reading and studying the material in this chapter, the student should*

Know the key legal terms used to describe the relationships among auditors, clients, and third parties.

Know the major events that shaped and changed auditors' legal relationships during the last 60 years.

Understand the legal climate in which the auditor operates in the present day.

Know the current guidelines for avoiding litigation.

This chapter uses a wide variety of legal terms and descriptions of legal relationships between auditors and clients and third parties. Therefore, we believe it is necessary to introduce these terms and descriptions before discussing the auditor's legal environment and the evolution of that environment.

Legal Terms and Legal Relationships Used in the Chapter[1]

The discussion in this section will follow this sequence.

1. We will first distinguish between common law and statutory law because auditors' potential legal liability may depend on the type of law involved.

---

[1] The following articles have been particularly helpful in preparing this section, and we gratefully acknowledge the authors' contributions to the literature.

Thomas A. Gavin, Rebecca L. Hicks, and Joseph D. Decosimo, "CPAs' Liability to Third Parties," *Journal of Accountancy* (June 1984), pp. 80–88.

Thomas A. Gavin, Rebecca L. Hicks, and James H. Scheiner, "Auditors' Common Law Liability: What We Should Be Telling Our Students," *Journal of Accounting Education,* Vol. 5 (1987), pp. 1–12.

2. Next, we will define and differentiate between the degrees of negligence because the outcome of litigation often "hinges" on the types of allegations against auditors.

3. Finally, we will discuss the relationships between auditors and the parties that might bring litigation against them, specifically clients and third parties. Again, the outcome of litigation may depend on the relationships that existed between the auditor and these parties when the alleged improper acts of the auditor occurred.

Common Law and Statutory Law

Common law is based on the precedents established from past judgments of courts, judgments that were sometimes made centuries ago. Common law has its basis in English law and is applied in court cases unless statutory law, passed by a legislative body, is applicable. For example, federal securities acts passed in 1933 and 1934 may be applied in some situations rather than common law precedents established in 1931 (this example is discussed at length later in the chapter).

On the other hand *statutory law* is based on law passed by a legislative body. Statutory law offers legal recourse in addition to common law for the specific areas covered by the statutes. For instance, common law precedents may not support a lawsuit brought against an auditor by a stockholder of the auditors' client because the allegation is ordinary negligence; however, a statute may have been enacted that allows the stockholder to recover from the auditor for ordinary negligence in situations specifically covered by that statute. In this case the stockholder may bring suit under either the statute or common law, but is more likely to select the statute because the chance of success is higher.

Ordinary Negligence

Ordinary negligence is sometimes thought of as simple carelessness without any attempt to deceive or commit fraud. For example, an auditor may have forgotten to inquire about contingent liabilities. A more formal definition and one that relates to accounting is that *ordinary negligence*

> represents a lack of due care in the performance of professional accounting tasks, due care implying the use of the knowledge, skill, and judgment usually possessed by practitioners in similar practice circumstances.

Until the last 20 or 30 years, it was generally believed that plaintiffs had to have a contractual or primary beneficiary relationship to successfully sue accountants for ordinary negligence under common law.

Gross Negligence

Gross negligence is more serious than ordinary negligence but is less serious than fraud. *Gross negligence* constitutes an extreme, flagrant, or reckless departure from the standards of due care and competence in performing professional duties.

In terms of auditor responsibility, gross negligence might be thought of as actions so reckless (failure to audit several significant accounts) that the auditor had no basis to believe in the fairness of the financial statements.

Fraud

Fraud is obviously the most serious of all and, if proven, allows a wide range of plaintiffs to successfully sue the auditor. *Fraud* involves

false representation of a material fact
deliberate intent to deceive
expectation of reliance by another
justifiable reliance
resulting damages

Assume that a set of financial statements had false representations (net income grossly overstated) and the auditor with this knowledge deceived the parties using the financial statements, thus inducing them to rely on the statements. Because of justifiable reliance by the parties, there were resulting damages to the parties. An action for fraud may successfully be brought against the auditors.

Privity Relationship

This term describes the common law relationship between auditors and their clients and is the relationship with which auditors have the most first-hand knowledge. We will define *privity* as

a contractual relationship between the auditor and the client for the performance of professional services.

Generally under common law, auditors can be sued successfully for ordinary negligence, gross negligence, or fraud by the parties with whom they have a privity relationship.[2]

Primary Beneficiary Relationship

Privity does not normally exist between auditors and third parties (e.g., creditors or investors). No contract for services has been entered into between auditors and these groups. Nevertheless, a third party could have what we call a *primary beneficiary* relationship with auditors, this relationship being

---

[2] Although a client may believe that its auditor committed gross negligence or fraud, the client would normally sue for ordinary negligence because it would be easier to prove (i.e., carelessness is usually easier to prove than recklessness or intent to deceive).

one in which the auditor knows the client has specifically engaged him or her to perform an audit for the benefit of an identified third party whose reliance is the aim of the engagement.

This relationship would occur when a client asks his or her auditor to attest to financial statements to be given to an identified prospective purchaser of the client's business. In this case the prospective purchaser is the third-party primary beneficiary even though no formal contract exists with the auditor.

Under common law, third-party primary beneficiaries have recourse against auditors similar to those of clients.

Foreseen Relationship

Until relatively recent times (30 years or so), third parties that did not have a primary beneficiary relationship with the auditor were unlikely to be successful in lawsuits involving ordinary negligence under common law. The relationship between the third parties and the auditors was too distant. In other words if a bank, not specifically known to the auditor (and thus without a primary beneficiary relationship), suffered a loss as a result of using audited financial statements of the auditor's client, that bank was unlikely to win a common law case against the auditor for ordinary negligence.

However, third parties of this type are beginning to win more cases if the courts construe them to be *foreseen parties* or

parties known to, or reasonably expected to be known to, the auditor who will rely on the auditor's work in making a particular business decision (e.g., a bank loan).

There are two keys that the courts use in defining foreseen parties.

1. The auditor's knowledge of the specific party, that is, persons or limited classes of persons (a particular creditor or a particular group of creditors), and
2. The auditor's knowledge of the specific transaction or substantially similar transactions (the use of an audit report for the granting of credit by a bank to the auditor's client).

It may not always be necessary that auditors know which bank is negotiating a loan with their client. If they simply know that their client is trying to secure a bank loan and is using the audited financial statements to do so, any particular bank that is used may become a foreseen party.

Foreseeable Relationship

A constantly shifting area of common law includes court decisions involving third-party suits against auditors by *foreseeable parties,* which are users of audited financial statements that are not specifically identified or who use the statements for transactions not specifically known to the auditor, but who may reasonably be expected to see the statements and to act or refrain from acting because of reliance on them.

Although a few courts have held that foreseeable parties could sue successfully for ordinary negligence, the majority have held that an auditor would be liable only if actual or constructive fraud (gross negligence) were proven.

Commentary on Legal Concepts

It is obvious, then, that under common law the proof of gross negligence or fraud by auditors (although difficult to prove) will allow various users of audited financial statements to collect damages. It is also obvious that parties that have the close relationship of privity or primary beneficiary with auditors can collect damages in common law cases if ordinary negligence, gross negligence, or fraud can be proved.

What is not so obvious are the damages that the ''somewhat remote'' foreseen and foreseeable parties may collect from auditors if they sue for ordinary negligence in common law cases. The present trend seems to favor foreseen but not foreseeable parties.

This, then, is a summary of the important terms, concepts, and relationships we will need to help us understand the complex world of the auditor's legal environment and the auditor's ever-changing responsibilities to the public. In the remainder of the chapter, we will trace the evolution of this environment from the early part of the century to the present time, discuss certain statutory laws, analyze some landmark cases, and see ''where we came from, where we are, and where we might be headed.''

The Auditing Function in the Early Years

To help provide a comprehensive view of the change that has taken place in the auditors' concept of their responsibility, it is desirable to examine a report style used in 1915.[3]

We have audited the books and accounts of the ABC Company for the year ended December 31, 1915, and we certify that, in our opinion, the above balance sheet correctly sets forth its position as at the termination of that year, and that the accompanying profit and loss account is correct.

[3]George Cochrane, ''The Auditor's Report: Its Evolution in the U.S.A.,'' *The Accountant* (Nov. 4, 1950), pp. 448–460.

Quite a difference from the present report we studied in Chapter 1. One might wonder whether the writers of a 1915 report conducted the same type of audit. In many respects, they did not. Examinations conducted in 1915 were different from those currently conducted in the following ways.

1. There were no laws requiring an audit, because the SEC had not been established. In many cases, reports were not issued to stockholders. If an audit was needed, the management or board of directors hired the auditor and the report was addressed to them.[4]

2. The audit was often performed for management. It was viewed as a type of guarantee or certification as to the correctness of the accounts; hence, the term *certificate*.

3. The audit in some cases was a complete one: all transactions were checked. In fact, fraud detection was the avowed purpose of some audits.

4. Because large-scale investment by absentee owners had not reached to-day's volume, the audit was centered on the balance sheet. For most companies this was the only published financial statement. Net income was one figure added to retained earnings in the balance sheet.

5. The concentration was on "certifying" the account balances that were on the books. Almost complete reliance was placed on use of internal evidence, that is, evidence that originates with or is held by the client. It was not standard practice to obtain independent evidence external to the client's accounting system.

6. Accounting and reporting principles were not defined as clearly as they are today. There was a widespread impression (as there still is) that the amounts in financial statements represented exactness. Because the auditor was often acting on behalf of management and because management wanted a certificate, it was natural that the auditor would attest to the "correctness" of the statements.[5]

Changes During the 1920s

As firms began to sell more securities to the public, ownership became more distinct from management and evolved into a separate class of proprietors called

---

[4]Today, stockholders often theoretically elect the auditors, but as a practical matter they usually only approve the recommendation of the board of directors.

[5]Cochrane, "The Auditor's Report."

third-party investors. Because the purpose of audits was often to satisfy groups that had a monetary interest in the enterprise, it was only natural for auditors' obligations to shift toward those third parties. The increase in size of many corporations made it impractical to audit every transaction. As a result of these changes, auditors were forced to rely more on samples. Determination that financial statements were in accordance with accepted accounting principles began to replace fraud detection as the major purpose of the audit.

In addition, a body of generally accepted accounting principles began to be developed. In 1929, the AICPA revised a bulletin called *Approved Methods for the Preparation of Balance Sheet Statements* which was first published in 1917. It stressed that because the income statement was of primary importance to stockholders, investors, and creditors, it should be prepared in detail, including comparative figures from prior years. Also, it pointed out that auditors should study the firm's financial system and use that study as a basis for testing rather than conducting a detailed examination of every transaction. In general, this decade can be characterized as an era in which the auditor's responsibility to *third parties* began to increase.

The *Ultramares* Case—Liability for Negligence Under Common Law

A vivid illustration of this increase in responsibility occurred during the 1920s, when a creditor of a client sued a CPA firm for negligence and fraud. The effect of the court's decision was so far-reaching that even today this case is considered a landmark with regard to third-party action against an accountant under common law. Following is a summary of the facts.

Touche, Niven & Co. (now Touche, Ross & Co.) were the auditors for Fred Stern & Co.[6] An audit was performed for the year ended December 31, 1923. The accountants knew that creditors of some type would use the balance sheet, but they were not aware of the specific creditor (thus the creditor was not a primary beneficiary of the audit). The audit was completed and the following report was issued:

> We have examined the accounts of Fred Stern & Co., Inc. for the year ending December 31, 1923, and hereby certify that the annexed balance sheet is in accordance therewith and with the information and explanations given us. We further certify that, subject to provision for federal taxes on income, the said statement, in our opinion, presents a true and correct view of the financial situation of Fred Stern & Co., Inc., as at Dec. 31, 1923.[7]

[6] All large CPA firms at one time or another have been involved in litigation, and the naming of any firm in this book is no reflection on that firm.

[7] *Ultramares Corporation v. Touche* (255 N.Y. 170, 174 N.E. 441, 1931).

The audited balance sheet showed total assets of approximately $2,500,000 and net worth of approximately $1,000,000. On the basis of these figures, the creditor lent the firm about $165,000.

In reality, the net worth of the company was virtually zero. Most of the overstatement was due to a large fictitious entry to accounts receivable. The auditors failed to investigate this entry.

When the overstatement was discovered, the client's creditor sued the auditors for both negligence and fraud.

In the original trial the judge disallowed the charge of negligence because there was a lack of privity or contractual relationship between the auditor and the client's creditor. In doing so, he followed the common law concept that had developed to that date, that is, only the party that contracted with the auditor could take action against the auditor for ordinary negligence. The auditor's lack of knowledge about the name of the creditor and the use that it would make of the statements prevented the primary beneficiary relationship. The charge of fraud was disallowed also.

On appeal the disallowance of the negligence charge was upheld with the following justification.

> If liability for negligence exists, a thoughtless slip or blunder, the failure to detect a theft or forgery beneath the cover of deceptive entries, may expose accountants to a liability in an indeterminate amount for an indeterminate time to an indeterminate class.[8]

However, the Court of Appeals ordered a new trial on the charge of fraud. In the opinion of the judge, the facts of the case had suggested a possibility that the negligence might be so serious as to constitute a form of fraud. The judge raised the question of whether the accountants had any basis for a genuine belief in the validity of the financial statements with the following quotation:

> Our holding does not emancipate accountants from the consequences of fraud. It does not relieve them if their audit has been so negligent as to justify a finding that they had no genuine belief in its adequacy, for this again is a fraud.[9]

The case ultimately was settled out of court, but important auditing implications were established. Although the common law precedent that disallows third-party action against an auditor for *ordinary* negligence was upheld, there was a new precedent that established the possibility of successful third-party action against an auditor for very serious (gross) negligence.

Although the court made no official comment, possibly the wording of the original audit report damaged the auditor's case, because it said that the auditor

[8] Ibid.

[9] Ibid.

certified (guaranteed) the statements to be true and correct (exact). The report might have been taken as a statement of fact, and not opinion.

Shortly after this decision the words *certify, true,* and *correct* were removed from the general report format.[10] A major result of *Ultramares* was the creation of a new theory of negligence under which third-party liability could be sustained in cases of gross negligence.

Generally, the results of the *Ultramares* case established, along with other cases, the common law relationships between auditors and clients and third parties that lasted for almost 40 years.

1. Auditors are liable to the client (who has a privity relationship) for ordinary negligence.

2. Auditors may be liable to a third party for ordinary negligence if they know that the examination is being performed for the primary benefit of that third party and the third party is known to the auditors (the primary beneficiary concept).[11]

3. Auditors are liable to a third party for gross negligence even if the third party is unknown to the auditor.

As we shall see later in the chapter, events occurred in the 1960s to erode the effect of the *Ultramares* case. The auditors' liability to third parties for ordinary negligence under common law has widened.

The Securities Act of 1933—Liability for Negligence Under Statutory Law

The *Ultramares* decision removed some common law protection that the auditor previously had enjoyed. In 1933, the U.S. Congress passed the Securities Act, which increased still further the auditor's potential liability to a certain class of third parties (but this time under statutory law not common law).

The purpose of the Securities Act is to regulate security offerings to the public through the mails or interstate commerce. A registration statement has to be filed with each new public offering of securities. Each registration statement includes financial statements that are audited by independent public accountants.

As far as accountants' potential liability is concerned, a significant part of the act is the provision giving third-party investors the right to claim money

---

[10] A number of current auditing pronouncements resulted from legal cases.

[11] A 1955 case, *C.I.T. Financial Corporation* v. *Glover, 224 F 2nd 44 (2nd Cir. 1955),* interpreted the *Ultramares* case to extend auditors' liability for ordinary negligence to third parties that have a primary beneficiary relationship.

damages against the auditor for ordinary negligence, regardless of the fact that they are not clients with a privity relationship or known third parties with a primary beneficiary relationship. For legal actions that come under this law, which is limited to financial statements included in registration statements for new public offerings of securities, the Securities Act provides a course of action in addition to the common law reaffirmed in the *Ultramares* case.

The money damages are the differences between (1) the amount the investor paid for the security and (2) the market price at the time of the suit or the sales price.

Additional provisions of the act have special applicability to auditors.

1. The third parties' prima facie case is an alleged false statement or misleading omission. They are not required to prove their accusation or to demonstrate that they relied on the financial statements.

2. The burden of proof is on the auditor to show that the third-party losses were caused by factors other than the auditor's negligence.

3. In addition, the potential liability extends to the effective date of the registration statement, which extends beyond the *date of the audit report*. Normally, the auditor's responsibility is limited to the audit report date.

4. However, accountants do have an ordinary negligence defense known as *due diligence* if they can show that after "reasonable investigation" they had reason to believe and did believe that the statements were true as of the effective date of the registration statement (*true* is the word used in the act).

A hypothetical example illustrates these four points. Assume that a CPA firm is engaged to audit the financial statements of a company that plans to sell stock to the public. These statements cover a period of three years, from January 1, 19X0 to December 31, 19X2.

The auditors finish the examination on February 15, 19X3, and the audit report bears this date. Because of the time involved in preparation, however, the registration statement becomes effective April 15, 19X3. Suppose that sometime in March 19X3 the company is sued for a sum that is quite large in relation to total assets and net income. No mention is made of this litigation in the financial statements that are included in the registration statement.

If investors buy the stock and the price drops after knowledge of the litigation becomes public, these third parties may sue the auditors to recover their lost investment. Their case is based on the disclosure omitted from the financial statements. The auditors cannot use the audit report date as a defense because their responsibility extends to April 15, 19X3. But if the auditors can show that they conducted a "reasonable investigation" of events up to April 15 and had no reason to suspect litigation, they may have a "due diligence" defense.

The Securities Exchange Act of 1934—Another Application of Statutory Law

When the Securities Act was passed, the Interstate Commerce Commission administered its provisions. In 1934, Congress passed the Securities Exchange Act to regulate public security trading and create the *Securities and Exchange Commission* (SEC) to replace the Interstate Commerce Commission as the regulatory agency for those acts.

Under the Securities Exchange Act, companies that are publicly held are required to file with the SEC, on a periodic basis, various types of financial information, including financial statements audited by independent public accountants. Publicly held companies are those with securities listed on a national or over-the-counter exchange.

For many years, it was unclear whether auditors and others were liable under a key provision of the 1934 act for misrepresentations or omissions that were negligent but not fraudulent. In the *Hochfelder* case discussed later in the chapter, the U.S. Supreme Court held that *scienter* (an intent to manipulate, deceive, or defraud) must generally be proven to successfully litigate under this key provision of the act. Therefore, it is generally held that a standard of fraud applies under this key provision of the statute.

In three ways, the Securities Exchange Act is less severe than the Securities Act.

1. The burden of proof to establish fraud under the 1934 act is greater than required to establish ordinary negligence under the 1933 act.

2. Under the 1933 act, the burden of proof is on the accountant to show that the third party's loss was not due to false or misleading statements. Under the 1934 act, some of the burden is shifted to the third-party plaintiff, who must prove that he or she relied on the financial statements and that the damages were caused by doing so.

3. The 1933 act relates to the registration of *new* public offerings of securities. The 1934 act is a separate piece of legislation and relates to continuous trading of securities with no effective registration date. Thus, there is no problem of determining the scope of audit procedures after the end of the field work.

Auditors' defense probably is easier under the 1934 act. If they can prove that they performed in *good faith* and had no knowledge that the statements were false or misleading, they can avoid liability. The 1934 act does not amend the 1933 act; the acts apply to different situations.

One of the controversial aspects of the 1934 act is the power granted to the Securities and Exchange Commission. In the wake of the criticism leveled against the profession during the early 1930s, Congress gave the SEC the authority to determine generally accepted accounting principles for publicly held companies. Although the SEC has influenced many reporting changes in the past, it has generally allowed the accounting profession to regulate itself so far.

The *McKesson & Robbins* Case—A Fraud that Changed Auditing Standards

Although the securities acts of 1933 and 1934 increased the auditor's responsibility to third parties, a famous fraud case in the late 1930s[12] served to remind the profession that their evidence-gathering techniques were inadequate.

McKesson & Robbins was a wholesale drug company whose securities were listed on the New York Stock Exchange and were registered under the Securities Exchange Act of 1934. One of the alleged activities of the firm was a foreign business carried on through a Canadian subsidiary. This separate subsidiary showed on its books sizable purchases, sales, and inventories, but, in fact, the transactions of this subsidiary were fictitious.

The fraud became known in 1939. In 1940, the Securities and Exchange Commission conducted an investigation. During the series of hearings, two questions were raised that had direct relevance both to Price Waterhouse, McKesson & Robbins' auditors, and to the auditing profession in general.

1. To what extent were contemporary acceptable auditing standards and procedures followed?

2. To what extent did the contemporary auditing standards and procedures provide necessary safeguards and ensure reliability of the financial statements?

Concerning the first question, the SEC believed that the auditors were negligent and that gross discrepancies of this type should have been detected. In general, however, it was conceded that the auditors had followed procedures that were acceptable at that time.

On the second question, the SEC was very critical of the scope of audit procedures followed by the entire profession. Although it declined to exercise the full authority granted by Congress, the SEC made several suggestions:

1. In the two important areas of accounts receivable and inventory, the SEC recommended that evidence of existence should be obtained from external and independent sources.

---

[12] Excerpts and paraphrases from the *Report on Investigation of the Securities and Exchange Commission in the Matter of McKesson & Robbins, Inc.,* December 1940.

2. The stockholders should elect the auditor.

3. The audit report should be addressed to the stockholders.

4. The auditors should attend stockholder meetings and answer questions from this group.

In their reply to the SEC, the McKesson & Robbins auditors maintained that their examination was not designed to detect fraud, particularly if collusion existed. But the SEC's first recommendation was followed explicitly in 1940. In this regard, the SEC amended its regulations to require the auditor's report to state whether the audit was made in accordance with generally accepted auditing standards applicable in the circumstances.

The AICPA issued a pronouncement requiring auditors to gather independent and external evidence on accounts receivable and inventory, if the amounts are *material*. (An amount is considered material if it would cause an informed reader to view the financial statements differently.) The evidence-gathering techniques that the accounting profession used to satisfy its auditing responsibility had undergone a permanent change. Today, it is routine procedure to seek independent verification of such accounts.

However, the SEC's other three suggestions have only been followed in part. Sometimes stockholders ratify the auditors, but this action is often a mere formality because the recommendation for the auditors comes from the board of directors or management. There is no SEC requirement concerning the addressee of the audit report, so the addressee can be the stockholders or the board of directors. Although the auditor's attendance at stockholder meetings is still optional, the SEC does require that the auditor be available to attend such meetings or that management disclose to stockholders that the auditor will not be available.

The *Barchris Construction Corporation* Case—Application of Statutory Law

The 1960s were characterized by rising prices for many corporate stocks, and many of the prices proved to be inflated. This decade also ushered in the "age of litigation." As a result of several lawsuits, coupled with an increasingly active role by the SEC, the auditor's expanded responsibility to third parties was confirmed. A major example is the *Barchris* case,[13] tried under the Securities Act of 1933. The importance of this particular lawsuit is that a favorable judgment was rendered for the third-party plaintiffs, who were bringing action under that portion of the law covering false statements and material omissions in the registration statement.

---

[13] Excerpts and paraphrases from *Escott* v. *Barchris Construction Corp.*, 283 F. Supp. 643, 701 (S.D.N.Y. 1968).

Because the registration statement included the most recently audited financial statements, the auditors, Peat, Marwick, Main & Co., were involved.

Barchris Construction Corporation was a builder of bowling facilities. Until 1961 the corporation had financed all of its needs from sources other than publicly traded securities. In the early part of 1961, the corporation filed a registration statement for the public sale of convertible bonds, which placed them under the provision of the federal securities act.

Late in 1962, Barchris went bankrupt. The purchasers of the bonds filed suit against the auditors, using the 1933 act as their basis for the suit. They claimed that the registration statement contained false statements and material omissions. The auditors attempted to use the "due diligence" defense provided in the act.

During the trial, a focus was on an apparent overstatement of earnings. Some of the alleged earnings overstatement was caused by recording the gain on a sale-leaseback as current revenue rather than amortizing it over the life of the lease.

As a result, the court ruled that the registration statement contained false statements of material facts. The "due diligence" defense was disallowed. Although damages were settled out of court, the case has important implications.

The court made the statement that "accountants should not be held to a higher standard than that recognized in their profession." Yet, in the case of the sale and leaseback, the gain on the sale was treated differently than the judge thought it should be. At the time of the audit, the only authoritative guide was *Accounting Research Bulletin No. 43*, which stated that there should be disclosure of the principal details of any important transactions concerning sale and leaseback. *APB No. 5*, issued by the Accounting Principles Board at a later time, specifies that material gains or losses on sale–leaseback operations should be deferred and amortized over the life of the lease. But at the time of the trial, *APB No. 5* had not been issued and both the immediate recognition and the deferral methods were being followed in practice. Therefore, the judge chose one method over the other.

The *Barchris* decision illustrated the use of the 1933 Securities Act to sue auditing firms. It also demonstrated that the courts are willing to choose between alternative accounting principles if they believe the application of a certain pronouncement does not result in fair statements (the court ruling on the sale and leaseback). This trend toward a separate definition of fairness by nonaccountants is continuing.

The Widening, Under Common Law, of Ordinary Negligence Liability to Third Parties

Although the extensive widening of ordinary negligence liability to third parties did not occur until the 1960s, the *C.I.T. Financial Corporation* case in the 1950s is acknowledged by many to be the beginning of the "erosion" of the precedent set in the *Ultramares* case. The judge in the *Ultramares* case had ruled that privity or a contractual relationship had to exist for the auditor to be liable for ordinary negligence under common law. As indicated earlier in the chapter, however, the *C.I.T. Financial Corporation* case extended the auditor's liability to third parties that had a primary beneficiary relationship (third parties known to the auditor to be beneficiaries of the audit).

In 1965, the American Law Institute published a second restatement of the law of torts. In the restatement, the liability of professionals to third parties for ordinary negligence was broadened to include foreseen parties.[14] These groups include more than the traditional primary beneficiary parties. Foreseen parties could include lenders who the auditors know will require an audit report before making or extending a loan or banks that make loans to the audit client, if the auditor knows the audit report will be used to obtain financing.

However, the 1965 restatement excluded foreseeable parties from those parties having to prove only ordinary negligence. These groups are potentially large numbers of people, unknown to auditors, who may foreseeably be expected to receive, use, and rely on the audit report—members of the investing public, for example.

A legal case in the late 1960s established that auditors' liability to third parties for ordinary negligence under common law may indeed be extended to foreseen parties. The case was *Rusch Factors, Inc., v. Levin.* Following are some of the pertinent facts.[15]

In late 1963 and early 1964, a corporation located in Rhode Island borrowed more than $300,000 from the plaintiff, a commercial bank. The plaintiff requested, received, and relied on audited financial statements in making the loan.

The Rhode Island corporation later declared bankruptcy and the lender recovered only part of the loan. The lender, in turn, sued the auditor and charged that reliance had been placed on audited financial statements that contained misrepresentations that the auditor had negligently failed to detect.

The auditor tried to have the case dismissed on the basis that no privity of contract existed with the bank. The judge refused to dismiss the case and stated that the bank was a party whose reliance was foreseen by the auditor. Of particular interest was a statement by the judge that the wisdom of the *Ultramares* case was doubted by the court.

The decision denied lack of privity as a defense against third-party action for ordinary negligence. However, the decision did not specifically overrule the *Ultramares* case. The judge believed that the plaintiff in the *Ultramares* case was a foreseeable rather than a foreseen party.

The decision widened the number of third-party groups that could sue auditors for ordinary negligence under common law. The decision opened the ques-

[14] Henry R. Jaenicke, *The Effect of Litigation on Independent Auditors,* Commission on Auditors' Responsibilities, Research Study No, 1, 1977, pp. 11–12.

[15] Excerpts and paraphrases from *Rusch Factors, Inc.* v. *Levin,* 284 F. Supp. 85 (D.R.I. 1968).

tion of whether common law would continue to evolve to allow foreseeable parties to sue auditors for ordinary negligence. The answer was yes!

In 1983 a New Jersey court extended the auditor's liability for ordinary negligence under common law to foreseeable parties. In this case, *Rosenblum* v. *Adler, 461 A. D. D. 2d 138 (N.J. 1983),* an entity agreed to give, as part payment, some of its common stock to purchase some of Rosenblum's business. The value of the common stock was to be determined by the purchaser's net income.

However, this net income had been overstated by recording fictitious assets and omitting liabilities, thus inflating the value of the common stock. Rosenblum attempted to regain the loss by filing suit against the purchaser's auditors and charging that the auditors were negligent by failing to detect the fictitious assets and omitted liabilities.

Even though the plaintiff was a foreseeable party, the court ruled that the auditors were liable for negligence. Two factors cited by the court were

1. The auditors had insurance to cover the liability risk (an apparent doctrine of "spreading" the liability risk to the public).

2. The moral responsibility of the auditors to serve the interests of strangers who rely on the audit opinion.

Clearly, this case extended the boundaries of liability for ordinary negligence under common law and could set precedents for the future.

It is still an open question as to how far the boundaries will be extended, however, because of the conflicting opinions that seem to be emerging from the courts. For example, a New York case in 1985, *Credit Alliance Corporation* v. *Arthur Andersen & Co., 493 N.Y. Supp. 2d 435 (1985),* apparently reversed this trend. This time, the court ruled for the defendent and in doing so returned to the precedent set in the *Ultramares* case. Also, the court seemed to affirm that liability to third parties would exist if the auditor's conduct was such that he or she was "linked" to the third party using the audit report.

Needless to say, the question of auditor liability for ordinary negligence under common law is very much an open issue, especially as it pertains to extension of liability to foreseeable parties.

Additional Cases that Changed Auditors' Legal Environment

During the 1960s and 1970s several additional cases made an impact on auditors' legal environment and auditors' views of their public responsibilities. Although these cases did not specifically alter the definitions of foreseen or foreseeable persons or change common law precedents, they were important landmarks in the evolution of auditors' legal liability and need to be discussed. In fact, two of the cases involved criminal liability and another affected a section of the Securities Exchange Act of 1934.

The *Continental Vending* Case—Criminal Exposure[16]

Continental Vending Machine Corporation (Continental) had an affiliate named Valley Commercial Corporation (Valley). Both companies were dominated by the president, who owned about 25 percent of the stock of Continental. He borrowed sums of money from Valley, which, in turn, borrowed the same amount from Continental. At the balance sheet date, approximately $3,500,000 appeared on the books of Continental as a receivable from Valley (in reality, a receivable from the president who was unable to repay it).

Adding to this financial complexity was the fact that Continental discounted notes to a bank through Valley. These notes appeared on the books of Continental as a note payable to Valley (actually a note to the bank). At the balance sheet date, the amount was about $1,000,000.

The notes to the financial statements contained an explanation that the $3,500,000 receivable, less the $1,000,000 payable, was secured on the date of the auditor's report by securities with a market value in excess of the net amount of the receivable. Coopers & Lybrand were aware of the details of these transactions when they issued their report on the financial statements.

Moreover, the collateral was worth only $2,900,000 on the report date, and because the offset of the $1,000,000 payable against the $3,500,000 receivable was improper, a shortage of approximately $600,000 resulted (the $3,500,000 gross receivable less the $2,900,000 of collateral).

If only a civil suit had been filed against the auditors, the accounting profession might not have given this case much attention. But the auditors were charged with conspiring and adopting a scheme to violate federal *criminal* statutes by certifying false and misleading financial statements. The following language was used by the court in stating the case that the government had to prove:

> Not to show that the defendants were wicked men, with designs on anyone's purse, which they obviously were not, but rather that they had certified a statement knowing it to be false.

Moreover, the court declared that proof of conformity with generally accepted accounting principles would constitute only *partial* evidence of financial statement fairness.

Three auditors of the CPA firm were found guilty and fined thus illustrating auditors' legal risk in the area of criminal conduct.[17] In addition, the concept of fairness began to broaden beyond the application of generally accepted accounting principles. Such a broadening trend is reflected in AU Section 411 (*SAS No. 5*) and is discussed in Chapter 19.

---

[16] Excerpts and paraphrases from *U.S.* v. *Simon,* 425 F.2d 796 (1969).

[17] For further insights into the implications of this case, see David B. Isbell, "The Continental Vending Case: Lessons for the Profession," *Journal of Accountancy* (August 1970), pp. 33–40.

In summary, auditors may be subject to criminal penalties under the federal securities acts if violations can be shown to be willful and intentional. Auditors may also be exposed to criminal penalties under the federal mail fraud and conspiracy statutes.

The *1136 Tenants' Corporation* Case—A Misunderstanding Resulting in Negligence

A cooperative apartment corporation hired a CPA to "perform all necessary accounting and auditing services," particularly as they related to the custodianship of the corporation's managing agent.[18]

Apparently, there was a misunderstanding between the corporation and the accountants as to the nature and extent of the services. No letter explaining the terms of the engagement had been written and sent to the owners of the apartment corporation. The owners apparently thought that an audit would be performed, whereas the CPA apparently understood that the services would be confined to "write-up" work consisting of maintenance of the books, preparation of financial statements, and preparation of related tax returns.

It was later determined that irregularities had been committed by the managing agent. When the irregularities were discovered, the client sued the accountants under common law for ordinary negligence in failing to uncover the fraud. The CPA, in turn, maintained that he had not been engaged to perform an audit.

The court decided that the weight of the argument was in favor of the client; money damages were awarded.

After the verdict was rendered, several articles appeared suggesting the use of safeguards to avoid this type of situation in the future. Chief among these safeguards is the realization that the concept of due care exists regardless of the type of work performed by the CPA. Also needed is a clearly worded engagement letter from the CPA to his or her prospective client stating specifically the scope of the proposed work.

The *Equity Funding* Case—More Criminal Exposure

In recent years a disturbing tendency has arisen (or surfaced) among some top corporation officials—the deliberate attempt to deceive auditors. An example is the *Equity Funding Corporation* case. The fraud in this case, like that in the *McKesson & Robbins* case, consisted of massive collusion on the part of higher management with the intent to falsify assets and earnings.

The major functions of Equity Funding Corporation were to sell insurance and mutual funds. During the 1960s, Equity Funding's earnings grew. However, when business faltered, dummy customers were made up, and false information was stored in the computer files.

To make the transactions appear real, a set of computer programs was used

---

[18]Excerpts and paraphrases from *1136 Tenants' Corp.* v. *Max Rothenberg & Co.*, 36 A.D. 2d 804, 319 N.Y.S.2d 1007 (1971).

which cleverly concealed the deception. It is now apparent that large-scale collusion occurred between officers and computer personnel.

Several CPA firms worked as auditors for Equity Funding at one time or another (Seidman & Seidman was the last auditor, having merged with a local firm that previously performed the audit), yet none was able to detect this fraud. When the facts finally became known in 1973, the case proved to be an embarrassment for the accounting profession. The auditor's assumption of top-level honesty has been reexamined. Chapter 6 contains suggestions on policies and procedures for acceptance and continuance of clients. There is more about this case in Chapters 11 and 14.

The *Hochfelder* Case—Liability for Fraud Under Statutory Law[19]

From the early 1960s to the mid-1970s, the frequency of liability suits filed against auditors under the Securities Exchange Act of 1934 increased. One example was a lawsuit brought against Ernst & Whinney (formerly Ernst & Ernst), a large CPA firm, by a group of investors that had placed sums of money in what they believed to be escrow accounts of First Securities Company of Chicago, a brokerage firm. The funds were used improperly by the president of First Securities Company and no accountability existed for them. The fraud was perpetrated by a so-called mail rule prohibiting anyone but the president from opening incoming mail. No record of the receipts was placed on the company's books. Ernst & Whinney failed to detect the irregularity.

When the fraud was uncovered, the investors sued the CPA firm for negligence under the Securities Exchange Act of 1934. Ernst & Whinney was not accused of participating willingly in the fraud but of negligent conduct because of its failure to discover the material weakness in controls resulting from the mail rule. However, the U.S. Supreme Court ruled for the CPA firm, and the suit was disallowed. The court stated that willful attempt to defraud *(scienter)* the investors, rather than simple negligence, must be proved.

As a result, it is more difficult for third parties to sue successfully on the basis of Section 10(b) of the Securities Exchange Act of 1934, unless more than simple negligence can be proved. But the ruling in the *Hochfelder* case has not prevented the SEC from using administrative proceedings to sanction auditors believed to be guilty of negligent conduct. An example of a sanction is the denial of a CPA or a firm the right to audit public clients for some period of time.

The Present-Day Situation

So where do auditors stand today as the result of 60 years of legal cases and other events that have significantly changed the perceptions of their responsibilities?

---

[19] Excerpts from *Ernst & Ernst* v. *Hochfelder*, 425 U.S. 185 (1976).

1. Today, auditors realize that their potential liability for ordinary negligence has extended beyond their clients who have a privity relationship with them. Third parties who have a primary beneficiary or foreseen (and possibly foreseeable) relationship with auditors can, in many cases, successfully litigate against auditors.

2. The Securities Act of 1933 has established the auditor's liability for ordinary negligence under statutory law and the Securities and Exchange Act of 1934 has provided a "watchdog" regulatory agency (the SEC).

3. Major frauds (unfortunately undiscovered by the auditors) have encouraged the accounting profession to take "fresh looks" at their auditing standards and their perceptions of due care.

However, auditors have responded by following tighter guidelines in

1. Selecting clients.

2. Making certain that generally accepted auditing standards are followed.

3. Defining the scope of their engagements and their understandings with clients.

Today, much of the public pressure on auditors is concentrated in the following areas:

1. The auditor's responsibility to detect and report errors and irregularities, including fraudulent financial reporting.

2. The auditor's responsibility to detect and report illegal acts.

In addition, auditors face a new danger of civil prosecution because of the passage of the Racketeer Influenced and Corrupt Organizations Act (RICO).

Each of these issues is discussed in the following subsections.

Errors and Irregularities

For many years, the accounting profession had debated the question of the auditor's responsibility to detect errors and irregularities committed by his or her audit clients.

Errors are unintentional misstatements or omissions in financial statements. They can be caused by

mistakes in gathering or processing accounting data (posting to wrong accounts), incorrect accounting estimates that are inadvertent (choosing a 10 percent rather than a 20 percent depreciation rate), or

mistakes in the application of accounting principles (incorrectly applying the lower of cost or market inventory valuation technique).

On the other hand,

irregularities are intentional acts such as falsification of financial statement amounts,

intentional omission of necessary financial statement information, or

misappropriation of assets.

A statement on auditing standards defines the auditor's responsibilities in each of these areas. Basically these responsibilities are as follows.

The auditor should assess the risk that errors and irregularities may cause the financial statements to contain a material misstatement. Based on that assessment, the auditor should design the audit to provide reasonable assurance of detecting errors and irregularities that are material to the financial statements.

This is a positive statement about an auditor's responsibilities to detect errors and irregularities, particularly compared with official pronouncements in previous years that severely limited auditor responsibility for the detection of fraud.

However, the statement on auditing standards goes on to point out that even a properly designed and executed audit may not detect a material irregularity caused by forgery and collusion. The statement also points out that an audit has inherent limitations, that the auditor is not an insurer, and that the audit report does not constitute a guarantee. This means that

the subsequent discovery that a material misstatement exists in the financial statements does not, in and of itself, evidence inadequate planning, performance, or judgment on the part of the auditor.

Taken together, the statement on auditing standards says this.

1. It is the auditor's task to design the audit program and conduct the audit in such a way that, if material errors or irregularities do exist in the financial statements being examined, there is a high probability that they will be detected.

2. For a variety of reasons, auditors may not detect material errors or irregularities in the financial statements being examined.

3. Therefore, if a material misstatement does occur in the financial statements that were examined, it is not *automatically* the fault of the auditor.

In studying the legal cases and the evolution of auditors' responsibilities described in this chapter, it is easy to see why the accounting profession is more positive than it used to be about its obligations to detect errors and irregularities.

More will be said in succeeding chapters about the auditor's detection and reporting responsibilities in this area.

Fraudulent Financial Reporting

The current environment of litigation and rising public expectations of fair financial reporting led to a strong initiative by the private sector of the accounting profession. In 1985 the National Commission on Fraudulent Financial Reporting (often referred to as the Treadway Commission) was created and funded by the AICPA and a number of other influential private-sector accounting and business organizations. The three-part objective of the Commission was as follows.

1. Consider the extent to which acts of fraudulent financial reporting undermine the integrity of financial reporting, what forces may have contributed to these acts, and how fraudulent financial reporting can be prevented or deterred.

2. Consider the role of the independent public accountant in detecting fraud and especially whether changes in auditing standards or procedures might reduce the extent of fraudulent financial reporting.

3. Identify attributes of corporate structure that may contribute to acts of fraudulent financial reporting or the failure to detect such acts promptly.

For purposes of the Commission's study, *fraudulent financial reporting* is defined as intentional or reckless conduct, whether act or omission, that results in materially misleading financial statements.

A number of recommendations were made in the report entitled *Report of the National Commission on Fraudulent Financial Reporting*. The ones that directly affect the role of the auditor revolve around these areas:

1. Change auditing standards to better recognize the independent public accountant's responsibility for detecting fraudulent financial reporting.

2. Take steps to improve audit quality.

3. Change the auditor's standard audit report to better communicate to the users of financial statements the role of the audit and its limitations.

4. Reorganize the process of setting auditing standards.

We can easily see from these recommendations that the accounting profession is responding to the changing audit environment, brought about, in part, by the events described in this chapter.

Illegal Acts

The accounting profession has also found it necessary to address the question of illegal acts by audit clients, a topical issue in view of the public's perceptions about this issue (many think it is the task of the auditor to detect illegal acts). Therefore, a recent statement on auditing standards was issued that defined the auditor's responsibilities in this area.

The statement defines *illegal acts* as violations of laws or governmental regulations by the audited entity or its management or employees acting on behalf of the entity. Nonbusiness personal misconduct by client personnel is not part of the definition of illegal acts.

Although auditors are in a position to detect the possibility of an illegal act (e.g., a pay rate for certain employees below the minimum wage), a person qualified in the law must make the final determination as to the illegality of the act.

What about the auditor's responsibility to detect illegal acts? The statement on auditing standards has this to say.

> . . . certain illegal acts have a direct and material effect on the determination of financial statement amounts. Other illegal acts . . . may in particular circumstances be regarded as having material but indirect effects on financial statements. The auditor's responsibility to detect and report misstatements resulting from illegal acts having a direct and material effect on the determination of financial statement amounts (except disclosure of contingencies) is the same as that for errors and irregularities. . . . The auditor should be aware of the possibility that (other) illegal acts (that have an indirect effect on financial statements) may have occurred. If specific information comes to the auditor's attention that provides evidence concerning the existence of possible illegal acts that could have a material indirect effect on the financial statements, the auditor should apply audit procedures specifically directed to ascertaining whether an illegal act has occurred. However, because of the characteristics of illegal acts (having an indirect effect) . . . , an audit made in accordance with generally accepted auditing standards provides no assurance that (such) illegal acts will be detected.

The auditor should assess the risk that illegal acts could have a direct and material effect on the financial statements (e.g., violation of federal income tax laws) and plan the audit to provide reasonable assurance of detecting such illegal acts. The auditor does *not* plan specific procedures to detect illegal acts that have an indirect effect on the financial statements (e.g., violations of laws relating to occupational safety and health, food and drug administration, or environmental protection), but should pursue them if they come to his or her attention.

Should the auditor determine that an illegal act has occurred, the auditor should consider the effect of the act on the financial statements (a modified audit report may be necessary) and other aspects of the audit (the reliability of management representations) and should determine that the audit committee of the board of directors has been adequately informed.

The Racketeer Influenced and Corrupt Organizations Act

No better example of the 60-year change in the auditor's legal environment can be furnished than a description of the potential liability that auditors are subject to under a federal law passed in 1970.

Congress, in an attempt to provide a strong antiracketeering law, passed the *Racketeer Influenced and Corrupt Organizations Act* (RICO). The statute is extremely broad and includes securities fraud and mail fraud in its definition of racketeering. The potential significance to the auditor is a part of the statute that provides for private civil lawsuits with triple damages to be awarded.[20]

The civil provision of the law is now being used as a basis for third-party lawsuits against accounting firms, as well as other types of businesses. Added to this is a Supreme Court decision that allows the private civil action part of the law to be applied to any commercial disputes.

The total impact of RICO on the legal liability of auditors is yet to be determined, and the law might be amended in the future. But the fact that such a statute can be used for third-party lawsuits is evidence of how much change has occurred since the *Ultramares* case limited the auditor's liability for ordinary negligence under common law to persons who have a privity relationship with the auditor.

Summary and Litigation Guidelines

One should not be left with the impression that the evolution of the audit process has been nothing more than a steady succession of court cases. It is true that legal cases and SEC actions have significantly changed auditors' concept of their responsibilities. These responsibilities have shifted, relatively, from clients to third-party investors. But the accounting profession has responded to the challenge and has increased the quality of its services. For every "landmark" case that has proved the auditors' fallibility, there are thousands of "clean" audits that have given the financial community much-needed reliance on financial statements.

One of the messages that should come from a discussion of the cases is that auditing is not like "other" jobs. This function involves unique risks and requires unique personal characteristics; both factors are covered in greater depth in other

---

[20] Newton N. Minow, "Accountants' Liability and the Litigation Explosion," *Journal of Accountancy* (September 1984), pp. 70–86.

chapters. For each example of poor judgment (which frequently results in national publicity), there are thousands of instances in which good judgment is used. For every case in which the client is able to compromise the auditor's independence, there are many more in which the auditors successfully assert their independence.

However, in view of the recent litigation and the changing public attitudes toward auditors, there are several options open to auditors to lower the chances of major lawsuits in the future.

1. Care should be taken in selection and retention of clients. Companies that have a history of financial difficulties are more likely than those without such difficulties to take measures to falsify earnings and hide events that should be disclosed in the financial statements. In general, CPA firms are giving attention to this matter and are "screening" prospective clients more carefully by investigating the backgrounds both of the company and its officers.

2. Auditors should make certain that generally accepted auditing standards are followed. The study of the cases in the chapter makes it obvious that one or more of these standards were violated in several instances. Auditors should always remember that the quality of their work is subject to review and will be scrutinized in the event of litigation.

3. Auditors should have a clear understanding with the client as to the scope of the engagement, the services that will be rendered, and the auditor's responsibility. Engagement letters (discussed in Chapter 6) help the auditor and client to avoid misunderstandings.

4. CPAs should consider realistically their expertise and competence before accepting a client. In some cases, CPAs may be well advised to avoid or discontinue a relationship unless they have the proper expertise and competence to do the work properly.[21]

Chapter 4
Glossary of Terms

(listed in the order of appearance in the chapter, with accompanying page references where the term is discussed)

Term		*Page in Chapter*
Common law law based on the precedents established from past court cases.		114
Statutory law law passed by a legislative body.		114

---

[21] Alan J. Winters, "Avoiding Malpractice Liability Suits," *Journal of Accountancy* (August 1981), pp. 69–74.

	Page in
Term	*Chapter*

Ordinary negligence   a lack of due care in the performance of professional accounting tasks, due care implying the use of the knowledge, skill, and judgment usually possessed by practitioners in similar practice circumstances.   114

Gross negligence   an extreme, flagrant, or reckless departure from due care in performing professional duties.   114

Fraud   knowledge of a false representation consisting of the following elements: false representation, deliberate intent to deceive, expectation of reliance by another, justifiable reliance, and resulting damages.   115

Privity   a contractual relationship between the auditor and the client for performance of professional services.   115

Primary beneficiary   a third party for whom the auditor knows the client has specifically engaged him or her to perform an audit for the benefit of an identified third party whose reliance is the aim of the engagement.   115

Foreseen parties   third parties known to or reasonably expected to be known to the auditor who will rely on the auditor's work in making a particular business decision.   116

Foreseeable parties   users of financial statements who are not specifically identified or who use the statements for transactions not specifically known to the auditor, but who may reasonably be expected to see the statements and to act or refrain from acting because of reliance on them.   116

Certificate   the term formerly used to describe the audit report.   118

Third parties   groups that have a vested interest in a company's financial statements and are not a part of management. Examples are creditors and stockholders.   119

Public companies   companies that sell their securities to the public or whose securities are traded on an exchange.   121

Auditors' due diligence defense   a defense that can be used by auditors against charges of ordinary negligence under the Securities Act of 1933. The auditors must have reason to believe and belief that the statements were true as of the effective date of a registration statement.   122

	Page in
Term	*Chapter*

Securities and Exchange Commission   the federal regulatory agency that regulates the public issuing and trading of securities.   123

Scienter   an intent to manipulate, deceive, or defraud.   123

Auditors' good faith defense   a defense that can be used by auditors against charges under the Securities Exchange Act of 1934. The defense is that the auditors performed in good faith and had no knowledge that the statements were false or misleading.   123

Material amount in the financial statements   an amount that would cause an informed reader to view the financial statements differently.   125

Errors   unintentional misstatements or omissions in financial statements.   132

Irregularities   intentional misstatement of financial statement amounts, intentional omission of necessary financial statement information, or misappropriation of assets.   133

Fraudulent financial reporting   intentional or reckless conduct, whether act or omission, that results in materially misleading financial statements.   134

Illegal acts   violations of laws or governmental regulations by the audited entity or management or employees acting on behalf of the entity.   135

Racketeer Influenced and Corrupt Organizations Act   a strong antiracketeering law passed by Congress that has been used as the basis for some civil lawsuits against auditors.   136

Chapter 4
References

American Institute of Certified Public Accountants. *Professional Standards:*

AU Section 230—*Due Care in the Performance of Work;*

The Auditor's Responsibility to Detect and Report Errors and Irregularities;

Illegal Acts by Clients.

Cochrane, George. "The Auditor's Report: Its Evolution in the U.S.A.," *The Accountant* (November 4, 1950).

Gavin, Thomas A., Hicks, Rebecca L., and Decosimo, Joseph D. "CPAs' Liability to Third Parties," *Journal of Accountancy* (June 1984), pp. 80–88.

Gavin, Thomas A., Hicks, Rebecca L., and Scheiner, James H. "Auditors' Common Law Liability: What We Should Be Telling Our Students," *Journal of Accounting Education*, Vol. 5 (1987), pp. 1–12.

Jaenicke, Henry R. The Effect of Litigation on Independent Auditors. New York: *Research Study No. 1, Commission on Auditors' Responsibilities*, 1977.

Mednick, Robert. "Accountants' Liability: Coping with the Stampede to the Courtroom," *Journal of Accountancy* (September 1987), pp. 118–122.

Minow, Newton N. "Accountants' Liability and the Litigation Explosion," *Journal of Accountancy* (September 1984), pp. 70–86.

Report of the National Commission on Fraudulent Financial Reporting. Washington, D.C.: National Commission on Fraudulent Financial Reporting, 1987.

Winters, Alan J. "Avoiding Malpractice Liability Suits," *Journal of Accountancy* (August 1981), pp. 69–74.

Chapter 4
Review Questions

4-1.   What is the difference between common law and statutory law?

4-2.   What is the difference between ordinary negligence, gross negligence, and fraud?

4-3.   What is the difference between a privity relationship and a primary beneficiary relationship?

4-4.   What is the difference between a primary beneficiary relationship and a foreseen party relationship?

4-5.   What is the difference between a foreseen party relationship and a foreseeable party relationship?

4-6.   Describe six major differences between the type of audit conducted in 1915 and the type conducted today.

4-7.   What common law relationships between auditors, clients, and third parties were established by the *Ultramares* case?

4-8.   What statutory law relationships between auditors and certain third parties were created with the Securities Act of 1933?

4-9.   What is the difference between the Securities Act of 1933 and the Securities Exchange Act of 1934?

4-10.   What is the "due diligence" defense that may be used by auditors under the Securities Act of 1933? What are the "good faith" and "no knowledge" defenses that may be used under the Securities Exchange Act of 1934?

4-11.   What recommendations were made by the SEC as a result of the hearings conducted on the *McKesson & Robbins* case.

4-12.   How did the *Barchris* case change the auditor's working climate?

4-13.   In what way did the *Rusch Factors* case change the relationship between auditors and third parties insofar as ordinary negligence under common law is concerned?

4-14.   In what way did the *Rosenblum* v. *Adler* case extend the auditor's liability for ordinary negligence under common law? What two factors were cited by the court to support its opinion?

4-15.   How does the *Continental Vending* case illustrate a different dimension of the auditor's legal risk?

4-16.   In the *1136 Tenants'* case, what was the difference between the client's and the CPA's view of the purpose of the professional services?

4-17.   What did the management of Equity Funding Corporation do to falsify its records and cover up the fraud?

4-18.   How did the *Hochfelder* case change the burden of proof under the Securities Exchange Act of 1934?

4-19.   What is the difference between errors and irregularities?

4-20.   Describe the auditor's responsibility to detect illegal acts?

4-21.   In the *Report of the National Commission on Fraudulent Financial Reporting* there were four major recommendations that directly affect the role of the auditor. What were these recommendations?

4-22.   In what way is the auditor potentially affected by the *Racketeer Influenced and Corrupt Organizations Act?*

4-23.   Describe four litigation guidelines.

**Chapter 4
Objective Questions**

4-24.   Which of the following is *least* likely to be an example of ordinary negligence?
a. The auditor misinterprets a transaction because he or she did not read the invoice carefully.
b. The auditor reads the minutes of the meetings of the client's board of directors and fails to note an important property acquisition approved by them.
c. The auditor omits the observation of the client's inventory that is material.
d. The auditor misreads the invoice and fails to note that an expenditure charged to an expense account should have been capitalized.

4-25.   Which of the following is *most* likely to be an example of fraud?
a. The auditor fails to properly determine the reason so many of the client's customers complain that they have been overcharged.
b. The auditor allows an important footnote on a large contingent liability to be omitted from the financial statements.
c. The auditor miscounts the amount in the client's petty cash funds.
d. The auditor forgets to observe inventory-taking at a client's place of business when inventory is a significant amount in the client's balance sheet.

4-26.   Which of the following *is* an example of a privity relationship?
a. A third party for whom the audit is being primarily conducted is known by the auditor.
b. A third party unknown specifically by the auditor but known to be a person to

whom the client might take the audited financial statements and apply for a loan.

    c. A third-party creditor unknown to the auditor who relies on the audited financial statements to make a credit decision concerning the auditor's client.

    d. The auditor's client with whom the auditor signed the agreement to perform the audit.

4-27.   Which of the following is *more* likely to be a foreseen party?

    a. The president of the auditor's client.

    b. A local bank that might be expected to lend the client money relying, in part, on the audited financial statements.

    c. The chairman of the board of directors of the auditor's client.

    d. A local bank that has never done business with the client and is unknown to the auditor.

4-28.   Which of the following is *more* likely to be a foreseeable party?

    a. A member of the general public, unknown to the auditor, who invests in stock of the auditor's client and relies on the audited financial statements for his or her investment decision.

    b. The controller of the auditor's client.

    c. A company that is interested in buying the client and that asks the client to provide it with audited financial statements.

    d. A local credit institution that has consistently done business with the auditor's client over the years and has relied on the audited financial statements in making credit decisions.

4-29.   In the *Ultramares* case the plaintiff's charge of negligence

    a. Was disallowed because the plaintiff was not a foreseen party.

    b. Was disallowed because the plaintiff had a privity relationship with the auditor.

    c. Was disallowed because the plaintiff did not have a privity relationship with the auditor.

    d. Was allowed.

4-30.   The Securities Act of 1933

    a. Extended the auditor's liability for ordinary negligence under common law.

    b. Created foreseen and foreseeable parties.

    c. Reversed the decisions made in the *Ultramares* case.

    d. Provided that third parties could sue the auditor for ordinary negligence under statutory law.

4-31.   The *Rusch Factors* case resulted in extending the auditor's liability to third parties for ordinary negligence under common law to

a. Foreseen parties.

b. Foreseeable parties.

c. Primary beneficiaries.

d. Those with privity relationships.

Chapter 4
Discussion/Case Questions

4-32.   Susan Jason, CPA, had been auditing the financial statements of Rosfeld Stores, Inc., a large department store, for several years. During the last two years a nationwide economic recession had affected Rosfeld's sales and net income severely. The company, looking for ways to lower operating expenses, constantly asked Jason how the audit fee could be reduced.

One day Rosfeld's president called Jason and suggested a method for saving money on the forthcoming audit. The president suggested that his personnel select the customer accounts on which confirmation letters would be sent. The same personnel would write and mail the confirmation letters. All of these procedures would be performed under the supervision of one of Jason's auditors.

Jason agreed to this procedure. As the auditor watched, two of Rosfeld's employees selected every fifth account, wrote a confirmation letter, and mailed the letters with the CPA firm's return address on the envelope. All of the confirmation letters were returned by the customers directly to the auditor with indications that the amount of accounts receivable on Rosfeld's books was correct. Jason issued a report with an unqualified opinion.

The next year it was discovered that Rosfeld Stores, Inc. had been inflating its sales by making up "dummy" customers, complete with assumed records and files. Rosfeld declared bankruptcy, and its creditors filed suit against Jason for negligence and fraud.

Required:

Answer the following questions.

a. Name the auditing standards that, in your opinion, were violated. Give reasons for your answers.

b. What conditions would have to exist for the creditors to be regarded by the court as primary beneficiaries?

c. What conditions would have to exist for the creditors to be regarded by the court as foreseen parties?

d. What conditions would have to exist for the creditors to be regarded by the court as foreseeable parties?

e. If the creditors were regarded as foreseen parties, would they probably win their negligence case? Give reasons for your answer.

f. Assume that Rosfeld Stores' securities are traded on the New York Stock

Exchange. In your opinion, would the creditors be able to prove that scienter existed? Give reasons for your answer.

4-33.   XYZ Oil Co. had been a problem for its auditor, Joe Jones, CPA, for several years. The Company's stock was traded in the over-the-counter market, and management was concerned with keeping net income as high as possible to support the stock price. Each year, the controller would refuse to record any of Jones's proposed entries if he could establish that they were not material. Accordingly, each year's net income was generally overstated by 5 to 10 percent, which Jones accepted on the basis that it was not material.

Of particular concern to Jones was a $10 million investment in an oil venture in South America; however, he had been unsuccessful to date in proving to the controller's satisfaction that a loss should be recorded on this investment.

During the current year's audit, Jones discovered a report indicating that the South American oil venture was worthless and had been for two years. When he discussed this report with the controller, the controller suggested that the investment be written off in equal amounts over the next ten years to prevent a significant effect in any year and to prevent embarrassment or liability to Jones from disclosing that past financial statements were misstated. The controller stated that recognition of the loss in the current year would mean bankruptcy for XYZ Oil Co. and certain liability for Jones.

Required:
Answer the following questions.
a. Assume that the stock is being offered for the first time and the provisions of the Securities Act of 1933 apply. If the investment was written off in ten installments and the company went bankrupt in one year, what prima facie case would plaintiff investors who lost money have against the auditor?
b. Assume the same situation as in a, above. How might the auditor prove that the investor losses were caused by other factors?
c. Assume the same situation as in a, above. In your opinion, would the auditor have a due diligence defense against the charge of ordinary negligence? Give reasons for your answers.
d. Assume that the stock has been on the market for several years and that the provisions of the Securities Exchange Act of 1934 apply. If the investment was written off in ten installments and the company went bankrupt in two years, what conditions would have to exist for investors who lost money to prove scienter?
e. Taking the case situation as stated, give reasons why the auditor should accept the controller's solution. What liability does he face if he does accept it? Give reasons why the auditor should not accept the controller's solution. What liability does he face if he does not accept it?
f. What should the auditor do? Give reasons for your answer.

4-34.   Mr. Clyde Neglent, CPA, was engaged to perform an audit of Hidden Records, Inc., a retail department store whose securities were traded actively on the New

York Stock Exchange. Mr. Neglent had made a review of the business and its owners before accepting the engagement and had found the following.

Hidden Records, Inc., securities were popular, particularly during the last two years when total assets had risen by 20 percent and earnings by 15 percent. The company appeared to have the characteristics of a solid commercial establishment. But one thing bothered Mr. Neglent. The president and other key officers had unstable records of employment. In addition, Mr. Neglent was puzzled by the sudden rise in profits during a period when retail sales in that region of the country had dropped. Nevertheless, the audit was taken and work soon commenced.

The company kept most of its records on computer files. The accounts receivable were maintained on magnetic disk. Mr. Neglent's knowledge of computer systems was minimal (another reason for his hesitation in accepting the engagement). Therefore, he decided to consult with the company's data-processing manager to determine the best way to audit the records stored in computer files.

Ms. Clev, the data-processing manager, made several suggestions on the various techniques that could be used to extract audit evidence. Most of them involved printouts of information stored in the computer. These suggestions all appeared to be reasonable and were followed by Mr. Neglent.

Mr. Neglent wished to send confirmation letters to a sample of the customers whose accounts made up the accounts receivable balance, because this amount represented approximately 20 percent of the total assets. Ms. Clev stated that she had a sampling plan that she used when it was necessary to select customer accounts randomly for various reasons. She offered to make this sample selection for Mr. Neglent and to print out confirmation requests. These requests would be given to Mr. Neglent, who, in turn, would mail them independently to the customers. Mr. Neglent agreed, and this procedure was carried out. Replies received from all the customers to whom letters were sent indicated that the account balances were correct.

All other phases of the examination went smoothly, and the audit report was issued routinely. The report contained an unqualified opinion. Several months later, Hidden Records, Inc., declared bankruptcy, and its securities were taken off the market. It appears that the company had inflated its earnings and assets by creating false sales and accounts receivable.

Required:
Answer the following questions.
a. Would third parties who relied on the financial statements and invested in the company's securities be able to successfully sue the auditor for ordinary negligence under the assumption that the investors constituted foreseen parties? Give reasons for your answer.
b. Would third-party investors qualify as foreseeable parties? Give reasons for your answer.
c. Would the investors be able to prove scienter and successfully sue the auditor? Give reasons for your answer.

d. Name any auditing standard or standards violated by the auditor. Give reasons for your answers.

e. All things considered, in what ways should the auditor have acted differently in this examination?

4-35. A colleague has read about the legal cases with which auditors have been involved in recent years. During a discussion, you consider it beneficial to summarize some highlights of auditors' legal liability during the past 60 years. Select six cases you think have had a major impact on audit practice and auditors' responsibility. In two or three sentences on each, explain the impact of these cases on the auditor's legal environment.

4-36. Refer to the example of an auditor's report issued in 1915. List the differences between the report styles in 1915 and today (refer to Chapter 1). Indicate in what ways this report would be deficient or misleading in light of modern auditing standards.

4-37. Answer the following questions or discuss the following statements.

a. It seems that every time a legal challenge is made to an audit, CPAs either lose the case or are embarrassed about the facts uncovered during the audit.

b. Is it possible to audit a company's financial statements if top management decides to be dishonest with the auditor?

c. Can financial statements be in accord with generally accepted accounting principles and not be fair?

d. In what ways have recent court cases changed the effects of the *Ultramares* case rulings? Name the cases and the specific effect of each case.

e. In what ways has the *Hochfelder* case limited auditors' legal liability? In what way has this case left their legal liability intact?

4-38. Indicate whether you think the following third-party groups would normally represent a (1) primary beneficiary, (2) foreseen party, or (3) foreseeable party. Give reasons for your answers.

a. A potential purchaser of a business who asks for audited financial statements of that business and is known to the auditor.

b. A potential purchaser of a business who asks for audited financial statements of that business and is unknown to the auditor. However, the auditor knows that his or her client has asked for an audit because of an intention to sell the business.

c. A purchaser of a business who, unknown to the auditor, relied on the audited financial statements to help make the decision to buy the business. The auditor had been led to believe that the client would use the financial statements only for a bank loan.

d. A local bank which, as a condition of a loan, requires that audited financial statements be furnished to it by the borrower's auditors. There is no other reason for the audit to be conducted.

e. An investor in securities of a public company.

f. A bank that makes loans to companies of the type audited by CPAs in that city. The auditor has never conducted business with that bank but does know that the bank makes these types of loans.

4-39.   Use and Dispose Company was organized to manufacture and sell inexpensive golf clubs that can be used during the golf round and then thrown away at the end of the round. In order to "keep the business in the family" the company never offered its stock to the public, thus avoiding the jurisdiction of the Securities and Exchange Commission.

The company was unable to sell much capital stock, but was successful in obtaining bank loans from several banks. Use and Dipose Company was able to obtain several bank loans without the knowledge of other banks. However, premium interest rates were charged on each loan.

Business was not particularly good in the first two years because most golfers preferred to play several rounds of golf with the same golf clubs. But the officers of the company were not discouraged and decided to renew all of their loans with each bank.

To the surprise of the officers, each bank asked for audited financial statements before making the decision to renew or call in the loans. The officers inquired of several CPAs about an audit, but the fees were either too high or the officers believed that the CPAs would be "too nosey." Finally, they found a CPA who would be willing to conduct the audit for a low fee. Conversations with the CPA led them to believe that he would "cooperate."

During the course of the audit, the CPA found a large receivable entitled "Receivables from Country Clubs." When the CPA asked for documentary evidence to support this receivable, the controller indicated that extensive conversations had been held with many country clubs and they had made "oral arrangements" to sell the disposable golf clubs to these organizations.

The CPA was a bit suspicious and decided to confirm the receivables with each country club. He was careless, however, and allowed the confirmation letters to be taken by the controller, who, in turn, signed them and mailed them back to the auditor as if they were legitimate confirmation replies. Each bank relied on the audited financial statements and extended the loans. The auditor did not know any of the banks, but he had reason to believe that Use and Dispose Company would submit the audited financial statements to creditors of this type with whom the company had done business since it was organized.

In addition, an individual, unknown to the auditor, purchased capital stock in the company, relying on the audited financial statements to make the decision.

Within a year, Use and Dispose Company declared bankruptcy and was unable to pay off any of the loans or return any money to the recent investor in capital stock. Each of the banks and the stock investor sued the CPA for ordinary negligence under common law.

Required:

Write a brief paragraph indicating the probable outcome of the lawsuit for (1) the banks and (2) the stock investor assuming each of these four situations (provide reasons for your opinions):

a. The only common law case that is used as a precedent in the lawsuit is the *Ultramares* case.

b. In addition to the *Ultramares* case, the *C.I.T. Financial Corporation* case is also used as a precedent in the lawsuit.

c. In addition to the *Ultramares* and *C.I.T. Financial Corporation* cases, the *Rusch Factors* case is also used as a precedent in the lawsuit.

d. In addition to the *Ultramares,* the *C.I.T. Financial Corporation,* and the *Rusch Factors* cases, the *Rosenblum* case is also used as a precedent in the lawsuit.

Materiality and Audit Risk

Learning Objectives   *After reading and studying the material in this chapter, the student should*

Be able to give an explanation of the audit function.

Understand the concept of materiality and how to relate it to planning and conducting an audit.

Understand the concept of audit risk and how to relate it to planning and conducting an audit.

Know the three components of individual audit risk.

Be able to describe how the use of sampling in testing relates to audit risk.

In Chapter 1 we introduced the subject of auditing, discussed it from a theoretical standpoint, and made distinctions between several types of auditing. In Chapter 3 we covered the auditor's ethical environment and showed how CPAs use ethical concepts and rules to guide them in their practice. In Chapter 4 we explored the evolution of the auditor's legal responsibilities and how this evolutionary process has influenced the nature and scope of modern-day audits.

We are now ready to discuss, in summary fashion, the subject of the audit, itself; that is, the concepts and means that auditors use to gather sufficient evidence to attest to the fairness of their client's financial statements. In succeeding chapters we will draw upon these concepts to explain how an audit is planned and conducted and how the auditor's opinion is derived.

In this chapter, we will make considerable use of and will reference two sections of *AICPA Professional Standards*, 1988. These are:

AU Section 312 [*SAS No. 47*]—Audit Risk and Materiality in Conducting an Audit.
AU Section 350 [*SAS No. 39*]—Audit Sampling.

An Explanation of the Audit Function

Remember from Chapter 1 that the purpose of the financial audit (which we will simply refer to as an audit) is to gather the necessary evidence to attest to the fairness of an entity's financial statements in conformity with generally accepted accounting principles. In this sense, then, an audit is an endeavor or an undertaking that requires the following:

1. The audit must be planned.

2. The audit must be conducted; that is, evidence must be gathered and evaluated.

3. A report of the audit results must be made to the appropriate person or groups.

We will not cover the audit report in this chapter, but we will discuss the basic elements of planning and conducting the audit so that we can better understand the material in Chapters 6 through 18 and the terms contained therein.

On pages 153 and 154 are two financial statements with which we can begin our discussion and continue to use throughout the chapter for teaching purposes. (We will disregard the statement of cash flows and the footnotes.)

What, in fact, are auditors attempting to do when they attest to the fairness of financial statements such as the income statement and balance sheets in Figures 5-1 and 5-2? Perhaps we should start with an explanation of what auditors *cannot* do when they perform the attest function. Auditors cannot *guarantee* to their client or any other users that the financial statements are *accurate*.

The operative words in this statement are *guarantee* and *accurate*. A guarantee would imply that the auditors examined every transaction during the accounting period and determined that all were properly recorded, summarized, classified, and compiled into the financial statements. As we know, such actions would be impracticable to carry out. Because of cost/benefit constraints, auditors often use a sampling process when examining evidence necessary to attest to the fairness of the financial statements. As we will learn later in this chapter, *sampling* is an examination of less than 100 percent of the items in a population. Accurate would imply that there is total exactness in the financial statements, an idea that we know to be untrue. Financial statements include opinions, estimates, and judgments that are often imprecise.

Given the preceding facts, then, what positive accomplishments can we attribute to the attest function? Or, put another way, what assurance can the auditors give the parties that rely on financial statements in making credit and investment decisions?

1. Auditors can give assurance that they know how the amounts and disclosures in the financial statements were recorded, summarized, classified, and compiled. For example, they understand how the $200,000 and $220,000

Begin Company
Income Statement
For the Year Ended December 31, 19X8

Revenues:		
Sales (Net)		$1,000,000
Cost of Goods Sold:		
Beginning Inventory	$300,000	
Purchases (Net)	580,000	
Cost of Goods Available for Sale	$880,000	
Less: Ending Inventory	280,000	600,000
Gross Margin		$ 400,000
Operating Expenses		300,000
Net Income Before Income Tax Expense		$ 100,000
Income Tax Expense		30,000
Net Income		$ 70,000

Figure 5.1 Income Statement.

amounts for Accounts Receivable shown in Figure 5.2 were derived. We should not underrate the importance of this assurance.

2. Auditors can give assurance that they gathered sufficient evidence to provide a reasonable basis for forming their opinion. In other words, they did obtain or examine evidence supporting the $220,000 of Accounts Receivable, the $280,000 of Inventory, and so on shown in Figure 5.2. It is necessary to gather evidence regarding the components of financial statements to form an overall opinion on these statements.

3. If their evaluation of the gathered evidence allows them to do so, the auditors can give assurance, in the form of an opinion (an informed one because of their qualifications), that the financial statements taken as a whole are fairly presented and are not *materially misstated* by errors or irregularities.

Such assurances are often important to the auditors' clients or third-party users of the financial statements. But two concepts underlie such assurances, concepts so important that they are used to establish

1. How much evidence auditors will obtain.

2. When and where they will obtain it.

3. What criteria will be used to evaluate it.

Begin Company
Balance Sheets
December 31, 19X7 and 19X8

	December 31	
	19X7	*19X8*
Assets		
Current Assets:		
Cash	$ 100,000	$ 150,000
Accounts Receivable (Net)	200,000	220,000
Inventory	300,000	280,000
Prepaid Expenses	10,000	20,000
Total Current Assets	$ 610,000	$ 670,000
Property and Equipment, net of Depreciation		
Equipment	$ 250,000	$ 280,000
Buildings	500,000	420,000
Net Property and Equipment	$ 750,000	$ 700,000
Total Assets	$1,360,000	$1,370,000
Liabilities and Stockholders' Equity		
Current Liabilities:		
Accounts Payable	$ 180,000	$ 120,000
Accrued Liabilities	220,000	220,000
Total Current Liabilities	$ 400,000	$ 340,000
Long-Term Liabilities:		
Notes Payable	$ 400,000	$ 450,000
Stockholders' Equity:		
Common Stock	$ 200,000	$ 200,000
Retained Earnings	360,000	380,000
Total Stockholders' Equity	$ 560,000	$ 580,000
Total Liabilities and Stockholders' Equity	$1,360,000	$1,370,000

Figure 5.2 Balance Sheets.

These concepts are materiality and audit risk, both of which will be explored in detail in the remainder of this chapter.

The Use of Materiality in Planning and Conducting an Audit

Let's look again at Figures 5.1 and 5.2 (remembering that these are only partial financial statement exhibits used for teaching purposes). We know that auditors cannot examine every transaction reflected in these financial statements, so they must be willing to accept some small amount of error. How much error or misstatement would auditors be willing to tolerate in these statements and still render an opinion that the statements are fairly presented and not misleading?

This is a difficult question. Perhaps we should frame the decision in the form of two examples.

1. A few days before the end of 19X8, a $100 expenditure for the repair of equipment was incorrectly charged to the equipment account in the balance sheet rather than to operating expenses in the income statement. As a result (ignoring depreciation), total assets should be stated at $1,369,900 rather than $1,370,000 and net income before taxes should be stated at $99,900 instead of $100,000. Are the financial statements still fairly presented and not misleading?

2. A few days before the end of 19X8, a $50,000 expenditure for the repair of equipment was incorrectly charged to the equipment account rather than to operating expenses. As a result (ignoring depreciation), total assets should be stated at $1,320,000 rather than $1,370,000 and net income before taxes should be stated at $50,000 instead of $100,000. Are the financial statements still fairly presented and not misleading?

In all likelihood the auditors would answer the question in the first example "yes" and the second example "no." Why? Because of the application of a concept called *materiality,* which is defined by the Financial Standards Accounting Board as

> the magnitude of an omission or misstatement of accounting information that, in light of surrounding circumstances, makes it probable that the judgment of a reasonable person relying on the information would have been changed or influenced by the omission or misstatement.

Put another way, the $100 misstatement is not likely to change or influence a reasonable person's judgment in this circumstance, but the $50,000 misstatement is likely to do so. Thus, materiality is a major factor that auditors consider when planning an audit and evaluating the evidence after the audit has been conducted. In the previously described example, the auditors would have to establish what is called a threshold of materiality by selecting some dollar figure as the amount by which the financial statements would be materially misstated if the total of the misstatements were above that amount.

Materiality Considerations

As we will see in the following discussion, there is much more to materiality decisions than arbitrarily selecting a single dollar amount for the financial statements. Consideration must be given to such factors as

1. The relationship of a misstatement to certain key amounts in the financial statements such as (this list is not exhaustive).

   a. Net income before taxes in the income statement.

   b. Total assets in the balance sheet.

   c. Total current assets in the balance sheet.

   d. Total stockholders' equity in the balance sheet.

   e. Certain accounts in the financial statements that are particularly important.

2. Qualitative factors such as (again, this list is not exhaustive)

   a. The probability that illegal payments might be made.

   b. The probability that irregularities might occur.

   c. Provisions in a client's loan agreement with a bank requiring that certain financial statement ratios be maintained at minimum levels.

   d. An interruption in a trend in earnings.

   e. Management's attitude about the integrity of the financial statements.

Refer to Figures 5.1 and 5.2 and we will apply the materiality criteria listed above.

The auditors may decide that any combination of misstatements that totals more than 8 percent of net income before taxes will ordinarily be material, subject to qualitative considerations. If the combination of misstatements is less than 3 percent of net income before taxes, the auditors will ordinarily consider them to be immaterial, subject to qualitative considerations. Misstatements that total between 3 and 8 percent will call for judgment on the part of the auditor. Therefore, the *materiality borders* for the income statement are between

$$\$3,000\ (\$100,000 \times 3\%) \text{ to } \$8,000\ (\$100,000 \times 8\%)$$

The auditors may apply a similar methodology to the materiality borders for total assets, current assets, and stockholders' equity in the balance sheet. Assume these materiality borders.

For total assets in the balance sheet:
$41,000 to $109,600

For current assets in the balance sheet:
$20,100 to $53,600

For total stockholders' equity in the balance sheet:
$17,400 to $46,400

In what way might the qualitative factors affect these materiality borders or guidelines? Management resistance to adjusting the accounting records for previously discovered errors might cause the auditors to lower the amounts in all of the materiality borders. The auditor should also remember that any illegal act or irregularity that is detected will probably be qualitatively material regardless of the dollar amount involved.

Another qualitative factor is a provision in one of the client's loan agreements that specifies that a minimum current ratio must be maintained. Look at Figure 5.2, and assume that the notes payable of $450,000 can be called if Begin Company does not maintain at least a 2:1 current ratio. The current ratio on the December 31, 19X8 balance sheet is barely under 2:1 (total current assets of $670,000/total current liabilities of $340,000). Begin Company may be tempted to increase current assets or reduce current liabilities. Therefore, the auditors may lower the materiality borders (in fact, the auditors may establish a very low materiality level on current assets and current liabilities because of this provision in the loan agreement).

On the other hand, there may have been an upward trend of net income in recent years, giving management less reason to try to overstate that figure. In this case, the materiality borders might be raised.

Preliminary Estimates of Materiality in Planning

Preliminary Estimates in the Total Financial Statements   There are two ways in which auditors use materiality. The first is in planning the audit and the second is in evaluating the evidence after conducting the audit. As far as planning is concerned, the auditors need to make preliminary estimates of materiality because there is an inverse relationship between the amounts in the financial statements that the auditors consider to be material and the amount of audit work necessary to attest to the fairness of the financial statements.

For example, if the auditor considers $8,000 to be material for the income statement, a certain amount of time and effort must be spent gathering evidence on the individual accounts. On the other hand, if that materiality threshold is lowered to $3,000, additional time and effort must be expended in gathering the necessary evidence. The reason is that it is more difficult to find a small error than a large error.

Therefore, auditors must give careful consideration to the setting of preliminary estimates of materiality in planning the audit. If the dollar amount of materiality is set too low, unnecessary audit effort will be expended. If the dollar amount of materiality is set too high, the auditors might overlook a significant misstatement and attest to financial statements that are materially misstated.

Even though the materiality borders illustrated on page 157 ($3,000 to $8,000 for the income statement, etc.) may be used to make the final decisions on acceptability of the fairness of the financial statements, the auditors may use the upper borders to set the **preliminary estimate** of materiality for planning purposes. The auditors might consider the following:

1. The financial statements will be materially misstated if the misstatement of net income before income taxes exceeds $8,000.

2. The financial statements will be materially misstated if the misstatement of total assets exceeds $109,600.

3. The financial statements will be materially misstated if the misstatement of total current assets exceeds $53,600.

4. The financial statements will be materially misstated if the misstatement of stockholders' equity exceeds $46,400.

The auditors should then choose $8,000 as their preliminary estimate of materiality for purposes of planning the amount of audit effort. This is the smallest materiality threshold and provides reasonable assurance that the auditors will gather enough evidence to make the following statement.

There is an acceptably low audit risk that net income before income taxes is not misstated by more than $8,000 and thus the financial statements are not materially misstated.

Why should the auditors select $8,000 as their materiality threshold? Because misstatements in one financial statement are likely to cause misstatements in other financial statements. By selecting $8,000 as the materiality threshold, the auditors are extending their audit effort and should also have an even lower audit risk that

total assets are not misstated by more than $109,600,

current assets are not misstated by more than $53,600, and

stockholders' equity is not misstated by more than $46,400.

Preliminary Estimates for Individual Accounts   Although auditors render an opinion on the financial statements taken as a whole, they must audit individual accounts to gather the necessary evidence to render this opinion. This means that the total preliminary estimate of materiality for planning purposes must be subdivided into amounts for individual financial statement accounts being examined. The portion of materiality allocated to individual accounts is referred to as *tolerable error* for that account.

There are several ways that materiality for the total financial statements can be assigned to individual accounts. One method is to assign the total materiality amount to accounts that would ordinarily be affected by any misstatements in the financial statements. Most of the balance sheet accounts fall into this category. Using Figure 5.2 as an example, then, the auditors could assign part of the total materiality of $8,000 to

Cash, Accounts Receivable, Inventory, Prepaid Expenses, Equipment, Buildings, Accounts Payable, Accrued Liabilities, Notes Payable, and Common Stock.

On what basis could the assignments be made? One possibility is to assign to each account the percentage of $8,000 that represents the percentage of that account balance to the total account balances. For example, if the cash account balance of $150,000 is 5 percent of the sum of all the account balances, then $400 ($8,000 × 5 percent) could be assigned to Cash.

Such an assignment method ignores several factors, however.

1. Some accounts may be more important than their dollar balance would imply because of the number of transactions that affect that account. A prime example is Inventory, which has a $280,000 balance in Figure 5.2. Even though the inventory balance is approximately 10 percent of the sum of all the account balances under consideration, its special importance might call for assigning it less than 10 percent of the $8,000 of materiality (thus necessitating more audit effort than normal on inventory).

2. Experience in prior-year audits might cause the auditors to believe that certain accounts are more or less likely to contain misstatements than other accounts. Accounts Receivable might be a case in point. The absence of detected misstatements in previous years might suggest that a higher than

normal amount of materiality be assigned to this account (thus lowering the amount of necessary effort).

After due consideration of all relevant factors, assume that the $8,000 of materiality is assigned to all the accounts listed previously. These assignments result in the following amounts for Accounts Receivable and Inventory (we will not show the hypothetical assignments to all the accounts).

Account Title	Account Balance	Amount of Materiality Assigned
	$	$
Accounts Receivable	220,000	1,500
Inventory	280,000	1,200
		$ 8,000

In auditing Accounts Receivable and Inventory the auditors will use the following planning guidelines.

1. Accounts Receivable—design audit procedures to detect errors of $1,500 or greater.

2. Inventory—design audit procedures to detect errors of $1,200 or greater.

It may seem a bit strange to plan to find relatively small errors in accounts with $220,000 and $280,000 balances, but remember these points.

1. Misstatements that affect Accounts Receivable and Inventory will probably affect net income before income taxes, and the overall materiality of $8,000 in the financial statements is based on the potential misstatement of net income before income taxes.

2. The amounts of $1,500 and $1,200 were assigned to Accounts Receivable and Inventory, respectively, because errors in these accounts must be aggregated with errors in other accounts and compared with the $8,000 materiality standard for the overall financial statements.

We will now turn our attention to the use of materiality estimates to evaluate audit evidence gathered during the conduct of the audit.

Use of Materiality in Evaluating Audit Evidence

We will not discuss the detail audit procedures used to collect evidence on each of the accounts examined. These procedures are illustrated in detail later in the text. For now, we will assume that audit evidence is gathered on each account and the uncorrected misstatements are tabulated for evaluation.

Assume, for example, that $2,000 of errors were found in the Inventory account. Would the auditors automatically assume that the financial statements taken as a whole were materially misstated? Not necessarily. The auditors might extend their audit effort on Inventory because of the particular importance of that account or because of the nature of the errors. However, the auditors would aggregate the $2,000 of errors with errors found in other accounts.

To illustrate, we can use this hypothetical schedule of errors found during the course of the audit.

Uncorrected errors in Inventory	$2,000
Uncorrected errors in the total of all other accounts	7,000
	$9,000

What would happen now? Again, there are several possibilities.

1. For a variety of reasons, the auditors may have revised their threshold of materiality upward from the preliminary estimate of $8,000 used for planning to $10,000 used to evaluate audit evidence. As an example, perhaps the client's cash flow situation has improved since the audit procedures were planned several months ago. In this case, the auditors would not automatically consider the financial statements to be materially misstated because the estimate of the total misstatements ($9,000) is less than revised materiality. (The authors believe that extreme care should be taken in making this type of revision.)

2. The auditors could conclude that the financial statements are not fairly presented because the total uncorrected errors ($9,000) exceed materiality of $8,000. We will leave for discussion in later chapters all of the alternatives available to the auditors. It is sufficient at this point to say that "something would have to be done," such as convincing the client to correct the errors or considering a modification of the audit report.

What if the estimate of the total misstatements was less than $8,000? The auditors might use the materiality borders on net income ($3,000 to $8,000 from page 157) to help them make a judgment as to whether the financial statements should be accepted as fair and not misleading.

Summary of Materiality Considerations

As we can see, considerations of materiality are inherent in the auditing process because they help set the guidelines as to the amount of evidence to gather and the decision of whether financial statements will be accepted as fairly presented. The auditors *must* use materiality because of the impossibility of providing a guarantee of exactness in the financial statements. The opinion on fairness expressed by the auditors assumes that materiality has been considered in arriving at that opinion.

The Use of Audit Risk in Planning and Conducting an Audit[1]

As important as materiality is, however, it must be coupled with considerations of audit risk in planning and evaluating an audit. It is not sufficient for the auditors to state the following:

> We will accept the financial statements as fairly presented and not materially misleading if
>
> net income before income taxes is not misstated by more than $3,000,
>
> total assets are not misstated by more than $41,100,
>
> current assets are not misstated by more than $20,100, and
>
> total stockholders' equity is not misstated by more than $17,400.

The auditors must make these types of statements.

> We will accept, *at a certain risk level,* the financial statements as fairly presented and not misleading if
> net income before income taxes is not misstated by more than $3,000,
>
> total assets are not misstated by more than $41,100,
>
> current assets are not misstated by more than $20,100, and
>
> total stockholders' equity is not misstated by more than $17,400.

The fact that auditors cannot guarantee the exactness of the financial statements implies considerations of both materiality and *audit risk,* the latter of which is defined as

[1]See "Audit Risk—Tracing the Evolution," by Janet L. Colbert in *Accounting Horizons* (September 1987), pp. 49–57 for an additional discussion of audit risk.

the risk that the auditor may unknowingly fail to appropriately modify his or her opinion on financial statements that are materially misstated.

But audit risk, like materiality, can be divided into two parts.

1. The overall audit risk that relates to the financial statements as a whole, the definition of which is shown above.

2. The *individual audit risks* that relate to each of the individual account balances that constitute the financial statements.

In keeping with this division of audit risks as suggested in *SAS No. 47,* we formulate in Figure 5.3, the steps that auditors can take concerning audit risk when planning the audit and evaluating the evidence obtained in conducting the audit. This is a conceptual approach; auditors often do not formalize many of the steps. In fact, there is little guidance in the professional standards or other auditing literature for allocating or aggregating audit risk. The first two steps relate to planning and are discussed in the following section. The next three steps relate to evaluation of evidence obtained during the audit and are explored in the subsequent section.

Decide on the **Overall Planned Audit Risk**

Assign the Overall Planned Audit Risk to **Individual Audit Risks** for the Individual Accounts

Ascertain the **Achieved Individual Audit Risks** for the Individual Accounts Obtained in Evaluating Evidence

Ascertain the **Achieved Overall Audit Risk** Obtained in Evaluating Evidence

Compare the Achieved Overall Audit Risk to the Planned Overall Audit Risk to Determine Whether to Accept the Financial Statements as Fairly Presented and not Materially Misstated.

Figure 5.3   Sequence of steps in considering audit risk.

Audit Risk in Planning the Audit

Decide on the Overall Planned Audit Risk

The auditor's first step is to consider the *overall planned audit risk* they are willing to take that they will attest to the fair presentation of the financial statements when, in fact, the financial statements are materially misstated. Considering the importance of this task, surprisingly few definitive guidelines exist on how the level of overall audit risk should be set. *SAS No. 47* merely states that the audit should be planned so that the audit risk will be limited to a low level.

Audit risk may be assessed in either quantitative or qualitative terms. We use a quantitative approach (e.g., a risk of 5 or 10 percent) to illustrate the concepts, although a qualitative approach (e.g., a low or moderate risk) may be more common in practice. We should remember that in setting a certain overall audit risk, the auditors are also expressing a certain level of confidence. For example, a 5 percent overall audit risk that the auditors will incorrectly accept the financial statements as fairly presented is also a 95 percent confidence level that the financial statements are fairly presented if indeed the auditors state that they are. A 10 percent risk level is a 90 percent confidence level, and so on.

By requiring that auditors set overall audit risk at a low level for purposes of planning their audit procedures, *SAS No. 47* implies that caution should be exercised. Remember that there is an inverse relationship between risk levels and the amount of necessary audit effort (lower risk levels mean more audit effort and higher risk levels mean less audit effort).

For example, auditors could use 5 percent as the overall risk level for planning purposes. (Could most of us "live" with a 95 percent confidence level that our business decisions are correct?) Using materiality amounts from the earlier part of the chapter, the auditors might use these decision guidelines.

1. At an overall audit risk of 5 percent, the financial statements will be accepted as fairly presented in all material respects if the overall misstatement in net income before income taxes is no more than $3,000.

2. At an overall audit risk of 5 percent, judgment will be applied to determine whether the financial statements are fairly presented in all material respects if the overall misstatement in net income before income taxes is between $3,000 and $8,000.

3. The financial statements will be considered to be materially misstated if the overall misstatement in net income before income taxes is more than $8,000.

Assign the Overall Audit Risk to Individual Accounts

Because an audit involves examinations of individual accounts, we "operationalize" the overall planned audit risk by dividing it into **individual audit risks** for Accounts Receivable, Inventory, and so on. Again, the auditing standards provide few definitive guidelines for doing this and thus leave it almost entirely to the judgment of the auditors.

However, the guidelines for allocating total materiality to individual accounts might be helpful (refer to page 159). If certain accounts are exceptionally important because of their size and/or the number of transactions affecting them during the accounting period (e.g., inventory), auditors may consider lower individual audit risks and, thus, more audit effort. On the other hand, favorable experience in examining other accounts in prior years might suggest higher individual audit risks and less audit effort.

One possibility is to assign to the individual accounts the same level as the overall audit risk (5 percent in this example). For teaching purposes, then, we will use 5 percent in our illustration.

Inherent Risk, Control Risk, and Detection Risk   Ultimately, auditors must determine audit effort for each account based on the risk they are willing to take that this audit effort will fail to detect material errors existing in the financial statements. At a micro level, this is the auditors' "ultimate fear," a fear that they will not detect what they should have.

To understand this, we need to subdivide further the audit risk for individual accounts into three components.

1. *Inherent risk,* as the name implies, is the inherent susceptibility of an account balance to material misstatement. This risk exists without regard to the audit of the financial statements. Generally speaking, inherent risk is greater with certain balances and transactions than others. Complex inventory calculations are more susceptible to misstatements than calculations of prepaid insurance. Cash and marketable securities are more likely to be stolen than land and buildings. There is more likely to be a misstatement in an estimate of allowance for doubtful accounts than in the capital stock account. Lack of management integrity also increases inherent risk.

2. *Control risk* is the risk that a material misstatement in a balance will not be prevented or detected on a timely basis by the internal control structure. Controls are discussed more fully in Chapters 7 and 8. Every organization has controls designed to prevent or detect errors. Such controls could range from the use of dual signatures on checks to elaborate controls over inventory counts. This risk also exists without regard to the audit of financial statements. The limitations of controls ensures that some control risk will usually exist. As discussed in Chapters 7 and 8, a strong system of controls lowers this risk.

3. *Detection risk* is the risk that the auditor will not detect a material misstatement in an account balance. Auditors' procedures may lead them to conclude that a material misstatement in the financial statements does not exist when, in fact, it does.

Detection risk can be controlled by auditors because it results from the following.

1. *Nonsampling risk.* Uncertainties still exist even if the auditor examines 100 percent of an account balance (examines all invoices for property additions, observes all inventory counts, receives confirmation letters from all customers, etc.). For example:

A. The auditor may not use the correct audit procedure. All vendor invoices supporting accounts payable may be examined, but confirmation letters should have been obtained from vendors.

B. The auditor may misapply an auditing procedure. Confirmation letters may be obtained from customers for recorded accounts receivable balances, but unrecorded balances are not detected.

C. The auditor may misinterpret an audit result. A letter received from a customer confirming an accounts receivable balance may appear to verify the balance on the books. In fact, the letter contradicts the book balance because the amount is noted by the customer as being in dispute.

These uncertainties can be reduced by proper audit training and supervision and by the use of quality-control measures discussed in Chapter 6.

2. *Sampling risk.* Uncertainties are implicit when the auditor examines less than 100 percent of an account balance. These uncertainties cannot be eliminated, but they can be controlled by careful attention to proper sampling techniques. Specific sampling techniques and their application to audit tests are discussed in Chapters 9 and 13.

Because detection risk is a component of the individual audit risk that can be controlled by the auditors, we use an *audit risk model* to provide guidelines for the level at which detection risk will be set. This audit risk model is derived from concepts illustrated in *SAS No. 47* and *SAS No. 39*.

$$\text{Individual audit risk} = \text{Inherent risk} \times \text{Control risk} \times \text{Detection risk}$$

The model may be restated as

$$\text{Detection risk} = \frac{\text{Individual audit risk}}{\text{Inherent risk} \times \text{Control Risk}}$$

Detection risk is then computed by (1) setting individual audit risk, inherent risk, and control risk through the application of judgment and (2) applying arithmetic.

Here is how the audit risk model could be used to set detection risk for the audit of the inventory account.

1. Judgmentally set individual audit risk for Inventory at 5 percent (perhaps because the overall audit risk is also set at 5 percent).

2. Judgmentally set inherent risk at 60 percent. The account is large, some calculations are complex, and a significant number of transactions are processed through this account each year.

3. Judgmentally set control risk at 30 percent because the control structure has been found to be effective in prior years and few errors were detected in tests of the controls.

Detection risk is then set at

$$\frac{.05}{.60 \times .30} = .27 \text{ or } 27 \text{ percent (rounded)}$$

A detection risk of 27 percent may provide guidance to the auditor in deciding how much audit effort to plan for the Inventory account.

If statistical sampling techniques are used, the 27 percent detection risk becomes a direct factor in determining sample size (this will be illustrated in Chapter 13). If nonstatistical sampling is used, the auditor would see that a relatively high detection risks could be taken (better than one chance in four) and therefore would plan only limited tests of inventory.

Quantifying judgmental factors is a difficult task and, for this reason, some auditors prefer to make only qualitative judgments as to the various risks illustrated previously. Others argue that the use of a quantitative approach forces auditors to give more thought to their audit judgments.

Audit Risk in Evaluating the Audit Findings

Ascertain the Achieved Individual Risks for the Accounts

During the audit, the auditors will have to decide, on the basis of evidence gathered and evaluated, whether there should be any change in inherent risk, control risk, or detection risk. If not, then the components of individual audit risk for the inventory account in our example would remain at

60 percent for inherent risk

30 percent for control risk

27 percent for detection risk

This means that the achieved individual audit risk for the Inventory remains at 5 percent as shown below.

$$\begin{array}{l}\text{Achieved individual} \\ \text{audit risk}\end{array} = \begin{array}{l}\text{Inherent} \\ \text{risk}\end{array} \times \begin{array}{l}\text{Control} \\ \text{risk}\end{array} \times \begin{array}{l}\text{Detection} \\ \text{risk}\end{array}$$

$$.05 \qquad = .60 \quad \times .30 \quad \times .27$$

As you can easily see, however, if either inherent risk, control risk, or detection risk is judged during the course of evidence gathering to be higher than originally planned, the achieved individual audit risk will be higher than 5 percent, and the auditor must consider what to do about it. The financial statements will not be considered misstated at this point, but the higher achieved individual audit risk will be considered in evaluating the *achieved overall audit risk*. Also, additional audit procedures might be performed on the inventory account, depending on the nature of the problems uncovered by the auditor.

For example, the auditors might have discovered control problems that cause him or her to revise the control risk judgment on Inventory to 80 percent. Then detection risk should be revised to 10 percent (.05/.60 × .80), which means that additional audit effort should be applied to the inventory account. It is always possible that unforeseen events may force the auditors to alter their judgments. Such is the nature of auditing.

Ascertain the Achieved Overall Audit Risk

Auditing standards provide little, if any, guidance on how to aggregate all the achieved *individual* audit risks into an achieved *overall* audit risk. But if the auditors have reason to believe that the financial statements may still be materially misstated due to further error remaining undetected, it is likely that the achieved overall audit risk will exceed the planned overall audit risk. The auditors will have to consider alternatives, the details of which are discussed at length in later chapters. Generally additional audit effort is required for the accounts where individual audit risk is unacceptably high.

Audit Sampling

We have shown how auditors must consider materiality and audit risk because of limitations of the audit function, that is, the inability of auditors to provide a guarantee of exactness in the financial statements. Some of the reasons for these limitations are inherent and could not be changed if the auditors examined 100 percent of all the available audit evidence. We covered this limitation when we discussed nonsampling risk earlier in the chapter. Other reasons for these limitations, however, relate to the fact that many audit tests are conducted by using sampling, that is, examination of less than 100 percent of the available audit evidence. Cost/benefit considerations dictate that sampling must sometimes be used.

In the remainder of this chapter, we will discuss the nature of audit sampling and some matters auditors must consider in performing some audit tests using sampling techniques. Detail illustrations of sampling will be left to later chapters, particularly Chapters 9 and 13.

The Nature of Audit Sampling

The third standard of field work refers to the gathering of sufficient and competent evidence to afford a reasonable basis for an opinion. The term *reasonable* implies that some uncertainty exists in auditors' opinions of the fair presentation of financial statements in accordance with generally accepted accounting principles. Part of this uncertainty exists because auditors apply some audit procedures to less than 100 percent of the items within an account balance when evaluating a characteristic of that balance. This is called audit sampling. Consider these alternatives:

1. Auditors can request confirmation letters from customers and vendors for every accounts receivable or accounts payable balance. Subject to the non-sampling risks discussed in the previous section, the auditor would have full assurance that these account balances contained no material errors. The alternative is to send letters to a sample of these customers and vendors. The sample results are assumed to be representative of the results that would be obtained if letters were sent to 100 percent of the customers and vendors, which would be more costly and time-consuming but would provide more assurance. A sample is less costly and time-consuming but provides less assurance.

2. Auditors can examine an invoice for every addition to property and equipment for the purpose of determining whether the expenditures should be capitalized or expensed, or they can examine a sample of invoices. Again, the sample results are assumed to be representative of 100 percent of the invoices, which would be more costly and time-consuming to examine but would provide more assurance than a less-than-100 percent examination.

In each case, the auditors must weigh the cost and time required to examine all the data against the adverse consequences of possible erroneous decisions based on examination of a sample of the data. The adverse consequences could be considerable and should not be taken lightly. An unqualified opinion on materially misstated financial statements could result in a lawsuit and loss of professional reputation.

For many auditing procedures, however, auditors decide that possible adverse consequences are more acceptable than the cost and time required to examine all of the data. A well-designed sample, properly executed and carefully evaluated, will furnish auditors with a significant degree of assurance. The cost and effort required to add an additional degree of assurance may not be acceptable to the auditor. Thus, the basic concept of sampling is well established in auditing practice.

Considerations in Using Audit Sampling

Many audit procedures do not require the use of audit sampling, including the following examples.

1. Some audit procedures involve inquiry, observation, or the completion of some form, such as

   A. Interviews with management personnel. Auditors inquire about such matters as inventory obsolescence and the status of overdue accounts receivable.

   B. Completion of questionnaires. When studying the control structure, auditors sometimes document their findings in the form of questions and answers on a questionnaire.

   C. Observation of client personnel. Auditors often need to ascertain whether certain duties are performed by different people.

   D. Inspection of assets. A count of marketable securities is a standard audit procedure.

2. Other audit procedures require the use of analytical procedures (discussed more fully in Chapter 12). Basically, such procedures involve reviews of the reasonableness of client information and do not require the use of sampling techniques.

3. Often, auditors examine 100 percent of the data comprising an account balance, for example, a 100 percent examination of additions to capital stock or confirmation of 100 percent of notes payable.

4. Sometimes auditors examine only a few items in an account balance, but the characteristic of the entire account balance is not evaluated. An example might be the examination of inventory items without activity in several months. The purpose of this procedure is to check for a possible inventory obsolescence problem, not to ascertain the fairness of the entire inventory balance. Such a procedure is not considered to be audit sampling and does not come under the guidelines we will discuss in the remainder of this chapter.

Sampling is used by a variety of scientific, professional, and governmental units. Audit sampling, however, is distinct in several ways.

1. Auditors corroborate and evaluate data already accumulated and summarized. This activity requires the use of audit sampling techniques different from those used when original data are gathered.

2. Accounting populations usually consist of a few large amounts, some fairly large amounts, and a considerable number of small amounts. Accounts receivable for wholesale and retail businesses is one example; checking accounts for banks is another example. Often, a 100 percent examination is made of the large and fairly large amounts. Audit sampling is then applied to the large block of small amounts.

3. A single audit procedure to which sampling is applied is seldom the sole source of audit evidence for a given account balance. Additional tests of the same account balance are usually made. The audit of inventory is a case in point. Auditors may observe the client's count of inventory at the end of the fiscal year, compare physical counts with perpetual records, test for inventory obsolescence, and inquire about consigned merchandise. The audit evidence gathered by applying audit sampling to one of these procedures (e.g., the comparison of inventory counts and perpetual records) is augmented by evidence obtained by the other procedures. This characteristic of audit sampling means that risk levels for some procedures can be higher than they would be without the "reinforcement" provided by other procedures applied to the same account balance.

In planning an audit sample, certain questions need to be answered.

1. What is the objective of the test for which audit sampling will be applied?

2. What is to be sampled? (How is the accounting population defined?)

3. What is the auditor looking for in the sample? (How is an error defined?)

4. How is the population to be sampled? (What is the sampling plan and the method of selection?)

5. How large is the sample? (How many sample items are to be subjected to the audit procedure?)

The answers to these questions provide a basis for applying audit sampling to certain tests and for controlling the sampling risks when audit sampling is used.

Statistical and Nonstatistical Sampling

Audit sampling can be performed by using statistical or nonstatistical techniques. The use of either technique is essentially a cost-benefit decision. The advantages of statistical sampling are as follows:

1. The design of a more efficient sample.

2. A more precise measurement of the sufficiency of audit evidence obtained.

3. A more precise quantitative evaluation of the sample results.

4. A quantitative measure of sampling risk.

On the other hand, the design and selection of the sample may be more costly if statistical sampling is used. Either systematic or pure random selection can be used for both statistical and nonstatistical techniques. When systematic selection is used, every fifth or tenth item, for example, is selected after a random start. When pure random selection is used, auditors refer to a table of randomly generated numbers and select the sample in such a way that every element in the population has an equal chance of selection.

A nonstatistical application may be designed that is equally effective and less costly than a statistical sampling application. However, nonstatistical sampling cannot quantitatively measure sampling risk. If this shortcoming is considered critical to the auditor, statistical sampling should be strongly considered.

In Chapters 9 and 13, we will contrast, in detail, these two techniques.

**Chapter 5
Glossary of Terms**

(listed in the order of appearance in the chapter, with accompanying page reference where the term is discussed)

| | Page in |
Term	Chapter
Sampling An examination of less than 100 percent of the items in a population.	152
Materially misstated When financial statements contain errors or irregularities whose effect is important enough to cause them not to be presented fairly in accordance with generally accepted accounting principles.	153
Materiality The magnitude of an omission or misstatement of accounting information that, in the light of surrounding circumstances, makes it probable that a reasonable person's judgment would have been changed or influenced by the omission or misstatement.	155

	Page in
Term	*Chapter*

Achieved individual audit risk   The audit risk achieved on individual accounts   167
after they are audited.

Achieved overall audit risk   The audit risk achieved on the total financial state-   168
ments after all accounts have been audited.

Chapter 5
References

American Institute of Certified Public Accountants. *Professional Standards:*

AU Section 312 [*SAS No. 47*]—*Audit Risk and Materiality in Conducting an Audit.*

AU Section 350 [*SAS No. 39*]—*Audit Sampling.*

Colbert, Janet L. "Audit Risk—Tracing the Evolution," *Accounting Horizons* (September 1987), pp. 49–57.

Jennings, Marianne, Kneer, Dan C., and Reckers, Philip M. S. "A Reexamination of the Concept of Materiality: Views of Auditors, Users, and Officers of the Court," *Auditing: A Journal of Practice and Theory* (Spring 1987), pp. 104–115.

Warren, Carl S., Yates, Stephen V. N., and Zuber, George R. "Audit Sampling: A Practical Approach," *Journal of Accountancy* (January 1982), pp. 62–72.

Chapter 5
Review Questions

5-1.   What is the purpose of a financial audit?

5-2.   Explain the limitations that auditors face when they perform the attest function.

5-3.   What three assurances can auditors give to the parties that rely on financial statements?

5-4.   What is materiality?

5-5.   Why is it necessary for the auditors to establish a threshold of materiality?

5-6.   What factors must auditors consider when making materiality decisions?

5-7.   Why do auditors make preliminary estimates of materiality for the total financial statements?

5-8.   Why do auditors make preliminary estimates of materiality for the individual accounts in the financial statements?

5-9.   Explain two alternative courses of action that the auditor can follow if the total misstatement in the financial statements is more than materiality for the total financial statements.

5-10.   In planning an audit and evaluating audit evidence what consideration must be coupled with materiality?

5-11.   What is the difference between overall planned audit risk and the individual audit risks?

5-12.   What are the following risks?
a. Inherent risk
b. Control risk
c. Detection risk

5-13.   What is the difference between the following?
a. Nonsampling risk
b. Sampling risk

5-14.   Give two versions of the audit risk model.

5-15.   Under what conditions would the achieved individual audit risk for an account be the same as the individual audit risk that is used to plan the audit of that account?

5-16.   What situation would have to exist for the achieved overall audit risk to exceed the planned overall audit risk?

5-17.   Describe four audit procedures that do not require the use of audit sampling.

5-18.   What five questions need to be answered in planning an audit sample?

5-19.   Describe four advantages of using statistical sampling.

Chapter 5
Objective Questions Taken from CPA Examinations

*5-20.   Which of the following is not an assurance that the auditors give to parties that rely on financial statements?
a. Auditors know how the amounts and disclosures in the financial statements were recorded, summarized, classified, and compiled.
b. Auditors give assurance that the amounts on the financial statements are accurate.
c. Auditors gathered sufficient evidence to provide a reasonable basis for forming their opinion.
d. If the gathered evidence allows them to do so, auditors can give assurance, in the form of an opinion, that the financial statements taken as a whole are fairly presented.

*5-21.   Which of the following phrases is not a part of the definition of materiality?
a. The magnitude of an omission or misstatement of accounting information that,
b. in light of surrounding circumstances,
c. makes it probable that the judgment of a reasonable person relying on the information,
d. would not have changed or been influenced by the omission or misstatement.

*5-22.   Which of the following is the reason preliminary estimates of materiality should be made by the auditor?
a. Materiality guidelines cannot be used after the audit procedures are conducted.
b. There is a direct relationship between the amounts in the financial statements that auditors consider to be material and the amount of audit work necessary to attest to the fairness of the financial statements.
c. There is an inverse relationship between the amounts in the financial statements that auditors consider to be material and the amount of audit work necessary to attest to the fairness of the financial statements.
d. Estimates of materiality will eliminate audit risk.

*Not a CPA examination question.

*5-23.   Which of the following is a correct statement?
   a. There is an inverse relationship between risk levels and the amount of necessary audit effort.
   b. There is a direct relationship between risk levels and the amount of necessary audit effort.
   c. There is no relationship between risk levels and the amount of necessary audit effort.
   d. Risk levels need not be considered by the auditor if estimates of materiality are made.

*5-24.   Which of the following is not a part of the audit risk model?
   a. Inherent risk.
   b. Control risk.
   c. Materiality risk.
   d. Detection risk.

5-25.   Which of the following best illustrates an error caused by sampling?
   a. A randomly chosen sample may not be representative of the population as a whole on the characteristic of interest.
   b. An auditor may select audit procedures that are not appropriate to achieve the specific objectives.
   c. An auditor may fail to recognize errors in the documents examined for the chosen sample.
   d. The documents related to the chosen sample may not be available for inspection.

5-26.   Which of the following is an error caused by sampling?
   a. Choosing an audit procedure that is inconsistent with the audit objective.
   b. Choosing a sample size that is too small to achieve the sampling objective.
   c. Failing to detect an error on a document that has been inspected by the auditor.
   d. Failing to perform audit procedures that are required by the sampling plan.

5-27.   The application of statistical sampling techniques is least related to which of the following generally accepted auditing standards?
   a. The work is to be adequately planned and assistants, if any, are to be properly supervised.
   b. In all matters relating to the assignment, an independence in mental attitude is to be maintained by the auditor or auditors.
   c. There is to be a proper study and evaluation of control risk as a basis for reliance thereon and for the determination of the resultant extent of the tests to which auditing procedures are to be restricted.
   d. Sufficient competent evidential matter is to be obtained through inspection,

*Not a CPA examination question.

observation, inquiries, and confirmation to afford a reasonable basis for an opinion regarding the financial statements under examination.

5-28.   Auditors who prefer statistical sampling to nonstatistical sampling may do so because statistical sampling helps the auditor
a. Measure the sufficiency of the evidential matter obtained.
b. Eliminate subjectivity in the evaluation of sampling results.
c. Reduce the level of tolerable error to a relatively low amount.
d. Minimize the failure to detect a material misstatement due to nonsampling risk.

Chapter 5
Discussion/Case Questions

5-29.   Audit risk and materiality should be considered when planning and performing an examination of financial statements in accordance with generally accepted auditing standards. Audit risk and materiality should also be considered together in determining the nature, timing, and extent of auditing procedures and in evaluating the results of those procedures.

Required:
a. 1. Define materiality.
2. Discuss the factors affecting its determination.
3. Describe the relationship between materiality for planning purposes and materiality for evaluation purposes.
b. 1. Define audit risk.
2. Describe its components of inherent risk, control risk, and detection risk.
3. Explain how these components are interrelated.
(*AICPA Adapted*)

*5-30.   Try-Hard Company was organized in early January of 19X7. The company is in the business of taking computer chips from discarded personal computers and making vases and other items that are used to decorate residences.

Try-Hard had managed to raise $200,000 from the sale of capital stock and $400,000 by borrowing on a long-term note. In 19X8, they borrowed another $50,000 on a long-term note. However, there are provisions in the notes that give the bank the right to call the notes if the current ratio falls below 2 to 1 in the balance sheet issued at the end of the second year of operations.

By using skillful marketing techniques and holding down expenses, the company was "in the black" by 19X8. However, federal authorities had cited

*This question requires you to make reasonable assumptions and to draw logical inferences from the material in the chapter.

Try-Hard several times for paying its employees less than the required minimum wage.

In late 19X8 Try-Hard engaged a CPA firm to audit their financial statements, parts of which are shown in Figures 5.1 and 5.2. During the planning stages of the audit, the CPA firm decided that the threshold of materiality" would be a misstatement of net income before income tax expense of $10,000.

Required

a. Using the amounts in Figures 5.1 and 5.2, assign the materiality of $10,000 to the appropriate accounts in the financial statements. Supply a written justification for the amount assigned to each account. If you did not assign some of the $10,000 to certain accounts, explain why.

b. For each of the accounts to which you assigned some of the $10,000 of materiality, indicate what steps you might take if the errors found in the account exceeded, by a small amount, the dollar amount of materiality assigned to that account.

c. Assume that, after aggregating the errors in each account, the total is $11,000. What are the possible actions you could take? Indicate the advantages and disadvantages of each possible course of action.

d. Assume that, after aggregating the errors in each account, the total is $15,000. In what way, if any, would your possible courses of action be different than the possible courses of action you might take in situation c., above?

*5-31   Take the same facts as Question 5-30, above. Using the audit risk model shown on page 166, calculate the detection risk for Inventory if the other risks are set at these levels.

a. Individual audit risk of 5 percent.
    Inherent risk of 50 percent.
    Control risk of 40 percent.

b. Individual audit risk of 5 percent.
    Inherent risk of 70 percent.
    Control risk of 20 percent.

Why might the inherent risk be set at 70 percent rather than at 50 percent? Why might the control risk be set at 20 percent rather than at 40 percent? Refer to situation A., above. What could cause the achieved individual audit risk on Inventory to be higher than the planned individual audit risk of 5 percent? What actions could the auditor take?

5-32.   For the following sets of circumstances, indicate whether the auditor would have a high or low risk of failing to detect these circumstances with appropriate audit procedures. Give reasons for your answers.

---

*This question requires you to make reasonable assumptions and to draw logical inferences from the material in the chapter.

a. When the company took a physical inventory on December 31, 19X6, one out of every ten items was miscounted by an average of 5 to 12 percent of its correct amount.

b. The allowance for doubtful accounts was stated at 2 percent of accounts receivable. The allowance should have been stated between 6 and 10 percent of accounts receivable. The dollar amount of accounts receivable is ten times as much as net income.

c. Accounts payable is understated by 3 percent as a result of leaving some accounts off the books at the end of the year. These accounts were not paid until 45 days after the end of the fiscal year. The dollar amount of accounts payable is $30,000, and the net income is $20,000.

5-33.   The auditor decided to examine 100 percent of the invoices supporting additions to property and equipment. Several months after the engagement was completed and the audit report was issued, significant amounts of expenditures were discovered to have been charged to the property and equipment accounts instead of repairs expense. Explain how these misclassifications could have been overlooked by the auditor.

5-34.   Rank the following conditions as having the most inherent risk (as discussed in the chapter), the second most inherent risk, and so on. Give reasons for your rankings.

a. The processing of charge sales transactions.

b. The processing of insurance expenditure transactions.

c. Calculation of inventory obsolescence.

d. The count of physical inventory items.

e. The physical security measures taken to guard equipment used in the plant.

f. The procedures used to maintain custody of the petty cash fund.

g. The tabulation of the records at the end of the year to determine the balance in accounts payable.

h. The calculation of the allowance for doubtful accounts.

5-35.   In each of the following situations, indicate the nature or type of nonsampling risk that caused the error to occur.

a. Letters were sent to accounts payable vendors for each amount recorded on the books. Later, a large amount of unrecorded accounts payable was discovered.

b. The auditor asked the custodian of the petty cash fund to sign a statement certifying that all disbursements from the fund were properly accounted for and documented. Later, it was discovered that large amounts of unauthorized expenditures had been made.

c. The auditor receives a letter from a bank official stating that the amount of cash on the client's books is on deposit at the end of the fiscal year. Later, it was discovered that the cash account was restricted.

5-36.   The auditor examined a sample of invoices supporting expenditures charged to repairs expense. No misclassification of any expenditure was found. Later, a material amount of expenditures was discovered to be inappropriately charged to repairs expense instead of to property and equipment. Discuss why this misclassification may have been overlooked.

5-37.   For each of the following procedures, indicate whether sampling would or would not be used. Give reasons for your answers.

a. Examinations of marketable securities.

b. Confirmation letters sent to accounts receivable customers. There are 400 customers and each balance is small.

c. Comparison of recorded expense account balances with budgeted amounts.

d. Observation of inventory counts made by the client when the physical inventory is counted at the end of the fiscal year.

e. Confirmation letters sent to accounts receivable customers. There are 40 customers, each with a large outstanding balance.

CHAPTER 6

The Framework of an Audit

Learning Objectives *After reading and studying the material in this chapter, the student should*

Know the process of arranging audit work with the client.

Understand how audit work is scheduled.

Understand the considerations in planning audit work.

Know the form and function of an audit program.

Understand how evidence is gathered and recorded in the form of audit working papers.

Be aware of the means of communicating audit findings.

This chapter summarizes the framework within which audit theory is applied and describes the setting in which the many audit procedures set forth elsewhere in this book are performed. The material in the chapter provides a background for consideration of the internal control structure (starting in Chapter 7) and evidence gathering for substantive tests of financial statement balances (starting in Chapter 12). Also, it shows how procedures discussed in those chapters are interrelated to form the total audit function.

Arrangement of the Audit

Sometimes one wonders how accounting firms obtain clients. The reputation of an accounting firm and its individual members for the performance of quality work is an important source of new clients. Quality audit work may be difficult for clients and others to recognize, but clients who are satisfied that they have received high levels of professional services at reasonable prices are important contributors to the development of a professional reputation.

Competition for clients among accounting firms has intensified in recent years. As a result, management of a potential client may select the accounting firm that proposes the lowest audit fee without considering other matters. Another factor in the selection of accounting firms that has become significant enough to attract the attention of the Auditing Standards Board and the SEC is the practice of "opinion shopping." A client wishing to employ an accounting method that is not acceptable to its present auditor may consult a number of other accounting firms until it finds one that will consider the method to be generally accepted. That firm would then be hired as the auditor. The client has shopped among the accounting firms until it has found one that will issue an unqualified opinion on financial statements that include the effect of a questionable accounting method. To discourage this practice the Auditing Standards Board has issued a statement requiring an accounting firm that is consulted regarding the acceptability of an accounting principle to consider all relevant facts and to communicate with the existing auditor.

Audit Committees

Increasingly important in selecting auditors and in maintaining auditor independence is the audit committee of the board of directors. Although audit committees have existed at some companies for many years, several events have increased their number and importance. The New York Stock Exchange now requires that all companies listed on that exchange have audit committees. Also, recommendations for the establishment of audit committees have been made by the AICPA, SEC, and professional and congressional committees.

Most recommendations for audit committees include the provision that members should be outside directors, although there is some diversity of opinion as to what constitutes an outside director. At a minimum, an outside director should not be an officer or employee of the company. Some recommendations go as far as to exclude a company's banker, investment adviser, and outside legal counsel. Although the duties of audit committees will vary among companies, they often include (1) nominating the independent auditors, (2) reviewing the plan for the audit and related services, (3) reviewing audit results and financial statements, and (4) overseeing the adequacy of the company's control structure. To aid the audit committee in performing these functions, auditors communicate with them regarding a number of matters that are discussed later in this chapter.

Audit committees may increase auditor independence by serving as an arbitrator of unsolved problems between management and the auditor. Because audit committee members (unlike management) have no direct responsibility for the results of a company's operations, they should be more objective in evaluating any disputes. Additionally, if the audit committee selects the auditor, management cannot threaten the auditor with dismissal, thereby reducing substantial pressure on the auditor's independence.

Acceptance of Clients

Although most auditors are eager to obtain new clients, both prudence and generally accepted auditing standards dictate that some investigation be made of prospective clients before they are accepted.

As a matter of prudence, many auditors discuss the business reputation of a prospective client with their acquaintances in the business community, such as bankers and attorneys. Others are known to use private detectives to investigate potential clients. Any indication of improper conduct by a company or its officers should cause the auditor to consider rejecting that company as a prospective client.

The matter of acceptance of new clients is included in *Statement on Quality Control Standard No. 1* and AU Section 315 (*SAS No. 7*). The former outlines quality-control considerations for accounting firms and includes the establishment of policies and procedures for deciding whether to accept or continue a professional relationship with a client to minimize the likelihood of associating with a company whose management lacks integrity. The latter states the requirements for communications between predecessor and successor auditors when a change of auditors occurs. It places the initiative for the communications with the successor auditor, who is required to make specific inquiry (after obtaining permission from the prospective client) of the predecessor auditor as to such matters as the integrity of management, disagreements with management about accounting principles, auditing standards, and other significant matters, and the reason for the change in auditors. The predecessor auditor should respond promptly and fully; any limitation on the response must be noted. A limited response or one that reflects adversely on the management of a prospective client must be given serious consideration in the decision to accept or reject the client. This type of communication between predecessor and successor CPAs is not required for engagements of lesser scope than an audit (compilations, reviews, etc.), but prudence dictates that it be followed anyway.

Auditors have become more selective in recent years in their acceptance of clients because lack of management integrity was a major factor in most important lawsuits against auditors (discussed in Chapter 4). A painful lesson learned from these criminal and civil suits was that an early evaluation of management integrity is as important to the assurance of fair financial statements as the time spent in performing audit procedures. The *Equity Funding* and *Continental Vending* cases discussed in Chapter 4 are prime examples.

Engagement Letters

The discussion of the *1136 Tenants' Corporation* case in Chapter 4 illustrates the danger of a misunderstanding between the accountant and the client when unaudited financial statements are prepared. To confirm the CPA's responsibility, an engagement letter should also be prepared for all audit engagements. These letters, normally addressed to the board of directors, the audit committee, or the chief executive officer, include (1) a confirmation of the audit engagement for the

Partner & Co.
100 Main Street
Fayetteville, Arkansas 72701

May 1, 19X8

Mr. Robert K. Luckey
Chairman of the Audit Committee
X Company
122 West Avenue
Center City, Arkansas 70000

Dear Mr. Luckey:

This will confirm our arrangements with you to audit the financial statements of X Company for the year 19X8. Our work is to consist of an audit of the balance sheet at December 31, 19X8, and the related statements of income, retained earnings, and cash flows for the year then ending in accordance with generally accepted auditing standards. Those standards require that we plan and perform the audit to obtain reasonable assurance about whether the financial statements are free of material misstatement. An audit includes examining, on a test basis, evidence supporting the amounts and disclosures in the financial statements. An audit also includes assessing the accounting principles used and significant estimates made by management, as well as evaluating the overall financial statement presentation.

We intend to assess the company's existing internal control structure. Primary reliance for the prevention and detection of errors and irregularities must be placed on this internal control structure because it is in constant operation and covers all periods and transactions; however, it cannot eliminate the possibility that errors and irregularities may occur. Although there can be no guarantee that such errors and irregularities will be detected by us, we will plan and perform our audit to find errors and irregularities that would have a material effect on the financial statements.

The charges for our services will be at our regular per diem rates plus out-of-pocket expenses. An interim billing of $30,000 will be delivered on or about November 30, 19X8, with a final billing on or about March 15, 19X9.

If these arrangements are in accordance with your understanding, please sign and return to us the enclosed copy of this letter. We appreciate this opportunity to be of service to you.

Sincerely,

Partner & Co.

Accepted by

_____

Robert K. Luckey

Figure 6.1   An audit engagement letter.

current year, (2) a statement of responsibility for detection of errors and irregularities, (3) fee and billing arrangements, and (4) other matters, if applicable, such
as reviews of financial statements included in SEC filings or preparation of income
tax returns. One form that an audit engagement letter might take is shown in
Figure 6.1.

Most accounting firms bill their clients on a per diem basis, that is, at daily
rates and fractions thereof. These rates depend on the experience and expertise of
the individuals working on the engagement (partners have the highest billing rates
and new staff members have the lowest), and the type of work being performed
(work on a registration statement requiring knowledge of SEC rules and regulations may be billed at a higher rate than regular audit work).

Scheduling the Audit Work

Efficient scheduling of audit work is the key to maximizing the effectiveness and
monetary return of an accounting firm. This fact becomes clear when one considers the economics of a public accounting practice.

The Economics of Public Accounting

Because a majority of businesses prepare financial statements on a calendar-
year basis, there is a greatly disproportional demand on auditors' time during the
early months of the year. An accounting firm must employ enough personnel to
meet the peak demands of its clients, which may occur in February. Consequently, in other months, such as May and June, the accounting firm will be
paying a number of personnel who are not producing revenue. Other functions can
be performed during these months, such as professional development and training, planning the next year's audits, and vacations; however, any audit time that
can be moved out of the peak period and into another time of the year will increase
the efficiency and monetary return of the accounting firm. Not all audit procedures must be performed after the end of the period being audited, and most
accounting firms strive to perform as much work at an interim date as possible.
This practice allows the accounting firm to reduce staff requirements and the
clients to issue financial statements and annual reports at an earlier date. Examples of audit procedures that can be carried out at different times of the year are
given in a separate section of this chapter.

The Audit Team

The number and experience of the individual auditors assigned to an engagement vary with the size and complexity of the audit.[1] In many cases, however, the
audit team will consist of the following personnel:

[1] The experience levels given in the following descriptions are generalizations; they vary widely
in practice.

1. One or more staff auditors, often with three years' experience or less, who perform audit procedures as directed by a senior auditor.

2. A senior or in-charge auditor with from two to six years' experience who performs difficult audit procedures requiring more subjective judgment, and who supervises and reviews the daily work of the staff auditors. The senior auditor may have special training or experience in the client's industry.

3. A manager or supervisor who may have from four to ten years' experience. The manager is responsible for arranging and requesting staff for each audit, reviewing the audit work performed by the staff and senior auditor, and billing and collecting the audit fee.

4. A partner with perhaps more than ten years' experience who has overall and final responsibility for the audit. The partner reviews the audit work of the staff, senior, and manager, resolves audit problems with the client, and approves the form of and signs the audit report.

There is normally some continuity of the audit team for a particular client from year to year, although terminations and promotions may result in some changes. To obtain a fresh look at each client periodically, many accounting firms require a complete change in the audit team for a particular client every five or so years. Some critics of the accounting profession have maintained that this change is not sufficient and that accounting firms should be rotated periodically, but this idea has not received wide acceptance.

Quality Control Considerations

A CPA's most valuable possession is his or her reputation for integrity and the performance of quality work. If a CPA firm has only a few partners and employees, direct and almost daily control can be exercised over the auditing practice. As CPA firms become larger, this control becomes more difficult and policies and procedures must be established to ensure quality work. To provide guidance in this area, the AICPA issued *Statement on Quality Control Standards No. 1,* which describes in general terms the elements of quality control and discusses matters relating to effective implementation of a system of quality control for an accounting firm.

Statement on Quality Control Standards No. 1 identifies nine elements of quality control and requires that policies and procedures be established to provide reasonable assurance that

1. *Independence* in fact and in appearance is maintained at all organizational levels—for example, maintaining records of audit clients and confirming

periodically with personnel that prohibited relationships with such clients do not exist.

2. *Personnel assigned to audit engagements* have the degree of technical training and proficiency required in the circumstances—for example, timely identification of staffing requirements so that enough qualified personnel can be made available.

3. Auditors, to the extent required, will *consult* and seek assistance from persons who have appropriate levels of knowledge, competence, judgment, and authority—for example, designating individuals who have expertise in SEC, specific industry, and general accounting and auditing areas to provide consultation and advice.

4. The conduct and *supervision* of work at all organizational levels meet the firm's standards of quality—for example, requiring that audit working papers be reviewed by supervisory personnel.

5. Personnel are *hired* who possess the appropriate characteristics to enable them to perform competently—for example, establishing minimum standards of academic preparation and accomplishment for recruiting at beginning levels.

6. Personnel will participate in sufficient *professional development* activities to provide them with knowledge for fulfilling their assigned responsibilities—for example, requiring personnel to attend training programs conducted by the firm, universities, state CPA societies, or the AICPA.

7. Personnel selected for *advancement* will possess the qualifications necessary to fulfill their increased responsibilities—for example, requiring supervisory personnel to furnish periodic appraisals of the work of assistants.

8. The *acceptance and continuance of clients* whose managements lack integrity are minimized—for example, inquiring of third parties, such as the proposed client's previous auditors, bankers, legal counsel, and others in the financial and business community, as to the reputation of the proposed client.

9. The elements of quality control are being effectively applied through *inspection*—for example, developing checklists or evaluation forms for use by designated persons in reviewing the quality control activities of the firm.

The nature and extent of a firm's quality control policies and procedures will depend on the size of the firm, its personnel's operating autonomy, the nature of its practice and organization, and cost-benefit considerations.

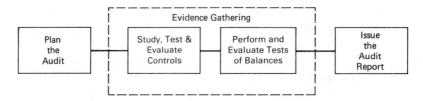

Figure 6.2   Major components of an audit. The Audit Risk Model.

Major Components of an Audit

Figure 6.2 presents in highly condensed form the major components of an audit. This chapter presents an overview of the audit and discusses the planning function. Preparation of audit working papers that are necessary to document the evidence-gathering techniques discussed in subsequent chapters is also covered.

The Audit Risk Model

As discussed in Chapter 5, audit risk is the risk that the auditor may unknowingly fail to qualify appropriately his or her report on financial statements that are materially misstated. Audit risk has several components including the risk that material errors will occur in the client's accounting system (inherent risk) and the risk that the client's control structure will not detect and correct material errors on a timely basis (control risk). The auditor assesses these risks by understanding the client's financial system and evaluating the client's controls. The auditor normally assumes that the less susceptible accounts are to error and the stronger the controls, the lower the risk that the client will prepare misstated financial statements. The other component of audit risk is the risk that, given that material errors exist in the financial statements, the auditor's substantive tests will fail to detect them (detection risk). The auditor controls this risk by varying the nature, timing, and extent of the tests of balances and disclosures, transactions that affect these balances and disclosures, and analytical procedures. Thus there is an inverse relationship between the strength of a client's controls and the effort an auditor expends in testing balances and disclosures in the financial statements. The relationships of these risks may be expressed in the form of the audit risk model,

$$AR = IR * CR * DR$$

where AR represents audit risk, IR represents inherent risk, CR represents control risk, and DR represents detection risk. The auditor considers the components of audit risk in planning the audit to reduce overall audit risk to an acceptably low level. These risks were discussed in detail in Chapter 5 and are summarized here because of their importance in the planning process.

The following examples illustrate how the audit risk model can be used to plan the extent of audit work to be performed.

Accounts Receivable   Accounts receivable consist of amounts due from the sale of a standard product to a few large companies under long-term contracts. Both quantity and price are established by contract, and customers remit weekly. Controls over shipping, billing, and collecting are strong and were tested with good results.

Because the account does not appear to be susceptible to error (low inherent risk) and controls appear to be strong (low control risk), the audit risk model may appear as follows:

$$AR = IR \quad * CR \quad * DR$$

$$LOW = LOW * LOW * ?$$

This assessment indicates that the auditor can plan to take a high risk of not detecting an error in this account because the probability of one occurring and not being detected is low. Therefore, the auditor would plan only limited substantive tests of the accounts receivable balance.

Inventory   Inventory consists of computer chips involving several stages of production. Standard costs are accumulated and transferred between stages. Exact specifications result in a high rate of rejection. Numerous differences are common between perpetual records and physical counts of inventory. Controls over the purchase and receipt of raw materials and the allocation of payroll costs are weak.

Because the account appears to be highly susceptible to error (high inherent risk) and controls are weak (high control risk) the audit risk model may appear as follows:

$$AR = IR \quad * CR \quad * DR$$

$$LOW = HIGH * HIGH * ?$$

This assessment indicates that the auditor should plan to take a low risk of not detecting an error in this account balance because the probability of one occurring and not being detected is high. Therefore, the auditor would plan extensive substantive tests of the inventory balance.

Tolerable Error

Also important in the planning process is the consideration of materiality and tolerable error. Materiality is considered at the overall financial statement level;

that is, a material error is one that would cause the financial statements taken as a whole to be misstated.[2] Tolerable error is the allocation of materiality to the individual account level for planning purposes. It is the amount of error that can be tolerated in one account which, when added to errors in other accounts, will not exceed materiality.

Tolerable error is a planning concept to assist auditors in determining how much work to plan for individual accounts. The less error that can be tolerated in a given account (i.e., the smaller the error the auditor must search for) the more work the auditor must perform.

Planning and Programming

Planning and programming are essential to the efficient conduct of an audit, regardless of its size. In addition, the first standard of field work requires that the work be planned adequately.

In planning an examination, an auditor should consider the following matters:

1. General business and industry conditions and peculiarities and the entity's accounting policies and procedures.

2. Anticipated reliance on the internal control structure.

3. Appropriate level of audit risk and preliminary judgments about materiality levels.

4. Potential problem areas in the financial statements and conditions that may require an extension or modification of anticipated audit procedures.

5. The type of audit report anticipated.

Information regarding some of these matters may be obtained from a review of prior-year reports and audit working paper files, discussions with client personnel, review of interim financial statements, consideration of recent professional pronouncements, and so on.

Levels of audit risk and materiality are based on the auditor's judgment. The auditor plans the audit to search for the smallest error that would be material to any one of the financial statements. Because planning ordinarily takes place before the financial statements have been prepared by the client, prior-year or annualized interim financial statements may be used for preliminary materiality judgments.

---

[2]Materiality for planning purposes may differ from materiality for final evaluation purposes because events can occur during the audit that affect this judgment. See Chapter 5 for a further discussion of materiality.

As noted previously, lower acceptable levels of both audit risk and materiality require that more work be planned on individual accounts; that is, more work must be performed both (1) to reduce the probability of not finding a material error and (2) to find smaller material errors.

As pointed out in the section on the economics of public accounting, both the auditor and the client benefit from as much of the audit as possible being performed outside the peak audit demand period. Several audit procedures can be performed at certain times other than after the end of the client's year.

The audit work can be divided in various ways, one of which is to split the work into the following phases.

Phase I—Planning and programming

Phase II—Interim audit work

Phase III—Year-end audit work

Phase IV—Final audit work

In Phase I, the auditor prepares a tentative plan for the audit. Different clients have different characteristics and risks that should be considered during this planning phase. The auditor's objective is to determine which accounts in the financial statements are subject to higher risk of material misstatement than others. The auditor then plans more extensive audit procedures for the high risk accounts.

To identify high risk accounts the auditor employs a number of techniques including:

1. Inquiry of management. The auditor often discusses with client management the effects on the financial statements of production and marketing operations, industry conditions, new accounting pronouncements, unusual accounting transactions, and so forth (e.g., if management states that the company was involved in a complex business combination during the year, the auditor would want to plan sufficient time to review the accounting for the transaction).

2. Evaluation of prior experience with the client. The auditor may review his or her prior year audit working papers to determine which accounts were found to have been in error last year. Unless the client has taken remedial steps, the same error may be present this year (e.g., if the provision for income taxes was materially misstated last year because the client lacked the expertise to make the calculation correctly, and if the expertise was not acquired during the current year, there is a high risk that the provision for income taxes may be materially misstated this year).

3. Performance of analytical procedures. The auditor should review the most recent interim financial statements available for unusual items. An

amount may be considered unusual if it varies significantly from a relationship that is expected to exist. Such a relationship may be with prior year or budgeted amounts, other financial statement amounts, industry data, or nonfinancial data such as units shipped.

After considering the potential risks of material misstatement of the financial statements, the auditor prepares an audit program containing detail audit procedures required to detect material misstatements in the financial statements.

In Phase I the auditor may also consider more efficient audit methods and procedures, opportunities for shifting more work out of the busy audit period, and the elimination of nonessential work, with primary emphasis on preparing or updating the audit program and reviewing prior-year audit working papers to find areas where the effectiveness of the audit work could be improved. The timing of this work is flexible, but the work should be completed before the beginning of the interim audit work.

More efficient audit methods and procedures might include the use of microcomputers or a generalized computer audit program (discussed in Chapter 14), more clerical assistance from clients, sampling techniques (discussed in Chapters 9 and 13), and better organization of audit working papers.

The shifting of additional work to an interim period requires understanding and careful evaluation of the internal control structure. If controls are strong, and the auditor's experience with the reliability of the accounting records and management's integrity has been good, some audit procedures normally performed after the end of the year may be moved to an interim date.

If the aforementioned factors are considered during the planning phase, the result should be a higher quality audit with a more efficient use of personnel.

Phase II, performed perhaps one to four months before the end of the client's year, consists of the execution of audit procedures that need not be performed at year end or during the final audit work. Remember that the auditor's objective is to move as much work as possible into Phase II. There are no specific rules or guidelines as to exactly what work can be performed at this time. Each engagement must be studied and the timing of the audit steps determined after careful consideration of the accounting procedures, controls, and other factors. Nevertheless, there are audit procedures that *usually* are done in Phase II, some that *may* be done, and others that *seldom* are done.

The assessment of control risk usually is performed in Phase II, because the extent and nature of subsequent audit procedures depend on the results of this assessment. One may wonder whether the auditor is required to perform the same assessment during Phase IV to cover the period from the interim audit work to year end, inasmuch as the entire year is the subject of the audit. In practice, auditors do make inquiries and limited reviews of procedures and controls during Phase IV, but not in as much depth as in Phase II.

Other procedures usually carried out in Phase II include a review of minutes of meetings of stockholders and board of directors (and any subcommittees thereof) and tests of additions to and reductions of accounts with balances that tend to carry forward rather than turn over rapidly. Examples are property and equipment, deferred charges, long-term debt, and stockholders' equity. Transactions in these accounts can be audited through an interim date and then audited from that date to year end in Phase IV. This approach is more efficient than auditing transactions for the entire year in Phase IV.

Audit procedures that *may* be performed in Phase II depend on the auditor's evaluation of the client's controls. If control risk is low, such procedures as confirmation of accounts receivable, observation of physical inventories, and confirmation of accounts payable may be performed in Phase II. If such procedures are performed in Phase II, the auditor must review transactions in the accounts from the interim date to year end to be satisfied of the validity of the account balances at year-end.

Some audit procedures are seldom performed in Phase II, because they would duplicate work done in Phase IV. For example, tests of accrued liabilities, review of loan agreements for compliance with restrictions, and examination of the stockbook normally are done at year end, and work done at an interim date would be an unnecessary duplication.

Phase III involves audit procedures that are performed at the end of a client's year. Examples of such procedures include observation of physical inventories, count of cash funds, and inspection of marketable or investment securities. This work often must be done on the specific year-end date, because it may not be possible otherwise to determine that the asset was actually on hand at that date. Certain techniques, such as the use of seals on cash boxes and the limitation of access to bank safety deposit boxes, may allow some of these procedures to be moved from year end to other dates.

Phase IV can begin as soon as the client has prepared and posted the final accounting entries and totaled, balanced, and closed the accounting records. This phase consists of execution of all audit procedures not previously performed and preparation and issuance of the audit report. Although sometimes pressured by a client to issue an audit report before all procedures have been completed, the auditor must insist on completing all aspects of the examination, no matter how minor, before issuing the report.

The Audit Program

The most important control mechanism in an audit is the audit program. It should be prepared in writing and outline all of the audit procedures that are considered necessary for an auditor to express an opinion on the client's financial statements. Although audit programs should be specifically tailored to each audit engagement, computer generated listings of audit procedures are sometimes utilized in audit program preparation.

An audit program that is properly prepared and used serves the following purposes:

1. Provides evidence of proper planning of the work and allows a review of the proposed scope of the audit. The program gives the partner, manager,

and other members of the audit team an opportunity to review the proposed scope of the audit *before* the work is performed, when there is still time to modify the proposed audit procedures.

2. Provides guidance to less experienced staff members. The specific audit steps to be performed by each staff person are indicated in the program.

3. Provides evidence of work performed. As each audit step is performed, the staff person signs or initials in a space beside that step on the program to indicate that it has been completed.

4. Provides a means of controlling the time spent on an engagement. The audit program usually includes the estimated time required to perform each audit step and a space in which the actual time required can be recorded. Thus, a staff member knows approximately how much time a certain audit step should require and can ask the senior for assistance if appreciably more or less time appears to be needed.

5. Provides evidence of the consideration of controls in designing the proposed audit procedures. Many programs include a brief summary of the important control features in each section of the audit and some evaluation of these controls. Thus, audit procedures can be restricted where controls are strong and expanded where they are weak.

The staff must keep in mind that the audit program is only a *tentative* program based on assumptions about the client's accounting procedures and controls. When the work begins, if the conditions are not as anticipated, the auditor may need to revise the audit program on the basis of conditions actually found. For example, if an auditor designs the audit program to confirm only a few accounts receivable balances because control risk is believed to be low (on the basis of past experience or a preliminary review), the program must be changed to confirm more accounts if the assessment of the level of control risk is increased.

An illustration of the property and equipment and accumulated depreciation section of an audit program is shown in the appendix to this chapter. The program has four major sections: (1) account description that states briefly the nature of the items included in the account, (2) evaluation of audit risk, that summarizes important controls and includes an evaluation of the component risks, (3) audit procedures, which outline the specific audit steps to be performed, who should perform them, and an estimate of the required time, and (4) conclusion, which represents the opinion of the staff as to whether the audit objectives have been accomplished.

The illustration indicates that inherent and control risks relating to property additions are low, but inherent and control risks relating to property retirements are relatively high because no periodic review is made for unreported retirements, and individual pieces of equipment are not tagged or otherwise specifically identified as belonging to the company. The low risks relating to additions does not mean that additions need not be audited, but the lower risks do allow the auditor to restrict the extent of the procedures and increase detection risk (by exclusion of property additions of less than $4,000 in this case). In contrast, an extended search for unrecorded retirements is performed because of higher risks in this area.

Finally, the audit program in the appendix illustrates the division of the audit work between interim and final. Some procedures are performed at an interim date and are updated through the end of the year during the final audit work (tests of property additions and maintenance expense by examination of vendor invoices, etc.). Other procedures are performed only once (preparation of lead schedule) to avoid unnecessary duplication.

Distinction Between Control Risk Assessment Procedures and Substantive Tests

There is a difference between evidence gathering for the purpose of assessing control risk and evidence gathering to evaluate the amounts and disclosures included in the financial statements on which the opinion is rendered. The former are called control risk assessment procedures, and the latter are called substantive tests.

The following chart shows the general relationship between these two types of evidence, and describes the two categories of substantive tests. Notice that the choices are to:

1. Perform *extensive* (many) substantive tests.

2. Perform *restricted* (some) substantive tests.

3. Perform minimum substantive tests.

Control risk assessment procedures are the steps the auditor takes to obtain evidence for the assessment of control risk, and include inquiry, observation, and inspection of documents. Evidence of the performance of these procedures may include memoranda, flowcharts, and listings of transactions as discussed in Chapter 8.

Tests of details of transactions and balances include such audit procedures as observation of inventories, confirmation of accounts receivable balances with customers, and examination of vendor invoices for operating expenses. Analytical procedures involve the study and comparison of relationships among data to identify fluctuations that are not expected, the absence of fluctuations that are expected, or other unusual items. Examples of analytical procedures may include comparison of account balances with prior-period, budgeted, or predicted amounts and comparison of operating and financial ratios with prior-period and industry ratios. All significant variations and fluctuations should be investigated

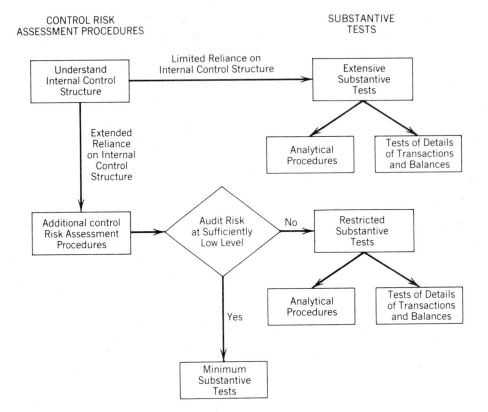

and resolved. Because analytical procedures are intended to disclose unusual items, they should be employed early in the audit so that audit programs can be designed to concentrate work in areas that appear unusual or out of line. They may be employed during the audit to obtain evidence and support or confirm other audit findings. They are necessary at the end of the audit to see that all unusual items were properly investigated.

In practice there is often some overlap between control risk assessment tests and substantive tests if auditors design procedures to achieve both objectives concurrently. For example, when auditors trace a sample of entries from the cash receipts listings to the customer ledger accounts, they may be accomplishing two objectives.

1. Auditors may be assessing the risk that the prescribed posting procedures are not functioning. If too many errors are found the auditors may conclude that the risk that the procedures are not functioning is high.

2. Auditors may be performing a substantive test to help them form a conclusion as to whether accounts receivable exist. If errors are found when the transactions are traced from the receipt listings to the customer ledger accounts, the auditor may conclude that the account balance is in error.

Working Papers

An auditor must gather evidence to support the review, test, and evaluation of inherent and control risks and the substantive tests performed directly on the amounts and disclosures shown in the financial statements. This evidence is accumulated in files of audit working papers.

Definition and Purposes of Working Papers

For auditors to conduct their examination properly and provide adequate support for their opinion, they must prepare audit working papers. A definition of working papers follows.

Working papers are records kept by the auditor of the procedures applied, the tests performed, the information obtained, and the pertinent conclusions reached in the engagement.

Working papers should be sufficient to show that the financial statements or other information on which the auditor is reporting were in agreement with (or reconciled with) the client's records. Listed below are *general* guidelines as to what working papers should include or show.

a. The work has been adequately planned and supervised, indicating observance of the first standard of field work.
b. The internal control structure has been studied and evaluated to the degree necessary to determine whether, and to what extent, other auditing procedures are to be restricted, indicating observance of the second standard of field work.
c. The audit evidence obtained, the auditing procedures applied, and the testing performed have provided sufficient competent evidential matter to afford a reasonable basis for an opinion, indicating observance of the third standard of field work.

In summary, properly prepared working papers are necessary for an auditor to demonstrate compliance with the standards of field work. They should show how the work was planned (primarily by the use of audit programs) and the extent of supervision of assistants (indication of reviews made by the auditor) and should contain sufficient, competent evidence (e.g., control risk checklists, confirmations from creditors, bank reconciliations) on which to base an opinion.

Ownership of Working Papers

Though there is some variation in state laws, working papers prepared by an auditor in connection with his or her examination of a client's financial statements are generally the property of the auditor. The client normally has no claim to the working papers, regardless of the fact that he or she paid the auditor to perform the audit for which the working papers are prepared. Working papers generally are not "privileged" in the manner of communications between an attorney and his or her client, and must be surrendered in response to a subpoena or other legal action. This means that information obtained by an auditor during an examination of financial statements could be used against the auditor or the client in a legal proceeding. Of course, even though the working papers belong to the auditor, he or she is required to comply with the confidentiality requirements of Rule 301 of the *AICPA Code of Professional Ethics,* as discussed in Chapter 3.

Importance of Working Papers

Because the audit working papers constitute the auditor's evidence of the work performed, they may be either helpful or detrimental if problems subsequently arise concerning the audited financial statements. They will become the most important documents involved in any subsequent litigation and, because they are subject to subpoena, they may provide evidence for the plaintiff or prosecution as well as for the auditor's defense.

It is unfortunate that the term *working papers* has evolved to describe the evidence that an auditor accumulates during an examination of financial statements. The term connotes an unfinished product such as an accumulation of preliminary notes and calculations on scratch pads. Though only a very imprudent auditor would prepare working papers in such a manner, many auditors are not as careful as they should be in this regard. For example, an auditor may spend many hours considering a serious accounting or reporting problem of a client, but make only a brief note of the conclusion once it is reached. Without evidence to show the careful consideration given the problem, it may appear later that only superficial thought was given to it. Even if working papers are complete, sloppy preparation with many erasures, misspelled words, and incomplete sentences will cast doubt on them. An adversary attorney might use such working papers to attempt to demonstrate a careless approach to the audit. Auditors must keep in mind that they may not be the only ones to read the working papers they prepare, and they must consider the impression others might gain from reading them.

Types of Working Papers

Auditors normally maintain two types of working paper files. One is referred to as a permanent or continuing audit file, and the other often is called the current-year audit file.[3]

Permanent Audit Files   The permanent audit file is composed of documents, schedules, and other data that will be of continuing significance to several

---

[3] In addition to audit working paper files, the auditor may maintain tax working paper files (for working papers developed in connection with the review or preparation of a client's tax returns), correspondence files (to maintain a record of all communications with each client), billing files (to maintain the current status and historical record of billings to and collections from each client), and client files (for developing a record of the relationship with each client).

years' audits. For example, an auditor must obtain a copy or extract of a client's articles of incorporation as evidence of the types (common and preferred), par values, and number of authorized shares of stock that the company may issue, as well as restrictions on payment of dividends, purchase of treasury stock, or other matters requiring disclosure in the financial statements. Rather than obtaining a copy or extract of the same document each year, the auditor places one copy in the permanent file, which is a part of each year's audit evidence. Of course, it is necessary to check each year for any amendment to the articles of incorporation and to indicate any changes on the document in the permanent file. Amendments normally would be detected by the auditor during his or her review of minutes of stockholders' and directors' meetings, because approval generally is required by one or both of these bodies.

Although the organization of permanent files varies, most would contain such sections as the following:

1. Historical information regarding the company. This section usually includes a memorandum describing the company and its operations, major plants and manufacturing processes, and products, distribution facilities, and important customers. An organization chart listing the names and positions of key officers and employees and any recurring audit administrative matters also are shown. This type of information is particularly important to auditors assigned to a client for the first time. It allows them to learn something of the operations of the company in a brief period of time and makes them aware of any unusual matters concerning the audit, such as timing deadlines and reporting requirements. The client is saved the task of acquainting different members of the auditing firm with basic information about the company. A partial example of such a memorandum follows.

X Co.
Company Operation
and
Audit Administration Memo

X Co. was formed in 19X0 by Mr. Fitzgerald and Mr. Hamilton, both of whom remain 50% stockholders. X Co. operates a 40,000 barrel per day refinery near Granville, Arkansas (also the location of its administrative offices), at the intersection of Highways 65 and 71. The President and Plant Manager is Mr. Foote and the Treasurer, with whom we arrange the timing of our work, is Ms. Johnson. The company acquires most of its raw materials (crude oil) in the open market and is subject to the regulations of the Department of Energy (a copy of the DOE regulations is filed behind this memo). The crude oil is refined into premium and regular gasoline, which is sold to a chain of independent gasoline stations. The company is on a December 31 fiscal year. Our audit report is to be delivered to the shareholders by February 10. In the past we have experienced difficulty and delay in obtaining confirmation of a significant accounts receivable from the chain of independent gasoline stations, so we must be sure to mail the confirmation at the earliest possible date and include sufficient details to . . . .

An auditor who had never worked on the X Co. engagement would know, by reading the memorandum, where the company is located and what it does, whom to contact at the company, what some of the important reporting and timing requirements are, and that he or she would need a knowledge of DOE regulations in the audit.

2. Company accounting procedures and the internal control structure. This material might consist of narrative descriptions of the client's control environment, accounting procedures and control procedures, internal control questionnaires, flowcharts, decision tables, or any combination of these items. A chart of accounts and samples of any records or forms that would aid in understanding company procedures also may be included. A brief example of a description of accounting procedures relating to notes payable and long-term debt is set forth below.

X Co.
Procedures for Notes Payable
and
Long-Term Debt

X Co. has outstanding a $5 million issue of 8% bonds due in installments of $500,000 per year beginning in 19X2. All refinery property and equipment is pledged to these bonds. The bond indenture restricts payment of dividends to $200,000 per year. The company also borrows on short-term notes for working capital purposes.

All borrowings are authorized by the Board of Directors, and the banks or other creditors are specifically mentioned in the minutes. Both the President and the Treasurer must sign any notes that are issued. The Treasurer maintains a schedule showing the due dates of all bond, note, and interest payments. . . .

Internal control questionnaires and flowcharts are shown in Chapter 8.

3. Corporate documents. In addition to the articles of incorporation, the permanent file normally contains copies or extracts of loan agreements, bond indentures, labor contracts, stock option plans, pension plans, important long-term operating agreements or contracts, and other documents. As all of these documents could significantly affect the company's operations and its financial statements, the auditor must have evidence of the provisions of these documents and of his or her reviews thereof.

4. Continuing analyses of certain accounts. It is often more efficient to maintain cumulative or carry-forward schedules in the permanent files for

certain accounts with little activity, or for which comparisons with several prior years are helpful, than to prepare such schedules each year in the current files. Continuing analyses might be used for capital stock, long-term debt, checklists for compliance with loan agreements, net operating loss carry-forward schedule, equity in earnings of subsidiaries, and gross profit ratios by major product class. An illustration of such an analysis is shown in the following table.

X Co.
Analysis of Uncollectible Accounts

For the year	19X5	19X6	19X7	19X8
Sales	$4,365,000	$5,837,000	$5,679,000	$5,928,000
Bad debt provision	54,000	68,000	63,000	71,000
Bad debt charge-offs	54,000	67,000	63,000	91,000
Balance 12-31				
Current	$372,000	$498,000	$501,000	$530,000
30–60 days	31,000	54,000	53,000	57,000
Over 60 days	2,000	19,000	16,000	52,000
Total	$405,000	$571,000	$570,000	$639,000
Allowance for doubtful accounts	$30,000	$35,000	$35,000	$15,000
Ratios—				
Bad debt charge-offs to sales	1.2%	1.1%	1.1%	1.5%
Allowance to total accounts receivable	7.4%	6.1%	6.1%	2.3%
Allowance to accounts receivable over 60 days	15.0	1.8	2.2	0.3
Days' sales in accounts receivable	33.9	35.7	36.6	39.3

This analysis should alert the auditor that there has been a deterioration in accounts receivable during the year, and should raise a question as to the adequacy of the allowance for doubtful accounts.

5. Audit planning. This section could include a master copy of the audit program (often on computer diskettes) that could be revised and mechanically copied each year rather than completely rewritten; schedules of plant

capacity and volumes of tanks, bins, and other containers (an auditor would be embarrassed to discover, after being satisfied as to inventory, that his or her client did not have the physical capacity to store the amount of inventory shown in the accounting records); and, if certain procedures are performed on a rotating basis, a record of the accounts (cost centers, bank accounts, etc.) or locations (branch offices, subsidiaries, etc.) tested each year to ensure that nothing is overlooked, or that the same account or location is not tested repeatedly year after year, while others are never tested.

The permanent audit file can be a very useful tool of the auditor if it is kept current and used. Occasionally, an auditor, in his or her haste to complete the current-year audit, will neglect to review and update the permanent file. When this happens, the file becomes less useful and less used each succeeding year, until it becomes a file of obsolete or superseded data. At that point, it becomes less than useless to the auditor; it becomes a threat because it is evidence of negligent and inadequate work.

Current Audit Files   The current audit files for each year contain the evidence gathered and the conclusions reached in the audit for that year. The material in the current files includes schedules and analyses of accounts, memoranda of audit work performed in certain areas and audit problems considered and resolved, an audit program, correspondence with third parties (banks, customers, creditors, legal counsel, etc.) confirming balances, transactions, and other data, a schedule of time spent on the engagement by individual auditors, and other documents. Examples of many of these items are provided in this and following chapters. Most of the working paper examples are prepared on a microcomputer because of the increasing use being made of this equipment in auditing. Although many types of microcomputers are used in practice, the working paper examples in this text were prepared on an IBM XT using the Lotus 1-2-3 electronic spreadsheet.

Working papers organized logically improve the efficiency of an audit and the effectiveness of its review. Although an auditor must be aware of the interrelationships among accounts (such as between sales and accounts receivable, or accounts payable, inventory, and cost of sales), and design his or her audit procedures accordingly, a logical approach to the organization of working papers is to begin with the financial statements on which the auditor expresses his or her opinion, which, of course, are the final product of the client's records and accounting system.

Using the financial statements as the apex, the auditor dissects the individual financial statement items to the point at which they are most efficiently and effectively audited. This point varies by company and by account. For example, it would be difficult to perform much effective auditing on the total accounts receivable balance shown in the financial statements. This account must first be broken down into subaccounts, such as customer, notes, officer and employees, interest, and other receivables on a schedule sometimes referred to as the lead schedule.

Then the more significant of the subaccounts would be analyzed further by customer, note, officer and employee, and so forth to obtain amounts that the auditor can subject to such audit tests as confirmation and aging. However, if all salespeople are paid a fixed commission on sales, it may be possible to test sales commission expense by multiplying total sales by the commission rate rather than analyzing commission expense by salespeople. Thus, the organization of working papers can be likened to the triangle shown below.

This concept is illustrated later in the discussion of indexing the working papers.

Although auditors would prefer to use the financial statements as the starting point for their audit, there are often practical reasons why they cannot. Sometimes the financial statements have not been prepared while the audit is in progress. In other cases auditors process adjusting entries as a result of their work, which would change any financial statements that have been prepared. Therefore, auditors normally prepare an audit trial balance, which resembles the financial statements (without footnotes) but contains columns for adjustments and reclassifications proposed as a result of the audit. The adjustments columns are for the posting of adjusting entries proposed by the auditors as a result of their work to correct errors in the accounting records. On many audit engagements auditors have no adjustments, whereas on others, numerous adjustments may be made. The reclassification columns are for the posting of reclassification entries; for example, entries to change the classification of an item for financial statement presentation purposes. Adjusting entries always must be posted to the accounting records by the client because they are corrections of errors in those records, but reclassification entries are not posted to the accounting records because they are only rearrangements of the ledger accounts for financial statement purposes.

The audit trial balance shown in Figure 6.3 contains certain adjusting and reclassifying entries (from Figures 6.4 and 6.5). The column entitled ''As adjusted and reclassified'' should agree with the amounts shown in the client's financial statements. The proposed adjusting and reclassifying entries must be concurred with by the client company's management, because the responsibility for the financial statements is theirs. If such entries are proposed by the auditor, the documentation and support for the entries must be included in the working pa-

X Co.
Audit Trial Balance
12-31-X8

TB-1

J. Jones
1-20-X9

	Index	As Adjusted 12-31-X7	Per Books 12-31-X8	Adjustments Dr.	Adjustments Cr.	As Adjusted 12-31-X8	Reclassifications Dr.	Reclassifications Cr.	As Adjusted and Reclassified 12-31-X8
Current Assets—									
Cash	A	73,430 ᴎ	65,141 √			65,141			65,141
Accounts receivable	B	121,189 ᴎ	140,767 √		(2) 6,000	134,767	(10) 18,797		153,564
Inventories	C	276,502 ᴎ	243,030 √			243,030			243,030
Prepayments	D	11,343 ᴎ	12,255 √			12,255			12,255
		482,464	461,193			455,193			473,990
Property and Equipment	E	581,750 ᴎ	604,988 √			604,988			604,988
Less Allowance for depreciation		89,266 ᴎ	108,716 √			108,716			108,716
		492,484	496,272			496,272			496,272
Other assets	H	17,392 ᴎ	16,629 √			16,629			16,629
		992,340	974,094			968,094			986,891

ᴎ Traced to prior year audit working papers.

√ Traced to general ledger.

Figure 6.3   Audit trial balance.

T/B-2

X Co.
Audit Trial Balance
Liabilities
12-31-X8

J. Jones
1-20-X9

	Index	As Adjusted 12-31-X7	Per Books 12-31-X8	Adjustments Dr.	Adjustments Cr.	As Adjusted 12-31-X8	Reclassifications Dr.	Reclassifications Cr.	As Adjusted and Reclassified 12-31-X8
Current Liabilities—									
Notes payable	M	50,000 M	60,000 √			60,000		(101) 50,000	110,000
Accounts payable	N	110,139 M	103,677 √		(1) 4,832	108,509		(102) 18,797	127,306
Accrued liabilities	P	80,623 M	81,778 √ (3) 5,000		4,832	76,778			76,778
		240,762	245,455	5,000	4,832	245,287		68,797	314,084
Long-term Debt		350,000 M	300,000 √			300,000	(10) 50,000		250,000
Stockholders' Equity—									
Common stock	S	100,000 M	100,000 √			100,000			100,000
Retained earnings—	T								
Beginning of year		282,263	301,578			301,578			301,578
Net income		69,315	77,061 √ 10,832	5,000	71,229				71,229
Dividends		(50,000) M	(50,000) √			(50,000)			(50,000)
End of year		301,578 M	328,639 √ 10,832	5,000	322,807				322,807
		401,578	428,639	10,832	5,000	422,807			422,807
		992,340	974,094			968,094	50,000	50,000	986,891

M *Traced to prior year audit working papers.*
√ *Traced to general ledger.*

Figure 6.3   Audit trial balance (*continued*)

TB-3

J. Jones
1-20-X9

X Co.
Audit Trial Balance
Revenue and Expense
12-31-X8

	Index	As Adjusted 12-31-X7	Per Books 12-31-X8	Adjustments Dr.	Adjustments Cr.	As Adjusted 12-31-X8	Reclassifications Dr.	Reclassifications Cr.	As Adjusted and Reclassified 12-31-X8
Sales	10	1,247,906 ⋏	1,417,232 M			1,417,232			1,417,232
Cost of goods sold	20	935,929 ⋏	1,055,838 ⋏	① 4,832		1,060,670			1,060,670
Gross profit		311,977	361,394			356,562			356,562
Selling expenses	30	88,497 ⋏⋏	106,236 ⋏	② 6,000		112,236			112,236
Administrative expenses	40	59,315 ⋏⋏	76,997 ⋏			76,997			76,997
Interest expense	40	34,850 ⋏⋏	31,100 ⋏			31,100			31,100
		182,662	214,333			220,333			220,333
Net income before income taxes		129,315	147,061			136,229			136,229
Federal and state income taxes		60,000 ⋏	70,000 ⋏		③ 5,000	65,000			65,000
		69,315	77,061			71,229			71,229

⋏ Traced to prior year audit working paper.

√ Traced to general ledger.

Figure 6.3 Audit trial balance (continued)

AJE
R. Senior
1-31-x9

X Co.
Audit Adjusting Entries
12-31-X8

Entry	Dr.	Cr.
(1)		
Cost of sales	4,832	
Accounts payable		4,832
To record purchases included in inventory but omitted from accounts payable. See C-1/3.		
(2)		
Bad debt expense	6,000	
Allowance for doubtful accounts		6,000
To increase the allowance for doubtful accounts. See B-1/1.		
(3)		
Accrued income taxes payable	5,000	
Income tax expense		5,000
To record income income tax effect of entries (1) and (2). See P.		

Figure 6.4 Audit adjusting entries.

pers. Therefore, the proposed entries usually are shown in three places: (1) the working paper schedule on which the entry is computed, (2) a schedule listing all such entries, and (3) the audit trial balance. Note that the entries in Figures 6.4 and 6.5 include references to working paper schedules in which the support for the entries can be found.

An example of the next level in the triangle, the lead schedule, is shown in Figure 6.6. It illustrates the division of the total inventory amount into subgroups by stage of completion. In other cases, the total inventory amount might be divided according to product lines, inventory storage location, or other criteria. The type of breakdown shown on the lead schedule is determined by the classifications used by each client in its accounting records. Thus, in this, as in many other aspects of auditing, no single format is applicable to all engagements; each must be tailored to the particular aspects of each audit.

The base of the working-paper triangle symbolizes the detail audit schedules—a myriad of schedules and documents, each representing a specific piece of evidence gathered during the audit. Examples of such schedules and documents are shown in the following chapters.

At this point, the concept of the working-paper triangle should be clear. From the audit trial balance consisting of three schedules, the accounts are analyzed on the lead schedules, of which, in this case, there would be approximately 15, and then each lead schedule is supported by several detail audit schedules. Thus, the base expands as accounts are analyzed in greater detail.

Form and Indexing

The examples in this and following chapters illustrate the methods of indicating the performance of audit work and the indexing of working papers.

The actual audit procedures performed can be indicated in several ways. First, Figure 6.6 illustrates a narrative documentation of evidence at ①. This inquiry of the plant manager could have been made in connection with an audit procedure to explain unusual variations in inventory balances between years (an analytical procedure). Note that the auditor confirmed the plant manager's explanation by examination of the sales backlog report. A second method of documenting the performance of audit procedures is the use of schedule headings to describe the examination of certain records and documents. For example, ''Per Vendor Invoice'' denotes the examination of invoices from vendors to obtain the information shown on the schedule. The third method, illustrated in Figure 6.6, is the use of the ''tick'' mark. In this case, the tick mark ✔ shows that the amount was traced to the general ledger. The type of tick mark used does not matter as long as the auditor and anyone reviewing the working papers can understand its meaning. Because these working papers are prepared on the auditor's microcomputer, they are automatically checked for clerical accuracy, so no notation of this check is necessary.

Other aspects of the form of working papers that can be noted from the foregoing illustrations are (1) each schedule has a heading consisting of the client's

RJE

R. Senior
1-31-X9

X Co.
Audit Reclassifying Entries
12-31-X8

	Entry	Dr.	Cr.
	(101)		
Long-term debt		50,000	
Notes payable			50,000

To reclassify as a current
liability the portion of long-term
debt due within one year.
See R.

	(102)		
Accounts receivable		18,797	
Accounts payable			18,797

To reclassify credit balances
in accounts receivable to
accounts payable. See B.

Figure 6.5   Audit reclassifying entries.

C

X Co.
Inventory Lead Schedule
12-31-X8

J. Jones
1-20-X9

	Index	As Adjusted 12-31-X7	Per Books 12-31-X8	Adjustments Dr.	Adjustments Cr.	As Adjusted 12-31-X8
Raw materials	C-1	76,425 ʌ	51,014 ✓			
Work in progress		29,760 ʌ	36,253 ✓			
Finished goods	C-2	151,903 ʌ	137,692 ✓			
Supplies	C-3	18,414 ʌ	18,071 ✓			
		276,502	243,030 (1)			
		TB-1	TB-1			

ʌ Traced to prior year working papers.
✓ Traced to general ledger.

(1) The plant manager stated that the decline in inventory was due to a decline in sales orders during the last quarter of this year. This was confirmed by examination of the sales backlog report as of 12-31-X8.

Figure 6.6 Inventory lead schedule.

name, a description of the information shown on the schedule, and the audit date, (2) each schedule is indexed, and (3) each schedule is signed and dated by the auditor performing the work.

To facilitate the organization and review of the working papers, auditors generally use some type of indexing or coding system to identify each schedule. One such indexing system, used in Figures 6.3 through 6.6, is the designation of each balance sheet account with a letter (such as "A" for cash, "B" for accounts receivable, etc.) and each income statement account group with a number (such as "10" for sales, "20" for cost of goods sold, etc.). These designations are modified further with numbers to provide the indexes of the detail audit schedules.

As shown in the illustrations, each account group listed on the audit trial balance is assigned a single letter or number that is also the index of the lead schedule for that account group. On the inventory lead schedule in the example, each subaccount is assigned an index consisting of the letter "C" (indicating that it is part of and should be filed in the inventory section) and a number (by type of inventory). Similar indexing would appear on other lead schedules. The schedules showing the detail audit work performed on each subaccount would be indexed with the subaccount number (indicating that the work relates to a particular subaccount) and an additional number to designate the schedule on which the work was performed. All schedules would be filed first in alphabetical order and then in numerical order. This type of indexing is simple and can be expanded in many ways.

The working-paper triangle with the indexes of the schedules described is shown in the following illustration.

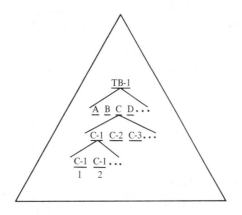

If a supervisor or other person had reason to review the audit work performed in the example on raw materials inventory, rather than look through what might be hundreds of pages of working papers, he or she would look first at the audit trial balance (Figure 6.3) to find the index of inventory (C).[4] The inventory

---

[4]In practice, most firms use a standard index system, and this first step would not be necessary; inventory always would be indexed as "C" or some other designation.

lead schedule (Figure 6.6) could then be found, and this would locate the index of raw materials (C-1). Considerable time can thus be saved if a logical indexing system is used.

Client Assistance

Clients often assist their auditors by preparing certain working-paper schedules. This practice can be advantageous to both auditors and clients. From the auditors' standpoint, the time spent on clerical and mechanical tasks is reduced and more important and significant aspects of the audit can be emphasized. Of course, the auditors must test the preparation of all such schedules to the extent necessary to satisfy themselves as to accuracy and credibility, but the time required to do so is normally much less than would be necessary for the initial preparation of the schedules. From the client's standpoint, any clerical work that can be shifted from the auditor to the client should reduce the total audit fee, which usually is based on the total time required to perform the audit.

To save time, auditors sometimes incorporate copies of client documents, schedules, and worksheets into their working papers. For example, rather than copy an inventory listing from the client's listing, the auditors may make a photographic copy of the client's listing and include it as a schedule in the working papers. This practice not only saves time, but also eliminates the possibility of an error in copying. The audit work would be performed on this copy. If the inventory information is maintained on data-processing equipment, the auditors might request a copy of the data-processing inventory listing for their working papers or access the client's computer file with their computer program and prepare their own listing. The fullest use should be made of mechanical aids and computer equipment.

According to AU Section 322 (*SAS No. 9*), auditors also may use the client's internal audit staff to assist in preparing working papers and performing audit procedures. Independent auditors should consider the competence and objectivity of the internal auditors and supervise and test their work to the extent they consider necessary. All judgments concerning the audit must be made by the independent auditor.

Security of Working Papers

Because auditors' working papers represent the support for their professional opinions and contain confidential information regarding their clients' operations, it is imperative that they maintain control of the working papers at all times. On the client's premises, they should use a trunk or briefcase that can be locked to secure the working papers at night, during lunch, or any other time they are not in use. Within their office, auditors normally maintain a fireproof safe for the protection and security of their working papers.

Communicating Audit Findings

Audit findings are communicated through the auditor's report and less formally by communications with the client's audit committee.

Issuing the Audit Report

Although the auditor prefers that the financial statements of the client be completed in final form before the audit commences, this is seldom done in practice. Even if the auditor has no adjustments to make in the financial records, certain financial statement classifications and disclosures may evolve from and during the audit. Thus, at the end of the audit, the auditors must review the financial statements to determine whether they are in accordance with generally accepted accounting principles and whether they contain all information necessary for a clear understanding of the company's operations and its financial position. If the company is subject to SEC regulations, the auditor also must determine that the financial statements comply with SEC accounting rules. Auditors often recommend additional footnote disclosure or clarification of footnote wording as a result of the review of the financial statements. Only after the financial statements are in final form can the auditor decide on the type of audit report to be issued (discussed in Chapters 19 and 20).

Once the financial statements and audit report are in final form, many accounting firms subject them to some type of quality-control review. Quality-control reviews take many forms. They often include (1) proofreading and clerical check, (2) tracing amounts and disclosures in the financial statements to the audit working papers to be sure that they are the same in both documents and have been subjected to audit, and (3) reading of the audit report and financial statements by another audit partner who was not associated with the engagement (some accounting firms carry this step further by requiring a complete review of the audit working papers by the second audit partner).

The first procedure listed involves a comparison of the final typed or printed copy of the audit report and financial statements with the draft copy to detect the omission of words or sentences and misspellings, and a check of the clerical accuracy of all totals. The second procedure is performed to determine that there is support in the audit working papers for all amounts and disclosures in the financial statements. This step is usually done by a senior or manager who has had no prior association with the engagement. The final procedure is sometimes thought of as a test to determine whether an individual knowledgeable about accounting but unfamiliar with the particular financial statements being reviewed finds the financial statements to be presented in a clear and understandable manner.

The auditor's report is signed and released to the client only after all of the foregoing procedures have been performed and all the questions or comments raised as a result have been cleared.

Communicating with the Audit Committee

In addition to the formal audit report, the auditor should determine that the audit committee[5] is informed of the following matters:

1. The initial selection of significant accounting policies, methods used to account for significant unusual transactions, and the effect of continuing accounting policies in controversial areas.

2. The processes used by management in formulating accounting estimates and the bases for the auditor's conclusions about the reasonableness of those estimates.

3. The implications of errors (both corrected and uncorrected), irregularities, and illegal acts discovered during the audit.

4. The auditor's responsibility for information other than the audited financial statements in documents such as corporate annual reports.[6]

5. The level of responsibility an auditor assumes under generally accepted auditing standards, that is, reasonable but not absolute assurance.

6. Any disagreements between the auditor and management, whether or not satisfactorily resolved.

7. Any major issues discussed by management and the auditor before the auditor was hired and issues on which other accountants were consulted.

8. Any serious difficulties the auditor encountered that were detrimental to the effective completion of the audit.

9. Significant deficiencies in the internal control structure (discussed in Chapter 8).

Audit committees may find the foregoing information useful in fulfilling their responsibilities for accounting and auditing matters.

---

[5] If a client does not have an audit committee, the communications should be to other financial oversight groups, such as finance or budget committees, if they exist.

[6] The auditor's responsibility for this other information is discussed in Chapter 19.

Chapter 6
Glossary of Terms

(listed in order of appearance in the chapter, with accompanying page reference where the term is discussed)

**Chapter 6
References**

Alderman, C. Wayne, and Deitrick, James W. "Auditors' Perceptions of Time Budget Pressures and Premature Sign-Offs: A Replication and Extension," *Auditing: A Journal of Practice and Theory* (Winter 1982), pp. 54–68.

American Institute of Certified Public Accountants. *Professional Standards*:
   AU Section 310—Adequacy of Planning and the Timing of Field Work;
   AU Section 311—Planning and Supervision;
   AU Section 315—Communications Between Predecessor and Successor Auditors;
   AU Section 322—The Effect of an Internal Audit Function on the Scope of the Independent Auditor's Examination;
   AU Section 339—Working Papers.
   AU Section 625—Reports on the Application of Accounting Principles;
   AR Section 400—Communications Between Predecessor and Successor Accountants;
   QC Section 200—Quality Control Policies and Procedures.

Deloitte Haskins & Sells. *Audit Committees*. 1981.

Kunitake, Walter K., Luzi, Andrew D., and Glezen, G. William. "Analytical Review in Audit and Review Engagements," *The CPA Journal* (April 1985), pp. 18–26.

McAllister, John P. and Dirsmith, Mark W. "How the Client's Business Environment Affects the Audit," *Journal of Accountancy* (February 1982), pp. 68–74.

Neumann, Frederick L. "Corporate Audit Committees and the Foreign Corrupt Practices Act," *Journal of Accountancy* (March 1981), pp. 78–80.

Ricchiute, David N. "A Case for Automated Workpapers," *Journal of Accountancy* (January 1981), pp. 71–75.

Schroeder, Mary S., Solomon, Ira, and Vickrey, Don. "Audit Quality: The Perceptions of Audit-Committee Chairpersons and Audit Partners," *Auditing: A Journal of Practice and Theory* (Spring 1986), pp. 86–94.

Scott, Richard A. and Dale, Donald M. "Interim Testing of Assets and Liabilities," *The CPA Journal* (November 1984), pp. 22–32.

Serlin, Jerry E. "Shopping Around: A Closer Look at Opinion Shopping," *Journal of Accounting, Auditing & Finance* (Fall 1985).

Urbancic, Frank R. "Professional Conduct in the Field," *Journal of Accountancy* (April 1981), pp. 74–75.

Van Son, W. Peter, Guy, Dan M., and Betts, J. Frank. "Engagement Letters: What Practice Shows," *Journal of Accountancy* (June 1982), pp. 72–80.

Van Son, W. Peter, and Winters, Alan J. "The Preaudit Conference: A Communication Tool," *Journal of Accountancy* (November 1982), pp. 86–93.

Weinstein, Stephen. "Survey on Chargeable Time," *Journal of Accountancy* (August 1982), pp. 87–90.

Zuber, George R., Elliott, Robert K., Kinney, William R., and Leisenring, James J. "Using Materiality in Audit Planning," *Journal of Accountancy* (March 1983), pp. 42–54.

**Chapter 6
Review Questions**

6-1.   What is meant by opinion shopping?

6-2.   Describe five potential duties of audit committees.

6-3.   Who has the responsibility to initiate communications when a change of auditors occurs? What specific inquiries should be made?

6-4.   List the matters normally included in an audit engagement letter.

6-5.   Why do auditors attempt to perform as much audit work as possible at an interim date?

6-6.   Describe the composition of the audit team and the responsibilities of its members.

6-7.   What are the nine elements of quality control identified in *Statement on Quality Control Standards No. 1*?

6-8.   What three risks does an auditor face when performing an audit? What is the combination of these risks called?

6-9.   What matters should an auditor consider when planning an audit?

6-10.   Why is an audit program considered tentative? What could cause it to be changed?

6-11.   What is the difference between control risk assessment procedures and substantive tests?

6-12.   What are the general guidelines as to what working papers should include?

6-13.   What is the significance of the lack of privileged communication between an auditor and his or her client?

6-14.   What are the two types of working paper files?

6-15.   What is the purpose of the permanent audit file?

6-16.   List six types of data found in the current audit files.

6-17.   Explain the general concept of the organization of working papers in the current files.

6-18.   Explain the difference between adjusting and reclassifying entries proposed by the auditor.

6-19.   What is a lead schedule?

6-20.   Who has the final responsibility for determining whether or not a proposed adjusting entry will be recorded?

6-21.   State three ways of indicating the performance of audit work in the working papers.

6-22.   What is the purpose of an index system for the working papers? Describe the system illustrated in the text.

6-23.   To what extent may an independent auditor use the client's internal audit staff?

6-24.   Explain three procedures often included in an accounting firm's quality-control review.

6-25.   What matters should be communicated by the auditor to the audit committee?

Chapter 6
Objective Questions Taken from CPA Examinations

*6-26.   If a CPA receives a request from an entity that is not a client to evaluate the use of an accounting principle, the CPA should
a. Consult with the entity's auditor as required by the Code of Professional Ethics.
b. Not consult with the entity's auditor because there is no requirement to do so.
c. Consult with the entity's auditor to ascertain all available facts relevant to forming a professional judgment.
d. Not consult with the entity's auditor because the evaluation should be made independently.

6-27.   As generally conceived, the "audit committee" of a publicly held company should be made up of
a. Representatives of the major equity interests (bonds, preferred stock, common stock).
b. The audit partner, the chief financial officer, the legal counsel, and at least one outsider.
c. Representatives from the client's management, investors, suppliers, and customers.
d. Members of the board of directors who are not officers or employees.

6-28.   The auditor will *not* ordinarily initiate discussion with the audit committee concerning the
a. Extent to which the work of internal auditors will influence the scope of the examination.
b. Extent to which change in the company's organization will influence the scope of the examination.
c. Details of potential problems the auditor believes might cause a qualified opinion.
d. Details of the procedures that the auditor intends to apply.

*Not a CPA examination question.

6-29.   Prior to the acceptance of an audit engagement with a client who has terminated the services of the predecessor auditor, the CPA should
   a. Contact the predecessor auditor without advising the prospective client and request a complete report of the circumstance leading to the termination with the understanding that all information disclosed will be kept confidential.
   b. Accept the engagement without contacting the predecessor auditor because the CPA can include audit procedures to verify the reason given by the client for the termination.
   c. Not communicate with the predecessor auditor because this would in effect be asking the auditor to violate the confidential relationship between auditor and client.
   d. Advise the client of the intention to contact the predecessor auditor and request permission for the contact.

6-30.   A prospective client's refusal to grant a CPA permission to communicate with the predecessor auditor will bear directly on the CPA's ability to
   a. Study and evaluate the client's internal control structure.
   b. Determine the integrity of management.
   c. Determine the beginning balances of the current year's financial statements.
   d. Establish consistency in application of GAAP between years.

6-31.   Engagement letters are widely used in practice for professional engagements of all types. The primary purpose of the engagement letter is to
   a. Remind management that the primary responsibility for the financial statements rests with management.
   b. Satisfy the requirements of the CPA's liability insurance policy.
   c. Provide a starting point for the auditor's preparation of the preliminary audit program.
   d. Provide a written record of the agreement with the client as to the services to be provided.

6-32.   Early appointment of the auditor enables interim work to be performed by the auditor which benefits the client in that it permits the examination to be performed in
   a. A more efficient manner.
   b. A more thorough manner.
   c. Accordance with quality control standards.
   d. Accordance with generally accepted auditing standards.

6-33.   In connection with the element of professional development, a CPA firm's system of quality control should ordinarily provide that all personnel
   a. Have the knowledge required to enable them to fulfill responsibilities assigned.
   b. Possess judgment, motivation, and adequate experience.

   c. Seek assistance from persons having appropriate levels of knowledge, judgment, and authority.

   d. Demonstrate compliance with peer review directives.

6-34.   Which of the following models expresses the general relationship of risks associated with the auditor's evaluation of inherent risk (IR), control risk (CR), and audit risk (AR), that would lead the auditor to conclude that only minimum substantive tests are necessary?

	IR	CR	AR
a.	20%	40%	10%
b.	20%	60%	5%
c.	10%	70%	4%
d.	30%	40%	5%

*6-35.   An auditor discovers evidence that raises a question as to management's integrity. As a result, the auditor's assessment of the audit risk model on this engagement is most likely to change as follows:

   a. Increase in control risk and decrease in detection risk.

   b. Increase in audit risk and decrease in inherent risk.

   c. Increase in inherent risk and decrease in detection risk.

   d. Increase in detection risk and decrease in audit risk.

*6-36.   When using the audit risk model for planning purposes, the auditor evaluates but cannot control

   a. Audit risk and inherent risk.

   b. Inherent risk and control risk.

   c. Control risk and detection risk.

   d. Detection risk and audit risk.

6-37.   Prior to beginning the field work on a new audit engagement in which a CPA does *not* possess expertise in the industry in which the client operates, the CPA should

   a. Reduce audit risk by lowering the preliminary estimates of materiality.

   b. Design special tests of financial statement balances to compensate for the lack of industry expertise.

   c. Engage financial experts familiar with the nature of the industry.

   d. Obtain a knowledge of matters that relate to the nature of the entity's business.

6-38.   The procedures specifically outlined in an audit program are primarily designed to

   a. Protect the auditor in the event of litigation.

*Not a CPA examination question.

    b. Detect errors or irregularities.

    c. Test control systems.

    d. Gather evidence.

6-39. An audit program provides proof that

    a. Sufficient competent evidential matter was obtained.

    b. The work was adequately planned.

    c. There was compliance with generally accepted standards of reporting.

    d. There was a proper study and evaluation of control risk.

6-40. Which of the following is ordinarily designed to detect possible material dollar errors on the financial statements?

    a. Control risk assessment procedures.

    b. Analytical procedures.

    c. Computer controls.

    d. Postaudit working-paper review.

6-41. The permanent file section of the working papers that is kept for each audit client most likely contains

    a. Review notes pertaining to questions and comments regarding the audit work performed.

    b. A schedule of time spent on the engagement by each individual auditor.

    c. Correspondence with the client's legal counsel concerning pending litigation.

    d. Narrative descriptions of the client's accounting procedures and internal control structure.

6-42. In planning a new engagement, which of the following is *not* a factor that affects the CPA's judgment as to the quantity, type, and content of working papers?

    a. The content of the client's representation letter.

    b. The type of report to be issued by the CPA.

    c. The CPA's estimated occurrence rate of attributes.

    d. The CPA's preliminary evaluations based on discussions with the client.

6-43. During an audit engagement, pertinent data are compiled and included in the audit working papers. The working papers primarily are considered to be

    a. A client-owned record of conclusions reached by the auditors who performed the engagement.

    b. Evidence supporting financial statements.

    c. Support for the auditor's representations as to compliance with generally accepted auditing standards.

    d. A record to be used as a basis for the following year's engagement.

6-44. In connection with a lawsuit, a third party attempts to gain access to the auditor's working papers. The client's defense of privileged communication will be successful only to the extent it is protected by the
a. Auditor's acquiescence in use of this defense.
b. Common law.
c. AICPA Code of Professional Ethics.
d. State law.

*6-45. An auditor should communicate to the audit committee all of the following matters except
a. The implications of errors discovered during the audit.
b. Unexpected account variations discovered during analytical procedures that were subsequently resolved.
c. Any disagreements between the auditor and management, whether or not satisfactorily resolved.
d. Any serious difficulties the auditor encountered that were detrimental to the effective completion of the audit.

Chapter 6
Discussion/Case Questions

6-46. For many years the financial and accounting community has recognized the importance of the use of audit committees and has endorsed their formation.

At this time the use of audit committees has become widespread. Independent auditors have become increasingly involved with audit committees and consequently have become familiar with their nature and function.

Required:
a. Describe an audit committee.
b. Identify the reasons audit committees have been formed and are currently in operation.
c. List the functions of an audit committee.
(*AICPA adapted*)

6-47. Joe Melton, CPA, has been contacted by the president of Mudalum Co. (a company developing a process to turn mud into aluminum) and asked to perform the company's audit for the current year. During a meeting with the president, Joe learned that the Securities and Exchange Commission had a suit pending against the company charging it with an illegal distribution of securities. The president

*Not a CPA examination question.

explained that it was an honest mistake by Mudalum because neither its former attorneys nor its former auditors informed him of the SEC registration requirements. For this reason, the president decided to change auditors and has threatened the former auditors with a lawsuit. Because of the threatened litigation, the former auditors refuse to discuss their audit of Mudalum Co. with Joe.

If you were Joe, would you accept Mudalum Co. as a client? Discuss your reasoning.

If you wished to make a further investigation of the situation, what would you investigate and what evidence would you gather?

May the former auditors properly refuse to discuss their audit of Mudalum Co. with Joe?

6-48.   Jones, CPA, is approached by a prospective client who desires to engage Jones to perform an audit that previously was performed by another CPA.

Required: .
Identify the procedures that Jones should follow in accepting the engagement.
(*AICPA adapted*)

6-49.   A CPA has been asked to audit the financial statements of a publicly held company for the first time. The preliminary verbal discussions and inquiries have been completed between the CPA, the company, the predecessor auditor, and all other necessary parties. The CPA is now preparing an engagement letter.

Required:
List the items that should be included in the typical engagement letter in these circumstances and describe the benefits to be derived from preparing an engagement letter.
(*AICPA adapted*)

6-50.   While planning the audit of Vicky King International Enterprises (VKIE), Jane Baldwin, CPA, is evaluating the preliminary levels of audit risk and materiality that should be used. VKIE is a public company in the home construction business. Because of high interest rates, business has been slow this year. Jane noted the following amounts in VKIE's prior-year financial statements:

Total assets	$75,000,000
Current assets	35,000,000
Current liabilities	20,000,000
Long-term debt	40,000,000
Stockholders' equity	15,000,000
Sales	65,000,000
Net income	1,000,000

Discuss the preliminary levels of audit risk and materiality that Jane should use for planning purposes and the effect of these matters on the amount of audit work Jane would plan to perform. If you would like additional information before establishing these levels, prepare a list of the information desired.

6-51. You have been assigned to the audit of Hogeye Ranch Co. In assessing audit risk for various accounts, you have gathered the following information.

Accounts receivable Accounts receivable consist of amounts due from the sale of cattle through six sale barns. All amounts are collected within one week. By state law, cattle cannot be sold without a certificate of inspection by a veterinarian, so all sales are easily accounted for by an examination of vet certificates. The number of cattle sold each month is reconciled with both vet certificates and sale barn receipts, and this control was tested with good results.

Cattle inventory The herd numbers 500 cows and bulls. Cattle records are kept on notepads by the cowboys. Deaths and births are not always recorded promptly. Ear tag identifications are sometimes lost so that specific animals may be difficult to identify. Also, a fence with a neighbor is in poor condition so that the client's and the neighbor's herds are sometimes mixed.

Property and equipment Property consists mainly of land, a barn, and fencing. Equipment consists of a truck, a tractor, and minor other items. No control risk assessment tests have been performed on controls relating to property and equipment.

Required:
For each account, assess each component of audit risk. Also indicate how your substantive tests will be affected.

6-52. Your knowledge of general economic conditions during the year ended December 31, 19X9, included the facts that inflation had been recorded at a high 12-percent rate, which caused a serious slowdown in business (real GNP declined 6 percent) and a steep drop in the stock market (approximately 25 percent). Unemployment was high, even though unions were demanding large wage increases. Because of high interest rates and the stock market decline, money supplies were tight, and long-term financing practically unavailable.

Discuss the effects of these conditions on your audits of the following companies for the year ended December 31, 19X9:

a. A construction contractor specializing in small office buildings on fixed-price contracts.

b. An investment company with 50 percent of its portfolio in common stocks and 50 percent in long-term bonds.

c. A manufacturing company that has always been only marginally profitable and whose 4-percent bonds mature January 1, 19X0.

d. A small finance company specializing in consumer loans.

e. A manufacturer whose warranty costs have historically averaged 5 percent of sales.

6-53. The first generally accepted auditing standard of field work requires, in part, that "the work is to be adequately planned." An effective tool that aids the auditor in adequately planning the work is an audit program.

Required:
What is an audit program, and what purposes does it serve?
(*AICPA adopted*)

6-54. Jane Grote, CPA, has conducted audits for more than 30 years and, because of her extensive experience, does not believe she needs an audit program to know what audit procedures to perform. Tom Prince, another CPA who recently became Jane's partner, believes that he should try to persuade Jane to use an audit program.
　　　　Is Tom right? If not, why not? If so, what reasons should he use?

6-55. Analytical procedures are useful tests of financial statement balances and transactions in the audit planning stage.

Required:
a. Explain why analytical procedures are considered substantive tests of financial statement balances and transactions.
b. Explain how analytical procedures are used in the audit planning stage.
c. Identify the analytical procedures that one might expect a CPA to use during an examination performed in accordance with generally accepted auditing standards.
(*AICPA adapted*)

6-56. Your client, Hogeye Ranch Co., has adopted an "Executive Bonus Plan" for its ranch foreman effective January 1, 19X6. The bonus is computed as 10 percent of net income before provision for income taxes and bonus. At December 31, 19X6 the client has accrued an estimated bonus of $24,000 ($2,000 per month). Net income for 19X6 after all adjustments except to income taxes and bonus is $119,327.15 and income tax expense is $122,000.00.
　　　　A copy of the plan has been obtained and filed in the permanent audit file. You find the following working paper in the accrued liability section.

Required:
Prepare a new schedule to more efficiently and effectively audit Accrued Bonus Expense.

Hogeye Ranch Co.

Accrued Bonus Expense

12-31-86

Balance at January 1, 1986				— 0 —	
Jan	JE # 4			200000 ✓	
Feb	JE # 8			200000 ✓	
Mar	JE # 14			200000 ✓	
Apr	JE # 20			200000 ✓	
May	JE # 24			200000 ✓	
Jun	JE # 30			200000 ✓	
Jul	JE # 36			200000 ✓	
Aug	JE # 42			200000 ✓	
Sept	JE # 50			200000 ✓	
Oct	JE # 55			200000 ✓	
Nov	JE # 60			200000 ✓	
Dec	JE # 67			200000 ✓	
Balance per general ledger Dec 31, 1986				2400000	
AJE # 6 Adjust accrual to requirement				253272	
				2653272	

✓ Examined properly approved journal entry.

6-57.   You have completed your audit of Ethridge Construction Company for the year ended November 30, 19X5, and have scheduled a meeting with the company's audit committee for the next day. The company builds small apartment buildings in a three-state area and has been only marginally profitable during the last five years. Ethridge uses the percentage-of-completion method to recognize revenue, and although you were generally satisfied with the overall fairness of the financial statements after your audit last year, you believe the company tends to be optimistic in estimating the stage of completion of its work-in-process.

You did not receive the assistance you anticipated from the company's internal auditor because she was working on a special project for the controller. This resulted in your performing more work, which resulted in a higher-than-anticipated audit fee. The client protested the higher audit fee but has agreed to pay it.

One of Ethridge's competitors issued its annual report a week before Ethridge. The president has asked that you complete next year's audit two weeks earlier than this year so that Ethridge can issue its annual report first. You worked an excessive amount of overtime just to meet this year's deadline.

Prepare an outline of all the points you would like to discuss with the audit committee.

Appendix to Chapter 6

Illustration of the Property and Equipment and Accumulated
Depreciation Section of an Audit Program

X Co.
Property and Equipment
12-31-X8

Account Description

This group of accounts represents the land, building, and equipment used in the company's manufacturing process, as well as the salespeople's automobiles. Annual straight-line depreciation rates are 15 percent for buildings, 20 percent for equipment, and 33⅓ percent for automobiles.

Evaluation of Audit Risk

A detailed ledger is maintained showing the individual items of property and equipment, and it is balanced with the control account monthly. Capital expenditures in excess of $5,000 require the approval of the board of directors in the capital expenditures budget. Formal policies have been established to distinguish between capital and maintenance charges. Retirements of property are reported by the shop supervisors, but no periodic review is made for unreported retirements and individual pieces of equipment are not tagged or otherwise specifically identified as belonging to the company.

Overall, inherent and control risks relating to property additions and the assertions of rights, completeness, valuation, and presentation are assessed as low. Inherent and control risks relating to property retirements and existence are assessed as medium to high.

To maintain audit risk at a low level, detection risk will be set high (limited work) for property additions and medium to low (expanded work) for property retirements.

Audit Procedures

| Time Required | | | Assigned | Performed |
Estimated	Actual	Audit Step	To	By
Interim—				
4		1. Review and assess inherent and control risk relating to property and equipment assertions and accumulated depreciation assertions (see separate programs).	Staff 1	
3		2. Analyze property and equipment additions through the interim audit date listing all additions in excess of $4,000. For all additions in excess of $4,000, examine vendor invoice, canceled check, and receiving report and determine if classification as a capital item is proper. Also indicate on schedule if the addition is a new or replacement item.	Staff 2	
3		3. Analyze maintenance expense through the interim audit date listing all charges in excess of $4,000. For all maintenance charges in excess of $4,000, examine vendor invoice, canceled check, and receiving report and determine if classification as an expense item is proper.	Staff 2	
1		4. Trace all additions in excess of $5,000 to capital budget approved by the board of directors.	Staff 2	
3		5. Analyze retirements of property and equipment through the interim audit date. Trace the original cost of items retired, together with dates acquired and retired, to the detailed property ledger. Test calculation of accumulated	Staff 1	

Audit Procedures (Continued)

Time Required				
Estimated	*Actual*	*Audit Step*	*Assigned To*	*Performed By*
		depreciation to date of retirement and trace any salvage proceeds to cash receipts book. Investigate any significant retirements for which there is no salvage. Recompute gain or loss on the retirement and relate to other income or expense account.		
2		6. Review and supervision.	Senior	
Final—				
1		1. Review and assess inherent and control risk relating to property and equipment and accumulated depreciation for any material changes from interim review.	Staff 1	
1		2. Prepare or obtain client-prepared lead schedule of property and equipment and accumulated depreciation.	Staff 2	
—		3. Trace beginning balances on lead schedule to prior-year audit working papers.	Staff 2	
1		4. Total the detailed property ledger and determine if it balances with the control account.	Staff 2	
2		5. Analyze property and equipment additions from interim to year end, listing all additions in excess of $4,000. Cross-reference the total of this schedule to the lead schedule. For all additions from interim date to year end in excess of $4,000, examine vendor invoice, canceled check, and receiving report and determine if classification as a capital item is proper. Also, indicate on schedule if the addition is a new or replacement item.	Staff 2	
1		6. Analyze maintenance expense from interim date to year end, listing all charges in excess of $4,000. Cross-reference the total of this schedule to the operating expense lead schedule. For all maintenance charges from interim date to year end in excess of $4,000, examine vendor invoice, canceled check, and receiving report and determine if classification as an expense item is proper.	Staff 2	
1		7. Trace all additions from interim date to year end in excess of $5,000 to capital budget approved by the board of directors.	Staff 2	

Audit Procedures (Continued)

Time Required		Audit Step	Assigned To	Performed By
Estimated	*Actual*			
1		8. Analyze retirements of property and equipment from interim date to year end. Cross-reference the total of this schedule to the lead schedule. Trace the original cost of items retired after interim date, together with dates acquired and retired, to the detailed property ledger. Test calculation of accumulated depreciation to date of retirement and trace any salvage proceeds to cash receipts book. Investigate any significant retirements for which there is no salvage. Recompute gain or loss on the retirement and relate to other income or expense account.	Staff 1	
		9. Perform a search for unrecorded retirements including the following:		
1		(a) Determine whether a retirement was recorded for each addition identified as a replacement.	Staff 1	
1		(b) Investigate any significant reduction in property insurance coverage or property tax assessments to determine if it resulted from property retirements.	Staff 1	
1		(c) Review miscellaneous and other income accounts for salvage credits or scrap sales that may indicate the disposal of retired property and equipment.	Staff 1	
1		(d) Discuss property and equipment retirements with the shop supervisors and the plant manager.	Staff 1	
2		(e) Select ten items of equipment from the detailed property and equipment ledger and locate them in the plant.	Staff 1	
1		(f) Write a memorandum outlining the work performed in the search for unrecorded retirements.	Staff 1	
		10. Test the current-year provision for depreciation:		
1		(a) Compare depreciation methods, estimated lives of assets, and estimated salvage values to prior year for consistency.	Staff 1	
2		(b) Make an overall test of depreciation expense by major asset category and investigate any significant variations.	Staff 1	

Audit Procedures (Continued)

Time Required		Audit Step	Assigned To	Performed By
Estimated	*Actual*			
1		11. Review the balances of accumulated depreciation at year end to determine the reasonableness of the undepreciated cost of the major assets in relation to their remaining depreciable lives. Consider such factors as obsolescence and technological changes, as well as physical characteristics.	Senior	
2		12. Review and supervision.	Senior	

Conclusion—

CHAPTER 7

Assessing Control Risk— Understanding the Internal Control Structure

---

Learning Objectives   *After reading and studying the material in this chapter, the student should*

Understand the general model that shows the relationship between control risk assessment and substantive tests of financial statement balances.

Be able to define an internal control structure and describe these three elements of an internal control structure:

>   The control environment.
>   The accounting system.
>   Control procedures.

Know the general procedures that are used to obtain an understanding of the internal control structure.

Be able to correlate the assessment of control risk with detection risk.

In Chapter 5 we discussed materiality and audit risk, two of the most important concepts that underlie financial auditing. We provided a general model of each of these concepts and indicated that we would illustrate them more fully in later chapters.

In Chapter 6 we provided the framework of an audit in which we listed the following steps (see Figure 6.2).

1. Plan the audit.

2. Gather the necessary evidence to form an opinion on the fairness of the financial statements in accordance with generally accepted accounting principles.

   a. Evidence is gathered by studying, testing, and assessing the client company's internal control structure.

   b. Evidence is gathered by performing and evaluating substantive tests of account balances and disclosures.

3. Issue the audit report that contains the audit opinion.

Chapter 6, covered step 1. In the remainder of the text we will cover

   step 2a in Chapters 7–11

   step 2b in Chapters 12–18

   step 3 in Chapters 19–21

In this chapter we concentrate on understanding the internal control structure. In the next chapter we illustrate methods of assessing control risk through detailed tests of controls.

The Relationship Between Control Risk Assessment and Substantive Tests of Financial Statement Balances

Why is it necessary for the auditor to assess control risk? Remember from Chapter 5 that detection risks for the audit of individual account balances are determined by application of the following model.

$$\text{Detection Risk} = \frac{\text{Individual audit risk}}{\text{Inherent risk} \times \text{Control risk}}$$

Assume that the auditor is considering how much testing of the accounts receivable balance is necessary to form an opinion as to the fairness of that account. He or she must determine a detection risk for that account, which is

the risk that the auditor's procedures will not detect material misstatements in the account.

The auditor must also assess control risk that relates to accounts receivable, which is the risk that a material misstatement in an account balance will not be prevented or detected on a timely basis by the internal control structure.

The "bottom line" is that assessments of control risk are necessary to help determine the nature, timing, and extent of substantive tests, as evidenced by the following diagram.

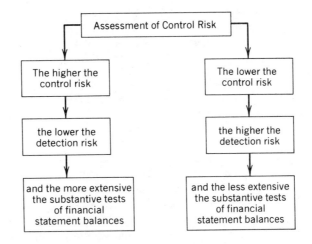

If we think of controls as types of safeguards, then it is easy for us to see the inverse relationship between controls and the extent of substantive tests of financial statement balances. Here are some examples.

1. If the auditor ascertains that customers' credit is investigated before credit sales are approved, the tests of allowance for doubtful accounts may be less extensive than they would be if no credit investigations were made.

2. If the auditor ascertains that perpetual inventory records are maintained and are periodically compared with independent inventory counts, the auditor's tests of the inventory records may be less extensive than they would be if this system of "checks and balances" did not exist.

With some exceptions as noted later, it is necessary, then, for the auditor to assess control risk to help determine the extent of substantive tests of financial statement balances.

Internal Control Structure

What does the auditor do when he or she assesses control risk?

> *Assessing control risk* is the process of evaluating the effectiveness of the internal control structure in preventing or detecting and correcting misstatements in the financial statements.

The form of assessment is optional with the auditor. A number (60 percent) may be assigned as we did in Chapter 5, or a qualitative (high) risk assessment may be made as we did in Chapter 6. In either case, the auditor is estimating the likelihood that the internal control structure will not prevent or detect and correct financial statement misstatements. Thus, the assessment process is essentially a judgment of the auditor.

> The *internal control structure* itself consists of the policies and procedures established to provide reasonable assurance that an entity's established objectives will be achieved.

This is a broad definition and covers areas that, in some cases, may be beyond the scope of the auditor's examination. For example, the auditor would not usually evaluate policies designed to improve employee morale.

On the other hand, the auditor *would* evaluate internal control structure policies and procedures that relate to the purpose of the audit of the financial statements. Specifically, the auditor would evaluate the policies and procedures of the internal control structure that, in his or her judgment, will *prevent* or *detect* and *correct* a misstatement in the financial statements, or reduce the risk of a misstatement in the financial statements.

The auditor must decide, then, whether it is appropriate to evaluate certain elements of the internal control structure and make an assessment (numerically or qualitatively) of the control risk of that element. Although the auditing standards contain few guidelines, it would be wise for the auditor to evaluate any part of the internal control structure that is likely to prevent or detect and correct financial statement misstatements.

Assume, for example, that the client has a budgeting system. The auditor may be inclined to ignore that part of the internal control structure because actual rather than budgeted dollar amounts are recorded in the financial statements. However, a budgeting system that provides for investigation of large deviations between actual and budgeted costs may reduce the risk of misstatement in the financial statements. How? By identifying some large deviations between actual and budgeted repair costs as expenditures misclassified as additions to property and equipment. Thus, the existence of this element of the internal control structure allows the auditor to assess a lower control risk for purposes of determining the detection risk for the audit of repairs expense and property and equipment.

To help in evaluating the internal control structure, the auditor divides it into these three elements.

1. The control environment.

2. The accounting system.

3. The control procedures.

In the remainder of this section, we will discuss each of these elements. In the next section, we will illustrate some general procedures that can be used to obtain an understanding of the internal control structure and make an assessment of control risk.

Control Environment

Perhaps no other element of the internal control structure has been given as much attention in recent years as the control environment.

> The *control environment* reflects the overall attitude, awareness, and actions of the board of directors, management, owners, and others concerning the importance of control and its emphasis in the entity.

To be more specific, control environment covers some of the following matters.

Management Philosophy and Operating Style   Each manager has his or her "ideas" as to how the operations of an entity should be conducted. Some managers pay close attention to financial reporting, prepare and use budgets, and place emphasis on meeting operating goals; other managers do not. Some managements are dominated by a few individuals; other managements are more decentralized.

The auditor's assessment of management philosophy and operating style (as difficult as it may sometimes be) could be a significant factor in the assessment of control risk. If current observation and prior experience convince the auditor that little importance is attached to proper financial reporting or if business risk is not adequately monitored, these may be early indications that control risk should be assessed at a high level.

Organizational Structure   The assignment of authority and responsibility within the company is also a criterion that the auditor will use in evaluating the control environment. Too much responsibility given to a few individuals may result in errors because of the excessive workload. Also, concentrated authority might create a climate in which irregularities are more likely to occur. The delegation of responsibility and authority for specific tasks should be clearly defined. An audit committee is an important control device in any organizational structure.

Remember from our discussions in earlier chapters that the auditor cannot observe the recording of every transaction. However, the more confidence the auditor has in the efficiency of the organizational structure, the more confidence he or she has that transactions have been properly recorded.

Management Control Methods   Management's control over company operations is another matter that the auditor must consider. Two effective methods of establishing this control are

> The use of budgets and standards, including investigation and timely action on variances
>
> An internal audit function with qualified personnel and the proper amount of authority

We have previously discussed how the use of budgets can improve the control structure and allow auditors to restrict substantive tests of account balances.

The existence and effective use of internal auditors by the company might be one of the most important elements of the control environment. Internal auditors (unlike external auditors) are able to observe and influence, on a daily basis, the financial reporting process of the company. In fact, many audit procedures performed by external auditors are also performed more extensively by internal auditors.

Personnel Management Methods   If the auditor has reason to believe that sufficient numbers of competent individuals are involved in the financial reporting system, he or she is more likely to assess a low risk to the probability that material misstatements exist in the financial statements because of the control environment. Again, the auditor's inability to observe the recording of every transaction places heavy emphasis on his or her assessment of company personnel.

Control Consciousness   Auditors should ask whether management has created a control environment in which people are motivated to comply with controls rather than to ignore them. Among other things, auditors should determine whether economic pressures on company personnel are likely to cause circumvention of the internal control structure. Here are some examples.

1. Very large bonuses for division heads depend, in part, on division operating profit. This practice may result in misstatement of the financial statements to increase profitability.

2. The pressure for a large dollar amount of sales is very intense. Such pressure may cause the credit department to accept business with high credit risks. This practice may result in large bad debt losses. Fictitious sales may also result.

One measure of management's *control consciousness* may be its reaction to control weaknesses pointed out by external or internal auditors. Quick corrective action by management might indicate its commitment to a sound internal control structure.

Summary of Control Environment We can easily see, then, that the auditor's assessment of the control environment is vitally important to his or her overall assessment of the internal control structure. Some auditors maintain that a poor control environment negates a good accounting system and sound control procedures. In fact, some auditors would argue that a company cannot have a reliable accounting system and control procedures without a high-quality control environment.

The Accounting System

The *accounting system* consists of the methods and records established to identify, assemble, classify, analyze, record, and report an entity's transactions and to maintain accountability for the related assets and liabilities.

The auditor must assess whether the client's accounting system is likely to produce reliable financial statements and other financial data. The less likely that the accounting system will accomplish this goal, the higher the risk assessment of this system.

In the next section of this chapter, we discuss methods of obtaining an understanding of the accounting system.

Control Procedures

Control procedures are those policies and procedures in addition to the control environment and accounting system that management has established to provide reasonable assurance that an entity's established objectives will be achieved.

Specifically, control procedures would include approval of transactions, segregation of duties, safeguarding of assets, proper recording techniques, and independent reconciliations.

Again, we will cover methods of obtaining an understanding of the control procedures in the next section.

Obtaining an Understanding of the Internal Control Structure

With definitions of the three elements of the internal control structure as a background, we will now turn our attention to discussions of the procedures that the auditor might use to obtain an understanding of this internal control structure.

Generally, the procedures used to obtain this understanding must be sufficient to accomplish these two goals.

1. The auditor should know the nature and design of the policies, procedures, methods, and records pertaining to each internal control structure element (control environment, accounting system, and control procedures).

2. The auditor should know whether these policies, procedures, and methods are operating effectively (or whether they are functioning as they are purported to function).

Put another way, in order for the auditor to assess the control risk as low on a given account, he or she must have the support to show that the internal control structure policies and procedures

are suitably designed to prevent or detect and correct misstatements in the financial statement account, and are operating in a manner consistent with the conclusion about control risk.

Assume, for example, that the auditor is assessing the control risk of accounts receivable for the purpose of determining the detection risk, which, in turn, determines the extent of substantive tests regarding the accounts receivable balance. To acquire an understanding of the design of the accounts receivable internal control structure (goal 1., above), the auditor might do the following (among other steps).

1. Determine that the control environment has appropriate policies and procedures by examining the organizational structure of the Billing Department, Credit Department, and so on.

2. Determine that the accounting system has appropriate policies and procedures by ascertaining that documents, journals, and ledgers, including control accounts and subsidiary ledgers, and so on do exist.

3. Determine that the control procedures include appropriate policies and procedures by inquiring as to whether the company performs credit checks, balances the accounts receivable control account with the subsidiary ledger, and so on.

To determine whether these policies and procedures are operating effectively (goal 2., above), the auditor might do the following (among other steps).

1. Make inquiries in the Billing and Credit Departments.

2. Examine some sales invoices and trace the processing of the transactions through the control account and the subsidiary ledger.

3. Examine some credit files for customer accounts where credit was extended, and observe that the accounts receivable control account was balanced with the accounts receivable subsidiary ledger.

In general, the auditor performs some combination of the following procedures to determine whether the internal control structure is suitably designed and operating properly.

Inquiries of appropriate company personnel

Inspection of documents and records

Observations of policies and procedures

Here are some examples of procedures that might be used in assessing the control risk for the control environment, accounting system, and control procedures. We will also provide illustrations of specific accounting systems and control procedures.

Obtaining an Understanding of the Control Environment

Unlike the accounting system and control procedures, there may be little documentary support for some parts of the control environment. The reason is that much of the control environment is attitude and philosophy. Much of what the auditor does, then, is to ask questions and make observations.

In some cases documents such as organizational charts, budgets, and written codes of conduct could be examined to ascertain that such items do, indeed, exist. In addition the auditor would ascertain that the organizational structure, budgeting process, and codes of conduct are actually operating as they should be.

In some cases a cursory examination of the control environment may be sufficient to determine that detection risk should be set low for certain elements of the financial statements. For example, management disregard of proper credit-granting policies may cause the auditor to plan extensive tests of the allowance for doubtful accounts. In this case the auditor will set a very high control risk for the valuation of accounts receivable without examining the accounting system or control procedures that relate to the granting of credit.

Obtaining an Understanding of the Accounting System and Control Procedures

Although there are differences between the accounting system and control procedures, they are so interrelated that often the auditor will study and evaluate them concurrently. Sometimes, descriptions of accounting systems include descriptions of controls that are designed to prevent and/or detect errors and irregularities. For example, the purchases system may call for one copy of a merchandise requisition to be sent to the Purchasing Department and one copy to be sent to the Accounts Payable Department. Sending copies of the requisition to two departments is part of the accounting system, but sending the copy to the Accounts Payable Department also establishes a control over the pending transaction.

For this reason, then, we will use the same illustrations to show how the auditor can obtain an understanding of both the accounting system and any control procedures that he or she has not studied in other parts of the audit process. These illustrations are general in nature. Detailed tests of controls are covered in Chapter 8.

Examples of Descriptions of Accounting Systems (and Related Controls) in the Areas of Purchases, Cash Disbursements, and Payroll

Here are some examples of information the auditor might obtain about purchases, cash disbursements, and payroll. Notice that in each case we are learning how the accounting system functions in general and are acquainting ourselves with some of the controls. In fact, these descriptions tell us the following about purchases, cash disbursements, and payroll.

1. How the transactions are initiated.

2. What accounting records are used in the transactions.

3. The accounting processes involved in the transactions.

In each of the accounting system descriptions we can see a number of controls that help to prevent and or/detect errors and irregularities. Examples are summarized for each type of system.

Example of Purchases Accounting System and Controls

1. When the Stores Department needs merchandise, two copies of a requisition are prepared. One copy is sent to the Accounts Payable Department and the other to the Purchasing Department.

2. Upon receipt of the requisition, the Purchasing Department, after obtaining competitive bids, initiates a five-copy purchase order.

3. One copy of the purchase order is sent back to the Stores Department, where the quantities and descriptions are verified.

4. Copies of the purchase order are sent to the Accounts Payable and Receiving Departments to serve as file copies and as notification that merchandise has been ordered.

5. Two copies of the purchase order are sent to the vendor, who acknowledges receipt by sending one copy back to the Purchasing Department.

6. The vendor ships the merchandise to the Receiving Department, where an independent count of the merchandise is made and three copies of a receiving report are prepared.

7. The merchandise, after being counted and inspected, is sent to the Stores Department, along with two copies of the receiving report. The Stores Department compares the merchandise with the listings on the receiving report and sends one copy of the receiving report to the Accounts Payable Department.

8. The third copy of the receiving report is sent from the Receiving Department to the Purchasing Department, where terms and other details are reviewed.

9. Two copies of an invoice are sent from the vendor to the Purchasing Department. The Purchasing Department retains one copy and sends the other copy to the Accounts Payable Department.

10. The Accounts Payable Department compares the details of the requisition, the purchase order, the invoice, and the receiving report. All four documents are filed together as documentation of the transaction.

Purchases

Description	Control
One copy of the requisition is sent to accounts payable.	Establishes control over the pending purchase transaction.
The purchasing agent obtains competitive bids.	Establishes control over prices.
The Receiving Department makes an independent count of incoming merchandise.	Establishes control over incoming merchandise.
The Stores Department compares merchandise with listings on the receiving report.	Continues the control over incoming merchandise.
The Accounts Payable Department compares the details of the requisition, the purchase order, the invoice, and the receiving report.	Establishes control over the entire purchase transaction and ensures that what was requested, ordered, received, and billed are the same.

Example of Cash Disbursements Accounting System and Controls

1. To initiate a cash disbursement, a voucher is prepared in the Accounts Payable Department. After the supporting documents (invoice, purchase order, requisition, and receiving report—see Purchases Accounting System and Controls) and the account distribution are verified, the voucher is approved for payment.

2. The amount of the voucher is entered in the voucher register in the Accounts Payable Department. Detail of the account distribution is sent to the General Accounting Department where the amounts are posted to the applicable subsidiary ledger accounts. The voucher along with the supporting documents is sent to the Cash Disbursements Department.

3. In the Cash Disbursements Department, the supporting documents are examined and the voucher is approved for payment.

4. A check is prepared and signed after inspection of the approved voucher. The check is mailed to the payee by the signer. The amount of the check is entered in the check register. The supporting documents are canceled after the check is signed.

5. The check number and the amount of the paid voucher are sent to the Accounts Payable Department and entered in the voucher register.

6. The General Accounting Department reconciles control totals from the subsidiary ledger accounts, the voucher register in the Accounts Payable Department, and the check register in the Accounts Payable Department. Periodically, the total of unpaid items in the voucher register is compared with the vouchers payable control account maintained in the General Accounting Department.

7. The bank sends the bank statement and canceled checks directly to the Internal Audit Department, where an independent bank reconciliation is performed.

Cash Disbursements

Description	Control
The cash disbursement voucher is approved for payment.	Ensures that goods or services were received before payment is made.
The supporting documents are canceled when the check is signed.	Ensures that the voucher is not paid twice.

Cash Disbursements

Description	Control
The total of unpaid items in the voucher register is compared with the vouchers payable general ledger control account.	Ensures agreement between the general ledger account and the voucher register.
The bank statement is sent directly to the Internal Audit Department, where an independent bank reconciliation is performed.	Ensures that unrecorded or inaccurately recorded cash disbursements are detected.

Example of Payroll Accounting System and Controls

1. The Timekeeping Department maintains two sets of time records. Employee clock cards, which originate in the Timekeeping Department, show the number of hours worked by each employee. Job time tickets, which come from the Shops Department, show the amount of time for each employee.

2. The Timekeeping Department reconciles the job time tickets with the employee clock cards. The job time tickets then are sent to the Cost Accounting Department. The employee clock cards are sent to the Payroll Department.

3. The Cost Accounting Department records the information from the job time tickets in a labor distribution journal. This journal is sent to the General Accounting Department, where an entry is made to a payroll clearing account.

4. The Payroll Department secures employment and rate authorization records and deduction slips from the Human Resources Department. These records and the employee clock cards are used to prepare the payroll register. A copy of the payroll register is forwarded to the Accounts Payable Department.

5. The Accounts Payable Department uses the payroll register to prepare a voucher that authorizes the writing of the payroll account reimbursement check. The voucher information is forwarded to the General Accounting Department for posting to the payroll clearing account. The voucher itself is forwarded to the Cash Disbursements Department.

6. The Cash Disbursements Department prepares the payroll account reimbursement check for the total amount of the payroll, as evidenced by the voucher received from the Accounts Payable Department. The check is sent to the bank.

7. The bank deposits the payroll check in an imprest payroll account. This account is used to write individual checks to employees.

8. The Payroll Department writes the individual payroll checks from the imprest payroll account. On occasion, the individual checks are distributed to employees by the Internal Audit Department. When this is done, identification is required of employees before payroll checks are released.

Payroll

Description	Control
The Timekeeping Department reconciles the job time tickets with the employee clock cards.	Ensures that all employees' time is accounted for.
The Payroll Department uses Human Resource Department records and employee clock cards to prepare the payroll register.	Ensures that proper data are used to prepare the payroll register.
The Cash Disbursements Department prepares one check for the total amount of the payroll.	Establishes control over the total amount of the payroll.
Individual checks are sometimes disbursed to employees by the Internal Audit Department.	Ensures that payroll checks are not being paid to improper or nonexistent employees.

The Flow of Transactions and Cycles

Another way to obtain an understanding of the accounting system and control procedures is to use the following three-step sequence.

1. Acquire an understanding of the flow of transactions through the accounting system.

2. Relate internal control structure objectives to points in the flow of transactions and handling of assets where errors or irregularities could occur.

3. Relate internal control structure procedures used by the company to control objectives satisfied by these procedures.

Each of these steps is discussed in the following sections.

The Flow of Transactions

To understand points in the accounting system where control measures *should* exist and whether the appropriate control measures *do* exist, the auditor may study the processing of transactions and the handling of assets within that accounting system.

Transactions may be studied according to some commonality, such as transaction cycle or business function. The understanding of these related classes of transactions can be obtained through inspection of written documentation, inquiries of client personnel, and observation of the processing of these transactions.

There are many ways to classify transactions within an accounting system. One method is to group transactions into the following four cycles.

1. The treasury cycle, which includes the following types of economic events.

   a. Funds received from equity investors and creditors.

   b. Funds temporarily invested until needed for operations.

2. The expenditure cycle, which includes the following types of economic events.

   a. Goods and services acquired from vendors and employees in exchange for obligations to pay.

   b. Obligations paid to vendors and employees.

3. The conversion cycle, which includes the following types of economic events.

   a. Holding resources.

   b. Using resources.

   c. Transforming resources.

4. The revenue cycle, which includes the following types of economic events.

   a. Distribution of resources to outsiders in exchange for promises of future payments.

   b. Receipts from outsiders for resources distributed to them.

A Brief Description of Some Functions of Each Cycle   The treasury cycle functions initiate the following accounting entries and use, in part, the following types of records and forms.

1. Incurrence and repayment of debts, using various types of commercial paper.

2. Issuance and retirements of stock, using stock certificates.

3. Purchases and sales of treasury stock.

4. Purchases and sales of investments, using stock and bond certificates.

5. Accruals, receipts, and payments of interest and dividends.

The part of the treasury cycle that deals with incurral of debt and investment of debt funds can be illustrated as follows.

Receipt of funds by incurring debt ← Repayment of debt

Purchase of investments with funds

Accrual and payment of interest on debt

Accrual and receipt of interest from investments

The expenditure cycle includes the acquisition of and the payment for fixed assets, inventories, labor (payroll), supplies, and a variety of other goods and services. The cycle initiates the following accounting entries and uses, in part, the following records and forms.

1. Purchases, using authorization for expenditures, purchase requisitions, purchase orders, receiving reports, and vendors' invoices.

2. Cash disbursements, using vouchers, check requests, and checks.

3. Adjustments, using debit and credit memos.

4. Payrolls and employee benefits paid, using time reports, clock cards, and checks.

The part of the expenditure cycle that deals with the acquisition of and payment for inventory can be illustrated as follows.

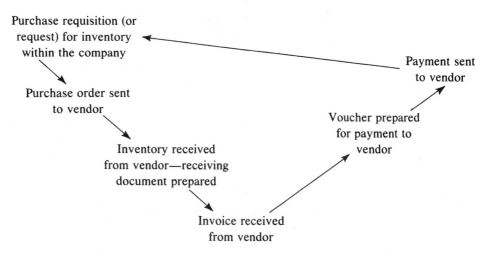

The conversion cycle includes such items as cost accounting, inventory management, and property accounting. The cycle initiates the following accounting entries and uses, in part, the following records and forms.

1. Depreciation and amortization, using appropriate worksheets or schedules.

2. Property retirements, using property files.

3. Transfers of inventory from raw materials to work in process to finished goods, using labor tickets, materials requisitions, and overhead rate worksheets.

The conversion cycle (as all the others) interfaces with other cycles. The part of the conversion cycle that includes use of property can be illustrated as follows.

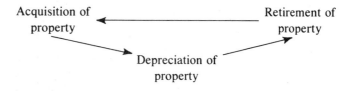

The revenue cycle includes such items as granting of credit, taking orders, shipping merchandise, billing, maintaining accounts receivable, and collecting cash receipts on account. The cycle initiates the following accounting entries and uses, in part, the following records and forms.

1. Sales, using credit files, price lists, customer orders, shipping documents, sales invoices, and accounts receivable subsidiary ledgers.

2. Cash receipts, using customer remittance advices and a cash receipts journal or record.

3. Sales returns and allowances, using customer adjustment forms.

4. Bad debt charges, write-offs, and recoveries, using aging schedules, credit files, and remittance advices.

The part of the revenue cycle that includes credit sales and cash receipts can be illustrated as follows.

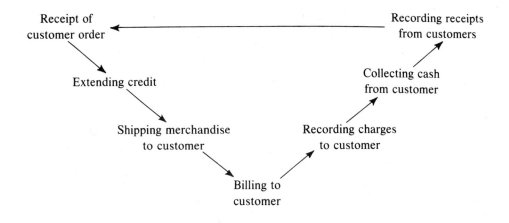

Internal Control Structure Objectives and Procedures

The auditor can identify the *internal control structure objectives* that relate to points in the processing of transactions and the handling of assets where errors or irregularities could occur.

Here are four internal control structure objectives.

1. Proper authorization of transactions and activities.

2. Design and use of adequate documents and records to record transactions and events, and segregation of duties so that procedures designed to detect misstatements are performed by persons other than those who are in a position to perpetrate them.

3. Adequate safeguards over access to and use of assets and records.

4. Independent checks on performance, reconciliations, and comparison of assets with recorded accountability.

This approach may help the auditor understand whether each cycle or group of transactions has internal control structure procedures designed to achieve the internal control structure objectives. Some examples of (1) transaction cycles, (2) the common internal control structure objectives within these cycles, and (3) the individual internal control structure procedures, are shown in Figures 7.1–7.4.

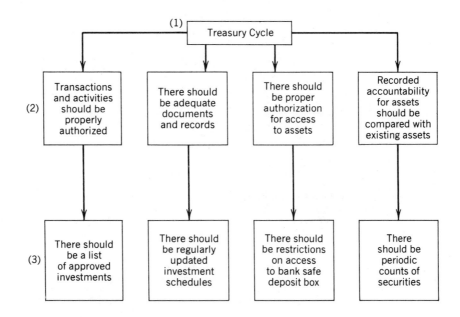

Figure 7.1 Treasury cycle

Correlating the Assessment of Control Risk with Detection Risk

So far, we have discussed the techniques by which the auditor gains an understanding of the internal control structure. In theory this step is followed by an assessment of control risk. This assessment is made by *tests of controls,* the purposes of which are to:

1. Ascertain that the internal control structure policies and procedures are properly designed.

2. Ascertain that the internal control structure policies and procedures are effectively operating, or operating as they are purported to operate.

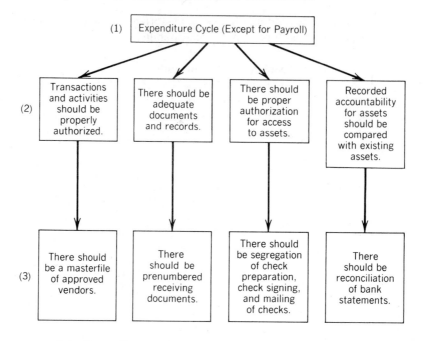

Figure 7.2   Expenditure cycle

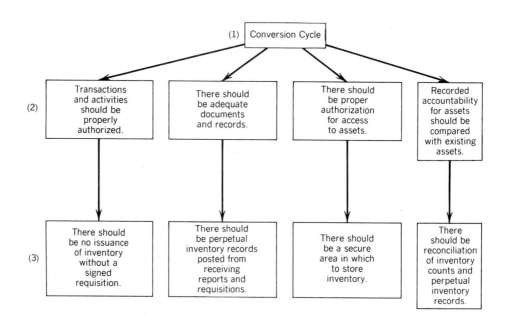

Figure 7.3   Conversion cycle

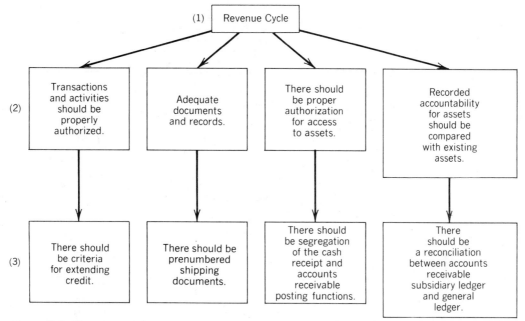

Figure 7.4   Revenue cycle

In practice, however, obtaining an understanding of the internal control structure, assessing control risk, and conducting tests of controls can be and often are performed concurrently. This is particularly true when the financial statements were audited in prior years by the same CPA firm and considerable information about the internal control structure has already been acquired. When an audit is being conducted for the first time, it might be necessary for the auditor to spend more than the usual amount of time acquiring a basic understanding of how the internal control structure is *supposed* to operate.

In making an assessment of control risk for the purpose of determining detection risk and the scope of related substantive tests, it is not necessary that the auditor conduct extensive or detailed tests of controls. In fact the auditor could make an assessment of control risk after acquiring only a *basic* understanding of the internal control structure and conducting some *basic* tests of controls. The material in this chapter assumes that the auditor has conducted only these basic tests.

On the other hand, the auditor could conduct more tests of controls with the use of techniques illustrated in Chapter 8. Then, another assessment of control risk would be made with the aid of the additional information obtained through the application of these detailed techniques.

The Auditor's Decision Model for the Assessment of Control Risk

The auditor must decide on the acceptable (or attainable) level of assessed control risk. The following chart is a model of this decision process.

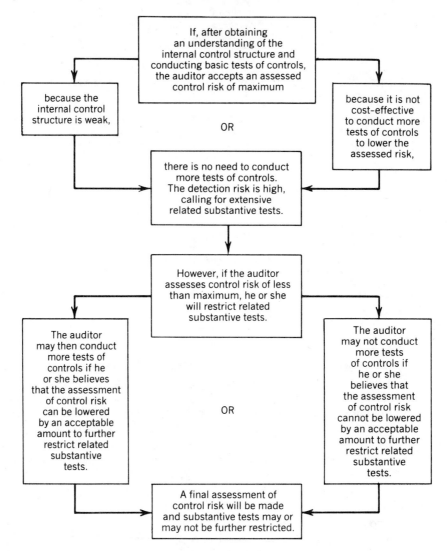

Assessing Control Risk by Assertion

The opinion on the fairness of financial statements is a composite of the opinions on the account balances that constitute the financial statements. In certain situations the auditor may make one assessment of control risk that affects several accounts. In the majority of cases, however, control risk assessments should be made for all financial statement assertions inherent in each account balance being audited.

> *Financial statement assertions* are management representations that are embodied in the account balance, transaction class, and disclosure components of financial statements. (Refer to Chapter 1 for a discussion of representations.)

These assertions include the following:

1. Existence or occurrence

2. Completeness

3. Rights and obligations

4. Valuation or allocation

5. Presentation and disclosure

We have extensive discussions and illustrations of these assertions and their relationships to substantive tests in Chapters 15–18. Our purpose in introducing them at this point is to emphasize that the assessment of control risk could be different for each assertion within an account balance, transaction class, or disclosure component.

In fact the assessed control risk (together with the inherent risk) for *certain* assertions embodied within an account balance could be sufficiently low to *eliminate* the need for substantive tests for these assertions. For example, the auditor could conclude that the control environment is good enough for the auditor to eliminate substantive tests on the accounts receivable disclosure assertion. On the other hand, the auditor might conclude that certain control procedures relating to extension of credit are weak, necessitating a relatively high control risk assessment on the valuation assertion for accounts receivable. This assessment, in turn, will require a lower detection risk for the accounts receivable valuation assertion and will prevent the auditor from restricting tests of the allowance for doubtful accounts.

Is it possible for the assessment of control risk on each assertion component of an account balance to be so low that it negates the necessity to perform any substantive tests on that account balance? As a practical matter this will not happen. Some substantive tests *should* be performed on every significant account balance or class of transactions, although in some cases the amount of substantive testing might be very small. Certain prepaid expenses or operating expenses are possible examples where only analytical procedures would be applied.

Summary

In this chapter we have covered the assessment of control risk that the auditor will make after obtaining an understanding of the internal control structure and conducting basic tests of controls. The audit procedures used to obtain this understanding and conduct these tests will ordinarily allow the auditor to lower his or her assessment of control risk below the maximum that would be necessary if these procedures were not conducted. This lowered assessment of control risk will, in turn, allow the auditor to raise detection risk and restrict the related substantive tests.

The auditor may decide to conduct more extensive and detailed tests of controls for the purpose of continuing to lower the assessment of control risk and further restrict related substantive tests. These detailed tests of controls are discussed and illustrated in Chapter 8, together with additional coverage of errors and irregularities. Chapter 8 will also cover reports on the internal control structure.

Chapter 7
Glossary of Terms

(listed in the order of appearance in the chapter, with accompanying page reference where the term is discussed)

Term	*Page in Chapter*
Assessing control risk the process of evaluating the effectiveness of an entity's internal control structure in preventing or detecting and correcting misstatements in the financial statements.	238
Internal control structure the policies and procedures established to provide reasonable assurance that an entity's established objectives will be achieved.	238
Control environment the overall attitude, awareness, and actions of the board of directors, management, owners, or others with similar authority concerning control and the emphasis given to it.	239
Accounting system the methods and records established to (1) identify, assemble, classify, analyze, record, and report an entity's transactions and (2) maintain accountability for the related assets and liabilities.	241

**Chapter 7
References**

American Institute of Certified Public Accountants. *Professional Standards:*

   Consideration of the Internal Control Structure in a Financial Statement Audit;

   AU Section 322—*The Effect of an Internal Audit Function on the Scope of the
   Independent Auditor's Examination.*

Loebbecke, James K., and Zuber, George R. "Evaluating Internal Control," *Journal of
   Accountancy* (February 1980), pp. 49–56.

Mock, T. J., and Willingham, J. J. "An Improved Method of Documenting and Evaluating a System of Internal Accounting Controls," *Auditing: A Journal of Practice & Theory* (Spring 1983), pp. 91–99.

Chapter 7
Review Questions

7-1.   Why is it necessary for the auditor to assess control risk?

7-2.   How does the internal control structure affect the assessment of control risk?

7-3.   Which types of internal control structure policies and procedures are evaluated by the auditor?

7-4.   Describe the three elements of the internal control structure.

7-5.   Describe five important elements of the control environment.

7-6.   Describe the two goals accomplished by the procedures used to obtain an understanding of the internal control structure.

7-7.   Name three steps that the auditor might follow to acquire an understanding of the design of the accounts receivable internal control structure.

7-8.   Name three steps that the auditor might follow to determine whether the policies and procedures of the accounts receivable internal control structure are operating as they are purported to operate.

7-9.   Describe the three-step sequence that an auditor follows to obtain an understanding of the accounting system and control procedures.

7-10.   Describe the types of economic events in each of the following cycles:
a. The treasury cycle.
b. The expenditure cycle.
c. The conversion cycle.
d. The revenue cycle.

7-11.   Name the four internal control structure objectives.

7-12.   What are the two purposes of tests of controls?

7-13.   At what two points can the auditor make an assessment of control risk?

7-14.   Describe the auditor's decision model for the assessment of control risk.

7-15.   Name the five financial statement assertions.

7-16.   Under what conditions could the auditor eliminate substantive tests for some account balance assertions?

Chapter 7
Objective Questions Taken from CPA Examinations

---

*7-17.   Which of the following is not a part of the equation used to determine detection risk?
a. Individual audit risk.
b. Inherent risk.
c. Overreliance risk.
d. Control risk.

*7-18.   Which of the following is an incorrect statement?
a. The higher the control risk, the higher the detection risk.
b. The higher the control risk, the lower the detection risk.
c. The lower the control risk, the higher the detection risk.
d. The lower the detection risk, the more extensive the substantive tests.

*7-19.   Which of the following is not a part of the internal control structure?
a. The control environment.
b. The accounting system.
c. The control procedures.
d. The control risk.

*Not a CPA examination question.

*7-20.   The control environment includes all of the following except:

a. Attitude and awareness concerning control and emphasis given to it.

b. Management philosophy.

c. Accounting system records.

d. Organizational structure.

*7-21.   In determining whether the internal control structure is suitably designed and properly operating, the auditor would usually have to use all of the following procedures except

a. Inquiry

b. Inspection.

c. Observation.

d. Sampling.

*7-22.   What control procedure would the auditor look for in a cash disbursements system to ensure that the voucher is not paid twice?

a. The voucher is approved for payment.

b. The supporting documents for the voucher are canceled when the check for the voucher is signed.

c. The bank statement is sent directly to the internal audit department.

d. The total of unpaid items in the voucher register is compared with the vouchers payable control account.

*7-23.   All of the following procedures should be used in a payroll system except the following:

a. The Timekeeping Department reconciles job time tickets with the employee clock cards.

b. The Payroll Department uses Human Resource Department records and employee clock cards to prepare the payroll record.

c. The Cash Disbursements Department prepares one check for the total amount of the payroll.

d. Individual checks are disbursed to employees by the member of the Payroll Department who prepares and signs the checks.

*7-24.   Which of the following internal control structure objectives is achieved with the internal control structure procedure of making periodic counts of securities?

a. Proper authorization of transactions and activities.

b. Adequate documents and records.

c. Proper authorization for access to assets.

d. Recorded accountability for assets compared with existing assets.

*Not a CPA examination question.

*7-25.   Which of the following internal control structure objectives is achieved with the internal control structure procedure of having criteria for extending credit?
   a. Proper authorization of transactions and activities.
   b. Adequate documents and records.
   c. Proper authorization for access to assets.
   d. Recorded accountability for assets compared with existing assets.

*7-26.   Which of the following is a proper reason for not conducting tests of controls?
   a. The internal control structure is strong.
   b. The procedures require more audit effort than the corresponding benefit obtained from lowering the control risk.
   c. The company does not have any flowcharts of the systems.
   d. The auditor prefers the control risk to be maximum.

7-27.   An independent auditor might consider the procedures performed by the internal auditors because
   a. They are employees whose work must be reviewed during substantive testing.
   b. They are employees whose work might be relied on.
   c. Their work affects the cost-benefit trade-off in evaluating inherent limitations.
   d. Their degree of independence may be inferred by the nature of their work.

7-28.   The primary purpose of the auditor acquiring an understanding of the internal control structure is to provide a basis for
   a. Determining whether procedures and records that are concerned with the safeguarding of assets are reliable.
   b. Constructive suggestions to clients concerning improvements in the internal control structure.
   c. Determining the extent of substantive tests to be applied.
   d. The expression of an opinion.

7-29.   Of the following statements about the internal control structure which one is *not* valid?
   a. No one person should be responsible for the custodial responsibility and the recording responsibility for an asset.
   b. Transactions must be properly authorized before such transactions are processed.
   c. Control procedures should be applied throughout the year.
   d. Control procedures reasonably ensure that collusion among employees cannot occur.

*Not a CPA examination question.

7-30. Which of the following would be *least* likely to suggest to an auditor that the client's management may have overridden the internal control structure?
   a. Differences are always disclosed on a computer exception report.
   b. Management does *not* correct internal control structure weaknesses that it knows about.
   c. There have been two new controllers this year.
   d. There are numerous delays in preparing timely internal financial reports.

7-31. Which of the following sets of duties would ordinarily be considered basically incompatible in terms of good internal control structure procedures?
   a. Preparation of monthly statements to customers and maintenance of the accounts receivable subsidiary ledger.
   b. Posting to the general ledger and approval of additions and terminations relating to the payroll.
   c. Custody of unmailed signed checks and maintenance of expense subsidiary ledgers.
   d. Collection of receipts on account and maintaining accounts receivable records.

7-32. Proper segregation of functional responsibilities calls for separation of the
   a. Authorization, recording, and custodial functions.
   b. Authorization, execution, and payment functions.
   c. Receiving, shipping, and custodial functions.
   d. Authorization, approval, and execution functions.

7-33. In a properly designed internal control structure the same employee should *not* be permitted to
   a. Sign checks and cancel supporting documents.
   b. Receive merchandise and prepare a receiving report.
   c. Prepare disbursement vouchers and sign checks.
   d. Initiate a request to order merchandise and approve merchandise received.

7-34. An auditor evaluates the existing internal control structure primarily to
   a. Ascertain whether employees adhere to managerial policies.
   b. Determine the extent of substantive tests that must be performed.
   c. Determine whether procedures and records concerning the safeguarding of assets are reliable.
   d. Establish a basis for deciding which tests of controls are necessary.

Chapter 7
Discussion/Case Questions

7-35.   During the course of acquiring an understanding of the internal control structure of her client, Consent Co., Ms. Search was pleased to discover that the record-keeping in general and the accountability for assets were good. Also, transactions were approved by the proper individuals and there was an adequate segregation of duties of sensitive responsibilities.

Ms. Search, however, was concerned about some aspects of the company's organizational structure and about the attitude of some of the company's top executives. For example:

1. The company used a system of budgets and standards but seemingly paid little attention to deviations unless they were extremely large.

2. The company had a credit manager who approved all credit sales above a certain amount. As far as Ms. Search could tell, the credit manager had no discernible criteria but simply approved or disapproved credit on an "intuitive" basis. Credit was rarely disapproved.

3. The yearly financial statements were always compiled within a few days after the end of the fiscal year. Many times, accruals were left out and were recorded only at the insistence of the auditor.

4. The internal auditors did little except routine clerical work and reported to the controller.

5. Department heads were assessed very large "bonus penalties" if the departmental physical inventory count was less than 99 percent of the amount on the departmental perpetual inventory records.

Required:
a. Give reasons why Ms. Search might assess the control risk at maximum and perform extensive substantive tests. Be specific as to which accounts (or account assertions) would require the most extensive substantive tests (you need not name the substantive tests).
b. Give reasons why Ms. Search might still assess the control risk below maximum.

7-36.   Review the narrative of (1) purchases, (2) cash disbursements, and (3) payroll on pages 244–247 and do the following for each of the three described systems:

a. Indicate alterations in the system (no receiving reports, for example) that could weaken the system and increase the assessment of control risk. Indicate why this alteration would have this effect.

b. Take all the alterations in each system and indicate whether you think that collectively this weakened system would call for assessing the control risks at maximum. Give reasons for your opinions.

7-37.   In 19X4 XY Company purchased over $10 million of office equipment under its "special" ordering system, with individual orders ranging from $5,000 to $30,000. "Special" orders entail low volume items which have been included in an authorized user's budget. Department heads include in their annual budget requests the types of equipment and their estimated cost. The budget, which limits the types and dollar amounts of office equipment a department head can requisition, is approved at the beginning of the year by the board of directors. Department heads prepare a purchase requisition form for equipment and forward the requisition to the Purchasing Department. XY's "special" ordering system functions as follows:

Purchasing: Upon receiving a purchase requisition, one of five buyers verifies that the person requesting the equipment is a department head. The buyer then selects the appropriate vendor by searching the various vendor catalogs on file. The buyer then phones the vendor, requesting a price quotation, and gives the vendor a verbal order. A prenumbered purchase order is then processed with the original sent to the vendor, a copy to the department head, a copy to receiving, a copy to accounts payable, and a copy filed in the open requisition file. When the buyer is orally informed by the Receiving Department that the item has been received, the buyer transfers the purchase order from the unfilled file to the filled file. Once a month the buyer reviews the unfilled file to follow up and expedite open orders.

Receiving: The Receiving Department receives a copy of the purchase order. When equipment is received, the receiving clerk stamps the purchase order with the date received, and, if applicable, in red pen prints any differences between quantity on the purchase order and quantity received. The receiving clerk forwards the stamped purchase order and equipment to the requisitioning department head and orally notifies the Purchasing Department.

Accounts payable: Upon receipt of a purchase order, the accounts payable clerk files the purchase order in the open purchase order file. When a vendor invoice is received, the invoice is matched with the applicable purchase order, and a payable is set up by debiting the equipment account of the department requesting the items. Unpaid invoices are filed by the due date and, at due date, a check is prepared. The invoice and purchase order are filed by purchase order number in a paid invoice file, and then the check is forwarded to the treasurer for signature.

Treasurer: Checks received daily from the Accounts Payable Department are sorted into two groups: those over $10,000 and those $10,000 and less. Checks for $10,000 and less are machine-signed. The cashier maintains the key and signature plate to the check-signing machine, and maintains a record of usage of the check-signing machine. All checks over $10,000 are signed by the treasurer or the controller.

Required
Describe the internal control structure weaknesses relating to the purchases and payments of "special" orders of XY Company for each of the following functions:
a. Purchasing
b. Receiving
c. Accounts payable
d. Treasurer
(*AICPA adapted*)

7-38. Assume that an independent auditor is examining the financial statements of a small not-for-profit institution. He finds that the accounting system is handled by one individual who writes checks, records and deposits the cash receipts, and records and posts all transaction entries. The independent auditor suggests that two additional people are needed to provide minimum control for the accounting system.
a. The directors of the institution agreed to hire two additional people. Suggest how the bookkeeping duties can be divided between the three individuals so as to maximize the probability that assets will be safeguarded and the accounting records will be reliable.
b. The directors reject the suggestion of hiring another individual. What effect would this have on substantive tests?

7-39. The following is a list of "tasks" that the independent auditor might ask the internal auditor to perform during the course of an audit. Indicate whether you think each task is a proper or improper function for the internal auditor. Give reasons for your answer.
a. Writing a narrative description of the system.
b. Designing a sample plan for examining payroll checks (the examination to be made by the independent auditor).
c. Testing individual perpetual inventory items based on sample selection made by the independent auditor (this same testing will not be performed by the independent auditor).

d. Constructing a systems flowchart that will be used later by the independent auditor in his or her assessment of control risk.

e. Providing answers to the independent auditor's internal control structure questionnaire.

7-40.   Listed hereafter are eight responsibilities that might be performed by individuals in an accounting system. Assume that five people are employed for the purpose of handling these eight responsibilities. No more than two jobs will be assigned to one person.

1. Responsible for the general ledger.

2. Responsible for the accounts receivable subsidiary ledger.

3. Responsible for deposit of cash receipts in the bank.

4. Responsible for the purchases journal.

5. Responsible for writing checks to creditors.

6. Responsible for the cash disbursements journal.

7. Responsible for the cash receipts journal.

8. Responsible for the payroll register.

Required:
a. Assuming that no employee will perform more than two jobs, list combinations of jobs for each of the five employees, considering the combinations that will safeguard assets and ensure reliability of the records. Support your listings with reasons.
b. List the *worst* combination of jobs that you can think of and support your reasoning.

7-41.   In a strong internal control structure, the following functions are separated: (1) authorizing a transaction, (2) recording a transaction, (3) maintaining custody of assets that result from a transaction, and (4) comparing assets with the related amounts recorded in the accounting records. In each of the following situations, indicate which functions are combined.
a. The payroll supervisor disburses the payroll checks.

b. The general ledger clerk maintains the accounts receivable subsidiary ledger.

c. The cashier maintains the cash receipts journal.

d. The accounts payable supervisor writes and mails the checks.

e. The storeroom clerks count the physical inventory.

f. The cashier reconciles the bank statements.

7-42. You have been engaged by the management of Alden, Inc. to review its internal control structure procedures over the purchase, receipt, storage, and issue of raw materials. You have prepared the following comments to describe Alden's procedures.

Raw materials, which consist mainly of high-cost electronic components, are kept in a locked storeroom. Storeroom personnel include a supervisor and four clerks. All are well trained, competent, and adequately bonded. Raw materials are removed from the storeroom only on written or oral authorization of one of the production supervisors.

There are no perpetual inventory records; hence, the storeroom clerks do not keep records of goods received or issued. To compensate for the lack of perpetual records, a physical inventory count is taken monthly by the storeroom clerks, who are well supervised. Appropriate procedures are followed in making the inventory count.

After the physical count, the storeroom supervisor matches quantities counted against a predetermined reorder level. If the count for a given part is below the reorder level, the supervisor enters the part number on a materials-requisition list and sends this list to the accounts payable clerk. The accounts payable clerk prepares a purchase order for a predetermined reorder quantity for each part and mails the purchase order to the vendor from whom the part was last purchased.

When ordered materials arrive at Alden, they are received by the storeroom clerks. The clerks count the merchandise and reconcile counts to the shipper's bill of lading. All vendors' bills of lading are initialed, dated, and filed in the storeroom to serve as receiving reports.

Required:

Describe the weaknesses in the internal control structure and recommend improvements to Alden's procedures for the purchase, receipt, storage, and issue of raw materials. Organize your answer sheet as follows:

Weaknesses	Recommended Improvements

(AICPA adapted)

7-43.   Trapan Retailing Inc. has decided to diversify operations by selling through vending machines. Trapan's plans call for the purchase of 312 vending machines, which will be situated at 78 different locations within one city and the rental of a warehouse to store merchandise. Trapan intends to sell only canned beverages at a standard price.

Management has hired an inventory control clerk to oversee the warehousing functions and two truck drivers, who will periodically fill the machines with merchandise and deposit the cash collected at a designated bank. The drivers will be required to report to the warehouse daily.

Required:
What internal control structure procedures should the auditor expect to find in order to ensure the integrity of the cash receipts and warehousing functions?
(*AICPA adapted*)

7-44.   The Art Appreciation Society operates a museum for the benefit and enjoyment of the community. During hours when the museum is open to the public, two clerks who are positioned at the entrance collect a $5 admission fee from each nonmember patron. Members of the Art Appreciation Society are permitted to enter free of charge on presentation of their membership cards.

At the end of each day one of the clerks delivers the proceeds to the treasurer. The treasurer counts the cash in the presence of the clerk and places it in a safe. Each Friday afternoon the treasurer and one of the clerks deliver all cash held in the safe to the bank and receive an authenticated deposit slip, which provides the basis for the weekly entry in the cash receipts journal.

The board of directors of the Art Appreciation Society has identified a need to improve its internal control structure relating to cash admission fees. The board has determined that the cost of installing turnstiles, sales booths, or otherwise altering the physical layout of the museum will greatly exceed any benefits that may be derived. However, the board has agreed that the sale of admission tickets must be an integral part of its improvement efforts.

Smith, CPA, has been asked by the board of directors of the Art Appreciation Society to review the internal control structure relating to cash admission fees and provide suggestions for improvement.

Required:
Indicate weaknesses in the existing internal control structure relating to cash admission fees that Smith should identify, and recommend one improvement for each of the weaknesses identified.

Organize the answer as indicated in the following example:

Weakness	Recommendation
1. There is no basis for establishing the documentation of the number of paying patrons.	1. Prenumbered admission tickets should be issued on payment of the admission fee.

(*AICPA adapted*)

7-45. Dunbar Camera Manufacturing, Inc., is a manufacturer of high-priced precision motion picture cameras in which the specifications of component parts are vital to the manufacturing process. Dunbar buys valuable camera lenses and large quantities of sheetmetal and screws. Screws and lenses are ordered by Dunbar and are billed by the vendors on a unit basis. Sheetmetal is ordered and billed by the vendors on the basis of weight. The receiving clerk is responsible for documenting the quality and quantity of merchandise received.

A preliminary review of the internal control structure indicates that the following procedures are being followed:

Receiving Report
Properly approved purchase orders, which are prenumbered, are filed numerically. The copy sent to the receiving clerk is an exact duplicate of the copy sent to the vendor. Receipts of merchandise are recorded on the duplicate copy by the receiving clerk.

Sheetmetal
The company receives sheetmetal by railroad. The railroad independently weighs the sheetmetal and reports the weight and date of receipt on a bill of lading (waybill), which accompanies all deliveries. The receiving clerk only checks the weight on the waybill against the purchase order.

Screws
The receiving clerk opens cartons containing screws, then inspects and weighs the contents. The weight is converted to number of units by means of conversion charts. The receiving clerk then checks the computed quantity against the purchase order.

Camera lenses
Each camera lens is delivered in a separate corrugated carton. Cartons are counted as they are received by the receiving clerk and the number of cartons is checked against purchase orders.

Required:
a. Explain why the internal control structure procedures as they apply individually to receiving reports and the receipt of sheetmetal, screws, and camera lenses are adequate or inadequate. *Do not discuss recommendations for improvements.*
b. What financial statement misstatements may arise because of the inadequacies in Dunbar's internal control structure procedures and how may they occur?
(*AICPA adapted*)

7-46.   Properly designed and utilized forms facilitate adherence to prescribed internal control structure policies and procedures. One such form might be a multicopy purchase order, with one copy intended to be mailed to the vendor. The remaining copies would ordinarily be distributed to the Stores, Purchasing, Receiving, and Accounting Departments.

The purchase order shown on page 273 is currently being used by National Industrial Corporation:

Required:

a. In addition to the name of the company, what other necessary information would an auditor recommend be included in the illustrative purchase order?

b. What primary internal control structure functions are served by the purchase order copies that are distributed to the Stores, Purchasing, Receiving, and Accounting Departments?

(*AICPA adapted*)

PURCHASE ORDER
SEND INVOICE ONLY TO:

297 HARDINGTEN DR., BX., NY 10461

TO _____   SHIP TO _____

_____   _____

_____   _____

DATE TO BE SHIPPED	SHIP VIA	DISC. TERMS	FREIGHT TERMS	ADV. ALLOWANCE	SPECIAL ALLOWANCE
QUANTITY		DESCRIPTION			

PURCHASE CONDITIONS

1. Supplier will be responsible for extra freight cost on partial shipment, unless prior permission is obtained.

2. Please acknowledge this order.

3. Please notify us immediately if you are unable to complete order.

4. All items must be individually packed.

Assessing Control Risk—Detailed Tests of Controls

Learning Objectives   *After reading and studying the material in this chapter, the student should*

Understand the audit procedures used to assess control risk by conducting detailed tests of controls.

Know the responsibilities the auditor has to detect errors and irregularities.

Know how to communicate internal control structure-related matters noted in an audit.

Know the general content of a report on the internal control structure.

In Chapter 7 we described the three elements of an internal control structure and covered the steps that the auditor takes in (1) acquiring an understanding of the internal control structure, (2) conducting tests of controls, and (3) assessing control risk. We pointed out that in practical audit situations these three steps are often carried out concurrently.

The tests of controls discussed and illustrated in Chapter 7 are not detailed but are designed to reduce the assessment of control risk from maximum to a lower level and to restrict related substantive tests. At that point the auditor decides whether it would be effective and efficient to conduct detailed tests of controls designed to bring the assessment of control risk to an even lower level and further restrict (or possibly eliminate for some assertions) related substantive tests.

This chapter covers some examples of these detailed tests of controls. For each of three systems of an internal control structure, we will illustrate how some tests of controls could be conducted using the following:

1. Flowcharts and internal control questionnaires to aid in determining whether the internal control policies and procedures are properly designed.

2. Examples of tests of control procedures designed to determine whether the internal control policies and procedures are operating effectively and operating as they are purported to operate.

We will also illustrate how the auditor could use all the evidence acquired to assess control risk by (1) considering the misstatements that could occur in the financial statement assertions, (2) identifying internal control structure policies and procedures relevant to the assertions, and (3) evaluating the effectiveness of these policies and procedures in preventing or detecting material misstatements in these assertions.

We will also include some discussions of the auditor's responsibility to detect errors and irregularities and how the auditor can communicate to the proper parties important internal control structure-related matters noted during the audit.

Documentation for Detailed Tests of Controls and Assessment of Control Risk

Flowcharts

Flowcharts are graphic descriptions of the information flow in a system or part of a system. The reader obtains a visual overview that may not be acquired from reading a narrative description of that same system. Thus, the auditor can often see strengths and weaknesses of system design in a quicker and an easier manner.

Flowcharts can be obtained from client personnel, if available, or the auditor can create them from observations, questions, and other available information. The advantages of obtaining client-prepared flowcharts are (1) time-saving and (2) possibly a more accurate overview of the system. The advantage of auditor-prepared flowcharts is the knowledge of the system obtained by the preparer.

Figure 8.1 shows the standard flowchart symbols normally used in flowcharts and the ones we will use in our illustrations.

Now look at Figure 8.2 for an illustration of a flowchart of a system of cash receipts on account. Notice that the flowchart is sectioned according to the areas where the events and information flows occur. These sections are as follows:

Basic Symbols

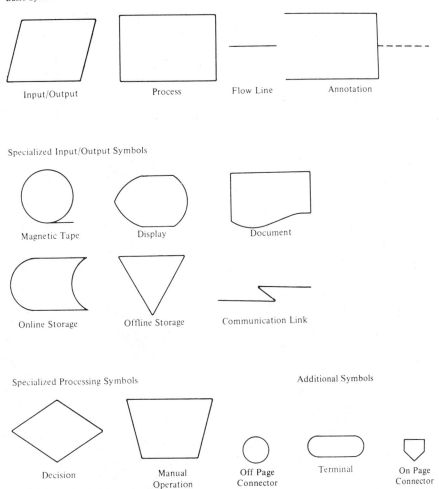

Figure 8.1   Standard Flowchart Symbols

1. The mail room where the checks and remittance advices are received from the customers.

a. The checks are endorsed and a two-part receipts listing is prepared. The checks are sent to the cashier.

b. Copies of both the receipts listing and the remittance advices are sent to the accounts receivable department.

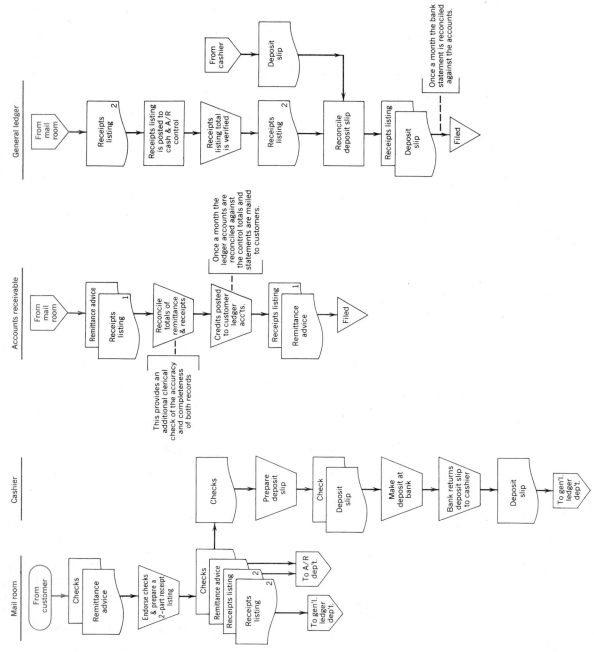

Figure 8.2 Flowchart for System of Cash Receipts on Account

    c. A copy of the receipts listing is sent to the General Ledger Department.

2. The Cashier Department where the checks are received from the mail room.

    a. A deposit slip is prepared and the checks are deposited at the bank.

    b. The bank returns the deposit slip to the cashier where it is forwarded to the General Ledger Department.

3. The Accounts Receivable Department where remittance advices and receipts listing are received from the mail room.

    a. The copy of the receipts listing and the remittance advices are reconciled and the information is posted to the individual customer ledger accounts.

    b. The remittance advices and receipts listing are filed.

    c. Once a month, the total of the customer ledger accounts is reconciled with the accounts receivable control total maintained in the General Ledger Department.

4. The General Ledger Department where the receipts listing is received from the mail room.

    a. Total receipts are verified and posted to the cash account and accounts receivable control account.

    b. The total of the receipts listing is reconciled with the total of the deposit slip.

    c. The receipts listing and the deposit slip are filed.

    d. Once a month, the bank statement is reconciled with the cash balance in the general ledger.

Internal Control Structure Questionnaires

In addition to examining a graphical design of the various systems of the internal control structure, the auditor might wish to ask and obtain answers to questions about these systems. Some of the answers might come from company employees and others from observations made while obtaining an understanding

Figure 8.3
An Internal Control Structure Questionnaire for Cash Receipts on Account

Question	Answer Yes	No	Comments
1. Do different people handle the cash and have access to the records of cash receipts?		✓	The mail room has access to cash receipts and prepares receipts listing, but customer statements are mailed in accounts receivable.
2. Is immediate control established over mail receipts?	✓		
3. Are deposits made intact daily?	✓		
4. Do different individuals handle the detail customer ledger accounts and control accounts?	✓		
5. Is the clerical accuracy of the cash receipts and remittance advices verified?	✓		
6. Is the bank-validated deposit slip returned to someone other than the cashier?		✓	The bank reconciliation is prepared in the General Ledger Department.
7. Is the total of the deposit slip reconciled with the remittance advice and receipt listing total before the deposit is made?		✓	No compensating strength found.

of the internal control structure. Other answers could be provided by examination of policy manuals and flowcharts.

Such questions and answers could be documented in *internal control structure questionnaires,* an example of which is in Figure 8.3. This questionnaire basically covers the system of cash receipts on account illustrated in the flowchart in Figure 8.2. Notice that check marks are placed in the Yes or No columns and, where applicable, additional information is added especially where there is a negative answer to the question.

Traditionally, internal control structure questionnaires have been an important element in the tests of controls of an internal control structure. Although other methods such as flowcharts have gained wide acceptance in recent years, the questionnaire approach is still popular among many CPA firms. The answers should be determined only after proper investigation of flowcharts, narratives, results of conversations, and so on.

Tests Directed Toward Operating Effectiveness of Controls

Not only is it necessary for the auditor to conduct tests of controls directed toward the design of internal control structure policies and procedures (flowcharts and internal control structure questionnaires), but he or she must also test the operating effectiveness of these policies and procedures. Put another way, the auditor must determine whether these policies and procedures are operating as they are designed to operate. Some means of conducting tests of controls are discussed in the following sections.

Inquiry of Appropriate Company Personnel   The auditor could interview the individuals who handle cash deposits, records of cash deposits, the accounts receivable subsidiary ledger, and the general ledger. From the interview, the auditor may determine whether the design of the internal control structure policies and procedures are operating effectively and as they are purported to operate according to the flowchart and internal control structure questionnaire (i.e., do different individuals actually handle the detail customer ledger accounts and the control accounts?).

Inspection of Documents   The auditor could also examine records that are part of the design of the internal control structure policies and procedures. For cash receipts on account, the auditor could examine copies of remittance advices, receipts listings, deposit slips, and entries to the accounts receivable subsidiary ledger and the general ledger. By doing so, the auditor would ascertain that the records *do exist*, have the proper format, and that the data are consistently recorded between records.

The auditor could also conduct a "*walkthrough*" by tracing one or more transactions from the receipt of cash to its deposit and to its recording in the subsidiary and general ledgers. The auditor is not conducting a scientific sample (as illustrated in Chapter 9) but is simply ascertaining whether the cash receipts transactions appear to be properly processed.

Observation of the Application of the Policy or Procedure   Sometimes the auditor might obtain evidence of operating effectiveness by watching the processing of the cash receipts transactions. To be most effective, this observation should probably be on a surprise basis.

Reperformance of the Application of the Policy or Procedure   One of the traditional methods that the auditor has used to test controls is to examine client policies and procedures as if he or she were applying the policies or performing the procedures. Instead of performing the processes, however, the auditor ascertains that client personnel performed them properly to a degree satisfactory to him or her.

For example, in checking the design of the cash disbursements system, the auditor observes that the system calls for all purchase invoices to be approved with a signature or initials by the controller before checks are prepared and issued to the vendor. The auditor could ascertain that this procedure is being applied by examining a sample of purchase invoices to see whether they contain the proper signature or initials.

Another test of controls that involves reperformance is the tracing of dollar amounts from one record to another (previously referred to as a test of transactions). These types of tests accomplish a dual purpose: (1) the auditor ascertains whether transaction processing procedures are carried out in accordance with the design of the system, and (2) the auditor checks the validity of dollar amounts being processed.

In the case of the cash receipts on account system we are using as an illustration, the auditor might decide to determine whether three controls are operating in this system. For each of these controls, a sample of information would be traced from one cash receipts record to another. Figure 8.4 is an example of three such tests (we will cover tests of controls using samples in more detail in Chapter 9).

Figure 8.4
Tests of Controls for Cash Receipts on Account

Control	Audit Test
Deposit of cash receipts on account	Trace information from the record of cash receipts to the record of deposits
Recording of cash receipts on account	Trace information from the record of deposits to the record of cash receipts
Postings of cash receipts on account	Trace postings from the cash receipts record to the customer ledger accounts

Considering Misstatements of Financial Statement Assertions

While conducting tests of controls, the auditor should include in his or her assessment of control risk a consideration of the following.

1. Consider the misstatements that could occur in the financial statement assertions.

2. Identify internal control structure policies and procedures relevant to these assertions.

3. Evaluate the effectiveness of such policies and procedures in preventing or detecting material misstatements in these assertions.

To relate these requirements to the cash receipts on account system we are illustrating, we have included in Figure 8.5 three possible misstatements (errors or irregularities) that could occur, one each in the three controls we have identified in the system. For each possible misstatement, we have also listed an internal control structure policy or procedure that is relevant to that misstatement.

Bear in mind that this is only a partial illustration of this type of documentation. Many possible misstatements would probably be listed for each system of the internal control structure.

Figure 8.5
Form for Assessing Control Risk by Considering Misstatements—Cash Receipts on Account

Misstatements that Could Occur in Completeness Assertion	Internal Control Structure Policies and Procedures
1. The cashier could withhold money from the daily deposit.	The deposit slip total is reconciled with the remittance advices and receipts listing total after the deposit is made.
2. The mail clerk could omit receipts from the receipts listing or fail to prepare a receipts listing.	Customers are sent monthly statements of their accounts by another party.
3. Posting could be omitted in the accounts receivable subsidiary ledger.	Different copies of receipts listings go to accounts receivable and general ledger. The accounts receivable subsidiary ledger and control account are reconciled monthly.

Tests of Controls of Purchases and Payroll Systems

The remainder of this section of the chapter is devoted to illustrations of the following for both purchases and payroll systems (see Figures 8.6 to 8.13):

1. A flowchart.

2. An internal control structure questionnaire.

3. Some detail tests of controls of the operating effectiveness and the purpose of these tests.

4. A form for assessing control risk by considering misstatements.

Remember that the purpose of each of these documents is the same for purchases and payroll as it is for the cash receipts system previously illustrated. This additional documentation is furnished to enhance the understanding of tests of controls.

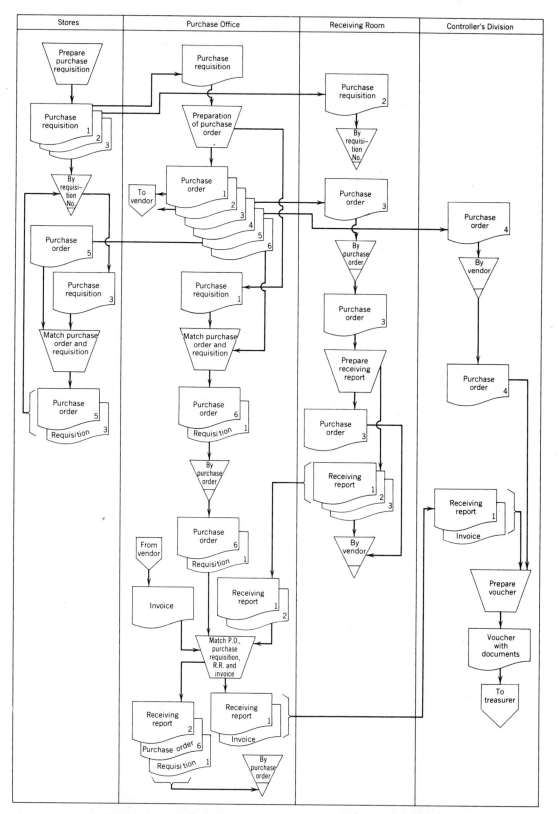

Figure 8.6 Flowchart for Purchases System

Figure 8.7
An Internal Control Structure Questionnaire for Purchases Controls

Question	Answer	Comments
1. Is there separation between authorizing, recording, and custody of merchandise purchases?	Yes	The Stores Department requests the merchandise, the Purchasing Department orders it, the Receiving Department receives it, and the Accounts Payable Department records the transactions.
2. Are steps taken to ensure the best prices for merchandise?	Yes	Competitive bids are required.
3. Is immediate control established over merchandise received from vendors?	Yes	A receiving report is prepared when merchandise is received.
4. Are receiving reports prepared after an independent count?	Yes	However, a copy of the purchase order showing quantities is held in the Receiving Department.
5. Are procedures used to ensure that merchandise ordered is received?	Yes	The receiving report is compared with the purchase order.
6. Are procedures used to ensure that merchandise invoiced by the vendor has been received?	Yes	The receiving report is compared with the invoice.

Figure 8.8
Tests of Controls for Purchases

Test	Purpose of the Test
1. Compare the Stores Department's purchase requisitions with receiving reports.	1. To determine that the items requested by the Stores Department were received from the vendor.
2. Compare invoice price with bids submitted by vendors.	2. To determine that competitive bidding procedures were followed.
3. Ascertain that the receiving reports are initialed or signed properly.	3. To determine that someone was taking responsibility for documenting independent counts.
4. Compare the vendor's invoice with a copy of the receiving report.	4. To ascertain that merchandise billed by the vendor was received by the company.
5. Compare the requisition, purchase order, invoice, and receiving report held in the Accounts Payable Department.	5. To ascertain that the entire transaction was accounted for properly.

Figure 8.9
Form for Assessing Control Risk by Considering Misstatements—Purchases

Misstatements That Could Occur	Internal Control Structure Policies and Procedures
1. The merchandise requested by the Stores Department could be different from that ordered and/or received.	1. The Purchasing Department compares receipt documents against the requisition.
2. Merchandise could be taken by individuals in the Receiving Department and no receiving report prepared.	2. The Accounts Payable Department matches the invoice with one of the Stores Department's copies of the receiving report. The Stores Department matches the receiving report with the merchandise.
3. The vendor could be overpaid for the merchandise.	3. The Receiving Department independently counts the merchandise but has no access to the invoice.

Detection of Errors and Irregularities

Although the assessment of control risk and its accompanying tests of controls are designed to consider the possibility of errors and irregularities, the auditor has special responsibilities that need to be explored. In recent years congressional committees, regulatory authorities, and the courts have imposed on the accounting profession more responsibility for the detection of errors and irregularities. The accounting profession has responded by using more definitive guidelines.

Definition of Errors and Irregularities

Errors are unintentional misstatements or omissions of amounts and disclosures in financial statements and consist of the following:

1. Mistakes in gathering or processing accounting data from which financial statements are prepared.

2. Incorrect accounting estimates arising from oversight or misinterpretation of facts.

3. Mistakes in the application of accounting principles.

On the other hand, *irregularities* are intentional misstatements or omissions of amounts or disclosures in financial statements and consist of the following:

1. Manipulation, falsification, or alteration of accounting records or supporting documents from which financial statements are prepared.

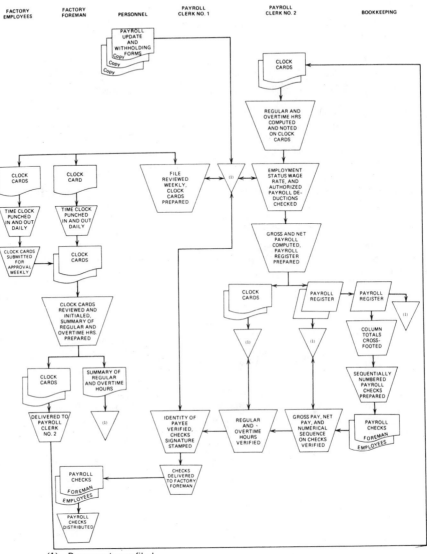

(1)   Documents are filed

Figure 8.10   Flowchart for Payroll System

2. Misrepresentation or intentional omission of events, transactions, or other significant information.

3. Intentional misapplication of accounting principles.

The difference between the two terms, then, relates to *intent*.

Figure 8.11

An Internal Control Structure Questionnaire for Payroll Controls

Question	Answer	Comments
1. Are duties of recording the payroll and disbursing the payroll checks separate?	Yes	The payroll is recorded in the Payroll Department. The checks are disbursed by the foreman.
2. Is an imprest payroll account used?	No	
3. Are steps taken to guard against paying checks to improper or fictitious employees?	Yes	Employment status is verified by another payroll clerk.
4. Are steps taken to ensure that the clock cards are accurate?	Yes	The clock cards are reviewed and initialed by the factory foreman.
5. Are employment records kept in a department separate from payroll preparation?	Yes	Employment and rate authorization records are kept in the Personnel Department.

Figure 8.12

Tests of Controls for Payroll

Test	Purpose of the Test
1. Inspect the job time tickets for proper approval by factory foreman.	1. To determine that proper supervisory personnel are aware of the time spent on jobs and that such time is approved by them.
2. Compare employee clock cards with the job time tickets.	2. To check the accuracy of the time records used to prepare the payroll. Also, to check compliance with the client's prescribed procedure.
3. Check the clerical accuracy of the payroll.	3. To ascertain the accuracy of the supporting documents for payroll checks.
4. For selected employees listed in the payroll register, examine the payee, amount, signature, and endorsement on the payroll check.	4. To determine that the payroll checks agree with the payroll register.
5. Trace pay rates and deductions to the authorizations and deduction slips kept in the Personnel Department.	5. To determine that proper rates and deductions are used in preparing the payroll.
6. Conduct a surprise payroll payoff by distributing payroll checks to employees who are identified properly.	6. To test for the possible existence of fictitious employees and to test the compliance with prescribed procedures for handling unclaimed checks.

Figure 8.13

Form for Assessing Control Risk by Considering Misstatements—Payroll

Misstatements That Could Occur	*Internal Control Structure Policies and Procedures*
1. The employee job time tickets could be inaccurate, resulting in an inaccurate payroll.	1. The employee clock cards are checked against the job time tickets.
2. Checks could be issued to fictitious employees (sometimes called payroll padding).	2. The payroll voucher is authorized in the Accounts Payable Department. The checks are prepared in the Payroll Department. The Internal Audit Department occasionally disburses checks.
3. Employees could be overpaid by the use of improper rates and deductions.	3. Rates, deductions, and other employment information are kept in the Personnel Department.
4. The payroll expense account(s) in the general ledger could be inaccurate.	4. A payroll clearing account is kept in the general ledger. Charges come from the labor distribution journal and credits from the payroll voucher.

The Auditor's Responsibility to Detect Errors and Irregularities

In previous years, the accounting profession was reluctant to take responsibility for the detection of errors or irregularities, preferring, instead, to relegate this responsibility entirely to management. Today, the profession's pronouncements about their own responsibilities are more definitive.

These four statements sum up the auditor's responsibilities.

1. The auditor should *assess* the risk that errors and irregularities may cause the financial statements to contain a *material misstatement*.

2. Based on that assessment, the auditor should *design* the audit to provide reasonable assurance of detecting errors and irregularities that are material to the financial statements.

3. The auditor should *exercise due care* in planning, performing, and evaluating the results of audit procedures, and maintain the proper degree of *professional skepticism* to achieve reasonable assurance that material errors or irregularities will be detected.

4. Since the auditor's opinion on the financial statements is based on the concept of *reasonable assurance*, the auditor is not an insurer and his or her report does not constitute a guarantee. Therefore, the subsequent discovery that a material misstatement exists in the financial statements *does not*, in and of itself, evidence inadequate planning, performance, or judgment on the part of the auditor.

Detection of Errors and Irregularities and the Internal Control Structure

How do these aforementioned responsibilities relate to the auditor's study of the internal control structure? During the course of this study, the auditor may identify an internal control structure policy or procedure that could permit an error or irregularity to occur repeatedly and the repeated occurrence could accumulate to a material amount. In such cases, the audit should be *planned to detect* that potential error or irregularity.

For example, the auditor might identify poor controls in the Credit Department. Traditionally, this assessment means that the scope of audit procedures that relates to the valuation assertion for accounts receivable must be larger than it would be with good controls. But if the auditor also identifies this absence of control as likely to permit a material error in the valuation of accounts receivable, he or she must design all the audit procedures necessary to give himself or herself reasonable assurance that any material error in this area is detected and the financial statements are corrected. It may be necessary to examine more credit files than is normally necessary to lower detection risk for the accounts receivable valuation assertion.

Communicating Internal Control Structure-Related Matters Noted in the Audit

As we know from our previous study of this chapter and Chapter 7, the major purpose of the auditor's study of the internal control structure is to assess the control risk for the purpose of determining the scope of related substantive tests. During the course of this study, however, the auditor will often (if not usually) find deficiencies in the internal control structure policies and procedures that are of interest to the company's audit committee. Such deficiencies are referred to as *reportable conditions*, which are defined as

> matters coming to the auditor's attention that in his judgment should be communicated to the audit committee because they represent significant deficiencies in the design or operation of the internal control structure that could adversely affect the organization's ability to record, process, summarize, and report financial data consistent with the assertions of management in the financial statements.

Examples of Reportable Conditions

Here are a few examples of reportable conditions:

1. Inappropriate segregation of duties (the same person deposits cash and records cash receipts, or the same person counts inventory and maintains perpetual inventory records).

2. Absence of approvals of transactions (no one approves credit extensions to customers, or no one approves invoices for cash disbursement).

3. No proper procedures for assessing and applying accounting principles (no policy for differentiating between capital and maintenance expenditures).

4. Evidence of intentional override of the internal control structure (the president insists that a check be prepared without the necessary documentation and approvals).

5. Failure to perform reconciliations (several months pass between reconciliation of the accounts receivable subsidiary ledger and the control account, and differences are ignored).

6. Falsification of accounting records (expenses are deliberately capitalized).

Communicating the Reportable Conditions

Generally accepted auditing standards require the auditor to communicate reportable conditions to the audit committee or another appropriate body of the client's organization. It is often preferable to communicate orally certain reportable conditions as soon as they are found. At the end of the audit a written report may be issued. The following is an illustration of the sections of such a report.

In planning and performing our audit of the financial statements of the ABC Corporation for the year ended December 31, 19X8, we considered its internal control structure. Our consideration was to determine our auditing procedures for the purpose of expressing our opinion on the financial statements and not to provide assurances on the internal control structure. However, in that connection, we noted certain matters involving the internal control structure and its operation that we consider to be reportable conditions under standards established by the American Institute of Certified Public Accountants. Reportable conditions involve matters coming to our attention relating to significant deficiencies in the design or operation of the internal control structure that, in our judgment, could adversely affect the organization's ability to record, process, summarize, and report financial data consistent with the assertions of management in the financial statements. These may involve aspects of (1) the control environment, (2) the accounting system, or (3) specific control procedures.

(Include paragraphs to describe the reportable conditions noted.)

This report is intended solely for the information and use of the audit committee, management, and others in the organization.

Engagements to Report on the Internal Control Structure

Separate engagements to report on a client's internal control structure (as opposed to reports made in connection with an audit) are relatively rare. However, the AICPA has provided guidelines for such reporting in AU Section 642. Generally, the accountant's report would (1) describe the scope of the engagement, (2) describe management's responsibility to establish and maintain the internal control structure, (3) describe the broad objectives and inherent limitations of the internal control structure, and (4) express an opinion on the internal control structure.

A report on the internal control structure must disclose any material weaknesses found during the engagement. Disclosure of immaterial weaknesses is optional. As a practical measure, however, the authors think that accountants may be well-advised to disclose *all* weaknesses and make a judgmental distinction in their report between those they do and those they do not consider material.

Restrictions on the scope of the accountant's engagement may require a qualified opinion or a disclaimer of opinion. When such restrictions are imposed by the client, a disclaimer is generally suggested.

Chapter 8
Glossary of Terms

(listed in the order of appearance in the chapter, with accompanying page reference where the term is discussed)

Term	*Page in Chapter*
Flowcharts a graphic description of the overall information flow in a system or part of a system	276
Internal control structure questionnaire a document that contains an auditor's questions about the internal control structure. Answers are obtained from a variety of sources such as inquiry, observation, and inspection of records, flowcharts and other documentation.	279
Walkthrough tracing one or more of the same type of transactions through a system to enhance an understanding of the internal control structure procedures.	281

Term	*Page in Chapter*

Errors   unintentional misstatements or omissions of amounts or disclosures in financial statements.   286

Irregularities   intentional misstatements or omissions of amounts or disclosures in financial statements.   286

Reportable conditions   matters coming to the auditor's attention relating to deficiencies in the design or operation of the internal control structure that, in the auditor's judgment, could significantly impair the organization's ability to record, process, summarize, and report financial data consistent with the assertions of management in financial statements.   290

**Chapter 8
References**

American Institute of Certified Public Accountants. *Professional Standards* AU Section 642 (*SAS No. 30*)—Reporting on Internal Accounting Control.

Libby, Robert, Artman, James T., and Willingham, John J. "Process Susceptibility, Control Risk, and Audit Planning," *The Accounting Review* (April 1985), pp. 212–228.

Loebbecke, James K., and Zuber, George R. "Evaluating Internal Control," *Journal of Accountancy* (February 1980), pp. 49–56.

Meservy, Rayman D., Bailey, Andrew D. Jr., and Johnson, Paul E. "Internal Control Evaluation: A Computational Model of the Review Process," *Auditing: A Journal of Practice and Theory* (Fall 1986), pp. 44–74.

Romney, Marshall B., Albrecht, W. Steve, and Cherrington, David J. "Auditors and the Detection of Fraud," *Journal of Accountancy* (May 1980), pp. 63–69.

Srinidhi, B. N., and Vasarhelyi, M. A. "Auditor Judgment Concerning Establishment of Substantive Tests Based on Internal Control Reliability," *Auditing: A Journal of Practice and Theory* (Spring 1986), pp. 64–76.

Willingham, John J., and Wright, William F. "Financial Statement Errors and Internal Control Judgments," *Auditing: A Journal of Practice and Theory* (Fall 1985), pp. 57–70.

**Chapter 8
Review Questions**

8-1.   Why are flowcharts used by the auditor?

8-2.   What are the advantages of the auditor obtaining client-prepared flowcharts?

8-3.   What are the sources of information used by the auditor to complete internal control structure questionnaires?

8-4.   Describe four ways that the auditor tests the operating effectiveness of internal control structure policies and procedures.

8-5.   What dual purpose is accomplished when the auditor traces dollar amounts from one record to another (sometimes called a test of transactions)?

8-6.   What is the three-step process that the auditor uses when he or she is considering misstatements during the assessment of control risk?

8-7.   What is the difference between errors and irregularities?

8-8.   What are the auditor's responsibilities to detect errors and irregularities?

8-9.   How does the auditor's responsibility to detect errors and irregularities relate to the auditor's assessment of the internal control structure?

8-10.   What is the term given to deficiencies in the internal control structure policies and procedures found by auditors during the course of the audit?

8-11.   Give six examples of the term referred to in Question 8-10.

8-12.   Describe the general content of the report on an entity's internal control structure.

8-13.   What types of weaknesses must be disclosed in a report on the internal control structure?

Chapter 8
Objective Questions Taken from CPA Examinations

*8-14.   Which of the following would not be a method used to conduct tests of controls?
a. Inquiry.
b. Walkthrough.
c. Confirmation.
d. Observation.

*8-15.   Which of the following is not a true statement regarding the auditor's consideration of misstatements?
a. Consider the misstatements that could occur.
b. Identify relevant internal control structure policies and procedures.
c. Test all internal control structure policies and procedures.
d. Evaluate the effectiveness of such policies and procedures in preventing or detecting material misstatements.

*8-16.   What is the reason for ensuring that every copy of a vendor's invoice has a receiving report?
a. To ascertain that merchandise billed by the vendor was received by the company.
b. To ascertain that merchandise received by the company was billed by the vendor.
c. To ascertain that the invoice was correctly prepared.
d. To ascertain that a check was prepared for every invoice.

*8-17.   Which of the following procedures is the best one to ensure that employee job time tickets are accurate?
a. Approve the payroll voucher in the Accounts Payable Department.
b. Keep employment information in the Human Resources Department.
c. Make sure that the number of hours per week on each employee's job time ticket is forty.
d. Check the employee clock cards against the job time tickets.

*8-18.   Which of the following is an irregularity?
a. Mistakes in gathering or processing accounting data.
b. Improperly altering accounting records.
c. Incorrect accounting estimates arising from misinterpretation of facts.
d. Mistakes in the application of accounting principles.

*Not a CPA examination question.

*8-19. Which of the following statements is not a part of the auditor's responsibilities to detect errors and irregularities?
   a. The auditor should assess the risk that errors and irregularities may cause the financial statements to contain a material misstatement.
   b. The auditor should plan the audit to provide full assurance of detecting errors and irregularities.
   c. The auditor should exercise due care in planning, performing, and evaluating the results of audit procedures.
   d. The auditor is not an insurer and his or her report does not constitute a guarantee.

8-20. Which of the following, if material, would be an irregularity as defined in Statements on Auditing Standards?
   a. Errors in the application of accounting principles.
   b. Errors in the accounting data underlying the financial statements.
   c. Misinterpretation of facts that existed when the financial statements were prepared.
   d. Misappropriation of assets.

8-21. An auditor's flowchart of a client's accounting system is a diagrammatic representation that depicts the auditor's
   a. Understanding of the system.
   b. Program for tests of controls.
   c. Documentation of the study and evaluation of the system.
   d. Understanding of the types of irregularities that are probable, given the present system.

8-22. The following are steps in the audit process:
      I. Prepare flowchart.
      II. Gather exhibits of all documents.
      III. Interview personnel.
   The most logical sequence of steps is
   a. I, II, III.
   b. I, III, II.
   c. III, II, I.
   d. II, I, III.

8-23. When assessing control risk, the completion of a questionnaire is most closely associated with which of the following?
   a. Separation of duties.
   b. Document verification.

c. Flowchart accuracy.

d. Tests of controls.

8-24.   When a customer fails to include a remittance advice with a payment, it is a common practice for the person opening the mail to prepare one. Consequently, mail should be opened by which of the following four company employees?

a. Credit manager.

b. Receptionist.

c. Sales manager.

d. Accounts receivable clerk.

8-25.   Which of the following symbolic representations indicate that a file has been consulted?

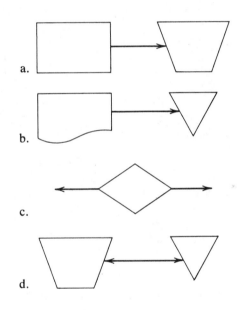

8-26.   Tracing copies of sales invoices to shipping documents will provide evidence that all

a. Shipments to customers were recorded as receivables.

b. Billed sales were shipped.

c. Debits to the subsidiary accounts receivable ledger are for sales shipped.

d. Shipments to customers were billed.

8-27.   A common audit procedure in the audit of payroll transactions involves tracing selected items from the payroll journal to employee time cards that have been approved by supervisory personnel. This procedure is designed to provide evidence in support of the audit proposition that

a. Only bona fide employees worked and their pay was properly computed.

b. Jobs on which employees worked were charged with the appropriate labor cost.

c. Internal controls relating to payroll disbursements are operating effectively.

d. All employees worked the number of hours for which their pay was computed.

8-28.   Which of the following is *not* an auditing procedure that is commonly used in performing tests of controls?

a. Inquiring.

b. Observing.

c. Confirming.

d. Inspecting.

8-29.   The accountant's report expressing an opinion on an entity's internal control structure would *not* include a

a. Description of the scope of the engagement.

b. An opinion on the internal control structure.

c. Brief explanation of the broad objectives and inherent limitations of internal control structure procedures.

d. Statement that the auditor is responsible for establishing and maintaining the internal control structure.

8-30.   The proper use of prenumbered termination notice forms by the Payroll Department should provide assurance that all

a. Uncashed payroll checks were issued to employees who have *not* been terminated.

b. Personnel files are kept up to date.

c. Employees who have *not* been terminated receive their payroll checks.

d. Terminated employees are removed from the payroll.

8-31.   A well-prepared flowchart should make it easier for the auditor to

a. Prepare audit procedure manuals.

b. Prepare detailed job descriptions.

c. Trace the origin and disposition of documents.

d. Assess the degree of accuracy of financial data.

Chapter 8
Discussion/Case Questions

8-32.   Long, a CPA, has been engaged to audit the financial statements of Maylou Corporation. While obtaining an understanding of Maylou's internal control structure procedures for purchases, Long was given the following document flowchart for purchases.

MAYLOU CORPORATION
DOCUMENT FLOWCHART FOR PURCHASES

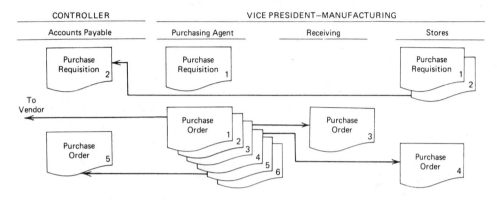

Required:

Identify the procedures, relating to purchase requisitions and purchase orders, that Long would expect to find if Maylou's internal control structure procedures for purchases are effective. For example, purchase orders are prepared only after giving proper consideration to the time to order and quantity to order. *Do not comment on the effectiveness of the flow of documents as presented in the flowchart or on separation of duties.*

(*AICPA adapted*)

8-33. A partially completed charge sales systems flowchart follows. The flowchart depicts the charge sales activities of the Bottom Manufacturing Corporation.

A customer's purchase order is received, and a six-part sales order is prepared from it. The six copies are initially distributed as follows:

Copy No. 1—Billing copy, to Billing Department.

Copy No. 2—Shipping copy, to Shipping Department.

Copy No. 3—Credit copy, to Credit Department.

Copy No. 4—Stock request copy, to Credit Department.

Copy No. 5—Customer copy, to customer.

Copy No. 6—Sales order copy, file in Sales Order Department.

BOTTOM MANUFACTURING CORPORATION
Flowchart of Credit Sales Activities

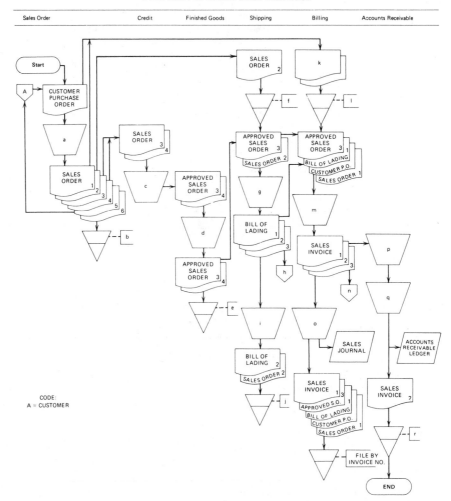

When each copy of the sales order reaches the applicable department or destination, it calls for specific internal control structure procedures and related documents. Some of the procedures and related documents are specified on the flowchart. Others are indicated only by the letters a to r.

Required:
List the procedures or the internal documents that are labeled letters c to r in the flowchart of Bottom Manufacturing Corporation's charge sales system.

Organize your answer as follows (note that an explanation of the letters a and b, which appear in the flowchart, are entered as examples):

Flowchart Symbol Letter	*Procedures or Internal Document*
a.	Prepare six-part sales order.
b.	File by order number.

Write a narrative describing the processes and information flows for the credit sales activities.

(AICPA adapted)

8-34.   The flowchart on page 302 depicts the activities relating to the shipping, billing, and collection processes used by Smallco Lumber, Inc.

Required:
a. Write a narrative describing the processes and information flows in the system.
b. Identify weaknesses in the internal control structure relating to the activities of (a) warehouse clerk, (b) bookkeeper #1, (c) bookkeeper #2, and (d) collection clerk.

(AICPA adapted)

8-35.   Cassandra Corporation, a manufacturing company, periodically invests large sums in marketable equity securities. The investment policy is established by the Investment Committee of the Board of Directors, and the treasurer is responsible for carrying out the Investment Committee's directives. All securities are stored in a bank safe deposit vault.

   The independent auditor's internal control structure questionnaire with respect to Cassandra's investments in marketable equity securities contains the following three questions:

   Is investment policy established by the Investment Committee of the Board of Directors?

   Is the treasurer solely responsible for carrying out the Investment Committee's directives?

   Are all securities stored in a bank safe deposit vault?

Required:
In addition to the preceding three questions, what questions should the auditor's internal control structure questionnaire include with respect to the company's investments in marketable equity securities?

(AICPA adapted)

8-36.   Harris, CPA, has been engaged to audit the financial statements of the Spartan Drugstore, Inc. Spartan is a medium-sized retail outlet that sells a wide variety of consumer goods. All sales are for cash or check. Cashiers utilize cash registers to

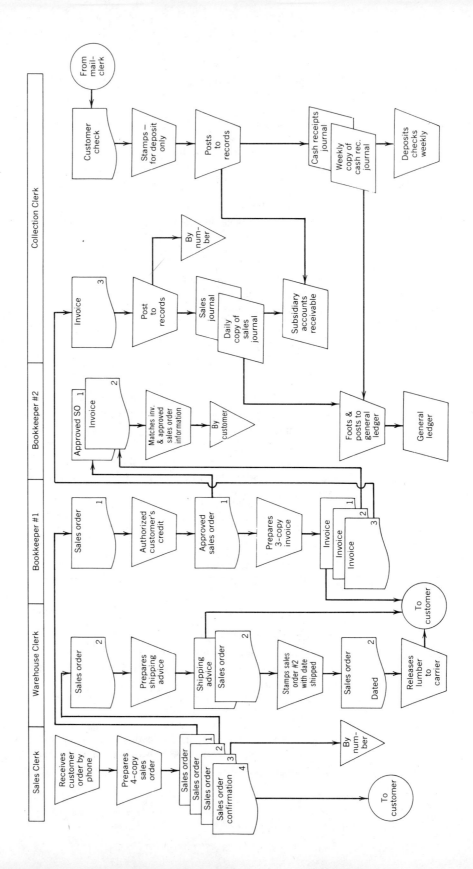

process these transactions. There are no receipts by mail and there are no credit card or charge sales.

Required:
Construct the "Processing Cash Collections" segment of the internal control structure questionnaire on "Cash Receipts" to be used in the evaluation of the internal control structure for the Spartan Drug Store, Inc. Each question should elicit either a yes or no response. Do *not* discuss the internal control procedures over cash sales.

(AICPA adapted)

8-37. Taylor, CPA, has been engaged to audit the financial statements of University Books, Incorporated. University Books maintains a large revolving cash fund exclusively for the purpose of buying used books from students for cash. The cash fund is active all year because the nearby university offers a large variety of courses with various starting and completion dates throughout the year.

Receipts are prepared for each purchase, and reimbursement vouchers are submitted periodically.

Required:
Construct an internal control structure questionnaire to be used in the evaluation of the internal control structure of University Books buying segment's revolving cash fund. The internal control structure questionnaire should elicit a yes or no response. Do not discuss the internal control structure procedures over the books that are purchased.

(AICPA adapted)

8-38. Certain audit tests consist of tracing dollar amounts from one document or record to another. The purpose of the audit test depends on the direction of the tracing. For each of the following sets of audit tests, indicate the difference in the purpose of each test.

a. Tracing amounts from the sales invoice to the accounts receivable subsidiary ledger, and vice versa.

b. Tracing amounts from the purchase invoice to the purchases journal, and vice versa.

c. Tracing amounts from the receipts listing to the duplicate deposit slip, and vice versa.

d. Tracing amounts from the payroll checks to the payroll register, and vice versa.

e. Tracing amounts from receiving reports to purchase invoices, and vice versa.

8-39. A feature of the internal control structure is considered weak if errors or irregularities could occur as a result of the feature's existence. For each of the following situations, indicate the error or irregularity that could occur.

a. Furnishing copies of fully completed purchase orders to the clerks who count incoming merchandise and fill out receiving reports.

b. Allowing the payroll supervisor to disburse payroll checks.

c. No reconciliation between the accounts receivable subsidiary ledger and the general ledger control account.

d. No credit check made before sales are made to customers.

e. Cancellation stamps are not placed on purchase invoices.

f. Payments are made by vendor monthly statements rather than vendor invoices.

g. Employees are paid in cash.

h. The person who handles cash receipts also approves accounts receivable writeoffs.

i. Extensions on sales invoices are not checked by another person.

j. The cashier reconciles the bank statement.

8-40. You were engaged to audit the financial statements of Blank City Newspapers, Inc., for the year ended December 31. The company publishes a newspaper with a daily circulation of aproximately 65,000.

During your examination of accounts receivable, certain unusual transactions were noted and discussed with company executives. When questioned about the transactions, the cashier admitted to a defalcation and gave company executives 298 remittance advices consisting of either the top half of the newspaper's monthly statement, the voucher portion of the customers' checks, or the cashier's memo of payment. The cashier said these remittance advices (amounting to $74,437.38) were the record of payments made by customers for which the checks had been deposited in the bank but no credit had been given in the customers' accounts. She had diverted some previous checks received by mail to an unauthorized bank account that she established in the company's name using a forged corporate resolution. Funds could be withdrawn upon her signature.

The company was shocked because the cashier was an old and faithful employee who was never sick and so interested in her work that she never took a vacation.

To conceal the irregularity, the cashier was lapping accounts receivable by withholding cash receipts from some customers and posting later cash receipts to these earlier customers' accounts. As the total misappropriated grew to a sizable amount, the process became so involved that most customers were receiving credit up to two weeks late.

A review of the company's internal control structure for cash receipts disclosed the following:

The cashier reported directly to the controller.

Mail was opened by another employee of the company. This employee did not prepare a record of the money and checks received before he distributed them.

All mail and over-the-counter receipts (cash sales and payments on accounts) were given to the cashier. Receipts included approximately $100 to $200 daily in currency.

The cashier prepared a daily report showing customer and amount of payment. She gave this report, together with remittance advices, to the Accounts Receivable Department for posting to the customers' accounts receivable ledger cards.

The cashier prepared the bank deposit and took the deposit to the bank. She obtained an authenticated deposit slip from the bank.

The cashier gave the authenticated deposit slip to the controller, who compared the total shown thereon with the total shown on the daily cash receipts report. These totals were always in agreement.

Your audit procedures included the confirmation of accounts receivable as of December 31. Most of the replies to the requests for confirmation were returned reporting no difference. However, the following replies were received from various customers:

"Less our ch #54818—$6,358.04, dated 12/23"

"Corrected statement received 1/8"

"$5,902.77 paid on our check #235043 dated 12/18"

"Payment on December 19th—$4,626.15 covering November"

Required:
a. Write a letter to the audit committee listing the reportable conditions noted in the company's accounting procedures for cash receipts and recommendations for improvement.
b. List the tests of controls that might have disclosed the irregularity by the cashier.
c. What should you do when you discover unusual items that might indicate an irregularity by one of the company's employees?

(Adapted and used with permission of Ernst & Whinney)

8-41. During the course of obtaining an understanding of a client's internal control structure, Mr. Inves, CPA, discovered that, in a number of instances, the pertinent information had not been posted from sales invoices to the customer ledger accounts. On inquiring about this situation, Mr. Inves was told by the controller that the posting had not been done because of a temporary shortage of personnel.

The controller suggested that Mr. Inves complete the posting himself, because 90 percent of it was already done.

Mr. Inves decided to follow this suggestion in order to expedite the audit. He completed the posting and balancing of the accounts receivable control account to the total of the customer ledger accounts. Mr. Inves considered the possibility of mentioning the posting deficiency in his formal letter to the audit committee, but he decided against including it because he considered it a minor matter and the client's shortage of personnel was the reason for the deficiency. No informal letter was issued to the controller.

Required:

a. What are the four conditions under which the AICPA approves bookkeeping services and audit services for the same client? (Refer to ethical rule on independence in Chapter 3.)

b. Do you think that Mr. Inves violated the AICPA Code of Ethics? Why or why not?

c. Assume that there were no bookkeeping/auditing provision in the AICPA Code of Ethics. Do you think that Mr. Inves violated the spirit of the rule on independence?

d. Do you think that Mr. Inves followed the right course of action in omitting the posting inadequacy from the letter to the audit committee? What would your answer be if Mr. Inves also issued an informal letter to the controller?

8-42.   During the audit of Clements Manufacturing Co., Bill Gahagan, CPA, noticed that scrap steel from the manufacturing process was piled in an unfenced vacant lot next to the plant. No records were kept of the amount of scrap generated in the manufacturing process or the amount on hand at any time. Scrap sales were recorded when made by the maintenance foreman.

Gahagan included these weaknesses in his report of reportable conditions to management, together with his recommendations for strengthening controls by fencing the area and weighing and recording the daily scrap production; however, the management of Clements took no action on the recommendations included in the report.

Six months later, it was discovered that the maintenance supervisor reported only a small portion of the actual scrap that was sold and had kept most of the proceeds from the scrap sales for himself. The president of Clements then called Gahagan and asked him why he had not caught the maintenance supervisor in his audit and suggested that he might hold Gahagan liable for the loss.

Discuss how Gahagan should handle this situation and how he would reply to the president. What liability do you think Gahagan would have in this situation? Would your answer be different if the letter was sent to the audit committee?

8-43.   During the course of an audit, Mr. Robin, CPA, observed that one of the clerks in the small toy department consistently was taking money from the customers in areas other than at the cash register. At the time, he gave little thought to this practice, because most items were priced in "whole dollars" and the customer did not need any change. He did mention this to the controller, who had the same reaction. The audit was completed and the report was issued.

The following year it was discovered that the clerk had been keeping the money from these "whole dollar purchases" rather than putting it in the cash register.

Required:

a. Could the auditor be held liable for failure to detect this fraud? Should his comment to the controller make any difference?

b. Assume that the auditor decided to include his observation in a letter of reportable conditions, along with his recommendation on how to eliminate this weakness and provide relative assurance that currency receipts are placed in the cash register drawer. Draft the relevant part of such a letter.

c. What tests of controls might have provided evidence that could have resulted in the detection of this fraud?

8-44. During an audit of a loan company, the auditor discovered that the recipient of a loan with a principal balance of $2,100 had received only $2,000 when the loan was written. The auditor checked the loan agreement and noted that it called for a $2,000 check and $100 in currency to be given to the customer who borrowed the money.

The auditor checked other loan agreements and found similar wording in each of them. When the controller was asked about this practice, she replied that this "service" was given to the customers so that they could have immediate access to currency. She thought that the $100 inconsistency was an error and could be corrected easily. The auditor decided to drop the matter.

Early the following year, a class-action lawsuit was brought against the loan company by several customers who discovered that they had received less than the principal amount of the loans. It was discovered that the controller had kept the currency. The company's board of directors notified the auditor that they would take legal action against him because of his failure to inform them of what he had learned about this matter.

Required:

a. Could the auditor be held liable for either ordinary negligence or gross negligence in this case?

b. Assume that the auditor chose to include this loan agreement practice in a letter of reportable conditions to the audit committee. Draft the relevant portion of such a letter. Include a recommendation of the controls that can be implemented to prevent such an occurrence.

c. What tests of controls might have detected this fraud?

CHAPTER 9

Tests of Controls—Nonstatistical and Statistical Sampling

Learning Objectives   *After reading and studying the material in this chapter, the student should*

Know the objectives of tests of controls.

Be able to define a deviation from a prescribed internal control structure procedure in a test of controls.

Be able to define a population for a test of controls.

Know how to apply the various methods of selecting samples for tests of controls.

Know how to determine the sample size, perform sampling plans, and evaluate sample results for tests of controls.

Understand the application of sampling for tests of controls using both nonstatistical and statistical sampling methods.

In Chapter 5, we discussed audit risk and pointed out that there is a risk that an auditor may unknowingly fail to modify appropriately an opinion on financial statements that are materially misstated. We also pointed out that audit risk exists, in part, because of audit sampling, which is the application of an auditing procedure to less than 100 percent of the items comprising the account balance or class of transactions.

In Chapter 7, we discussed the general concept of tests of controls and indicated that they may be performed as the auditor acquires an understanding of the internal control structure or as a basis for further restricting the substantive tests of financial statement assertions.

In this chapter, we will discuss tests of controls in depth and demonstrate how such tests are planned, executed, and evaluated. The discussion will cover the following subjects:

1. How the objectives of tests of controls are determined.

2. The definition of a deviation from an internal control structure procedure and conditions that indicate whether a deviation has or has not occurred.

3. How a population from which a sample is taken is defined.

4. Comparison of different methods available to select the sample.

5. Factors to consider in determining the sample size.

6. How to perform the sampling plan.

7. How to evaluate the sampling results.

8. How to document the sampling procedure.

Using Step 8 as a guideline, we will then illustrate tests of controls using both nonstatistical and statistical techniques.

Determining the Objective of a Test of Controls

The objectives of *tests of controls* are to enable auditors to assess whether an internal control structure policy or procedure is properly designed and is operating effectively (i.e., a credit extension control that relates to valuation of accounts receivable).

Here are some examples of detail tests of controls and their purposes. The tests are grouped by inventory purchase controls, cash disbursement controls, and payroll controls.

Some Tests of Controls for Inventory Purchases Controls

Test	Purpose of the Test
1. Compare the Stores Department's purchase requisitions with properly prepared receiving reports.	1. To determine whether the items requested by the Stores Department were received from the vendor (existence).

Some Tests of Controls for Inventory Purchases Controls (Continued)

Test	Purpose of the Test
2. Compare invoice price with bids submitted by vendors.	2. To determine whether competitive bidding procedures are followed (valuation).
3. Compare the vendor's invoice with the receiving report.	3. To ascertain whether merchandise billed by the vendor was received by the company (existence).
4. Compare the purchase order with the vendor's invoice.	4. To ascertain whether the purchase was properly authorized (existence and valuation).

Some Tests of Controls for Cash Disbursement Controls

Test	Purpose of the Test
1. Trace entries in the voucher register to the vouchers.	1. To ascertain whether the entries were properly recorded (valuation and presentation).
2. Compare vouchers with supporting vendor invoices and canceled checks.	2. To determine whether goods recorded are owned and properly valued (rights and valuation).
3. Compare vouchers with supporting receiving reports.	3. To determine whether goods paid for were received (existence).
4. Examine supporting documents for indication of cancellation.	4. To ascertain that the probability of duplicate payment to creditors has been minimized (existence).
5. Trace entries in the voucher register to the general ledger.	5. To check the accuracy of postings from books of original entry to the general ledger (valuation and presentation).

Some Tests of Controls for Payroll Controls

Test	Purpose of the Test
1. Inspect the job time tickets for proper approval by authorized official.	1. To determine whether the time spent on jobs is approved (occurrence).
2. Compare employee clock cards with the payroll register.	2. To determine whether the time for which employees are paid agrees with the time cards (occurrence).
3. Check the clerical accuracy of the payroll register.	3. To ascertain whether the payroll was properly summarized (valuation).
4. Compare the payee and amount on the payroll check to the payroll register and examine signature and endorsement.	4. To determine whether the payroll checks agree with the payroll register (obligations and completeness).

Some Tests of Controls for Payroll Controls (Continued)

Test	Purpose of the Test
5. Trace rates and deductions on the payroll to the authorizations and deduction slips kept in the Personnel Department.	5. To determine whether proper rates and deductions are used in preparing the payroll (valuation).
6. Conduct a surprise payroll payoff by distributing payroll checks to employees who are identified properly.	6. To test for the possible existence of fictitious employees and to test procedures for handling unclaimed checks (occurrence).

Notice that the purpose of each listed test of controls is to determine whether "what is supposed to be in operation actually is in operation." For example, the auditor might be told or might determine from flowcharting the inventory purchases system that client personnel in the Accounts Payable Department compare all the relevant documentation for purchase transactions. However, the auditor needs to "prove it" by comparing requisitions (what was requested by the Stores Department), purchase orders (what was ordered from the vendor), invoices (what was billed by the vendor), and receiving reports (what was received by the company).

It is not necessary that all the year's requisitions, purchase orders, invoices, and receiving reports be examined and compared. As we explain later in the chapter, some tests may be conducted on a sample basis. The sample results would then be used by the auditor to draw inferences about the effectiveness of the internal control structure procedures.

The Definition of a Deviation from an Internal Control Structure Procedure

To conduct an effective test of controls, the auditor must be able to identify a *deviation,* which is a departure from the prescribed internal control structure procedure. The deviation must relate to the specific control structure procedure being tested. Assume, for example, that the purpose of comparing the vendor's invoice with a copy of the receiving report is to ascertain whether all purchased merchandise is received. A deviation exists when a receiving report does not contain the same items as the invoice. It is assumed that the control procedure calls for the same items to be on the invoices and receiving reports.

Care must be taken not to improperly define a deviation. Assume that in the previous example, the purpose of the test is to ascertain whether invoices are accompanied by proper receiving reports. In this case, a deviation is a missing receiving report, a receiving report with quantities different from those shown on the invoice, or a receiving report with different types of items from those shown on the invoice.

Definition of the Population

For the tests of controls to accomplish the audit objective, the *population* to which the test is applied must be appropriately defined. Referring to an earlier example, an auditor might compare items on the receiving report with items on the vendor invoice. If the audit objective is to determine that all merchandise billed from vendors was received (i.e., accounts payable are owed), the population consists of all vendor invoices recorded during the year. If the audit objective is to determine that all received merchandise was billed by the vendors (i.e., accounts payable are complete), the population consists of all receiving reports prepared during the year. Likewise, assume that the auditor examines supporting documents for canceled checks for the objective of determining whether proper goods or services were received for money paid to vendors. The population for this test is all checks issued during the year.

Ideally, tests of controls should be applied to a sample of all the applicable transactions in the audit period. For example, if the audit is for the calendar year 19X5, the sample should be drawn from items (receiving reports, time tickets, etc.) for the entire period of January through December.

Sometimes, tests must be applied to transactions in periods of less than a year. To make more efficient use of time, auditors often obtain an understanding of the internal control structure at an interim date. In such cases, it is not always necessary to conduct tests of controls covering the remainder of the year. If the interim date were late in the year (November for a December 31 year end) and if the test results in the interim period were satisfactory, additional tests might be bypassed if the auditor is able to satisfy himself or herself that no changes in the internal control structure have occurred. This satisfaction could be obtained by means of other auditing procedures such as inquiry.

Sample results in the interim period may lead the auditor to conclude that the operation of internal control structure procedures is unsatisfactory for the year. This conclusion would be based on the large number of deviations found in the interim period. In such a case, tests for the interim period are sufficient.

The auditor must be careful to define the unit that will be sampled within the population. For example, a *sampling unit* may be

1. A document, such as an invoice.

2. An entry, such as a posting to a subsidiary ledger.

3. A line within a document, such as lines within an invoice.

In deciding whether to sample a document or a line, the auditor considers the objective of the test. Again, let us refer to an earlier example. Assume that the purpose of comparing vendor invoices and receiving reports is to ascertain whether there is a receiving report to match each invoice. A deviation is a missing receiving report; therefore, the sampling unit is the invoice. But what if the purpose of this test is to ascertain whether all items on the invoice are matched by items on a receiving report? In this case, the sampling unit may be the line, not the invoice.

Note that the size of the population differs if the auditor defines lines rather than invoices as sampling units. For instance, 2,000 invoices processed during the year constitute a population of 2,000. If there is an average of 10 lines per invoice, the population of invoice lines is 20,000.

Methods of Selecting the Sample

Auditors are not required to use one particular method to select a sample. However, items should be selected in such a way that the sample is representative of the population. Otherwise, auditors cannot draw definitive conclusions about internal control structure procedures. For a sample to be representative of the population, every item in the population must have an opportunity to be selected.

Two of the less rigorous sampling methods are (1) a block sample and (2) a haphazard sample. A *block sample* is the selection of a group of consecutive transactions, such as for a month of the year. Another type of block sample is the selection of transactions for groups of days, such as March 5, June 19, and so on. Block sampling is convenient but may not be representative of the population.

Haphazard sampling is a method of selection that has no particular pattern or conscious bias toward selecting or omitting any particular items. For example, in examining a sample of checks for supporting documentation, no attempt is made to select or omit checks with an unusual volume of supporting documents. Like block sampling, this method is convenient and could produce a sample that is representative of the population. Its major drawbacks are that there is no scientific basis for judging sample results, and, without proper care the sample may contain significant bias.

Sampling Methodology—Random Numbers

Unrestricted random selection means that every element in the population has an equal chance of being selected. In a population of 200 lines, each one has a $\frac{1}{200}$ chance of appearing in the sample. If the method is to be statistically defensible, a tested table of random numbers should be used. Such a table is illustrated in Table 9.1C in Appendix B of this chapter.

A random number table can be read vertically, horizontally, or diagonally, and the user can pick the left-hand, middle, or right-hand portion of the number. These methods are illustrated in the following partial reproduction of a random number table.

Table Numbers		Can Be Read						
		Vertically			*Horizontally*		*Diagonally*	
10480	15011	104	048	480	104	150	104	048	480
22368	46573	223	236	368	048	501	465	657	573
24130	48360	241	413	130	480	011			

Care must be taken, however, to discard unusable numbers read from the table. For example, in a population of 200 lines, three-digit sets should be used, and any three-digit number over 200 should be discarded because it exceeds the population total. Assume that the first number selected from the table is 192; this means that the 192nd line of the array of population items is selected. If the next number is 419, it should be omitted. This process continues until the sample is chosen. An alternative procedure is to subtract the population total, or a multiple of this total, from three-digit numbers that are too high. For example, if the three-digit number 220 is chosen, it becomes 20 (220 minus 200). If 419 is chosen, it becomes 19 (419 minus 400). By this method, no three-digit number is discarded. Whatever method is used, it is important for the auditor to fully document the sample selection.

What if a number is selected again? If the sample size determination table for this type of test calls for *sampling with replacement* (replacing the item before continuing with the sample), the number should be reused. If the table calls for *sampling without replacement* (not replacing the item before continuing with the sample), the number should be ignored.[1] Audit samples are normally selected without replacement. The sample size is lower and auditors have no need to examine a document or item more than once.

It is often more convenient to use computer-generated random numbers. They are sometimes referred to as pseudorandom numbers because they have all the characteristics of random numbers, although they are not generated randomly.

Sampling Methodology—Systematic Sampling

Unrestricted random sampling is not the only method available for selecting items to be examined. *Systematic sampling* can be used and every *n*th element selected. If such a technique is used, however, the auditor should ascertain that the population from which the sample is taken does not contain unusual items that appear at fixed intervals.

For instance, assume that during certain days of each week invoices are

---

[1] The analogy of drawing marbles from a jar is often used to illustrate these terms. Assume that a jar contains ten marbles, and one is drawn out. If sampling with replacement is used, the marble is replaced in the jar before another sample item is drawn, so ten marbles are always left in the jar. If sampling without replacement is used, the marble is not replaced, and the number of marbles in the jar is lowered when a subsequent sample item is drawn.

processed by a part-time employee who makes an unusually large number of mistakes. As a result, approximately every tenth invoice contains a clerical deviation. If the auditors selected every tenth invoice as their sampling interval, the sampling results would not provide a good estimate of the deviations in the population.

Systematic sampling is easy to use and might provide results comparable to those gained from unrestricted random sampling. But the auditor should take care to avoid using the method with populations that might contain nonrandom deviations.

To introduce randomness into the selection, a random starting point should be used; for example, by a blind stab into a random number table.

Determining the Sample Size

The size of the sample should provide an acceptable risk that the population deviation rate does not exceed the tolerable rate. Acceptable risk levels and tolerable population deviation rates are matters of audit judgment and could vary with each test.

Whether statistical or nonstatistical sampling is used, auditors should consider a number of factors in deciding on the size of the sample:

1. The risk of overreliance.

2. The tolerable rate.

3. The expected deviation rate in the population.

Risk of Overreliance

The *risk of overreliance* relates to the effectiveness of the audit. The *risk of overreliance* is the risk that the sample results support the planned degree of reliance on the control when the true population deviation rate is large enough not to justify such reliance. For the following reasons, the risk of overreliance is kept at a relatively low level by auditors (if statistical sampling is used, 10 percent is normally the maximum).

1. A test of controls is the best source of evidence that the control procedure is operating as prescribed.

2. The auditor wants high assurance that the test results are representative of the true deviation rate in the population.

If statistical sampling is used, the auditor must quantify the risk level. Risk levels of 1, 5, and 10 percent are examples. If nonstatistical sampling is used, the risk levels can be described as low, moderate, or high (relatively high).

Whether statistical or nonstatistical sampling is used, there is an inverse relationship between the risk of overreliance and the sample size. Under certain conditions, for example, raising the risk level from low to moderate, or from 1 to 5 percent, will reduce the sample size by almost 50 percent. Raising the risk level from moderate to high, or from 5 to 10 percent, could reduce the sample size another 10 percent (approximately).

When determining the appropriate risk level, auditors consider the reliance to be placed on a control. Reliance, as the term is used in planning a sample, does not refer to the strength of a control; reliance refers to the importance of a control in determining the extent to which substantive tests will be restricted. If a control on which auditors place heavy reliance is functioning properly, substantial restriction is placed on substantive tests of balances. On tests of controls of this type, auditors will set the risk of overreliance at a low level. On the other hand, if a control on which auditors place little reliance is functioning properly, only a small restriction is placed on substantive tests of balances. On tests of controls of this type, auditors will set the risk of overreliance at a higher level.

It may sometimes be difficult to decide whether risk levels should be low, moderate, or high (or 1, 5, or 10 percent). For this reason, the same risk level is sometimes used for all tests of controls. This means that the sample size depends on the factors discussed in the next two subsections.

Acceptable Tolerable Rates

The *tolerable rate* is the maximum rate of deviations auditors will accept without altering the planned substantive testing of an assertion regarding a balance or class of transactions. Thus, altering the evaluation of a control results in altering substantive tests on the account balances to which that control relates.

In setting the tolerable rate, the auditor considers how materially the financial statements would be affected if the control does not function properly. The auditor will set a relatively low tolerable rate on controls more likely to prevent or detect material errors in the financial statements; likewise, the auditor will set a relatively high tolerable rate on controls less likely to prevent or detect material errors in the financial statements.

To illustrate, let us compare two controls. One control is designed to prevent or detect errors in pricing sales invoices (the test is comparing invoice prices to the master price list). The other control is designed to prevent or detect the recording of a sale when the merchandise has not been shipped (the test is comparing sales invoices to shipping documents).

For several reasons, the pricing control might be less likely to prevent material errors in the financial statements than the sales recording control. In the first place, repetitive errors in invoice pricing may produce lower dollar errors than repetitive errors in recording sales. In the second place, pricing errors may be easier to correct before financial statements are prepared. Therefore, the auditor would set a relatively high tolerable rate on the pricing test and a relatively low tolerable rate on the sales recording test. The difference in rates is the auditor's assessment that errors in the pricing control are less likely to cause material errors in the financial statements.

If statistical sampling is used, tolerable rates must be quantified: 1 to 4 percent might be considered low; 5 to 9 percent could be considered moderate; 10 percent is probably considered high.

There is an inverse relationship between the tolerable rate and the sample size. Under certain conditions, a change in the tolerable rate from low (4 percent) to moderate (8 percent) reduces the sample size by approximately 50 percent.

Expected Population Deviation Rate

As the estimate of the population deviation rate approaches the tolerable rate, there is more need for precise information from the sample. Therefore, as the expected population deviation rate increases, the sample size increases if all other factors remain constant.

The estimate of the population deviation rate is a matter of audit judgment. The sample deviation rate in the prior-period audit is one basis for making this judgment; a preliminary sample (e.g., 20 items) is another basis.

There is a direct relationship between the estimate of the population deviation rate and the sample size. For example, under certain conditions, an increase in the estimate from 2 to 3 percent increases the sample size by approximately 100 percent. An increase of this size will certainly lower the sampling risk. However, care should be taken not to "overaudit."

Performing the Sampling Plan

Performance of the sampling plan is essentially an application of the appropriate audit procedure to the elements in the sample (comparison of invoices and receiving reports, examination of time tickets for proper approval, etc.). Here are some guidelines to use in performing the sampling plan.

1. Select extra sample items to use as "replacements" in case a voided or unusable document is found.

2. Consider terminating the sampling process and drawing conclusions if too many errors are found early in the sampling process. For instance, assume that 5 checks with missing documentation are found in the first 50 checks examined. It might be obvious that the operation of that control is unsatisfactory even if no missing documentation is found for the remaining 50

checks to be examined. The test can be terminated and the auditors can conclude that the control cannot be relied on.

3. Unlocated documents should ordinarily be considered a deviation.

Evaluating the Sample Results

The first step in evaluating sample results is to calculate the deviation rate in the sample. Five missing authorizations on 100 time tickets constitute a 5 percent deviation rate and is now the best estimate of the actual population deviation rate. From here, a set of decision rules can be followed.

1. If the *sample deviation rate (calculated estimate of the population deviation rate)* is higher than the tolerable rate, the audit risk is not at a sufficiently low level to additionally restrict substantive tests of the financial statement assertions that relate to this control.

2. If the sample deviation rate is less than the tolerable rate, consider that these sample results could have occurred even if the actual population deviation rate is higher than the tolerable rate. Here are some additional guidelines.

a. If the sample deviation rate is considerably lower than the tolerable rate (e.g., 1 percent compared to 8 percent), assume that audit risk is at a sufficiently low level to additionally restrict substantive tests of financial statement assertions that relate to this control.

b. If the sample deviation rate is barely lower than the tolerable rate (e.g., 7 percent compared to 8 percent), generally conclude that the audit risk is not at a sufficiently low level to additionally restrict substantive tests of financial statement assertions that relate to this control.

c. If the sample deviation rate is higher than the estimate of the population deviation rate used to plan the sample size, the sample results should generally be interpreted to mean that audit risk is not at a sufficiently low level to additionally restrict substantive tests of financial statement assertions that relate to this control. Assume that in planning a sample the auditor estimated the deviation rate in the population to be 3 percent and found that the sample deviation rate was 4 percent (4 missing receiving reports for 100 invoices examined). The audit risk is unacceptably high.

We can summarize by stating that if

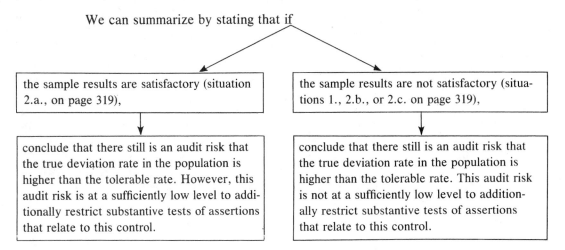

the sample results are satisfactory (situation 2.a., on page 319),

conclude that there still is an audit risk that the true deviation rate in the population is higher than the tolerable rate. However, this audit risk is at a sufficiently low level to additionally restrict substantive tests of assertions that relate to this control.

the sample results are not satisfactory (situations 1., 2.b., or 2.c. on page 319),

conclude that there still is an audit risk that the true deviation rate in the population is higher than the tolerable rate. This audit risk is not at a sufficiently low level to additionally restrict substantive tests of assertions that relate to this control.

Bear in mind that there may still be some restriction on substantive tests of financial statement assertions because of the control risk assessment made when the auditors acquired an understanding of the internal control structure and conducted basic tests of controls. These detail tests of controls are designed to ascertain whether the internal control structure procedures are operating effectively. If these control test results are acceptable, the substantive tests of certain financial statement assertions may be further restricted. If these control test results are not acceptable, further planned restriction of substantive tests would have to be reconsidered.

Example of a Test of Controls—Nonstatistical Sampling

To illustrate the concepts discussed in the previous section, we will now cover a test of controls and demonstrate how to (1) determine the sample size for the test, (2) apply a sampling technique to the test, and (3) evaluate the sampling results. In this section we will use nonstatistical techniques. In the following section we will cover the same test of controls with the use of statistical sampling.

Assume that we have already acquired an understanding of the internal control structure of purchases controls by using techniques illustrated in Chapters 7 and 8. As a result of our favorable impressions gained during this study, we plan to extend reliance on the internal control structure and restrict substantive tests of certain financial statement assertions for the Purchases and Accounts Payable accounts that relate to purchases controls. We wish to ascertain, however, that these controls are operating effectively and as prescribed by conducting several detail tests of controls. On the basis of these test results, we will decide whether audit risk is sufficiently low to additionally restrict substantive tests of certain financial statement assertions for the Purchases and Accounts Payable accounts.

Refer to pages 310–311, which contain examples of tests of controls for inventory purchases controls. Notice that the third listed test is a comparison of the vendor's invoice with the receiving report, the purpose being to ascertain whether merchandise billed by the vendor was received by the company (relates to the assertions that the Accounts Payable exist and the Purchases occurred).

We will assume that the population consists of the vendor's invoice file for the year or to the date we conduct this test. A sample of invoices is to be compared with the related receiving reports. No deviation exists if we find the following.

1. A receiving report exists for each invoice and is attached or appropriately filed with the invoice.

2. The vendor's name, description of merchandise, and quantity received are the same on the invoice and the receiving report (or a satisfactory explanation is obtained if the information is different).

Otherwise a deviation exists for that invoice.

Determination of Sample Size

Our first step is to determine the number of invoices we will compare with a related receiving report. Assume that the client company processed 2,000 invoices during the year or the period covered by our test. How many should we select?

Generally, the size of the sample in a test of controls is based on the following three factors.

1. Tolerable rate (the highest deviation rate that the auditor will tolerate).— Missing or improper receiving reports could indicate billed merchandise has not been received (i.e., purchases have not occurred and accounts payable do not exist). We will assume that the auditor accepts a high rate of error for this control because he or she believes that the accounts are unlikely to be misstated by nonexistent purchases or accounts payable. Tolerable rate is set at 8 percent. If the sample results indicate that audit risk is sufficiently low that the deviation rate in the population of invoices is no more than 8 percent, the sample results are acceptable.

2. Risk of overreliance.—The auditor must consider the reliance he or she plans to place on this purchase control for the purpose of restricting the substantive tests. In other words, if this control is weak or nonexistent, how much effect would it have on the related substantive tests of financial statement assertions? Heavy reliance calls for a relatively low risk of overreliance, whereas a small amount of reliance calls for a relatively high risk. For planning purposes, this risk is set at a moderate level to provide moderate reliance that the deviation rate in the sample is a reliable predictor of the deviation rate in the population.

3. Expected population deviation rate—This rate could be based on the deviation rate found in the sample for the same test performed in the previous audit, or it could be based on a preliminary sample. For our purposes, we will assume a 2 percent rate.

The relationships between sample size and these three factors are shown in the following table.

	Factor		Sample Size	
	Higher	*Lower*	*Larger*	*Smaller*
Tolerable rate	X			X
		X	X	
Risk of overreliance		X	X	
	X			X
Estimate of the population deviation rate	X		X	
		X		X

When nonstatistical sampling is used, it is not necessary that an amount be assigned to the risk of overreliance. Because auditors use judgment to determine an appropriate sample size, they could set this risk nonquantitatively at high, moderate, or low. For purposes of this illustration, we will assume a sample size of 100 or 5 percent of the population.

Method of Sample Selection

On pages 314–316 we discussed various selection methods and the advantages and disadvantages of each. Systematic sampling is sometimes used because it is easy to apply. If the auditor believes that deviations are randomly scattered throughout the population, this method should not produce biased results.

We will assume the use of systematic sampling in which every twentieth invoice is selected to ascertain whether it is accompanied by a matching and properly completed receiving report.

Evaluation of Sample Results

The auditor will use his or her judgment in deciding whether the sample results are acceptable or unacceptable. But the auditor can and probably should use the decision rules discussed on page 319 of this chapter.

In the following illustration we will assume several sampling results and will explain why each of these results would be acceptable or unacceptable using these decision rules. An acceptable sampling result means that audit risk is at a sufficiently low level to additionally restrict substantive tests of assertions that relate to this purchases control. An unacceptable sampling result means that audit risk is not at a sufficiently low level to additionally restrict substantive tests of assertions that relate to this purchases control.

Evaluation of Sampling Results on the Assessment of Control Risk

Tolerable Rate—8 percent

Risk of Overreliance—Moderate

Estimate of Deviation Rate in the Population—2 percent

	Sample Size	Number of Deviations	Sample Deviation Rate (Number of Deviations Divided by the Sample Size)
Test Result 1	100	10	10%
Test Result 2	100	0	0%
Test Result 3	100	6	6%

In all likelihood, the first test result shown above would be considered unacceptable because the sample deviation rate (the calculated estimate of the deviation rate in the population) is 10 percent and the tolerable rate is 8 percent. There is an unacceptably high risk that the true deviation rate in the population of 2,000 invoices is larger than 8 percent.

The second test result would probably be considered acceptable because the sample deviation rate is 0 percent and is considerably lower than the tolerable rate of 8 percent. There is an acceptably low risk that the true deviation rate in the population is not higher than 8 percent.

What about the third test result? The sample deviation rate is slightly lower than the tolerable rate of 8 percent, but is higher than the 2 percent estimate of the population deviation rate. Although auditor judgment is always the ultimate criterion, this test result would probably be considered unacceptable. The sample deviation rate is too close to the tolerable rate and is higher than our estimate of the population deviation rate.

Other Considerations in Evaluating the Sample Results

The auditor should look beyond the sample deviation rate and examine the types of deviations found. For example, six missing receiving reports might be more serious than six receiving reports that include all but a few minor items shown on the related invoice. Qualitative factors would be a part of the auditor's judgment as to whether audit risk is at a sufficiently low level to additionally restrict substantive tests of assertions related to this control.

Example of a Test of Controls—Statistical Sampling

In the previous section we discussed the use of nonstatistical sampling to perform a test of controls. In this section, we will demonstrate the same type of test using statistical sampling.

Actually, the objective of the test of controls is the same regardless of the sampling method selected. Also, systematic or random sampling techniques are just as applicable to nonstatistical as to statistical sampling. The factors that are different, however, are the ways in which (1) the size of the sample is determined, and (2) the sampling results are evaluated. We will cover each of these factors in the following subsections (remember that the objective of comparing the invoices with the receiving reports is still to determine whether this particular purchases control is operating effectively and as prescribed).

Determination of Sample Size

Because we are looking for an *attribute* (a properly completed receiving report for each invoice), we will make use of statistical sampling tables that assume the use of the technique called *estimation sampling for attributes*. For given risk levels (risk of overreliance), we can determine the optimum sample size for given tolerable rates and estimates of the expected deviation rate in the population.

In fact, an examination of Tables 9.1 and 9.2 shows that a wide variety of sample sizes can be ascertained by (1) referring to the appropriate risk level table (Table 9.1 for 5 percent and Table 9.2 for 10 percent), (2) selecting the desired tolerable rate, and (3) using the estimate of the deviation rate in the population. These two tables are adapted from statistical sampling tables published by the American Institute of Certified Public Accountants. The adaptation is done to make the tables easier to read and use. The complete tables appear in Appendix B.

Notice that in each table we have larger sample sizes as the tolerable rates become smaller with the same estimate of the population deviation rate. This is simply a quantitative expression of the inverse relationship between the tolerable rate and the sample size. If the auditor wants a "tighter tolerance" or "more precise estimate," he or she must take a larger sample.

If the auditor uses a tolerable rate that is not shown in the table, two alternatives are available.

1. The auditor can find the next lowest listed tolerable rate below the one he or she wishes to use. The sample size for that listed tolerable rate is the one used for the test. Look at Table 9.2 and note the tolerable rates of 7.6 and 5.2 associated with the expected population deviation rate of 2.0. If the auditor's tolerable rate is 6.0, a sample size of 100 can be selected because 5.2 is the next lowest listed tolerable rate below 6.0.

2. The auditor can interpolate. Using the same example as above, the following calculation would be made.

$$n = 50 + \frac{7.6 - 6.0}{7.6 - 5.2} \times 50$$

$$n = 84$$

Table 9.1
Determination of Sample Size—Risk of Overreliance of 5 Percent

If the Expected Deviation Rate in the Population Is	If the Tolerable Rate Is	The Sample Size Is
2.0	9.1	50
2.0	6.2	100
2.0	5.1	150
2.0	4.5	200
2.0	4.2	250
3.0	7.6	100
3.0	5.8	200
4.0	12.1	50
4.0	8.9	100
4.0	7.7	150
4.0	7.1	200
4.0	6.7	250
5.0	10.2	100
5.0	8.3	200
6.0	14.8	50
6.0	11.5	100
6.0	10.2	150
6.0	9.5	200
6.0	9.1	250
7.0	13.0	100
7.0	10.8	200
8.0	17.4	50
8.0	14.0	100
8.0	12.6	150
8.0	11.9	200
8.0	11.4	250

Method of Sample Selection

As pointed out earlier in the chapter, either systematic or unrestricted random number sampling can be used for tests of controls. Although unrestricted random number sampling may be theoretically preferable, systematic sampling is acceptable as long as there is a random start and the auditor believes that no deviation patterns exist in the population (i.e., every tenth invoice has a missing or improperly completed receiving report).

Evaluation of Sample Results

Although qualitative factors are considered by auditors when evaluating sample results for both statistical and nonstatistical sampling, statistical sampling

Table 9.2
Determination of Sample Size—Risk of Overreliance of 10 Percent

If the Expected Deviation Rate in the Population Is	If the Tolerable Rate Is	The Sample Size Is
2.0	7.6	50
2.0	5.2	100
2.0	4.4	150
2.0	4.0	200
2.0	3.7	250
3.0	6.6	100
3.0	5.2	200
4.0	10.3	50
4.0	7.8	100
4.0	6.9	150
4.0	6.4	200
4.0	6.1	250
5.0	9.1	100
5.0	7.6	200
6.0	12.9	50
6.0	10.3	100
6.0	9.3	150
6.0	8.8	200
6.0	8.4	250
7.0	11.7	100
7.0	10.0	200
8.0	15.4	50
8.0	12.7	100
8.0	11.6	150
8.0	11.0	200
8.0	10.7	250

tables are available to provide auditors with a quantitative evaluation of the sample results. Table 9.3 is an adaptation of a statistical sampling table published by the American Institute of Certified Public Accountants. Once again, we are using an adaptation to make it easier to read. The published table appears in Appendix B.

Note that we must now quantify the risk of overreliance. We will assume a 5 percent risk of overreliance for our example.

As noted in Table 9.3, the numbers in the two right-hand columns represent the achieved tolerable rates at given risk levels if a certain number of deviations is found when a certain sample size is used. The *planned tolerable rate* (8 percent in our example) is the planned highest deviation rate in the population that the auditor can accept and still conclude that the control is operating as prescribed.

Table 9.3

Evaluation of Sample Results for Tests with Risks of Overreliance of 10 Percent and 5 Percent

		The Achieved Tolerable Rate Is	
If the Sample Size Is	*If the Number of Deviations Is*	*If Risk of Overreliance Is 10%*	*If Risk of Overreliance Is 5%*
100	0	2.28	2.95
100	1	3.83	4.66
100	2	5.23	6.16
100	3	6.56	7.57
100	4	7.83	8.92
100	5	9.08	10.23
150	0	1.52	1.98
150	1	2.57	3.12
150	2	3.51	4.14
150	3	4.40	5.09
150	4	5.26	6.00
150	5	6.10	6.88
200	0	1.14	1.49
200	1	1.93	2.35
200	2	2.64	3.11
200	3	3.31	3.83
200	4	3.96	4.52
200	5	4.59	5.18

The *achieved tolerable rate* is based on the sample results and is the highest probable deviation rate in the population at a designated risk of overreliance.

For example, look at the left-hand column of Table 9.3 and note that with a sample size of 100, a risk of overreliance of 5 percent, and one deviation, the achieved tolerable rate is 4.66 percent. If the auditor takes a sample of 100 and finds one improperly completed receiving report, there is only a 5 percent risk that the true deviation rate in the population exceeds 4.66 percent.

Therefore, in using Table 9.3 to evaluate the sampling results quantitatively, we use these decision guides.

1. If the achieved tolerable rate is equal to or lower than the planned tolerable rate, the sampling results are acceptable and audit risk is sufficiently low to additionally restrict the substantive tests of assertions that relate to the purchases control.

2. If the achieved tolerable rate is higher than the planned tolerable rate, the sampling results are not acceptable and audit risk is not sufficiently low to

additionally restrict the substantive tests of assertions that relate to the purchases control.

We can look at Table 9.3 and easily tell what our sampling results will be for various deviation rates that we might find. With a sample size of 100, we must find three deviations or less for our sampling results to be acceptable.

Stop-or-Go Sampling

If the cost of obtaining evidence is high, or if for any other reason the auditor wishes to guard against overauditing, the *stop-or-go* method may be used. Using this technique, the auditor selects a minimum sample size that, if few or no deviations are found, will satisfy sampling needs. The achieved tolerable rate is calculated at a given risk percentage. If the achieved tolerable rate is no higher than the planned tolerable rate, the auditor might accept the sample results and discontinue any additional sampling. If the achieved tolerable rate is higher than the planned tolerable rate, the auditor will examine the apparent causes of the deviations. If the deviations appear to be random, an additional sample is taken and the same evaluations made.

For example, refer to Table 9.3. Assume that for a given test of controls the auditor takes a 10 percent risk of overreliance and uses a planned tolerable rate of 4 percent. A sample of 100 is drawn and no deviations are found. The achieved tolerable rate is 2.28 percent. The auditor might stop at this point and accept the sampling results. If two deviations are found and the achieved tolerable rate is 5.23 percent, the auditor may take another sample of 100. If the achieved tolerable rate of all 200 items does not exceed 4 percent, the auditor might accept the sample results. It is suggested that final sample conclusions be made no later than the point at which the sample size is three times its initial amount.

Stop-or-go sampling may be more efficient than the estimation sampling for attributes statistical method illustrated earlier in the chapter. The initial sample size, however, is probably smaller than an optimum sample size used in the estimation sampling method. Therefore, no valid estimate of the actual population deviation rate can be made from the initial minimum sample size.

Summary

1. The auditor obtains an understanding of the internal control structure and what procedures should be in place by inquiries and observations, and perhaps by detailed study of documents, flowcharts, and narrative descriptions of the system.

2. Tests of controls, some of which are illustrated in this chapter, determine whether certain of these procedures are properly designed and actually in place.

3. Before detail tests of controls are conducted, the auditor has already acquired a basic understanding of the internal control structure and has determined whether limited or extended reliance can be placed on it.

   a. If the auditor places limited reliance on the internal control structure, extensive substantive tests of financial statement assertions will be conducted.

   b. If the auditor places extended reliance on the internal control structure, restricted substantive tests of financial statement assertions will be conducted.

   (1) If detail tests of controls are performed and are acceptable, the auditor can additionally restrict the substantive tests of financial statement assertions that relate to the controls being tested.

   (2) If detail tests of controls are performed and are unacceptable, the auditor will reevaluate the nature, timing, and extent of planned substantive tests.

Appendix A to Chapter 9

Discovery Sampling for Attributes

Introduction

Chapter 9 concerns attribute sampling for the purpose of estimating the rate of deviations in the population. There is another form of attribute sampling in which the purpose is to "discover" at least one deviation if the percentage of such deviations in the population is at or above a certain level (generally very low). *Discovery sampling,* as it is popularly known, is designed to be used in the testing of critical deviations, such as fictitious payroll checks or important missing documents.

Because discovery sampling for attributes has not gained much appeal in public practice, it is not used as commonly as estimation sampling. Nevertheless, auditing students should become familiar with these techniques to increase their academic knowledge of statistical sampling.

An Example of the Methodology

The methodology for using the discovery sampling tables is similar to that employed for the estimation sampling tables. The major difference is that separate tables are used for different population sizes.

The following steps are based on the use of Table 9.1A. However, the same procedures can be followed with Table 9.1B, although different numerical answers are derived.

1. Decide what risk of overreliance is acceptable (assume 5 percent).

2. Decide what tolerable rate is acceptable at a risk of 5 percent (assume .5 percent). Normally, the rate will be lower than used in estimation sampling for attributes because the deviations are more serious.

Table 9.1A
Discovery Sampling for Attributes for Populations between 5,000 and 10,000

Required Sample Size	If the Population Deviation Rate Is:							
	.1%	*.2%*	*.3%*	*.4%*	*.5%*	*.75%*	*1%*	*2%*
	The Probability of Discovering at Least One Deviation in the Sample Is:							
50	5%	10%	14%	18%	22%	31%	40%	64%
60	6	11	17	21	26	36	45	70
70	7	13	19	25	30	41	51	76
80	8	15	21	28	33	45	55	80
90	9	17	24	30	36	49	60	84
100	10	18	26	33	40	53	64	87
120	11	21	30	38	45	60	70	91
140	13	25	35	43	51	65	76	94
160	15	28	38	48	55	70	80	96
200	18	33	45	56	64	78	87	98
240	22	39	52	62	70	84	91	99
300	26	46	60	70	78	90	95	99+
340	29	50	65	75	82	93	97	99+
400	34	56	71	81	87	95	98	99+
460	38	61	76	85	91	97	99	99+
500	40	64	79	87	92	98	99	99+
600	46	71	84	92	96	99	99+	99+
700	52	77	89	95	97	99+	99+	99+
800	57	81	92	96	98	99+	99+	99+
900	61	85	94	98	99	99+	99+	99+
1000	65	88	96	99	99	99+	99+	99+
1500	80	96	99	99+	99+	99+	99+	99+
2000	89	99	99+	99+	99+	99+	99+	99+

Note: 99+ indicates a probability of 99.5 percent or greater. Probabilities in these tables are rounded to the nearest 1 percent, Copyright © (1968) by the American Institute of Certified Public Accountants, Inc., reprinted with permission.

Table 9.1B

Discovery Sampling for Attributes for Populations between 2000 and 5000

Required Sample Size	If the Population Deviation Rate Is:							
	.3%	.4%	.5%	.6%	.8%	1%	1.5%	2%
	The Probability of Discovering at Least One Deviation in the Sample Is:							
50	14%	18%	22%	26%	33%	40%	53%	64%
60	17	21	26	30	38	45	60	70
70	19	25	30	35	43	51	66	76
80	22	28	33	38	48	56	70	80
90	24	31	37	42	52	60	75	84
100	26	33	40	46	56	64	78	87
120	31	39	46	52	62	70	84	91
140	35	43	51	57	68	76	88	94
160	39	48	56	62	73	80	91	96
200	46	56	64	71	81	87	95	98
240	52	63	71	77	86	92	98	99
300	61	71	79	84	92	96	99	99+
340	65	76	83	88	94	97	99+	99+
400	71	81	88	92	96	98	99+	99+
460	77	86	91	95	98	99	99+	99+
500	79	88	93	96	99	99	99+	99+
600	85	92	96	99	99	99+	99+	99+
700	90	95	98	99	99+	99+	99+	99+
800	93	97	99	99	99+	99+	99+	99+
900	95	98	99	99+	99+	99+	99+	99+
1000	97	99	99+	99+	99+	99+	99+	99+

Note: 99+ indicates a probability of 99.5 percent or greater. Probabilities in these tables are rounded to the nearest 1 percent.
Copyright © (1968) by the American Institute of Certified Public Accountants, Inc., reprinted with permission.

3. Refer to Table 9.1A. Look down the .5 percent column until the next highest percentage over 95 (for a 5 percent risk) is found (96). Look across that row and find the necessary sample size (answer—600).

4. Take the sample of 600. The sampling method is *without* replacement. If no deviations are found, the following statements can be made (reading from the .5 percent column to the right).

a. There is a 96 percent probability that the deviation rate in the population is less than .5 percent (or 4 percent risk that it is equal to or more than .5 percent).

b. There is a 99 percent probability that the deviation rate in the population is less than .75 percent (about a 1 percent risk that it is equal to or more than .75 percent).

c. There is a 99 + percent probability that the deviation rate in the population is less than 1 percent (about a 1 percent risk that it is equal to or more than 1 percent).

5. If an error is found, some other auditing technique should be applied. Therefore, no table of evaluation of sample results is used with this method.

The following example is part of Table 9.1A showing the route that is taken to locate the sample size for a 96 percent reliability (4 percent risk) and a .5 percent deviation rate.

Required Sample Size	Deviation Rate		
	.3%	.4%	.5%
50			
60			
600			96

Although the discovery sampling tables have limited use, a study of the numbers is helpful academically because it shows the relationships among sample size, risk, and deviation rates.

Appendix B to Chapter 9

Table of Random Numbers and Sampling Tables

This appendix contains the following:

1. Table 9.1C, which is a table of random numbers. The concept of random sampling is discussed in the body of the chapter.

Table 9.1C
Table of random numbers.

Line	(1)	(2)	(3)	(4)	(5)	(6)	(7)	(8)	(9)	(10)	(11)	(12)	(13)	(14)
							Column							
1	10480	15011	01536	02011	81647	91646	69179	14194	62590	36207	20969	99570	91291	90700
2	22368	46573	25595	85393	30995	89198	27982	53402	93965	34095	52666	19174	39615	99505
3	24130	48360	22527	97265	76393	64809	15179	24830	49340	32081	30680	19655	63348	58629
4	42167	93093	06243	61680	07856	16376	39440	53537	71341	57004	00849	74917	97758	16379
5	37570	39975	81837	16656	06121	91782	60468	81305	49684	60672	14110	06927	01263	54613
6	77921	06907	11008	42751	27756	53498	18602	70659	90655	15053	21916	81825	44394	42880
7	99562	72905	56420	69994	98872	31016	71194	18738	44013	48840	63213	21069	10634	12952
8	96301	91977	05463	07972	18876	20922	94595	56869	69014	60045	18425	84903	42508	32307
9	89579	14342	63661	10281	17453	18103	57740	84378	25331	12566	58678	44947	05585	56941
10	85475	36857	53342	53988	53060	59533	38867	62300	08158	17983	16439	11458	18593	64952
11	28918	69578	88231	33276	70997	79936	56865	05859	90106	31595	01547	85590	91610	78188
12	63553	40961	48235	03427	49626	69445	18663	72695	52180	20847	12234	90511	33703	90322
13	09429	93969	52636	92737	88974	33488	36320	17617	30015	08272	84115	27156	30613	74952
14	10365	62219	87529	85689	48237	52267	67689	93394	01511	26358	85104	20285	29975	89868
15	07119	97336	71048	08178	77233	13916	47564	81056	97735	85977	29372	74461	28551	90707
16	51085	12765	51821	51259	77452	16308	60756	92144	49442	53900	70960	63990	75601	40719
17	02368	21382	52404	60268	89368	19885	55322	44819	01188	63255	64835	44919	05944	55157
18	01011	54092	33362	94904	31273	04146	18594	29852	71585	85030	51132	01915	92747	64951
19	52162	53916	46369	58586	23216	14513	83149	98736	23495	64350	94738	17752	35156	35749
20	07056	97628	33787	09998	42698	06691	76988	13602	51851	46104	88916	19509	25625	58104
21	48663	91245	85828	14346	09172	30168	90229	04734	59193	22178	30421	61666	99904	32812
22	54164	58492	22421	74103	47070	25306	76468	26384	58151	06646	21524	15227	06909	44592
23	32639	32363	05597	24200	13363	38005	94342	28728	35806	06912	17012	64161	18296	22851
24	29334	27001	87637	87308	58731	00256	45834	15398	46557	41135	10367	07684	36188	18510
25	02488	33062	28834	07351	19731	92420	60952	61280	50001	67658	32586	86679	50720	94953
26	81525	72295	04839	96423	24878	82651	66566	14778	76797	14780	13300	87074	79666	95725
27	29676	20591	68086	26432	46901	20849	89768	81536	86645	12659	92259	57102	80428	25280
28	00742	57392	39064	66432	84673	40027	32832	61362	98947	96067	64760	64584	96096	98253
29	05366	04213	25669	26422	44407	44048	37937	63904	45766	66134	75470	66520	34693	90449
30	91921	26418	64117	94305	26766	25940	39972	22209	71500	64568	91402	42416	07844	69618
31	00582	04711	87917	77341	42206	35126	74087	99547	81817	42607	43808	76655	62028	76630
32	00725	69884	62797	56170	86324	88072	76222	36086	84637	93161	76038	65855	77919	88006
33	69011	65795	95876	55293	18988	27354	26575	08625	40801	59920	29841	80150	12777	48501
34	25976	57948	29888	80604	67917	48708	18912	82271	65424	69774	33611	54262	85963	03547
35	09763	83473	73577	12908	30883	18317	28290	35797	05998	41688	34952	37888	38917	80050
36	91567	42595	29758	30134	04024	86385	29880	99730	55536	84855	29080	09250	79656	73211
37	17955	56349	90999	49127	20044	59931	06115	20542	18059	02008	73708	83517	36103	42791
38	46503	18584	18845	49618	02304	51038	20655	58727	28168	15475	56942	53389	20562	87338
39	92157	89634	94824	78171	84610	82834	09922	25417	44137	48413	25555	21246	35509	20468
40	14577	62765	35605	81263	39667	47358	56873	56307	61607	49518	89656	20103	77490	18062
41	98427	07523	33362	64270	01638	92477	66969	98420	04880	45585	46565	04102	46880	45709
42	34914	63976	88720	82765	34476	17032	87589	40836	32427	70002	70663	88863	77775	69348
43	70060	28277	39475	46473	23219	53416	94970	25832	69975	94884	19661	72828	00102	66794
44	53976	54914	06990	67245	68350	82948	11398	42878	80287	88267	47363	46634	06541	97809
45	76072	29515	40980	07391	58745	25774	22987	80059	39911	96189	41151	14222	60697	59583
46	90725	52210	83974	29992	65831	38857	50490	83765	55657	14361	31720	57375	56228	41546
47	64364	67412	33339	31926	14883	24413	59744	92351	97473	90297	38931	04110	23726	51900
48	08962	00358	31662	25388	61642	34072	81249	35648	56891	69352	48373	45578	78547	81788
49	95012	68379	93526	70765	10592	04542	74663	54328	02349	17247	28865	14777	62730	92277
50	15664	10493	20492	38391	91132	21999	59516	81652	27195	48223	46751	22923	32261	85653

Source: Interstate Commerce Commission, *Table of 105,000 Random Decimal Digits* Washington, D.C.: Bureau of Transport, Economics and Statistics, 1949).

Table 9.1D

Determination of Sample Size—Tabular Form—One-Sided Overreliance Risk Level (10 percent)

Sample Size	0.0	.5	1.0	2.0	3.0	4.0	5.0	6.0	7.0	8.0	9.0	10.0	12.0	14.0	16.0	18.0	20.0	25.0	30.0	40.0	50.0
50	4.5		7.6		10.3		12.9		15.4			17.8	20.1	22.7	24.7	27.2	29.1		39.8	50.0	59.9
100	2.3		3.3	5.2	6.6	7.8	9.1	10.3	11.7	12.7	14.0	15.0	17.3	19.6	21.7	24.0	26.1	31.4	36.6	46.9	56.8
150	1.5			4.4		6.9		9.3		11.6		13.9	16.1	18.4	20.5	22.7	24.8		35.2	45.5	55.4
200	1.1	1.9	2.6	4.0	5.2	6.4	7.6	8.8	10.0	11.0	12.2	13.3	15.5	17.7	19.8	22.0	24.0	29.3	34.5	44.4	54.4
250	.9			3.7		6.1		8.4		10.7		12.9	15.1	17.2	19.3	21.5	23.6		33.7	43.7	53.7
300	.8		2.2	3.5	4.7	5.9	7.0	8.2	9.3	10.4	11.5	12.6	14.7	16.9	19.0	21.1	23.2	28.2	33.2	43.2	53.2
350	.7			3.3		5.7		8.0		10.2		12.3	14.5	16.7	18.8	20.9	22.8		32.8	42.8	52.8
400	.6	1.3	2.0	3.2	4.4	5.6	6.7	7.8	8.9	10.0	11.1	12.2	14.3	16.5	18.5	20.5	22.5	27.5	32.5	42.5	52.5
450	.5			3.1		5.5		7.7		9.9		12.0	14.2	16.3	18.3	20.3	22.3		32.3	42.3	52.2
500	.5		1.8	3.1	4.2	5.4	6.5	7.6	8.7	9.8	10.9	11.9	14.1	16.1	18.1	20.1	22.1	27.1	32.1	42.1	52.0
550	.4			3.0		5.3		7.5		9.7		11.8	13.9	15.9	17.9	19.9	21.9		31.9	41.9	51.9
600	.4	1.1	1.7	2.9	4.1	5.2	6.3	7.4	8.5	9.6	10.7	11.7	13.7	15.7	17.7	19.7	21.7	26.7	31.7	41.7	51.7
650	.4			2.9		5.2		7.4		9.5		11.6	13.6	15.6	17.6	19.6	21.6		31.6	41.6	51.6
700	.3		1.7	2.9	4.0	5.1	6.2	7.3	8.4	9.5	10.5	11.5	13.5	15.5	17.5	19.5	21.5	26.5	31.5	41.5	51.5
750	.3			2.8		5.1		7.3		9.4		11.4	13.4	15.4	17.4	19.4	21.4		31.4	41.4	51.4
800	.3	1.0	1.6	2.8	3.9	5.0	6.1	7.2	8.3	9.3	10.3	11.3	13.3	15.3	17.3	19.3	21.3	26.3	31.3	41.3	51.3
850	.3			2.8		5.0		7.2		9.2		11.2	13.2	15.3	17.3	19.3	21.3		31.3	41.3	51.3
900	.3		1.6	2.7	3.9	5.0	6.0	7.1	8.2	9.2	10.2	11.2	13.2	15.2	17.2	19.2	21.2	26.2	31.2	41.2	51.2
950	.2			2.7		4.9		7.1		9.1		11.1	13.1	15.1	17.1	19.1	21.1		31.1	41.1	51.1
1000	.2	.9	1.5	2.7	3.8	4.9	6.0	7.1	8.1	9.1	10.1	11.1	13.1	15.1	17.1	19.1	21.1	26.1	31.1	41.1	51.1
1500	.2		1.4	2.5	3.6	4.7	5.7	6.7	7.7	8.7	9.7	10.7	12.7	14.7	16.7	18.7	20.7	25.7	30.7	40.7	50.7
2000	.1	.8	1.3	2.5	3.5	4.5	5.5	6.5	7.5	8.5	9.5	10.5	12.5	14.5	16.5	18.5	20.5	25.5	30.5	40.6	50.6
2500	.1		1.3	2.4	3.4	4.4	5.4	6.4	7.4	8.4	9.4	10.4	12.4	14.4	16.4	18.4	20.4	25.4	30.4	40.4	50.4
3000	.1	.7	1.3	2.4	3.4	4.4	5.4	6.4	7.4	8.4	9.4	10.4	12.4	14.4	16.4	18.4	20.4	25.4	30.4	40.4	50.4
4000	.1	.7	1.2	2.3	3.3	4.3	5.3	6.3	7.3	8.3	9.3	10.3	12.3	14.3	16.3	18.3	20.3	25.3	30.3	40.3	50.3
5000	.0	.7	1.2	2.3	3.2	4.2	5.2	6.2	7.2	8.2	9.2	10.2	12.2	14.2	16.2	18.2	20.2	25.2	30.2	40.2	50.2

Note: The numbers in the first column represent sample sizes (50, 100, etc.). The numbers in the first row represent deviation rates (0.0, .5, 1.0, etc.). The rest of the numbers represent tolerable rates.

2. Table 9.1D, which is a table used to determine sample size when the risk of overreliance is 10 percent.

3. Table 9.1E, which is a table used to determine sample size when the risk of overreliance is 5 percent.

4. Table 9.1F, which is a table used to evaluate sample results for different sample sizes and risk levels.

Table 9.1E
Determination of Sample Size—Tabular Form—One-Sided Overreliance Risk Level (5 percent)

Sample Size	Tolerable Rates for Various Deviation Rates																				
	0.0	.5	1.0	2.0	3.0	4.0	5.0	6.0	7.0	8.0	9.0	10.0	12.0	14.0	16.0	18.0	20.0	25.0	30.0	40.0	50.0
50	5.8			9.1		12.1		14.8		17.4		19.9	22.3	25.1	27.0	29.6	31.6		42.4	52.6	62.4
100	3.0		4.7	6.2	7.6	8.9	10.2	11.5	13.0	14.0	15.4	16.4	18.7	21.2	23.3	25.6	27.7	33.1	38.4	48.7	56.8
150	2.0			5.1		7.7		10.2		12.6		15.0	17.3	19.6	21.7	24.0	26.1		36.7	47.0	56.6
200	1.5	2.4	3.1	4.5	5.8	7.1	8.3	9.5	10.8	11.9	13.1	14.2	16.4	18.7	20.9	23.1	25.2	30.5	35.7	45.7	55.6
250	1.2			4.2		6.7		9.1		11.4		13.7	15.9	18.1	20.3	22.4	24.6		34.8	44.8	54.7
300	1.0		2.6	3.9	5.2	6.4	7.6	8.8	10.0	11.1	12.2	13.3	15.5	17.7	19.8	22.0	24.1	29.1	34.1	44.1	54.1
350	.9			3.7		6.2		8.5		10.8		13.0	15.2	17.4	19.5	21.7	23.6		33.6	43.6	53.6
400	.7	1.6	2.3	3.6	4.8	6.0	7.2	8.3	9.5	10.6	11.7	12.8	15.0	17.2	19.2	21.2	23.2	28.2	33.2	43.2	53.2
450	.7			3.5		5.9		8.2		10.4		12.6	14.8	16.8	18.9	20.9	22.9		32.9	42.9	52.9
500	.6		2.1	3.4	4.6	5.8	6.9	8.0	9.2	10.3	11.4	12.5	14.6	16.7	18.6	20.7	22.6	27.6	32.6	42.6	52.6
550	.5			3.3		5.7		7.9		10.1		12.3	14.4	16.4	18.4	20.4	22.4		32.4	42.4	52.4
600	.5	1.3	2.0	3.2	4.4	5.6	6.7	7.8	9.0	10.0	11.2	12.2	14.2	16.2	18.2	20.2	22.2	27.2	32.2	42.2	52.2
650	.5			3.2		5.5		7.7		10.0		12.1	14.1	16.1	18.1	20.1	22.1		32.1	42.1	52.1
700	.4		1.9	3.1	4.3	5.4	6.6	7.7	8.8	9.9	10.8	11.9	13.9	15.9	17.9	19.9	21.9	26.9	31.9	41.9	51.9
750	.4			3.1		5.4		7.6		9.8		11.8	13.8	15.8	17.8	19.8	21.8		31.8	41.8	51.8
800	.4	1.1	1.8	3.0	4.2	5.3	6.4	7.5	8.7	9.7	10.7	11.7	13.7	15.7	17.7	19.7	21.7	26.7	31.7	41.7	51.7
850	.4			3.0		5.3		7.5		9.6		11.6	13.6	15.6	17.6	19.6	21.6		31.6	41.6	51.6
900	.3		1.7	3.0	4.1	5.2	6.3	7.5	8.5	9.5	10.5	11.5	13.5	15.5	17.5	19.5	21.5	26.5	31.5	41.5	51.5
950	.3			2.9		5.2		7.4		9.4		11.4	13.4	15.5	17.4	19.5	21.4		31.5	41.5	51.5
1000	.3	1.0	1.7	2.9	4.0	5.2	6.3	7.4	8.4	9.4	10.4	11.4	13.4	15.4	17.4	19.4	21.4	26.4	31.4	41.4	51.4
1500	.2		1.5	2.7	3.8	4.9	5.9	6.9	7.9	8.9	9.9	10.9	12.9	14.9	16.9	18.9	20.9	25.9	30.9	40.9	50.9
2000	.1	.8	1.4	2.6	3.7	4.7	5.7	6.7	7.7	8.7	9.7	10.7	12.7	14.7	16.7	18.7	20.7	25.7	30.7	40.7	50.7
2500	.1		1.4	2.6	3.6	4.6	5.6	6.6	7.6	8.6	9.6	10.6	12.6	14.6	16.6	18.6	20.6	25.6	30.6	40.6	50.6
3000	.1	.8	1.4	2.5	3.5	4.5	5.5	6.5	7.5	8.5	9.5	10.5	12.5	14.5	16.5	18.5	20.5	25.5	30.5	40.5	50.5
4000	.1	.7	1.3	2.4	3.4	4.4	5.4	6.4	7.4	8.4	9.4	10.4	12.4	14.4	16.4	18.4	20.4	25.4	30.4	40.4	50.4
5000	.1	.7	1.3	2.3	3.3	4.3	5.3	6.3	7.3	8.3	9.3	10.3	12.3	14.3	16.3	18.3	20.3	25.3	30.3	40.3	50.3

Note: The numbers in the first column represent sample sizes (50, 100, etc.). The numbers in the first row represent deviation rates (0.0, .5, 1.0, etc.). The rest of the numbers represent tolerable rates.

Table 9.1F
Evaluation of Sample Results

	Number of Deviations	Risk Level 10%	5%	1%		Number of Deviations	Risk Level 10%	5%	1%
Sample	0	8.80	11.29	16.82	Sample	0	1.83	2.37	3.62
Size	1	14.69	17.61	23.75	Size	1	3.08	3.74	5.19
25	2	19.91	23.10	29.59	125	2	4.20	4.95	6.55
	3	24.80	28.17	34.88		3	5.27	6.09	7.81
	4	29.47	32.96	39.79		4	6.29	7.17	9.00
Sample	0	4.50	5.82	8.80		5	7.29	8.23	10.15
Size	1	7.56	9.14	12.55		6	8.27	9.25	11.26
50	2	10.30	12.06	15.77		7	9.24	10.26	12.34
	3	12.88	14.78	18.72		8	10.19	11.25	13.40
	4	15.35	17.38	21.50		9	11.13	12.23	14.14
	5	17.76	19.88	24.15		10	12.06	13.19	15.47
	6	20.11	22.32	26.71		11	12.98	14.15	16.48
	8	24.69	27.02	31.61		12	13.89	15.09	17.47
Sample	0	3.02	3.92	5.96		13	14.80	16.03	18.45
Size	1	5.09	6.17	8.53		19	20.14	21.50	24.16
75	2	6.94	8.16	10.74	Sample	0	1.52	1.98	3.02
	3	8.69	10.01	12.78	Size	1	2.57	3.12	4.34
	4	10.38	11.79	14.70	150	2	3.51	4.14	5.49
	5	12.02	13.51	16.55		3	4.40	5.09	6.54
	6	13.62	15.18	18.34		4	5.26	6.00	7.54
	7	15.20	16.82	20.08		5	6.10	6.88	8.50
	8	16.75	18.42	21.77		6	6.92	7.74	9.44
	12	22.78	24.63	28.25		7	7.72	8.59	10.35
Sample	0	2.28	2.95	4.50		8	8.52	9.42	11.24
Size	1	3.83	4.66	6.45		9	9.31	10.24	12.12
100	2	5.23	6.16	8.14		10	10.09	11.05	12.98
	3	6.56	7.57	9.70		11	10.86	11.85	13.83
	4	7.83	8.92	11.17		12	11.62	12.64	14.67
	5	9.08	10.23	12.58		13	12.39	13.43	15.50
	6	10.29	11.50	13.95		14	13.14	14.21	16.32
	7	11.49	12.75	15.29		15	13.89	14.98	17.13
	8	12.67	13.97	16.59		16	14.64	15.75	17.94
	9	13.83	15.18	17.87		23	19.79	21.02	23.42
	10	14.99	16.37	19.13					
	11	16.13	17.55	20.37					
	15	20.61	22.15	25.18					

Table 9.1F (Continued)
Evaluation of Sample Results

	Number of Deviations	Risk Level				Number of Deviations	Risk Level		
		10%	5%	1%			10%	5%	1%
Sample	0	1.31	1.70	2.60	Sample	0	1.14	1.49	2.28
Size	1	2.20	2.68	3.73	Size	1	1.93	2.35	3.27
175	2	3.01	3.55	4.72	200	2	2.64	3.11	4.14
	3	3.78	4.37	5.63		3	3.31	3.83	4.93
	4	4.52	5.15	6.49		4	3.96	4.52	5.69
	5	5.24	5.91	7.32		5	4.59	5.18	6.42
	6	5.94	6.65	8.12		6	5.21	5.83	7.13
	7	6.63	7.38	8.91		7	5.82	6.47	7.82
	8	7.32	8.10	9.68		8	6.42	7.10	8.50
	9	8.00	8.80	10.43		9	7.01	7.72	9.16
	10	8.67	9.50	11.18		10	7.60	8.33	9.82
	11	9.33	10.19	11.91		11	8.18	8.94	10.46
	12	9.99	10.87	12.64		12	8.76	9.54	11.10
	13	10.65	11.55	13.36		13	9.34	10.14	11.73
	14	11.30	12.22	14.07		14	9.91	10.73	12.36
	15	11.95	12.89	14.77		15	10.48	11.31	12.98
	16	12.59	13.55	15.47		16	11.04	11.90	13.59
	17	13.23	14.21	16.16		17	11.61	12.48	14.20
	18	13.87	14.87	16.85		18	12.17	13.05	14.81
	27	19.51	20.64	22.84		19	12.73	13.63	15.41
						20	13.28	14.20	16.01
						21	13.84	14.77	16.60
						30	18.75	19.79	21.82

Chapter 9
Glossary of Terms

(listed in the order of appearance in the chapter, with accompanying page reference where the term is discussed)

Term	*Page in Chapter*
Test of controls a test designed to provide auditors with reasonable assurance that the internal control structure policies and procedures are properly designed and operating.	310
Deviation a departure from a prescribed internal control procedure.	312
Population the complete group of items with similar characteristics of interest from which the sample is drawn.	313
Sampling unit the characteristic being sampled, such as a document, an entry, or a document line.	313
Block sample the selection of a group of consecutive transactions.	314
Haphazard sampling a method of sample selection that has no particular pattern or conscious bias toward selecting or omitting any particular item.	314
Unrestricted random selection selection of a sample in such a way that every sampling unit in the population has an equal chance of being selected.	314
Sampling with replacement a sample selection method where as each sampling unit is selected, it is replaced in the population so that it is subject to being selected again.	315
Sampling without replacement a sample selection method where a selected sampling unit is not replaced in the population and therefore is not subject to being selected again.	315
Systematic sampling a sample selection method where sampling units are selected at fixed intervals in a population (e.g., selecting every fifth item in a population).	315
Risk of overreliance the risk that the sample results support the planned degree of reliance on the control when the true deviation rate in the population is so large as to not justify such reliance.	316

	Page in
Term	*Chapter*

Tolerable rate   the maximum rate of deviations an auditor will accept without altering planned reliance on a control.   317

Calculated estimate of the population deviation rate   the same as the sample deviation rate, the best estimate of the deviation rate in the population.   319

Attribute   a condition in the population that does or does not exist (such as a matching receiving report for an invoice or a signature on a payroll check).   324

Estimation sampling for attributes   sampling to ascertain whether an attribute does or does not exist for the purpose of estimating the rate of attribute deviations in the population.   324

Achieved tolerable rate   the tolerable rate that is based on the sample results.   327

Stop-or-go sampling   sampling in intervals; at the end of one interval, an evaluation of the sample results is made. A decision is made to stop the sampling or to proceed with another interval.   328

Discovery sampling   a type of statistical sampling in which the purpose is to "discover" at least one deviation if the percentage of such deviations in the population is at or above a certain level.   329

**Chapter 9
References**

Akresh, Abraham D., and Zuber, George R. "Exploring Statistical Sampling," *Journal of Accountancy* (February 1981), pp. 50–56.

American Institute of Certified Public Accountants. *Audit and Accounting Guide—Audit Sampling* (New York: AICPA, 1983).

American Institute of Certified Public Accountants. *Professional Standards* AU Section 350 [*SAS No. 39*]—Audit Sampling.

Warren, Carl S., Yates, Stephen V. N., and Zuber, George R. "Audit Sampling: A Practical Approach," *Journal of Accountancy* (January 1982), pp. 62–72.

Chapter 9
Review Questions

9-1.   In what way does a test of controls affect the substantive tests of financial statement assertions?

9-2.   Give two tests of controls and the purpose of these two tests of controls for each of the following:
a. Purchase controls.
b. Cash disbursement controls.
c. Payroll controls.

9-3.   What is the difference between a population and a sampling unit? Give three examples of sampling units.

9-4.   What is the difference between a block sample and a haphazard sample?

9-5.   What is the difference between unrestricted random selection and systematic sampling? What characteristic of the population could make systematic sampling unreliable?

9-6.   What is the risk of overreliance?

9-7.   What does the term *reliance* mean as it is used in planning a sample?

9-8.   What does the auditor consider when setting the tolerable rate?

9-9.   Why does the sample size increase when the expected population deviation rate increases?

9-10.   Name three guidelines to use in performing the sampling plan.

9-11.   Name the decision rules to use in evaluating sample results.

9-12.   What two matters will be decided on the basis of the results of tests of controls?

9-13.   The size of the sample in a test of controls is based on three factors. Name these three factors.

9-14.   What is the relationship between each of the following and sample size in a test of controls?
a. Tolerable rate.
b. Risk of overreliance.
c. Estimate of the population deviation rate.

9-15.   Two factors are different when a test of controls is conducted using nonstatistical or statistical sampling. Name these two factors.

9-16.   What is the difference between the planned tolerable rate and the achieved tolerable rate?

9-17.   What two decision guides are used to quantitatively evaluate the sampling results when statistical sampling is used for conducting tests of controls?

9-18.   Describe how stop-or-go sampling may be more efficient than estimation sampling for attributes when statistical sampling is used for conducting tests of controls.

9-19.   What is the purpose of discovery sampling?

9-20.   For what types of tests of controls is discovery sampling designed to be used?

Chapter 9
Objective Questions Taken from CPA Examinations

9-21.   If all other factors specified in a statistical sampling plan remain constant, changing the risk of overreliance from 10 to 5 percent would cause the required sample size to
a. Increase.
b. Remain the same.
c. Decrease.
d. Become indeterminate.

9-22.   If all other factors specified in a statistical sampling plan remain constant, changing the tolerable rate from 8 to 12 percent would cause the required sample to
a. Increase.
b. Remain the same.
c. Decrease.
d. Become indeterminate.

9-23.   If all other factors specified in a statistical sampling plan remain constant, changing the estimated deviation rate from 2 to 4 percent would cause the required sample size to
a. Increase.
b. Remain the same.
c. Decrease.
d. Become indeterminate.

9-24.   An example of estimation sampling for attributes in a test of controls would be estimating the
a. Quantity of specific inventory items.
b. Probability of losing a patent infringement case.
c. Percentage of overdue accounts receivable.
d. Dollar value of accounts receivable.

9-25.   If certain forms are *not* consecutively numbered
a. Selection of a random sample probably is *not* possible.
b. Systematic sampling may be appropriate.
c. Stratified sampling should be used.
d. Random number tables *cannot* be used.

9-26.   In estimation sampling for attributes, which one of the following must be known in order to appraise the results of the auditor's sample?
a. Estimated dollar value of the population.
b. Standard deviation of the value in the population.
c. Actual deviation rate of the attribute in the population.
d. Sample size.

9-27.   Which of the following sample selection techniques is most likely to create sample bias?
a. Systematic selection.
b. Haphazard selection.
c. Block selection.
d. Unrestricted random selection.

9-28.   The tolerable rate for tests of controls necessary to justify reliance on the internal control structure depends primarily on which of the following?
a. The cause of errors.
b. Financial statement effect of improperly functioning control.
c. The amount of any substantive errors.
d. The limit used in audits of similar clients.

9-29.   An auditor compares information on canceled checks with information contained
in the cash disbursement journal. The objective of this test is to determine that
a. Recorded cash disbursement transactions are properly authorized.
b. Proper cash purchase discounts have been recorded.
c. Cash disbursements are for goods and services actually received.
d. No discrepancies exist between the data on the checks and the data in the
journal.

9-30.   The tolerable rate of deviations for a test of controls is generally
a. Lower than the expected deviation rate in the related accounting records.
b. Higher than the expected deviation rate in the related accounting records.
c. Identical to the expected deviation rate in the related accounting records.
d. Unrelated to the expected deviation rate in the related accounting records.

9-31.   If the auditor is concerned that a population may contain exceptions, the determination of a sample size sufficient to include at least one such exception is a characteristic of
a. Discovery sampling.
b. Variables sampling.
c. Random sampling.
d. Dollar-unit sampling.

9-32.   At times a sample may indicate that the auditor's planned degree of reliance on a
given control is reasonable when, in fact, the true deviation rate does not justify
such reliance. This situation illustrates the risk of
a. Overreliance.
b. Underreliance.
c. Incorrect precision.
d. Incorrect rejection.

Items 33 and 34 are based on the following information:

The diagram below depicts the auditor's estimated deviation rate compared with
the tolerable rate, and also depicts the true population deviation rate compared
with the tolerable rate.

	True State of Population	
	Deviation Rate Exceeds Tolerable Rate	Deviation Rate Is Less Than Tolerable Rate
Auditor's Estimate Based On Sample Results		
Deviation Rate Exceeds Tolerable Rate	I.	II.
Deviation Rate Is Less Than Tolerable Rate	III.	IV.

9-33.   In which of the situations would the auditor have properly relied on internal control?
a. I.
b. II.
c. III.
d. IV.

9-34.   As a result of a test of controls, the auditor does not rely on a properly functioning control and thereby unnecessarily increases substantive testing. This is illustrated by situation.
a. I.
b. II.
c. III.
d. IV.

*9-35.   Which of the following does not have to be considered when deciding on the size of a sample for a test of controls?
a. The risk of overreliance.
b. The standard deviation of the population.
c. The tolerable rate.
d. The expected deviation rate in the population.

*Not a CPA examination question.

*9-36.   Which of the following statements is not true?
   a. There is an inverse relationship between the risk of overreliance and the sample size.
   b. There is an inverse relationship between the tolerable rate and the sample size.
   c. There is an inverse relationship between the estimated deviation rate in the population and the sample size.
   d. There is a positive relationship between the estimated deviation rate in the population and the sample size.

*9-37.   In which of the following cases are the sampling results in a test of controls most likely to be acceptable?
   a. The tolerable rate is 6 percent and the sample deviation rate is 7 percent.
   b. The tolerable rate is 6 percent and the sample deviation rate is 5 percent.
   c. The tolerable rate is 6 percent and the sample deviation rate is 2 percent.
   d. The estimate of the deviation rate in the population is 4 percent and the sample deviation rate is 5 percent.

Chapter 9
Discussion/Case Questions and Problems

9-38.   During the course of an audit engagement, Ms. Command, the senior, decided to use nonstatistical sampling (per the *SAS No. 39* guidelines) on a certain test of controls. The sampling plan included the following.

1. The tolerable rate was set at 6 percent because only a moderate effect on the financial statements would occur if the control being tested did not function properly.

2. The risk of overreliance was set at 5 percent because of the need for high assurance that the control was functioning as prescribed.

3. The estimated deviation rate in the population was set at 2 percent, based on the deviation rate found in the prior year.

Although nonstatistical sampling was used, Ms. Command computed a sample size based on numerical guidelines in the auditing literature. The performance of the test of controls was assigned to Mr. Critical, an assistant.

*Not a CPA examination question.

Mr. Critical selected and audited the sample and calculated a sample deviation rate of 2.5 percent. However, he was puzzled as to how to evaluate the sample results. He remembered reading the guidelines in the auditing literature. If the sample deviation rate is far enough below the tolerable rate, there is an acceptably low risk that the true deviation rate in the population exceeds the tolerable rate; 2.5 percent seemed to be sufficiently low to accept the sampling results.

The auditing literature, however, also suggests that the sampling results would not generally be accepted if the sample deviation rate exceeded the preliminary estimate of the deviation rate in the population (2.5 percent compared to 2 percent).

Mr. Critical took the question to Ms. Command, who seemed annoyed. Ms. Command responded by stating that the sampling results should be accepted and related substantive tests restricted.

Mr. Critical questioned whether the sampling results should be accepted if the sample deviation rate is 2.5 percent. It seemed that the "careful" course of action was to expand the substantive tests. To accept the results seemed "out of line" with guidelines in the auditing literature. Ms. Overhear, another assistant, injected an opinion. She thought that the sample should be expanded. Her reasoning was that the sample deviation rate "should be 2 percent or under" based on knowledge of the population characteristics and prior-year audits.

Required:
Evaluate the strengths and weaknesses of each person's arguments.

9-39.   Reproduced below are two sections of Table 9.1F in Appendix B (evaluation of sample results).

Table 9.1F
Extracts

	Number of Deviations	Achieved Tolerable Rates for these Risk Levels		
		10%	*5%*	*1%*
Sample	0	3.02	3.92	5.96
Size	1	5.09	6.17	8.53
75	2	6.94	8.16	10.74
	3	8.69	10.01	12.78
Sample	0	2.28	2.95	4.50
Size	1	3.83	4.66	6.45
100	2	5.23	6.16	8.14
	3	6.56	7.57	9.70

Required:

1. Explain why the achieved tolerable rates become larger as we move across the rows from left to right in each sample size block (3.02 to 3.92, etc.).

2. Explain why the achieved tolerable rates become larger as we move down the columns from top to bottom in each sample size block (3.02 to 5.09, etc.).

9-40. Using the attribute sample size and sample evaluation tables in the chapter, place a number in the blank in each of the following situations.

	A	B	C	D
Risk of overreliance	5%	10%	5%	10%
Tolerable rate	6%	8%	6%	10%
Estimated deviation rate	2%	3%	3%	5%
Sample size	—	—	—	—
Number of deviations found in the sample	2	1	3	2
Achieved tolerable rate	—	—	—	—

9-41. An auditor is applying statistical sampling for attributes to the testing of extensions on sales invoices. There are 250 invoices with an average of four sales on each invoice. The auditor uses 1,000 as the population total and classifies each extension mistake as a deviation. The auditor decides to use a 10 percent risk of overreliance, a tolerable rate of 5.2 percent, and an estimated deviation rate of 2 percent.

Assume that the following deviation condition exists in the population (the invoices are numbered 1–250; the lines are numbered 1–1,000).

Invoice No.	Line No.	Amount of Deviation	Error Results in Overstatement (O) or Understatement (U) of Sales
10	39	$ 100	U
21	81	350	O
51	202	900	O
53	220	700	O
61	240	950	O
70	291	300	U
102	410	410	U
103	413	850	O
150	600	1000	O
170	674	150	O
192	798	500	O
203	840	350	O
210	855	520	U
215	890	925	O
224	906	820	O
225	908	1000	O
231	930	800	O
250	971	900	O

Required:

a. Calculate the sample size.

b. Take the sample using random selection. Identify the numbers in the random number set with the lines 1–1,000. For example, random number 102 is line 102, and so on. If you select a line number listed in the preceding deviation chart, assume that a deviation is located.

c. Quantitatively evaluate your sample results. If you incorrectly rejected the sample results, why did this happen?

d. Would the dollar amount of the deviations you found change the evaluation of your results? Why or why not?

9-42.   Levelland, Inc., a client of your firm for several years, uses a voucher system for processing all cash disbursements, which number about 500 each month. After carefully reviewing the company's internal control structure, your firm decided to sample the vouchers for nine specific characteristics to test the operation of the voucher system against the client's representations as to the system's operation. The characteristics to be evaluated are listed on the voucher test worksheet.

Levelland, Inc. Voucher Test Worksheet—Years Ended December 31

Characteristics	Column A Estimated Deviation Rate (%)	Column B Tolerable Rate (%)	Column C Risk of Overreliance (%)	Column D Assumed Sample Size	Column E Number of Deviations Found
Invoice in agreement with purchase order or check request	1.1	3	5	460	4
Invoice in agreement with receiving report	.4	2	5	340	2
Invoice mathematically accurate—					
Extensions	1.4	3	5	1000	22
Footings	1.0	3	5	460	10
Account distributions correct	.3	2	5	340	2
Voucher correctly entered in voucher register	.5	2	5	340	1
Evidence of accounting department checks—					
Comparison of invoice with purchase order or check request	2.0	4	5	240	2
Comparison of invoice with receiving report	1.3	4	5	160	2
Proving mathematical accuracy of invoice	1.5	3	5	340	10

Required:

Assume the use of nonstatistical sampling on the nine tests. For each test, compare the sample deviation rate with the tolerable rate and explain why you would or would not accept the results of the test.

(*AICPA adapted*)

9-43.   Some auditors maintain that the extension of a sample beyond its original size when the original sample result is unsatisfactory is evidence that the auditor is abandoning objectivity. Give reasons for and against this contention.

9-44.   Examine the following list of procedures and indicate whether sampling could or could not be used with each procedure. Support your reasons.

a. Review of flowcharts.

b. Completing internal control structure questionnaires.

c. Examining payroll checks for proper date, amount, signature, and endorsement.

d. Oral inquiries of client personnel.

e. Testing calculations on sales invoices.

f. Examining purchase invoices for proper payment authorization.

9-45.   The setting of the tolerable rate for tests using sampling for attributes depends in part on the auditor's assessment of the critical nature of the potential deviations. For example, many auditors would probably consider an invoice pricing deviation to be less critical than a missing invoice. The following are lists of potential deviations in the areas of sales, payroll, and disbursements. Rank each set of deviations from "most critical" to "least critical" and justify your ranking.

Sales	*Payroll*	*Disbursements*
1. Pricing error in the sales invoice	1. Improper endorsement on the payroll check	1. Invoice not approved for payment
2. No shipping document to match the sales invoice	2. No dual signature on the payroll check	2. No cancellation stamp on paid invoice
3. No sales invoice to match the shipping document	3. Error in the gross pay calculation	3. No receiving report to match paid purchase invoice
4. Error in posting amount from sales invoice to the accounts receivable subsidiary ledger	4. Amount of the check different from the amount in the payroll register	4. Posting error from the invoice to the purchases journal
5. Making sales without prior credit approval	5. No employee receipt for disbursement of payroll in currency	5. No purchase requisition to match purchase invoice

9-46.   Jiblum, CPA, is planning to use attribute sampling to determine the degree of reliance to be placed on an audit client's internal controls over sales. Jiblum has begun to develop an outline of the main steps in the sampling plan as follows:

1. State the objective or objectives of the audit test (e.g., to test the reliability of internal control over sales).

2. Define the population (define the period covered by the test; define the completeness of the population).

3. Define the sampling unit (e.g., client copies of sales invoices).

Required:
a. What are the remaining steps in the above outline that Jiblum should include in the statistical test of sales invoices? Do not present a detailed analysis of tasks that must be performed to carry out the objectives of each step. Parenthetical examples need not be provided.
b. How does statistical methodology help the auditor to develop a satisfactory sampling plan?
(AICPA adapted)

9-47. During the review of the internal control structure of a client's system of cash disbursements, an auditor decided to test the controls by taking a sample of purchase invoices and examining them to determine whether they were properly approved for payment. Therefore, a deviation would be an examined invoice with no evidence of approval prior to payment.

The population of invoices is shown on pages 352–354. A check mark in the deviation column beside an invoice number means that no approval was indicated for that invoice and, if the auditor includes that invoice in his or her sample, a deviation will be recorded. (As we can see, there are deviations in 22 of the invoices.)

Assume that the auditor decides on a risk of overreliance of 10 percent, a tolerable rate of 8 percent, and estimates that the deviation rate in the population is 2 percent. The selected sample size is 50.

Required:

a. Assume that nonstatistical sampling is used and that a systematic sampling technique is employed. Using a one-digit number from the table of random numbers in Appendix B as a starting point (number 2 means invoice no. 02362), list the 50 invoice numbers that would be examined. Indicate how many deviations were found, the sample deviation rate, and whether you consider the sampling results to be acceptable or unacceptable. Given the deviation rate in the population, did the sampling results lead you to the correct conclusion?

b. Assume that statistical sampling is used and that the random number sampling technique is employed. Using the table of random numbers in Appendix B, list the 50 invoice numbers that would be examined. Indicate how many deviations were found, the sample deviation rate, the achieved tolerable rate, and whether you consider the sampling results to be acceptable or unacceptable. Given the deviation rate in the population, did the sampling results lead you to the correct conclusion?

The Population of Invoices

Invoice No.	Deviation (no approval)	Sample Selection	Invoice No.	Deviation (no approval)	Sample Selection
02359			02400		
60			01		
61			02		
62			03		
63			04		
64			05		
65			06	✓	
66			07		
67			08		
68	✓		09		
69			10		
70			11	✓	
71			12		
72			13		
73			14		
74			15		
75			16		
76			17		
77			18		
78			19		
79			20	✓	
80	✓		21		
81			22		
82			23		
83			24		
84			25		
85			26	✓	
86			27		
87			28		
88			29		
89			30		
90			31		
91			32		
92	✓		33		
93			34	✓	
94			35		
95			36		
96			37		
97			38		
98			39		
99			40		

The Population of Invoices (Continued)

Invoice No.	Deviation (no approval)	Sample Selection	Invoice No.	Deviation (no approval)	Sample Selection
41			83		
42			84		
43			85		
44			86		
45			87		
46			88	✔	
47			89		
48			90		
49	✔		91		
50			92		
51			93		
52			94		
53			95		
54			96	✔	
55			97		
56			98		
57			99		
58			02500		
59			01		
60			02		
61			03		
62			04		
63			05		
64	✔		06		
65			07	✔	
66			08		
67			09		
68			10		
69			11		
70			12		
71			13		
72			14		
73			15		
74			16		
75			17		
76	✔		18	✔	
77			19		
78			20		
79			21		
80			22		
81			23		
82			24		

The Population of Invoices (Continued)

Invoice No.	Deviation (no approval)	Sample Selection	Invoice No.	Deviation (no approval)	Sample Selection
25			67		
26			68		
27			69	✓	
28			70		
29			71		
30			72		
31			73		
32			74		
33			75		
34	✓		76		
35			77		
36			78		
37			79		
38			80		
39			81	✓	
40			82		
41			83		
42			84		
43			85		
44			86		
45			87		
46			88		
47			89		
48			90		
49	✓		91		
50			92		
51			93	✓	
52			94		
53			95		
54			96		
55			97		
56			98		
57			99		
58			02600	✓	
59			01		
60			02		
61	✓		03		
62			04		
63			05		
64			06		
65			07		
66			08		

Internal Control Structure in a Computer Environment

Learning Objectives   *After reading and studying the material in this chapter, the student should*

Understand the impact that computers have on internal control structures.

Be able to describe the general controls used in a computerized internal control structure.

Be able to describe the application controls used in a computerized internal control structure.

Be able to distinguish between batch processing and online processing in a computerized internal control structure.

Understand the unique internal controls that the auditor must consider when auditing minicomputer systems, microcomputer systems, and electronic funds transfer systems.

The Impact of the Computer

General Similarities and Differences

The use of computers in profit-oriented companies began in the early 1950s. Their accounting use was so limited in those early days that auditors paid little attention to them. In the late 1950s and early 1960s, increased use of computers stimulated the publication of numerous books and articles on new audit tools that should be developed to meet the challenge of different systems. As time passed, however, it became apparent that much of auditors' traditional work remained unchanged.

Today, it is generally acknowledged that the audit of financial statements compiled from computer-generated records is in many ways similar to, and different from, the audit of financial statements compiled from manually created documents. Some general similarities and differences are shown below.

Similarities	*Differences*
1. No new auditing standards are required.	1. Some new auditing procedures are used.
2. The basic elements of a strong internal control structure are the same.	2. There are differences in the techniques of maintaining a strong internal control structure.
3. The major purpose of obtaining an understanding of the internal control structure and assessing the control risk is to determine whether substantive tests will be extensive or will be restricted.	3. There is some difference in the manner in which an understanding of the internal control structure is acquired.

Different Control Techniques

Computers may be programmed to detect many data processing errors. In this sense, they have a distinct advantage over manual processing. But computer systems also require that data be converted to machine-readable form before it is processed. Since computers process input exactly as prepared, it is essential that controls exist to ensure that this input is complete, correct, and valid.

Magnetic tape, magnetic disk, and other computer data files are generally faster, more efficient, and more durable than data files used in manual processing. At the same time, however, it may be easier for unauthorized persons to access and alter such files. For this reason, access to data files should be controlled and tight security measures used.

The Internal Auditing Function in a Computer System

In many organizations, there is a trend toward separate internal computer audit staffs. This type of specialization allows internal auditors to acquire an extensive knowledge of the computer system and to test it regularly.

Because of this trend, the external auditor can often place substantial reliance on the work of internal auditors. Such reliance, of course, must be in accord with the pronouncements of *SAS No. 9* regarding the external auditor's supervision and review of the internal auditor's work.

Other Distinctions Between Computer Processing and Manual Processing

A number of other control procedures vary when computer systems are used rather than manual processing.

1. The traditional audit trails that are familiar in manual systems may exist in computer systems only for a short time in computer-readable form. An *audit*

trail can be described as a chain of evidence provided through coding, cross-references, and documentation connecting account balances and other summary results with orginal transactions and calculations. Here is an example of an audit trail in a manual system.

In a computer system, the cash receipts data are transformed into machine-readable form soon after the transaction occurs. In certain types of computer systems, the data may be transcribed from a remittance advice (a form of source document) to a magnetic tape storage device. The data appear as output in the form of a computer printout, representing a combination of a sales journal and a cash receipts journal. The general ledger data may be stored on magnetic tape. In other computer systems, the data are transformed into machine-readable form and processed into a general ledger entry as the cash receipts transaction occurs.

2. Computer programming instructions process similar transactions in the same way. Random error associated with manual processing does not exist. However, incorrect programming instructions will always result in incorrect processing of transactions. In auditing computer systems, auditors usually pay more attention to the accuracy and validity of the programming process than to casual errors normally created in a manual system.

3. Procedures performed by separate individuals in a manual system are often performed by one person in a computer system. Therefore, the segregation of duties control that auditors rely on in manual systems simply does not exist in its traditional form when a computer system is used. Other segregation of duties (such as within the computer processing activities) must be substituted for the traditional ones.

4. Data stored in machine-readable rather than visible form can be inappropriately accessed or altered. Because the data are processed with a relatively small amount of human involvement, the potential for observing errors or irregularities is less than in a manual system.

5. A computer system can produce a wide variety of information used by management to more effectively supervise the operations of the company. A wider variety of information is also available to the auditor, analytical information being a prime example.

6. In a manual system, transactions are usually authorized before they are executed and recorded. Checks to vendors and write-offs of accounts receivable are examples. In a computer system, some transactions are automatically executed and recorded without explicit management authorization. In accepting the design of the computer system, management implicitly grants its authorization to these transactions. For instance, accounts receivable may be automatically written off if the customer's credit status reaches a certain point. In approving the

computer program that executes and records this write-off, management authorizes this type of transaction.

In the remainder of this chapter, we will describe controls in a computer system that are designed to prevent or detect errors or irregularities caused by some of these problems. In Chapter 11, we will discuss methods used to review and evaluate these controls. Some of these methods are similar to those used to review and evaluate controls in a manual system; other methods are unique to the audit of controls in a computer system.

Computer Controls

Sometimes organizations find it convenient to divide computer controls into two groups—general controls and application controls. Such a division may help the auditor organize the review process more efficiently. The auditor should recognize, however, that the objective of an internal control structure is the same as that described in Chapters 7 and 8.

General controls are defined as follows:

1. The plan of organization and operation of the EDP activity.

2. The procedures for documenting, reviewing, testing, and approving systems or programs and changes thereto.

3. Controls built into the equipment by the manufacturer (commonly referred to as ''hardware'' controls).

4. Controls over access to equipment and data files.

5. Other data and procedural controls that affect overall EDP operations.

Application controls are more specific. Their function is to provide reasonable assurance that the recording, processing, and reporting of specific data processing applications (e.g., credit sales and cash receipts) are properly performed.

For discussion, these controls are divided into the following categories.[1]

General Controls

1. Organization and operation controls.

2. Systems development and documentation controls.

---

[1] *Audit and Accounting Guide—The Auditor's Study and Evaluation of Internal Control in EDP Systems* (New York, AICPA, 1977).

3. Hardware and systems software controls.

4. Access controls.

5. Data and procedural controls.

Application Controls

1. Input controls.

2. Processing controls.

3. Output controls.

In the remainder of this section we will discuss these controls. The auditor's understanding of the internal control structure will be taken up in Chapter 11.

Organization and Operation Controls

Organization and operation controls consist of the general plan designed to effect a smooth operation, accomplish the assigned tasks, and minimize the opportunity for errors or irregularities in the system. Some examples, such as proper job segregation, periodic rotation of duties, and effective operational supervision, are conceptually the same as those used in a manual system. Others, such as proper scheduling of computer operations and proper control over program changes, are unique to computer systems.

Different Job Responsibilities

One obvious difference in the organization and operation controls of a computer system is the functions performed by personnel who operate the system. Although there is much diversity in practice, a computer system may involve the following positions.

1. Systems analyst

   a. Reviews potential applications of data processing and works with users in defining information and control requirements.

   b. Designs and reviews the documentation for computerized systems.

   c. Designs the various computerized and manual controls.

   d. Monitors the program maintenance function and maintains systems documentation.

2. Programmer

  a. Codes (not designs systems for) various computerized applications.

  b. Codes the computer procedures for programmed controls.

  c. Maintains the computer programs by coding, testing, and debugging modifications.

3. Machine operator

  a. Operates equipment and in general maintains custody of the computer hardware.

  b. Provides physical security over data and program files that are in an operational mode.

4. Control group (this function is often performed in the various user departments such as shipping, payroll, and accounts payable)

  a. Monitors manual input from the user areas. This position includes the origination or comparison of control totals.

  b. Monitors computer output and reconciles this output with the manual input, including control totals.

5. Input data operator (this function is often performed in the various user departments such as shipping, payroll, and accounts payable)

  a. Converts manual input to machine-readable form.

  b. Verifies the machine-readable data produced from manual input.

6. Internal auditor (not a position in a computer department)

  a. Provides assistance in defining system controls.

  b. Performs audit functions to ensure integrity and continuity of system.

No one of the listed groups should have direct and complete access to the record-keeping system. The systems analysts and programmers should have no control over the day-to-day computer operations. The machine operator's knowledge of detailed programs and records should not be comprehensive. Output controls should be maintained by the control group or user department.

Unique Computer Control Problems

In addition to different job responsibilities, unique control problems exist in a computer system. To visualize these problems clearly, we should review some elements of a manual system.

Assume that credits are posted to the customers' ledger accounts by individuals in one department, and cash is deposited in the bank by an individual in another department. Thus, a proper segregation of duties exists, because the functions of cash recording and cash custody are separated.

What comparable control features should exist in a computer system? First, it is important to understand that the basic objective of segregation of duties is equally applicable here. But the segregation is carried out differently from that in a manual system. The "posting" of credits to customer ledger accounts is accomplished through computer programs under the control of operators and is based on computer instructions coded by programmers. In many cases, the cash deposits are processed in the same manner as they are in a manual system. Thus, it would seem that a proper segregation of duties requires that neither programmers nor machine operators have access to cash; this is a logical assumption, and such segregation is common.

But access to assets is a different problem in computerized installations, because such access can exist *without* the individuals maintaining *physical* contact with the items. For example, computer personnel have access to assets if the computer activity includes the preparation or processing of documents that lead to the use or disposition of the assets. Computer personnel have direct access to cash if the computer activity includes the preparation and signing of disbursement checks. Sometimes access by computer personnel to assets may not be readily apparent because the access is indirect. For example, computers may generate payment orders authorizing issuance of checks, shipping orders authorizing release of inventory, or authorization of other transactions.

What can be done to improve the internal control structure when computer personnel have this type of indirect access to assets? Several steps are advisable.

1. Access to computer programs should be limited so that only authorized changes can be made. Normally, the computer programmers should not be allowed to make changes without proper approval (a program change control).

2. The programmers themselves should not operate the computers.

3. All programs should be documented with flowcharts, listings of the programs, and input, output, and file descriptions. Periodic runs should be made by independent personnel to ensure that the actual programs are processing as described in the listings and flowcharts.

4. Errors or exceptions that are detected by the computer should be communicated to the appropriate person who has the responsibility to correct them. Operator errors are normally detected by the system aborting, a message printed by the computer, or the reconciliation of controls by the control group. Routine errors or exceptions resulting from conditions tested by the computer programs should be reported to the control group for disposition. Errors resulting from hardware or vendor software failures should be reported to management.

5. Records should be kept of all processing actions involving the computer to lower the probability of unauthorized operation and to provide a documented log for management.

6. Job rotation among computer operators is desirable. If one operator were running a deliberately altered program, collusion might be necessary to continue the irregularity.

Some of these safeguards (job rotation, for example) are also applicable to manual systems. The techniques for carrying out these safeguards are different in a computer system, however.

The basic objective of comparing recorded accountability with a physical count of assets does not change when a computer system is used. The major difference is that the recorded accountability is produced by the computer and thus is more reliable *if* proper control measures are followed. For example, one can assume that the cash receipts tallied in the mail room are posted accurately both to the customer ledger accounts and to the accounts receivable control account if prescribed procedures are followed.

Other Considerations for Organization and Operation Controls

Segregation between Computer Department and Users   To the extent possible, there should be a segregation of functions between the computer department and users of computer processed data. Specifically, those who perform computer functions should not

1. Authorize transactions.

2. Correct errors in transactions.

3. Initiate the preparation of data.

4. Have custody or control over assets.

5. Be able to change the controls.

6. Originate changes in master files (such as files for accounts receivable customers).[2]

Controls that separate the authorizing and recording of transactions are valid both for manual and computer processing. If we think of users as people who could authorize transactions and members of the computer department as people who record transactions, the reason for separation of these duties becomes more obvious.

In smaller companies, the computer function may be a part of a user department. Also, the increasing use of minicomputers and microcomputers have made the separation of use of data and computer processing of data more difficult.

Segregation of Functions within the Computer Department   To the extent possible, the following policies should be followed within the computer department:

1. Separate people should write the programs and operate the equipment.

2. An independent control group should exist.

3. Machine operators should be rotated.

4. Vacations for all employees should be required.

Reasons for these separate functions have been explained in previous sections. Basically, the internal control structure should minimize the possibility of unauthorized and undetected modifications in the computer programs.

Consequences of Weak Organization and Operation Controls

Organization and operations controls are so vital that major weaknesses could cause the auditor to have serious reservations about the reliability of results produced by the system. A programmer who operates the computer and has unlimited access to computer files might be in a position to commit and conceal a variety of irregularities. Strong controls in other areas may not completely compensate for this weakness. For these reasons, the auditor should consider the strength of organization and operation controls when reviewing other controls, particularly application controls.

[2]Gordon B. Davis, Donald L. Adams, and Carol A. Schaller, *Auditing and EDP,* 2nd ed. (New York, AICPA, 1983).

Systems Development and Documentation Controls

Documentation controls consist of procedures designed to ensure the integrity of computer storage devices and systems documentation. Some examples follow.

1. Data are stored magnetically on tapes or disks. Since the information on the tape or disk will be machine-read, there is always the possibility that an incorrect file will be processed. To detect this, a magnetized internal label corresponding to the external label should be the first record of the file so that it can be properly identified by the computer during initial file processing.

2. The grandfather-father-son principle can be used with magnetic tape so that if one tape becomes unreadable, a backup tape will be available. The transaction tape of a processing run is called the ''father,'' the output master tape is called the ''son,'' and the master tape produced by the previous updating is called the ''grandfather.''

3. Access to computer documentation should be controlled, with records maintained of each usage and each modification.

4. Nonresident files should be stored in a secure, fireproof storage area under the strict control of a person charged with these responsibilities—copies of critical files should be stored at off-site locations.

5. Computer programs stored on magnetic devices should be duplicated with a securely stored backup file, and strict control over changes should be followed.

In addition, computer documentation should consist of at least the following items.

1. Program listing—a listing of a program that shows steps written by the programmer in the specific computer language.

2. Error listing—a list of all types of errors a program has been designed to detect, the probable causes of such errors, and the most likely necessary corrective actions. This listing is prepared by the programmer when he or she writes the program.

3. Log—a listing of the detail of all computer runs. The logs include (a) errors detected and printed out by the computer; (b) everything pertinent to a machine run, such as identification of the run, setup actions taken, input–output files used, and actions taken by the operator each time the machine

halted; (c) an accounting of all machine time, including productive time, idle time, rerun time, and so forth; and (d) a listing of all tapes used, showing date, time, and files processed.

4. Record layout—a listing of all fields of information in a record and how they are arranged in the record. For example, each set of meaningful columns may be a field.

5. Flowcharts (discussed and illustrated in the next four subsections).

Flowcharts

Flowcharts are diagrams of sequence, data flow, and processing logic in information processing. They can be used to describe the proposed design of a computer application and to document the completed application itself. Auditors often find flowcharts useful for documenting controls about which they are obtaining an understanding.

Flowcharts are generally divided into two categories.[3]

1. A *systems flowchart* describes the sequence of major processing operations (both manual and computer) and the data flow to and from the files used in processing. This type of flowchart is an overview of the system.

2. A *program flowchart* describes the sequence of operations and logic in a computer program. This type of flowchart shows the detail of computer processing referenced in a systems flowchart.

Illustration of a Systems Flowchart

Figure 10.1 on pages 366–367 is an example of a systems flowchart for the processing of credit sales, noncash credits, and cash receipts on account. It is very general and simply shows the processing operations and flow of data from source document to computer-generated output. The application controls used in a system of this type are omitted in order to concentrate on the data flows. Here is a description of the flowchart. (A more detailed description of this flowchart is given in Question 10-44 in the end-of-chapter Discussion Questions):

1. Data from sales invoices, credit memos, and remittance advices (all in manual form) are entered at a terminal in the respective departments and recorded on a transactions tape (in magnetic tape form).

2. A *computer edit program* checks the data on the transactions tape for accuracy, validity, reasonableness, and completeness. Exception reports are printed.

[3] Ibid., p. 345.

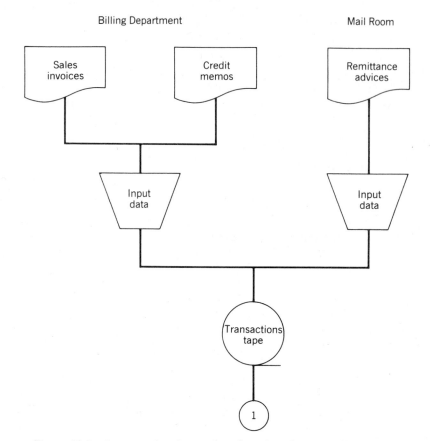

Figure 10.1   An example of a systems flowchart for a computer system

3. A computer update program takes data from the edited transactions tape and the master file and generates an updated master file, a printed transaction register, and printed exception reports.

Note that two program flowcharts are written for the two computer processing steps.

Partial Illustration of a Program Flowchart

Figure 10.2 is a partial example of a program flowchart for the computer edit program shown in the systems flowchart. A more comprehensive example of this flowchart is illustrated in Question 10-45 in the end-of-chapter Discussion Questions.

The computer program steps illustrated in this flowchart are as follows:

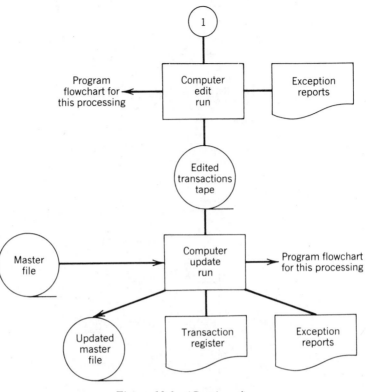

Figure 10.1   (Continued)

1. Read a record on the transactions tape. A record is a charge sale, a noncash credit, or a cash receipt on account.

2. Determine whether the customer number field is greater than zero. Print an error message if the field is zero.

3. The same as in Step 2 for posting source numbers on the record.

4. Check the price for reasonableness on a charge sale record; print an error message if the price is over an established limit.

5. Check the total amount of the sale on a charge sale record and print an error message if the price multiplied by the number of items on the record does not equal the amount.

6. Test to see whether all records have been processed; if they have, certain totals are printed; if not, another record is read.

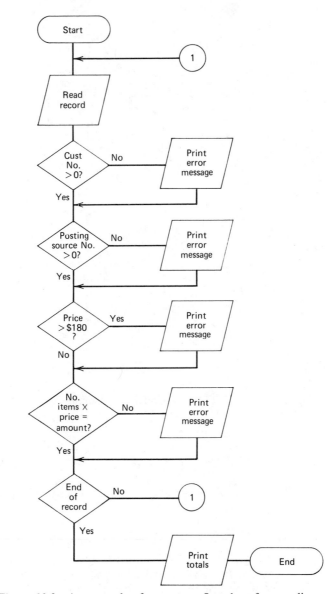

Figure 10.2   An example of a program flowchart for an edit program.

Note that a program flowchart usually contains a number of decisions. The computer makes comparisons and takes alternative procedure routes, depending on the results of the comparisons.

Value of Flowcharts

Auditors do not always use flowcharts to review documentation of a computer system; auditing standards do not require this. But a systems flowchart can be a useful tool for understanding the overall processing flow of a computerized credit sales, purchases, or payroll system. Auditors should probably use systems flowcharts unless alternative documentation is available to aid them in obtaining a reliable overview of the processing flows in a computer system.

Program flowcharts are not as popular as they once were for designing computer program logic. Program flowcharts for complex applications can be time-consuming to prepare and difficult to read. Flowcharts can be useful, however, for documenting the logic of short computer programs or for part of a larger computer program. They are also useful as a device for identifying the controls being tested by a computer program (our reason for illustrating program flowcharts). There is a trend toward using structured computer programs as a substitute for program flowcharts. This trend may continue.

Hardware and System Software Controls

These controls are built into the equipment itself, in contrast with processing or programming controls that make use of computer programs. There are a number of such controls, one of which is explained below.

Parity Check   This is an internal computer check against malfunction in the machine's movement of data. For example, assume that the internal storage of a computer consists of "bits" that are magnetized positively to represent the number 1 and are magnetized negatively to represent the number zero. This binary digit characterization is shown with an illustration of 1s and zeros.

Parity check bit	0	0	1	1
Bits representing	0	1	0	0
numbers, letters,	0	0	1	1
and other characters	0	0	1	0
	1	0	0	1

Notice that the parity check bit is magnetized zero if all other bits have an odd number of 1s, and 1 if all other bits have an even number of 1s. In effect, this is an odd parity check system (there can also be even parity check systems), so that in normal functioning all combinations of bits have an odd number of magnetized 1s. If a malfunction occurs so that zeros are changed to 1s or vice versa and an even number of 1s is created, the machine signals an error.

Systems Software   It is important that the integrity of a systems program, such as a compiler, be maintained. There should be a formal procedure for requesting, authorizing, and approving all changes to systems programs.

If systems software does not function properly, the computer programs will not process data accurately. This inaccuracy in data processing could affect the degree of reliance that the auditor places on the system's processing and output.

Access Controls

Access controls are designed to help prevent or detect deliberate or accidental errors caused by (1) improper use or manipulation of data files, (2) unauthorized or incorrect use of a computer program, or (3) improper use of computer resources or a combination of these. In some ways, these controls are similar to the systems development and documentation controls. Access controls, however, emphasize ways to prevent or detect improper or incorrect use of computer resources.

A number of individual controls have been suggested to implement the broad objective of access controls. Here are some of them.

1. Access to program documentation should be limited to those persons who require it in the performance of their duties. Unlimited access to program documentation could result in unauthorized changes to computer programs and data files. Placing specific people in charge of the documentation and maintaining logs of program and data use are some ways to prevent improper or incorrect program changes.

2. Access to data files and programs should be limited to those individuals authorized to process or maintain particular systems. Data files should be restricted to computer operators; computer program documentation should be restricted to people authorized to make modifications to programs.

3. Access to computer hardware should be limited to computer operators. Physical security devices can be used to partially implement this control. In addition, reviews of utilization reports and console logs can be made on a regular basis.

In general, access controls are simply sets of operating procedures designed to prevent unauthorized modifications to data files and programs or misuse of computer hardware. Weaknesses in these controls affect the integrity of the entire computer system. Such weaknesses should be considered when reviewing related application controls.

Data and Procedural Controls

Data and procedural controls provide a framework for controlling daily operations and establishing safeguards against processing errors. They are designed to ensure prompt and accurate processing of data. Although there is some duplication between data and procedural controls and other general controls, some procedures need to be discussed separately.

1. A control function of some type should

   a. Ensure that all authorized data are accurately processed.

   b. Follow up on errors detected during processing and ascertain that transactions with errors are corrected and resubmitted by the proper party.

   c. Verify the proper distribution of output.

   Obviously, these tasks are very important and should be performed by either user departments or an independent group within the computer department. If this control function is assigned to a group within the computer department, it is vitally important that this group be organizationally independent of systems analysis, programming, and machine operations. Otherwise, there will be an improper segregation of duties that could affect a number of other controls. A control group of the type discussed earlier in the chapter would be appropriate.

2. There should be a written manual of systems and procedures for all computer operations. This manual should provide for management's general or specific authorizations to process transactions. For example, if management authorizes write-offs of customer accounts that are outstanding for more than 120 days, this policy should be in the systems and procedures manual so that computer personnel will follow this authorization in processing transactions.

3. Internal auditors or some other independent group within the organization should review and evaluate proposed systems at critical stages of development.

4. Internal auditors or some other independent group within the organization should review and test computer processing activities (such as computer programs).

Like other general controls, data and procedural controls are important to the auditor's reliance on computer processing. This processing, in turn, produces results used to prepare financial statements. Therefore, data and procedural controls relate directly to application controls and should be considered when reviewing them.

Commentary on General Controls

It should be apparent that general controls must be in place for application controls to be effective. It would be of little benefit to the company to have computer programs that edit input data for accuracy, validity, and completeness if these same computer programs could be improperly altered by a variety of personnel. Likewise, it would be of limited benefit to the company to have verification of input data if verification was performed by the same personnel who authorized the transactions.

In studying application controls in the next sections of the chapter, remember that these controls can be effective only if they are backed up by effective general controls.

Input, Processing, and Output Controls

Application controls have been defined as follows.

Input controls are designed to provide reasonable assurance that data received for processing by computers have been properly authorized, converted into machine sensible form and identified, and that data (including data transmitted over communication lines) have not been lost, suppressed, added, duplicated, or otherwise improperly changed. . . .

Processing controls are designed to provide reasonable assurance that electronic data processing has been performed as intended for the particular application. . . .

Output controls are designed to assure the accuracy of the processing result (such as account listings or displays, reports, magnetic files, invoices, or disbursement checks) and to assure that only authorized personnel receive the output.

Input and Output Control Terms

1. *Batch control*   This is a technique to help ensure that data flowing through the system are complete and accurate. At an early point in the system, independent totals of documents are accumulated by a unit of the company, such as a control group, and are later matched against totals derived from the processing of the same documents by the computer department. The three most common types of batch totals are the following:

a. Control total—usually a meaningful dollar total such as total charge sales.

b. Hash total—a total that need not have any significance other than as a batch total. The total of customer account numbers is an example.

c. Record count—a count of the number of documents or transactions processed.

The three types of batch totals (control total, hash total, and record count) are illustrated in the following table.

If the Following Receipts Were Processed on a Given Day	Customer Number	Customer Name	Amount
	0053	Leven Bros.	$ 590.00
	0007	Alpha	3,525.00
	0056	Wolsey	480.00
	0081	Eastgate	347.00
	0036	Keller-Goodman	480.00
	0012	Gamma	5,210.00
	0043	Bart Bros.	288.00
	0008	Griffin	750.00
	0057	Cardwell	1,020.00
	0063	Mann's	2,820.00
The control total would be			$15,510.00
The hash total would be	416 (the sum of customer numbers)		
The record count would be		10 (the number of documents)	

2. *Check digit*   An extra digit of an identification number that is algebraically computed from the other digits and serves to detect certain types of data transmission or conversion errors.

Processing Control Terms   Processing controls are program steps to ascertain that predetermined conditions will be detected and certain types of errors in the input records will be detected when computer processing occurs. The major categories are as follows:

1. *Completeness test*   A test to ascertain that all information fields are complete.

2. *Validation test*   A test to ascertain that all information fields contain valid data. A dollar amount field should not contain alphabetic characters, for example.

3. *Sequence test*   A test to ascertain that data being processed are in the correct sequence.

4. *Limit or reasonableness test*   A matching of certain data in the input records being processed against a predetermined limit in the computer program. The purpose is to detect data above or below this limit. For example,

number of hours worked falling outside certain upper and lower limits would be listed for investigation.

Discussion of Input Controls

As indicated in the previous section, input controls are designed to provide reasonable assurance that computer input is entered into the computer system accurately and completely. In particular, the following four types of input transactions need to be controlled.

1. *Transactions entered into the system.* Transactions of this type often represent the largest volume of activity, and, therefore, can generate the largest number of errors. Inventory purchases and merchandise sales are prime examples.

2. *Transactions that update or maintain files.* Examples are changes of credit status on accounts receivable master files and changes in inventory purchase prices on master files for pricing inventory. Failure to properly update files can have far-reaching effects on the reliability of the accounting records. In the first example, the effect could be an understated allowance for doubtful accounts because of sales to poor credit risks. In the second example, the effect could be a materially misstated inventory account because of incorrect pricing of inventory items.

3. *Transactions that inquire into the status of records on computer files.* An inquiry, in itself, does not change a file. However an inquiry that produces an incorrect response about a record in a file could result in an incorrect decision concerning a transaction. If an inquiry into the credit status of a customer produces incorrect information, an incorrect decision to extend credit might be made.

4. *Transactions that correct errors made in previously entered transactions.* An example is a transaction to change an expenditure from a fixed-asset addition to repairs expense. Correction of an error is often more complex than the original transaction and, if not handled properly, can create additional errors.

There are other types of input transactions, but control over these is particularly important because of their volume, complexity, or potential to materially misstate the financial statements. As we discuss individual input controls, remember that their purpose is to prevent or detect errors in transactions of the type described here.

Individual Input Controls

Only transactions that have management's general or specific authorization should be accepted for processing by the computer department. If a transaction is supported by a document, some evidence of approval is needed. Time cards and purchase invoices are examples. If a transaction is entered without a supporting document, a terminal user identification or some other means of authorization should be used. The procedure of requiring authorization for transactions is conceptually no different in computerized than in manual processing. In a computer system, however, unauthorized input may be harder to trace and correct.

Conversion of data into machine-readable form should be controlled. The use of control totals, hash totals, and record counts will help to detect errors made when data from source documents are transferred to magnetic tape, or some other device that can be read by a computer. When data are entered directly into a computer storage device through a terminal, a computer edit program will help to detect errors.

Movement of data between one processing step and another, or between departments, should be controlled. When data are moved, they can be lost, added, or altered. Control totals, hash totals, and record counts are also helpful here.

Discussion of Processing Controls

Processing controls are sometimes called programming controls. They consist of computer application programs that read the input data, test it for certain types of errors, and print out messages if such errors are found in the data. These computer programs also check for certain error conditions in files as updating runs are made.

In general, processing controls are designed to prevent or detect the following types of errors:

1. Incomplete or duplicate processing of input transactions.

2. Processing and updating of the wrong files.

3. Processing of illogical, incomplete, or unreasonable input.

4. Loss or distortion of data during processing.

Processing controls can also be used in manual processing by reviewing the source documents, journals, and other material that comprise the transaction trail. In a manual system, however, these controls would have to be applied without the aid of the computer, which would be very tedious. Therefore, manual systems usually depend on other means to accomplish what the computer can accomplish in a computer system by checking detailed items of every input transaction.

Individual Processing Controls

Control totals should be produced at an early point in the application by originators of source documents or by a control group. They should not be forwarded to the computer department. The computer then produces its own set of control totals; an independent group (the control group, for example) reconciles the two sets of totals.

Limit and reasonableness checks should be incorporated into the computer programs that edit the input data for errors. In this application, the computer program checks the input data for illogical conditions that should not exist. Some examples are 120 hours on a weekly time card, inventory quantity reduced to a negative value, an unusually large check issued to a small-volume vendor, or acceptance of a credit sale for a closed account. The logic tests contained in a computer program could include the following:

1. Comparison of data to a limit.

2. Test of data for illogical amounts in data fields.

3. Test for alphabetic data in a numeric field, or vice versa.

4. Test of logical relationships between fields.

Discussion of Output Controls

Output controls are designed to ensure that (1) the processing results are accurate and (2) only authorized personnel receive the output. A control group may be given the responsibility for implementing this control. They see that input data with errors are returned to the original source, properly corrected, and resubmitted. A control group reconciles control totals generated by the computer with the same totals originated at an earlier point in this system. Finally, the control group sees that output reports are given to the appropriate personnel. As can easily be seen, output controls are closely related to input and processing controls.

Individual Output Controls

Some examples of individual output controls include the following:

1. Output control totals should be reconciled with input and processing controls.

2. Output should be scanned and tested by comparison to original source documents.

3. Output should be distributed only to authorized users.

Overall Controls

In addition, the computerized system should have this overall control.

	Amounts	*File*	
	Beginning balance	from	Master file
Plus	Today's input	from	Transaction file
Minus/plus	Errors/rejects	from	Edit file
Plus	Internally generated amounts, such as late charge, should equal ending balance, which becomes tomorrow's *beginning* balance	from	Master file

Note: The master file should also have a computer-generated record count (in and out), as well as a control total(s) over selected dollar amount(s).

Difference Between Batch Processing and Online Processing

The systems flowchart illustrated in Figure 10.1 is an example of *batch processing*. A review of that flowchart shows that source documents are created when the charge sales, noncash credits, and cash receipts transactions occur. Data from these source documents are periodically transferred to magnetic tape. After the data on the tape (transactions tape) are edited, a periodic computer processing is performed that creates an updated accounts receivable master file, as well as other output. Thus, a batch processing system is sometimes called a method of periodic preparation and periodic processing.

If there is no need for frequent inquiry of a record, batch processing can be a feasible and relatively inexpensive method of entering and processing transactions for some applications. The sales and accounts receivable application shown in the flowchart assumes that periodic updating of the accounts receivable master file is sufficient. There is no need to know a customer's balance immediately after a transaction is executed.

Online processing (to be illustrated in the next section) does not require that data from source documents be transferred to machine-readable form before computer processing takes place. In fact, it is not necessary that a source document be created when an online system is used (though one may be created). When the transaction occurs, such as a charge sale, the data are entered through a terminal into the permanent record, often maintained on magnetic disk. A record inquiry can be made at any time.

In the sales and accounts receivable application illustrated in the next section (Figure 10.3), customers may be given the balance in their account immediately after a charge sale, noncash credit, or cash receipts transaction is entered. For this reason, an online processing system is sometimes called a method of terminal entry and immediate processing.

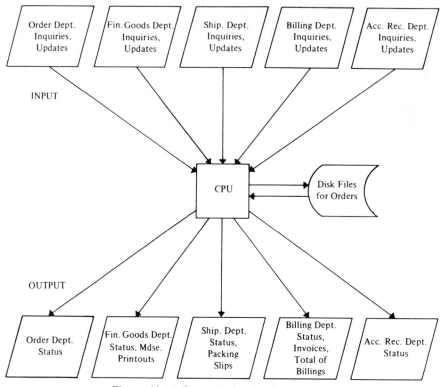

Figure 10.3 Computerized-online system.

Controls in Online Systems

Some Differences Between Batch and Online Controls

Although the concepts discussed in the section on application controls are based on a batch-processing system, many of the concepts are equally applicable to online systems. Separation of duties is still important, program changes should be approved, and independent groups should periodically test programs.

However, the different structure of online systems calls for a change in the emphasis placed on some controls. For instance, it would be more important to limit access to terminals in an online system than to restrict use of the key to tape machine in a batch-processing system. An unauthorized tape record has more chances to be detected before the data on the record enter the computer files. Machine verification and preliminary edit programs are examples of checkpoints. But with the exception of edit programs designed to reject certain types of improper input, these checkpoints may be lacking in an online system. Therefore, it is important that access to computer terminals be considerably restricted.

A hypothetical illustration of how an online system might function is shown in Figure 10.3. Each department has a terminal with direct access to the CPU and the magnetic disk storage files so that inquiries can be made on the status of customer invoices and orders; a terminal with a display screen shows these data. In addition, updates can be made to a customer's account balance directly from the accounts receivable department. Because disk storage is used, random access processing can be employed, making it unnecessary to process records in sequence.

Types of Online Systems

Actually, an online system could be one of three types.

1. Online inquiry, batch data entry, and batch file updating.

2. Online inquiry, online data entry, and batch file updating.

3. Online inquiry, online data entry, and online file updating (illustrated in the computerized-online system in Figure 10.3).

The first type limits the use of the terminals to inquiry of the status of an account or some other information such as reservations. The second type permits status inquiries and entry of transactions, but master files are updated by a batch method (such as in some department stores). The third type permits inquiry and the file is updated as the transactions are entered. The third type is the most complex system of the three, and also requires the most extensive controls because of the possibility of erroneous or unauthorized file alterations.

Appropriate Controls for the Online System

For the first type of online system (inquiry only), the traditional batch-processing methods are appropriate. In addition, access to the terminal should be controlled through use of periodically changed passwords. Unsuccessful attempts to access the system should be monitored.

For the second type (inquiry and entry), the traditional batch-processing methods are also appropriate. In addition to password and monitoring controls, this type of system should do the following:

1. Permit terminal operators only to enter or recall data. No terminal operator should have access to files or programs.

2. Contain appropriate edit steps in the computer programs so that unauthorized or improper transactions are rejected. Control totals of transactions should also be a part of the computer programs. These control totals could be compared with similar totals generated when files are updated.

For the third type (inquiry, entry, and updating), batch control methods are not appropriate. To create an audit trail, therefore, all processed transactions and master file changes should be recorded on another set of files accessible only to authorized personnel. For example, a record of every transaction and every master file change could be recorded on magnetic tape. Such a tape could be used to review transactions and recreate master files.

The third type of online system also needs at least the same access and edit controls required by the second type.

Control Considerations in Newer Systems

In recent years computer technology has produced a number of systems that can be used by both large and small businesses. However, special audit control problems are created with these systems. The three that are discussed in this section are minicomputers, microcomputers, and electronic funds transfer systems.

Characteristics of Minicomputers

Minicomputers are physically small but powerful computer systems that are somewhat comparable to single applications used in larger systems. For example, a company may have a minicomputer to handle its accounts receivable or payroll function. These types of computers are often operated by a small staff of personnel that are computer users rather than computer professionals. Minicomputer systems often lack the physical security of larger computer systems. In addition, minicomputer systems make considerable use of online entry and online updating.

Control Considerations in Minicomputer Systems

The controls that auditors should evaluate in a minicomputer system depend on the type of system in use. Some minicomputer systems operate from a central computer with data stored in a central location. Each minicomputer in the system updates the central data base, as well as maintains files in its own areas. In this regard, a minicomputer system has some of the same characteristics as online systems with terminals at various locations, a significant difference being the processing and data storage capability of a minicomputer.

Other minicomputer systems have their own independent equipment and files. These files are updated when processing takes place; there is no updating of a central data base. Audit trails must be created (if at all) on printed output rather than through magnetic media. To provide an adequate audit trail for logging transactions, it might be necessary to add a magnetic tape or disk storage device to the system.

If the minicomputer system is connected to a central computer, the auditor's control considerations are not significantly different from those already discussed in this chapter. The control considerations depend on whether online entry and online updating are performed, or whether some form of batch processing is used.

If the minicomputer system has independent equipment and files, each mini-computer location may have its own set of controls. In the remainder of the discussion on minicomputers, we will assume the use of an independent system.

Given these characteristics, independent minicomputers have special control problems that may not exist in larger installations. In general, some of these potential problems are as follows:

1. Lack of segregation of duties among programming, operations, and control of data within the computer department.

2. Inadequate processing controls in programs furnished by vendors, especially controls applicable to online processing.

3. Access to data files and programs by a number of individuals.

4. Lack of control over program changes, caused by the fact that the same person who makes program changes in a minicomputer installation often controls data files and enters transactions.

Specifically, the control problems in a minicomputer system can be divided into the following categories (note that the same control classifications are used for systems with centralized processing):

1. *General controls*

   a. *Segregation of functions between the computer department and users.* In independent minicomputer systems, this segregation of functions often does not exist because users also perform computer functions. Some segregation of functions between users may be feasible; for example, having one person enter and process data and another person maintain a control log.

   b. *Segregation of functions within the computer department.* If the users perform computer functions, the segregation of functions suggested in (a) above may be applicable. If computer processing and use of the computer is separated (unlikely in many systems), programming and machine operations should be segregated. If packaged software from a manufacturer is used, this segregation of duties may occur automatically. If programs are developed by the company, programming and machine operations are often performed by the same person.

2. *Application controls*

   a. *Control of conversion of data into machine-readable form.* If some form of batch processing is used in the minicomputer system, this control could take the form of batch totals. If input data are entered, without conversion, at a terminal, this conversion control is not necessary. However, the use of a terminal to enter input data increases the importance of controlling these data. Some form of batch controls might still be feasible. A powerful computer edit program is also desirable.

b. *Limit or reasonableness checks*. This control can often be accomplished by selecting appropriate application software packages.

c. *Control over distribution of output to authorized users*. In small minicomputer systems, the familiarity of personnel makes it likely that output will be distributed correctly.

Given these problems, there are limited, but nevertheless vital, controls that an auditor should look for in reviewing independent minicomputer systems.

If there is a segregation of functions between the computer department and users, the user departments should do the following:

1. Authorize transactions.

2. Use batching or other appropriate procedures to determine that all input is processed.

3. Have control over changes to master files and resubmission of transactions rejected by computer edit programs.

4. Balance master files from one processing cycle to another.

If the minicomputer system uses online updating, there should be limited access to the terminals and use of passwords. It is also advisable for user departments to keep transaction and master file totals and to periodically balance these totals with those generated by the computer system.

If there is no segregation of functions between the computer department and users (often the case), the auditor may have to rely on extensive substantive tests.

Controls in Microcomputer Systems

Microcomputers are personal computers that perform a variety of functions on a "stand alone" basis. They have some of the same characteristics as independent minicomputers; the machines and files are independent of a central processor (although they may be connected in a local area network). Minicomputers, however, are often used for one application in each location. In a small company, one microcomputer may be used for such applications as accounts receivable, inventory, and payroll. Microcomputers are also used in such nonaccounting applications as word processing.

When used to process accounting data, microcomputers have the following control problems.[4]

1. There is no separate computer staff. Microcomputer users are trained to perform certain applications.

2. Microcomputers are not in a controlled area in a computer center. Among other things, this causes a problem of physical security.

3. Files are often stored on removable disks (floppy diskettes).

We should not assume, however, that no control can be exercised over the use of microcomputers. Some of the control problems just described can be addressed by the following means:

1. Adequate training of personnel who use microcomputers. The duties of these personnel should be documented.

2. Labeling of diskettes and separate secure storage.

3. Making of backup diskettes for all files.

4. Protection of critical software stored on microcomputers.

5. Frequent printouts of data processed on the microcomputer.

Many of these controls are applicable to other forms of computer processing. However, as companies continue to make more use of microcomputers, it may be necessary to devise new control procedures that are totally different from those used for centralized processing.

Electronic Funds Transfer System (EFTS)

EFTS has been defined as a computer-based network that allows payment/ receipt types of transactions to be approved, executed, and recorded with electronic impulses and machine-sensible data, rather than with paper.

A widely used example of EFTS is the remote banking services currently in use. Bank customers can insert a plastic card into a remote terminal and enter a personal identification number and the desired type of transaction. The transaction will then be completed and the card returned. A number of functions can be performed at a remote bank terminal, such as deposits of cash, withdrawals of cash, transfers between accounts, and payment of bills.

A major control problem in the use of EFTS, therefore, is the fact that

---

[4] See Davis, Adams, and Schaller, *Auditing and EDP*.

accounting transactions originate at remote terminals operated by customers. Another control problem is the lack of documents evidencing the transactions. Still another problem is the ease with which any users, authorized or unauthorized, can create a transaction if they have a personal identification number.

However, there are a number of EFTS controls that, if used, will decrease the probability of material errors or irregularities.

1. Neither cards nor personal identification numbers should be issued by computer programmers or operators.

2. No one person should have complete knowledge of or access to an entire system.

3. Distribution of cards should be carefully controlled and supplies of cards and equipment should be guarded very carefully.

4. There should be a control group, independent of computer operations, that is responsible for application controls.

5. A log of each transaction should be created both at the main computer and at the terminals. These logs provide a primary and a backup audit trail and should be monitored for unusual activity.

6. Methods should be devised to ensure that no user can initiate a transaction at a terminal unless a valid identification number is used. The terminals should be programmed to recognize and confiscate any stolen or counterfeit cards.

7. Transactions improperly entered at the terminals should be corrected either by the originator of the transaction or by an independent third party. Some terminals are programmed to refuse a transaction once it has been improperly entered a certain number of times.

8. Mailing of customer statements and handling of customer inquiries should be performed by individuals independent of EFTS processing.

Summary of Control Considerations in Newer Systems

Clearly, newer computer systems such as minicomputers, microcomputers, and EFTS have provided more efficient ways for many businesses to create records and to process transactions. At the same time, though, certain control problems have been created that must be addressed by auditors. In many cases, the traditional audit trail no longer exists for these newer systems. This means that auditors should be particularly careful to review the controls that do exist and to ascertain that the controls are being followed as prescribed.

Chapter 10
Glossary of Terms

(listed in the order of appearance in the chapter, with accompanying page reference where the term is discussed)

	Page in
Term	*Chapter*

unauthorized or incorrect use of a computer program, or (3) improper use of computer resources.

Data and procedural controls   controls that provide a framework for controlling daily operations and establishing safeguards against processing errors.   370

Input controls   controls designed to provide reasonable assurance that data received for processing by computer have been properly authorized, converted into machine-sensible form, and identified, and that data have not been lost, suppressed, added, duplicated, or otherwise improperly changed.   372

Processing controls   controls designed to provide reasonable assurance that data have been properly processed in a particular application.   372

Output controls   controls designed to ensure the accuracy of the processing result and limit output to authorized personnel.   372

Batch control   a technique to help ensure that data flowing through the system are complete and accurate.   372

Control group   a group of independent employees that performs tests of the accuracy of data flow to and from the computer and sees that output is distributed properly.   375

Batch processing   processing of similar data at intervals or in batches.   377

Online processing   processing of data as transactions occur; processing usually takes place when data are entered at a terminal.   377

Minicomputers   physically small but powerful computer systems that are often used for single applications in larger systems.   380

Microcomputers   personal computers that perform a variety of functions; the equipment and files can be independent of a central processor.   382

Electronic funds transfer system   a computer-based network that allows payment/receipt types of transactions to be approved, executed, and recorded with electronic impulses and machine-sensible data rather than with paper.   383

Chapter 10
References

American Institute of Certified Public Accountants. *Audit and Accounting Guide—The Auditor's Study and Evaluation of Internal Control in EDP Systems.* (New York, AICPA, 1977).

American Institute of Certified Public Accountants. *Professional Standards* AU Section 1030—The Effects of Computer Processing on the Examination of Financial Statements.

Davis, Gordon B., Adams, Donald L., and Schaller, Carol A. *Auditing and EDP,* 2nd ed. (New York, American Institute of Certified Public Accountants, 1983).

Davis, Gordon B. and Weber, Ron. "The Impact of Advanced Computer Systems on Controls and Audit Procedures: A Theory and an Empirical Test," *Auditing: A Journal of Practice and Theory* (Spring 1986), pp. 35–49.

Guide to Accounting Controls—EDP (New York, Price Waterhouse, 1979).

Chapter 10
Review Questions

10-1.   Describe three general similarities between the audit of computer systems and the audit of manual systems. Name three differences.

10-2.   Briefly describe six control procedures that are different when a computer is used rather than manual processing.

10-3.   Name and briefly describe
a. The five general computer controls.
b. The three application computer controls.

10-4.   Name six tasks that should not be performed by those who perform computer functions.

10-5.   What are flowcharts?

10-6.   Distinguish between a systems and a program flowchart.

10-7.   Describe the three most common types of batch totals.

10-8.   Describe the function of a control group.

10-9.   What function is performed by the edit program described in the systems flow-chart?

10-10.   Describe the difference between batch processing and online processing.

10-11.   Describe three types of online systems.

10-12.   What is a minicomputer? Describe four potential control problems in a minicomputer system.

10-13.   What four functions should be assigned to user departments in a minicomputer system?

10-14.   Describe four potential control problems in a microcomputer system.

10-15.   Describe five ways that control problems in a microcomputer system can be addressed.

10-16.   What is a major control problem in the operation of an EFTS?

10-17.   Describe eight controls that can be used in an EFTS operation.

Chapter 10
Objective Questions Taken from CPA Examinations

10-18.   First Federal S & L has an online real-time system, with terminals installed in all of its branches. This system will not accept a customer's cash withdrawal instructions in excess of $1,000 without the use of a "terminal audit key." After the transaction is authorized by a supervisor, the bank teller then processes the transaction with the audit key. This control can be strengthened by
a. Online recording of the transaction on an audit override sheet.
b. Increasing the dollar amount to $1,500.

    c. Requiring manual, rather than online, recording of all such transactions.

    d. Using parallel simulation.

10-19.   A computer input control is designed to ensure that

    a. Machine processing is accurate.

    b. Only authorized personnel have access to the computer area.

    c. Data received for processing are properly authorized and converted to machine-readable form.

    d. Computer processing has been performed as intended for the particular application.

10-20.   Which of the following is an example of a check digit?

    a. An agreement of the total number of employees to the total number of checks printed by the computer.

    b. An algebraically determined number produced by the other digits of the employee number.

    c. A logic test that ensures all employee numbers are nine digits.

    d. A limit check that an employee's hours do *not* exceed 50 hours per work week.

10-21.   Which of the following activities would most likely be performed in the computer department?

    a. Initiation of changes to master records.

    b. Conversion of information to machine-readable form.

    c. Correction of transactional errors.

    d. Initiation of changes to existing applications.

10-22.   For control purposes, which of the following should be organizationally segregated from the computer operations function?

    a. Data conversion.

    b. Surveillance of CRT messages.

    c. Systems development.

    d. Minor maintenance according to a schedule.

10-23.   Which of the following *best* describes a fundamental control weakness often associated with computer systems?

    a. Computer processing equipment is more subject to systems error than manual processing is subject to human error.

    b. Computer processing equipment processes and records similar transactions in a similar manner.

    c. Computer processing procedures for detection of invalid and unusual transactions are less effective than manual control procedures.

d. Functions that would normally be separated in a manual system are combined in the computer system.

10-24. Matthews Corp. has changed from a system of recording time worked on clock cards to a computerized payroll system in which employees record time in and out with magnetic cards. The computer system automatically updates all payroll records. Because of this change
a. A generalized computer audit program must be used.
b. Part of the audit trail is altered.
c. The potential for payroll related fraud is diminished.
d. Transactions must be processed in batches.

10-25. An auditor's investigation of a company's computer processing control procedures has disclosed the following four circumstances. Indicate which circumstance constitutes a weakness in internal control structure procedures.
a. Machine operators do not have access to the complete run manual.
b. Machine operators are closely supervised by programmers.
c. Programmers do not have the authorization to operate equipment.
d. Only one generation of backup files is stored in an off-premises location.

10-26. Which of the following is an example of application controls in computer processing systems?
a. Input controls.
b. Hardware controls.
c. Documentation procedures.
d. Controls over access to equipment and data files.

10-27. In its computer processing system a company might use check digits to detect which of the following errors?
a. Assigning a valid identification code to the wrong customer.
b. Recording an invalid customer's identification charge account number.
c. Losing data between processing functions.
d. Processing data arranged in the wrong sequence.

10-28. So that the essential accounting control features of a client's computer processing system can be identified and evaluated, the auditor must, at a minimum, have
a. A basic familiarity with the computer's internal supervisory system.
b. A sufficient understanding of the entire computer system.
c. An expertise in computer systems analysis.
d. A background in programming procedures.

10-29. Program controls, in a computer processing system, are used as substitutes for human controls in a manual system. Which of the following is an example of a program control?
a. Dual read.
b. Echo check.
c. Key verification.
d. Limit and reasonableness test.

10-30. Some computer processing internal control structure procedures relate to all computer activities (general controls), and some relate to specific tasks (application controls). General controls include
a. Controls designed to ascertain that all data submitted to the computer system for processing have been properly authorized.
b. Controls that relate to the correction and resubmission of data that were initially incorrect.
c. Controls for documenting and approving programs and changes to programs.
d. Controls designed to ensure the accuracy of the processing results.

10-31. Which of the following employees normally would be assigned the operating responsibility for designing a computer processing installation, including flowcharts of data-processing routines?
a. Computer programmer.
b. Data-processing manager.
c. Systems analyst.
d. Internal auditor.

10-32. When an online computer system is in use, the internal control structure can be strengthened by
a. Providing for the separation of duties between data input and error listing operations.
b. Attaching plastic file protection rings to reels of magnetic tape before new data can be entered on the file.
c. Preparing batch totals to provide assurance that file updates are made for the entire input.
d. Making a validity check of an identification number before a user can obtain access to the computer files.

10-33. When erroneous data are detected by computer program controls, such data may be excluded from processing and printed on an error report. The error report should probably be reviewed and followed up by the
a. Supervisor of computer operations.
b. Systems analyst.

    c. Control group.

    d. Computer programmer.

10-34.   Which of the following would *lessen* internal control in a computer processing system?

    a. The custodian of computer records maintains custody of computer program instructions and detailed listings.

    b. Computer operators have access to operator instructions and detailed program listings.

    c. The control group is solely responsible for the distribution of all computer output.

    d. Computer programmers write and debug programs that perform routines designed by the systems analyst.

10-35.   The computer system most likely to be used by a large savings bank for customers' accounts would be

    a. An online system.

    b. A batch-processing system.

    c. A generalized utility system.

    d. A direct-access data base system.

10-36.   One of the major problems in a computer system is that incompatible functions may be performed by the same individual. One compensating control for this is use of

    a. A tape library.

    b. A self-checking digit system.

    c. Computer-generated hash totals.

    d. A computer log.

10-37.   Which of the following is not a characteristic of a batch-processing computer system?

    a. The collection of like transactions that are sorted and processed sequentially against a master file.

    b. Keying of transactions, followed by machine processing.

    c. The production of numerous printouts.

    d. The posting of a transaction, as it occurs, to several files, without intermediate printouts.

10-38.   If a control total were to be computed on each of the following data items, which would best be identified as a hash total for a payroll computer application?

    a. Net pay.

    b. Department numbers.

    c. Hours worked.

    d. Total debits and total credits.

10-39.   In the weekly computer run to prepare payroll checks, a check was printed for an employee who had been terminated the previous week. Which of the following controls, if properly utilized, would have been most effective in preventing the error or ensuring its prompt detection?

    a. A control total for hours worked, prepared from time cards collected by the timekeeping department.

    b. Requiring the treasurer's office to account for the numbers of the prenumbered checks issued to the computer department for the processing of the payroll.

    c. Use of a check digit for employee numbers.

    d. Use of a header label for the payroll input sheet.

Chapter 10
Discussion/Case Questions

10-40.   For a number of years, the Keep Company had used a computer batch entry and batch-processing system for its credit sales transactions. As clerks made credit sales, a copy of the sales invoice was given to the customer and another copy was placed in the register drawer. At the end of each day, these sales invoice copies were batched by a control group. The data on the invoices were keyed into a transactions tape. As the keying took place, an edit program checked data for certain error conditions and calculated batch totals. The control group checked the computer-generated batch totals with their own, and also made sure that rejected data were rekeyed. The file updating was performed in a manner similar to that shown in the systems flowchart in this chapter. The system seemed to work well and there were few complaints from customers.

    However, Ms. Change, a new employee who worked in the computer department, suggested that an online-entry and online-updating system be installed. She contended that the batch-entry and batch-processing system was too slow and inefficient. Under her suggested system, a terminal would be located in each department that sold merchandise. As a credit sale was made, the clerk would key the transaction at the terminal and the data would update the customer's account, which would be maintained on magnetic disk files. A sales invoice would be prepared and a copy given to the customer; but nothing would be done with the store's copy, except to place it in a file.

    Ms. Hold, another computer employee, suggested that a system of online entry and batch processing should be used initially. If this system worked, a conversion could be made to the online-entry and online-processing system.

    However, Mr. Keep, the owner, decided to follow Ms. Change's suggestion. The change was made, and for a short time everything seemed to work well.

Several months later, numerous customers began to complain of wrong account balances. Some customers said that all items they purchased had not been charged to them. Other customers claimed that incorrect charges had been made to their accounts.

In an attempt to correct the problems, the controller tried to reconstruct all sales transactions made since the new system was installed. He discovered that all sales invoice copies had been thrown away and no separate computer record of the sales transactions had been made.

When the independent auditor (who had not been told of the change) performed a study of the internal control structure, she did not rely on any controls in the system and assessed control risk at 100 percent. An unusually large number of substantive tests were performed, including 100 percent confirmation of all accounts-receivable balances. The auditor also wrote a long letter to the owner suggesting a number of controls for the new system.

Required:

a. Describe how this situation could have occurred (what improper functions were performed or what proper functions were not performed).

b. What controls were probably suggested by the auditor? Give reasons for each suggested control.

c. How could the temporary use of an online-entry and batch-processing system have avoided some of the problems?

10-41.   Mr. Traditional had a modest accounting practice consisting, for the most part, of local clients. None of the firms he serviced had a computer system, although several of them had talked of obtaining one.

In early March, Mr. Traditional received a telephone call from Unlimited Horizons, Inc., one of his clients that had undergone considerable growth within the last few years. The client indicated that there were tentative plans to acquire computer equipment and to convert part of the accounting system from manual to computer processing. The purpose of the call was to solicit Mr. Traditional's help in installing a suitable system. As the client's controller put it, "You will be auditing it later this year, so this will be a good opportunity to familiarize yourself with the characteristics of the new setup."

Mr. Traditional hesitated to accept the engagement, but decided to do so to avoid losing the client to another CPA firm. He consulted an up-to-date auditing text and found that a proper segregation of duties calls for a separation among (1) systems analyst, (2) computer programmer, (3) computer operator, (4) input data operator, (5) file maintenance, and (6) control group.

When Mr. Traditional suggested this type of job segregation to the controller of Unlimited Horizons, Inc., it was rejected as being too expensive. The controller decided that one person could design systems, program, and operate the computer, and he also felt that a control group could be omitted. It was left to Mr. Traditional to decide what other controls would be built into the system.

Later in the year, Mr. Traditional was asked to conduct the audit of Unlimited Horizons, Inc., but he felt that because he had participated in the design and installation of the system, a senior in the firm should do the field work. Mr. Traditional would still review the audit and sign the report. This arrangement was carried out, and the audit was completed with an unqualified opinion.

Several months later, Unlimited's programmer confessed to fraud. He had perpetrated a scheme to have the computer print out checks far in excess of the purchase amount to several vendors, who then gave the programmer a kickback of part of the excess payment.

Upon learning of this confession, Mr. Traditional called in the senior and asked her about the situation. The senior replied that she had used all the auditing techniques that she considered appropriate. The senior did indicate that she had "wondered" about the lack of segregation between the duties of programming, machine operation, and systems design. The senior also had noticed that the programmer was the only person who ever handled computer output, including error messages. However, she was reluctant to say anything to Mr. Traditional, because Mr. Traditional had aided in setting up the system.

Required:
a. What do the official pronouncements of the AICPA state about auditors' responsibility for fraud detection?
b. Do you believe that either Mr. Traditional or the senior will be able to use these official pronouncements as a defense in the event of a lawsuit?
c. Do you think that either Mr. Traditional or the senior violated any auditing standards? If so, which one(s)? Why?
d. Assume that you were the senior and had reported these control deficiencies to Mr. Traditional. Assume that Mr. Traditional dismissed them as minor. What would you do?

10-42. Talbert Corporation hired an independent computer programmer to develop a simplified payroll application for its newly purchased computer. The programmer developed an online, data-based microcomputer system that minimized the level of knowledge required by the operator. It was based upon typing answers to input cues that appeared on the terminal's viewing screen, examples of which follow:

a. Access routine:
  1. Operator access number to payroll file?
  2. Are there new employees?

b. New employees routine:
  1. Employee name?
  2. Employee number?
  3. Social security number?
  4. Rate per hour?

   5. Single or married?
   6. Number of dependents?
   7. Account distribution?

c. Current payroll routine:
   1. Employee number?
   2. Regular hours worked?
   3. Overtime hours worked?
   4. Total employees this payroll period?

The independent auditor is attempting to verify that certain input validation (edit) checks exist to ensure that errors resulting from omissions, invalid entries, or other inaccuracies will be detected during the typing of answers to the input cues.

Required:
Identify the various types of input validation (edit) checks the independent auditor would expect to find in the computer system. Describe the assurances provided by each identified validation check. (One example is a password. Another example is a limit check.)

(*AICPA adapted.*)

10-43. It is sometimes asserted that a programmer in an EDP system *could* be in a unique position to perpetrate fraud that remains undetected. Indicate three ways that a programmer could take assets from the company through unauthorized programming activities. Describe the lack of controls that might make it possible for the loss of assets to go undetected.

10-44. Examine the systems flowchart shown on pages 397–398.
Part 1—Write a detailed narrative of the procedures shown in the flowchart.

Part 2—For items A through G on page 399, put the word input, processing, or output in the blank provided. Explain in the space provided why you classified the control as you did.

10-45. Examine the program flowchart on pages 400–401 and write a narrative description of the computer processing shown. Include in your narrative a general description of the error messages.

10-46. A weak internal control structure may allow errors or irregularities to occur. For each of the following situations, indicate the error or irregularity that could occur.
a. The computer operator, who has some knowledge of programming, is allowed unlimited access to programs.

b. The control totals are forwarded to the computer operator.

c. Magnetic tapes are not properly labeled.

d. The computer program has no programming controls.

e. No log is kept of computer runs.

10-47.   Mr. A. O. Steady, a programmer for One Corporation, had been employed in his job for a number of years. He was the only programmer. There was a separate computer operator and input data operator.

   The computer system provides for data from purchase invoices to be entered at a terminal. The data are processed through the computer, and checks for vendors are printed by the computer. Each check is manually compared with the purchase invoice by another individual before mailing.

   One day it was discovered that Mr. Steady had been receiving kickbacks from a company that had received money from One Corporation without sending them any merchandise. The president of the company was puzzled about how Mr. Steady could have perpetrated this fraud. There seemed to be a proper segregation of duties, and the programmer never handled the checks that were printed by the computer.

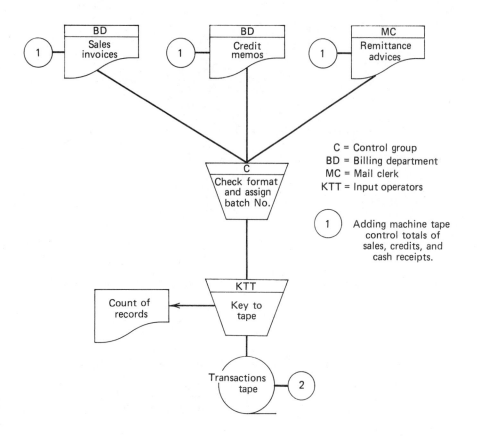

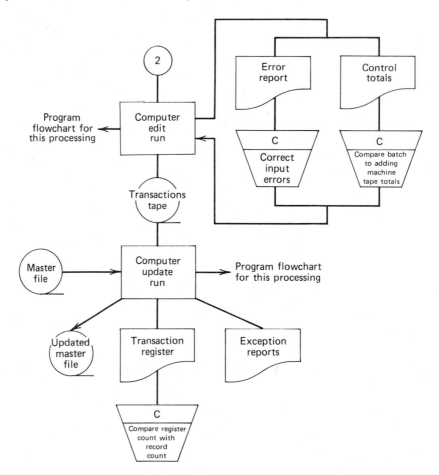

Required:
a. Explain how this fraud may have occurred and remained undetected.
b. Discuss some controls, including noncomputer types, that might have prevented or uncovered the fraud.

10-48.   George Beemster, CPA, is examining the financial statements of the Louisville Sales Corporation, which recently installed a computer. The following comments have been extracted from Mr. Beemster's notes on computer operations and the processing and control of shipping notices and customer invoices:

> To minimize inconvenience, Louisville converted without change its existing data-processing system. The computer vendor supervised the conversion and has provided training to all computer department employees (except input data operators) in systems design, operations, and programming.

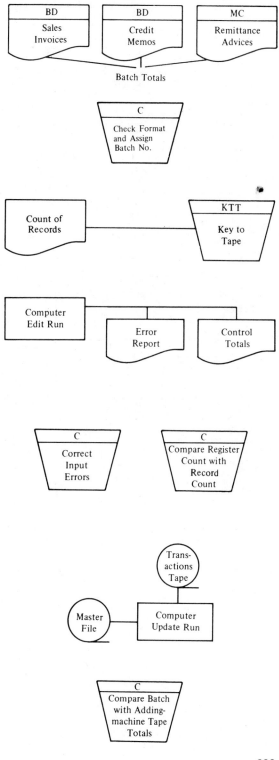

BD	BD	MC
Sales Invoices	Credit Memos	Remittance Advices

Batch Totals

C
Check Format and Assign Batch No.

Count of Records

KTT
Key to Tape

Computer Edit Run

Error Report

Control Totals

C
Correct Input Errors

C
Compare Register Count with Record Count

Transactions Tape

Master File

Computer Update Run

C
Compare Batch with Adding-machine Tape Totals

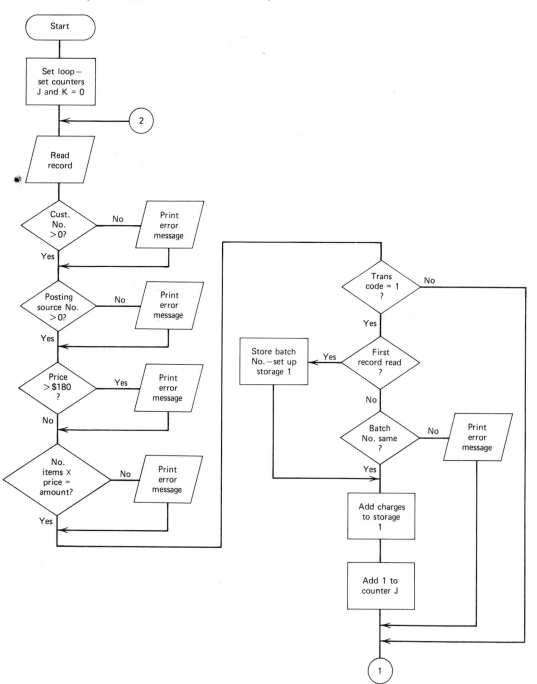

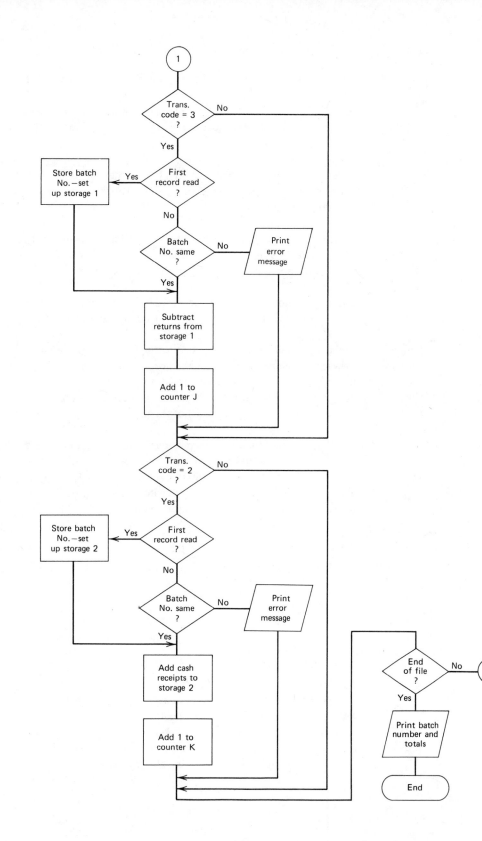

Each computer run is assigned to a specific employee, who is responsible for making program changes, running the program, and answering questions. This procedure has the advantage of eliminating the need for records of computer operations, because each employee is responsible for his or her own computer runs.

At least one computer department employee remains in the computer room during office hours, and only computer department employees have keys to the computer room.

System documentation consists of those materials furnished by the computer vendor—a set of record formats and program listings. These and the tape library are kept in a corner of the computer department.

The corporation considered the desirability of programmed controls but decided to retain the manual controls from its existing system.

Company products are shipped directly from public warehouses, which forward shipping notices to general accounting. There a billing clerk enters the price of the item and accounts for the numerical sequence of shipping notices from each warehouse. The billing clerk also prepares daily adding machine tapes ("control tapes") of the units shipped and the unit prices.

Shipping notices and control tapes are forwarded to the computer department for data entry and processing. Extensions are made on the computer. Output consists of invoices (in six copies) and a daily sales register. The daily sales register shows the aggregate totals of units shipped and unit prices, which the computer operator compares to the control tapes.

Required:
Indicate the weaknesses that you see in the system and your recommendations for correcting these weaknesses.

(AICPA adapted)

10-49.   You are reviewing audit work papers containing a narrative description of the Tenney Corporation's factory payroll system. A portion of that narrative is as follows:

Factory employees punch timeclock cards each day when entering or leaving the shop. At the end of each week, the timekeeping department collects the time cards and prepares duplicate batch-control slips by department showing total hours and number of employees. The time cards and original batch-control slips are sent to the payroll accounting section. The second copies of the batch-control slips are filed by date.

In the payroll accounting section, payroll transaction data from the information on the time cards are keyed through a terminal to a transactions tape and a batch total for each batch is keyed from the batch-control slip. The time cards and batch-control slips are then filed by batch for possible reference. The payroll transaction data and batch total data are sent to data processing. Each batch is edited by a computer program that checks the validity of the employee number against a master employee tape file and the total hours and number of employees against the batch total data. A detail printout by batch and employee number indicates batches that do not balance and invalid employee numbers. This printout is returned to payroll accounting to resolve all differences.

In searching for documentation, you found a flowchart of the payroll system that included all appropriate symbols (American National Standards Institute, Inc.) but was only partially labeled. The portion of this flowchart just described appears on page 404.

Required:

a. Number your answers 1 through 17. Next to the corresponding number of your answer, supply the appropriate labeling (document name, process description, or file order) applicable to each numbered symbol on the flowchart.

b. Flowcharts are one of the aids an auditor may use to determine and evaluate a client's internal control structure. List advantages of using flowcharts in this context.

(AICPA adapted)

10-50.   When auditing a computer accounting system, the independent auditor should have a general familiarity with the effects of the use of computers on the various characteristics of the internal control structure. The independent auditor should be aware of those control procedures that are commonly referred to as "general" controls and those that are commonly referred to as "application" controls. General controls relate to all computer activities and application controls relate to specific accounting tasks.

Required:

a. What are the general controls that should exist in computer based accounting systems?

b. What are the purposes of each of the following categories of application controls?

(1) Input controls.

(2) Processing controls.

(3) Output controls.

(AICPA adapted)

TENNEY CORPORATION
FLOW CHART OF FACTORY PAYROLL SYSTEM

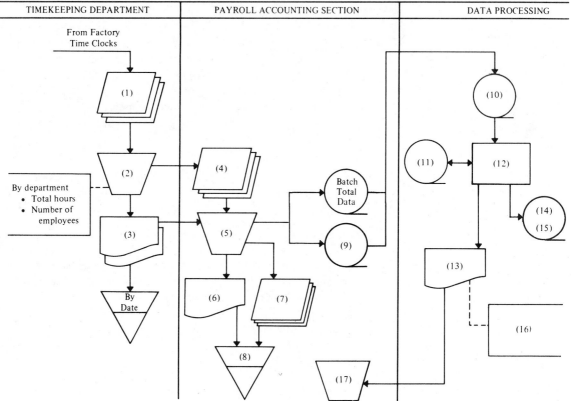

10-51.   Complete the following chart.

System	Important System Controls*
a. A batch entry and batch processing system.	
b. A minicomputer system that is connected to a central computer and uses online entry and online updating.	
c. A microcomputer system.	

*For b, emphasize controls not relevant to a; for c, emphasize controls not relevant to a or b.

10-52.   Smaller Company is a manufacturer of plastic golf balls. Since the company was organized, it had used central processing for all of its computerized accounting operations. Early this year management decided to use microcomputers to process inventory transactions and maintain inventory records in the branch offices.

Several operators (who had previous word processing experience with microcomputers) were hired in each branch office. A number of programmers and computer operators in central processing were terminated. The newly hired microcomputer operators were given a two-week training course in the use of the appropriate software to process inventory transactions.

The microcomputers were located wherever they "would fit" in the respective branch offices. Floppy diskettes were used and were stored in the same file drawers as the printouts of inventory transactions and records. All employees had access to the files. Only one set of diskettes was maintained.

The auditor for Smaller Company had not been consulted about the change to microcomputers for processing inventory transactions at the branch offices. Therefore, when he arrived late in the year to update his understanding of the internal control structure, he discovered the following:

1. No one at the branch offices knew the correct amount of inventory for each type of plastic golf ball. The inventory amounts on printouts did not match the inventory control account in the general ledger maintained in the central accounting offices.

2. Diskettes were not labeled and no one seemed to know the contents of each diskette.

3. Discounts were being lost because no one in the branch offices had the necessary invoice information to know when merchandise orders had been filled by vendors.

Because of this and other microcomputer inventory problems at the branches, the auditor was considering assessing a 100 percent control risk to inventory controls and performing extensive substantive tests on inventory.

Required:
a. Give probable reasons why the auditor found the previously described conditions.
b. What controls should now be put in or strengthened?
c. What potential problems are inherent in the use of microcomputers for accounting applications of this type?

CHAPTER 11

Understanding the Internal Control Structure and Testing the Controls in a Computer System

---

Learning Objectives   *After reading and studying the material in this chapter, the student should*

Know how to obtain a basic understanding of the internal control structure in a computer system.

Know how to identify the computer controls on which the auditor might rely in restricting substantive tests.

Know how to obtain a detailed understanding of the general and application computer controls and to assess control risk.

Understand the tests of general and application computer controls and some of the special techniques used to test these controls.

In Chapter 10, we discussed and illustrated examples of controls in a computer system. Conceptually, these controls accomplish the same objectives in any type of accounting system, and they essentially include the following characteristics:

1. Qualified and properly trained personnel.

2. Proper segregation of functions.

3. Execution of transactions by authorized personnel.

4. Accurate recording of transactions.

5. Access to assets limited to authorized personnel and to someone other than those who authorize transactions and record transactions.

6. Periodic comparison of recorded accountability with assets.

In this chapter we will describe and illustrate the techniques used by the auditor to acquire an understanding of the internal control structure and to test controls in a computer system.

Chapter 10 should be covered before the material in this chapter is studied. It would also be helpful to review Chapters 7 and 8, which cover the general concepts of an internal control structure.

Understanding the Internal Control Structure and Testing the Controls in a Computer System—An Overview of the Model

Although acquiring an understanding of the internal control structure and testing the controls in a computer system can be a complex task, there is a general model that will provide a good overview of the process. Each step is described below. Later in the chapter, we will discuss these steps in detail.

1. Obtain a *basic* understanding of the internal control structure.

   a. Purpose—To become familiar with the control environment, the accounting system, and the individual controls in which computers play a significant role.

   b. Methods—Inquiry and discussion; observation; review of documentation and reports; examination of transaction flows.

2. Identify the computer controls on which the auditor might rely in restricting substantive tests.

   a. Purpose—To decide on which computer controls the auditor will concentrate.

   b. Method—Judgment.

3. Obtain a *detailed* understanding of the computer controls identified in 2., above (both general and application as discussed in Chapter 10).

   a. Purpose—To determine, in detail, how these controls operate to decide whether

(1) limited reliance should be placed on these controls and extensive substantive tests conducted, or

(2) extended reliance should be placed on these controls and restricted substantive tests conducted.

b. Methods—Detailed examination of documentation; interview of internal auditors and computer personnel; observation of the operation of general and application controls.

4. Assess the control risk for the general and application controls in 3., above, to determine whether

(1) control risk is *not* sufficiently low and extensive substantive tests must be conducted or

(2) control risk is sufficiently low and restricted substantive tests can be conducted.

5. Test those general and application controls where it is believed that the assessment of control risk may be further lowered (conduct additional tests if some testing was done in 3., above).

a. Purpose—To determine whether the assessment of control risk may be further lowered and substantive tests of financial statement assertions further restricted.

b. Methods—Detailed examination of records; detailed tests of control procedures; inquiry; observation.

6. Reassess the control risk for the general and application controls in 3., above, to determine whether control risk is assessed sufficiently lower as the result of the tests of controls to *additionally* restrict substantive tests of financial statement assertions affected by those controls.

Detailed Discussions of the Model

With some exceptions, the review, assessment, and testing model described in the previous section is similar to the one shown in Chapter 7. The most notable exception is the separate reviews of general and application controls. There is some danger in separating the review process in this way because the effectiveness of application controls depends on proper general controls. In fact, without adequate general controls, many application controls may not be effective.

Therefore, in dividing the review process into review of general and application controls, bear in mind that the two types of controls are closely related. They are discussed separately because many companies divide their computer controls in this way and because they were discussed separately in Chapter 10.

Obtain a Basic Understanding of the Internal Control Structure

This part of the review is designed to give the auditor an understanding of the following.

1. The control environment.

2. The flow of transactions through the accounting system.

3. The extent to which computers are used in each significant accounting application.

4. The basic structure of accounting control.

The review is macro in nature and is conducted in enough depth to allow the auditor to assess which computer controls might be relied on in restricting substantive tests. For this reason, both computer and noncomputer portions of the accounting system are reviewed together.

The methods of conducting this phase of the review are similar to those used in the review of manual systems. The auditor asks questions, makes observations, and reviews documentation.

To gain an understanding of the flow of transactions, the auditor may (among other things) do the following:

1. Examine some of the source documents.

2. Determine how data are converted into machine-readable form in a batch-entry system or how data are entered at a terminal in an online entry system.

3. Find out what master files are used.

4. Find out how errors in the system are detected and corrected.

To determine the extent to which computers are used in each significant accounting application, the auditor may (among other things) do the following:

1. Observe the types of transactions processed.

2. Determine which transaction flows involve computer activities and which do not.

To gain an understanding of the basic structure of accounting controls, the auditor may (among other things) do the following:

1. Identify the controls existing in the system.

2. Determine which controls are manual and which are computerized.

During this phase of the review, the auditor should find out whether each general and application control appears to accomplish its purpose. In particular, the auditor should determine whether duties are adequately segregated within the computer department and between the computer department and users (remember that in some minicomputer and microcomputer systems no segregation of duties may exist).

The auditor should also determine the extent of systems documentation, control over computer program changes, and restrictions on access to data files and computer programs.

If general controls of the type described in the two preceding paragraphs do not exist, the auditor might find it difficult to justify continuation of the review process.

Identify the Appropriate Computer Controls

The assessment of the basic understanding is generally the same for a computer system as for a manual system. The auditor may decide to rely on all or some of the computer controls for purposes of restricting substantive tests.

For those controls on which some reliance may be placed, tests of controls may be performed. For example, the auditor may decide that segregation of functions between the computer department and computer users is a control that might be relied on. A detailed review of these two areas might be made and tests conducted. If, at the end of the review and testing process, substantial reliance is placed on this control, the auditor would restrict related substantive tests.

There are three reasons why the auditor might not perform detailed reviews and tests of some computer controls.

1. The auditor is unable to rely on a particular computer control because it is not effective.

2. More audit effort may be required to complete the review and conduct tests of a particular control than the saved audit effort of reducing substantive tests.

3. The computer control is redundant because other controls exist.

In any of these three circumstances, the auditor would have to depend more heavily on substantive tests to gather evidence.

Obtain a Detailed Understanding of Computer Controls

For the computer controls on which some reliance is placed, a detailed understanding is obtained by examining documentation, interviewing personnel, and observing operations. If the auditor wishes, this phase could be divided into a review of general and application controls (remembering, again, the relationship between the two types of controls).

For general controls, it is particularly important that the auditor obtain answers to the following question. How is segregation of functions within the computer department and between the computer department and users organized and supervised? (Remember that the auditor has already determined in the basic review that reliance might be placed on this control. The answer to this question will help to determine how much reliance may be placed on this control.)

For the application controls, the auditor may use detailed flowcharts to identify specific controls. In addition, discussions with systems analysts, computer programmers, users, and computer operators might be helpful. Here, the ability of the auditor to converse in technical computer terms will be beneficial.

Table 11.1 includes some questions that might be asked during the review process.

Assessment of Control Risk

After the review of individual controls, the auditor would make an assessment of the degree of reliance to be placed on each control. Those controls on which the auditor still plans to rely may be tested, unless to do so is not considered cost-effective. No reliance is placed on controls considered to be too weak; substantive tests are extensive.

Table 11.2 shows how some controls may be assessed.

Tests of Controls

Tests of controls have the same purpose in a computer system as they do in manual systems. Some of the tests in a computer system, however, may be performed using the computer. These types of tests are described in detail later in the chapter. Tests of general controls require questions and observations, such as those that ascertain whether segregation of functions is being followed as prescribed.

Reassess Control Risk

The auditor makes a reassessment of computer controls on which some reliance is to be placed and which were tested. If the tests confirm the reliance, additional restrictions of substantive tests may be made. If the tests show that a particular control is not functioning, the reassessment of that control may change and substantive tests may not be additionally restricted or may be expanded.

Table 11.1

Questions to Ask in Obtaining a Detailed Understanding of Computer Controls

Question	Reason for the Question
Is there a separation between the functions of programming and computer operation?	If these functions are combined, the programmer might be able to place some substitute steps in the program, instructing the computer to branch around an important edit check. An example is the total number of hours worked. The program steps could branch around the edit of a certain employee's time records and ignore the excessive hours recorded for this individual. The use of a separate operator would not ensure that an irregularity of this type would not occur, but it would improve the chances, particularly if the programmer had no further access to the program.
Are programs periodically tested by a control group or an internal audit group?	Program steps that are run on the computer may not be the same as the steps shown on the program listing. They should be tested occasionally by an outside group for intentional or unintentional changes. Standard procedures should be used for initiating and reviewing program changes.
Are programmers or machine operators allowed to correct input errors and reconcile control totals?	Allowing the programmer to perform these functions is similar to allowing an accounts receivable clerk to maintain the general ledger control account. Because errors or irregularities could be covered up, a separate person or group (preferably a member of a control group) should perform this function.
Is there controlled access to data files and other computer documentation?	Unauthorized access to programs or files could result in improper alterations. Limited access to ledgers and journals is required in a manual system, but in a computer system, alteration might be more difficult to detect.

Documentation of the Review and Assessment of Computer Controls

A wide variety of documentation can be used by the auditor in the review and assessment process. Some of the documentation is the same as the type used in reviewing and assessing controls in a manual system. Generally, the documentation could include such items as narratives, flowcharts, descriptions of computer controls, questionnaires, and computer printouts. The amount and type depend on the judgment of the auditor.

Table 11.2
Assessment of Computer Controls

Errors or Irregularities that Could Occur in the System	Internal Control Procedures (if any) that Should Prevent or Detect These Errors or Irregularities	Internal Control Procedures that Are Documented as Part of the System
The machine operator could make unauthorized changes to the programs that would result in such things as duplicate payments to vendors.	The functions of programmer and machine operator should be separated.	These functions are separate.
Errors could occur when machine-readable data are created from source document information.	There should be verification of the source document data and a system should be used to utilize the computer to detect errors missed in the verification.	There is a machine verification, but a check digit system for source documents is not used.
Errors could occur when data are processed by the computer.	Batch controls should be established over the source documents before they are released for further processing.	Batch totals are accumulated where the source documents are created. These totals are matched with the computer output by the control group.
Blank fields, illogical conditions, and out-of-limit figures could occur even after verification takes place.	The data should be processed through a computer program that contains programming controls.	The data are processed through a computer edit program that tests for certain error conditions.

Examples of Review Procedures and Tests of Controls

To provide specific examples of the assessment process just described, we have compiled a list of possible review procedures and related tests of controls for selected computer controls. This list is contained in Table 11.3.

Methods to Test Computer Programs

As part of the tests of controls described in the previous sections, auditors may wish to test the computer programs, themselves. Such methods are sometimes referred to as *through the computer approaches*. Some of the techniques, such as test data, test the functioning of computer programs on a "static" basis, that is, the program is not being processed by the client at the time it is tested. Other techniques, such as parallel simulation and integrated test facilities, test the func-

Table 11.3
Review Procedures and Related Tests of Computer Controls

Review Procedures	Tests of Controls

Organization and Operation Controls

Review Procedures	Tests of Controls
Review organization charts and job descriptions for evidence of proper segregation of duties between the computer department and computer users.	Observe the actual operation.
Inquire as to whether there is a policy prohibiting the computer department from initiating or authorizing transactions.	Observe the reconciliation of control totals with computer processing results.
Review appropriate documentation and make inquiries for evidence of proper segregation of duties within the computer department.	(a) Observe the actual operation. (b) Examine usage records for evidence of proper authorization for use of data files. (c) Examine time logs to determine that computer operators' duties are rotated.
Review the organizational structure and relationships of the control group or control function.	Examine, on a test basis, reconciliation of control totals by the control group.
Discuss with internal auditors their procedures for viewing and testing computer processing activities.	Examine internal auditors' reports and workpapers.

Systems Development and Documentation Controls

Review Procedures	Tests of Controls
Review plans for controlling the conversion from one computer record to another to prevent unauthorized changes on master and transaction files.	(a) Observe conversion procedures. (b) Trace detailed records from old files to new ones.
Interview appropriate personnel to determine whether computer program changes have been authorized, tested, and documented.	Trace selected computer program changes to the appropriate supporting records and approvals.
Review documentation standards to determine whether they appear to provide for adequate documentation.	Examine selected documentation to assess conformance with the documentation standards.
Review the methods for determining that access to data files and programs are limited to authorized individuals.	Examine the console log and program access records.

Input Controls

Review Procedures	Tests of Controls
Review procedures for determining that only properly authorized and approved input is accepted for computer processing.	(a) Examine, on a test basis, evidence of transaction authorization. (b) Investigate exceptions in the authorization process.

Table 11.3 (Continued)

Review Procedures	Tests of Controls
Review the procedures for controlling the conversion of input to machine-readable form.	(a) Observe verification procedures. (b) Compare edited transactions to original input. (c) Use test data to test certain control features.
Review the procedures used to determine that data movement from one processing step to another does not result in lost, added, or altered data.	(a) Observe the procedures for moving data from one processing step to another. (b) Trace a group of transactions through the system.

Processing Controls

Review the controls used to prevent processing the wrong file or to detect errors in file manipulation.	Examine the console log for error messages and determine how errors are resolved.
Review the documentation to determine what edit checks are in programs.	(a) Use computer audit software to check the data recorded on output files. (b) Use test data to test the edit checks.
Review the control totals used to verify data at appropriate points in the processing.	(a) Observe the procedures for reconciling control totals. (b) Test the reconciliation of control totals.

Output Controls

Review the procedures for reconciling output with control totals.	(a) Observe the reconciliations. (b) Test the reconciliations.
Review the procedures for scanning output and comparing it to original source documents.	(a) Observe the verification procedures. (b) On a test basis, compare output with source documentation.
Review the procedures for determining that output is distributed only to authorized users.	(a) Observe the distribution of the output. (b) Test the distribution of the output and determine that recipients are authorized personnel.

tioning of the computer programs as the programs are being processed by the client.

Auditing standards do not require that tests of controls include tests of computer programs, but if the auditor intends to rely on certain application controls, one or more of these techniques may prove useful. Before any of these techniques are implemented, however, the auditor should either possess the required technical knowledge or have it available.

Test Data

The accounting profession has devised methods of testing "through the computer" itself. One technique, which involves the use of *test data*, was designed for batch systems. The method operates as follows.

1. Client documentation is reviewed and controls are identified.

2. Simulated transactions, including records with errors, are created and entered in the system to test the identified controls.

3. These transactions are entered on the auditor's worksheet, along with the predetermined computer results.

4. The simulated transactions are processed with the client's computer program, and the computer results are compared with the predetermined results. If the two sets match, the client's program is assumed to be functioning as called for in the program documentation.

The test data procedure is depicted in the following diagram. The diagram shows the auditors' data being entered from magnetic tape. If they wish, auditors could create the transactions in the source documents, which would be tantamount to testing the client's data entry technique.

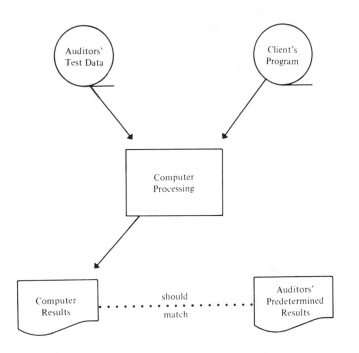

What assurance do auditors have that they are using the correct program? If a different program is being used to perpetuate an irregularity, the client might furnish the auditors with a program that correctly processes the test data, while he or she uses the other program to process the real data. There is no assurance that this substitution will not occur, but precautionary steps can be taken to lower the probability of such an occurrence.

For instance, the test data could be run on a surprise basis. However, a more practical approach might be for auditors to copy the client's program in advance of the test data run. Then, at the client's convenience, the test data could be processed, and the program used in this processing could be compared with the copy of the program obtained earlier.

An Example of Test Data

The foregoing discussion provides a background for a specific illustration of the test data procedure. Reference to the systems flowchart in Chapter 10 (Figure 10.1) shows that there are two computer programs. The first program is an edit program designed to (1) print an error message for certain inaccurate or invalid data on the invoices, credit memos, and remittance advices, and (2) print control totals for comparison with similar totals produced in the billing department and the mail room. The second program is an updating program that incorporates current transactions into the master file records. Though both computer programs should be tested by the auditor, the illustration can be simplified by confining the discussion of test data to the edit program.

There are some edit tests incorporated in the program flowchart in Figure 10.2.

1. A completeness test of the customer and posting source numbers. If the computer reads a record that has a blank or zeros in either of these fields, an error message is printed.

2. A limit test of the price. The price of the most expensive item sold by the client is $180. If the computer reads a record that has a price in excess of this amount, an error message is printed.

3. A validity test of the amount. If the computer reads a record that contains an extension error on the total amount of the sale, an error message is printed.

Next, there are three sets of the batch numbers (not shown in Figure 10.2). If this number is incorrect for any or all of the transaction codes, an error message or messages are produced. Finally, totals are accumulated for all records that contain the daily batch numbers.

Following are partially completed illustrations of (1) test data designed by auditors, (2) auditors' predetermined results, and (3) the actual computer output. Observe that auditors enter one input record without errors to test the program output under conditions in which there are no inaccuracies. In addition, auditors enter one record for every type of error condition tested in the edit program. Because seven errors are possible, eight records are illustrated.

Examples of Test Data Designed by Auditors

Type of Error	Transaction Code	Batch No.	Customer No.	Source No.	Name	Date	Description	No. of Items	Price	Amount
No errors	1	501	07	2102	Alpha	X91003	DXl sofa	12	180.00	2160.00
Invalid customer No.										
Invalid source No.										
Excess price										
Extension error										
Billing batch No. in error										
Billing batch No. in error										
Mail room batch No. in error										

Examples of Predetermined Output Designed by Auditors

The first record's processing should not show any errors.

The second record's processing should produce an error message: Invalid customer number.

The third record's processing should produce an error message; Invalid source number.

The fourth record's processing should produce an error message: Price in excess of limit.

The fifth record's processing should produce an error message: Extension error.

The sixth record's processing should produce an error message: Incorrect billing batch number.

The seventh record's processing should produce an error message: Incorrect billing batch number.

The eighth record's processing should produce an error message: Incorrect mail room batch number.

The batch totals produced by the computer should be

(1) Billing Dept record count _____ Control total _____

(2) Mail Room record count _____ Control total _____

Form of Output for Computer Edit Program for Customer Charges and Credits

Transaction Code	Batch No.	Customer No.	Document No.	Date	No. of Items	Price	Amount
Invalid customer No.							
Invalid document No.							
Price over limit							
Incorrect extension							
Incorrect billing batch No.							
Incorrect billing batch No.							
Incorrect mail room batch No.							
	Billing Batch No.		Mail Room Batch No.		No. Records		Total

Critique of the Test Data Approach

What, then, is the major advantage of using test data, particularly in comparison with an around-the-computer approach, to test controls? A major benefit is the greater assurance that is gained about the reliability of the client's computer programs. The auditors have reasonable assurance that the client's programs they test function as prescribed, even though they may not be completely certain that they are testing the right programs.

However, the use of test data does have certain limitations.

1. For instance, a successful test data run does not necessarily indicate a strong internal control structure because other types of errors or irregularities could occur outside the computer processing area. A prime example is the failure of a mail clerk to report all cash receipts.

2. Test data determine whether the program that has been *furnished* the auditor is functioning as it should. The auditor cannot be *certain* that this is the same program used in daily operations, although proper precautions can greatly increase that assurance.

3. The test data approach is limited to a test of the functions in the *client's* program, and that program may be inadequate to edit the client's machine-readable records.

4. The test data approach was designed for a batch-processing system. There is some question as to its suitability for the newer online systems where there is no intermediate processing between the input devices and the central processing unit, and where more continuous processing takes place.

5. Developing test data can be time-consuming and the test data must be tailormade for every application.

Despite these drawbacks, the use of test data is definitely a step in the direction of going through the computer and, with proper safeguards, can provide auditors with insights into the computer system that are not gained by ignoring the computer.

Parallel Simulation

In the *parallel simulation* method shown in Figure 11.1, both simulated data and actual client data are run simultaneously with the client's program, and computer results are compared with auditors' predetermined amounts. A theoretical advantage of this method over the traditional test data approach is the ability of auditors both to check the functioning of the client's program and to test the accuracy of the client's output.

Auditors can also run the client's program with actual data several times during the year. The purpose of this procedure is to provide relative assurance that the client's records have been processed consistently during the year.

This approach is a computer counterpart of the traditional test of transactions in a manual system, in which data are traced, for selected time periods, from source documents to journals and ledgers. In both procedures, auditors are attempting to satisfy themselves that record-keeping procedures are employed consistently. Undoubtedly, there are benefits to be gained from monitoring of this sort, but it could prove costly.

Online Audit Monitor

In Chapter 10, we described an online-entry system as one in which transactions are entered at a terminal as they occur. If such a system is properly designed, it will include edit programs that test the accuracy, validity, and completeness of all transactions entered at the terminal. In such a system, batch entry is not used; therefore, traditional testing techniques, such as test data, may not be feasible.

A testing technique has been devised to test transactions as they are entered into the system on an online basis. This technique is called an *online audit monitor*[1] and is shown in Figure 11.2. Basically, this monitor is a set of auditor's criteria that is added to the computer edit programs used by the client to check

[1] Gordon B. Davis, Donald L. Adams, and Carol A. Schaller, *Auditing and EDP,* 2nd ed. (New York, AICPA, 1983).

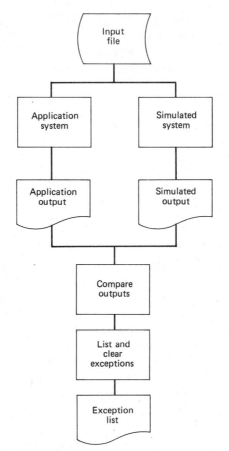

Figure 11.1   Parallel processing flowchart. *Source:* Gordon B. Davis, Donald L. Adams, and Carol A. Schaller, *Auditing and EDP*, 2nd ed., 1983. Copyright © (1983) American Institute of Certified Public Accountants, Inc., reprinted with permission.

transactions entered into the system through a terminal. The criteria might call for certain transactions entering the system to be "flagged" and printed out (or written on disk or tape) for review by the auditor. For example, the auditor may designate that every charge sale entered at a terminal is to be flagged if that sale was made to a customer who already had an outstanding balance for more than 90 days. The auditor can follow up to see if these sales are a violation of the credit limit policy (a test of controls of credit policy procedures).

Online audit monitoring generally follows this sequence.

1. As a transaction is entered into the system, the standard edit program checks are applied to the data (checking the proper number of numeric characters, for example).

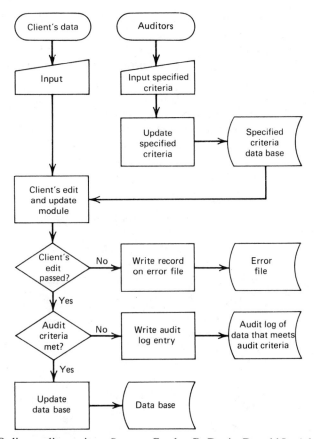

Figure 11.2   Online audit monitor. *Source:* Gordon B. Davis, Donald L. Adams, and Carol A. Schaller, *Auditing and EDP*, 2nd ed., 1983. Copyright © (1983) American Institute of Certified Public Accountants, Inc., adapted and reprinted with permission.

2. When the standard edit checks are completed, the auditor's specified criteria are applied to the transaction. In our example, all charge sales would be edited to ascertain if they were made to customers who already have a balance in excess of 90 days old.

3. Any transaction that meets the auditor's criteria is flagged and written on a disk or tape log, or is printed on an online terminal located in the auditor's office.

4. The transaction is marked on a disk or tape log with a special character or code that identifies it as a transaction subject to auditor's review.

5. The transaction is released for normal processing.

Online audit monitoring has a number of advantages. First, it can be used with a system that enters transactions at a terminal as they occur (online entry). Also, this technique can be used without interfering with the client's normal processing routine. In fact, auditors can enter criteria from their own terminal if proper arrangements are made with the client.

If too many transactions are selected by the auditor, however, there could be serious impact on the client's normal processing. There is also the possibility that terminal operators might alter transactions that they know will be subjected to the auditor's edit process. For this reason, the auditor's edit criteria should be kept confidential or revealed only to selected client personnel.

The Auditor's Program

Sometimes, the *auditors'* computer programs can be run with actual client data. The computer results are compared with actual client output to test its validity. If the computer output matches the previously processed client output, the client's computer processing is accepted.

This method is illustrated in the following diagram compared with the diagram for the test data approach.

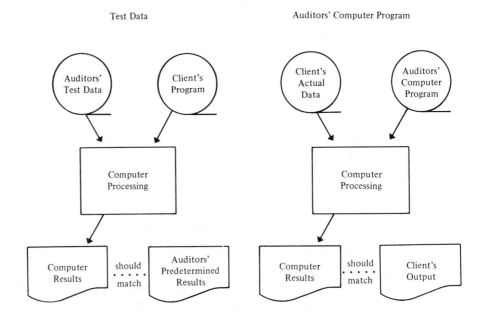

Several advantages of this approach are apparent. First, auditors can be almost certain that the correct program is being run because it is designed either by them or by their firm. With the test data approach, auditors have only relative assurance that the client program being processed is the correct one.

Another advantage of auditors' programs is that tests can be made of the controls that auditors believe are important in the client's system. If auditors use their own program, they can test for *any* condition, regardless of whether or not that condition is tested in the client's edit program. For example, auditors may wish to check for alphabetic data in the customer number. A program run using actual client data should detect errors of this sort.

To explain this concept more fully, the auditors' program technique is illustrated in the following diagram with an example of sales invoice data that are extended improperly.

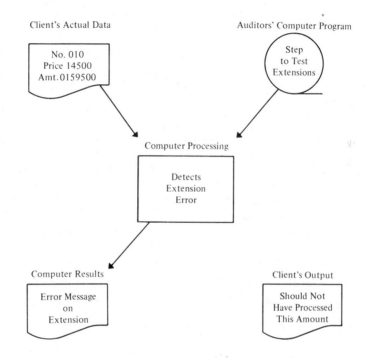

There is also a disadvantage to the auditors' use of their own programs, namely, the cost of writing and periodically modifying them. In fact, many firms do not have either the money or the expertise to use this technique.

Auditors' Participation in Computer System Design

Discussion of audit techniques for tests of controls in a computer system must include examination of auditors' participation in the design of such systems. As explained in Chapter 1, there is a sharp distinction between accounting and auditing. Accounting is a process of compiling information and is essentially a record-keeping function. Auditing is an analytical process of reviewing, observing, calculating, and so on to ascertain the fairness of the amounts that are recorded by the company.

In manual systems, this separation of activities has not presented any technical problem because auditors, trained extensively in the function of recording manual transactions, are generally able to acquire fairly quickly the tools to audit such systems. Thus, with the proper training and experience, auditors can function adequately without participating in the design of a manual accounting system.

In contrast, as computer systems become more complicated, auditors may not be able to conduct an audit without extensive knowledge of the system. In the opinion of some practitioners, this knowledge can be gained only through participation in the system's design. Such an opinion was expressed by an AICPA task force on computer auditing.

> The auditor's participation in the system design will become more critical in the case of an advanced system. This involvement will enable the auditor to provide a valuable contribution, particularly from the control standpoint to the company's new systems and will, since new audit requirements can be specified during the initial design phase, decrease the chance of an "unauditable" system being developed.

Although the possibility is not mentioned in the foregoing comments, participation by auditors in computer systems design might lower the probability of computer frauds because better accounting controls may be installed at the outset. Participation of this sort also should enable auditors to use better evidence-gathering techniques and should improve the probability of detecting situations similar to that in the *Equity Funding* case (in which computers were used to process a large volume of false data).

But it is also possible that certain ethical considerations eventually will arise concerning independence. The question is interesting and demonstrates the complexity of the environment in which auditors operate, particularly in the audit of financial statements generated by computer systems.

Chapter 11
Glossary of Terms

(listed in the order of appearance in the chapter, with accompanying page reference where the term is discussed)

Term	Page in Chapter
Through the computer approaches testing the computer programs.	414
Test data simulated transactions created by the auditor and processed by the client's computer program(s). The computer output is compared with the auditor's predesigned output.	417

Term	Page in Chapter

Parallel simulation   simulated data and actual client data are run simultaneously with the client's program, and computer results are compared with auditors' predetermined amounts.   421

Online audit monitor   a set of auditor's criteria that is added to the computer edit programs used by the client to check transactions entered into the system through a terminal.   421

**Chapter 11
References**

American Institute of Certified Public Accountants. *Audit and Accounting Guide—The Auditor's Study and Evaluation of Internal Control in EDP Systems.* (New York, AICPA, 1977)

Davis, Gordon M., Adams, Donald L., and Schaller, Carol A. *Auditing and EDP,* 2nd ed., 1983, American Institute of Certified Public Accountants, New York.

Loebbecke, James K., Mullarkey, John F., and Zuber, George R. "Auditing in a Computer Environment," *Journal of Accountancy* (January 1983), pp. 68–78.

**Chapter 11
Review Questions**

11-1.   Name the six characteristics of strong computer controls listed at the beginning of the chapter.

11-2.   Describe the six steps in the general model used to acquire an understanding of the internal control structure and test the controls in a computer system.

11-3.   Give three reasons why the auditor might not perform a detailed review of some computer controls.

11-4.   What is an important question to an auditor acquiring a detailed understanding of computer general controls?

11-5.   What is the objective of the assessment of control risk in the detailed review of computer controls?

11-6.   What is the purpose of reassessing control risk after the tests of controls are conducted?

11-7.   Contrast the purpose of and the methods of conducting the three following tests of controls in a computer system.
a. Test data.
b. Parallel simulation.
c. Online audit monitor.

11-8.   What are some of the limitations of using test data?

11-9.   Describe advantages and disadvantages of using online audit monitoring.

11-10.   Describe how the use of auditors' programs differ from the use of test data.

11-11.   Describe some advantages of auditors' participation in the design of computer systems.

Chapter 11
Objective Questions Taken from CPA Examinations

11-12.   Which of the following client computer systems generally can be audited without examining or directly testing the computer programs of the system?
a. A system that performs relatively uncomplicated processes and produces detailed output.
b. A system that affects a number of essential master files and produces a limited output.
c. A system that updates a few essential master files and produces *no* printed output other than final balances.
d. A system that performs relatively complicated processing and produces very little detailed output.

11-13.   Internal control structure procedures within the computer activity may leave *no* visible evidence indicating that the procedures were performed. In such instances, the auditor should test these accounting controls by
a. Making corroborative inquiries.

b. Observing the separation of duties of personnel.

c. Reviewing transactions submitted for processing and comparing them to related output.

d. Reviewing the run manual.

11-14. Tests of controls of a computer system

a. Can be performed using only actual transactions because testing of simulated transactions is of *no* consequence.

b. Can be performed using actual transactions or simulated transactions.

c. Are impractical because many procedures within the computer activity leave *no* visible evidence of having been performed.

d. Are inadvisable because it may distort the evidence in master files.

11-15. In a daily computer run to update checking account balances and print basic details on any customer's account that was overdrawn, the overdrawn account of the computer programmer was never printed. Which of the following control procedures would have been *most* effective in detecting this irregularity?

a. Use of the test data approach by the auditor in testing the client's program and verification of the subsidiary file.

b. Use of a running control total for the master file of checking account balances and comparison with the printout.

c. A program check for valid customer code.

d. Periodic recompiling of programs from documented source programs, and comparison with programs currently in use.

11-16. After obtaining an understanding of a client's computer controls, an auditor may decide not to perform tests related to the control procedures within the computer portion of the client's internal control structure. Which of the following would *not* be a valid reason for choosing to omit tests?

a. The controls appear adequate.

b. The controls duplicate operative controls existing elsewhere in the system.

c. There appear to be major weaknesses that would preclude reliance on the stated procedure.

d. The time and dollar costs of testing exceed the time and dollar savings in substantive testing if the tests of controls show the controls to be operative.

11-17. When erroneous data are detected by computer program controls and printed on an error report, the internal control structure would be *most* adversely affected by having which of the following areas follow up on the error report?

a. Computer control group.

b. System analyst.

c. Supervisor of computer operations

d. Computer programmer.

11-18.   Assume that an auditor estimates that 10,000 checks were issued during the accounting period. If a computer application control that performs a limit check for each check request is to be subjected to the auditor's test data approach, the sample should include
   a. Approximately 1,000 test items.
   b. A number of test items determined by the auditor to be sufficient under the circumstances.
   c. A number of test items determined by the auditor's reference to the appropriate sampling tables.
   d. One transaction.

11-19.   Which of the following is likely to be of least importance to an auditor in obtaining an understanding of the internal control structure in a company with computer processing?
   a. The segregation of duties within the computer center.
   b. The control over source documents.
   c. The documentation maintained for accounting applications.
   d. The cost-benefit ratio of computer operations.

11-20.   Auditing by testing the input and output of a computer system instead of the computer program itself will
   a. Not detect program errors that do not show up in the output sampled.
   b. Detect all program errors, regardless of the nature of the output.
   c. Provide the auditor with the same type of evidence.
   d. Not provide the auditor with confidence in the results of the auditing procedures.

11-21.   Which of the following is *not* among the errors that an auditor might include in test data when auditing a client's computer system?
   a. Numeric characters in alphanumeric fields.
   b. Authorization code.
   c. Differences in description of units of measure.
   d. Illogical entries in fields whose logic is tested by programmed consistency checks.

11-22.   In auditing through a computer, the test data method is used by auditors to test the
   a. Accuracy of input data.
   b. Validity of the output.
   c. Procedures contained within the program.
   d. Normalcy of distribution of test data.

11-23.   Smith Corporation has numerous customers. A customer file is kept on disk storage. Each customer file contains name, address, credit limit, and account balance. The auditor wishes to test this file to determine whether credit limits are being exceeded. The best procedure for the auditor to follow would be to

a. Develop test data that would cause some account balances to exceed the credit limit and determine whether the system properly detects such situations.

b. Develop a program to compare credit limits with account balances and print out the details of any account with a balance exceeding its credit limit.

c. Request a printout of all account balances so they can be manually checked against the credit limits.

d. Request a printout of a sample of account balances so they can be individually checked against the credit limits.

11-24. When an auditor tests a computerized accounting system, which of the following is true of the test data approach?

a. Test data are processed by the client's computer programs under the auditor's control.

b. Test data must consist of all possible valid and invalid conditions.

c. Testing a program at year end provides assurance that the client's processing was accurate for the full year.

d. Several transactions of each type must be tested.

11-25. When auditing "around" the computer, the independent auditor focuses solely upon the source documents and

a. Test data.

b. Computer processing.

c. Compliance techniques.

d. Computer output.

Chapter 11
Discussion/Case Questions

11-26. Johnson, CPA, was engaged to audit the financial statements of Horizon Incorporated, which has its own computer installation. While obtaining a basic understanding of the internal control structure, Johnson found that Horizon lacked proper segregation of the programming and operating functions. As a result, Johnson itensified the assessment of the internal controls surrounding the computer and concluded that the existing compensating general controls provided reasonable assurance and that the objectives of the internal controls were being met.

Required:

a. In a properly functioning computer environment, how is separation of the programming and operating functions achieved?

b. What are the compensating general controls that Johnson most likely found? Do not discuss hardware and application controls.

c. If no compensating general controls were found by the auditor, should the review process be continued or should no reliance be placed on computer controls and complete reliance be placed on substantive tests? Give reasons for and against continuing the assessment process.

(AICPA adapted)

11-27.   Refer to Question 10-48 in Chapter 10. For each weakness noted in the question, indicate a general control or an application control that would overcome that weakness. Be specific in discussing the type of control (for example, an access control relating to access to computer programs or a processing control that edits the data, etc.). Give reasons the controls that you describe relate to the weaknesses.

11-28.   During an audit of a company that uses computers, Mr. Sure, the auditor, decided to process test data with some of the client's computer programs. The computer output matched his predesigned output. Later, however, Mr. Sure discovered that some of these computer programs were producing improper output. Indicate reasons that this could have happened.

11-29.   The following five topics are part of the relevant body of knowledge for CPAs who have field work or immediate supervisory responsibility in audits involving a computer:

1. Computer equipment and its capabilities.

2. Organization and management of the computer function.

3. Characteristics of computer-based systems.

4. Fundamentals of computer programming.

5. Computer center operations.

CPAs who are responsible for computer audits should possess certain general knowledge on each of these five topics. For example, on the subject of computer equipment and its capabilities, the auditor should have a general understanding of computer equipment and should be familiar with the uses and capabilities of the central processor and the peripheral equipment.

Required:
For each of the topics 2 through 5, describe the general knowledge that should be possessed by those CPAs who are responsible for computer audits.

(AICPA adapted)

11-30.   James, who was engaged to audit the financial statements of Talbert Corporation, is about to audit the payroll. Talbert uses a computer service center to process the weekly payroll as follows.

Each Monday, Talbert's payroll clerk inserts data in appropriate spaces on the preprinted service center-prepared input form, and sends the form to the service center by messenger. The service center extracts new permanent data from the input form and updates master files. The weekly payroll data are then processed. The weekly payroll register and payroll checks are printed and delivered by messenger to Talbert on Thursday.

Part of the sample selected for audit by James includes the input form and payroll register shown below.

Talbert Corporation Payroll Input—Week Ending Friday, Nov. 23, 19X9

| | Employee Data—Permanent File | | | | Current Week's Payroll Data | | | | |
| | | | | | Hours | | Special Deductions | | |
Name	Social Security	W-4 Information	Hourly Rate	Reg	OT	Bonds	Union	Other
A. Bell	999-99-9991	M-1	$10.00	35	5	$18.75		
B. Carr	999-99-9992	M-2	10.00	35	4			
C. Dawn	999-99-9993	S-1	10.00	35	6	18.75	$4.00	
D. Ellis	999-99-9994	S-1	10.00	35	2		4.00	$50.00
E. Frank	999-99-9995	M-4	10.00	35	1		4.00	
F. Gillis	999-99-9996	M-4	10.00	35			4.00	
G. Hugh	999-99-9997	M-1	7.00	35	2	18.75	4.00	
H. Jones	999-99-9998	M-2	7.00	35			4.00	25.00
J. King	999-99-9999	S-1	7.00	35	4		4.00	
New Employee								
J. Smith	999-99-9990	M-3	7.00	35				

Talbert Corporation Payroll Register—Nov. 23, 19X9

| | | Hours | | Payroll | | Gross | Taxes Withheld | | | Other | Net | Check |
Employee	Social Security	Regular	OT	Regular	OT	Payroll	FICA	Federal	State	Withheld	Pay	No.
A. Bell	999-99-9991	35	5	$350.00	$75.00	$425.00	$26.05	$76.00	$27.40	$18.75	$276.80	1499
B. Carr	999-99-9992	35	4	350.00	60.00	410.00	25.13	65.00	23.60		296.27	1500
C. Dawn	999-99-9993	35	6	350.00	90.00	440.00	26.97	100.90	28.60	22.75	260.78	1501
D. Ellis	999-99-9994	35	2	350.00	30.00	380.00	23.29	80.50	21.70	54.00	200.51	1502
E. Frank	999-99-9995	35	1	350.00	15.00	365.00	22.37	43.50	15.90	4.00	279.23	1503
F. Gillis	999-99-9996	35		350.00		350.00	21.46	41.40	15.00	4.00	268.14	1504
G. Hugh	999-99-9997	35	2	245.00	21.00	266.00	16.31	34.80	10.90	22.75	181.24	1505
H. Jones	999-99-9998	35		245.00		245.00	15.02	26.40	8.70	29.00	165.88	1506
J. King	999-99-9999	35	4	245.00	42.00	287.00	17.59	49.40	12.20	4.00	203.81	1507
J. Smith	999-99-9990	35		245.00		245.00	15.02	23.00	7.80		199.18	1508
	Totals	350	24	3080.00	333.00	3,413.00	209.21	540.90	171.80	159.25	2,331.84	

Required:

a. Describe how James should verify the information in the illustrated payroll input form.

b. Describe (but do *not* perform) the procedures that James should follow in the examination of the November 23, 19X9, payroll register.

(AICPA adapted)

11-31.   Three auditors for the CPA firm of Alford & Alford were engaged in a discussion about the best way to test the computer controls of their client, Mod-Comp., Inc. Jane Tester contended that the traditional test data method would be best because the client's computer system still used batch processing in some of its applications. Bill Oline maintained that the online audit monitor technique was best because some online processing was now being used by the client. Jim Progemer stated that they should develop their own computer program so that they would have more flexibility in testing the client's computer controls.

Required:

(If you wish to test only the general knowledge in the chapter, cover only requirement a; requirement b. is complex.)

a. Discuss the advantages and disadvantages of the three techniques advocated by each of the three auditors. (*Note:* Try to develop some answers in addition to those you obtain from reading the appropriate sections of the chapter.)

b. Show how each of these techniques would operate by developing your own data, such as the following:

(1) Develop five items of test data, the predetermined output, and the form of the computer output for the test data approach (use pages 419 and 420 as a guide).

(2) Develop 20 items of client input data and five items of auditor's specified criteria (i.e., sale made to a customer with a long outstanding balance). Develop an audit log of data that meets the audit criteria (use page 423 as a guide).

(3) Develop five items of client's actual data and develop a description of the auditors' computer program that would test these data. Show the form of the computer results and the client's output and indicate why they do or do not match (use page 425 as a guide).

CHAPTER 12

Evidence of Financial Statement Assertions

Learning Objectives   *After reading and studying the material in this chapter, the student should*

Know the professional guidelines on competency and sufficiency of audit evidence.

Understand how audit objectives are related to management assertions in the financial statements.

Know how audit procedures are derived from audit objectives.

Appreciate the need for an understanding of the client's business.

Understand how to determine known and likely error.

In this chapter we explore the general characteristics of evidence gathering techniques. Comprehensive coverage of selected audit procedures is included in subsequent chapters.

The Philosophy of Evidence Gathering

The Third Standard of Field Work

AU Section 326 (*SAS No. 31*) describes the third standard of field work as follows:

Sufficient competent evidential matter is to be obtained through inspection, observation, inquiries, and confirmations to afford a reasonable basis for an opinion regarding the financial statements under examination.

Although the term *evidence gathering* may be used in a narrow sense to refer to the acquisition of evidence regarding year-end financial statement balances, in a broader context the term represents most of the acts performed by auditors to form an opinion as to the fairness of financial statements. In the latter sense, then, evidence gathering includes the study of the internal control structure.

Guidelines for Evidence Gathering

Auditors need guidelines to help them decide on the competency and sufficiency of audit evidence. Competency refers to the validity and relevance of the evidence, whereas sufficiency refers to the amount of evidence to be obtained. Some *general* guidelines are furnished in *SAS No. 31,* but otherwise auditors must apply their own judgment in selecting specific audit procedures and deciding the amount and types of evidence to be gathered.

The Competency of Audit Evidence

Certain types of audit evidence may be more competent, that is, more valid and relevant, than others. The following guidance assists auditors in evaluating the competency of various types of audit evidence.

Evidence from Independent Sources   AU Section 326 (*SAS No. 31*) states that

When evidential matter can be obtained from independent sources outside an entity, it provides greater assurance of reliability for the purposes of an independent audit than that secured solely within the entity.

Although this statement would seem to be axiomatic in today's audit environment, remember that two landmark fraud cases (*Ultramares* and *McKesson & Robbins*) might not have occurred, or the frauds might have been detected in the audits, if evidence of accounts receivable and inventory had been acquired from independent outside sources. More recently, as a result of the *Equity Funding* case, a suggestion has been made by a special committee of the AICPA that independent confirmations be obtained of an insurance company's insurance in force if the amount is material.

Therefore, there is probably little opposition to the theoretical guideline that "outside" evidence should be obtained, if possible. The auditors' practical problem, however, is determining the specific outside evidence that should be gathered. Discussion of certain accounts shows which ones might be susceptible to outside verification.

The key, of course, is whether the information in question is known by some outside party. For example, the amounts of cash and marketable securities probably can be verified independently if they are held by outside entities. In contrast, deferred income taxes and goodwill are created as the result of internal calculations, and outside confirmation of authenticity cannot be obtained by auditors.

Accounts receivable and accounts payable usually qualify for independent outside verification because they represent individual balances owed by customers and to creditors. Sales and cost of products sold typically do not qualify for the same basic reason that deferred income tax and goodwill do not—these two income statement accounts cannot be authenticated by outside entities in the aggregate.

As a general rule, then, auditors will attempt to confirm with an independent outside source (1) tangible assets held by outside organizations, (2) debts owed to or by the client, and (3) other information that there is reason to believe an outside source can verify.

Evidence and Control Risk   Another auditing standard guideline provides that when accounting data and financial statements are developed under conditions of low control risk there is more assurance about their reliability than when they are developed under conditions of high control risk.

The question of how much or what type of audit scope adjustment to make for the quality of the internal control structure is a matter of judgment for which there are few definite criteria. Some auditors might confine tests of certain accounts to analytical procedures if the control structure is exceptionally strong. Other auditors might take a different viewpoint and make only a small change in the amount of testing, regardless of the control structure.

The inventory account can be used to illustrate the inverse relationship between internal control structure and substantive testing. The inventory account often constitutes a significant portion of both current and total assets and has an important effect on net income. Thus, it is natural to assume that inventories are given substantial testing by auditors.

What change can auditors make in the nature, timing, or extent of inventory testing if control structure is strong? One answer is that the client's inventory count may be observed at times other than year end *if* an accurate perpetual inventory system is in use. An illustration of this concept is shown on page 438.

If the auditors observed the client's inventory count at November 30 and a review of the inventory system and tests of the perpetual inventory records gave them relative assurance that these records were reliable, a December 31 balance of $20,800 probably would be acceptable. Some review would be made of the intervening transactions in the client's perpetual inventory records from November 30 through December 31. But because the reliability of the inventory records already has been established, this would not be a detailed review.

Date	Perpetual Inventory Records (in dollars) from 11-30 through 12-31			Physical Inventory Count (in dollars) as of 11-30
	Purchases	Issues	Balance	
11-30	$	$	$20,000	$20,000 (inventory count
12-3	1000[a]		21,000	observed by auditors)
12-5		500[a]	20,500	
12-10		400[a]	20,100	
12-15	1000[a]		21,100	
12-20	500[a]		21,600	
12-27		800[a]	20,800	? (not taken by client)

[a]Transactions reviewed by auditors.

If, on the other hand, the internal control structure relating to inventories contains many weaknesses, an extensive year-end inventory observation by the auditor might not produce audit evidence as competent as the preceding interim observation.

Evidence from Direct Personal Knowledge   The third *SAS No. 31* guideline for judging the competency of audit evidence is as follows:

> The independent auditor's direct personal knowledge, obtained through physical examination, observation, computation, and inspection, is more persuasive than information obtained indirectly.

Inventories again provide an example of the relative competency of evidence. Assume that this account consists of inventories held for the client by a public warehouse. A letter from the warehouse attesting to the existence and ownership of the inventories furnishes auditors with persuasive evidence that the inventories do exist and that they are owned by the client. However, physical observation of the inventories may give auditors *more* persuasive evidence of existence and ownership.

Even physical examination of the inventories may not furnish auditors with completely reliable evidence, however. For example, the inventory may consist of grain stored in a storage silo, and an auditor may be unable to distinguish his or her client's grain from that owned by others. Therefore the term *persuasive* is used rather than *convincing*.

One can easily ascertain some accounts that are suitable for evidence gathering through direct personal knowledge:

1. Marketable securities can be examined.

2. The client's count of physical inventories can be observed.

3. Taxes on income can be computed and compared with the client's computation.

4. Depreciation and amortization can be computed (probably on a test basis) and compared with the client's computation.

Direct personal knowledge by the auditor may not produce competent evidence if specialized knowledge is required. In this case, the auditor may consider the use of a specialist. Specialists may be used to value works of art, estimate mineral reserves, make actuarial determinations, and so forth. If a specialist is used, the auditor must be satisfied with his or her professional reputation and should review any methods or assumptions that materially affect the specialist's findings. Normally, an auditor does not refer to the work of a specialist in the audit report.

The Sufficiency of Audit Evidence

The Persuasiveness of Evidence   SAS No. 31 also contains criteria for judging the sufficiency of audit evidence; that is, how much and what type should be gathered. One guideline relates to persuasiveness:

> The amount and kinds of evidential matter required to support an informed opinion are matters for the auditor to determine in the exercise of his professional judgment after a careful study of the circumstances in the particular case. In the great majority of cases, the auditor finds it necessary to rely on evidence that is persuasive rather than convincing.

A good illustration of the difficulty of gathering convincing evidence is the process of determining the fairness of the allowance for doubtful accounts. Consider the reason for the account and its composition. The purpose of the account is to reduce the accounts receivable balance to its estimated realizable amount. The estimate is based on the client's judgment as to which accounts or what percentage of the accounts receivable balance may be uncollectible.

There is no way to confirm the collectibility of the account balance with an independent source, and it cannot be verified by inspection. Auditors usually find out what method the client used to calculate the allowance (perhaps from an aging schedule). Next, the auditors test the accuracy of the client's calculations. Finally, the auditors render a *judgment* as to whether the client's assumptions are sound. In all likelihood, some of the best evidence that auditors can acquire is a summary of the collection history and some opinions (often from the client) on the collectibility of slow paying accounts. This evidence may be persuasive, but far from convincing.

Another prime example of the difficulty of gathering convincing evidence is the process of evaluating contingent liabilities arising from pending or threatened lawsuits against the client. Normally, auditors do not have the expertise to make a reasonable prediction of the outcome of unsettled litigation, and typically they turn to the client's lawyer for an opinion. The lawyer's response is important evidence because his or her opinion might cause the auditors to request an entry to record a liability on the client's books. The lawyer's response is also important in determining the type of opinion the auditors will render on the company's financial statements. In certain situations, auditors may be forced to give a qualified opinion if the lawyer is unwilling to give an evaluation of the probable outcome of the litigation pending against the client.

Evidence obtained from legal counsel on matters discussed in the preceding paragraph is persuasive but not convincing, because it is entirely possible that the lawyer may be unable to give a firm opinion or the opinion may be wrong. In addition, any response received from the client's lawyer may contain some bias because of the lawyer's vested interest in receiving a favorable verdict from the courts.

The Cost of Obtaining Evidence   Another guideline on the sufficiency of evidence is contained in *SAS No. 31*.

> An auditor typically works within economic limits; his opinion, to be economically useful, must be formed within a reasonable length of time and at reasonable cost. . . . As a guiding rule, there should be a rational relationship between the cost of obtaining evidence and the usefulness of the information obtained.

This guideline suggests that auditors should consider the relationship between (1) the value of additional assurance that can be obtained by gathering further evidence and (2) the cost of gathering such evidence. For example, assume that an audit client has 1,000 individual customer accounts that comprise total accounts receivable. The auditor has decided to gather evidence regarding the existence of accounts receivable by confirmation procedures and considers the following sample sizes and related levels of assurance (these levels of assurance may be considered implicitly and may not be quantified).

Number of Confirmations	*Level of Assurance*	*Increase in*	
		Confirmations	*Assurance*
100	80%	100	80%
200	90	100	10
300	95	100	5
400	97	100	2
500	98	100	1
.	.	.	.
.	.	.	.
.	.	.	.
1000	99+	100	—

As can be seen, each additional 100 confirmations, at approximately the same cost, provides less and less *additional* assurance. An auditor uses professional judgment to determine the point at which additional confirmations cost more than the value of the additional assurance obtained. It is not unlikely that different auditors may select different cutoff points because professional judgments may vary.

Another example of the cost-benefit relationship of evidence gathering is the audit of property and equipment accounts. Except, possibly, for initial examinations, auditors generally do not conduct a physical inspection of the fixed assets that constitute the beginning balance in the client's balance sheet. They usually confine their audit procedures to the additions and retirements that are recorded, and should have been recorded, during the year.

Though an annual inspection of property and equipment would provide auditors with additional evidence of the accounts' validity, the cost of such a procedure in most cases would greatly outweigh the benefit. The turnover rate of property and equipment is usually low, and evidence of the authenticity of these accounts can be gathered with other audit procedures.

Although an auditor considers the cost of obtaining evidence in relation to its usefulness, it is equally important to note that the difficulty and expense involved in testing a particular item do not constitute valid reasons for omitting a test that, in the auditor's judgment, is required. For example, if a significant portion of inventory is stored at a remote location, the extra time and expense required to observe that inventory would not justify omitting the procedure if the auditor believed that observation was necessary.

The Evaluation of Evidence

A criterion for the evaluation of audit evidence is contained in *SAS No. 31.*

> In developing his opinion, the auditor should give consideration to relevant evidential matter regardless of whether it appears to corroborate or to contradict the assertions in the financial statements.

Auditors may be tempted to search for evidence that confirms their beliefs about the accounting records. For example, if an auditor believes that the error rate in a population is 5 percent, he or she is likely to be satisfied with the result of a sample that indicates an error rate of 5 percent or less. On the other hand, if the result of a sample indicates a 6-percent error rate, the auditor may be tempted to increase the sample by the number of items which, if they contain no errors, will reduce the sample error rate to 5 percent. This practice seems contrary to the preceding criterion. The auditor should not attempt to convert contradictory evidence to corroborative evidence or vice versa. If the preceding sample size was originally too small, it should have been increased regardless of the sample outcome, not because of it. Auditors should maintain an attitude of *professional skepticism* toward the evidence they obtain and client assertions in the financial statements.

Evidence Gathering

The collective purpose of all audit procedures is to gather sufficient competent evidence to form an opinion regarding the financial statements taken as a whole. In a narrower sense, however, the individual audit procedures depend on the nature of the account under examination, the objectives of auditing that account, the risks associated with that account, and the documents or records used to compile the account balance.

For example, certain accounts, such as sales and expenses, represent totals of transactions for a certain period, usually a year. Other accounts, such as property and equipment, represent accumulated balances from several years. Still other accounts represent balances with a rapid turnover, such as cash and accounts receivable. Other aspects of an account that influence audit procedures are volume of transactions (usually small for capital stock and long-term debt and large for cash and accounts payable), and verifiability (such as physical observation of inventories and calculation of deferred charges).

A discussion of evidence gathering, then, must include consideration of the following factors:

1. The means of gathering audit evidence.

2. The characteristics of such evidence.

3. The objectives of auditing a particular account (including their relationship to management assertions regarding that account).

4. The audit procedures required to satisfy the objectives.

The first two factors are generally applicable to the audit of any account, whereas the last two are unique to each account.

The Means of Gathering Audit Evidence

Generally, evidence gathering techniques can be categorized as follows (all may not be applicable to each account):

1. Observation—auditors observe or watch the performance of some function.

2. Confirmation—auditors obtain acknowledgments in writing from third parties of transactions, balances, and other information.

3. Calculation—auditors recompute certain account balances.

4. Analysis—auditors combine or decompose amounts in meaningful ways to allow the application of audit judgment.

5. Inquiry—auditors question client personnel about transactions and balances.

6. Inspection—auditors examine documents relating to transactions and balances.

7. Comparison—auditors relate two or more transactions or balances.

For the audit of certain accounts, all seven techniques might be used. The inventory account serves as an example.

1. Normally, inventory quantities are counted by the client at year end. The evidence of the validity of these quantities can be obtained by *observation* of the client's count.

2. Some of the year-end inventory may be on consignment or in public warehouses. Evidence of the existence of this merchandise can be acquired by *confirmation* from the party holding the inventory.

3. Evidence that inventory listings have been properly extended and totaled is acquired by *calculation*.

4. For inventory to be stated fairly at the balance sheet date, a proper year-end cutoff (a determination that only goods on hand at the end of the year are included in inventory and that all liabilities for goods on hand are recorded properly) should be made by the client. To determine that a proper inventory cutoff is made, the auditors use *analysis*.

5. During the process of observing the client's inventory count, auditors sometimes have questions about the manner in which various quantities are determined and the possible obsolescence of certain items. The auditors may attempt to obtain answers to these questions by *inquiry* of client personnel.

6. The testing of inventory transactions represented by vendor invoices, material issue tickets, shipping records, and so on is a necessary part of determining the reliability of the records that support the inventory account. These documents can be tested by *inspection*.

7. Inventory should be priced at the lower of cost or market. Auditors can gather evidence that this procedure is used by making *comparisons* of inventory cost to vendor invoices and price lists.

The auditor uses the seven techniques to design the specific audit procedures to be applied in each area of the audit.

The Characteristics of Audit Evidence

The auditor should appreciate the different characteristics of audit evidence and the reliance that can be placed on each type. Audit evidence can be characterized as one of the following types:

1. Generated and held by the client.

2. Received from outside parties and held by the client.

3. Determined or received directly by the auditor by independent means or from independent parties.

The first type consists of the client's books and records (the general ledger, etc.) as well as corroborating documents such as client sales invoices, disbursement checks, and purchase orders. Minutes of meetings of the board of directors and stockholders also are examples of this type of evidence.

The second category of evidence includes purchase orders from customers, purchase invoices from vendors, bank statements, titles to properties, insurance policies, and so forth. The fact that independent parties prepare the documents and send them to the client adds reliability to this type of evidence. Client custody of these documents takes away some of their reliability.

Generally, the third classification of evidence is considered the most reliable, because the auditors obtain this evidence from independent parties and control its use. The most common type of independent evidence consists of letters obtained from customers, creditors, insurance companies, lawyers, and others concerning the status of certain financial information.

An auditor normally prefers evidence of the third type if available, but in many situations it is impossible or impracticable to obtain (as in the audit of deferred income taxes, payroll expense, unamortized debt discount, etc.). In using evidence of the first type, the auditor must be particularly alert and consider, among other things, the source from which the evidence originated within the client company. For example, more reliance may be placed on a sales invoice supported by a shipping ticket from the shipping department than on a journal entry prepared within the accounting department. Similarly, an auditor may place more reliance on an explanation for a variation in annual sales received from a plant manager than on a similar explanation received from the chief accountant. The reason for this bias is that the chief accountant generally will give an explanation to support the amounts shown in the accounting records, whereas the plant manager, who may be unaware of what is shown in the accounting records, is more likely to base the explanation on actual operating factors. The auditor attempts to obtain the most independent evidence that is available. As mentioned earlier, however, the auditor's decisions concerning what evidence to gather are complicated by time constraints and cost-benefit considerations.

In the case of an examination of accounts receivable, the auditors could use the third type of evidence to satisfy the objective of ascertaining the existence of the balances that constitute this account. Evidence of proper valuation, however, would require some use of the first and second evidence categories.

Audit Objectives

Before beginning the examination, the auditor must define carefully the audit objectives for each account. Although this statement may sound rather basic, auditors sometimes tend to begin their work by mailing confirmations to customers, examining invoices and canceled checks, and performing numerous other tasks without first considering what they are attempting to accomplish for each account and then determining the best, most efficient way to proceed. Only by knowing what the objectives are can an auditor know whether they have been accomplished. For example, an auditor may decide that one objective in auditing cash is to determine that it is not restricted and is subject to immediate withdrawal; but if this objective is not specified, the auditor may omit the audit steps necessary to accomplish it. Similarly, by establishing objectives, the auditor may avoid excess work that does not contribute to their accomplishment.

An auditor determines the objectives of auditing each account by relating them to the assertions, either explicit or implicit, that management makes regarding that account. The general assertions that may be made regarding an account are introduced in Chapter 8 and discussed more fully here.

1. *Existence or occurrence*—for example, that accounts such as inventories and accounts payable actually exist at a given date and that transactions such as sales and expenses actually occurred during a given period.

2. *Rights and obligations*—for example, that accounts such as inventories are actually owned and accounts payable are actually owed.

3. *Completeness*—for example, that all inventories and accounts payable that exist are included in the balance sheet and that all sales and expenses that occurred are included in the income statement.

4. *Valuation or allocation*—for example, that inventories are recorded at the lower of cost (determined in accordance with generally accepted ac-

counting principles) or market and that allocations of cost in the form of depreciation are made to the appropriate period.

5. *Presentation and disclosure*—for example, that inventory classified as a current asset is expected to be sold within one year or the normal operating cycle and that any pledging of inventory to collateralize debt is adequately disclosed.

Thus, the auditor's objectives in the audit of each account are to determine whether management's assertions concerning the account are appropriate. Within this general framework, each individual account may be analyzed to determine specific objectives.

In some cases, the auditor must determine the proper accounting treatment for the financial statement item either by reference to official pronouncements or by a knowledge of the "generally accepted" accounting principle in order to establish his or her objective. As an example, Section I 78 of FASB *Accounting Standards* contains these comments on inventory.[1]

Cost Principle

Cost is defined as the sum of the applicable expenditures and charges directly or indirectly incurred in bringing inventories to their existing condition and location.

Pricing Options

Cost for inventory purposes shall be determined under any one of several assumptions as to the flow of cost factors (such as first-in first-out, average, and last-in first-out); the major objective in selecting a method shall be to choose the one that most clearly reflects periodic income.

Lower of Cost or Market Principle

A departure from the cost basis of pricing the inventory is required when the utility of the goods is no longer as great as its cost. If the utility of goods is impaired by damage, deterioration, obsolescence, changes in price levels, or other causes, a loss shall be reflected as a charge against the revenues of the period in which it occurs. The measurement of such losses shall be accomplished by applying the rule of pricing inventories at (lower of) cost or market.

One specific objective in auditing inventory, then, is to ascertain that the amount of inventory shown on the balance sheet is stated at the lower of cost or market, by use of one of the generally accepted pricing methods. This objective, in turn, relates to the broad objective of determining that the inventory is valued properly.

[1] All accounting references are to *Accounting Standards* published by the Financial Accounting Standards Board.

In other cases, the specific objectives flow naturally from the broad ones. Again with inventory as an example, the broad objective of authenticating existence leads to the specific objective of determining that the inventory amount on the balance sheet is represented by physical items actually on hand, in transit, or on consignment. By this approach, the auditor can arrive at the following specific objectives for the audit of inventories.

1. Determine whether the inventory amount on the balance sheet is represented by all physical items actually on hand, in transit, or on consignment (existence and completeness).

2. Determine whether the inventory is calculated properly at the lower of cost or market in accordance with generally accepted accounting principles consistently applied (valuation).

3. Determine whether the inventory belongs to the company and whether any liens on the inventory are disclosed properly (rights and disclosure).

4. Determine whether any excess, slow-moving, or special-purpose items are properly valued and classified (valuation and presentation).

A similar approach may be used to arrive at the audit objectives for other financial statement amounts.

Audit Procedures

After the audit objectives have been determined, the next step is to define the audit procedures that will accomplish the specified objectives. There is no one set or official list of audit procedures that can be used on each engagement, because the nature of the accounts and their materiality vary. For example, the procedures for the audit of inventory existence and valuation of a manufacturer of a complex product with several stages of production and a sophisticated standard cost system would be different from those for a company whose inventory consists of a large pile of coal. Also, if inventory is an immaterial amount in the financial statements, only a few limited procedures may need to be applied to this account. Finally, inherent and control risks are important determinants of both the extent and nature of auditing procedures in a particular engagement.

As pointed out previously, the greater the inherent and control risks, the more reliance the auditor must place on the related tests of balances and transactions and analytical procedures. There is no precise scale with which these risks can be measured; neither is there a related table indicating the percentage of inventory items to be counted or accounts receivable to be confirmed. Some accounting firms have developed structured decision aids to attempt to quantify the effectiveness of the control structure and the extensiveness of audit procedures. Judgment, however, with a tempering of experience, remains the basis for both the evaluation of controls and the determination of the extent of audit procedures. Exercise of this judgment, of course, is one trademark of a professional.

Although an all-inclusive list of audit procedures cannot be prepared, the following procedures are representative of those often followed in the audit of inventories. Note that the procedures are keyed to the objectives (assertions) to which they relate.

1. Review, test, and evaluate the inherent and control risks relating to inventories. (Normally this would include controls in the purchasing and payroll areas.)

2. At year end, *observe* the client's inventory counting and recording procedures to determine whether they are adequate to result in an accurate inventory. Make and record test counts of inventory and compare them with those made by the client. Recount any items for which differences are found (existence and completeness).

3. *Confirm* the existence and ownership of inventory held on consignment or in public warehouses (existence and rights).

4. Test the propriety of the cutoff of inventory shipments and receipts by recording the numbers and descriptions of the last five shipping and receiving reports during the year-end inventory observation, and at a later date, *inspect* the first five shipping and receiving documents after the end of the year. *Analyze* the sales and purchase invoices that correspond with those shipping and receiving documents and determine whether (a) items recorded as sales in the current period were excluded from inventory, (b) items recorded as sales in the subsequent period were included in inventory, (c) items recorded as purchases in the current period were included in inventory, and (d) items recorded as purchases in the subsequent period were excluded from inventory (existence, completeness, and rights).

5. During the inventory observation, look for and *inquire* about any excess, slow-moving, obsolete, or unsalable inventory. Indications of such items would be a covering of dust or rust, or prior-year inventory tags (valuation and presentation).

6. *Account for* all prenumbered inventory tags before and after the physical inventory (existence and completeness).

7. Obtain a copy of the final inventory listing and test *clerical accuracy*. *Compare* inventory prices with purchase invoices. *Test the calculation* of the inventory amount on the basis of the method used (i.e., FIFO, LIFO, average) and *compare* with market—the lower of replacement cost or net realizable value (valuation and rights).

8. Review *confirmations* received from banks and other creditors and *minutes* of the board of directors for indications of pledges or assignments of inventories (rights and disclosures).

9. Apply *analytical procedures* to the inventory balance in relation to sales, production, shipments, and purchases and compare with prior year and budget (existence, completeness, and valuation).

These procedures are necessarily more general than those in an actual audit engagement, but they demonstrate how audit procedures are designed to accomplish the audit objectives. Normally, several procedures are required to achieve an objective fully, and, in many cases, one procedure will contribute to the fulfillment of more than one objective.

Auditing Accounting Estimates

Accounting estimates present special challenges to auditors because they are based on subjective as well as objective factors. The subjective factors increase the opportunity for intentional and unintentional bias in the estimates. The subjective factors also make controls more difficult to establish over accounting estimates. Examples of accounting estimates include allowances for doubtful accounts, inventory obsolescence, and warranty costs.

Auditors should identify all relevant estimates and then determine whether they are properly presented.

The need for accounting estimates may be identified from a knowledge of the client's business and a review of pertinent documentation. For example, an auditor may know from prior experience or a review of sales contracts that a client provides a warranty on its product. This would identify a need for an estimate for an allowance for warranty costs for products sold as of the balance sheet date.

To determine a reasonable amount or range of amounts for an identified estimate, the auditor may consider relevant historical data and events occurring subsequent to the balance sheet date. For example, historical data may indicate that one-tenth of 1 percent of all sales are returned for repair or replacement within a 30-day warranty period. The auditor may estimate an allowance for warranty costs at the balance sheet date as one-tenth of 1 percent of sales for the last month of the year. This estimate could then be evaluated for reasonableness by comparing it with warranty costs recorded in the first month of the following year.

Some estimates, such as a potential loss from litigation, are very difficult to estimate because there are no relevant historical data or subsequent transactions. In these cases disclosure may be all that is required by generally accepted accounting principles.

A Business Approach to Auditing

It is important that auditors maintain an overall perspective of the financial statements they are examining. They may easily become involved in the details and forget to ask, "Does this answer or presentation make good sense in light of present industry and economic conditions?" To be able to answer that question adequately, auditors must understand the client's business operations and have some knowledge of industry and economic conditions. This means that auditors must be more than number checkers; they must develop business judgment and knowledge equal to or greater than those of the clients they serve.

This knowledge will help auditors identify audit areas needing special consideration and determine the appropriateness of accounting principles and the adequacy of disclosure. Also, they will be in a better position to evaluate the reasonableness of estimates and representations made by management.

Auditors acquire an understanding of the client's business operations by discussions with operating personnel as well as with financial personnel. During the audit, they should not isolate themselves in the accounting department, but should seek explanations for variations in the client's operations from engineers, operation managers, marketing managers, and others. After all, it is the client's business operations that are reflected in the financial statements. Who could be more qualified to discuss and explain them than the people directly involved? Such discussions are useful not only to provide audit evidence, but also to broaden auditors' understanding of the operation of business in general and the client's business in particular. This understanding allows them to use such techniques as operating and financial ratio analyses as more effective audit tools and to detect financial statement items that appear unusual. Audit work then can be concentrated on these items. Analytical procedures are applications of the business approach.

Auditors have many sources from which to gain knowledge of a particular industry and general economic conditions. Periodicals and other publications are available for almost every industry, and government agencies publish a wide range of business statistics. Knowledge of general economic conditions can be secured by reading such publications as *The Wall Street Journal* and *Business Week*.

The application of operating, industry, and general economic knowledge to the audit of financial statements sometimes is referred to as "the business approach" to an audit. Some examples of how this could be useful follow.

1. You are reviewing the audit trial balance of a sugar refiner at the beginning of an audit, and you are surprised by a large increase in sales during the current year. Because of your knowledge of the industry, you know the approximate average price per pound of sugar during the year; dividing this price into total sales gives you approximately 10 million pounds sold during the year. You recall that the production capacity of your client's plant is only 6 million pounds per year. Though there may be a reason for this

difference (reduction of inventory, purchase of refined sugar from others for resale, etc.), you make a note to consider expanding your audit work in the sales area.

2. In your audit of a manufacturing company, you note that the gross profit ratio has increased from 20 to 30 percent, but you know that because of overcapacity in the industry, several sales price reductions were made during the year which alone would result in a decline in the gross profit ratio. When the client is unable to explain the increase satisfactorily, you revise your audit program to increase tests of inventory (for possible overstatement), accounts payable (for possible unrecorded purchases), and sales (for possible price allowances).

3. While reviewing the audit trial balance, you note that interest income on short-term investments has increased from that of the prior year. You mentally calculate that the average rate of interest received during the year, based on an average of the beginning and ending amounts invested, was 12 percent; however, from your knowledge of general economic conditions, you know that short-term interest rates did not exceed 10 percent during the entire year. You recompute interest income for the year because you believe it is overstated and find that the client did make an error by accruing interest receivable for the last quarter of the year twice. Your new assistant thinks that you have some strange, mystical, extrasensory power.

Ratio Analysis

One specific application of a business approach to auditing is the calculation and evaluation of certain financial statement ratios. These data should not be computed and appraised mechanically without regard for the business and industry environment in which the client operates. But if such computations are used properly and are integrated with pertinent information obtained from other sources, they can be valuable tools in allocating more efficiently the auditor's time and efforts.

As an illustration, assume the calculation of the following ratios for the client's current and prior years' financial statements (the current year's statements are preliminary, and audit adjustments have not been made).

Ratio	19X8	19X9
Gross profit	32.1	27.3
Accounts receivable turnover	5.5	4.2
Inventory turnover	6.3	7.2

What audit significance can be attached to these ratios? Taken in the abstract, they probably mean little. But coupled with business information obtained from other sources, they could show the auditor where to concentrate audit effort. Here are some examples.

1. For an auditor to evaluate properly the decline in the gross profit ratio several factors must be considered, such as (a) variations in sales volume, (b) relationships of fixed and variable costs, (c) variations in sales price, (d) variations in production costs, (e) variations in production volume, and (f) method of inventory computation. The decline in the gross profit rate could properly result from such factors as lower sales volume, higher production costs, and lower sales prices. The auditor is concerned that it did not result from understated inventory, overstated purchases, or understated sales.

2. Accounts receivable turnover decreased from 19X8 to 19X9. In 19X9, credit sales increased, credit terms remained the same, and a new system of more rapid billing was introduced. Under these conditions, the auditor concludes that accounts-receivable turnover *should* have increased in 19X9 unless slow-paying customers caused collections to falter. The auditor should expand the scope of the work in auditing the allowance for doubtful accounts.

3. The inventory turnover increased in 19X9. But considering the introduction of a new line of high-turnover merchandise, the increase appears modest. During the inventory observation, it was noted that there were unusually large stocks of certain lines of merchandise on hand. The auditor should devote special attention to audit procedures designed to detect obsolete inventory.

The foregoing examples are only a few of the many that could be presented. Effective use of ratio analysis may help to point out critical areas and thus result in a better-quality audit.

Regression Analysis

Another specific application of the business approach to auditing is the use of regression analysis to predict the dollar amount of an account. If this predicted amount is materially different from the actual amount recorded on the client's records, special audit effort is devoted to that account. Regression analysis measures the rate at which a dependent variable changes in relation to an independent variable. For simple linear regression, the analysis is illustrated in the graph on page 453.

The independent variable can be expressed as number of units, number of hours, number of dollars, and so forth. The dependent variable can also be expressed as one of several measures. Some examples of independent and dependent variables are (1) machine hours and repair expenses, (2) direct labor costs and indirect labor costs, and (3) sales dollars and delivery expenses. We will use the third example for illustration.

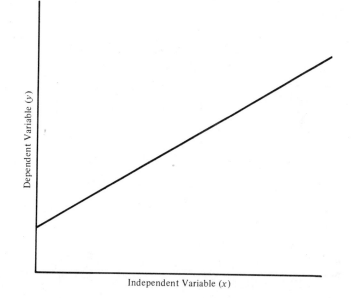

A first-order regression function[2] may be expressed as

$$E(Y) = B_0 + B_1X$$

where

    $E(Y)$ is the expected value of Y (the account to be predicted).
    X is the account believed to have a relationship with Y.
    B_0 is often thought of as the fixed element of the account to be predicted, but it may have no particular meaning as a separate term in the regression function.
    B_1 is the rate of change of Y for each unit change in X.

    The auditor may believe that there should be a close relationship between the client's dollar sales for the year and delivery expense and decide to predict the amount of delivery expense by using simple linear regression analysis.

    To predict the delivery expense rate of variability in relation to dollar sales, the auditor collects the actual dollar amounts of both accounts for the previous ten years. (In practice, three years of monthly data are often used.) It is assumed that the dollar relationships that exist between these accounts for the ten-year period are typical of the relationship that should exist in the current year.

    Sales and delivery expense for the ten-year period follow.

[2] For information regarding the use of regression analysis in auditing, see Kenneth W. Stringer and Trevor R. Stewart, *Statistical Techniques for Analytical Review in Auditing* (New York: Wiley, 1986).

Year	Sales (in thousands of dollars)	Delivery Expense (in thousands of dollars)
19W9	$10,019	$ 78
19X0	11,904	94
19X1	13,638	110
19X2	15,622	127
19X3	19,431	151
19X4	22,774	175
19X5	26,058	183
19X6	31,354	210
19X7	35,900	255
19X8	41,895	317

By use of the ordinary least squares statistical technique, the auditor calculates the estimated fixed portion of delivery expense at $10,000 and the estimated variable portion at $.007 per sales dollar. The auditor could plot the data on a chart and draw the calculated variable expense line. Such a graph follows on page 455.

An examination of the graph shows that the correlation between sales and delivery expense appears to be very high (the coefficient of determination is .98). Unless the auditor has other evidence to contradict the appearance of high correlation, he or she may assume that $10,000 plus $.007 per sales dollar is a good predictor of delivery expense.

The next step is to calculate the predicted amount of delivery expense for the current year and compare it with the actual figure on the client's 19X9 income statement. If, in the auditor's judgment, the difference is too large, more than the usual amount of audit effort should be directed at this account.[3]

Assume that 19X9 sales are $45,000,000 and 19X9 delivery expense is $300,000. The predicted delivery expense is $325,000 [$10,000 + (.007 × $45,000,000)]. The auditor must make a judgment on the materiality of this difference. If he or she considers the $25,000 to be material, he or she might examine a significant portion of the evidence supporting the delivery expense account. Such an examination could reveal misclassifications of expenditures between delivery expense and other accounts. Another possibility is that sales are overstated.

A decision to concentrate audit effort in this direction might have been made by a cursory examination of delivery expense and sales for the prior ten years. Regression analysis techniques refine the process. The methodology is easy to apply and with the advent of sophisticated microcomputers, the calculations can be made quickly.[4] However, the auditor should be aware that a number of statisti-

---

[3] The auditor may calculate confidence intervals at a certain risk level to aid in identifying large variations.

[4] See Terry L. Brock, "Multiple Regression on Lotus 1-2-3," *Journal of Accountancy* (July 1986), pp. 106–110.

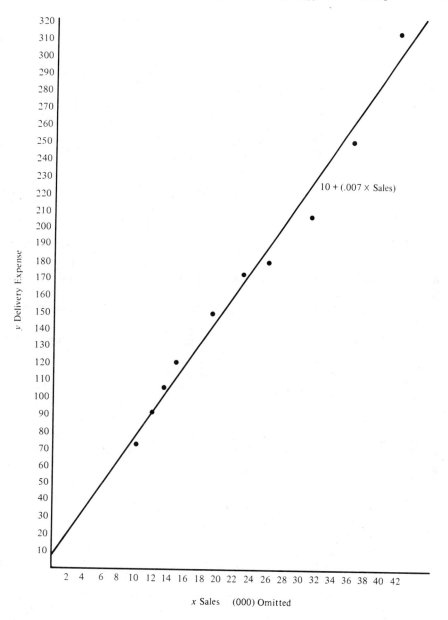

x Sales   (000) Omitted

cal assumptions are involved in the use of regression analysis and that violation of these assumptions may bias the results. These assumptions are not reviewed here, but may be found in most basic statistics books.

Relationships among Accounts

Auditors must be aware of the natural flow of funds through a set of financial statements while performing their audit work. This flow of funds and the resulting

Table 12.1
Accounts on Which Audit Work Is Often Performed Simultaneously

Balance Sheet Accounts	Income Statement Accounts
Accounts receivable	Sales and bad debt expense
Inventories	Cost of goods sold
Investment securities	Other income (dividends and interest)
Property and equipment	Maintenance and depreciation expense
Prepaid insurance	Insurance expense
Notes payable	Interest expense
Accrued income taxes	Income tax expense

relationships are such that evidence gathered to support the propriety of one account often contributes to the accomplishment of the audit objectives for another account. For example, audit procedures performed and evidence gathered in the audit of inventory, cash, and accounts payable contribute to the audit of cost of goods sold. Likewise, the auditor who has satisfactorily tested the client's procedures for recording sales and cash transactions has a certain amount of evidence in support of accounts receivable before performing any audit procedures listed in that section. Table 12.1 illustrates pairs of accounts on which audit work is often performed simultaneously.

Many of the balance sheet accounts listed in Table 12.1 can be confirmed by outside parties (accounts receivable and notes payable) or observed by the auditor (inventories and investment securities). Many of the income statement accounts, because they represent a large number of individual items flowing through the accounts during the year (sales and cost of goods sold), require great reliance on tests of the procedures for recording income and expense and the internal control structure. These two approaches, however, are complementary; confirmation and observation contribute to the audit of the income statement accounts, and the tests of controls add assurance to the audit of the balance sheet accounts. In fact, the double-entry accounting system allows accounts to be audited from two directions.

Consider sales, for example. This account can be, and to some extent is, audited by examining evidence to support the amounts recorded in the account, such as sales invoices and shipping documents. This is only a portion of the evidence gathered for the audit of sales, however. The following equation

$$\begin{matrix} \text{Accounts} \\ \text{receivable} \\ \text{at beginning} \\ \text{of a period} \end{matrix} + \begin{matrix} \text{Credit} \\ \text{sales} \\ \text{for a} \\ \text{period} \end{matrix} - \begin{matrix} \text{Cash} \\ \text{collections} \\ \text{of accounts} \\ \text{receivable} \end{matrix} = \begin{matrix} \text{Accounts} \\ \text{receivable} \\ \text{at end of a} \\ \text{period} \end{matrix}$$

can be rewritten as

$$\begin{array}{c} \text{Credit} \\ \text{sales} \\ \text{for a} \\ \text{period} \end{array} = \begin{array}{c} \text{Accounts} \\ \text{receivable} \\ \text{at end of} \\ \text{a period} \end{array} + \begin{array}{c} \text{Cash} \\ \text{collections} \\ \text{of accounts} \\ \text{receivable} \end{array} - \begin{array}{c} \text{Accounts} \\ \text{receivable} \\ \text{at beginning} \\ \text{of a period} \end{array}$$

Because it is a common practice in many companies to record all sales through accounts receivable, credit sales are often equivalent to total sales. In these cases, by auditing the accounts receivable balance at the end of a period (assuming that the balance at the beginning of the period was audited in the prior year), and by testing the controls over recording cash receipts, the auditor adds evidence to the audit of sales without gathering any evidence in direct support of the amounts recorded in the sales account.

Related Party Transactions

When auditors examine or obtain evidence from a third party, such as vendor invoices, confirmations, or sales agreements, they normally assume that the third party is independent of the client. If this assumption is invalid, the evidence will be less reliable. Also, the audit risk associated with related party transactions may be higher because of the possibility that the parties to the transactions are motivated by reasons other than those that may exist for most business transactions. Auditors have been victimized on several occasions by clients who recorded large sales that later turned out to have been made to undisclosed related parties. As the sales agreements were not with outside parties and sometimes contained contingencies that later led to reversal of the sale, they were improperly recorded as revenue and earnings. Related party transactions continue to create problems for auditors and are often difficult to detect.

Related parties include affiliated companies, owners, management, and any other party that does not fully pursue its own separate interests. The auditor attempts to determine the existence of related parties by inquiry of management and predecessor auditors and review of stockholder listings, SEC filings, and material investment transactions. If related parties are detected, the auditor attempts to identify transactions with such parties by the review of minutes, accounting records for large or unusual transactions, confirmations and loan agreements for the existence of guarantees, and "conflict-of-interest" statements obtained by the company.

If related party transactions are identified, the auditor must first gain an understanding of the business purposes of the transactions. The auditor cannot complete the audit until he or she understands the business sense of material related party transactions. The auditor should also be aware that the substance of a related party transaction may be significantly different from its form and that financial statements should recognize the substance of transactions rather than their legal form. If valid business purposes exist, the auditor should examine or obtain appropriate evidence of the transactions and determine that they have been approved by the board of directors or other appropriate officials.

The following illustration of a related party transaction is condensed from an actual case reported by the SEC. Company A, a real estate broker, purportedly sold properties to Company B, an unaffiliated company, for $5,400,000 and recognized profit of $550,000 from the transaction. However, a provision of the agreement guaranteed Company B that it would suffer no loss from operation of the properties and that it could sell the properties back to Company A. Later Company B did request that Company A take back the properties. At this point Company A formed two companies, undisclosed related parties, to purchase the properties from Company B. Company A knew that no profit could be recognized if it took the properties back, but by transferring the properties to undisclosed related parties it concealed the fact that no income should have been recognized because the risk of loss from the properties remained with it. The SEC concluded that the auditors failed to review adequately the agreements related to this transaction or to pursue the implications of the disposition of the properties by Company B.

If related party transactions are material, the auditor should determine whether the financial statements disclose the nature of the relationships and a description of the transactions including dollar volume and year-end balances.

The Risk of Insufficient or Incompetent Evidence

There is always a risk that evidence gathered during the examination is insufficient or incompetent to provide auditors with an adequate basis for an opinion on the client's financial statements. Thus, auditors must constantly be aware of the possibility that they may have formed wrong conclusions about the financial statements.

To *reduce* (not completely eliminate) the probability of forming invalid conclusions, auditors exercise judgment in the selection of the type and amount of evidence they gather to support an opinion. Sometimes this judgment proves to be faulty, and as a result, auditors may suffer the consequences of a lawsuit for negligence. The *Barchris Construction Corporation* case is an illustration. Apparently, the auditors believed that the evidence they gathered on events occurring after the balance sheet date was sufficient to sustain an opinion that the financial statements were fair. According to the court's comments, the auditors should have detected a deteriorating financial condition that existed after the balance sheet date.

The courts have sometimes taken the position that the auditors' judgment was so faulty that a form of fraud was committed. An early trend was established for judicial positions of this type when the judge ordered a new trial in the *Ultramares* case on the basis that gross negligence may have occurred. Inadequate evidence of the existence and rights of accounts receivable had been gathered by the auditors. Several years later, the AICPA established an expanded criterion for competency of evidence when they required direct confirmation with the client's customers.

Review and Evaluation of Evidence

The auditor must remain keenly alert while performing audit procedures, no matter how routine a step appears to be. One brief period of carelessness can have a devastating effect on the quality of the audit. Although the senior, manager, and partner will review the audit working papers prepared by the staff, none of these people will see the invoice, canceled check, or other document that actually was examined. Therefore, a basic responsibility for the audit rests with the staff.

The staff is assisted in meeting this responsibility by senior supervision. The senior should explain the purpose and means of accomplishing the audit steps assigned to the staff. Though the staff may be encouraged to develop their own solutions to problems encountered on the engagement, the senior should review the soundness of these solutions with them and assist them when they encounter significant difficulties.

Each firm should establish a formal set of procedures to be followed if differences of opinion concerning accounting or auditing issues arise among firm personnel involved in an examination. These procedures should enable the staff to document the reason for disagreement and, if necessary, to be disassociated from the resolution of the issue.

The review process provides the means for controlling the performance of the audit procedures. The audit working papers should be reviewed at each level of responsibility from the senior through the partner. In other words, the senior reviews the working papers prepared by the staff, the manager reviews the working papers prepared by the staff and the senior, and the partner reviews all of the working papers, including any prepared by the manager. As the reviews are conducted at each level, the reviewer makes notes or points about the audit work. These notes may be answered or cleared either personally or by someone at a lower level. Satisfactory disposition must be made of all such notes before the audit can be considered complete.

In reviewing the audit work, the supervisors must be satisfied that the working papers contain evidence that the scope of the work was adequate and that the work was actually performed using appropriate care and skill. For example, each level of supervision must be satisfied that an adequate *number* of confirmations of accounts receivable was obtained and that *care and skill* were employed in obtaining, recording, reconciling, and evaluating the confirmations received. The supervisors must also concentrate on the meaning of the *audit findings* and their implications with respect to the financial statements and the auditor's report. For example, if the auditor does not receive an adequate response to accounts-receivable confirmation requests or finds material unreconcilable differences between the client and customer records, consideration must be given to proposing an adjustment to the financial statements or modifying the auditor's report.

Audit findings may be recorded in the working papers in (1) notes or points made by reviewers, (2) memoranda regarding specific audit and reporting problems encountered and their disposition, (3) audit staff conclusions on various working papers, and (4) support for adjusting and reclassifying entries. Should any audit finding made by the audit team indicate that an error or irregularity may have occurred, the finding should be investigated until the facts that are reasonably obtainable have been assembled or until it becomes clear that the matter is immaterial. Such findings should immediately be reported to the audit partner, who must review the available evidence, consider its implications, consult with other designated partners, if necessary, and discuss the matter and the extent of further investigation with an appropriate level of management.

In evaluating audit findings, the auditor considers both known and likely errors. Known errors are those specifically identified in the audit process. Likely errors consist of the auditor's best estimate of the total errors in an account balance. They include (1) errors projected to a total account balance from auditing only a sample of the individual items included in the account, (2) unreasonable estimates affecting an account balance, and (3) prior-period errors that affect the current period. An example of the computation of likely error for accounts receivable (net of allowance for doubtful accounts) is shown in the following table.

| | Effect On | |
| | Accounts Receivable | Net Income[a] |
Error		
Known error—invalid accounts receivable detected by sending confirmations to all accounts in excess of $50,000	$40,000	$26,000
Known error—invalid accounts receivable detected by sending confirmations to a sample of 20% of all accounts below $50,000	2,000	1,300
Likely error—projection of confirmation sample results to remaining 80% of all accounts below $50,000	8,000	5,200
Likely error—difference between estimated allowance for doubtful accounts per books ($200,000) and nearest reasonable estimate by auditor ($230,000)	30,000	19,500
Likely error—difference between estimated allowance for doubtful accounts per books at end of prior year ($150,000) and nearest reasonable estimate by auditor at end of prior year ($170,000) that was accepted by auditor as immaterial	—	(13,000)
Total likely error	$80,000	$39,000

[a] The effect on net income is reduced by 35 percent to allow for the estimated income tax effect.

In evaluating the materiality of total likely error, the auditor should consider the risk of even further error due to sampling risk and the imprecise nature of certain audit procedures.

All likely errors that are determined to be immaterial should be reported to the client's management to determine whether they want to correct them. Clients often wish to correct minor errors so they can begin a new year with a more accurate set of accounting records. The auditor will prepare a schedule summarizing all uncorrected errors to be reasonably assured that, in the aggregate, they do not have a material effect on the financial statements. This schedule often is called a summary of immaterial entries or a summary of entries passed. Figure 12.1 is an example of such a schedule. The net amount of the entries not made is compared with the amounts to be shown in the financial statements to determine whether it is material in the aggregate. In determining materiality, the auditor must keep in mind all aspects of the audit. For example, if a company's loan agreement provides that the company will maintain an excess of current assets over current liabilities of at least $100,000 or be in default, and if current assets total $200,100, and current liabilities total $100,000, a $101 adjustment could be material. Normally, the senior, manager, and partner assigned to the audit state or approve the conclusion that the entries not recorded are not material.

Consideration of an Entity's Ability to Continue as a Going Concern

In addition to the requirement that an auditor evaluate evidence regarding amounts shown in the client's financial statements, professional standards require an overall evaluation of the client's ability to continue as a going concern. This evaluation relates to the viability of the entity, not just whether its assets are recoverable and its liabilities are properly classified. This is an important extension, because for the first time auditors are charged with the responsibility under professional standards of interpreting financial statements in addition to expressing an opinion as to whether or not they conform with generally accepted accounting principles. Although different auditors may place different degrees of importance on the following events and factors, they are illustrative of the matters considered.

The first indication of a problem is often an operating loss by the client in the current year. This may lead the auditor to consider whether (1) operating losses have occurred in prior years, (2) cash flows from operations have been positive or negative in the current and prior years, and (3) key financial ratios such as the current ratio, quick ratio, and debt to equity ratio exhibit adverse trends. Other indicators are defaults under loan agreements, denial of normal trade credit from suppliers, and the necessity to restructure debt or seek new sources of financing. Additionally, factors that may not have an immediate effect on solvency might include work stoppages; legal proceedings; loss of important franchises, patents, customers, or suppliers; and uninsured catastrophes.

If conditions or events such as these are identified, the auditor should consider whether management has plans for and the ability to implement alternative means of maintaining adequate cash flows. Examples include plans and the ability to (1) dispose of assets, (2) renew or extend existing loans, (3) reduce or dispose of operations producing negative cash flows, and (4) obtain new equity capital and reduce dividend payments. The auditor should attempt to examine evidence to support management's ability to carry out these plans. Examples of such evidence

PJE

R. Smith
2-1-X9

X Co.
Summary of Entries Passed
12-31-X8

Increase/(Decrease) in

Index	Description	Current Assets	Current Liabilities	Long-term Assets	Long-term Liabilities	Stockholders Equity	Net Income
10 / B	Sales Accounts receivable To record credit memo issued in Jan,X9 applicable to Dec,X8 sales	(350)					(350)
F / 20	Accumulated depreciation Depreciation expense To correct error in calculation of depr.			200			200
P / 20	Accrued liabilities Property tax expense To correct overaccrual of property taxes		(230)				230
	Total	(975)	(650)	200	0	0	(125)
	Income tax effect	0	(60)		0	0	60
	Net	(975)	(710)	200	0	0	(65)
	Per Audit Trial Balance	473,990	314,084	512,901	250,000	422,807	71,229

In my opinion, the entries passed are immaterial in relation to the financial statements.

R. Senior   M. Manager   P. Partner

Figure 12.1   X Co. Summary of entries passed 12-31-X8.

would be appraisals or bids for assets held for disposition and correspondence from banks indicating an agreement to renew or extend loans.

If the necessary evidence to support management's plans cannot be obtained or if substantial doubt remains about the client's ability to continue as a going concern, the auditor should evaluate whether the matter is adequately disclosed in the financial statements and consider whether his or her audit report requires modification. The appropriate audit report modification in these circumstances is discussed in Chapter 20.

Omitted Audit Procedures

Occasionally, usually as the result of a peer review, an auditor may become aware after an audit report has been delivered that a necessary audit procedure was not performed during the audit. If the auditor believes that the omission of the procedure impairs his or her ability to support the previously expressed opinion and that shareholders, creditors, or others are continuing to rely upon the opinion, the omitted procedure should be performed.

Appendix to Chapter 12

General Tools Used for the Preparation of Audit Programs

Audit Tools	Potential Uses
Confirmation	Evidence of existence (or ownership) of cash in bank, accounts receivable, inventory on consignment, insurance coverage, accounts payable, long-term debt, capital stock outstanding, contingent liabilities, and pension commitments
Observation	Evidence of existence of inventories, cash on hand, notes receivable, investment securities, loan collateral, and property and equipment
Inspection	Evidence of ownership, existence, and valuation represented by vendor invoices, receiving reports, purchase orders, sales invoices, and shipping documents
Inquiry	Evidence of ownership, existence, completeness, valuation, and classification represented by oral and written communications with clients
Calculation	Evidence of existence and valuation of accrued liabilities, deferred income taxes, depreciation expense, and interest expense
Comparison	Evidence of ownership, existence, valuation, and classification represented by changes from the prior year or budgeted amounts, ratio analysis, and regression techniques
Analysis	Evidence of ownership, existence, valuation, and classification represented by reviews for reasonableness and predictable relationships among accounts

Chapter 12
Glossary of Terms

(listed in order of appearance in the chapter, with accompanying page reference where the term is discussed)

Chapter 12
References

American Institute of Certified Public Accountants. *Professional Standards*.

AU Section 326—Evidential Matter.

AU Section 336—Using the Work of a Specialist.

Brumfield, Craig A., Elliott, Robert K., and Jacobson, Peter C. "Business Risk and the Audit Process," *Journal of Accountancy* (April 1983), pp. 60–68.

Canfield, Gary A. "A Guide for Effectively Questioning Clients," *Journal of Accountancy* (September 1985), pp. 162–168.

Craig, Thomas R. "Audit Circularization Checklist," *Journal of Accountancy* (October 1983), pp. 123–124.

Holstrum, Gary L., and Mock, Theodore J. "Audit Judgment and Evidence Evaluation," *Auditing: A Journal of Practice and Theory* (Fall 1985), pp. 101–108.

Hylas, Robert E., and Ashton, Robert H. "Audit Detection of Financial Statement Errors," *The Accounting Review* (October 1982), pp. 751–765.

Mock, Theodore J., and Wright, Arnold. "Evaluating the Effectiveness of Audit Procedures," *Auditing: A Journal of Practice and Theory* (Fall 1982), pp. 33–44.

Schramm, Ronald. "Reviewing Audit Workpapers," *Journal of Accountancy* (June 1981), pp. 50–52.

Whittington, Ray, Zulinski, Marilyn, and Ledwith, James W. "Completeness—The Elusive Assertion," *Journal of Accountancy* (August 1983), pp. 82–92.

Chapter 12
Review Questions

12-1.   What is the third standard of field work?

12-2.   How does the auditor evaluate the competency of audit evidence obtained from outside sources?

12-3.   Describe the relationship between reliability of accounting data and the internal control structure.

12-4.   Differentiate the competency of audit evidence gained through personal knowledge of the auditor and evidence obtained indirectly.

12-5.   What is the difference between convincing and persuasive audit evidence?

12-6.   How does the cost of obtaining evidence affect its sufficiency?

12-7.   How does an auditor make an objective evaluation of audit evidence?

12-8.   List and describe seven techniques for gathering audit evidence. State how each could be applied to the audit of inventory.

12-9.   List the three characteristics of audit evidence and give an example of each.

12-10.   Which characteristic of audit evidence is considered the most reliable? Why?

12-11.   Why should the auditor consider the objectives of auditing each account before beginning his or her work?

12-12.   What are the five broad objectives of auditing a given account?

12-13.   How is the effectiveness of a client's internal control structure related to the extensiveness of substantive tests?

12-14.   How does an auditor identify relevant accounting estimates?

12-15.   How does an auditor evaluate the reasonableness of the amount of an accounting estimate?

12-16.   What is the "business approach" to an audit?

12-17.   How does an auditor gain knowledge of his or her client's business operations?

12-18.   How is ratio analysis used in an audit?

12-19.   How does the auditor use regression analysis?

12-20.   List six pairs of accounts on which audit work is often performed simultaneously.

12-21.   Explain how audit evidence relating to sales can be obtained without examining documents in support of amounts recorded in the sales account.

12-22.   Describe a related party and the effect it may have on audit evidence.

12-23.   Explain the review process for audit working papers.

12-24.   Where may audit findings be documented?

12-25.   Differentiate between known and likely errors.

Chapter 12
Objective Questions Taken from CPA Examinations

12-26. Which of the following *best* describes the element of relative risk that underlies the application of generally accepted auditing standards, particularly the standards of field work and reporting?
a. Cash audit work may have to be carried out in a more conclusive manner than inventory audit work.
b. Intercompany transactions are usually subject to less detailed scrutiny than arm's-length transactions with outside parties.
c. Inventories may require more attention by the auditor on an engagement for a merchandising enterprise than on an engagement for a public utility.
d. The scope of the examination need *not* be expanded if errors that arouse suspicion of fraud are of relatively insignificant amounts.

12-27. Of the following which is the *least* persuasive type of audit evidence?
a. Documents mailed by outsiders to the auditor.
b. Correspondence between auditor and vendors.
c. Copies of sales invoices inspected by the auditor.
d. Computations made by the auditor.

12-28. Although the validity of evidential matter is dependent on the circumstances under which it is obtained, there are three general presumptions that have some usefulness. The situations given below indicate the relative reliability a CPA has placed on two types of evidence obtained in different situations. Which of these is an exception to one of the general presumptions?
a. The CPA places more reliance on the balance in the scrap sales account at Plant A, where the CPA has made limited tests of transactions because of good controls, than at Plant B, where the CPA has made extensive tests of transactions because of poor controls.
b. The CPA places more reliance on the CPA's computation of interest payable on outstanding bonds than on the amount confirmed by the trustee.
c. The CPA places more reliance on the report of an expert on an inventory of precious gems than on the CPA's physical observation of the gems.
d. The CPA places more reliance on a schedule of insurance coverage obtained from the company's insurance agent than on one prepared by the internal audit staff.

12-29. Audit evidence can come in different forms with different degrees of persuasiveness. Which of the following is the *least* persuasive type of evidence?
a. Vendor's invoice.
b. Bank statement obtained from the client.

    c. Computations made by the auditor.

    d. Prenumbered client invoices.

12-30.   The auditor is most likely to seek information from the plant manager with respect to the

    a. Adequacy of the provision for uncollectible accounts.

    b. Appropriateness of physical inventory observation procedures.

    c. Existence of obsolete machinery.

    d. Deferral of procurement of certain necessary insurance coverage.

12-31.   The independent auditor's plan for an examination in accordance with generally accepted auditing standards is influenced by the possibility of material errors. The auditor will therefore conduct the examination with an attitude of

    a. Professional skepticism.

    b. Subjective mistrust.

    c. Objective indifference.

    d. Professional responsiveness.

12-32.   Each of the following might, in itself, form a valid basis for an auditor to decide to omit a test *except* the

    a. Relative risk involved.

    b. Relationship between the cost of obtaining evidence and its usefulness.

    c. Difficulty and expense involved in testing a particular item.

    d. Degree of reliance on the relevant controls.

12-33.   Which of the following is *not* a specialist upon whose work an auditor may rely?

    a. Actuary.

    b. Appraiser.

    c. Internal auditor.

    d. Engineer.

12-34.   Which of the following elements ultimately determines the specific auditing procedures that are necessary in the circumstances to afford a reasonable basis for an opinion?

    a. Auditor judgment.

    b. Materiality.

    c. Relative risk.

    d. Reasonable assurance.

12-35.   Confirmation is most likely to be a relevant form of evidence with regard to assertions about accounts receivable when the auditor has concerns about the receivables'

a. Valuation.
b. Classification.
c. Existence.
d. Completeness.

12-36. An auditor would be *least* likely to use confirmations in connection with the examination of
a. Inventories.
b. Refundable income taxes.
c. Long-term debt.
d. Stockholders' equity.

12-37. An auditor usually examines receiving reports to support entries in the
a. Voucher register and sales returns journal.
b. Sales journal and sales returns journal.
c. Voucher register and sales journal.
d. Check register and sales journal.

12-38. An auditor, in gathering evidence regarding an estimate of the allowance for doubtful accounts, may apply all of the following procedures except
a. Review of the collection history of accounts receivable.
b. Confirmation of accounts receivable.
c. Review of credit files.
d. Examination of collection of accounts receivable after the audit date.

12-39. The auditor notices significant fluctuations in key elements of the company's financial statements. If management is unable to provide an acceptable explanation, the auditor should
a. Consider the matter a scope limitation.
b. Perform additional audit procedures to investigate the matter further.
c. Intensify the examination with the expectation of detecting management fraud.
d. Withdraw from the engagement.

12-40. As a result of analytical procedures, the independent auditor determines that the gross profit percentage has declined from 30 percent in the preceding year to 20 percent in the current year. The auditor should
a. Document management's intentions with respect to plans for reversing this .trend.
b. Evaluate management's performance in causing this decline.
c. Require footnote disclosure.
d. Consider the possibility of an error in the financial statements.

12-41.   Which of the following *best* describes the most important stage of an auditor's statistical analysis of significant ratios and trends?
a. Computation of significant ratios and trends.
b. Interpretation of significant variations and unusual relationships.
c. Reconciliation of statistical data to the client's accounting records.
d. Comparison of statistical data to prior-year statistics and to similar data published by government and private sources.

12-42.   An independent auditor finds that Simner Corporation occupies office space, at no charge, in an office building owned by a shareholder. This finding indicates the existence of
a. Management fraud.
b. Related party transactions.
c. Window dressing.
d. Weak internal controls.

12-43.   The existence of a related party transaction may be indicated when another entity
a. Sells real estate to the corporation at a price that is comparable to its appraised value.
b. Absorbs expenses of the corporation.
c. Borrows from the corporation at a rate of interest that equals the current market rate.
d. Lends to the corporation at a rate of interest that equals the current market rate.

12-44.   The audit work performed by each assistant should be reviewed to determine whether it was adequately performed and to evaluate whether
a. There has been a thorough documentation of the internal control structure.
b. The auditor's system of quality control has been maintained at a high level.
c. The assistants' preliminary judgments about materiality differ from the materiality levels of the persons who will rely on the financial statements.
d. The results are consistent with the conclusions to be presented in the auditor's report.

12-45.   In the course of the examination of financial statements for the purpose of expressing an opinion thereon, the auditor will normally prepare a schedule of unadjusted differences for which the auditor did not propose adjustment when they were uncovered. What is the primary purpose served by this schedule?
a. To point out to the responsible client officials the errors made by various company personnel.
b. To summarize the adjustments that must be made before the company can prepare and submit its federal tax return.

    c. To identify the potential financial statement effects of errors or disputed items that were considered immaterial when discovered.

    d. To summarize the errors made by the company so that corrections can be made after the audited financial statements are released.

Chapter 12
Discussion/Case Questions

12-46.   In each of the following cases, rank the various items of evidence on a scale from most persuasive to least persuasive. Furnish support for your rankings.

    a. Evidence to support the cash account.

      (1) Bank reconciliation prepared by the client.

      (2) A written confirmation of the bank balance, sent directly to the auditor.

      (3) Written certification by the client that the bank balance is correct.

      (4) Oral assurance by the client that the bank balance is correct.

      (5) The year's canceled checks and validated deposit slips held by the client.

    b. Evidence to support accounts receivable (not including the allowance for doubtful accounts).

      (1) Sales invoices held by the client.

      (2) Written certification by the client that the balance is correct.

      (3) Written confirmation of the balances, sent by the customers directly to the auditor.

      (4) An accounts receivable aging schedule.

      (5) Shipping documents held by the client, showing the dollar amount of merchandise sent to customers.

      (6) Deposit slips held by the client, showing the cash received from customers during the month after year end.

    c. Evidence to support inventory quantities.

      (1) Purchase invoices held by the client.

      (2) Checks issued to vendors during the month following year end.

      (3) Observations of the client's physical count.

      (4) A written certification from the client that the amount shown as inventory is correct.

12-47.   One of the audit clients of Brown and Brown, CPAs, is We-Fit Manufacturing Company, makers of shirts, sweaters, and other clothing items. The finished goods inventory consists of merchandise placed in hundreds of sealed boxes on the warehouse floor. The client's inventory count consists of a count of boxes that are supposed to contain a standard number of shirts or sweaters. The only way the auditors can be certain about the contents of the boxes is to break them open and count the pieces of clothing. They do not wish to use this method of verification except on a few selected boxes.

Required:

a. What criterion would you use in deciding how many boxes to open, if any, during the inventory observation?

b. What are the possible legal implications associated with a massive number of empty boxes?

c. Would you seek extra audit evidence on the validity of inventory simply as a result of the client's count procedure? If so, what types?

12-48. One of the clients of Mr. Cain, CPA, is a local financial institution. As a part of the standard audit procedures, Mr. Cain sent accounts receivable confirmations to 50 of the 200 customers.

Although a return envelope was sent with the confirmations, most of the customers chose to bring the letter to the office. Mr. Cain was interrupted constantly to explain orally the nature of the confirmation letter. He would tell the customers that their signatures were to be placed on the letter without any additional comment only if they agreed that they owed the amount printed on the letter. Otherwise, the customers were asked to indicate the amount they believed they owed.

Few of the customers seemed to understand the oral instructions given by Mr. Cain, and most merely signed the letter and left it. Mr. Cain was perplexed by these responses, but he did not know whether to send additional letters, look for alternative types of evidence, or simply accept these signatures without additional audit procedures.

Required:

a. Which of the three courses of action would you recommend? If you reject all three courses of action, what would you recommend?

b. Comment in general on the validity and limitations of audit evidence gained from confirmation letters sent to the public.

12-49. Auditors frequently refer to the terms *standards* and *procedures*. Standards deal with measures of the quality of the auditor's performance. They refer specifically to the ten generally accepted auditing standards. Procedures relate to those acts that are performed by the auditor while trying to gather evidence. They refer specifically to the methods or techniques used by the auditor in the conduct of the examination.

Required:

List at least seven different types of procedures that an auditor would use during an examination of financial statements. For example, a type of procedure that an auditor would frequently use is the observation of activities and conditions. *Do not discuss specific accounts.*

(*AICPA adapted*)

12-50.   Classify the following items of audit evidence from most reliable (1) to least reliable (18). Discuss the reasons for your classifications.

a. Canceled payroll check.

b. Client sales invoice.

c. Request for a travel advance.

d. Client-prepared receiving report for merchandise.

e. Client-prepared depreciation worksheet.

f. Journal entry to correct an account classification.

g. Board of director minutes signed by the corporate secretary.

h. Vendor invoice for merchandise purchased.

i. Client-prepared purchase order for merchandise.

j. Copy of client articles of incorporation.

k. Bank statement.

l. Cutoff bank statement received directly by the auditor.

m. Positive accounts receivable confirmation.

n. Negative accounts receivable confirmation.

o. Client-prepared inventory count sheet.

p. Oral client representations.

q. Written client representations.

r. Representation letter from client's attorney.

12-51.   You are the auditor of Star Manufacturing Company. A trial balance taken from the books of Star at year end follows:

Account	Dr. (Cr.)
Cash in bank	$ 87,000
Trade accounts receivable	345,000
Notes receivable	125,000
Inventories	317,000
Land	66,000
Buildings, net	350,000
Furniture, fixtures, and equipment, net	325,000
Trade accounts payable	(235,000)
Mortgages payable	(400,000)
Capital stock	(300,000)
Retained earnings	(510,000)
Sales	(3,130,000)
Cost of sales	2,300,000
General and administrative expenses	622,000
Legal and professional fees	3,000
Interest expense	35,000

There are no inventories consigned either in or out.

All notes receivable are due from outsiders and held by Star.

Required:

a. Which accounts should be confirmed with outside sources?

b. Describe by whom they should be confirmed and the information that should be confirmed.

c. Organize your answer in the following format.

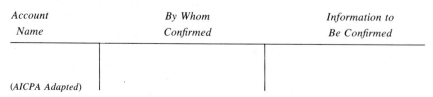

Account Name	By Whom Confirmed	Information to Be Confirmed

(AICPA Adapted)

12-52. Bill Kelting, audit senior from New York City, was assigned to be in charge of the Hogeye Ranch Co. audit. Before this engagement the only cows Bill had seen were in pictures. However, Bill knew how to perform an audit. A large sample of sales was traced to sales barn receipts, and expenses were traced to vendor invoices. Cattle were accounted for as purchased, sold, or on hand. All amounts in the financial statements were tied down to Bill's satisfaction. While reviewing the audit working papers on the last day of field work, the manager inquired as to what happened to the calves. Bill replied that there were no calf transactions because no calves had been purchased during the year. The manager reminded Bill that calves could be acquired on a ranch without being purchased. Bill spent three days past the expected end of the job reviewing birthing records and accounting for the calves. The calves had been exchanged in one transaction for "next-spring-delivery" of heifers, but the transaction had not been recorded. Substantial changes were required in the financial statements and tax returns and a large time overrun occurred.

How might this problem have been avoided?

12-53. The auditor should obtain a level of knowledge of the entity's business, including events, transactions, and practices, that will enable the planning and performance of an examination in accordance with generally accepted auditing standards.

Required:

How does knowledge of the entity's business help the auditor in the planning and performance of an examination in accordance with generally accepted auditing standards?

(AICPA adapted)

12-54. Trend and Jones, CPAs, were planning their initial audit of Kargo Corporation, whose stock was traded actively on the New York Stock Exchange. Although the partners had consulted with the predecessor auditor and had reviewed prior-year working papers, they still had a number of questions about the areas that should be given special attention in the engagement. To provide them with more insight, Ms. Trend and Mr. Jones decided to take the published financial statements of Kargo Corporation for the last two years and the statements for the first quarter of this year and develop some ratios. They calculated the following amounts.

	19X6	19X7	1st Quarter 19X8
Current ratio	2.1 to 1	2.0 to 1	1.8 to 1
Accounts receivable turnover	8.3	8.4	8.6[a]
Inventory turnover	7.4	9.2	10.8[a]
Times interest earned	1.7	1.6	1.4
Earnings per share	10.50	11.62	3.45
Debt/equity ratio	.95	1.20	1.24
Dividends per share	2.50	3.00	.90

[a] Annualized.

In addition to these ratios, the following information is available.

1. Kargo's credit terms are 30 days net.

2. The Kargo Corporation has a loan restriction that requires it to maintain at least a 2 to 1 current ratio.

3. The "normal" inventory turnover for the industry in which Kargo Corporation operates is 10.

Required:
a. Indicate the areas in which the auditors should concentrate special effort. Consider only the areas revealed by the ratio analysis. Do not name specific audit procedures.
b. Discuss actions that the management of Kargo might be inclined to take to cover up any possible adverse effects of these listed ratios. What could the auditors do to provide reasonable assurance that they found these actions?

12-55. Joyce Cover, CPA, was engaged to examine the financial statements of Extensive, Inc., a first-time audit client. The engagement is for the year ended December 31, 19X6. The study and evaluation of the internal control structure was conducted during the late fall of 19X6 and, with the exception of accounts receivable and sales, substantial reliance was placed on all controls.

In January, 19X7, Extensive, Inc. compiled the following financial statement data as of December 31, 19X6 and for the year 19X6.

Sales		$800,000
Cost of goods sold		500,000
Gross margin		$300,000
Operating expenses:		
Salaries	$ 60,000	
Depreciation on equipment	40,000	
Uncollectible accounts	20,000	
Commissions	8,000	
Supplies	12,000	
Travel	15,000	
Miscellaneous	15,000	$170,000
Net income before tax		$130,000
Income tax expense		60,000
Net income		$ 70,000

Assets

Current assets:		
Cash	$ 2,000	
Marketable securities	5,000	
Accounts receivable (net of allowance		
for doubtful accounts of $22,000)	78,000	
Inventory	50,000	$135,000
Long-term assets:		
Equipment	$200,000	
Less: Accumulated depreciation	80,000	$120,000
Other assets		17,000
Total assets		$272,000

Liabilities and Equities

Current liabilities:		
Accounts payable	$ 15,000	
Accrued expenses	2,500	$ 17,500
Long-term liabilities:		
Notes payable		$110,000
Total liabilities		$127,500
Capital stock	$100,000	
Retained earnings	44,500	$144,500
Total liabilities and equities		$272,000

Required:

a. On which of the above accounts would evidence be obtained through

   (1) Inspection

   (2) Observation

(3) Inquiry

(4) Confirmation

(The same account may be listed more than once. Give reasons for your listings.)

b. On which of the above accounts could evidence be obtained from independent outside sources? Name the independent outside sources for each listed account.

c. On which accounts would the evidence gathered be affected by the relatively poor quality of controls? Give reasons for your answers.

d. On which accounts is the evidence gathered likely to be most persuasive? Least persuasive? Give reasons for your answers.

e. On which accounts is the cost of obtaining evidence likely to be the highest? The lowest? Give reasons for your answers.

f. On which accounts is the evaluation of evidence likely to be the most subjective? The least subjective? Give reasons for your answers.

CHAPTER 13

Sampling for Substantive Tests of Account Balances— Nonstatistical and Statistical

---

Learning Objectives   *After reading and studying the material in this chapter, the student should*

Know the sampling objectives of a substantive test.

Be able to define the population for a substantive test.

Be able to choose an appropriate audit sampling technique to use for a substantive test.

Be familiar with the factors needed to determine, and be able to determine, the necessary sample size for a substantive test.

Know the methods of selecting samples for substantive tests.

Be able to perform the sampling plan and evaluate the sample results for a substantive test.

Understand the differences between nonstatistical sampling, classical statistical sampling, and probability proportional to size statistical sampling.

In Chapter 9, we discussed tests of controls that require the use of sampling techniques, both nonstatistical and statistical. Chapter 9 followed two chapters (7 and 8) that were devoted to the study of the internal control structure and general concepts of tests of controls.

In this chapter we discuss substantive tests of account balances that also require the use of sampling techniques, both nonstatistical and statistical. This chapter also follows a chapter devoted to the underlying concepts of substantive testing.

The sequence of this chapter will follow the historical development of sampling for substantive tests.

1. Nonstatistical sampling was the traditional method for many years and is still widely used. The auditor uses his or her judgment in determining the sample size, applying the sampling methodology, and evaluating the sample results.

2. About 20 to 25 years ago, classical statistical sampling, which employs concepts of normal distribution theory, began to be used. Estimation sampling was introduced, followed by tests of hypothesis.

3. About 10 to 15 years ago, the method of probability proportional to size statistical sampling (PPS) became popular because of its appeal to the auditor seeking ways to find large overstatements of account balances, if the population contained such overstatements.

The chapter will begin with discussions and illustrations of the general concepts of sampling for substantive tests, followed by the application of these concepts to the three techniques.

Sampling for Substantive Tests

The overall purpose of substantive tests is to gather evidence as to the propriety of account balances and disclosures. For analytical procedures and some tests of details, nonsampling techniques are applicable. Some examples are (1) comparison of current and prior years' recorded expenses and (2) examination of insurance policies or stock certificates.

There are a number of substantive tests, however, that lend themselves to the use of sampling methods. Confirmation of accounts receivable, comparison of physical inventory counts and perpetual inventory records, and examination of invoices for additions to fixed assets are examples discussed in Chapters 15 through 18. When the auditor decides that sampling is appropriate for a given substantive test, the objective is to test the reasonableness of the amount on the client's records. The audit procedure is a form of hypothesis test.

As a case in point, assume that the auditor is testing the clerical accuracy of the client's perpetual inventory records that support the inventory account in the balance sheet. The hypothesis (statistically called null hypothesis) is that the evidence supports the recorded inventory amount; the dollar difference between the recorded amount and the correct amount is not enough when added to errors in other accounts to make the financial statements materially misleading. The sample results will lead the auditor to either accept or reject the hypothesis.

Thus, the acceptance or nonacceptance of the hypothesis carries with it two sampling risks.

1. The *risk of incorrect rejection* is the risk that the auditor will incorrectly reject the hypothesis that the evidence supports the account balance. The sampling results could lead the auditor to believe incorrectly that the account balance contains more error than can be tolerated.

2. The *risk of incorrect acceptance* is the risk that the auditor will incorrectly accept the hypothesis that the evidence supports the account balance. The sampling results could lead the auditor to believe incorrectly that the account does not contain more errors than can be tolerated.

Therefore, when sampling is used as a hypothesis test, the sampling objectives are twofold:

1. To determine by *estimation sampling* techniques the estimated account balance the auditor considers to be correct.

2. To determine whether the difference between the estimated amount and the recorded amount allows the auditor to accept the evidence as supporting the account balance.

In most audit sampling applications, the characteristic of interest is the *projected error,* that is the difference between the estimated and recorded amounts. In testing the accuracy of inventory records, for example, assume that the recorded amount on the client's records is $100,000. As a result of the sample, the auditor estimates the inventory to be $90,000. Considering all available evidence, the auditor must make a judgment as to whether this projected error of $10,000 is so large as to cause rejection of the hypothesis that the evidence supports the account balance. The discussion in the remainder of this chapter illustrates the sampling tools and other guidelines used to aid the auditor in making these types of judgments.

Defining the Population

After determining the sampling objectives of the substantive test, the auditor defines the population on which the test will be performed, including the sampling unit. Basically, this seems to be a fairly simple task; *the population* consists of all the items in the account balance. If the records show 1,000 accounts receivable balances, the population may be defined as 1,000 units.

In defining the population, however, the auditor should consider a number of situations.

1. If the objective of the test is to detect unrecorded items (completeness), the population is not the items recorded on the client's books. Accounts payable is a case in point. For purposes of confirmation requests, the population may not be the recorded amounts, but the list of vendors that did business with the client during the audit period. For purposes of testing subsequent disbursements, the population is the record of cash disbursements for a period following the end of the year.

2. Debit and credit balances may have to be classified differently for sampling purposes. Credit balances in accounts receivable should generally be treated as current liabilities; likewise, debit balances in accounts payable are generally considered to be current assets.

3. The physical representation of the population may not include all items in the population. If this is true, then a sample of items from the physical representation may not be representative. In testing the proper classification of additions to fixed assets, the auditor may be shown a file drawer of invoices supporting this class of transactions. The auditor should determine that this file drawer of invoices is, indeed, the complete population of additions to fixed assets.

It may be necessary or desirable to test 100 percent of some part of an account balance. Many accounting populations consist of a few large amounts, a moderate number of reasonably large amounts, and a large number of small amounts. A few large accounts receivable may need to be confirmed on a 100 percent basis. A few large inventory balances may need to be compared to the physical count on a 100 percent basis. Sampling techniques discussed in this chapter are not applicable to these types of tests.

Sampling units are individual elements in the population and, for sampling purposes, could consist of the following:

1. An account balance.

2. A transaction that comprises an account balance.

3. A document evidencing a transaction.

In defining the sampling unit, the auditor must consider the objective of the sample and the likelihood of obtaining usable results. In recent years, consideration has been given to confirming individual accounts receivable invoices rather than the account balances themselves. If the auditor believes that there will be a large number of differences between the recorded amounts and confirmation replies and that these differences will be difficult to resolve, consideration might be given to defining individual invoices as the population.

Sampling Techniques

Basically, there are three techniques for sampling for a substantive test.

1. The auditor can use *nonstatistical sampling techniques,* which require the use of judgment in determining the sample size and evaluating the sample results. Although tables are available to aid the auditor in deciding on the size of the sample, it is not necessary to use these tables. Nonstatistical sampling is convenient and does not require knowledge of statistical methods. If the auditor has a thorough understanding of the objective of the test and a good knowledge of the population characteristics, a nonstatistical sample may produce reliable results.

2. *Classical statistical sampling techniques* may be used. The auditor needs some understanding of normal distribution theory (or available help from other auditors) to effectively use these methods. The auditor couples judgmental factors with statistical equations and tables to determine the sample size and quantitatively evaluate the sample results. As pointed out later in the chapter, classical statistical sampling may be useful when the population contains many differences between the recorded and audited amounts.

3. An increasingly popular statistical sampling technique is *probability proportional to size sampling.* Although some knowledge of statistical theory is desirable, the formulas are relatively easy to use and tables are available to aid in determining the sample size and quantitatively evaluating the sample results. This technique is particularly useful when the population contains a small number of large dollar overstatements. However, if the population contains a large number of small overstatements and understatements, classical statistical sampling or nonstatistical sampling may be more useful.

Determining the Sample Size

Whether nonstatistical or statistical sampling methods are used in the substantive test, the auditor must make a number of judgments to determine an optimum sample size. The following factors must be considered:

1. The variation in the population.

2. Risk levels the auditor is willing to accept.

3. The tolerable error the auditor is willing to accept.

4. The dollar error the auditor expects to exist in the population.

In the remaining subsections, we will discuss each of these judgmental factors in sequence.

Variation in the Population

Many accounting populations have a high variability (or dispersion). Statistically, this variability is measured by the *standard deviation*. Nonstatistically, it is measured judgmentally by a review of the dispersion of the numbers. For example, an inventory population may have the following characteristics:

20 items each with dollar amounts over $40,000;

100 items each with dollar amounts between $10,000 and $39,999;

1,000 items each with dollar amounts under $10,000.

Such a wide variation necessitates a relatively large sample for the sample to be representative of the population. If all other factors remain the same, wider variations in the population call for larger sample sizes, and vice versa. Generally, the sample size can be smaller and more efficient if a population with high variability is stratified into meaningful groups. Then, a sample or a 100 percent test is taken from each group (or stratum).

An obvious basis for dividing the population shown above is the recorded dollar amount. The auditor could do the following:

1. Test all 20 items over $40,000.

2. Select a relatively large sample of items with dollar amounts between $10,000 and $39,999.

3. Select a relatively small sample of items with dollar amounts under $10,000.

Recorded dollar amount is not the only basis for dividing the population into groups or strata. Another basis is the likelihood of error. Prior experience may have shown that a certain group of the above-listed inventory items consistently contain differences between the perpetual records and the physical counts. In this case, the auditor may wish to test these error-prone items on a 100 percent basis.

The variation in the population may be estimated judgmentally, by measuring the variation of the recorded amounts, or by conducting a pilot sample. A pilot sample is conducted by performing actual audit procedures on a small preliminary sample of population items. Such a sample enables the auditor to gain a better understanding of the difference in variation between recorded and audited amounts. For example, a test of 30 inventory items may show that the physical counts of these items vary more widely than the amounts on the perpetual records. This may demonstrate to the auditor a need for a larger sample size than originally planned.

If the auditor has no reason to believe that there are significant differences between recorded and audited amounts, an estimate of the variability of the recorded amounts might be sufficient. If statistical sampling is used, this variability is measured by computing the standard deviation of the recorded amounts (or the standard deviation of a sample of the recorded amounts if this is less time-consuming and reasonably reliable). If nonstatistical sampling is used, the estimated variability can be measured by the standard deviation of recorded amounts or by the use of judgment.

In the latter part of this chapter, we demonstrate how stratification can be used in nonstatistical sampling and classical statistical sampling. For example, on pages 494–498 we demonstrate with nonstatistical sampling how approximately 60 percent of the recorded population can be 100 percent tested and a sample taken from the other 40 percent of the recorded population. Also, on page 504 (Table 13.2) and page 505 we show a different type of stratification. Here, 15 of the original 100 accounts are eliminated, 16 of the remaining accounts with large recorded balances are 100 percent tested, and the remaining 69 accounts are sampled.

Stratification is not necessary when probability proportional to size sampling is used because stratification is inherent in this sampling technique. We illustrate this on pages 512–522 by showing that the probability proportional to size sampling technique assigns a higher probability of selection to accounts with large recorded balances than to accounts with small recorded balances.

Considerations in Setting the Risk of Incorrect Acceptance

Audit risk is a combination of the risk that material errors will occur in the accounting process used to develop the financial statements and the risk that these errors will not be detected by the auditor. Audit risk is also described as the risk that there is a total monetary error in an account balance greater than is tolerable and that the auditor fails to detect this monetary error. *Tolerable error* relates to materiality and is the maximum monetary error that may exist in an account balance which, when added to errors in all other accounts, will not cause the financial statements to be materially misstated.

Audit risk is controlled by three factors that have been discussed in earlier chapters.

1. Inherent risk—the risk that errors will occur in the accounting process. The auditor judgmentally assesses this risk.

2. Control risk—the internal control structure is assessed to evaluate the risk that errors will occur and not be detected or that monetary errors that are more than tolerable do exist. The auditor judgmentally assesses this risk.

3. Detection risk—substantive tests are used to control the risk that monetary errors that are more than tolerable are not detected by the auditor. These substantive tests consist of

    a. Tests of details of account balances (such as accounts receivable) and classes of transactions (such as charges to an expense account).

    b. Analytical procedures.

The professional standards do not specify the relative degree of reliance that should be placed on each factor. That decision is made in the context of a specific audit situation. The descriptive relationships among these factors, sample size, and planned sampling risk of incorrect acceptance are shown in the following table (for simplicity, assume no nonsampling risk).

Factor	*Sample Size of Substantive Test of Details*	*Planned Sampling Risk of Incorrect Acceptance*
1. Reliance on lack of susceptibility of account balance to error		
a. Greater	Smaller	Larger
b. Lesser	Larger	Smaller
2. Reliance on the internal control structure related to the account		
a. Greater	Smaller	Larger
b. Lesser	Larger	Smaller
3. Reliance on analytical procedures and other substantive tests of details related to the account balance		
a. Greater	Smaller	Larger
b. Lesser	Larger	Smaller

If the auditor wishes to quantify the risk of incorrect acceptance as a planning tool for a substantive test of details, the following equation may be used.

$$R = IR \times CR \times APR \times TD$$

$$TD = \frac{R}{IR \times CR \times APR}$$

where:

R = audit risk.
IR = inherent risk.
CR = control risk.
APR = the risk that analytical procedures and other related substantive tests of details will not detect errors greater than are tolerable.
TD = the allowable risk of incorrect acceptance on a substantive test of details.

For example, assume that an auditor accepted an audit risk of 5 percent that an account balance or class of transactions contained monetary errors that when added to errors in other accounts or classes of transactions would cause the financial statements to be materially misstated. Assume, also, that *IR, CR,* and *APR* were set at 100 percent each. The *TD* risk is computed as follows:

$$TD = .05/(1.00 \times 1.00 \times 1.00)$$

$$TD = .05 \text{ or } 5 \text{ percent}$$

The auditor is assigning no reliance to the lack of susceptibility of the account balance to error, the internal control structure, analytical procedures, or other substantive tests. The risk of incorrect acceptance is low and the sample size is large. Such a situation might occur in a small organization without adequate accounting expertise, without segregation of duties, and where there are no reliable amounts with which to perform analytical procedures. In this case, the auditor might lower the sampling risk and send a large number of accounts receivable confirmations.

The following analysis shows the value of *TD* using additional sets of values for *IR, CR,* and *APR*

1. R = .05

   IR = 1.0 (very susceptible to error)

   CR = .30 (moderate risk that the internal control structure will not detect material errors—or moderate reliance on the internal control structure)

APR = .30 (moderate risk that analytical procedures or other substantive tests of details will not detect material errors—or moderate reliance on analytical procedures or other substantive tests of details)

TD = .05/(1.0 × .30 × .30)

= .55 or 55 percent

2. R = .05

IR = .50 (moderate risk or moderate reliance)

CR = .20 (low risk or high reliance)

APR = .10 (low risk or high reliance)

TD = .05/(.50 × .20 × .10)

= 5.0 (this particular substantive test may not be necessary)

If the auditor did not wish to quantify the risk associated with the planned substantive test of details, the following nonquantitative set of decision rules could be used, assuming that audit risk is kept at a low level.

1. If there is no reliance on inherent processes, the internal control structure, or other substantive tests, set the risk of incorrect acceptance at a very low level.

2. If there is moderate reliance on inherent processes, the internal control structure, and other substantive tests, set the risk of incorrect acceptance at a moderate level.

3. If there is high reliance on inherent processes, the internal control structure, and other substantive tests, consider omitting the planned substantive test or selecting a very small sample.

4. If there is moderate reliance on the inherent processes and the internal control structure and low reliance on other substantive tests, or vice versa, set the risk of incorrect acceptance somewhere between moderate and low.

Illustration of Setting the Risk of Incorrect Acceptance

Assume that the auditor sets an audit risk (R) of 5 percent. The planned substantive test using sampling is a test of the clerical accuracy of the physical inventory listings. There are several hundred listings and a sample will be taken.

Assume that the inherent processes and internal control structure procedures that relate to inventory summarization are reliable in some respects. However, some weaknesses exist relating to the audit objective of determining whether inventory listings are accurately compiled. For example, inexperienced personnel count the inventory and some problems have been encountered with accounting for inventory listings. On this basis, the auditor assigns *IR* a risk factor of .80 and *CR* a risk factor of .60

Most of the analytical procedures are designed to test for proper valuation and disclosure of inventories. However, the auditor does conduct another test of details by tracing test counts made during the physical inventory observation to the inventory listings. The auditor also accounts for physical inventory count sheets. On this basis, the auditor assigns *APR* a risk factor of .50.

The risk that the auditor may incorrectly accept the inventory listings as being accurately compiled is calculated as follows:

$$TD = R/(IR \times CR \times APR)$$

$$TD = .05/(.80 \times .60 \times .50)$$

$$TD = .20 \text{ or } 20 \text{ percent}$$

Considerations in Setting the Risk of Incorrect Rejection

The consequences of incorrectly rejecting an account balance are additional audit cost or an incorrect audit adjustment. Therefore, these two consequences should be prime factors in deciding on the appropriate risk level. Consideration should be given to the type of audit procedure used and the viable alternatives should the audit procedure result in a rejection of the account balance. For example, the auditor may examine the client's shipping records if the evaluation of the confirmation requests results in a conclusion that the client's accounts receivable balance might be materially misstated. If the examination of shipping records is not a costly audit procedure, the risk of incorrect rejection is set at a relatively high level.

Similarly, if observation of the client's physical inventory results in a conclusion that the client's inventory balance might be materially misstated, the auditor may reexamine the control procedures in the purchases/inventory cycle. If this reexamination is a costly process, the risk of incorrect rejection may be kept at a relatively low level and the sample size of the clerical tests may be set at a relatively high level.

Tolerable Error the Auditor Is Willing to Accept

Recall from Chapter 9 that in conducting tests of controls the auditor is required to estimate the highest population deviation rate than can be tolerated without altering planned reliance on the internal control structure procedure being tested. This deviation rate is called the tolerable rate.

In conducting substantive tests, the auditor is required to estimate the dollar error that can exist in an account balance which, when added to the errors in all other accounts, will not cause the financial statements to be materially misstated. This estimate is called the *tolerable error* and is related to the auditor's estimate of materiality. Materiality, as we know, is an extremely difficult item to measure, but to determine sample size an estimate must be made.

Although the dollar amount of a potential error is only one measure of materiality, let us use it for illustrative purposes. Assume that recorded net income before income taxes is $500,000. The auditor has determined that the financial statements are materially misstated if there is an error in net income before income taxes of more than $40,000. Assume, also, that the auditor is conducting a substantive test of the clerical accuracy of the perpetual inventory records. To determine a sample size, an estimate of tolerable error must be made for this account balance. The auditor might follow this line of reasoning.

1. There is reason to believe that errors in other account balances could create an error in net income before income taxes as high as $30,000. The tolerable error for inventory should be set in such a way that materiality for the entire financial statements does not exceed $40,000.

2. Based on these prior estimates and the auditor's estimate of materiality, the tolerable error for inventory might be set at $10,000.

The auditor must give careful consideration to the dollar amount of tolerable error for a given substantive test of an account balance. A higher tolerable error causes the sample size to decrease and a lower tolerable error causes the sample size to increase. A smaller sample size lowers the probability of detecting a given error; a sample size that is too large is an inefficient use of time.

The Expected Error in the Population

Recall, again, from Chapter 9 that as the expected amount of deviation in the population approaches the tolerable rate, there is need for precise information on the characteristics of the population. In conducting substantive tests, the same logic is applied to the auditor's estimate of the expected dollar error in the population. As this estimate increases, the sample size of the substantive test increases.

An estimate of the dollar amount of error in the population can be made in a number of ways (note some similarity to the ways of estimating the deviation rate in the population).

1. Information from the prior year's audit may be used.

2. The auditor may consider the type of account being examined. For example, the customer billing process may be less effective than the methods of calculating perpetual inventory amounts. Therefore, on the basis of this

information, the auditor may estimate a higher dollar error in accounts receivable than in inventory.

3. The auditor may use similar tests to estimate the dollar error. In examining the documentation supporting additions to a certain fixed-asset account, the auditor may estimate the dollar error in this class of transactions to be the same as the dollar error found when documentation supporting additions to another account was examined.

Method of Sample Selection

In substantive testing, as in testing of controls, the sample should be selected in such a way that it is expected to be representative of the population. We discussed several methods in Chapter 9; in this section we will briefly review these methods.

1. The sample could be selected judgmentally in such a way that no obvious or apparent bias exists. In some cases, lack of bias may be harder to avoid for substantive tests than for tests of controls. Some tests of controls consist of examination of documents, many of which are almost identical in appearance. On the other hand, in many substantive tests, which require selection of dollar amounts, it may be more difficult to avoid bias. The auditor may be tempted to ignore an accounts receivable that has no distinguishing characteristics, such as being large, small, or in dispute.

2. Systematic sampling can be used. As pointed out in Chapter 9, this sampling method is convenient and under certain conditions can produce sampling results as reliable as random number sampling.

3. Random number sampling can be used. Each time a sample item is selected, every item in the population has an equal chance of selection. However, random number sampling might be inconvenient and difficult to apply.

Performing the Sampling Plan

After selecting the sample, the applicable audit procedure should be applied to each sample item. In this respect, there is no difference between nonstatistical, classical statistical, and probability proportional to size sampling. The audit procedure is the same regardless of which sampling technique is used.

What if a sample item is missing, such as an invoice? In this case, the auditor must exercise judgment and take one of two courses of action.

1. If the auditor believes the evaluation of error in the account balance would not be altered if the missing item were examined, alternative procedures may be omitted.

2. If the auditor believes the evaluation of error in the account balance might be altered if the missing item were examined, alternative procedures should be used.

The decision on the use of alternative procedures depends on the auditor's assessment of the importance of the missing item. A missing page from an inventory listing that represents 20 percent of the total account balance would be assessed differently from a missing purchase invoice that supports a small addition to fixed assets.

Evaluating Sample Results

Quantitative Evaluation

After the sample is selected and the audit procedure performed, the last step is to evaluate the sample results. If statistical sampling is used, part of the evaluation will be made with the aid of tables and computations. With nonstatistical sampling, only professional judgment is used to make the quantitative and qualitative evaluations.

First, the audited values should be compared with the recorded values and errors compiled. The auditor should be certain that differences between the audited and recorded values are errors. For example, any difference between an accounts receivable confirmation reply and the amount on the books should be reviewed for possible reconciling items. If the difference can be resolved (a payment in transit by a customer), it is not considered an error.

Next, the error results of the sample should be projected to the population. These techniques for projecting errors and computing likely errors are explained and illustrated on pages 460–461 of Chapter 12 and should be reviewed. Note that the projected error is more than the sum of the errors found in the sample. If the auditors find $300 of errors in the sample, the projection of the error results is more than this amount. The projection is actually an estimate of what the error in the population would be if every item were examined.

To illustrate, we will assume that no items are examined on a 100 percent basis. A sample of 100 items is taken from a population of 2,500 items; 4 percent of the population items (10 percent of the dollar amount of the population) is sampled. The total error in the sample is $1,000.

There are two ways to calculate a projected error in the population.

1. Divide the total error in the sample by the percentage of dollars in the population that was sampled. In this illustration, the projected error is

$10,000 ($1,000 error divided by 10 percent dollar percentage of the population in the sample).

2. Calculate an average error per sampled item and multiply it by the number of items in the population. In this illustration, the projected error is $25,000 ($1,000 error divided by 100 items in the sample = $10, the average error per sampled item, times 2,500, the number of items in the population).

This difference between the two projected errors results because 10 percent of the dollar amount but only 4 percent of the number of items in the population are sampled. Which method should be used? The decision depends on whether the errors in the sample relate better to the dollar amount of the items sampled or are fairly constant among all items. If the former is true, the projected error should be $10,000; if the latter is true, the projected error should be $25,000.

To elaborate further, assume that individual accounts receivable are tested. A $110 error is found in a recorded amount of $1,000, a $45 error is found in a recorded amount of $500 and so on. It appears that errors relate to recorded dollar amounts and that $10,000 is a more reliable projected error. However, assume that individual inventory amounts are tested. The amount of the errors ranges from $8 per sample item to $12 per sample item. In this case, the amounts of the errors appear to be fairly constant and $25,000 appears to be a more reliable projected error.

If the illustration had assumed that both 4 percent of the items and 4 percent of the dollar amount of the population were sampled, the projected error is the same using either method. Under method 1, the projected error is $25,000 ($1,000/.04). Under method 2, the projected error is $25,000 ($1,000/100 = $10 × 2,500 = $25,000).

When the auditor is satisfied that differences between recorded and audited amounts in the sample are errors, the client should be asked to adjust the recorded amounts. After calculating the projected error, any adjustments agreed on and recorded by the client can be subtracted from this projected error. The remaining part of the projected error is used to determine the likely error, illustrated in Chapter 12.

Even if the likely error is less than the tolerable error, the auditor should not pass the likely error off as immaterial and forget about it. All likely errors in all audit tests should be combined and a decision made as to whether the financial statements taken as a whole are materially misstated. Errors in individual accounts may be singularly immaterial, but collectively all the errors may prove to be otherwise. See page 462 of Chapter 12 for an example of an audit working paper that combines such immaterial errors.

Qualitative Evaluation

In addition to projecting sample errors and quantitatively evaluating sample results, the auditor should make qualitative evaluations. Consideration should be given to the cause and nature of sample errors and the relationship of sample errors to other phases of the audit.

For example, the likely error may be small, but the errors occurred in a clustered group of items. All the errors found in the sample may be of a certain type, giving the auditor reason to believe that there may be an error pattern in the population.

If many significant unexpected errors are found, the auditor may change the reliance placed on the internal control structure that produced the account balance. This reevaluation may, in turn, require an expanded sample or an extension of other related tests on the same account balance.

An Illustration of a Substantive Test Using Nonstatistical Sampling

The Sampling Plan

For our illustration of nonstatistical sampling, we will use Table 13.1, that contains the following information for 99 accounts receivable amounts:

1. Account numbers (number 30 is omitted because it is a credit balance and classified as a current liability).

2. Client book or recorded amounts.

3. The audited amounts or the amounts that would be confirmed by the customers if confirmation letters were sent to them.

4. The differences or errors in the account balances. For purposes of this illustration, assume that no differences can be resolved by the auditor and all of them are classified as errors.

The audit test consists of positive confirmation requests sent to a sample of the 99 accounts. This small population is used only for teaching purposes and does not represent the typical size of an accounts receivable population on which sampling techniques would be used.

The objective of the test is to ascertain whether the accounts exist and are owned by the client. Other substantive tests of accounts receivable are also performed, but we will concentrate only on this one.

A 100 percent test is conducted on the 16 accounts with recorded balances of $3,000 or more. Positive confirmation requests are sent to all 16 of these customers. By doing this, the auditor will conduct a 100 percent test of $90,758 of the

Table 13.1
Information for Nonstatistical and Classical Sampling Illustrations

Account Number	Client Book Amount	Audit Confirmation Amount	Difference	Account Number	Client Book Amount	Audit Confirmation Amount	Difference
1	$1,020	$1,020	$ —	41	$ 988	$ 988	$ —
2	696	1,534	838	42	306	306	—
3	208	218	10	43	—	—	—
4	1,847	1,907	60	44	5,551	5,551	—
5	—	—	—	45	2,652	2,016	(636)
6	1,240	1,240	—	46	195	195	—
7	5,391	5,418	27	47	950	950	—
8	1,190	1,190	—	48	306	306	—
9	2,554	2,554	—	49	—	—	—
10	218	218	—	50	2,605	2,605	—
11	5,000	4,027	(973)	51	3,196	2,836	(360)
12	4,606	5,360	754	52	850	850	—
13	2,106	2,106	—	53	—	—	—
14	402	402	—	54	3,722	3,722	—
15	1,335	1,335	—	55	14,522	14,522	—
16	3,240	3,240	—	56	—	—	—
17	2,507	2,507	—	57	—	—	—
18	2,824	2,794	(30)	58	582	582	—
19	650	650	—	59	14,941	14,977	36
20	—	—	—	60	1,780	890	(890)
21	144	144	—	61	3,008	3,008	—
22	669	669	—	62	3,329	3,329	—
23	543	543	—	63	3,175	2,975	(200)
24	730	730	—	64	1,080	1,080	—
25	770	385	(385)	65	425	425	—
26	145	145	—	66	569	569	—
27	7,049	7,193	144	67	2,064	2,064	—
28	640	640	—	68	—	—	—
29	890	890	—	69	1,860	1,860	—
31	238	238	—	70	660	760	100
32	742	724	(18)	71	200	200	—
33	480	—	(480)	72	2,455	2,455	—
34	240	240	—	73	3,950	4,050	100
35	480	480	—	74	—	—	—
36	—	774	774	75	906	906	—
37	845	845	—	76	100	100	—
38	345	345	—	77	1,041	1,041	—
39	1,030	1,030	—	78	1,190	1,190	—
40	2,035	2,035	—	79	576	576	—

Table 13.1 (cont.)

Account Number	Client Book Amount	Audit Confirmation Amount	Difference	Account Number	Client Book Amount	Audit Confirmation Amount	Difference
80	$ —	$ —	$ —	91	$ 5,218	$ 5,218	$ —
81	10	10	—	92	119	119	—
82	4,860	4,860	—	93	720	720	—
83	885	885	—	94	—	—	—
84	104	104	—	95	975	975	—
85	—	—	—	96	1,160	1,160	—
86	2,940	2,940	—	97	540	540	—
87	576	576	—	98	145	145	—
88	1,020	1,020	—	99	710	710	—
89	—	—	—	100	360	360	—
90	873	873	—				
				Totals	$155,998	$154,869	$(1,129)

$155,998 recorded balance, and the variability of the other accounts will be lowered considerably.

No letters will be sent to the 14 accounts with zero balances. The auditor is concerned with existence (possible overstatement of accounts receivable rather than understatement). The zero balance amounts cannot be overstated (except for a credit balance), and a professional judgment leads the auditor to believe that any possible understatement of the recorded amounts would not be significant. The completeness assertion is the subject of other audit tests.

Confirmation letters are sent to a sample of the other 69 accounts. Judgmental sampling techniques are used to select the sample and evaluate the sampling results. A projected error of the population of 69 accounts is calculated and combined with other errors found in the 16 accounts tested on a 100 percent basis. This total likely error in accounts receivable is aggregated with likely errors in all other accounts to help the auditor determine whether the financial statements are materially misstated.

After considering possible errors in the other account balances and a materiality level for the financial statements taken as a whole, the auditor sets $10,000 as the tolerable error for accounts receivable. Based on prior years' audits and professional judgment, the auditor estimates the actual dollar error in the population to be $1,000.

In the professional judgment of the auditor, there is a moderate risk that errors greater than the tolerable amount will occur and that internal control structure procedures and other substantive tests will not detect them. Therefore, the auditor decides to set a moderate risk of incorrect acceptance.

If the sampling decision results in rejection of the hypothesis that the evidence supports the account balance, alternative procedures to determine whether this is an incorrect rejection will be costly and time-consuming. Therefore, the auditor decides on a low risk of incorrect rejection to increase the sample size and more effectively guard against this possibility.

After considering all of these factors, the auditor uses professional judgment to decide on a sample size of 23 of the 69 accounts. Systematic sampling is used with a random start.

Selection of the Sample

Examination of Table 13.1 shows that the following 16 accounts have a recorded balance of $3,000 or more. Confirmation requests are sent to 100 percent of these accounts. Here are the results.

Account Number	Recorded Amount	Audit Amount	Difference
7	$ 5,391	$ 5,418	$ 27
11	5,000	4,027	(973)
12	4,606	5,360	754
16	3,240	3,240	—
27	7,049	7,193	144
44	5,551	5,551	—
51	3,196	2,836	(360)
54	3,722	3,722	—
55	14,522	14,522	—
59	14,941	14,977	36
61	3,008	3,008	—
62	3,329	3,329	—
63	3,175	2,975	(200)
73	3,950	4,050	100
82	4,860	4,860	—
91	5,218	5,218	—
	$90,758	$90,286	$(472)

The projected error for these 16 accounts is $472, the net difference between the recorded and audited amounts.

Confirmation requests are sent to 23 of the remaining 69 accounts with balances in excess of zero. A letter is sent to every third customer beginning with customer number 2. In selecting every third account, the amounts of $3,000 or more are omitted because they are included in the 16 accounts audited on a 100 percent basis. Following are the sample results.

Account Number	Recorded Amount	Audit Amount	Difference
2	$ 696	$ 1,534	$ 838
6	1,240	1,240	—
10	218	218	—
15	1,335	1,335	—
19	650	650	—
23	543	543	—
26	145	145	—
31	238	238	—
34	240	240	—
38	345	345	—
41	988	988	—
46	195	195	—
50	2,605	2,605	—
60	1,780	890	(890)
66	569	569	—
70	660	760	100
75	906	906	—
78	1,190	1,190	—
83	885	885	—
87	576	576	—
92	119	119	—
96	1,160	1,160	—
99	710	710	—
	$17,993	$18,041	$ 48

The confirmation results are summarized in the table below.

The likely error of $298 is well below the tolerable error of $10,000. The hypothesis that the evidence supports the account balance is not rejected. However, the $298 is combined with likely errors found in other account balances so that the total can be considered in the aggregate.

Group	Total Recorded Amount on Books	Recorded Amount of Group	Audit Amount of Group	Difference
100% tested	$90,758	$90,758	$90,286	$(472)
Sample of 23	65,240	17,993	18,041	$ 48
Projected Error { 100% tested				$(472)
Sample of 23 ($17,993/$65,240 = .276)(48/.276) =				174
Total likely error				$(298)

Qualitative Evaluation of Sample Results

Although the likely error is relatively small, several qualitative factors should be considered by the auditor. Following are two examples:

1. Out of 39 accounts examined, errors were found in 11. One reason for the relatively low likely error is the offset effect of the overstatements and understatements. The auditor might wish to investigate this large percentage of errors.

2. If none of the errors was corrected on the books by the client, this might indicate an unwillingness to concede that errors exist in the population. This attitude could be a source of auditor–client conflict in other phases of the audit.

Classical Statistical Sampling Methods

Although some numerical guides are available, the nonstatistical sampling techniques illustrated in the previous section do not require knowledge of statistical theory or application of statistical concepts. Classical statistical sampling, on the other hand, uses normal distribution theory for determining sample sizes and quantitatively evaluating sample results. Therefore, *some* knowledge of statistical theory and application of statistical concepts is helpful.

Statistical sampling is sometimes more difficult to use than nonstatistical sampling. However, the former provides a scientific basis for evaluating sampling risk, whereas the latter does not. Classical statistical methods may be efficient for sampling populations that contain a number of differences between recorded and audited amounts. The illustration we are using (Table 13.1, used to demonstrate nonstatistical sampling) contains several overstatements and understatements.

Generally, auditors use one of three statistical methods to estimate the dollar amount of a population:

1. Mean estimation or simple extension estimation.

2. Ratio estimation.

3. Difference estimation.

Mean Estimation

In mean estimation a sample mean of the audited values is calculated. The sample mean is multiplied by the number of elements in the population to obtain an estimate of the total dollar amount in the population.

The optimum sample size for estimating the dollar amount of the population can be found by using the following four items.

1. An estimate of the standard deviation of the population. Estimates may be obtained from prior-year audits. Also, if significant errors are not anticipated, the standard deviation of the recorded amounts in the population may be used as an estimate.

2. The auditor's desired levels of sampling risks. Risk of incorrect rejection is based on the difficulty and cost of additional investigation. Risk of incorrect acceptance is derived from the audit risk model.

3. The auditor's desired *allowance for sampling risk,* which is the acceptable difference between the expected error (see page 490) and the tolerable error. In classical sampling, this allowance is sometimes called precision.

4. The number of elements in the population.

The effect of each of these four items on sample size is demonstrated in the following table.

	Factor		Sample Size	
	Higher	*Lower*	*Larger*	*Smaller*
1. Estimated standard deviation of the population.	X		X	
		X		X
2. Desired levels of sampling risks.		X	X	
	X			X
3. Desired allowance for sampling risk	X			X
		X	X	
4. Number of elements in the population	X		X	
		X		X

The following steps are used to obtain the sample results.

1. Compute the mean of the sample and multiply it by the number of elements in the population. The result is an estimate of the total dollar amount of the population (sometimes called the point estimate).

2. Compute the achieved allowance for sampling risk (sometimes called achieved precision) around the population estimate, expressed as, for example, ± $10,000.

3. Add the allowance to and subtract the allowance from the estimate of the dollar amount in the population. The result is the allowance interval at a specified risk level.

Mean estimation may be used to estimate the dollar amount of a population without book values. Some examples are as follows:

1. Estimation of supplies inventory whose records consist only of quantities.

2. Estimation of supplies inventory when the dollar amount in the ledger is kept constant and all supply expenditures are charged to expense during the year.

3. Estimation of allowance for doubtful accounts.

Mean estimation can also be used when the dollar amount of the population contains book values, such as recorded accounts receivable balances. In this case the auditor must control the risk of incorrect acceptance because a decision will be made as to whether or not the evidence supports acceptance of a book value. This risk is controlled by adjusting the relationship of the allowance for sampling risk to tolerable error when determining sample size. This technique is illustrated beginning on page 506. Ratio and difference estimation usually provide more reliable estimations of book values in this circumstance.

Generally, mean estimation, as well as ratio and difference estimation, provide more efficiency if the population is stratified into subgroups.

Ratio Estimation

Ratio estimation is appropriate when the auditors want to estimate a population value based on the ratio of recorded amounts and audited amounts. In unstratified populations, the standard deviation of ratios is usually smaller than the standard deviation of account balances, thus resulting in smaller sample sizes. Although the method is suitable for such procedures as tests of extension of inventory amounts and confirmation of accounts receivable, it is not compatible with procedures in which no book value for individual items exist.

For an example of *ratio estimation,* assume that a client-furnished figure is $100,000. The auditors sample $20,000 of this amount, and their calculated audit figure is $21,000 or 105 percent of the sampled book figure. They then estimate the population figure as $105,000 (105 percent of $100,000).

Ratio estimation can be used most effectively when the calculated audit figures are approximately proportional to the client-furnished book figures. For example, the following situation is appropriate for ratio estimation because the ratios of audited to book figures are fairly consistent.

Book Figures	Audited Figures	Difference	Ratio
$ 8,000	$ 7,900	$(100)	.99
10,000	10,250	250	1.03
12,000	11,700	(300)	.98
9,000	9,300	300	1.03
$39,000	$39,150	$ 150	

Conversely, the following situation would *not* be as suitable for ratio estimation because the relationship between book and audited figures is not proportional, and the audit to book ratios are not consistent. These figures might be used more appropriately with difference estimation, discussed in the next section.

Book Figures	Audited Figures	Difference	Ratio
$ 8,000	$ 8,050	$ 50	1.01
10,000	8,600	(1,400)	.86
12,000	11,800	(200)	.98
9,000	10,700	1,700	1.19
39,000	$39,150	$ 150	

If a small number of audit/book differences exist in the population, the use of ratio estimation may not be appropriate. A relatively large sample would be necessary to ensure that the differences between book and audited values found are representative of the population. Such a large sample would erase much of the benefit of ratio estimation. However, stratification of the population may be useful in this situation.

Difference Estimation

The objective of *difference estimation* is to estimate a population value based on the difference between the client's book amount and the audited amount (same as ratio estimation), but the method is *slightly* different because the auditor uses dollar rather than ratio differences. Difference estimation is also incompatible with procedures in which no book value for individual items exist.

As an example, assume that a book figure is $100,000 for a population of 1,000 accounts. A sample of $20,000 of this book amount revealed an audited amount of $21,000. The sample size is 100. The total difference in the sample is $1,000 or an average difference of $10 ($1,000 difference ÷ the sample size of 100). To estimate the population difference, the auditors multiply the average difference of $10 by the population total of 1,000. The estimated population difference is $10,000, and the estimate of the population total is $110,000.

Difference estimation may be used if the dollar amount (not ratios) of audit/ book differences is fairly consistent. Otherwise, the method's advantages and disadvantages are essentially the same as for ratio estimation.[1]

Application of Mean Estimation

Steps in Applying Mean Estimation

Mean estimation, as well as other classical statistical sampling techniques, can be applied more efficiently by following a sequence of logical steps. These steps are outlined in the following list and discussed more fully in the remainder of the section.[2]

1. Determine the distribution of the account balances to assess the need for stratification.

2. Stratify the accounts if high variability is a problem.

3. Determine the appropriate sample size by

   a. Determining the desired risks of incorrect acceptance and incorrect rejection.

   b. Determining the desired allowance for sampling risk and the tolerable error.

   c. Estimating the population standard deviation.

4. Select the sample and perform the necessary audit procedures.

5. Quantitatively evaluate the sample results by estimating the population total, calculating an achieved allowance for sampling risk, and accepting or rejecting the hypothesis that the evidence supports the recorded amount.

6. Perform a qualitative evaluation of the sample results.

---

[1] For further comparisons of the variable sampling techniques discussed in this chapter, see John Neter and James K. Loebbecke, *Behavior of Major Statistical Estimators in Sampling Accounting Populations—Auditing Research Monograph No. 2*, published by the AICPA.

[2] Auditors would not commonly select the mean estimation method for auditing accounts with recorded balances. However, it illustrates estimation sampling concepts and avoids some of the complications of ratio and difference estimation techniques. If mean estimation is understood, other techniques will not be difficult to comprehend.

Estimation of an Accounts Receivable Balance

Distribution of the Account Balances   Assume that the auditors wish to estimate the balance of accounts receivable and test the hypothesis that the evidence supports the recorded balance. Logically, one of the first steps taken by the auditors is to review the numerical distribution of the accounts. Such a distribution is shown in Table 13.2.[3]

Table 13.2
Distribution of the Accounts

Range of Account Balances	Number of Accounts	Total Dollar Amount of Accounts
$ 0– 999	60	$ 23,705
1,000– 1,999	13	16,793
2,000– 2,999	10	24,742
3,000– 3,999	7	23,620
4,000– 4,999	2	9,466
5,000– 5,999	4	21,160
6,000– 6,999	0	0
7,000– 7,999	1	7,049
8,000– 8,999	0	0
9,000– 9,999	0	0
10,000–10,999	0	0
11,000–11,999	0	0
12,000–12,999	0	0
13,000–13,999	0	0
14,000–14,999	2	29,463
	99	$155,998

It is obvious that the distribution of the 99 accounts is skewed heavily, and also that it has a relatively high standard deviation. Following is some information about the population of accounts receivable (although the auditors may not know all these facts):

1. The mean is $1,576.

2. The total is $155,998.

3. The standard deviation is $2,413.

[3] This distribution is taken from Table 13.1. This table was used to illustrate nonstatistical sampling. It is also used to illustrate classical statistical sampling so that the results may be compared.

Any attempt to determine a statistically derived sample size for this accounts-receivable distribution would be ineffective because the size of such a sample probably would be very large.

Stratification—A Solution to High Variability   How can statistical sampling methods be applied to a distribution of accounts-receivable balances with such a large variability? One possibility is to stratify the accounts into two or more subgroups and then treat each subgroup as a separate population. Review of the distribution of accounts shows the strata into which each dollar group can be placed.

One first notices two very large account balances totaling $29,463 (out of a population total of $155,998). Clearly, these two accounts could and should be audited separately with positive confirmation requests. By doing this, one reduces the variability in the remaining population of 97 and covers approximately 20 percent of the total dollar balance in accounts receivable.

A further examination of the account balance distribution shows that an additional 14 accounts are listed in the dollar categories starting at $3,000 and ending at $7,999. Positive confirmation requests on a 100 percent basis also might be appropriate for these balances.

Among the 60 accounts listed in the $0–999 classification are 14 with zero balances. Extracting these accounts will lower the variability of the remaining distribution.

After separation of the accounts according to the criteria explained in the foregoing paragraphs, the following groups emerge.

Type of Account	Number of Accounts	Type of Evidence
Balances ≥ $3,000	16	Positive confirmation on a 100 percent basis
Balances between $1 and $2,999	69	Positive confirmation on a sample of accounts—statistical sampling techniques applied

The new population to which variable sampling methods can be applied has a different and more suitable set of statistical measures.

1. The mean is $946.

2. The total is $65,240.

3. The standard deviation is $754.

Note the distribution of the new population as shown in the table on page 506.

Range of the 69 Remaining Account Balances after Stratification	Number of Accounts	Total Dollar Amount of Accounts
$ 1– 499	21	$ 5,170
500– 999	25	18,535
1,000–1,499	10	11,306
1,500–1,999	3	5,487
2,000–2,499	4	8,660
2,500–2,999	6	16,082
		$65,240

Audit Risks   Using the equation, $TD = R/[IR \times CR \times APR]$, discussed earlier in the chapter, the auditor has a 20 percent risk of incorrect acceptance calculated by assigning the values .05 to R, 1.0 to IR, .50 to CR, and .50 to APR, as follows:

$$.20 = .05/[1.0 \times .50 \times .50]$$

Using judgment, the auditor sets the risk of incorrect rejection at 5 percent.

Allowance for Sampling Risk   Using judgment, the auditor sets the tolerable error at $21,000. The allowance for sampling risk is calculated by reference to Table 13.3. This table gives the ratio of desired allowance for sampling risk to tolerable error for several combinations of risks of incorrect acceptance and incorrect rejection. The table factor of .700 is multiplied by $21,000 to calculate an allowance (or precision) of $14,700. This amount is usually expressed as ± $14,700. If the recorded amount is within ±$14,700 of the estimated amount, the auditor can state, at a 20 percent risk of incorrect acceptance, that the recorded amount is not in error by more than $21,000.

Estimation of the Population Standard Deviation   The auditors also need a reasonably good estimate of the population standard deviation to determine an optimum sample size. The standard deviation is a measure of variability in the numerical distribution. The higher this variability, the larger the sample size necessary to increase the probability of drawing samples whose characteristics are close to those of the population.

In this case the auditors use a microcomputer program to calculate the standard deviation of the recorded amounts. The standard deviation of the 69 recorded amounts in this illustration is estimated to be $790.

Use of the Variables to Determine Sample Size   The desired risks of 20 and 5 percent, the desired allowance for sampling risk of $14,700, a $790 estimate of the population standard deviation, and the population size of 69 can be used to derive a sample size. If sampling is conducted with replacement, the equation is

Table 13.3
Ratio of Desired Allowance for Sampling Risk to Tolerable Error[a]

Risk of Incorrect Acceptance	Risk of Incorrect Rejection			
	.20	.10	.05	.01
.01	.355	.413	.457	.525
.025	.395	.456	.500	.568
.05	.437	.500	.543	.609
.075	.471	.532	.576	.641
.10	.500	.561	.605	.668
.15	.511	.612	.653	.712
.20	.603	.661	.700	.753
.25	.653	.708	.742	.791
.30	.707	.756	.787	.829
.35	.766	.808	.834	.868
.40	.831	.863	.883	.908
.45	.907	.926	.937	.952
.50	1.000	1.000	1.000	1.000

[a]This table is derived from *Statistical Auditing* by Donald Roberts (New York: AICPA, 1978). Copyright © (1978) American Institute of Certified Public Accountants, Inc., reprinted with permission. For further information on the hypotheses underlying this measure of the risk of incorrect rejection, see *Statistical Auditing*, pp. 41–43.

$$\text{Sample size} = \left(\frac{\left(\begin{array}{c} \text{Estimate of the} \\ \text{population} \\ \text{standard deviation} \end{array} \right) \left(\begin{array}{c} \text{Reliability} \\ \text{coefficient} \end{array} \right) \left(\begin{array}{c} \text{Population} \\ \text{size} \end{array} \right)}{\text{Desired allowance for sampling risk}} \right)^2$$

The reliability coefficient refers to a standard deviation multiple associated with a certain reliability (the complement of risk). See Table 13.4, which provides a list of reliability factors. A 5 percent of incorrect rejection is a 95 percent reliability. The two-sided factors from the table are used for the risk of incorrect rejection.

Table 13.4
Reliability Factors

Reliability	One-Side or One-Tailed Factor	Two-Side or Two-Tailed Factor
80	.84	1.28
85	1.04	1.44
90	1.28	1.64
95	1.64	1.96
99	2.33	2.58

The statistical notation is

$$n = \left(\frac{s \times U_R \times N}{A} \right)^2$$

$$n = \left(\frac{790 \times 1.96 \times 69}{14,700} \right)^2$$

$$n = 53$$

As applied to confirmation requests, sampling with replacement does not mean that two letters are mailed to the same customer if the same number is selected in the random sample. It simply means that a larger sample must be selected to overcome the possible obstacle of choosing the same number more than once when only one letter is circularized.

A more practical approach is to sample without replacement and thus derive *n* separate customer numbers. If this method is adopted, the following correction factor is applied to the sample of 53.

$$n' \text{ (without replacement)} = \frac{n \text{ (with replacement)}}{1 + \dfrac{n \text{ (with replacement)}}{N}}$$

$$n' = \frac{53}{1 + \dfrac{53}{69}}$$

$$n' = 30 \text{ (without replacement)}$$

Selecting the Sample and Performing the Audit Procedures   Once the sample size is derived, the sample itself is selected. It should be emphasized that the audit procedures are *no different* when statistical sampling is used than when judgmental sampling is employed. In this illustration, the auditors mail 30 confirmation requests to randomly selected customers.

There are two fairly common techniques for deriving a set of random numbers. One method is to draw samples from a random number table by the techniques described in Chapter 9. Another is to list the numbers from a computer-generated random number program. Assume that the latter method is used. Because accounts receivable customer numbers are available, they can be identified easily with the numbers produced by the computerized random number generator.

Once the 30 customer numbers are selected, confirmation requests are sent and the auditors wait for replies. If a letter is forwarded by a customer and contains an indication of a disagreement with the book balance, the auditors seek to find the reason for this difference. A satisfactory resolution of this discrepancy is tantamount to a satisfactory reply from the customer.

But what if the auditors are unable to reconcile the difference between the balance listed on the client's records and the amount confirmed by the customer? If it is determined that the client's amount is wrong, use the customer amount to estimate the population total.

Assume that the sample is drawn, the confirmation letters are mailed, and the customer replies are received. Table 13.5 lists the 30 customers receiving confirmation requests. Assume that unresolved discrepancies are errors in the records; therefore, to estimate the population total, the amount confirmed by the customer is used as the correct amount.

Estimate of the Population Total—Allowance for Sampling Risk Range
The next step for the auditor is to use the tally of confirmation results to make an estimate of the population total. A range is developed around this estimate, and the auditor may then accept, at a 20 percent risk of incorrect acceptance, if the book value falls within the range, or reject, at a 5 percent risk of incorrect rejection, if the book value falls outside the range.

These sets of calculations are performed by taking the $29,448 total of the confirmation results and developing the sample mean.

$$\$29{,}448 \div 30 = \$982$$

Then an estimate of the population total is made.

$$\$982 \times 69 = \$67{,}758$$

It should be pointed out that $67,758 is only one of *many* population estimates that could have been derived by the auditors. How many could be selected if, from a population of 69, a random sample of 30 is selected without replacement? The answer is

$$\frac{69 \ (\text{Factorial})}{30 \ (\text{Factorial}) \ (69 \ - \ 30) \ (\text{Factorial})}$$

(31,627,280,000,000,000,000). The reason statisticians consider 30 to be a large sample is that there are so many population estimates (and sample means) that the sample distribution is expected to be fairly close to normal, even if the population from which the sample is taken is skewed.

The achieved allowance for sampling risk (A') is developed by use of the following equations and calculations on this page and page 511.

A' (achieved allowance for sampling risk) $= s_{\bar{x}} \times U_R \times N$

$$s_{\bar{x}} = \frac{s}{\sqrt{n}}$$

$$s_{\bar{x}} = \frac{783}{\sqrt{30}} = 143$$

Table 13.5
Customers Receiving Confirmation Requests

Random Number	Customer Number	Book Balance	No Error Indicated	Amount of Customer Reply (error in records)	Amount Used in Population Estimate
1	1	$1,020	x		$ 1,020
2	2	696		$1,534	1,534
10	14	402	x		402
11	15	1,335	x		1,335
14	19	650	x		650
15	21	144	x		144
17	23	543	x		543
22	29	890	x		890
34	45	2,652		2,016	2,016
37	48	306	x		306
38	50	2,605	x		2,605
43	65	425	x		425
44	66	569	x		569
45	67	2,064	x		2,064
46	69	1,860	x		1,860
49	72	2,455	x		2,455
50	75	906	x		906
51	76	100	x		100
52	77	1,041	x		1,041
53	78	1,190	x		1,190
54	79	576	x		576
57	84	104	x		104
58	86	2,940	x		2,940
59	87	576	x		576
61	90	873	x		873
62	92	119	x		119
65	96	1,160	x		1,160
66	97	540	x		540
67	98	145	x		145
69	100	360	x		360
					$29,448

$A' = 143 \times 1.96 \times 69 = 19{,}339$ (achieved allowance for sampling risk with replacement)[4]

This allowance is multiplied by a finite correction factor because sampling is done without replacement.

$$19{,}339 \times \sqrt{\frac{N - n}{N - 1}}$$

$$19{,}339 \times \sqrt{\frac{69 - 30}{69 - 1}} = 14{,}658 \text{ (achieved allowance for sampling}$$
$$\text{risk without replacement).}$$

The auditors then have the following range: $53,100 ($67,758, the population estimate, minus $14,658) to $82,416 ($67,758, the population estimate, plus $14,658).

The achieved allowance for sampling risk will be larger than the desired allowance if the sample standard deviation is larger than the estimated population standard deviation used to compute the sample size. If this occurs, a new and larger sample size could be computed by using the standard deviation of the first sample.

However, in this example, the achieved allowance of $14,658 is less than the desired allowance of $14,700. The reason is that the sample standard deviation of $783 is smaller than the estimated population standard deviation of $790.

The following graph describes the normal distribution into which the population estimates of the sample of 30 are assumed to fall. The population estimate of the sample is $67,758, and the sample mean is $982. The allowance for sampling risk (or precision) range is $53,100 to $82,416.

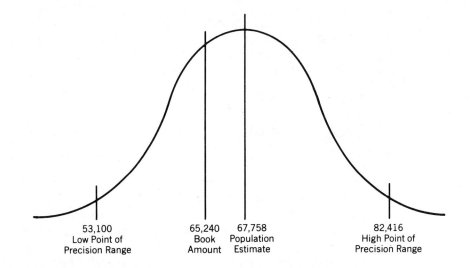

53,100	65,240	67,758	82,416
Low Point of	Book	Population	High Point of
Precision Range	Amount	Estimate	Precision Range

[4] The $783 standard deviation of the sample is different from the $790 standard deviation of the recorded amounts.

The Decision to Reject or Not Reject the Hypothesis that the Evidence Supports the Recorded Balance   For the $65,240 recorded amount, the following decision criteria would be used.

1. If the client's recorded balance falls within the achieved allowance (or precision) range (as it does in the preceding graph) and if the achieved allowance is smaller than the desired allowance, the auditor will generally accept (not reject) the hypothesis that the evidence supports the recorded balance. This acceptance is at a risk of incorrect acceptance equal to or less than 20 percent. One way of describing the risk is as follows. There is one chance in five or less that the recorded balance is in error by more than the $21,000 tolerable error and that an incorrect acceptance is made.

2. If the likely error of $2,518 ($67,758, population estimate, minus $65,240, the recorded balance) plus the achieved allowance for sampling risk of $14,658 is equal to or less than the tolerable error, the hypothesis that the evidence supports the recorded balance would still be accepted (not rejected). The likely error of $2,518 plus the allowance of $14,658 equals $17,176, which is less than the tolerable error of $21,000. Therefore, the hypothesis is accepted with a risk of incorrect acceptance of 20 percent or less.

3. If the likely error plus the allowance for sampling risk is more than the tolerable error, the hypothesis that the evidence supports the recorded balance would be rejected. A 5 percent risk of incorrect rejection accompanies the decision to reject the hypothesis. One way of describing the risk is that there is 1 chance in 20 that the recorded balance is not in error by more than $21,000 and that an incorrect rejection is made.

To evaluate the entire accounts-receivable balance of $155,998, the auditor must combine the errors found in the 16 accounts tested 100 percent with the projected error calculated in the sample. This total likely error is aggregated with errors in other accounts and compared with materiality for the overall financial statements.

Probability Proportional to Size Sampling

Sometimes the auditor may decide to use statistical sampling on populations of account balances or classes of transactions that normally contain a few overstatements, some of which may be large. Accounts receivable and inventory are two examples. In auditing these types of populations the major criterion is to ascertain, at a desired risk level, whether the dollar overstatement does or does not exceed a certain amount.

Unless the population is stratified, the classical statistical sampling procedures discussed so far in this chapter may not be appropriate. Mean estimation sometimes proves to be unreliable. Allowance for sampling risk intervals cannot be calculated on ratio and difference estimation unless differences between book and audited amounts are found in the sample. For a population with few errors, a small sample may produce no differences. Even if differences are found, they may be the smaller ones and the population estimate may be poor.

Probability proportional to size sampling, sometimes called dollar-unit sampling, overcomes these potential problems with these types of populations. In fact, even if the dollar amount of the errors is not large and the errors are few, probability proportional to size sampling (PPS) has some advantages over mean, ratio, and difference estimation. The sampling method is more likely to result in selection of a few large dollar overstatements should such a condition exist in the population.

Characteristics of PPS

PPS uses each dollar in the population as a separate sampling unit, as contrasted with mean, ratio, and difference estimation, which use such items as account balances as the sampling unit. Each dollar has an equal chance of selection. However, if any dollar portion of an account balance is selected, the entire balance is sampled (e.g., a confirmation letter sent, physical and perpetual inventory compared, etc.). This procedure results in large recorded dollar balances in the population having a greater chance of being selected and audited. If such selected dollar balances are overstated, they will be detected (unless a nonsampling error occurs).

PPS is performed on the assumption that no recorded dollar balance is overstated by more than its recorded amount. For instance, it assumes that a recorded accounts receivable balance of $10,000 could not actually be as low as $-\$5,000$ (or a $5,000 credit balance).

To determine an appropriate sample size for this type of PPS illustration, the following items are needed.

1. The tolerable error.

2. Risk of incorrect acceptance.

3. The number of errors to be allowed in the sample.

4. Recorded book value of the population.

An Illustration of PPS—Assuming No Errors Are Found

The mechanics of selecting and evaluating a PPS sample can be shown by reference to Table 13.1, used to illustrate nonstatistical and classical statistical sampling. The 99 accounts are listed in Table 13.6. Note that some audit amounts are changed to create a population that consists for the most part of a few large

Table 13.6
Information for Probability Proportional to Size Sampling Illustration

Account Number	Client Recorded Amount	Audit Confirmation Amount	Difference	Account Number	Client Recorded Amount	Audit Confirmation Amount	Difference
1	$ 1,020	$ 1,020	$ —	41	$ 988	$ 988	$ —
2	696	696	—	42	306	306	—
3	208	208	—	43	—	—	—
4	1,847	1,847	—	44	5,551	5,551	—
5	—	—	—	45	2,652	2,016	(636)
6	1,240	1,240	—	46	195	195	—
7	5,391	5,418	27	47	950	950	—
8	1,190	1,190	—	48	306	306	—
9	2,554	2,554	—	49	—	—	—
10	218	218	—	50	2,605	2,605	—
11	5,000	4,027	(973)	51	3,196	2,836	(360)
12	4,606	4,606	—	52	850	850	—
13	2,106	2,106	—	53	—	—	—
14	402	402	—	54	3,722	3,722	—
15	1,335	1,335	—	55	14,522	14,522	—
16	3,240	3,240	—	56	—	—	—
17	2,507	2,507	—	57	—	—	—
18	2,824	2,824	—	58	582	582	—
19	650	650	—	59	14,941	14,941	—
20	—	—	—	60	1,780	890	(890)
21	144	144	—	61	3,008	3,008	—
22	669	669	—	62	3,329	3,329	—
23	543	543	—	63	3,175	3,175	—
24	730	730	—	64	1,080	1,080	—
25	770	385	(385)	65	425	425	—
26	145	145	—	66	569	569	—
27	7,049	7,049	—	67	2,064	2,064	—
28	640	640	—	68	—	—	—
29	890	890	—	69	1,860	1,860	—
31	238	238	—	70	660	760	100
32	742	742	—	71	200	200	—
33	480	—	(480)	72	2,455	2,455	—
34	240	240	—	73	3,950	3,950	—
35	480	480	—	74	—	—	—
36	—	—	—	75	906	906	—
37	845	845	—	76	100	100	—
38	345	345	—	77	1,041	1,041	—
39	1,030	1,030	—	78	1,190	1,190	—
40	2,035	2,035	—	79	576	576	—

Table 13.6 (cont.)

Account Number	Client Recorded Amount	Audit Confirmation Amount	Difference	Account Number	Client Recorded Amount	Audit Confirmation Amount	Difference
80	$ —	$ —	$ —	91	$ 5,218	$ 5,218	$ —
81	10	10	—	92	119	119	—
82	4,860	4,860	—	93	720	720	—
83	885	885	—	94	—	—	—
84	104	104	—	95	975	975	—
85	—	—	—	96	1,160	1,160	—
86	2,940	2,940	—	97	540	540	—
87	576	576	—	98	145	145	—
88	1,020	1,020	—	99	710	710	—
89	—	—	—	100	360	360	—
90	873	873	—				
				Totals	$155,998	$152,401	$(3,597)

dollar overstatements. The audit procedure selected is a positive confirmation request. The objective of the audit procedure is to determine whether the amounts exist and are owned by the client. The following data are assumed:

1. Tolerable error—$10,000.

2. Risk of incorrect acceptance—15 percent.

3. Number of errors allowed—0.

4. Recorded book amount—$155,998.

The sample size is computed by using the equation

$$n = \frac{\text{Reliability factor for errors of overstatement (per table)}}{TE/BV}$$

The numerator is a table factor based on an assumption of a certain number of errors and a risk of incorrect acceptance (see Table 13.7). In this case zero errors and 15 percent provide a table factor of 1.90.

The denominator is the tolerable error (*TE*) divided by the recorded book value (*BV*). In this case $10,000 ÷ $155,998. Therefore

$$n = \frac{1.90}{10,000/155,998} = 30 \text{ (rounded)}$$

Table 13.7
Probability-Proportional-to-Size Sampling Tables: Reliability Factors for Errors of Overstatement

Number of Over-statement Errors	Risk of Incorrect Acceptance								
	1%	*5%*	*10%*	*15%*	*20%*	*25%*	*30%*	*37%*	*50%*
0	4.61	3.00	2.31	1.90	1.61	1.39	1.21	1.00	.70
1	6.64	4.75	3.89	3.38	3.00	2.70	2.44	2.14	1.68
2	8.41	6.30	5.33	4.72	4.28	3.93	3.62	3.25	2.68
3	10.05	7.76	6.69	6.02	5.52	5.11	4.77	4.34	3.68
4	11.61	9.16	8.00	7.27	6.73	6.28	5.90	5.43	4.68
5	13.11	10.52	9.28	8.50	7.91	7.43	7.01	6.49	5.68
6	14.57	11.85	10.54	9.71	9.08	8.56	8.12	7.56	6.67
7	16.00	13.15	11.78	10.90	10.24	9.69	9.21	8.63	7.67
8	17.41	14.44	13.00	12.08	11.38	10.81	10.31	9.68	8.67
9	18.79	15.71	14.21	13.25	12.52	11.92	11.39	10.74	9.67
10	20.15	16.97	15.41	14.42	13.66	13.02	12.47	11.79	10.67

Source: Audit and Accounting Guide—Audit Sampling (AICPA, 1983). Copyright © (1983) American Institute of Certified Public Accountants, Inc., reprinted with permission.

The sampling method is systematic and the sampling interval is computed as follows:

$$\$155,998 \div 30 = \$5,200 \text{ (rounded)}$$

The sample is taken by assuming that there are 155,998 sampling units and that every 5,200th unit is selected. The chart below shows some of the selection process from the 99 accounts in Table 13.6. Assume a random start at the 1,000th unit with the 6,200th unit being the second unit selected.

Recorded Amount	Cumulative Recorded Amount	Sampling Interval	Recorded Amount of Account Selected
$1,020	$ 1,020	$1,000	$1,020
696	1,716		
208	1,924		
1,847	3,771		
1,240	5,011		
5,391	10,402	6,200	5,391

The next account selected would be the account that falls into the $11,400 cumulative book amount ($6,200 + $5,200). As can be seen, the largest account balances have the largest chance of selection.

For simplicity, assume that the population either contains no errors or no errors are detected in the sample. The auditor could then state with a 15 percent risk that the maximum dollar overstatement in the population does not exceed $10,000.

A More Detailed Illustration of PPS

In the previous illustration, the sample results were assumed to be satisfactory because the upper limit on net overstatement (or maximum dollar overstatement in the population) was not in excess of the tolerable error. There was a 15 percent risk that the true overstatement in the population was in excess of the tolerable error and that the auditor incorrectly accepted the estimate of error in the account. The results occurred because no errors were anticipated in determination of the sample size and no errors were found when the sample was taken.

In the illustration in Table 13.8, we also assume a 15 percent risk of incorrect acceptance, a tolerable error of $10,000, no anticipated errors, a sample size of 30, and a sampling interval of $5,200. However, all 99 account balances (except zero

Table 13.8
Illustration of PPS Using All Population Items[a]

Recorded Amount	Cumulative Recorded Amount	Sampling Interval	Recorded Amount of Account Selected	Audit Amount
$ 1,020	$ 1,020	$ 1,000	$ 1,020	$ 1,020
696	1,716			
208	1,924			
1,847	3,771			
1,240	5,011			
5,391	10,402	6,200	5,391	5,418
1,190	11,592	11,400	1,190	1,190
2,554	14,146			
218	14,364			
5,000	19,364	16,600	5,000	4,027
4,606	23,970	21,800	4,606	4,606
2,106	26,076			
402	26,478			
1,335	27,813	27,000	1,335	1,335
3,240	31,053			
2,507	33,560	32,200	2,507	2,507
2,824	36,384			
650	37,034			
144	37,178			
669	37,847	37,400	669	669
543	38,390			

Table 13.8 (cont.)

Recorded Amount	Cumulative Recorded Amount	Sampling Interval	Recorded Amount of Account Selected	Audit Amount
$ 730	$ 39,120			
770	39,890			
145	40,035			
7,049	47,084	$ 42,600	$ 7,049	$ 7,049
640	47,724			
890	48,614	47,800	890	890
238	48,852			
742	49,594			
480	50,074			
240	50,314			
480	50,794			
845	51,639			
345	51,984			
1,030	53,014	53,000	1,030	1,030
2,035	55,049			
988	56,037			
306	56,343			
5,551	61,894	58,200	5,551	5,551
2,652	64,546	63,400	2,652	2,016
195	64,741			
950	65,691			
306	65,997			
2,605	68,602	68,600	2,605	2,605
3,196	71,798			
850	72,648			
3,722	76,370	73,800	3,722	3,722
14,522	90,892	79,000	14,522	14,522
14,522[b]	90,892[b]	84,200	14,522	14,522
14,522[b]	90,892[b]	89,400	14,522	14,522
582	91,474			
14,941	106,415	94,600	14,941	14,941
14,941[b]	106,415[b]	99,800	14,941	14,941
14,941[b]	106,415[b]	105,000	14,941	14,941
1,780	108,195			
3,008	111,203	110,200	3,008	3,008
3,329	114,532			
3,175	117,707	115,400	3,175	3,175
1,080	118,787			
425	119,212			
569	119,781			

Table 13.8 (cont.)

Recorded Amount	Cumulative Recorded Amount	Sampling Interval	Recorded Amount of Account Selected	Audit Amount
$ 2,064	$121,845	$120,600	$ 2,064	$ 2,064
1,860	123,705			
660	124,365			
200	124,565			
2,455	127,020	125,800	2,455	2,455
3,950	130,970			
906	131,876	131,000	906	906
100	131,976			
1,041	133,017			
1,190	134,207			
576	134,783			
10	134,793			
4,860	139,653	136,200	4,860	4,860
885	140,538			
104	140,642			
2,940	143,582	141,400	2,940	2,940
576	144,158			
1,020	145,178			
873	146,051			
5,218	151,269	146,600	5,218	5,218
119	151,388			
720	152,108	151,800	720	720
975	153,083			
1,160	154,243			
540	154,783			
145	154,928			
710	155,638			
360	155,998			

[a] Zero balances are not used because the purpose of the test is to detect overstatements.

[b] These accounts are selected three times because of their dollar size. The PPS sampling method takes this into account and the method should not be altered because this occurs. The accounts would be audited only once.

balances) are used to select the sample. By doing this, we will demonstrate how a PPS systematic sample is drawn from an unstratified population, how the projected error is calculated, and how the sample results are evaluated.

Note that the PPS method does not require the division of the population into strata, which is generally required when classical statistical sampling is used on populations with high variability. Note also that all accounts with balances of $5,200 or more are selected when a sampling interval of $5,200 is used.

When a dollar in the sampling interval is selected for examination, the entire account balance containing that dollar is examined. This automatic selection of large balances is popular with many auditors because these accounts are more likely to contain large overstatements.

Following is a summary of the errors found in the sample:

Recorded Amount	Audited Amount	Error
$5,391	$5,418	$ 27
5,000	4,027	(973)
2,652	2,016	(636)
Net overstatement found in the sample		$(1,582)

Because the sampling interval started at $1,000, 30 accounts were selected. Only 26 different accounts were used, however. Two accounts, $14,522 and $14,941, are so large that the sampling interval caused each of them to be selected three times. The sample size without replacement is 26, and this is the number of confirmation requests sent to customers.

If errors occur in recorded amounts that are equal to or greater than the sampling interval of $5,200, the entire amounts of the errors are classified as projected errors. Thus, the $27 understatement in $5,391 is classified as a projected error of $27. Errors in recorded amounts below the sampling interval of $5,200 have a "tainting" factor. Any error relates to the entire sampling interval of $5,200. For example, if an audited amount was 20 percent less than its recorded amount, it is "tainted" by 20 percent; the projected error is $1,040, or $5,200 times .20.

The following table is a compilation of the likely error (sum of the total projected errors) in the population based on the three errors found in the sample.

Recorded Amount	Audit Amount	Tainting[a]	Sampling Interval	Projected Error[b]
$5,391	$5,418	—	$ —	$ 27
5,000	4,027	20%	5,200	(1,040)
2,652	2,016	24	5,200	(1,248)
Total likely overstatement				$(2,261)

[a] The recorded amount minus the audit amount divided by the recorded amount, or the error divided by the recorded amount.

[b] The sampling interval times the tainting percentage.

As in nonstatistical sampling, this likely error is aggregated with errors in all other accounts and compared with materiality for the overall financial statements.

In probability proportional to size sampling, an allowance for sampling risk can be calculated and added to the likely error to derive an upper limit on net overstatement. This upper limit can then be compared to the tolerable error. Remember from our discussion of classical statistical sampling that the same comparison can be made.

In PPS sampling, the allowance for sampling risk has two parts:

1. An allowance based on the projected errors under the sampling interval. Each projected error is multiplied by an increment in the table of reliability factors (see Table 13.7). Notice that the projected errors are listed in descending dollar order.

2. A "basic" allowance (or basic precision). This allowance is the sampling interval times the factor for the specified risk of incorrect acceptance and no errors. This factor is taken from the same table of reliability factors used to calculate the sample size (Table 13.7).

Following are calculations of the *upper limit on net overstatement.*

Projected Error under the Sampling Interval		*Reliability Factor Increment (from Table 13.7)*		*Projected Error Plus Allowance for Sampling Risk*
$1,248	×	1.48[a]	=	$1,847 (rounded)
1,040	×	1.34[b]	=	1,394 (rounded)
$2,288				$3,241

[a]Table 13.7. The factor for a 15 percent risk of incorrect acceptance for one error (3.38) minus the factor for a 15 percent risk of incorrect acceptance for no errors (1.90).

[b]The table factor for 15 percent risk and two errors (4.72) minus the table factor for 15 percent risk and one error (3.38).

The allowance for sampling risk based on increments of projected error under the $5,200 sampling interval is:

$$\$3,241 - \$2,288 = \$953$$

The basic allowance for sampling risk is the sampling interval times the factor for 15 percent and no errors taken from Table 13.7:

$$\$5,200 \times 1.90 = \$10,000 \text{ (rounded)}$$

Total allowance for sampling risk	$10,953
Total likely overstatement (from page 520)	2,261
Upper limit on net overstatement	$13,214

The sample results are not acceptable because the tolerable error is $10,000. No errors were anticipated in the sample but three errors, with a net overstatement of $1,582, were found. The actual overstatement in the population is $3,597; therefore, the account balance is incorrectly rejected.

To avoid the possibility of an incorrect rejection for this reason, a larger sample could be taken. One or more errors could be anticipated when the sample size is determined, thus lowering the upper limit on net overstatement.

Summary

When the auditor decides to use sampling to conduct a substantive test of details, either nonstatistical or statistical methods may be used. The major advantages of nonstatistical sampling are its convenience and the fact that no special knowledge of statistical theory is required. Its major disadvantage is that no scientific evaluation of sampling risk can be made. However, a nonstatistical sampling plan that is well designed and executed can produce reliable results.

If the auditor decides to use statistical sampling, two methods are generally available. Classical statistical sampling requires some knowledge of normal distribution theory or the availability of other people who understand such theory and can review the plan. This sampling method could be useful for populations that contain a large number of small dollar understatements or overstatements. With large variation in the population, stratification is usually necessary if mean estimation is used. There is less need for stratification if either ratio estimation or difference estimation is employed.

The other statistical sampling method is probability proportional to size sampling. The availability of tables makes the determination of the sample size and the evaluation of sample results generally easier than classical statistical sampling. Also, PPS is more effective for finding large dollar overstatements in the population. For this reason, PPS is often preferred when the population is believed to contain a few, if any, large dollar overstatements. It is not necessary to stratify the population when PPS is used.

There are concepts common to all of these techniques. The sequence of steps discussed in the first part of this chapter is a logical way to sample for substantive tests.

Chapter 13
Glossary of Terms

(listed in the order of appearance in the chapter, with accompanying page reference where the term is discussed)

Term	*Page in Chapter*
Risk of incorrect rejection the risk that the auditor will incorrectly reject the hypothesis that the evidence supports the account balance.	481
Risk of incorrect acceptance the risk that the auditor will incorrectly accept the hypothesis that the evidence supports the account balance.	481
Estimation sampling taking a sample and using the sample results to estimate the characteristic or the dollar amount of the population from which the sample is taken.	481
Projected error the difference between the estimated and recorded amount of a population; projected from the errors found in the sample.	481
Population all the units in an account balance or class of transactions.	481
Sampling unit individual elements in a population that contain the characteristic of interest.	482
Nonstatistical sampling techniques sampling techniques that require only the use of judgment in determining sample size and evaluating sample results.	483
Classical statistical sampling techniques sampling techniques that use normal distribution theory in determining sample size and evaluating sample results; judgmental factors are combined with statistical equations, tables, or both.	483
Probability proportional to size sampling sampling techniques designed to detect large overstatements in the population; judgmental factors are combined with statistical equations, tables, or both.	483
Standard deviation statistical measure of variability in a population; used in classical statistical sampling to determine sample size.	484
Audit risk a combination of the risks that material errors will occur in the accounting process used to develop the financial statements and that these errors will not be detected by the auditor.	485

	Page in
Term	*Chapter*

Tolerable error   the dollar error that can exist in an account balance which, when added to errors in all other accounts, will not exceed materiality for the overall financial statements.   490

Mean estimation   a technique of estimating the dollar amount of a population by calculating the mean of the sample and projecting this mean to the population. This technique can be used in classical statistical sampling.   499

Allowance for sampling risk   the acceptable difference between the expected error and the tolerable error.   500

Ratio estimation   a technique of estimating the dollar amount of a population by calculating the ratio between the audited and recorded amounts in the sample and using this ratio to make the estimate. This technique can be used in classical statistical sampling.   501

Difference estimation   a technique of estimating the dollar amount of a population by calculating the average difference between the audited and recorded amounts in the sample and projecting this difference to the population. This technique can be used in classical statistical sampling.   502

Stratification   dividing the population into subgroups or strata and treating each subgroup as a separate population.   505

Upper limit on net overstatement   a term used in probability proportional to size sampling to indicate the projected error plus the allowance for sampling risk. This term is similar to upper limit of the allowance for sampling risk (precision) range used in classical statistical sampling.   520

**Chapter 13
References**

American Institute of Certified Public Accountants. *Professional Standards*

AU Section 350 [*SAS No. 39*]—Audit Sampling.

AU Section 312 [*SAS No. 47*]—Audit Risk and Materiality in Conducting an Audit.

Neter, John, and Loebbecke, James K. *Behavior of Major Statistical Estimators in Sampling Accounting Populations—Auditing Research Monograph No. 2* (New York: AICPA, 1975).

Chapter 13
Review Questions

13-1.   When sampling is used to test the hypothesis that the evidence supports the account balance, what are the two parts of the sampling objective?

13-2.   In most audit sampling situations, what is the characteristic of interest?

13-3.   What situations should the auditor consider when defining the population for a substantive test?

13-4.   In what three ways could the sampling unit be defined for a substantive test?

13-5.   What three sampling techniques can the auditor use for a substantive test?

13-6.   What four items must the auditor consider to determine the sample size when using statistical or nonstatistical sampling methods for a substantive test?

13-7.   What two methods can be used to measure variation in a population?

13-8.   What factors can be used to control audit risk?

13-9.   If other factors are held constant, what happens to the sample size of substantive tests of details (becomes larger or smaller) when
a. Reliance on the internal control structure increases?
b. Reliance on analytical procedures and other substantive tests of details decrease?

13-10.   What are the consequences of incorrectly rejecting a hypothesis that the evidence supports an account balance?

13-11.   Explain how the auditor might determine tolerable error.

13-12.   What is the relationship between tolerable error and sample size?

13-13.   Why does the sample size of a substantive test increase as the estimate of the dollar error in the population goes up?

13-14.   Discuss the three ways that a sample can be selected in substantive testing.

13-15.   Describe two ways to calculate a projected error in the population when nonstatistical sampling is used.

13-16.   In each of the following cases, indicate what conclusion the auditor might draw (These answers must be thought out—study pages 492–493).
a. The likely error is more than the tolerable error.
b. The likely error is considerably lower than the tolerable error.
c. The likely error is lower than, but close to, the tolerable error.
d. The likely error is more than the preliminary estimate of the population error.

13-17.   Nonstatistical sampling is used. The recorded amount on the books is $100,000, the recorded amount of the sample is $40,000, and the audit amount of the sample is $35,000. Calculate the projected error. Show the calculations.

13-18.   What three methods can be used to estimate the dollar amount of a population when classical statistical sampling is used?

13-19.   In classical statistical sampling, what four items are used to obtain the optimum sample size for estimating the dollar amount of a population?

13-20.   In classical statistical sampling, what three steps are used to obtain the sample results?

13-21.   In classical statistical sampling, what six steps should be followed in applying mean estimation?

13-22.   Explain how the desired allowance for sampling risk is determined in classical statistical sampling (use numbers if necessary).

13-23.   In classical statistical sampling, what is compared to the tolerable error to determine whether the auditor accepts the hypothesis that the evidence supports the account balance?

13-24.   What four items are needed to determine the sample size when probability proportional to size sampling is used?

13-25.   Probability proportional to size sampling is used. The sampling interval is $6,000. One error is found. The recorded amount of the account in which the error was found is $5,000, and the audited amount is $3,500. Calculate the projected error. Show the calculations.

Chapter 13
Objective Questions Taken from CPA Examinations

---

*13-26. The relationship between the sampling risk of incorrect acceptance and the sample size of substantive tests is
   a. Positive.
   b. Inverse.
   c. Indeterminate.
   d. None of the above.

*13-27. Probability proportional to size sampling (PPS) is normally used when it is thought that the population contains
   a. A few understatements.
   b. A large number of understatements.
   c. A few overstatements.
   d. A large number of overstatements.

13-28. To determine the number of items to be selected in a sample for a particular substantive test of details, the auditor should consider all of the following *except*
   a. Tolerable error.
   b. Deviation rate.
   c. Allowable risk of incorrect acceptance.
   d. Characteristics of the population.

13-29. Statistical sampling provides a technique for
   a. Exactly defining materiality.
   b. Greatly reducing the amount of substantive testing.
   c. Eliminating judgment in testing.
   d. Measuring the sufficiency of evidential matter.

13-30. Using statistical sampling to assist in verifying the year-end accounts payable balance, an auditor has accumulated the following data:

	Number of Accounts	Book Balance	Balance Determined by the Auditor
Population	4,100	$5,000,000	?
Sample	200	$ 250,000	$300,000

*Not a CPA examination question.

Using the ratio estimation technique, the auditor's estimate of year-end accounts payable balance would be
a. $6,150,000.
b. $6,000,000.
c. $5,125,000.
d. $5,050,000.

13-31. Hill has decided to use Probability Proportional to Size (PPS) sampling, sometimes called dollar-unit sampling, in the audit of a client's accounts receivable balances. Hill plans to use the following PPS sampling table:

Table
Reliability Factors for Errors of Overstatement

Number of over-statement errors	Risk of Incorrect Acceptance				
	1%	*5%*	*10%*	*15%*	*20%*
0	4.61	3.00	2.31	1.90	1.61
1	6.64	4.75	3.89	3.38	3.00
2	8.41	6.30	5.33	4.72	4.28
3	10.05	7.76	6.69	6.02	5.52

Additional Information

Tolerable error	$ 24,000
Risk of incorrect acceptance	5%
Number of errors allowed	0
Recorded amount of accounts receivable	$240,000
Number of accounts	360

What sample size should Hill use?
a. 120
b. 108
c. 60
d. 30

13-32. In assessing sampling risk, the risk of incorrect rejection of an account balance relates to the
a. Efficiency of the audit.
b. Effectiveness of the audit.
c. Selection of the sample.
d. Audit quality controls.

13-33. If the achieved allowance for sampling risk of a statistical sample is greater than the desired allowance for sampling risk, this is an indication that the
a. Standard deviation was larger than expected.
b. Standard deviation was less than expected.
c. Population was larger than expected.
d. Population was smaller than expected.

13-34. In the application of statistical techniques to the estimation of dollar amounts, a preliminary sample is usually taken primarily for the purpose of estimating the population
a. Variability.
b. Mode.
c. Range.
d. Median.

13-35. From prior experience, a CPA is aware that cash disbursements contain a few usually large disbursements. In using classical statistical sampling, the CPA's best course of action is to
a. Eliminate any unusually large disbursements that appear in the sample.
b. Continue to draw new samples until no unusually large disbursements appear in the sample.
c. Stratify the cash-disbursements population so that the unusually large disbursements are reviewed separately.
d. Increase the sample size to lessen the effect of the unusually large disbursements.

13-36. An important statistic to consider when using a classical statistical sampling audit plan is the population variability. The population variability is measured by the
a. Sample mean.
b. Standard deviation.
c. Standard error of the sample mean.
d. Estimated population total minus the actual population total.

13-37. Use of the ratio estimation sampling technique to estimate dollar amounts is *inappropriate* when
a. The total book value is known and corresponds to the sum of all the individual book values.
b. A book value for each sample item is unknown.
c. There are some observed differences between audited values and book values.
d. The audited values are nearly proportional to the book values.

13-38.   In classical statistical sampling, which of the following must be known in order to estimate the appropriate sample size required to meet the auditor's needs in a given situation?
a. The total amount of the population.
b. The desired standard deviation.
c. The desired risk levels.
d. The estimated rate of error in the population.

13-39.   An auditor selects a preliminary sample of 100 items out of a population of 1,000 items. The sample statistics generate an arithmetic mean of $60, a standard deviation of $6, and a standard error of the mean of $0.60. If the sample was adequate for the auditor's purposes and the auditor's desired allowance for sampling risk was plus or minus $1,000, the *minimum* acceptable dollar value of the population would be
a. $61,000.
b. $60,000.
c. $59,000.
d. $58,800.

13-40.   The major reason that the difference and ratio estimation methods would be expected to produce audit efficiency compared to mean estimation is that the
a. Number of members of the populations of differences or ratios is smaller than the number of members of the population of book values.
b. Risk of incorrect acceptance may be completely ignored.
c. Calculations required in using difference or ratio estimation are less arduous and fewer than those required when using direct estimation.
d. Variability of populations of differences or ratios is less than that of the populations of book values or audited values.

Chapter 13
Discussion/Case Questions and Problems

13-41.   During the course of an audit engagement, Mr. Command, the senior, decided to use nonstatistical sampling on a certain substantive test. The sampling plan included the following:

1. The tolerable error was set at $10,000 based on overall materiality.

2. The risk of incorrect acceptance was set at 20 percent, based on high reliance on internal control structure procedures and other substantive tests of the same account balance.

3. The estimated dollar error in the population was $2,000, based on errors assumed to exist in populations of this type.

Although nonstatistical sampling was used, Mr. Command selected a sample size based on numerical guidelines in the literature. The performance of the audit procedures on the sample items was assigned to Mr. Critical, an assistant.

Mr. Critical audited the sample and calculated a likely error of $2,500. However, he was puzzled as to how to evaluate the sample results. He remembered reading the guidelines in the auditing literature. If the likely error is far enough below the tolerable error, there is an acceptably low risk that the true dollar error in the population exceeds the tolerable error. It seemed that $2,500 was sufficiently low to accept the sampling results.

However, the auditing literature also suggests that the sampling results would not generally be accepted if the likely error exceeded the preliminary estimate of the dollar error in the population.

Mr. Critical took the question to Mr. Command, who seemed annoyed. Mr. Command responded by stating that the sampling results should be accepted.

Mr. Critical questioned whether the sampling results should be accepted if the likely error is $2,500. The "careful" course of action would seem to be to expand the substantive tests. To accept the results seemed "out of line" with guidelines in the auditing literature.

Required:
Evaluate the strengths and weaknesses of each person's contention.

13-42.   Discuss each of the following questions.
a. If numerical guidelines are desirable in determining a sample size for a nonstatistical substantive test, why not use statistical sampling and determine the sample size with tested tables?
b. Evaluating a nonstatistical substantive test by comparing the likely error to the tolerable error is too vague. Why not use a statistical sampling approach and calculate an allowance for sampling risk?

13-43.   Assume that a population has the following characteristics:

> Number of items in the population—300
>
> Population recorded amount—$600,000
>
> Sample size—100

Required:
a. If the sample mean is $1,800 and mean estimation is used, the estimate of the population total is $_____.
b. If ratio estimation is used and (1) the recorded amount of the sample is

$200,000 and (2) the audit amount of the sample is $210,000, the estimate of the population total is $_____.

c. If difference estimation is used and (1) the recorded amount of the sample is $200,000 and (2) the audit amount of the sample is $195,000, the estimate of the population total is $_____.

13-44.   The following data for a substantive test using sampling are available:

> Population recorded amount—$200,000
>
> Tolerable error—$10,000
>
> Number of items in the population—200
>
> Risk of incorrect acceptance—20 percent
>
> Estimated dollar error in the population—$2,000

Required:

a. Assume the use of nonstatistical sampling and a sample size of 50. Assume that the recorded amount of the sample is $40,000 and the audited amount of the sample is $35,000. Calculate the projected error using the two methods illustrated in the chapter. Using both methods, indicate why the sampling results are acceptable or unacceptable.

b. Assume the use of PPS sampling with zero estimated errors.

(1) Calculate the sample size using the equations and tables illustrated in the chapter. (Round up the sample size, if necessary, to the next highest number.)

(2) Disregarding Problem (1), assume a sample size of 40. What is the sampling interval? If an error is found in an account with a recorded balance of $50,000, would "tainting" have to be used to calculate a projected error? Why or why not? Calculate the projected error if a $400 overstatement is found in an account with a recorded balance of $4,000.

13-45.   Take the population in the table on pages 533–534 and perform the following (use sampling without replacement and a standard deviation of the recorded amounts of 20)

a. Determine the sample size without replacement. Assume a tolerable error of $2,000, a risk of incorrect rejection of 20 percent, and a risk of incorrect acceptance of 10 percent.

b. Take the sample without replacement. Assume that the recorded and audited amounts are the same except for the following.

Account Number	Recorded Amount	Audited Amount
1	$218	$118
20	211	0
27	224	37
68	202	0
69	207	407
126	173	373
143	198	98

c. Calculate a projected error. Calculate an allowance for sampling risk and an allowance (precision) range.

d. Indicate whether the sampling results are acceptable or unacceptable. Explain your reason.

Number	Amount	Number	Amount	Number	Amount
1	218	29	215	57	191
2	209	30	208	58	180
3	200	31	200	59	181
4	196	32	193	60	182
5	170	33	183	61	209
6	178	34	203	62	208
7	180	35	181	63	214
8	199	36	228	64	188
9	201	37	230	65	193
10	230	38	232	66	196
11	228	39	188	67	194
12	212	40	199	68	202
13	197	41	187	69	207
14	190	42	212	70	206
15	202	43	230	71	184
16	196	44	201	72	182
17	233	45	214	73	178
18	181	46	215	74	175
19	196	47	189	75	209
20	211	48	178	76	213
21	210	49	234	77	215
22	208	50	204	78	231
23	186	51	205	79	232
24	190	52	220	80	175
25	191	53	198	81	176
26	183	54	169	82	178
27	224	55	234	83	180
28	226	56	190	84	182

Number	Amount	Number	Amount	Number	Amount
85	185	124	170	163	171
86	188	125	172	164	240
87	189	126	173	165	235
88	191	127	174	166	234
89	193	128	175	167	190
90	195	129	176	168	182
91	197	130	177	169	203
92	199	131	178	170	171
93	202	132	179	171	220
94	204	133	180	172	198
95	206	134	118	173	233
96	208	135	180	174	202
97	210	136	191	175	197
98	212	137	192	176	196
99	215	138	193	177	102
100	218	139	194	178	198
101	220	140	195	179	195
102	221	141	196	180	206
103	224	142	197	181	206
104	226	143	198	182	205
105	228	144	199	183	205
106	230	145	200	184	174
107	232	146	201	185	174
108	234	147	202	186	180
109	235	148	203	187	179
110	210	149	204	188	188
111	190	150	205	189	178
112	185	151	206	190	196
113	220	152	207	191	206
114	215	153	208	192	216
115	210	154	209	193	226
116	205	155	210	194	236
117	200	156	211	195	196
118	195	157	212	196	186
119	190	158	213	197	185
120	185	159	214	198	184
121	185	160	215	199	183
122	180	161	216	200	186
123	175	162	158		

Total	$39,816
Mean	$199.08

13-46.   The following list of tests is typical of those usually performed by auditors in gathering evidence to ascertain the fairness of financial statement balances. For each listed test, indicate whether it might be useful to apply sampling techniques. Support your *yes* or *no* answers with reasons.

a. Confirming accounts receivable.

b. Observing physical inventory counts.

c. Confirming insurance information with the client's insurance agent.

d. Testing the clerical accuracy of the accounts receivable aging schedule.

e. Examining invoices that support the repairs and maintenance expenses in the income statement.

f. Examining securities in the client's safety deposit box.

g. Testing the clerical accuracy of the client's bank reconciliations.

h. Ascertaining the reasonableness of the fixed-asset depreciation rates.

i. Examining the invoices that support the additions to fixed assets.

13-47.   During the planning of the audit of Strong Company, the partner in charge of the audit was discussing sampling plans with a manager and a senior. The discussion centered on the potential use of sampling in testing the clerical accuracy of the perpetual inventory records.

   The senior maintained that a classical statistical sampling technique was the appropriate method. Experience has shown that the dollar amounts of clerical errors in the inventory records are small, although the number of errors is often large.

   The manager disagreed with the suggestion. He contended that increasing numbers of auditors are using PPS, which does not require stratification. If a few large dollar errors existed in the population and none was found in the sample, the results could be misleading.

   The senior believed that the potential problem presented by the manager was overrated. Experience shows that perpetual inventory records contain small dollar errors.

   At this point, the audit partner became a bit impatient. She was anxious to complete the planning of the audit and start the field work. She suggested that the group confer with a newly promoted senior who had recently taken an up-do-date auditing course and had attended a company-sponsored professional development course in statistical sampling.

Required:

Assume that you are the newly promoted senior and have been asked to suggest a sampling plan for the inventory testing.

a. Summarize the merits and flaws in each argument.

b. Suggest the conditions under which either classical statistical sampling or PPS might be appropriate.

13-48.   You desire to estimate the amount of the inventory of your client, Draper, Inc. You satisfied yourself earlier as to the inventory quantities. During the audit of the pricing and extension of the inventory, the following data were gathered using appropriate unrestricted random sampling with replacement procedures.

*Total items in the inventory (*N*)	12,700
*Total items in the sample (*n*)	400
*Total audited value of items in the sample	$38,400

Required:
a. According to the sample results, what is the estimate of the total value of the inventory using mean estimation? Show computations in good form where appropriate.
b. Independent of your answer to problem a, assume that the book value of Draper's inventory is $1,700,000, and on the basis of the sample results, the estimated total value of the inventory is $1,690,000. The tolerable error is $15,000 and the achieved allowance for sampling risk is $8,000. Discuss the audit and statistical considerations the auditor must evaluate before deciding whether to accept the hypothesis that the evidence supports the book value.
(*AICPA adapted*)

13-49.   One argument that has been given against the use of statistical sampling for conducting audit tests is that auditors are "sticking their necks out." Why not confine judgments to general statements and avoid that problem? In the event of a lawsuit, wouldn't the auditor have a better defense by stating that judgment was used rather than having to justify certain percentages? Reply to this statement.

13-50.   Smith, CPA, has decided to rely on an audit client's internal control structure procedures affecting receivables. Smith plans to use sampling to obtain substantive evidence concerning the reasonableness of the client's accounts receivable balances. Smith has identified the first few steps in an outline of the sampling plan as follows:
a. Determine the audit objectives of the test.
b. Define the population.
c. Define the sampling unit.
d. Consider the completeness of the population.
e. Identify individually significant items.

Required:
Identify the remaining steps that Smith should include in the outline of the sampling plan. Illustrations and examples need not be provided.
(*AICPA adapted*)

13-51.   Edwards has decided to use Probability Proportional to Size (PPS) sampling, sometimes called dollar-unit sampling, in the audit of a client's accounts receivable balance. Few, if any, errors of account balance overstatement are expected.

Edwards plans to use the following PPS sampling table:

Table
Reliability Factors for Errors of Overstatement

Number of Over- statement Errors	Risk of Incorrect Acceptance				
	1%	*5%*	*10%*	*15%*	*20%*
0	4.61	3.00	2.31	1.90	1.61
1	6.64	4.75	3.89	3.38	3.00
2	8.41	6.30	5.33	4.72	4.28
3	10.05	7.76	6.69	6.02	5.52
4	11.61	9.16	8.00	7.27	6.73

Required:
a. Identify the advantages of using PPS sampling over classical statistical sampling.

> *Note:* Requirements b and c are *not* related.

b. Calculate the sampling interval and the sample size Edwards should use given the following information:

Tolerable error	$15,000
Risk of incorrect acceptance	5%
Number of errors allowed	0
Recorded amount of accounts receivable	$300,000

> *Note:* Requirements b and c are *not* related.

c. Calculate the total projected error if the following three errors were discovered in a PPS sample:

	Recorded Amount	Audit Amount	Sampling Interval
1st error	$ 400	$ 320	$1,000
2nd error	500	0	1,000
3rd error	3,000	2,500	1,000

(*AICPA adapted*)

13-52.   Take the illustration of probability proportional to size sampling (PPS) starting on page 514 of the chapter material and do the following.

a. Assume a tolerable error of $15,000 instead of $10,000, leaving all other variables on page 515 the same.

b. Calculate the sample size and the sampling interval as illustrated on pages 515–516 of the chapter material. Round the sample size and the sampling interval to the next highest number.

CHAPTER 14

The Use of Computers to Gather and Document Audit Evidence for Substantive Testing

---

Learning Objectives   *After reading and studying the material in this chapter, the student should*

Be able to define, discuss the functions of, and describe generalized computer audit programs.

Understand the capabilities of generalized computer audit programs in gathering audit evidence.

Know the audit evidence acquired when a generalized computer audit program is used to gather and document audit evidence for a given account in the financial statements.

Be able to describe the documentation that can be created when microcomputers are used to gather and document audit evidence.

This chapter is a continuation in the sequence of chapters on gathering audit evidence for substantive testing (Chapters 12–18). In Chapter 12, we discussed the general nature of evidence gathering. In Chapter 13, we covered sampling, both nonstatistical and statistical. In this chapter we will show how computers can be used to gather audit evidence.

Although it is a bit of an oversimplification, the auditors' relationship with computers might be described as falling into one or both of the following categories:

1. Obtaining an understanding of the internal control structure, assessing the control risk, and testing the controls of a company that uses computers to process its accounting data.

2. The use of computer hardware and software to gather and document evidence used for substantive tests of financial statement account assertions.

The material in Chapter 11 contains descriptions of the first category. The material in this chapter contains descriptions of the second category.

Definition of Generalized Computer Audit Programs

A *generalized computer audit program* is designed to perform, for the benefit of the auditor, certain data-processing functions, such as (1) reading computer files, (2) selecting information, (3) performing calculations, and (4) printing reports in a format specified by the auditor.[1] Such programs are useful because auditors can learn to use them quickly, they allow direct access to the data, and documentation is often a by-product of their use.

Detailed Functions of Generalized Computer Audit Programs

Many detailed functions can be performed by a generalized computer audit program. Here is a fairly comprehensive, but not exhaustive, list of these program capabilities. Many of the audit procedures are discussed in Chapters 15 through 18.

1. Scanning or examining computer records for exceptional or unusual characteristics and obtaining a list of these characteristics. Some examples are as follows:

a. Accounts receivable balances over a certain amount, over the credit limit, or containing a credit balance.

b. Unusually large inventory balances.

c. Unusual payroll situations such as terminated employees or excessive overtime.

2. Making or checking computations and obtaining for the auditors' review computations that are incorrect. Some examples are as follows:

[1] American Institute of Certified Public Accountants. *Audit and Accounting Guide—Computer Assisted Audit Techniques* (AICPA, 1979).

    a. Payroll calculations.

    b. Interest calculations.

    c. Depreciation calculations.

    d. Calculations of various prepaid items.

3. Comparing data on different records or files and listing unusual or irregular results, such as the following:

    a. Comparing accounts receivable master file balances between two dates with accounts receivable debits and credits contained in detail transaction files between the same dates.

    b. Comparing items on the master payroll files with items on personnel records.

4. Selecting and obtaining various types of samples. Included among these might be the following:

    a. Accounts receivable and accounts payable confirmations.

    b. Fixed-asset changes.

    c. Inventory items.

    d. Selected items from an expense account.

5. Preparing various analyses and listings that facilitate the examination of certain accounts. Some of these are the following:

    a. Accounts receivable aging schedules.

    b. Analysis of inventory by date of purchase.

    c. Statistics relating to various accounts, such as accounts receivable and inventory turnover.

    d. Trial balances and lead schedules.

All of these listed capabilities of generalized computer audit programs have one common trait. The auditors employ a developed series of computer programs to acquire various lists, analyses, and so on from data maintained on the client's computerized files. Access to this information is considered essential, or certainly desirable, to perform the audit. If the client employed a manual system, some of this same information would be gained without the aid of computers. If a computer system were used and no generalized computer audit programs were available, printouts of data would probably be obtained from the computer files. Manual analyses would then be made from such data.

Description of Generalized Computer Audit Programs

Generalized computer audit programs should not be thought of as mysterious and difficult to understand. Although training is necessary to apply the programs in actual audit practice, the concepts can be illustrated in chart and narrative form. For example, the diagram below shows the *general* method that is employed, although individual systems differ from one CPA firm to the next.

The *auditors' specifications* are the descriptions of the audit objectives and the types of files to be used in computer processing. The generalized computer audit program is written for the individuals performing the audit. It is not necessary for the auditors to understand the minute features of the programming techniques, but they need to be knowledgeable of the audit objectives and the characteristics of the client's system from which the information is taken.

Although the client's files are assumed to be on magnetic tape, they could be on disk or other types of storage devices. The computer output to be used by the

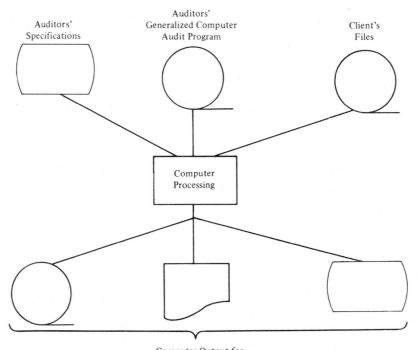

Auditors'
Specifications

Auditors'
Generalized Computer
Audit Program

Client's
Files

Computer
Processing

Computer Output for
Auditors' Use

auditors in meeting audit objectives might be tape, printed material, visual display, or other types of output. Whatever the form, the auditors have a tool that is very usable, one that is not accessible in a manual system.

An added feature sometimes used is a special software processor that converts the auditors' specification data into a problem-oriented or high-level language program. This program, in turn, processes the client's files, producing the desired information to be used in the examination of the appropriate account. A technique such as this reduces the auditors' need for firsthand knowledge of the programming language. It does, however, sharpen the necessity of understanding the audit objectives and the manner in which the data are stored in the client's computer files.

Audit Objectives and Computer Capabilities

One should not be left with the impression that a generalized computer audit program produces all of the necessary evidence in the audit of a company's financial statements. Although it is true that computations, comparisons, and other clerical functions may be performed with this computerized process, it also remains for the auditors to use much of the output in conducting the *same* procedures that they would have if the information had been acquired through manual methods.

To illustrate this point, let us relist some of the output obtained from the processing of the client's files by a generalized computer audit program. To the right of each listing are descriptions of appropriate audit steps to be taken *with* the information produced by computer processing.

Output Produced by the Generalized Computer Audit Program	*Audit Procedures Performed with This Output*
1. Listing of accounts receivable balances that exceed the credit limit.	1. Discussions with client personnel on causes, and effect on allowance for doubtful accounts.
2. Listing of accounts receivable credit balances.	2. Inquiries concerning the question of reclassifying such balances as current liabilities.
3. Listing of unusually large inventory balances.	3. Investigation for possible obsolescence and errors in computation; observation of client's inventory count.
4. Listing of recently terminated employees.	4. Investigation of the disposition of unclaimed payroll checks.
5. Accounts receivable and accounts payable confirmations.	5. A tally of confirmation results and follow-up of customer's exceptions.
6. Listing of property and equipment additions.	6. Examination and analyses of source documents supporting such additions.

Certainly, this tabulation demonstrates that generalized computer audit programs produce necessary information for the conduct of an audit, but in many instances additional work must be performed. Such programs provide the most aid in phases of the audit that call for calculations, listings, clerical comparisons, and so on. On the other hand, although computer printouts furnish information that can be *used* to make inquiries and conduct observations, this computer output is no *substitute* for these audit procedures themselves.

Gathering Information from an Accounts Receivable Master File

Description of the System

The basic functions of generalized computer audit programs, along with explanations of their advantages and limitations, have been discussed. The next step is to provide a relevant example of an application. Although many illustrations could be chosen, we have selected one that is both easily identifiable and integrated with material in previous chapters.

Assume that the client processes accounts receivable charges and credits on a computerized batch-processing system, which includes magnetic tape as the storage device for the master files. As credit sales, cash receipts, and noncash credits are read into computer memory, the data on the master tape are also entered. One of the ouputs of the computer processing is a new master tape containing updated data on each customer's account.[2]

This data-processing function can best be illustrated by referring to examples from three accounts receivable records, Block Wholesale Company, Xanthos Bros. Furniture Company, and Urban Home Furnishing. Their manually determined ledger account balances and their records on the master tape file as of October 31, 19X9 are shown below.

Customer Number	Name	Balance Notation	Date	Posting Source	Debit	Credit	Balance
0001	Block Wholesale Co.	Bal. 9-30-X9			$	$	$ 940.00
			10-10-X9	S-02117	1,020.00		1,960.00
			10-12-X9	R-02375		940.00	1,020.00
0037	Xanthos Bros. Furn. Co.		8-18-X9	S-01937	1,190.00		1,190.00
			10-15-X9	R-02054		200.00	990.00
			10-22-X9	CM-00375		145.00	845.00
0091	Urban Home Furnish.		5-15-X9	S-01308	1,010.00		1,010.00
			6-20-X9	S-01526	1,010.00		2,020.00
			10-10-X9	S-02114	3,198.00		5,218.00

[2]For an overview of the entire process, see the systems flowchart in Figure 10.1.

If these same balances were kept on magnetic tape, they might appear as in the following table.

Records on Master Tape File

Customer Account No.	Name	Credit Status[a]	Current Charges	Current Cash Receipts	Current Sales Returns	Total Balance	Current Balance	Balance 31–60 Days	Balance 61–90 Days	Balance Over 90 Days
000001	Block Whole-sale Co.	1	0102000	0094000	0000000	0102000	0102000	0000000	0000000	0000000
000037	Xanthos Bros. Furn. Co.	2	000000	0020000	0014500	0084500	0000000	0000000	0084500	0000000
000091	Urban Home Furnish.	3	0319800	0000000	0000000	0521800	0319800	0000000	0000000	0202000

[a]1—Unlimited Credit.

2—$500 or more balance over 60 days—credit limit of $2,000.

3—$1,000 over 90 days—no additional credit given.

The credit status exists after the current month's processing. Customer No. 37's balance does not exceed the credit limit, but it would have if current charges had exceeded $1,155.00 ($2,000.000—$845.00). Customer No. 91's credit limit has been exceeded since there is a $2,020.00 balance in the over-90-day category, and current charges were made to the account.

Before an application of the generalized computer audit program is made, the objectives of the computer processing will be defined. For illustration, we can list some objectives that are similar to those sought in an actual engagement.

1. The auditors wish to select for positive confirmation accounts receivable balances that have certain characteristics.

a. One such characteristic is the dollar amount. Positive confirmations may be circularized on large account balances for the reasons enumerated in Chapter 12—more competent audit evidence is obtained for accounts receivable that exceed tolerable error. We will assume that the auditor instructs the computer program to select for positive confirmation all balances in excess of $5,000.

b. Another characteristic is the age of the account. The auditors wish to establish, as firmly as possible, the authenticity of accounts with older balances. Therefore, we assume that another audit procedure is to send positive confirmations to all customers whose balances, or any portion thereof, are in excess of 90 days.

2. The auditors wish to select for negative confirmation requests a systematic sample of accounts other than those selected for positive confirmation

requests. We will assume that every third account is selected starting with the first customer number. If an account is already chosen for a positive request, it will be skipped for a negative request.

3. The third and last auditors' objective is to produce a report of special account characteristics for further analysis or investigation. Within the accounts receivable master file, there are many information items that auditors might find useful. We will confine our output to the following:

a. A list of accounts with balances that exceed the credit limit. This list will be discussed with the credit manager or other appropriate personnel.

b. A list of accounts with all or any portion of the balance in the 61- to 90-day category and in which current charges were made. Accounts such as this are not necessarily doubtful of collection but may furnish the auditors with information on the company's handling of slow-paying accounts. This list may also be discussed with the client.

c. A list of accounts that have had credit balances for a period in excess of 30 days. If the total of these accounts is considered material, the auditors may wish to propose a reclassification entry reclassifying such balances as a current liability.

d. A list of accounts with all or any portion of the balance in excess of 90 days. The auditors will probably discuss the collectibility of such accounts with appropriate client personnel and examine credit files as a basis for evaluating collectibility. Ultimately, this information may be used as partial support for a proposed adjusting entry to the allowance for doubtful accounts.

The accounts receivable aging schedule could be printed by the computer on which the generalized computer audit program is run. Whether this would be a part of the auditors' objective or not depends on the client's computer output. If such a schedule is furnished by the client, the auditors may wish to have it test-checked as a part of their procedures.

A Program Flowchart of the Auditors' Objectives

Any reasonably complicated computer program is supported by a flowchart detailing the logic operations of the routine being processed. By way of review we might remember that a systems flowchart shows the overview of the data movement from one process to another. Conversely, a program flowchart (exhibited here) contains descriptions of the computer-processing logic and is used to code the computer program itself as well as to provide needed documentation.

On page 547 is a program flowchart for this hypothetical application of a generalized computer audit program.

PROGRAM FLOWCHART FOR THE
PROGRAM TO READ MASTER FILES

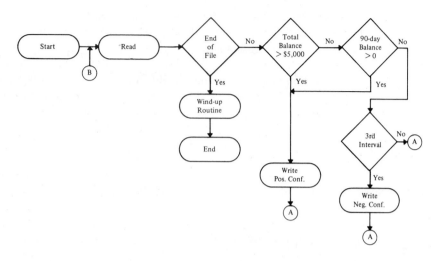

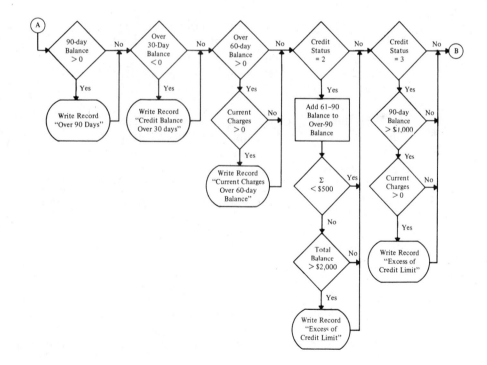

Input and Output of the Generalized Computer Audit Program

On top of page 549 is a tabulation of selected accounts receivable data. The numbers in the columns are arranged as if the data were stored on magnetic tape. These particular customers are selected because their files contain all of the characteristics specified in the list of auditors' objectives (balance over 90 days, etc.).

We will assume that the master file data are stored on magnetic tape and are read into the main memory of the computer as the client's input file.

The three tables at the bottom of page 549 and on page 550 illustrate the output that would be generated by the application of the generalized computer audit program to a selected group of accounts.

Characteristics of Programs Used in Audit Practice

Some CPA firms have developed their own packages of generalized computer audit programs with these common attributes:

1. The ability to read client data stored on computer files and perform certain audit procedures such as footings and extensions.

2. The ability to select computerized client data with certain characteristics and print the data for the auditor's scrutiny and review.

3. The ability to select samples based on a predesigned plan and perform certain statistical sampling calculations.

The third type could be a series of computer programs designed to allow auditors to use statistical sampling techniques on clients' computerized files (such as accounts receivable, inventory, etc.). The statistical sampling method used in these programs could be classical statistical sampling or probability proportional to size sampling, both of which are discussed in Chapter 13. Applications can be made on a wide variety of computer equipment common to the business world.

The Use of Microcomputers to Gather and Document Audit Evidence

Since the early 1980s when they were first introduced into commercial use, auditors have developed numerous applications for the use of microcomputers to gather and document audit evidence for substantive testing. The use of spreadsheets has been particularly prevalent because many audit working papers are in this form.

Here are some descriptions of spreadsheet working papers now being used by many CPA firms that are also illustrated in Chapters 15–18 of this text. As we list each type of working paper, we will briefly describe its use and will also refer

Master File Data for Auditor's Program

Customer Account Number	Credit Status	Current Charges	Current Cash Receipts	Current Sales Returns	Current Write-Offs	Total Balance	Current Balance	Balance 31–60 Days	Balance 61–90 Days	Balance Over 90 Days
0001(3)	1	0102000	0094000	0000000	0000000	0102000	0102000	0000000	0000000	0000000
0003	1	0020800	0000000	0000000	0000000	0020800	0020800	0000000	0000000	0000000
0004(3)	1	0174700	0092000	0000000	0000000	0184700	0174700	0010000	0000000	0000000
0005	1	0000000	0000000	0014500	0000000	0000000	0000000	0000000	0000000	0000000
0007(1)	1	0541800	0325000	0000000	0000000	0541800	0541800	0000000	0000000	0000000
0009(1)(5)	1	0516000	0000000	0000000	0000000	0619800	0516000	0094800	0009000	0000000
0015	1	0133500	0102500	0000000	0000000	0133500	0133500	0000000	0000000	0000000
0016(2)(5)(4)	2	0271500	0010000	0000000	0000000	0324000	0271500	0000000	0032000	0020500
0025(3)	1	0038500	0000000	0000000	0000000	0077000	0038500	0038500	0000000	0000000
0027(1)(5)	1	0470900	0000000	0000000	0000000	0704900	0470900	0204000	0030000	0000000
0030(6)	1	0000000	0000000	0000000	0000000	−092000	0000000	−092000	0000000	0000000
0044(1)(2)(4)	2	0505100	0020000	0000000	0000000	0555100	0505100	0000000	0000000	0050000
0090	1	0051600	0000000	0000000	0000000	0087300	0051600	0035700	0000000	0000000
0091(2)(4)(1)	3	0319800	0000000	0000000	0000000	0521800	0319800	0000000	0000000	0202000

Characteristics that the generalized computer audit program will identify for each account illustrated:

(1) Over $5,000—for positive confirmation.

(2) Over 90 days—for positive confirmation and an exception report.

(3) Every third account—for negative confirmation.

(4) Over the credit limit—for an exception report.

(5) Balance 61–90 days with current charges—for an exception report.

(6) Credit balance over 30 days—for an exception report.

Accounts for Positive Confirmation
Criteria: Total Balance in Excess of $5,000.00, or Any Part in Excess of 90 Days

Customer Account Number	Credit Status	Current Charges	Current Cash Receipts	Current Sales Returns	Write-Offs	Total Balance	Current Balance	Balance 31–60 Days	Balance 61–90 Days	Balance Over 90 Days
7	1	$5,418.00	$3,250.00	0.0	0.0	$5,418.00	$5,418.00	0.0	0.0	0.0
9	1	5,160.00	0.0	0.0	0.0	6,198.00	$5,160.00	948.00	90.00	0.0
16	2	2,715.00	100.00	0.0	0.0	3,240.00	2,715.00	0.0	320.00	205.00
27	1	4,709.00	0.0	0.0	0.0	7,049.00	4,709.00	2,040.00	300.00	0.0
44	2	5,051.00	200.00	0.0	0.0	5,551.00	5,051.00	0.0	0.0	500.00
91	3	3,198.00	0.0	0.0	0.0	5,218.00	3,198.00	0.0	0.0	2,020.00

Accounts for Negative Confirmation
Criteria: Every Third Account, Excluding Accounts for Positive Confirmation[a]

Customer Account Number	Credit Status	Current Charges	Current Cash Receipts	Current Sales Returns	Write-Offs	Total Balance	Current Balance	Balance 31–60 Days	Balance 61–90 Days	Balance Over 90 Days
1	1	$1,020.00	$ 940.00	0.0	0.0	$1,020.00	$1,020.00	0.0	0.0	0.0
4	1	1,747.00	920.00	0.0	0.0	1,847.00	1,747.00	100.00	0.0	0.0
25	1	385.00	0.0	0.0	0.0	770.00	385.00	385.00	0.0	0.0

[a]If all 100 accounts were processed, additional accounts would be illustrated.

Exception Listings

Customer Account Number	Credit Status	Current Charges	Current Cash Receipts	Current Sales Returns	Write-Offs	Total Balance	Current Balance	Balance 31–60 Days	Balance 61-90 Days	Balance Over 90 Days
9	1	$5,160.00	0.0	0.0	0.0	$6,198.00	$5,160.00	$ 948.00	$ 90.00	0.0
9		61–90 balance with current charges								
16	2	2,715.00	100.00	0.0	0.0	3,240.00	2,715.00	0.0	320.00	205.00
16		Balance exceeds credit limit								
16	2	2,715.00	100.00	0.0	0.0	3,240.00	2,715.00	0.0	320.00	205.00
16		61–90 balance with current charges								
16	2	2,715.00	100.00	0.0	0.0	3,240.00	2,715.00	0.0	320.00	205.00
16		Balance exceeds 90 days								
27	1	4,709.00	0.0	0.0	0.0	7,049.00	4,709.00	2,040.00	300.00	0.0
27		61–90 balance with current charges								
30	1	0.0	0.0	0.0	0.0	−920.00	0.0	−920.00	0.0	0.0
30		Credit balance exceeds 30 days								
44	2	5,051.00	200.00	0.0	0.0	5,551.00	5,051.00	0.0	0.0	500.00
44		Balance exceeds credit limit								
44	2	5,051.00	200.00	0.0	0.0	5,551.00	5,051.00	0.0	0.0	500.00
44		Balance exceeds 90 days								
91	3	3,198.00	0.0	0.0	0.0	5,218.00	3,198.00	0.0	0.0	2,020.00
91		Balance exceeds credit limit								
91	3	3,198.00	0.0	0.0	0.0	5,218.00	3,198.00	0.0	0.0	2,020.00
91		Balance exceeds 90 days								

you to the appropriate page in the text. Discussions in Chapters 15–18 will provide detailed explanations of how these working papers are used to document the evidence gathered and the substantive testing performed on the various financial statement accounts.

Spreadsheet Working Paper	Use Made of Working Paper	Text Reference
Customer trade receivables aged listing	To document customers to whom accounts receivable confirmations are sent and to aid in ascertaining the reasonableness of Allowance for Doubtful Accounts	Page 584 in Chapter 15
Accounts payable confirmation control	To document the vendors to whom accounts payable confirmations are sent and to describe the audit procedures performed on these accounts	Page 626 in Chapter 16
Equipment additions	To document the individual additions to equipment selected for testing and to describe the audit procedures performed on these additions	Page 652 in Chapter 17
Analysis of legal expense	To document the detail of the expenditures for legal expense and to describe the auditing procedures performed on these expenditures	Page 696 in Chapter 18

In Chapters 15 through 18 some examples of working papers are shown that are not created by the use of a microcomputer. In fact, many working papers are written manually. Once again, this indicates that there is a limit to the aid that computer software can give to auditors.

Systems Evaluation Approach–Computerized Audit Support

The Systems Evaluation Approach–Computerized Audit Support (SEACAS) is a computer system that can be carried to an audit engagement and set up quickly for onsite work. This tool may eventually automate most aspects of the audit.

A microcomputer-based audit tool developed by Peat, Marwick, Main & Co., SEACAS assists auditors in gathering, analyzing, and distributing information for a variety of uses but primarily for auditing. SEACAS capitalizes on the development of the microcomputer, which permits a variety of computer applications to be performed on equipment that can be transported easily and set up on a desktop. SEACAS enables auditors to complete more quickly and efficiently many time-consuming functions that have traditionally been performed manually. It improves the quality of audits by allowing auditors to use more time to solve complex auditing problems.

SEACAS is a stand-alone computer system. It does not require any connection with client computer systems; the client does not need to have any accounting operations computerized. The auditor uses SEACAS to accumulate, analyze, and evaluate data.

The following descriptions show some of the uses of SEACAS.

1. Trial balance and financial statement processing. SEACAS permits the preparation and processing of trial balances, including posting audit adjustments and reclassifications, and the drafting of financial reports to be accomplished more efficiently and reliably.

2. Audit programming. SEACAS will assist in designing for each client an efficient and complete audit program that takes into consideration all relevant factors. Through its integration of a variety of audit information, SEACAS will be able to consolidate and analyze data developed from such diverse sources as the trial balance, various client files, workpapers, and public databases.

3. Detailed workpaper preparation. Auditors have traditionally spent considerable time preparing detailed spreadsheet analyses. SEACAS will assist in this preparation by providing automated mechanisms to handle detailed clerical functions. With an automated spreadsheet, auditors can improve the reliability of such workpapers and reduce preparation time.

4. Audit confirmations. Confirmation preparation and control represent a time-consuming audit task that will be assisted by computerization. Statistics regarding confirmations that have been mailed and received, or are still outstanding, can be analyzed quickly; and additional information reports can be generated as needed.

5. Statistical sampling. Statistical sampling capabilities that were previously available only from a timesharing network or had to be produced manually can be applied by auditors using SEACAS to provide timely and accurate information needed to prepare audit samples, analyze results, and complete audit test work.

6. Database retrieval. Data related to the client's industry, including financial or product news and other relevant information, can be obtained quickly and efficiently by using SEACAS to draw directly on public databases. This capability will assist auditors in pricing client investment portfolios, comparing client and industry data, and preparing background information for client reports.

7. Engagement management. Audit administration will also benefit from SEACAS. Through access to operating office scheduling and time-gathering databases, audit managers will have the tools available for better execution of their engagement responsibilities.

8. Word processing. SEACAS word processing can be used by auditors for preparing audit and client memoranda, correspondence, and reports more efficiently.

Considerations in Deciding to Use Generalized Computer Audit Programs

Audit software should be considered when the procedures are especially time-consuming or complex. Client cooperation may be necessary for the effective use of computer audit programs. Proper facilities need to be provided, copies of files need to be available, and assistance with the computer may be needed.

Also, the auditor should consider the cost-benefit relationship of using computer audit programs. In some cases, the audit procedures may be performed more economically by doing them manually.

Critique of Generalized Computer Audit Programs

The Auditors' Computer Proficiency

Now that conceptual discussions and illustrations of generalized computer audit programs have been presented, we turn to broad considerations of the role of computer training for auditors. One question that should be asked immediately is how much computer programming proficiency, if any, auditors need to use the tools illustrated in this chapter. The answer generally given by CPA firms is that little is necessary, although familiarity with microcomputers and programming knowledge is desirable.

It seems logical, however, to assume that the most efficient use of these software packages occurs when the users comprehend the computer system in use. To possess this understanding, auditors should have a workable computer "vocabulary" [3] and should be familiar with the way data are processed on machine-readable records and stored in computerized files.

Auditors also need an understanding of flowcharting and should be able to read various types of documentation, such as record layouts. Perhaps of primary importance is the desirability for auditors to visualize their objectives, the file systems used by the client, and the output required from application of the generalized computer audit program to these files.

Fraud Detection

There seems to be little question but that a proper application of a generalized computer audit program will enhance the quality of an audit. However, can the use of these software systems increase the probability of detecting fraud? This would be a difficult question to answer even if actual case studies were available. Generalized computer audit programs are generally not designed to detect fraud.

At the same time, it should be acknowledged that the use of auditors' software provides some advantages over manual auditing should certain types of fraud exist in the client's organization. If computers are being employed to perpetrate irregularities, an "around-the-computer" approach is less likely to provide evidence of these occurrences.

One of the most publicized frauds in recent years is the *Equity Funding* case. As indicated in Chapter 11, this case is not technically a computer fraud but an irregularity aided and partially concealed through the *use* of computers. In this case the company maintained a set of fictitious insurance policies on machine-readable files (accessible for manual scrutiny only through printouts).

Through the use of some clever programming techniques, Equity Funding restricted the policy information shown on the printouts, so that all such policies had the appearance of legitimacy. Also, other measures were taken by the client to hamper the auditors' evidence gathering. Germane to this discussion, however, is the point that client computer printouts of data stored in the files did not provide sufficient evidence to detect the irregularity.

It is mere conjecture to speculate on whether the correct application of a generalized computer audit program would have caught or prevented the fraud. Whenever data are stored on magnetized "invisible" devices, the application of a CPA firm's own program would be expected to produce more reliable results. An

[3]See terminology in Chapters 10 and 11.

important question is whether the cost of developing and applying such methods is worth the benefit to be derived.

At the present time, many CPA firms have the resources and the expertise to develop and use generalized computer audit programs. Supervisory responsibility for program operation is placed on specially trained individuals who acquire the necessary computer knowledge either through in-house seminars or prior academic background. However, the option of using such programs is evolving into a necessity as more companies develop computerized systems. Understanding of generalized computer audit programs is becoming more commonplace.

Expert Systems

As computer power is enhanced and auditors are faced with making decisions in more complex environments, some accounting firms have begun to develop expert systems to assist their personnel in the audit process. An expert system is a complex system of computer programs that models the decision process of a human expert. The psychological methods used to gain an understanding of the human expert's decision processes and the conversion of these decision processes into mathematical equations and computer programs is far beyond the scope of this text. However, auditing students should be aware that such systems are under development and, in some cases, in limited use. Some of the initial expert systems are used to assess control risk, evaluate loan collectibility, and evaluate whether a company can continue as a going concern. Additional expert systems may be developed to support other auditor judgments.

**Chapter 14
Glossary of Terms**

(listed in the order of appearance in the chapter, with accompanying page reference where the term is discussed)

Term	*Page in Chapter*
Generalized computer audit program a program or series of programs designed by the auditor to gather evidence.	540
Auditors' specifications descriptions of the audit objectives and the types of files to be used in computer processing.	542

Chapter 14
References

American Institute of Certified Public Accountants. *Audit and Accounting Guide—Computer-Assisted Audit Techniques* (New York: AICPA, 1979).

Davis, Gordon B., Adams, Donald L., and Schaller, Carol A. *Auditing & EDP,* 2nd ed. (New York: AICPA, 1983).

Chapter 14
Review Questions

14-1.   Name two categories into which auditor/EDP relationships fall.

14-2.   What are generalized computer audit programs?

14-3.   Give five examples of functions that can be performed by a generalized computer audit program.

14-4.   What is the common trait of all the generalized computer audit program capabilities listed in the chapter?

14-5.   Reproduce and label the flowchart or diagram that shows the general method used to operate a generalized computer audit program.

14-6.   Name three types of storage devices that can be used for client files that are processed with generalized computer audit programs.

14-7.   Take the following examples of output produced by generalized computer audit programs and list a possible audit procedure that would be performed with each item of output.
a. Listing of accounts receivable balances that exceed the credit limit.
b. Listing of unusually large inventory balances.
c. Listing of fixed-asset additions.

14-8.   Name four types of spreadsheet working papers that can be produced with microcomputers.

14-9.   What items should auditors consider when deciding whether to use generalized computer audit programs?

14-10.   Name three items of knowledge that auditors should possess to comprehend the computer system used by the client.

Chapter 14
Objective Questions Taken from CPA Examinations

14-11.   The purpose of using generalized computer audit programs is to test and analyze a client's computer
a. Systems.
b. Equipment.
c. Records.
d. Processing logic.

14-12.   An auditor can use a generalized computer audit program to verify the accuracy of
a. Computer controls.
b. Accounting estimates.
c. Totals and subtotals.
d. Account classifications.

14-13.   An auditor obtains a magnetic tape that contains the dollar amounts of all client inventory items by style number. The information on the tape is in no particular sequence. The auditor can best ascertain that no consigned merchandise is included on the tape by using a computer program that
a. Statistically selects samples of all amounts.
b. Excludes all amounts for items with particular style numbers that indicate consigned merchandise.
c. Mathematically calculates the extension of each style quantity by the unit price.
d. Prints on paper the information that is on the magnetic tape.

14-14.   A primary advantage of using a generalized computer audit program in the audit of an advanced computer system is that it enables the auditor to
a. Substantiate the accuracy of data through self-checking digits and hash totals.
b. Utilize the speed and accuracy of the computer.
c. Verify the performance of machine operations that leave visible evidence of occurrence.

d. Gather and store large quantities of supportive evidential matter in machine-readable form.

14-15. Which of the following is an advantage of generalized computer audit programs?
a. They are all written in one identical computer language.
b. They can be used for audits of clients that use different computer equipment and file formats.
c. They have reduced the need for the auditor to study input controls for computer related procedures.
d. Their use can be substituted for a relatively large part of the required tests of controls.

14-16. Which of the following is true of generalized computer audit programs?
a. They can be used only in auditing online computer systems.
b. They can be used on any computer without modification.
c. They each have their own characteristics, which the auditor must carefully consider before using in a given audit situation.
d. They enable the auditor to perform all manual tests of controls less expensively.

14-17. The most important function of a generalized computer audit program is the capability to
a. Access information stored on computer files.
b. Select a sample of items for testing.
c. Evaluate sample test results.
d. Test the accuracy of the client's calculations.

14-18. A primary advantage of using generalized computer audit programs in auditing the financial statements of a client that uses a computer system is that the auditor may
a. Check the accuracy of data through computer input controls.
b. Access information stored on computer files without a complete understanding of the client's hardware and software features.
c. Reduce the level of required testing to a relatively small amount.
d. Gather and permanently store large quantities of supportive evidential matter in machine readable form.

14-19. Which of the following audit procedures would an auditor be least *likely* to perform using a generalized computer audit program?
a. Searching records of accounts receivable balances for credit balances.
b. Investigating inventory balances for possible obsolescence.
c. Selecting accounts receivable for positive and negative confirmation.
d. Listing of unusually large inventory balances.

14-20.   The least likely use by the auditor of a generalized computer audit program is to
  a. Perform analytical procedures on the client's data.
  b. Access the information stored on the client's computer files.
  c. Identify weaknesses in the client's computer controls.
  d. Test the accuracy of the client's computations.

Chapter 14
Discussion/Case Questions

14-21.   The auditors of Update Company were considering the use of a generalized computer audit program to gather and document evidence from their client's computerized files. Most of the transactions, including accounts receivable and inventory, were processed by Update Company's computer system.

  One of the auditors, Ms. Current, suggested that as much information as possible be taken from Update Company's computerized system by the use of a generalized computer audit program. She made a list of each financial statement account on which information could be taken from computerized files with the use of a generalized computer audit program. She also made a list of the information for each account that could be taken from the computer files in this manner. The other auditor, Mr. Leave, agreed that much information could be obtained from Update Company's computer files in an efficient way by using the generalized computer audit program. He contended, however, that the information, itself, was not an audit procedure and that audit procedures would have to be performed on each item of information taken from the computer files. He wondered whether it would be more efficient simply to obtain printouts of the computer files and select the information they needed from these printouts to conduct the necessary audit procedures.

  Required:
  a. List the accounts and the information for each account that Ms. Current probably had in mind. (*Hint:* Consider each account on which computer files are probably maintained, and list the information the auditor would probably need; there are no "right" answers to this requirement.)
  b. List the audit procedures that Mr. Leave probably has in mind that will be conducted with the use of the information taken (at Ms. Current's suggestion) from Update Company's computer files (again, there are no "right" answers to this requirement).
  c. What potential problems could the auditor have if no generalized computer audit program is used?

14-22.   A CPA's client, Boos & Baumkirchner, Inc., is a medium-sized manufacturer of products for the leisure-time activities market (camping equipment, scuba gear, bows and arrows, etc.). A computer system maintains inventory records of finished goods and parts. The inventory master file is maintained on a disk. Each record of the file contains the following information:

Item or part number

Description

Size

Unit of measure code

Quantity on hand

Cost per unit

Total value of inventory on hand at cost

Date of last sale or usage

Quantity used or sold this year

Economic order quantity

Code number of major vendor

Code number of secondary vendor

In preparation for year-end inventory, the client has two identical sets of preprinted inventory count cards prepared. One set is for the client's inventory counts and the other is for the CPA's use to make audit test counts. The following information has been recorded on records that can be scanned:

*Item or part number

*Description

*Size

*Unit of measure code

In taking the year-end inventory, the client's personnel will write the actual counted quantity on the face of each record. When all counts are complete, the counted quantity will be processed against the disk file, and quantity-on-hand amounts will be adjusted to reflect the actual count. A computer listing will be prepared to show any missing inventory count records and all quantity adjustments of more than $100 in value. These items will be investigated by client personnel, and all required adjustments will be made. When adjustments have been completed, the final year-end balances will be computed and posted to the general ledger.

The CPA has available a generalized computer audit program that will run on the client's computer and can process disk files.

Required:

a. In general and without regard to the preceding facts, discuss the nature of generalized computer audit programs and list the various types and uses of such programs.

b. List and describe at least five ways a generalized computer audit program can be used to assist in all aspects of the audit of the inventory of Boos & Baumkirchner, Inc. (For example, the program can be used to read the disk inventory master file and list items and parts with a high unit cost or total value. Such items can be included in the test counts to increase the dollar coverage of the audit verification.)

(*AICPA adapted*)

14-23.   The following is a list of tasks performed by auditors in gathering evidence to support their opinion. For each task, indicate whether a generalized computer audit program could be used. Indicate the reasons for your answer.

a. Selecting accounts receivable confirmations.

b. Comparing subsidiary amounts to general ledger control amounts.

c. Investigating accounts receivable confirmation responses.

d. Inquiries on the collectibility of customer accounts.

e. Extracting important items from the minutes of meetings of the board of directors.

f. Preparing a list of property and equipment additions in excess of a certain dollar amount.

g. Comparing capital stock issuances with legal authorizations.

h. Determining the adequacy of insurance coverage.

i. Test checking the accounts receivable aging schedule with supporting documents.

14-24.   In many cases the output of a generalized computer audit program is used by the auditor for the same purpose as if the output were obtained through manual means. For each of the following examples of generalized computer audit program output, indicate the use that the auditor would make of the output in conducting the audit. For example, a computer-generated list of unusually large inventory balances might be used to test for possible inventory obsolescence.

a. Bank reconciliations for all the company's cash accounts.

b. An aged accounts receivable schedule.

c. A list of unusually large inventory balances (list a procedure other than testing for possible inventory obsolescence).

d. A list of property and equipment additions and retirements.

e. A list of vendors from whom large dollar purchases were made during the year.

f. A list of employees who have received overtime pay in excess of a certain amount.

g. A set of comparative financial statements for the two previous years.

14-25.   Refer to the program flowchart to read accounts receivable master files, located on page 547. The following is an explanation of the flowchart logic with certain steps left blank. Fill in the blank steps.

a. Start.

b. Read a record.

c. If it is the end of the file, end the process. If not, go to the next step.

d. _____

_____

_____

e. If all or part of the account has a balance greater than 90 days old, write a positive confirmation and go to the next step Ⓐ. If not, go to the next step.

f. If this is the third interval of accounts, write a negative confirmation and go to the next step Ⓐ. If not, go to the next step Ⓐ.

g. _____

_____

h. If there is a credit balance in the over-30-day category, write a record and go to the next step. If not, go to the next step.

i. _____

_____

j. _____

_____

k. If the credit status is 2, add the 61–90-day balances to the over-90-day balances. If not, go to the step that tests for credit status of 3.

l. _____

_____

_____

m. If the sum of the 61–90-day balances plus the over-90-day balances is greater than $2,000, write a record and go to the next step. If not, go to the next step.

n. _____

_____

o. If the 90-day balance is greater than 0, test for current charges. If not, read another record.

p. _____

_____

_____

14-26.   Refer to the master file data for the auditor's program on top of page 549. Assume the following information about three customer accounts.

a. Customer No. 500 has an $8,000 balance, of which $6,000 is current, $1,000 is 31–60 days old, and $1,000 is 61–90 days old.

b. Customer No. 501 has a $4,000 balance, of which $3,500 is current and $500 is over 90 days old.

c. Customer No. 502 has a $3,000 balance, all of which is current.

Required:

Using the program flowchart to read accounts receivable master files, located on page 547, indicate which accounts would have positive confirmations sent by the auditors. Also indicate the exception messages, if any, that would be sent on these three accounts.

14-27.   An auditor accesses a magnetic file that contains the dollar amounts of all client inventory items by style number. The information on the disk is in no particular sequence. By use of a generalized computer audit program, how can the auditor best ascertain that no consigned merchandise is included in the file?
(*AICPA adapted*)

14-28.   An auditor's client has a magnetic disk that contains the detail of its customers' insurance policies by policy number. Unknown to the auditor is the fact that many of the policies are for nonexistent customers. To prevent these nonexistent policies from being printed and tested by the auditors, a special code was placed in the account number of fictitious policies. When the computer read this code, the policy data associated with it were not printed.

Required:

Indicate how the auditor could have used a generalized computer audit program to detect this coverup.

14-29.   Roger Peters, CPA, has audited the financial statements of the Solt Manufacturing Company for several years and is making preliminary plans for the audit for the year ended June 30, 19X9. During this audit, Mr. Peters plans to use a set of generalized computer audit programs. Solt's computer manager has agreed to prepare special tapes of data from company records for the CPA's use with the generalized audit programs.

The following information is applicable to Mr. Peters' audit of Solt's accounts payable and related procedures:

1. The formats of pertinent tapes are shown on page 563.

2. The following monthly runs are prepared:
    a. Cash disbursements by check number.
    b. Outstanding payables.
    c. Purchase journals arranged (1) by account charged and (2) by vendor.

3. Vouchers and supporting invoices, receiving reports, and purchase order copies are filed by vendor code. Purchase orders and checks are filed numerically.

4. Company records are maintained on magnetic tapes. All tapes are stored in a restricted area within the computer room.

MASTER FILE—VENDOR NAME

Card Code 100

| Vendor Code | Record Type | Space | Vendor Name | Blank |

MASTER FILE—VENDOR ADDRESS

Card Code 120

| Vendor Code | Record Type | Space | Address—Line 1 | Address—Line 2 | Address—Line 3 | Blank |

TRANSACTION FILE—EXPENSE DETAIL

Card Code 160

| Vendor Code | Record Type | Voucher Number | Blank | Batch | Voucher Number | Voucher Date | Vendor Code | Invoice Date | Due Date | Invoice Number | Purchase Order Number | Debit Account | Prd Type | Product Code | Blank | Amount | Quantity |

TRANSACTION FILE—PAYMENT DETAIL

Card Code 170

| Vendor Code | Record Type | Voucher Number | Blank | Batch | Voucher Number | Voucher Date | Vendor Code | Invoice Date | Due Date | Invoice Number | Purchase Order Number | Check Number | Check Date | Blank | Amount | Blank |

Required:

Prepare a schedule for the computer manager outlining the data that should be included on the special tape for the CPA's audit of accounts payable and related procedures. This schedule should show the

    (1) Client tape from which the item should be extracted.

    (2) Name of the item of data.

(AICPA adapted)

14-30.   An auditor is conducting an audit of the financial statements of a wholesale cosmetics distributor with an inventory consisting of thousands of individual items. The distributor keeps its inventory in its own distribution center and in two public warehouses. An inventory computer file is maintained on a computer disk and at the end of each business day the file is updated. Each record of the inventory file contains the following data:

    Item number

    Location of item

    Description of item

    Quantity on hand

    Cost per item

    Date of last purchase

    Date of last sale

    Quantity sold during year

The auditor is planning to observe the distributor's physical count of inventories as of a given date. The auditor will have available a computer tape of the data on the inventory file on the date of the physical count and a generalized computer audit program.

Required:

The auditor is planning to perform basic inventory auditing procedures. Identify the basic inventory auditing procedures and describe how the use of the generalized computer audit program and the tape of the inventory file data might be helpful to the auditor in performing such auditing procedures.

    Organize your answer as follows:

Basic Inventory Auditing Procedure	*How Generalized Computer Audit Program and Tape of the Inventory File Data Might Be Helpful*
Observe the physical count, making and recording test counts where applicable.	Determine which items are to be test counted by selecting a random sample of a representative number of items from the inventory file as of the date of the physical count.

(AICPA adapted)

14-31.   In the past, the records to be evaluated in an audit have been printed reports, listings, documents, and written papers, all of which are visible output. However, in fully computerized systems that employ daily updating of transaction files, output and files are frequently in machine-readable forms such as tapes or disks. Thus, they often present the auditor with an opportunity to use the computer in performing an audit.

Required:
Discuss how the computer can be used to aid the auditor in examining accounts receivable in such a fully computerized system.
(*AICPA adapted*)

14-32.   After determining that computer controls are valid, Hastings is reviewing the sales system of Rosco Corporation to determine how a computerized audit program may be used to assist in performing tests of Rosco's sales records.

Rosco sells crude oil from one central location. All orders are received by mail and indicate the preassigned customer identification number, desired quantity, proposed delivery date, method of payment, and shipping terms. Since price fluctuates daily, orders do not indicate a price. Price sheets are printed daily and details are stored in a permanent disk file. The details of orders are also maintained on a permanent disk file.

Each morning the shipping clerk receives a computer printout that indicates details of customers' orders to be shipped that day. After the orders have been shipped, the shipping details are entered into the computer, which simultaneously updates the sales journal, perpetual inventory records, accounts receivable, and sales accounts.

The details of all transactions, as well as daily updates, are maintained on disks that are available for Hastings' use in the performance of the audit.

Required:
a. How may Hastings use a generalized computer audit program to perform substantive tests of Rosco's sales records in their machine-readable form? *Do not discuss accounts receivable and inventory.*
b. After having performed these tests with the assistance of the computer, what other auditing procedures should Hastings perform to complete the examination of Rosco's sales records?
(*AICPA adapted*)

14-33.   Microcomputer software has been developed to improve the efficiency and effectiveness of the audit. Electronic spreadsheets and other software packages are available to aid in the performance of audit procedures otherwise performed manually.

Required:
Describe the potential benefits to an auditor of using microcomputer software in an audit as compared to performing an audit without the use of a computer.
(*AICPA adapted*)

Auditing the Working Capital Cell—Part I

Learning Objectives *After reading and studying the material in this chapter, the student should*

Know the characteristics of the cash, accounts receivable, and prepayments accounts.

Understand how important features of the internal control structure associated with each account affect the scope of audit procedures for that account.

Know the audit objectives of each account.

Be able to determine and apply the audit procedures necessary to accomplish the audit objectives of each account.

Understand the preparation of audit working papers to document the audit procedures for each account.

Chapter 12 covers the conceptual approaches to gathering evidence. The purpose of this chapter and the following three chapters is to provide examples of audit objectives, procedures, and working papers that illustrate specific evidence gathering and working paper preparation techniques. Because the emphasis is on learning techniques rather than memorizing procedures or formats, a complete set of working papers is not considered necessary and is not included. This chapter and the following chapter include a discussion of the objectives, procedures, and selected working paper examples for the working capital accounts shown on the audit trial balance in Chapter 6.

Accounts in the working capital cell tend to turn over rapidly, so the balance at the end of a period contains few if any elements that were included in the balance at the beginning of the period. Thus, audit emphasis is placed on the ending account balance rather than on changes in the account during the period being audited.

Current Assets

Although assets may be understated as well as overstated, auditors normally find few cases of unrecorded or understated assets. Management's desire for increased earnings tends to result in more auditor-proposed adjustments to reduce earnings and assets than to increase them (though there may be exceptions motivated by income tax factors). Thus, auditors place primary emphasis on verifying recorded amounts (existence, ownership, and valuation) when they audit assets. (The emphasis is different in the audit of liabilities.)

Cash

Although the cash balance often is not one of the larger amounts on the balance sheet, the volume and dollar amount of transactions flowing through the cash account usually is greater than for any other account, because most business transactions ultimately are settled in cash. Also, being the most liquid of all assets, cash is very susceptible to defalcation (high inherent risk). For these reasons, the audit procedures applied to cash are often more extensive than the dollar size of the balance sheet account might seem to warrant.

Most business transactions are carried out by check, although businesses commonly maintain small petty cash funds for minor disbursements. Unless the balance or volume of transactions in a petty cash fund is large, the auditor seldom makes a count of the fund. Cash may be counted, however, if it is material or if unusual circumstances exist.

Unless otherwise disclosed in the financial statements, the cash balance included in current assets is considered to be unrestricted and available for immediate withdrawal. Restrictions on cash can take many forms, from an informal agreement with a bank to maintain an average balance above a certain amount to support borrowing and other credit arrangements (referred to as a compensating balance) to formally restricted escrow or other accounts from which immediate withdrawal cannot be made. Compensating balance arrangements should be disclosed in a note to the financial statements, whereas formally restricted accounts may be classified as noncurrent assets.

A general concept of the control structure—the separation of responsibilities for recording transactions affecting an asset from custody of the asset—has special applicability to cash. The implementation is sometimes referred to as a separation of the treasury and accounting functions. In large companies, these functions frequently are separated into different departments, with a treasurer supervising the custody function and a controller supervising the recording function. Even if such a complete separation of functions is not possible, certain specific duties can be separated among the available personnel to achieve the strongest control possible under the circumstances. For example, an employee who receives and deposits cash and checks should not prepare sales invoices, post detail accounts receivable records, reconcile the detail of accounts receivable to the control account, prepare or mail customer statements, approve write-offs of customer accounts, or receive or reconcile the bank statements. Similarly, an authorized check-signer should not receive or reconcile the bank statement, open the mail, approve vouchers for payment, and so on. All elements of strong internal control procedures will not be present in every company, and the auditor's evaluation of the nature and effectiveness of existing controls serves as the basis for determining the scope of his or her substantive tests.

An earlier chapter notes that no account is audited in a vacuum; that is, evidence gathered in the examination of one account may be applicable to other accounts as well. Audit procedures applied to other accounts often generate evidence concerning the cash account that supplements the evidence gathered in the cash section. Thus, procedures listed in this section do not generate the only evidence related to cash.

Audit Objectives

The objectives (assertions) in the audit of cash are as follows:

1. To determine whether the amount shown as cash in the financial statements constitutes all (completeness) cash on hand, in banks, or in transit (existence) that is owned (rights) by the company.

2. To determine whether any restricted cash is properly classified and disclosed (presentation and disclosure).

Note that cash is generally asserted to be valued at face amount so that no specific audit objective is shown for this assertion. There could be exceptions to this general assertion, as in the case of translation of foreign currencies.

Audit Procedures and Working Papers

The first procedure to accomplish these objectives should be a review of the internal control structure relating to cash. Control risk assessment related to cash receipts is often tested in a cash receipts test, such as that illustrated in Chapter 8. A cash disbursement test (see Chapter 8) is used to assess control risk for cash payments. The "proof of cash" or "block reconciliation" described later in this section is a dual-purpose test (both internal controls and account balances are tested). The result of these tests determines the extensiveness of other cash audit procedures.

The following are some examples of the control structure that would be considered by the auditor in determining the scope of tests of cash: (1) receipt and

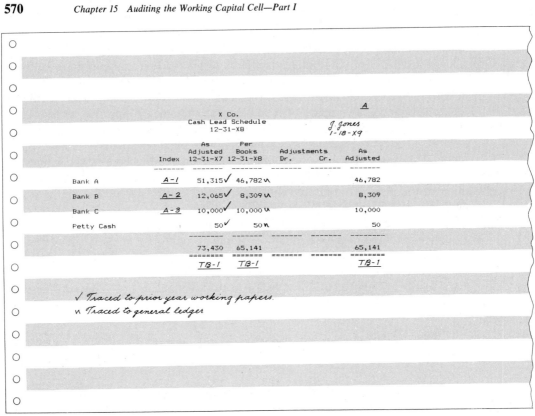

Figure 15.1 Cash lead schedule.

reconciliation of monthly bank statements by parties with no other cash duties may allow the auditor to reduce the number of bank reconciliations tested, limit the extent of audit procedures applied, and perform the bank reconciliation work at an interim date; (2) the comparison of checks to supporting documentation, such as a vendor's invoice, by the check signer may reduce the number of such comparisons made by the auditor; or (3) lack of segregation of check preparation and check signing functions may increase the number of checks and supporting documentation examined by the auditor. Other examples of audit procedures that can be varied in scope on the basis of the auditor's evaluation of the internal control structure are presented throughout this section.

The next procedure could be to prepare a lead schedule analyzing the amount shown in the audit trial balance by bank account (Figure 15.1). The amounts on the lead schedule should be compared with the general ledger and prior-year working papers.

Analytical Procedures The auditor may review changes in bank balances during the audit period for reasonableness and compare ending balances with cash

A-1

X Co.
Cash in Bank A
12-31-X8

J. Jones
1-18-X9

Balance per bank				59,650
Deposits in transit- Dates deposited				
Per Books	Per Bank			
12-30-X8	1-2-X9	606		
12-31-X8	1-2-X9	5,879		
				6,485
Outstanding Checks				(19,353) (1)
Other reconciling items				0
				46,782
				A

List of Outstanding Checks

Check No.	Amount
3014	3
3175	416
3180	2,650
3181	718
3183	4,377
3184	8,288
3185	1,935
3186	966
	19,353 (1)

Figure 15.2 Cash in Bank A.

budget balances; explanations should be obtained for significant or unusual variations.

Bank Reconciliations and Cutoff Statements The auditor then can prepare or obtain a copy of the client's bank reconciliation for each account. The reconciliation for Bank A is shown in Figure 15.2. Similar reconciliations also would be prepared or obtained for Banks B and C. The company's procedures provide that only a limited number of very minor items may be purchased with petty cash. The auditor's review of procedures indicates that this policy is being followed, and therefore no additional work will be performed on the petty cash balance.

The bank reconciliation provides the auditor with an important means of accomplishing certain objectives regarding cash—to determine that the cash is represented by deposits in banks or in transit (existence) and is owned (rights) by the company. If the amount shown as the balance in the bank is confirmed directly with the bank, and if the reconciling items (deposits in transit and outstanding checks) are audited satisfactorily, substantial persuasive evidence will have been accumulated in support of the cash balance shown in the accounting records. These procedures might appear in the audit program as follows.

1. Foot the bank reconciliation and any supporting details (performed by microcomputer when the schedule was prepared).

2. Confirm the balance per bank directly with the bank by means of a standard bank confirmation (indicated by Ç in Figure 15.3; also see Figure 15.4).

3. Obtain a cutoff bank statement directly from the bank for the period from 1-1-X9 to 1-15-X9.

4. Trace the balance per bank in the reconciliation to the year-end bank statement and the beginning balance of the cutoff bank statement (indicated by ✓ and ⊘ in Figure 15.3).

5. Trace the balance per books to the cash book (indicated by ∧ in Figure 15.3).

6. Trace the dates and amounts of deposits in transit to the cutoff bank statement obtained directly from the bank (indicated by ⊘ in Figure 15.3).

7. For canceled checks received in the cutoff bank statement and dated on or before the audit date, perform the following steps (indicated by ⊘ in Figure 15.3).

   a. Trace to the outstanding checklist supporting the bank reconciliation to determine whether they are shown properly.

   b. Compare the signature with the list of authorized check signers in the permanent audit file.

   c. Examine the endorsement to see that the check is endorsed by the payee and that there are no unusual second endorsements.

   d. Review payees for any that appear unusual such as checks payable to cash.

   e. Compare with cash book as to date, number, payee, and amount.

8. For checks received in the cutoff bank statement and dated after the audit date, examine the first bank endorsement to see that it does not precede the audit date (indicated by Note 1 in Figure 15.3).

A-1

X Co.
Cash in Bank A
12-31-X8

J. Jones
1-18-X9

List of
Outstanding Checks

Check No.	Amount
3014	3
3175	416
3180	2,650
3181	718
3183	4,377
3184	8,288
3185	1,935
3186	966
	19,353

Balance per bank   59,650

Deposits in transit—
Dates deposited

Per Books	Per Bank	
12-30-X8	1-2-X9	606
12-31-X8	1-2-X9	5,879
		6,485

Outstanding Checks   (19,353)

Other reconciling items   0

46,782

A

Note 1 - The first bank endorsements of all checks clearing with the cutoff bank statement were examined; none preceded the audit date.

Note 2 - Numbers of all checks issued during the month of December, 19X8 were accounted for as clearing with the December bank statement or as being on the outstanding check list.

C Confirmed by bank - See A-1/

√ Traced to December bank statement

(w) Traced to cutoff statement received directly from bank.

√ Traced to cash book.

(v) Examined cancelled check and compared with cash book as to date, number, payee, and amount. Also examined endorsement and compared signature with authorized signers.

(x) Compared with cash book as to check number and amount.

Figure 15.3   Cash in Bank A.

**STANDARD FORM TO CONFIRM ACCOUNT
BALANCE INFORMATION WITH FINANCIAL INSTITUTIONS***

Instructions to auditor: This form has been designed for use by auditors when confirming deposit and loan balance information with financial institutions. Please check *one* of the boxes below if confirmation of deposit balances only or loan balances only is desired. For more complex or detailed accounts and transactions the auditor should indicate in a separate communication the information that is desired from the financial institution.

Instructions to financial institution: Your completion of the following report is appreciated. We have listed below from our records the account number and description for balances to our credit/debit. Please confirm deposit balances only □ or loan balances only □. Please use the enclosed envelope to return the original directly to our accountant (see name below).

X Company   Fayetteville, Arkansas
(ACCOUNT NAME PER BANK RECORDS)   (CLIENT ADDRESS)

By _Bruce Lee_
    Authorized Signature

RETURN	[Partner & Co.]	[ ]	Balances intentionally left
TO	[100 Main Street]		blank, form mailed prior to
	Fayetteville, AR		balance date for your prompt
			processing.

REPORT FROM
FINANCIAL   [Bank A   ]
INSTITUTION [Fayetteville, AR]

1. At the close of business on Dec. 31, 19 X8 our records showed the following balance(s) to our credit.

ACCOUNT NAME	ACCOUNT NO.	AMOUNT
Regular	10 0000	$59,650

2. According to our records, we were directly liable to you at the close of business on Dec. 31, 19 X8 as follows:

ACCOUNT NO./ DESCRIPTION	AMOUNT	DATE DUE	INTEREST RATE	PAID TO	DESCRIPTION OF COLLATERAL
Note	$300,000	12-1-Y4	8%	12-1-X8	Land and Buildings
Note	60,000	10-30-X9	8%	12-31-X8	Accounts Receivable

EXCEPTIONS:

The foregoing is in agreement with our records except as noted.

Bank _R. Lorneff_   _1-16-X9_
     Authorized Signature   Date

* Approved 1988 by American Bankers Association, American Institute of Certified Public Accountants and Bank Administration Institute.
  Additional forms available from:

AICPA — ORDER
P.O. Box 1003   Original
New York, NY 10108-1003   To be mailed to accountant

Figure 15.4   Bank A confirmation.

9. For checks on the outstanding checklist that did not clear with the cutoff bank statement, compare check number and amount with cash book and investigate any that have been outstanding for an unusually long time (indicated by ⓧ in Figure 15.3).

10. Account for all check numbers issued during the month as having cleared with the year-end bank statement or as being on the outstanding checklist (indicated by Note 2 in Figure 15.3).

The desirability of a separation between authorization of cash disbursements, signing and mailing checks, and preparation of the bank reconciliation is pointed out in Chapter 8. If such separation exists, audit procedures 7 through 10 might be applied on a test basis. Auditors sometimes use a minimum dollar amount as a basis for selecting the items to be tested in this type of situation to be sure of testing all significant items. Other types of sample selection previously discussed could also be used.

The foregoing procedures include two requests from the bank: a bank confirmation and a cutoff bank statement. Both items are necessary because the information requested in each is different. The bank confirmation includes data about direct liabilities as well as the account balance. The cutoff bank statement contains canceled checks, debit memos, and credit memos, as well as a listing of transactions.

Because of the large number of companies being audited each year, the requests impose a considerable burden on the banks, particularly after the end of the calendar year. The standard bank confirmation (Figure 15.4) was designed to facilitate the furnishing of information by banks to auditors, and should be used whenever possible. The auditor sends these forms *directly* to the bank or other financial institution and receives them *directly* back. The auditor normally sends confirmation requests to every bank with which the client has an account or has done recent business. This helps to detect unrecorded bank accounts (completeness) and direct liabilities. Note that Item 2 on the form is a request for information on outstanding loans that the client has with the bank as of the balance sheet date. Thus, this form can serve as a working paper for both cash and liabilities. The auditor may also wish to confirm with the bank other transactions and agreements between the client and the bank, but this request should be conveyed in a separate letter rather than as part of the standard bank confirmation. Examples of such transactions and agreements include certificates of deposit, collateral and pledged assets, compensating balance requirements, contingent liabilities, letters of credit, loan agreements, securities held in safekeeping, and repurchase/reverse repurchase transactions.

The auditor also may ask banks with accounts that were closed during the year and show a zero book balance whether they have been notified formally of the closing of the accounts (often they are not) and whether there have been any transactions after the date of the last book entry. Unless the necessary formal steps are taken by the client to close such accounts they could be used for unauthorized deposits and subsequent misappropriation of funds.

The cutoff bank statement is a normal bank statement that has been cut off as of some date during the month following the audit date. The length of the period is based on the auditor's judgment as to the time required for year-end reconciling items to clear the bank. The auditor requests that the cutoff statement be sent directly to him or her for use in testing the propriety of reconciling items at year end.

If an auditor has reason to suspect lapping (an irregularity involving the substitution of cash items to cover misappropriated funds and the delayed posting of collections to the detail accounts receivable records), authenticated deposit slips may be requested from the bank. Authenticated deposit slips are copies of deposit slips that are mailed to the bank for comparison with copies in its files. The bank indicates on the deposit slip that this has been done (authenticates the deposit slip) and mails it directly to the auditor. The effectiveness of this procedure is limited, however, if details of the deposit are not included on the deposit slip or if the bank does not make an item-by-item comparison of the deposit slip (banks sometimes decline to do so). Lapping is illustrated on page 587.

Interbank Transfers   The foregoing procedures would provide evidence of the individual cash account balances, but the auditor also must consider the effect of transactions between accounts, often referred to as *interbank transfers*. (Intrabank, interdivision, and intercompany transfers also should be tested.) Companies often have several bank accounts (some for special purposes such as payroll), and transfers among them are common. The objective of testing interbank transfers is to determine that for each transfer near the end of the year, the amount added (deposited) to one account was subtracted (withdrawn) from another account during the same year (existence and completeness). For example, if a transfer is added to one account on December 31 and subtracted from another on January 2, the cash balance as of December 31 would be overstated by the amount of the transfer (another account such as vouchers payable also would be overstated). This practice, sometimes called *kiting,* has been used by companies to conceal weak cash positions and to increase their current ratios (if current liabilities exceed current assets, an equal increase in each will improve the current ratio). Auditors test interbank transfers with an interbank transfer schedule such as that shown in Figure 15.5. The time period covered by this schedule depends on the normal time for a check to clear the banks involved. One or two weeks is not unusual.

The first transfer in Figure 15.5 was recorded on the books and cleared both banks in the same year and therefore is not a reconciling item. The second transfer was recorded on the books in one year and cleared both banks in the subsequent year. Therefore, it should appear in Bank A's reconciliation as a deposit in transit (as in Figure 15.3) and in Bank B's reconciliation as an outstanding check.

Kiting may also be used to temporarily conceal a cash shortage. If a bookkeeper misappropriates funds from a bank account or petty cash fund by unau-

			Dates of						
		Deposits		Withdrawals					
Check Number	Description	Per Books	Per Bank	Per Books	Per Bank	Bank A	Bank B	Bank C	
3183	Transfer from A to B	12-30-X8 ✓	12-30-X8 ⋀	12-30-X8 ✓	12-31-X8 ⋀		(10,000)	10,000	
0613	Transfer from B to A	12-31-X8 ✓	1-2-X9 ⋀	12-31-X8 ✓	1-3-X9 ⋀	5,879	(5,879)		
						A-1	A-2		

X Co.
Interbank Transfer Schedule
For the Period 12-22-X8 to 1-10-X9
12-31-X8

J. Jones
1-19-X9

$\frac{A}{7}$

✓ Traced to cash book.
⋀ Traced to bank statement.

Figure 15.5   Interbank transfer schedule.

thorized withdrawals, the shortage may be covered at the audit date by writing, but not recording, a check on another company bank account, preferably in a distant city to increase the time required for clearance. The concealment is temporary because the unrecorded check will clear the bank after the audit date and create another shortage. Auditors trace canceled checks dated prior to the audit date and returned with the cutoff bank statement to the list of outstanding checks supporting the bank reconciliation to detect this type of kiting. This step is indicated by $\oslash$ in Figure 15.3.

Testing Cash Transactions   In addition to applying audit procedures to the year-end cash balance, auditors sometimes test the recording of cash transactions for some period during the year. To do this, they prepare what is known as a *block reconciliation* or *proof of cash* for the period selected. An example of a block reconciliation is shown in Figure 15.6 (the month ending on the audit date is used to relate it to the previous examples, but any one or more months within the period being audited could have been selected). The reconciliation must balance, that is, the amounts in each column must sum to the total of the column and the amounts in each row must sum to the balance at the end of the period. This form of reconciliation "blocks in" a period, so that all cash transactions in a particular account for the period can be accounted for and tested.

Audit procedures that could be applied to the amounts in the block reconciliation are listed below (the letters correspond to those in Figure 15.6).

a. Confirm with bank and trace to ending balance on November bank statement and beginning balance on December bank statement.

b. Trace to December bank statement.

c. Obtain or prepare a list of outstanding checks; determine whether each check on the list (1) cleared with December bank statement (by examination of canceled check) or (2) was listed as outstanding at December 31.

d. Compare with general ledger or cash book.

e. Prepare a listing of deposits from bank statement and indicate date of each deposit (see f).

f. Prepare a listing of deposits from cash book and indicate date of each deposit; compare this listing with that prepared in step e and investigate any significant delays between dates deposits were recorded in cash book and by bank.

g. Trace to cutoff bank statement.

h. Prepare and total a listing of canceled checks included with bank statement.

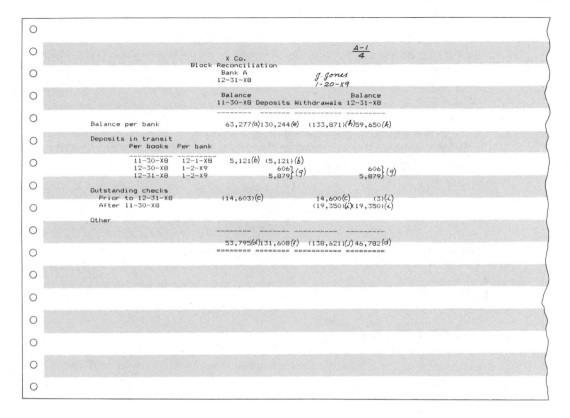

Figure 15.6 Block reconciliation.

i. Same as steps 7, 8, and 9 listed previously as applicable to year-end bank reconciliation.

j. Prepare and total a listing of disbursements from cash book and (1) account for serial numbers of all checks issued during the period; and (2) examine canceled checks clearing during the month for signatures and endorsements and compare with cash book as to date, number, payee, and amount.

k. Confirm with bank and trace to ending balance on December bank statement and beginning balance on cutoff bank statement.

Classification and Disclosure   Most of the procedures discussed previously in this section relate to the objective of determining the existence, completeness, and rights regarding the cash balance. To determine that restricted cash is properly classified and disclosed, the auditor must gather additional evidence. This evidence may take the form of answers to inquiries of management (sometimes included in the management representation letter) and a special confirmation letter to each bank requesting specific confirmation of compensating balances and other agreements between the bank and the client. Another source for detection of restrictions on cash is the audit of liabilities, particularly the review of the provisions of lease and loan agreements and related documents. Board of director minutes may also disclose restrictions of cash.

Managements of companies occasionally attempt to "window dress" their cash balance by borrowing funds immediately prior to year end and repaying the loans immediately after year end so that a large cash balance will appear in the financial statements. This practice is not improper as long as it is adequately disclosed.

SUMMARY OF IMPORTANT AUDIT PROCEDURES FOR CASH

- Review and evaluate the effect of the internal control structure on the scope of cash work.

- Perform analytical procedures.

- Obtain or prepare copies of bank reconciliations, and
    foot the reconciliations,
    confirm the bank balance,
    trace the bank balance to year-end and cutoff bank statements,
    trace balance per books to cash book,
    trace deposits in transit to cutoff bank statements,
    compare outstanding checklist with canceled checks included with the cutoff bank
        statement and examine checks for date, number, payee, amount, signature, and
        endorsement
    examine canceled checks included with the cutoff bank statement dated after the audit
        date for date of first bank endorsement,
    investigate any long outstanding checks, and
    account for all check numbers issued during the month ending on the audit date.

- Schedule and review interbank transfers.

- If considered necessary, test cash transactions with a block reconciliation for a selected period.

- Inquire of management and review special bank confirmations, lease and loan agreements, and minutes for restrictions on cash that may require reclassification or disclosure.

Receivables

Receivables usually represent uncollected revenues, but may include other items such as claims and other credits due from vendors, amounts due from sale of scrap or assets not held for resale, and accrued income such as interest and unbilled construction contract work (accounted for on the percentage-of-completion basis).

Accounts receivable included in current assets are considered to be collectible within one year or during a company's natural operating cycle. Other receivables are classified as long-term assets. Notes or accounts receivable due from officers, employees, or affiliated enterprises should be shown separately and not included under a general heading, such as notes receivable or accounts receivable. Also, amounts due from or to related parties and the terms and manner of settlement should be disclosed. Therefore, the segregation of certain receivables, if material, is necessary for a proper classification.

Receivables are sometimes pledged as collateral for a loan, and sometimes discounted or sold (with or without recourse). Disclosure is required of the direct or contingent liabilities that may arise from such transactions.

Receivables, like all other assets, should not be stated at an amount in excess of net realizable value. An allowance account is used to reduce the receivable balance to the amount expected to be realized. The allowance for doubtful accounts should be sufficient to cover not only losses from accounts known to be uncollectible, but also an estimate of current receivables that subsequently will become uncollectible. In addition, the account should be adequate to cover discounts and other allowances.

The internal control structure relating to accounts receivable is discussed in Chapter 8. The basic concept of segregation of duties requires that such responsibilities as maintaining detail receivable ledgers, receiving cash, maintaining the receivable control account, preparing sales documents, writing off bad debts, and approving credit be separated to the extent possible.

Audit Objectives

The objectives (assertions) in the audit of receivables are as follows:

1. To determine whether the amount shown as receivables in the financial statements represents all (completeness) bona fide amounts due from others (existence) and owned by the client (rights).

2. To determine whether receivables are stated at net realizable value (valuation).

3. To determine whether receivables are classified properly (presentation).

4. To determine whether all liens on and pledges of receivables are disclosed properly (disclosures).

Audit Procedures and Working Papers

The auditor should begin work in this section with a review of the client's internal control structure relating to sales, shipping, billing, and accounts receivable. An example of some of these controls is shown in Chapter 8. The evaluation of these controls should affect directly the work performed in this section and particularly the scope of one of the most important procedures in this section—the direct confirmation of account balances.

A strong internal control structure, such as that shown in the cash receipts system in Chapter 8, might allow the auditors to reduce the number of confirmations sent. Other examples of controls that would affect the nature, timing, and extent of substantive tests of accounts receivable are (1) lack of a policy to reconcile detail accounts receivable records to the general ledger control account or an out-of-balance condition should cause the auditor to significantly increase the number of confirmations requested, (2) periodic confirmation by internal auditors may allow the external auditor to reduce the number of confirmations requested, and (3) the existence of a separate credit and collections department with effective procedures for collecting customer accounts may allow the auditor to reduce the extent of his or her analysis and tests of the aging schedule and to perform them at an interim date.

The auditor must prepare a lead schedule for receivables to determine types and amounts of major subaccounts. Figure 15.7 shows that X Co.'s receivables consist primarily of customer accounts receivable. The officer and employee and other accounts should be reviewed to determine that there were no significant transactions through them during the year. If there were none, no additional work normally would be performed on these accounts, because they are clearly immaterial.

Analytical Procedures   Numerous opportunities exist to employ analytical procedures to accounts receivable. Some of the more common comparisons are (1) current year balance to current year budget and prior year actual, (2) number of days' sales in accounts receivable for current and prior year, (3) accounts receivable turnover ratio for current and prior year, (4) ratio of bad debt expense to sales for current and prior year, (5) ratio of allowance for doubtful accounts to accounts receivable for current and prior year, and (6) ratio of past due accounts receivable to total accounts receivable for current and prior year. Unusual and unexplained variations may raise questions as to the propriety of the accounts receivable balance and the adequacy of the allowance for doubtful accounts (existence and valuation).

The Aging Schedule   The auditor ordinarily would obtain a listing of the individual customer trade receivables in order to have sufficiently detailed information to which he or she can apply audit procedures. Because using one audit schedule for two tests is more efficient than preparing separate schedules, a detail listing of customer trade receivables is combined with an aging schedule in Figure 15.8. Note the following audit procedures that have been performed on this schedule.

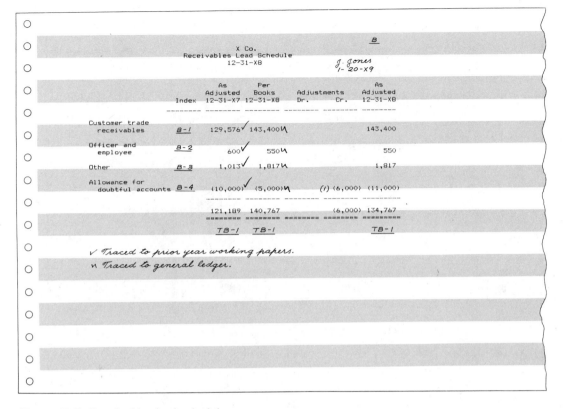

Figure 15.7 Receivables lead schedule.

1. The listing was totaled by the microcomputer and determined to be in agreement with the general ledger (by cross-referencing to the lead schedule where the balance had been traced to the general ledger).

2. Customer account balances were confirmed on a test basis (related to existence and rights of the receivable).

3. Alternative procedures (the examination of invoice, shipping documents, and remittance advice evidencing subsequent payment by the customer) were applied to customer balances selected for confirmation but for which no reply was received (relates to existence of the receivable).

4. The adequacy of the allowance for doubtful accounts was tested by (a) review of credit files and discussions of the collectibility of all accounts over $2,000 with the credit manager, (b) review of subsequent collection of account balances, and (c) comparison with the prior year of the percentage of accounts receivable in each of the aging categories (valuation at net realizable value and proper classification).

B-1

J. Jones
1-20-x9

X Co.
Customer Trade Receivables
Aged Listing
12-31-X8

Account No.	Customer Name	Balance 12-31-X8	Current	30-60 Days	60-90 Days	Over 90 Days	Subsequent Collections	Comments
1103	Cunningham Inc.	5,630 ⌀	5,630				0	
1110	Litton & Co.	1,935	1,860		75		1,860	
1112	La Fleur & Sons, Ltd.	278				278	0	Bankrupt
1120	March Co.	3,811 v	2,701	1,110			3,811	

Total		B 143,400	110,745	18,759	8,286	5,610	64,423	
Percent of total		100%	77%	13%	6%	4%		
Prior year percentages		100%	83%	11%	5%	1%		

C Confirmed by customer - see B-1
√ Second request mailed.
√ Non-reply. Examined invoice, shipping documents, and remittance advice for subsequent collection.

Client computes allowance for doubtful accounts as 100% of accounts over 90 days old. I reviewed credit files and discussed all accounts over $2000 with the credit manager and noted approximately $6000 of accounts in the 30-60 and 60-90 day columns that are doubtful. Recommend the following adjustment:

Bad debt expense   6000
* Allowance for doubtful accounts   6000*

J. Jones
1-20-x9

Figure 15.8 Customer trade receivables aged listing.

Confirmations   AU Section 331.01 (*SAS No. 1*) states the following:

Confirmation of receivables and (observation of inventory) are generally accepted auditing procedures. The independent auditor who issues an opinion when he has not employed them must bear in mind that he has the burden of justifying the opinion expressed.

Figure 15.9 is an example of a *positive* confirmation request in which the customer is asked to return the confirmation directly to the auditor, indicating thereon agreement or disagreement with the amount shown on the client's records. Often the confirmation request is accompanied by a statement showing the detail of the accounts receivable balance, which allows the customer to determine agreement or disagreement more accurately. Positive confirmations are preferable when individual account balances are relatively large or when the internal control structure is weak and there is reason to believe that there may be a substantial number of errors in the accounts.

A negative confirmation request contains much of the same wording as a positive request, except that the customers are asked to return the confirmation directly to the auditor *only* if they disagree with the amount shown in the client's records. Therefore, the auditor cannot be completely sure that customers do not return negative confirmations because they (1) agree with the clients' balances, or (2) neglect to give them proper consideration. Negative confirmations may be used when there are a large number of relatively small account balances, the internal control structure is believed to be strong, and the individuals receiving the confirmation requests are likely to give them adequate consideration.

Note that the letter is addressed from the client to the customer in such a way as to convey the message that a confirmation to the auditor is requested, rather than a payment to the company. This point is particularly important if the customers are members of the general public who are not used to receiving this type of letter and are likely to misconstrue it as a payment request. Occasionally, a note is printed in boldface type at the top of the letter stating that it is *not* a request for payment.

If a positive confirmation request is sent and no reply is received within a reasonable period of time, a second request is sent. If a reply is not received after the second request, the auditors will apply alternative procedures (inspection of internal records such as copies of sales invoices, shipping documents, and evidence of payment). Once an account has been selected for verification, some type of evidence should be obtained. The matter may not be dropped simply because a reply is not received to a confirmation request.

The auditor should investigate all exceptions to both positive and negative confirmation requests. Often the difference between the client's records and the customer's reply can be explained by a cash receipt in transit or a late charge by the client. Sometimes the client has made an error, in which case an adjusting entry would be proposed if the difference is material. Not only exceptions but also gratuitous comments should be investigated. For example, if the comment "Paid

X CO.
122 WEST AVE.
FAYETTEVILLE, ARKANSAS

January 19, 19X9

Cunningham, Inc.
423 Best Road
Fayetteville, Arkansas 72701

Gentlemen:

Our auditors, Partner & Co., are now engaged in an audit of our
financial statements. In connection therewith, they desire to
confirm the balance due us on your account as of December 31,
19X8, which was shown on our records (and the enclosed statement)
as $5,630.00. _B-1_

Please state in the space below whether or not this is in agreement with your records at that date. If not, please furnish any
information you may have which will assist the auditors in reconciling the difference. After signing and dating your reply,
please mail it directly to Partner & Co., 100 Main Street, Fayetteville, Arkansas 72701. A stamped, addressed envelope is enclosed for your convenience.

It is very important that Partner & Co. receive your prompt reply. We sincerely appreciate your assistance and will return the
courtesy extended to us whenever X Co. receives your corresponding audit request.

Very truly yours,

Bruce Lee

_B-1_   Bruce Lee
                          Controller

The above balance of $ _5,630.00_ due X Co. agrees with our
records at December 31, 19X8 with the following exceptions (if
any):

none

Date _1-20-X9_   Signed _Harold Cunninghan_

Figure 15.9 Accounts receivable confirmation.

in full on January 8, 19X9'' were added by a customer to a confirmation as of December 31, 19X8, the auditor should trace the payment to cash receipts on or near January 8, 19X9.

Auditors often send confirmations to 100 percent of the accounts that exceed tolerable error and to a sample of all others. In determining the size of the sample, the auditor would consider factors discussed in Chapter 13 such as the amount of tolerable error, the risk of incorrectly accepting a materially incorrect amount, variation in the population, and so forth.

The auditor should understand that a confirmation is evidence of the existence of a receivable, but is *not* evidence of its collectibility. A customer may agree completely that a balance is due, but may be without funds to make payment. Similarly, the collection of a receivable after the audit date is evidence of its collectibility but may not be evidence of its existence at the audit date (the receivable and related sale actually may have occurred after the audit date).

Confirmation of accounts receivable may disclose an irregularity referred to as lapping. If an individual has access to both cash receipts and accounts receivable, cash receipts from one customer may be diverted to personal use and a subsequent cash receipt for a second customer posted to the account of the first customer. This leaves an incorrect balance in the account of the second customer that must be covered by the cash receipt from a third customer, and so on. Naturally, this type of irregularity is not permanently concealed and must be continually manipulated. However, some significant losses have occurred because of lapping.

Lapping may be temporarily concealed by changing the client's copy of the deposit slip to show what was improperly posted to customer accounts rather than what was actually received. Additionally, monthly statements to customers may be prepared to show a balance different from the incorrect balance shown in the ledger. Here is a brief example of how the accounts could be manipulated.

| | | *Customers* | | | | | |
| | | *A* | | *B* | | *C* | |
	Theft	*Book Balance*	*Correct Balance*	*Book Balance*	*Correct Balance*	*Book Balance*	*Correct Balance*
Balance		$400	$400	$600	$600	$200	$200
Receipt from A	400		(400)				
Balance	400	400	—	600	600	200	200
Receipt from B	200	(400)			(600)		
Balance	600	—	—	600	—	200	200
Receipt from C				(200)			(200)
Balance	600	—	—	400	—	200	—

Lapping may come to light when it breaks down due to its complexity. Note that because the shortage is continually being shifted among accounts, the bookkeeper cannot afford to take a vacation or otherwise allow others to post the receipts. This is one reason that lapping is sometimes discovered when a "loyal, hard-working" employee becomes seriously ill or is otherwise prevented from performing his or her job. In addition to the confirmation of the balance of a customer's account that is being manipulated (customers B and C in the preceding example), the tracing of individual amounts shown on deposit slips authenticated or obtained directly from the bank (see page 576) to the cash book may disclose this irregularity. Lapping may be deterred by a separation of the cashier and accounts receivable functions.

Valuation of Receivables   Because the determination of the adequacy of the allowance for doubtful accounts can be very subjective, the exercise of good business judgment by the auditor is crucial in this area. An auditor cannot automatically accept amounts computed by standard client procedures (such as a percentage of sales, a percentage of accounts past due, etc.), even if such procedures produced the proper results in the past. Conditions change, and procedures that produced reliable results at one time may not do so later. Among the factors an auditor would consider in evaluating the adequacy of the allowance for doubtful accounts are (1) a review of the effectiveness of the client's current credit and collection policies, (2) statistical analyses such as number of days' sales in accounts receivable, bad debts written off as a percentage of sales, bad debt expense as a percentage of sales, and percentage of accounts receivable in each aging category (most useful if the volume of accounts is high and the dollar value of individual accounts is low), (3) review of credit files and payment histories of individual accounts (a very effective procedure but possibly impractical if more than a few large accounts are involved), (4) review of subsequent collections (also an effective procedure, but many collectible accounts may not be paid in the normal course of business before the audit is completed), and (5) consideration of general economic and industry conditions, the business approach (e.g., an auditor would intuitively expect the allowance for doubtful accounts of a consumer loan company to be higher during a period of recession and high unemployment, because many customers would be out of work and unable to repay their loans). The auditor must require the client to bear the burden of justifying the adequacy of the allowance for doubtful accounts.

The auditor's earlier evaluation of the internal control structure for credit sales might affect the scope of audit work in this area. For example, if compliance with the credit policy has been violated consistently, and customers with questionable credit have been sold merchandise, the auditor may do more investigation of slow paying accounts.

Matters Requiring Disclosure   To meet the objective of adequate disclosure of liens or pledges of receivables, the auditor would (1) inquire of management as to any financial arrangements made to assign, discount, or pledge receivables, (2) inspect loan agreements for the existence of and minutes for the approval of such financial arrangements, and (3) request confirmation of the existence of such arrangements from financial institutions with which the client transacts business. The business approach is also useful here. For example, an auditor should know that a client company that is short of cash and already has pledged its property and equipment is much more likely to have pledged its receivables than a client with an adequate cash flow.

SUMMARY OF IMPORTANT AUDIT PROCEDURES FOR ACCOUNTS RECEIVABLE

- Review and evaluate the effects of the internal control structure on the scope of accounts receivable work.

- Perform analytical procedures.

- Obtain and test the clerical accuracy of an account receivable trial balance.

- Send confirmations (positive or negative) to selected customers; send second requests to customers who fail to respond to first requests for positive confirmations.

- Perform alternative procedures for customers who fail to respond to second requests for positive confirmations.

- Obtain and test accuracy of an aged trial balance, and evaluate adequacy of allowance for doubtful accounts by
  comparison with prior year of percentages and amounts in each aging category, examination of credit files and payment histories for large delinquent accounts, and review of subsequent collection of account balances.

- Inquire of management and review agreements and minutes for liens or pledges of accounts receivable that may require disclosure.

Prepayments

Prepayments represent costs incurred that are applicable to future periods. Prepayments are short term in nature and usually are associated with services to be received within the next year, such as prepaid insurance, rent, and taxes.

Audit Objectives

The objectives (assertions) in the audit of prepayments are as follows:

1. To determine whether the amounts shown as prepayments in the financial statements constitute all such prepayments (completeness), are computed in accordance with generally accepted accounting principles (valuation), and are applicable to future periods (existence and rights).

2. To determine whether the amounts can reasonably be expected to be realized (valuation).

3. To determine whether the amounts are classified properly in the financial statements and whether disclosure is adequate (presentation and disclosure).

Audit Procedures and Working Papers

The control procedures to be considered by the auditor in the examination of prepayments include those applicable to cash disbursements, the client's policies regarding the kinds of costs that are subject to deferral, and the systematic procedure for amortizing such costs to expense. Cash disbursement procedure tests are illustrated in Chapter 8. Tests of the procedures for proper deferral and amortization, described in this section, are dual-purpose tests. The evaluation of the effectiveness of these procedures is a significant factor in determining the scope of the auditor's work in this area. For example, a consistently followed policy of deferring the cost of only certain appropriate items might enable the auditor to substantially limit his or her examination of invoices supporting additions to the prepayments account. Additionally, the test of prepayment amortizations by internal auditors should allow the external auditor to restrict substantive tests in this area.

After the auditor's assessment of the internal control structure, the next step normally would be the preparation of a lead schedule. In the X Co. example, however, there is only one prepayment account. A standard lead schedule containing only one account would be pointless; therefore, in this case, the auditor would reference directly from the detail audit schedule for prepaid insurance (Figure 15.10) to the audit trial balance. This schedule (unlike working papers in the cash, accounts receivable, and inventory sections) shows the transactions for the year that affect prepaid insurance and insurance expense (the procedures result in evidence about an expense account as well as an asset account).

Analytical Procedures   The auditor should compare current-year prepayment balances by major category (insurance, rent. etc.) with the prior year. Because prepayment balances often apply to a specific period at the end of each year (e.g., an insurance policy covers the period July 1 to June 30 so that there are always six months of unexpired premium each December 31), variations in balances may relate primarily to variations in cost. This allows the auditor to make

D

J. Jones
1-22-X9

X Co.
Analysis of Prepaid Insurance and Expense
12-31-X8

Description	Prepaid Balance 12-31-X7	Current Premium	Amortization to Expense	Prepaid Balance 12-31-X8
Policy No. REC 12233 for fire and extended coverage on building and contents in the amount of $600,000 for the year from 6-30-X7 to 6-30-X8	5,742	0	(5,742)	0
Increase in above policy to $625,000 and extension to 6-30-X9	0	12,624 ✓	(6,312) ✗	6,312
Policy No. WC 22244 for workman's compensation coverage of $100,000 from 1-1-X8 to 12-31-X8 ✓	0	3,291 ✓	(3,291)	0
Policy No. CC 3719 – Blanket fidelity bond coverage in the amount of $200,000 from 1-1-X8 to 12-31-X8 ✓	0	1873 ✓	(1,873)	0
	11,343	37,898	36,986	12,255
	TB-1	20 / 40	29,704 / 7,282 = 36,986	TB-1

✓ Examined insurance policy noting provisions of the policy and annual premium.

√ Examined insurance company invoice and cancelled check.

✗ Checked calculation of amortization.

I discussed the Company's insurance coverage with Mr. Lee, Controller. He is satisfied that insurance coverage is adequate to cover the replacement cost of the assets and anticipated liability claims. I noted no significant omissions or inadequacies of insurance coverage.

J. Jones
1-22-X9

Figure 15.10 Prepayments.

effective tests of balances of prepayments by using analytical procedures. Any new categories of prepayments in the current year should be investigated to determine whether their deferral is appropriate (existence).

Tests of Balance and Amortization   Under generally accepted accounting principles, assets generally are stated at cost. The auditor has tested this aspect in Figure 15.10 by examination of invoices from insurance companies and the related canceled checks (see ∧). Additional evidence of the annual premium cost is obtained from examination of the insurance policy (see √). The auditor must be aware that the premium on certain types of policies, such as workman's compensation, sometimes are based on the injury experience of the insured and are subject to retroactive adjustment. In this case, a review of the client's injury experience and consultation with the client's insurance agent may be necessary to arrive at an estimate of the final premium. The applicability of the prepaid portion of the cost to future periods is tested by calculation of the current-year amortization on the basis of the percentage of the total policy period included in the current year (see ✗). An examination of the policy periods shown in the description column indicates that all will expire within one year and that the classification of the prepaid balance as a current asset is proper. The objective of determining that the amounts can reasonably be expected to be realized is usually self-evident with prepaid insurance, because the balance generally is refunded on cancellation of the policy if not utilized in the future. This is not the case for all prepaid items, however. Consider prepaid rent on a plant that is shut down permanently. Although the cost in this case may apply to some future period, prepayments must generate some future benefit or value at least equal to their cost to be classified properly as assets. If such items do not produce revenues to absorb their costs, they will not be realized.

Review of Insurance Coverage   On Figure 15.10 is a notation of a review of the company's insurance coverage with the controller and the auditor's observation of no significant omissions or inadequacies in the coverage. Disclosure of significantly inadequate insurance coverage may be necessary for a fair presentation of financial statements. The auditor is not an insurance expert with the qualifications to reach an informed opinion about insurance coverage, although he or she should be familiar with typical business insurance coverage. For example, most businesses maintain fidelity bond coverage to insure against loss from embezzlement and theft, and auditors consider this coverage in their overall evaluation of the internal control structure. The auditor should recommend that the client consult with an insurance representative about any obvious deficiencies in coverage. Important audit information sometimes can be obtained from a review of insurance coverage. A reduction in insurance coverage of property and equipment, for example, may lead the auditor to an unrecorded property retirement, and the existence of a loss-payable clause in a policy could result in the detection of an unrecorded liability.

The audit procedures for other types of prepayments are similar to those for prepaid insurance and are not illustrated in detail. A common problem in auditing prepayments is the auditor's tendency to perform excessive work on relatively immaterial balances. This problem is due in part to the usually uncomplicated and easily verifiable nature of the accounts. An auditor must resist the temptation to dwell on immaterial and uncomplicated accounts and concentrate on the more difficult audit areas.

SUMMARY OF IMPORTANT AUDIT PROCEDURES FOR PREPAYMENTS

• Review and evaluate the effect of the internal control structure on the scope of prepayments work.

• Perform analytical procedures.

• Examine invoices and other documents for additions to prepayments.

• Test calculation of amortization for the period and ending balances.

• Review insurance coverage.

Chapter 15
Glossary of Terms

(listed in order of appearance in the chapter, with accompanying page reference where the term is discussed)

Term		*Page in Chapter*
Cutoff bank statement	a bank statement, usually for a portion of a month, sent directly from the bank to the auditor for use in testing the validity of certain cash balances and transactions.	576
Kiting	the practice of (1) recording an interbank transfer as a deposit in one period and as a disbursement in the subsequent period to improperly inflate the cash balance or (2) covering a cash shortage with an unrecorded check on an out-of-town bank.	576

| | Page in |
| Term | Chapter |

Lapping   an irregularity involving the substitution of cash items to cover mis-   576
appropriated funds and the delayed posting of collections to the detail
accounts receivable records.

Block reconciliation (proof of cash)   a form of bank reconciliation that "blocks   578
in" a period so that all cash transactions for that period can be accounted
for and tested

Alternative procedures   procedures employed when the audit procedure pro-   585
ducing the most competent evidence cannot be completed, for example,
internal documents such as sales invoices, shipping documents, and evidence of collection may be examined if a customer fails to reply to accounts receivable confirmation requests.

Chapter 15
References

American Institute of Certified Public Accountants. *Professional Standards*.

AU Section 331—Receivables and Inventories.

Ashton, Robert H., and Hylas, Robert E. "Increasing Confirmation Response Rates,"
Auditing: A Journal of Practice & Theory (Summer 1981), pp. 12–22.

Bailey, Charles D., and Ballard, Gene. "Improving Response Rates to Accounts Receivable Confirmations: An Experiment Using Four Techniques," *Auditing: A Journal of
Practice & Theory* (Spring 1986), pp. 77–85.

Compton, John C., and Van Son, W. Peter. "Check Truncation: The Auditor's Dilemma,"
Journal of Accountancy (January 1983), pp. 36–38.

Johnson, Johnny R., Leitch, Robert A., and Neter, John. "Characteristics of Errors in
Accounts Receivable and Inventory Audits," *The Accounting Review* (April 1981),
pp. 270–293.

Krogstad, Jack L., and Romney, Marshall B. "Accounts Receivable Confirmation—An
Alternative Auditing Approach," *Journal of Accountancy* (February 1980), pp. 68–
74.

Walther, L. M. "Evaluating the Adequacy of a Client's Insurance Coverage," *Journal of
Accountancy* (June 1980), pp. 36–39.

Chapter 15
Review Questions

15-1. Why are assets more likely to be overstated than understated, and what effect does this have on the auditor's emphasis in the audit of assets?

15-2. Explain why the audit procedures applied to cash are usually more extensive than might seem warranted by the size of the cash balance.

15-3. Give an example and explain the importance of restrictions on cash.

15-4. State the objectives in the audit of cash.

15-5. What analytical procedures may an auditor apply to cash?

15-6. In an examination of a bank reconciliation, the auditor gathers evidence regarding the amounts shown therein. Indicate the evidence he or she would gather or examine in support of
a. The bank balance.
b. The book balance.
c. Deposits in transit.
d. Outstanding checks.

15-7. List two requests an auditor will make of a bank in connection with his or her audit of cash.

15-8. The standard bank confirmation provides the auditor with evidence relating to accounts other than cash. State how this is done.

15-9. What is the purpose of obtaining authenticated deposit slips from the bank? Explain the limitations on the effectiveness of this procedure.

15-10. What is the objective of testing interbank transfers?

15-11. Explain what is meant by "kiting."

15-12. What is the purpose of a block reconciliation or proof of cash?

15-13. State the objectives in the audit of receivables.

15-14.   Give three examples of the internal control structure that may affect the scope of substantive tests of accounts receivable.

15-15.   How can analytical procedures be applied to accounts receivable?

15-16.   What are "alternative procedures" and when are they performed?

15-17.   To which audit objectives are the procedures for the test of the allowance for doubtful accounts related?

15-18.   To which audit objective is the confirmation of accounts receivable related?

15-19.   List the factors an auditor would consider in evaluating the adequacy of the allowance for doubtful accounts.

15-20.   Discuss the audit procedures an auditor would employ to detect liens on or pledges of receivables.

15-21.   State the objectives in the audit of prepayments.

15-22.   Explain how the internal control structure relating to prepayments could affect the scope of the auditor's work in that section.

15-23.   What analytical procedures may an auditor apply to prepayments?

15-24.   What evidence would an auditor examine in support of additions to prepaid insurance?

15-25.   Why does an auditor review a client's insurance coverage?

Chapter 15
Objective Questions Taken from CPA Examinations

15-26.   To gather evidence regarding the balance per bank in a bank reconciliation, an auditor would examine all of the following *except*
a. Cutoff bank statement.
b. Year-end bank statement.

    c. Bank confirmation.

    d. General ledger.

15-27.   As one of the year-end audit procedures, the auditor instructed the client's personnel to prepare a standard bank confirmation request for a bank account that had been closed during the year. After the client's treasurer had signed the request, it was mailed by the assistant treasurer. What is the major flaw in this audit procedure?

    a. The confirmation request was signed by the treasurer.

    b. Sending the request was meaningless because the account was closed before the year end.

    c. The request was mailed by the assistant treasurer.

    d. The CPA did *not* sign the confirmation request before it was mailed.

15-28.   An unrecorded check issued during the last week of the year would most likely be discovered by the auditor when the

    a. Check register for the last month is reviewed.

    b. Cutoff bank statement is reconciled.

    c. Bank confirmation is reviewed.

    d. Search for unrecorded liabilities is performed.

15-29.   Listed in the table are four interbank cash transfers, indicated by the numbers 1, 2, 3, and 4, of a client for late December 19X8 and early January 19X9. Your answer should be selected from this list.

	Bank Account 1 Disbursement Date (Month/Day)		Bank Account 2 Deposit Date (Month/Day)	
	Per Bank	*Per Books*	*Per Bank*	*Per Books*
1.	12/31	12/30	12/31	12/30
2.	1/2	12/30	12/31	12/31
3.	1/3	12/31	1/2	1/2
4.	1/3	12/31	1/2	12/31

    a. Which of the cash transfers indicates an error in cash cutoff at December 31, 19X8?

    b. Which of the cash transfers would appear as a deposit in transit on the December 31, 19X8, bank reconciliation?

    c. Which of the cash transfers would *not* appear as an outstanding check on the December 31, 19X8, bank reconciliation?

15-30.   The cashier of Rock Company covered a shortage in the cash working fund with cash obtained on December 31 from a local bank by cashing, but not recording, a check drawn on the company's out-of-town bank. How would the auditor discover this manipulation?

a. Confirming all December 31 bank balances.

b. Counting the cash working fund at the close of business on December 31.

c. Investigating items returned with the bank cutoff statements.

d. Preparing independent bank reconciliations as of December 31.

15-31. Which of the following is one of the better auditing techniques that might be used by an auditor to detect kiting?

a. Review composition of authenticated deposit slips.

b. Review subsequent bank statements and canceled checks received directly from the banks.

c. Prepare a schedule of bank transfers from the client's books.

d. Prepare year-end bank reconciliations.

15-32. An auditor who is engaged to examine the financial statements of a business enterprise will request a cutoff bank statement primarily in order to

a. Verify the cash balance reported on the bank confirmation inquiry form.

b. Verify reconciling items on the client's bank reconciliation.

c. Detect lapping.

d. Detect kiting.

15-33. The auditor should ordinarily mail confirmation requests to all banks with which the client has conducted any business during the year, regardless of the year-end balance, because

a. The confirmation form also seeks information about indebtedness to the bank.

b. This procedure will detect kiting activities that would otherwise not be detected.

c. The mailing of confirmation forms to all such banks is required by generally accepted auditing standards.

d. This procedure relieves the auditor of any responsibility with respect to non-detection of forged checks.

15-34. On the last day of the fiscal year, the cash disbursements clerk drew a company check on Bank A and deposited the check in the company account in Bank B to cover a previous theft of cash. The disbursement has not been recorded. The auditor will best detect this form of kiting by

a. Comparing the detail of cash receipts as shown by the cash receipts records with the detail on the authenticated duplicate deposit tickets for three days prior to and subsequent to year end.

b. Preparing from the cash disbursements books a summary of bank transfers for one week prior to and subsequent to year end.

    c. Examining the composition of deposits in both Bank A and Bank B subsequent to year end.

    d. Examining paid checks returned with the bank statement of the next accounting period after year end.

15-35.   Auditors may use positive and/or negative forms of confirmation requests for accounts receivable. An auditor most likely will use
    a. The positive form to confirm all balances regardless of size.
    b. A combination of the two forms, with the positive form used for large balances and the negative form for small balances.
    c. A combination of the two forms, with the positive form used for trade receivables and the negative form for other receivables.
    d. The positive form when the internal control structure related to receivables is satisfactory, and the negative form when the internal control structure related to receivables is unsatisfactory.

15-36.   In the confirmation of accounts receivable the auditor would most likely
    a. Request confirmation of a sample of the inactive accounts.
    b. Seek to obtain positive confirmations for at least 50 percent of the total dollar amount of the receivables.
    c. Require confirmation of all receivables from agencies of the federal government.
    d. Require that confirmation requests be sent within one month of the fiscal year end.

15-37.   When scheduling the audit work to be performed on an engagement, the auditor should consider confirming accounts receivable balances at an interim date if
    a. Subsequent collections are to be reviewed.
    b. Control over receivables is good.
    c. Negative confirmations are to be used.
    d. There is a simultaneous examination of cash and accounts receivable.

15-38.   An auditor should perform alternative procedures to substantiate the existence of accounts receivable when
    a. No reply to a positive confirmation request is received.
    b. No reply to a negative confirmation request is received.
    c. Collectibility of the receivables is in doubt.
    d. Pledging of the receivables is probable.

15-39.   Lapping would most likely be detected by
    a. Examination of canceled checks clearing in the bank cutoff statement.
    b. Confirming year-end bank balances.
    c. Preparing a schedule of interbank transfers.
    d. Investigating responses to accounts receivable confirmations.

15-40.   Which of the following statements regarding the audit of negotiable notes receivable is *not* correct?

a. Confirmation from the debtor is an acceptable alternative to inspection.

b. Materiality of the amount involved is a factor considered when selecting the accounts to be confirmed.

c. Physical inspection of a note by the auditor does not provide conclusive evidence.

d. Notes receivable discounted with recourse need to be confirmed.

15-41.   An aged trial balance of accounts receivable is usually used by the auditor to

a. Verify the validity of recorded receivables.

b. Ensure that all accounts are promptly credited.

c. Evaluate the results of tests of controls.

d. Evaluate the provision for bad debt expense.

15-42.   Returns of positive confirmation requests for accounts receivable were very poor. As an alternative procedure, the auditor decided to check subsequent collections. The auditor has satisfied himself that the client satisfactorily listed the customer name next to each check listed on the deposit slip; hence, he decided that for each customer for which a confirmation was not received, he would add all the amounts shown for that customer on each validated deposit slip for the two months following the balance sheet date. The major fallacy in the auditor's procedure is that

a. Checking of subsequent collections is not an acceptable alternative auditing procedure for confirmation of accounts receivable.

b. By looking only at the deposit slip, the auditor would not know if the payment was for the receivable at the balance sheet date or a subsequent transaction.

c. The deposit slip would not be received directly by the auditor, as a confirmation would be.

d. A customer may not have made a payment during the two-month period.

15-43.   Once a CPA has determined that accounts receivable have increased because of slow collections in a "tight money" environment, the CPA would be likely to

a. Increase the balance in the allowance for bad debts account.

b. Review the going concern ramifications.

c. Review the credit and collection policy.

d. Expand tests of collectibility.

15-44.   To conceal defalcations involving receivables, the auditor would expect an experienced bookkeeper to charge which of the following accounts?

a. Miscellaneous income.

b. Petty cash.

c. Miscellaneous expense.

d. Sales returns.

15-45.   When auditing the prepaid insurance account, which of the following procedures would generally *not* be performed by the auditor?

a. Recompute the portion of the premium that expired during the year.

b. Prepare excerpts of insurance policies for audit working papers.

c. Confirm premium rates with an independent insurance broker.

d. Examine support for premium payments.

Chapter 15
Discussion/Case Questions and Problems

15-46.   In your audit of Ryan Company for the year ended December 31, 19X8, you note that the bank reconciliation for the Third National Bank Account contains a large unlocated difference, as shown in the following table.

Balance per bank statement	$142,267
Deposit in transit	3,864
Outstanding checks	(40,793)
Unlocated difference	10,846
Balance per general ledger	$116,184

From the bank statements (including the cutoff statement you received directly) and cash records, you determine the following:

1. A deposit in the amount of $3,678 of Rain Co. was credited against the company's account in error in December.

2. A check in payment of an advertising invoice cleared the bank in December in the amount of $10,318 that was recorded in the cash book at $1,318.

3. Unrecorded bank service charges for December amounted to $25.

4. Proceeds of a bank loan on December 1, 19X8, discounted for three months at 8 percent, had not been recorded by the company in the amount of $9,800.

5. No entry had been made to record the return for NSF of a customer's check of $7,898.

6. A deposit for the collection of accounts receivable was recorded as $21,079 whereas the actual deposit in the bank was $13,678.

7. A check for a salesperson's expenses recorded in the cash disbursement books and shown on the outstanding checklist as $612 cleared with the cutoff bank statement and was noted to be in the amount of $216.

8. The company is required by an informal agreement with the bank to maintain a compensating balance of $100,000.

Required:
a. State the objectives for the audit of cash.
b. State the procedures you would consider using to accomplish the objectives (the final determination would depend on your evaluation of the internal control structure, although it appears to be weak from some of the items noted above).
c. Prepare the adjusting entry and footnote disclosures necessary for a fair presentation of cash.

15-47.   The following interbank transfer schedule has been prepared in connection with the audit of Panther Creek Properties, Inc.

Deposit Date		Withdrawal Date		Amount of Deposit/ (Withdrawal)		
Per Books	Per Bank	Per Books	Per Bank	First Bank	Second Bank	Third Bank
12/31	12/31	12/30	1/2	(3,500)		3,500
12/30	1/2	12/31	1/3		5,000	(5,000)
12/29	1/2	12/31	12/31	9,000		(9,000)
12/31	1/2	1/2	1/3	3,000	(3,000)	

Complete the following summary as of December 31, assuming no deposits in transit or outstanding checks other than any that would result from the above transfers.

	First Bank	Second Bank	Third Bank
Total deposits in transit	_____	_____	_____
Total outstanding checks	_____	_____	_____
Total over/(under) statement of cash	_____	_____	_____

15-48.   During the year Strang Corporation began to encounter cash flow difficulties, and a cursory review by management revealed receivable collection problems. Strang's management engaged Stanley, CPA, to perform a special investigation. Stanley studied the billing and collection cycle and noted the following:

The accounting department employs one bookkeeper who receives and opens all incoming mail. This bookkeeper is also responsible for depositing receipts, filing remittance advices on a daily basis, recording receipts in the cash receipts journal, and posting receipts in the individual customer accounts and the general ledger accounts. There are no cash sales. The bookkeeper prepares and controls the mailing of monthly statements to customers.

The concentration of functions and the receivable collection problems caused Stanley to suspect that a systematic defalcation of customers' payments through a delayed posting of remittances (lapping of accounts receivable) is occurring. Stanley was surprised to find that no customers complained about receiving erroneous monthly statements.

Required:

Identify the procedures that Stanley should perform to determine whether lapping exists. *Do not discuss deficiencies in the internal control structure.*

(AICPA adapted)

15-49.   Your firm has been engaged to audit the financial statements of RST Inc. for the year ending December 31. RST Inc. is a medium-sized manufacturing company that has approximately 400 open trade accounts receivable and does not prepare monthly statements. The manager assigned to the engagement has decided to circularize the trade accounts receivable as of September 30 (three months before year end). The senior on the job asks you to be at the company on Wednesday morning, October 1, to mail requests for confirmation. He tells you to ask the company's personnel to prepare 25 positive confirmation requests and 100 negative confirmation requests. He further asks you to obtain an aged trial balance as of September 30, to trace the balances of the open accounts to the trial balance from the subsidiary ledgers, to test the aging, to foot the trial balance, and to compare the total of the trial balance with the accounts receivable control account in the general ledger. The senior also informs you that detailed tests of sales and cash receipts will be made for the month of September.

Required:

a. Enumerate the types of accounts you would want to include in your selection of accounts to be circularized by the positive method.

b. Enumerate the types of accounts you would want to include in your selection of accounts to be circularized by the negative method.

c. Outline a plan for maintaining adequate control over confirmation requests.

d. Outline the additional audit steps that should be undertaken at December 31, in support of the amounts shown as accounts receivable; the company is preparing for your use an aged trial balance of accounts receivable as of that date.

(Used with permission of Ernst & Whinney)

15-50.   Susan Start, a newly hired staff assistant of a CPA firm, was assigned to the audit team examining the financial statements of Rel-Hep Finance Company. The senior in charge of the engagement decided to assign Susan to the audit of the allowance for doubtful accounts.

During the course of this work, Ms. Start noticed that the allowance for doubtful accounts figure was only 1 percent of the accounts receivable balance, despite the fact that many large accounts were very old. She passed this information on to the senior who, in turn, asked the client about the low allowance percentages.

The client indicated that there was no particular problem, because the company's policy was to refinance slow paying customers. For example, if Customer A had not made any recent monthly payments on a $500 one-year note, the company would refinance the note over a two- or three-year period, thus lowering the monthly payments. Generally, additional credit was not refused a customer, regardless of the status of payments on an existing account. The client maintained that this policy made possible a low allowance because few accounts had to be written off.

Required:

a. If you were suspicious of the small size of the allowance account, what evidence would you gather to verify or alleviate your suspicions?

b. With accounts that are constantly being refinanced, what evidence can be gathered to develop a reasonable assurance that these accounts are collectible?

15-51.   The CPA firm of Wright & Co. is in the process of examining William Corporation's 19X4 financial statements. The following open matter must be resolved before the audit can be completed.

No audit work has been performed on nonresponses to customer accounts receivable confirmation requests. Both positive and negative confirmations were used. A second request was sent to debtors who did not respond to the initial positive request.

Required:

What alternative audit procedures should Wright consider performing on the nonresponses to customer accounts receivable confirmation requests?

(AICPA adopted)

15-52.   Com-See-Me, a retail furniture company, made a practice of assigning certain customer account balances to a local bank which, in turn, advanced the furniture company money. When the designated customers paid their bills, these amounts were forwarded to the bank.

As a condition of this financing arrangement, the bank required an annual audit by a CPA firm. During the course of the audit, the senior in charge was informed by the company controller that no circularization of accounts receivable confirmations would be allowed, because the company did not wish their customers to find out about the financing arrangements with the bank.

Selected financial data are shown below.

Accounts Receivable 12-31	$ 50,000
Total Current Assets 12-31	$ 500,000
Total Assets 12-31	$1,000,000
Net Income for Year Ended 12-31	$ 300,000

After consulting with the partner in charge of the audit, the senior informed the controller that no confirmation letters would be sent.

Required

a. Do you think that the CPA firm lost its independence by agreeing to this restriction on the scope of the audit procedures?

b. Without considering Question a, indicate whether you think this restriction should warrant an unqualified opinion, a qualified opinion, or a disclaimer of opinion. *AICPA Professional Standards,* Volume A (*SAS No. 2*), requires one of these types of opinions.

c. What evidence would you attempt to acquire in place of accounts receivable confirmations?

15-53.   You have been assigned to the audit of a medium-sized manufacturer of machine parts whose fiscal year ends October 31. You and the senior arrive at the same time on Monday, November 13, to start the field work for the completion of the audit. The controller gives the senior a package of working papers which he has had prepared for your use in connection with the audit. The senior gives you a copy of the accounts receivable aging schedule prepared by the company, the audit program, the internal control structure evaluation, and a file containing all working papers in connection with confirmation of receivables mailed on November 2. The file contains the following information:

Computer listing of accounts receivable at October 31.

A working paper showing the name, address, and balance of 12 customers to whom positive requests for confirmation were mailed.

Four customers' statements marked across the face "Do not mail."

Five positive requests that have been returned by customers confirming the balances as being correct.

Eight negative confirmations that have been returned with notations made thereon by customers.

Two positive and one negative requests returned by the post office marked "unknown" or with a similar designation.

The senior introduces you to the credit manager, the accounts receivable bookkeeper, and the billing clerk. She then instructs you to proceed with the tests of the aging schedule and completion of the audit work on accounts receivable, as outlined in the audit program, and advises that she will return the next day to answer any questions you have with respect to the accounts receivable and to review any items you think should be discussed with her.

The senior informs you that the computer listing of accounts receivable was prepared by the accounts receivable bookkeeper for your use in sending out the confirmations. Your representative checked the customers' statements against the listing and the accounts receivable detail ledger, but did not check the total of the listing. However, you note that the total at the bottom of the listing does agree with the total shown on the aging schedule prepared by the company. You are told that either positive or negative requests were sent to all of the 50 accounts.

The aging schedule is shown on page 607. You are to assume that the internal control structure is adequate. You should study the aging schedule and answer the questions that follow. The normal credit terms are net 30.

Required:

a. What auditing procedures should the audit program call for with respect to the aging schedule?

b. Which items on the aging schedule would you select for additional auditing procedures, why would you select them, and what procedures would you use?

c. What would you do with the computer listing prepared at the time the confirmations were mailed?

d. What would you do with the statements marked "Do not mail"?

e. Which items would you select for discussion with the senior?

f. What would you do with the five positive requests that were returned indicating no exceptions?

g. In examining these positive requests, what would you look for?

h. What would you do with the requests returned by the post office marked "Unknown" or with a similar designation?

i. What would you do with the negative requests returned with notations made by customers?

(*Used with permission of Ernst & Whinney*)

15-54.   Taylor Wholesalers distributes golf equipment to about 100 retail sporting goods stores. At June 30, 19X7, the end of the company's fiscal year, the distribution of the accounts receivable balances was as follows:

10 accounts over $50,000	$ 780,000
60 accounts under $50,000	1,100,000
30 accounts with zero balances	—
	$1,880,000

Aged Trial Balance—Accounts Receivable October 31

	Balance Dr.	Balance Cr.	Oct.	Sept.	Aug.	May– June–July	Prior
Allied Products Co.	$ 12,618.32				$12,618.32		
American Manufacturing Co.		$ 612.00					
B & D Machinery, Inc.	57,538.79		$ 35,123.76	$10,078.12	6,312.45	$ 6,024.46	
Best Equipment, Inc.	1,098.45		198.45				$ 900.00
Cooper, Frank M. (employee)	5,000.00					5,000.00	
Chalmers Motors, Inc.	7,445.83			1,263.17	2,376.28	3,806.38	
Davidson Engineering Company	3,573.35					3,573.35	
Drake Press Division	78,396.21		78,396.21				
Erie Machine Works, Inc.	6,215.63						6,215.63
Evans and Co. (deposit)	10,000.00		10,000.00				
Franklin Motors, Inc.	17,624.91		11,784.16	5,840.75			
Franklin Motors, Inc. (note)	25,000.00				25,000.00		
Globe Machinery, Inc.	30,248.65		25,932.40				4,316.25
Globe Machinery, Inc. (consignment)	103,487.98		50,116.73	28,745.27	12,678.93	8,319.00	3,628.05
Goldman Sachs	14,750.00		14,750.00				
Watkins Company	4,728.16		4,728.16				
Whitman, Inc.	16,512.54		16,512.54				
Young Machinery Co.	8,378.05		6,873.00	1,505.05			
	$495,444.00	$5,612.00	$328,577.92	$53,932.36	$66,768.91	$31,104.88	$15,059.93

No accounts receivables are past due. The internal control structure affecting accounts receivable is considered to be very strong. You have been furnished with the following audit program for substantive tests of accounts receivable.

1. Foot the detail accounts receivable ledger and compare the total with the balance in the accounts receivable control account.

2. Using customer numbers, randomly select 50 accounts for positive confirmation. Send second requests and perform alternative procedures where necessary.

3. Obtain a detail aged trial balance and test the schedule to the detail accounts receivable ledger. Select every third account and discuss its collectibility with the credit manager.

4. Examine all subsequent collection of accounts receivable during the month of July, 19X7.

What changes to the program, if any, would you suggest?

15-55.   During an audit of the financial statements of Gole Inc., Robbins, CPA, requested and received a client-prepared property casualty insurance schedule, which included appropriate premium information.

Required:
a. Identify the type of information, in addition to the appropriate premium information, that would ordinarily be expected to be included in a property casualty insurance schedule.
b. What are the basic audit procedures that Robbins should perform in examining the client-prepared property casualty insurance schedule?

(*AICPA adapted*)

Auditing the Working Capital Cell—Part II

Learning Objectives *After reading and studying the material in the chapter, the student should*

Know the characteristics of the inventory and current liabilities accounts.

Understand how important features of the internal control structure associated with each account affect the scope of substantive tests of that account.

Know the audit objectives of each account.

Be able to determine and apply the audit procedures necessary to accomplish the audit objectives of each account.

Understand the preparation of audit working papers to document the audit procedures for each account.

This chapter continues the discussion of the audit objectives, procedures, and selected working paper examples of the working capital accounts.

Inventories

Inventories is one of the most significant accounts for many industrial and commercial companies. Because of its effect on both working capital and gross profit the determination of inventory amounts can involve some of the most complex calculations in a company's accounting process. Also, the susceptibility of inventories to misappropriation and misstatement (high inherent risk) often requires extensive audit procedures if the amounts are material.

Inventories consist of physical goods to be sold, or consumed in the production of goods to be sold, in the ordinary course of business. In practice, materials and supplies that can be used in construction of property and equipment also are included in inventories.

The valuation of inventories has been the subject of several accounting pronouncements. Basically, these statements provide that inventories should be stated at cost, that cost may be determined under any one of several assumptions as to the flow of cost factors (first-in first-out, last-in first-out, average, etc.), and that inventories should not be valued in excess of market (generally the lower of replacement cost or net realizable value). The relationship between these accounting principles and the determination of audit objectives for inventories is illustrated in Chapter 12.

Though the principles appear to be straightforward, the auditor will encounter many situations that do not fit precisely within the principles. An auditor earns a professional reputation by arriving at an informed judgment as to the proper accounting in these circumstances. Consider the following examples. A plant, because of lack of sales orders, operates below capacity. Is the increased fixed cost per unit a properly inventoriable cost or is it an excess capacity cost that should be charged to expense as incurred? A client markets a new product that fails to gain customer acceptance and is selling very slowly. What is the net realizable value of the 100,000 units on hand when only 100 are sold each week at a retail price of $50 per unit? The client sells a chemical, the price of which fluctuates widely in the open market. Shortly after the end of the year, the price drops sharply. Should the client reduce the value of inventory to reflect the lower market price, or ignore the price drop on the basis that such fluctuations are normal and expected?

Because of the complexities of inventory calculations, the auditor must be particularly alert for inconsistencies in the inventory procedures. A change from the last-in first-out to the average cost method of pricing inventories would be apparent; changes in the method of determining quantities (i.e., the inclusion of goods in the current year that were excluded in the prior year because of obsolescence) and in the application of pricing methods (i.e., the inclusion of the storeroom operating cost in inventory one year and not in the next) can be less obvious, but still have a significant effect on net income.

An auditor normally reviews and tests the client's cost accounting system in the tests of inventory pricing. To do so, the auditor must be knowledgeable of the most generally used cost accounting systems, including process cost, job order cost, and standard cost systems. The auditor also must understand the physical flow of material and labor through the client's facilities to fully understand the operation of the cost system. Thus, it is necessary to look beyond the numbers. The internal control structure for inventories is closely related to purchasing, receiving, and accounts payable. Ordinarily, the responsibilities for ordering, receiving, storing, shipping, and accounting for the goods should be separated to the extent possible. In addition, the client should adopt procedures to ensure an accurate physical inventory (including specific written instructions, prenumbered inventory cards or listings, double counts of inventory items, etc.) and pricing. Because the internal control structure of several areas affect inventories, the auditor must consider the result of several tests of controls in evaluating the effectiveness of the internal control structure related to inventories. Tests of purchasing (purchasing and receiving), cash disbursements (accounts payable), payroll (labor costs), and sales (shipping) affect inventories and are illustrated in Chapter 8. Dual-purpose tests in the inventory area include physical inventory test counts and inventory pricing tests, both of which are illustrated later in this section. The auditor's evaluation of these controls determines the extent of subsequent audit procedures. As an example, the authorization of purchases, the recording of purchases, and the custody of the assets resulting from purchases should be separated. If such segregation of duties exists, the auditors might be willing to reduce the audit procedures that test inventory quantities.

Audit Objectives

The objectives (assertions) in the audit of inventories are as follows:

1. To determine whether the amount shown as inventories in the financial statements is represented by all (completeness) physical items on hand, in transit, or on consignment (existence).

2. To determine whether the inventory is calculated properly at the lower of cost or market in accordance with generally accepted accounting principles consistently applied (valuation).

3. To determine whether the inventory belongs to the company and whether any liens on the inventory are disclosed properly (rights and disclosure).

4. To determine whether any excess, slow-moving, or special-purpose items are properly valued and classified (valuation and presentation).

Audit Procedures and Working Papers

The first step is to review the internal control structure relating to inventories and to evaluate the results of tests of controls for the purchasing, receiving, shipping, cash disbursement, and cost accounting systems. As a result of this review, the auditor establishes the scope of work in this section. For example, if perpetual records are kept and inventory is maintained in secure storage areas under the control of a storekeeper with no incompatible duties, the auditor would perform a more limited inventory observation and make fewer test counts than if all employees had unrestricted access to inventory. Additionally, an auditor would perform more limited inventory pricing tests where a current, effective, and integrated cost accounting system was in operation than where such a cost system did not exist. Finally, the auditor would perform more extensive inventory cutoff

```
                                                                    C
                                 X Co.
                        Inventory Lead Schedule              J. Jones
                              12-31-X8                      1-20-X9

                                 As                              As
                            Adjusted Per Books             Adjusted
                   Index   12-31-X7 12-31-X8   Dr.    Cr.   12-31-X8

    Raw Materials      C-1    76,425 ✓ 51,014 ᴎ

    Work in process    C-2    29,760 ✓ 36,253 ᴎ

    Finished goods     C-3   151,903 ✓ 137,692 ᴎ

    Supplies           C-4    18,414 ✓ 18,071 ᴎ


                              276,502  243,030 ①

                               TB-1    TB-1

    ①  The plant manager stated that the decline in inventory
        was due to a decline in sales orders during the last
        quarter of 19X8. This was confirmed by examination of
        the sales backlog report as of 12-31-X8.

    ✓  Traced to prior year working papers.
    ᴎ  Traced to general ledger.
```

Figure 16.1   Inventory lead schedule.

procedures where there is no separate receiving department and prenumbered receiving reports are not used than where such controls did exist.

An illustration of the inventory lead schedule is shown in Figure 16.1, and the amount of finished goods is analyzed further by item in the summary of finished goods inventory shown in Figure 16.2. This illustration provides an example of how auditors satisfy themselves as to a total amount by systematically analyzing and auditing the components of that amount. By totaling the amount column, the auditor determines that the amount shown as finished goods is correct, *provided that* the individual amounts are correct. The individual amounts are determined by (a) the number of units, (b) the unit cost, and (c) the multiplication of the two. Thus, if the auditor is satisfied as to these three factors, he or she is satisfied as to the total finished goods inventory. Conversely, if any step is omitted (such as totaling the amount column), a link between the amount shown on the audit trial balance (and ultimately the financial statements) and the detail audit work (such as physical observation of the inventory) is broken. In this case, the auditor has no assurance that the individual amounts audited are represented in the financial statements. If they are not, any audit procedures performed on them

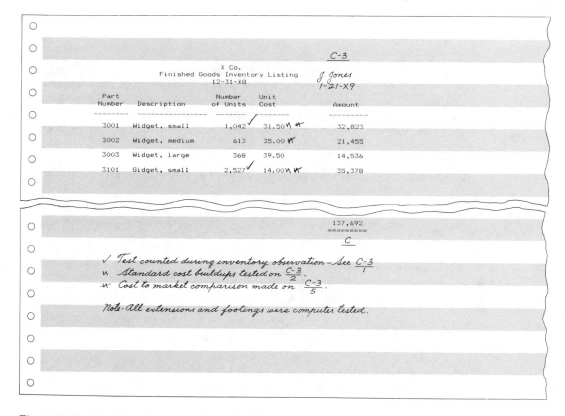

Figure 16.2   Finished goods inventory listing.

are meaningless. Therefore, it is important that the auditor maintain the audit link between the amounts audited and the amounts shown in the financial statements.

Analytical Procedures   The auditor may place considerable reliance on analytical procedures in the inventory area. Some important comparisons (by department or product line) that are often made include (1) gross profit ratios in current and prior year, (2) inventory turnover in current and prior year, (3) inventory and cost of sales in current year with current-year budget and prior-year actual, and (4) standard and unit costs of major items of inventory in current and prior years. Significant and unusual variations should alert the auditor to possible errors or inconsistencies in counting (existence), pricing, including obsolescence (valuation), or summarizing (completeness) inventories.

The Inventory Observation   The number of units is tested in the observation of the physical inventory to determine existence. This audit procedure is important enough to consider in some detail. AU Section 331.01 (*SAS No. 1*) states, ''. . . and observation of inventories are generally accepted auditing proce-

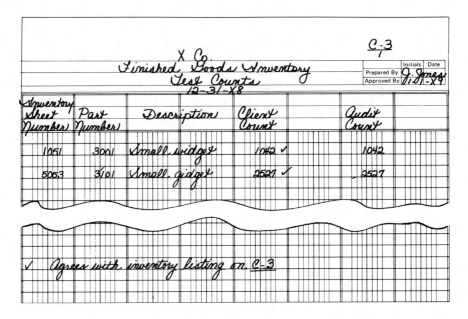

Figure 16.3   Finished goods inventory test counts.

dures. The independent auditor who issues an opinion when he has not employed them must bear in mind that he has the burden of justifying the opinion expressed.''

The client has the responsibility for *taking* an accurate physical inventory. Auditors *observe* this inventory-taking to satisfy themselves that it is accurate. This distinction is important, because if auditors take, rather than observe, the inventory, they assume the responsibility for a significant item involved in the preparation of the financial statements. Their independence regarding those statements therefore would be jeopardized.

Before the start of the physical inventory, auditors should review the client's written inventory instructions, looking for procedures that promote a complete and accurate inventory count by the client. To the extent they find such controls as double counts of high-value items, identification procedures to prevent double counting, or procedures for accurate recording and collecting of count totals, the auditors adjust the scope of the observation procedures.

During the actual inventory, auditors' emphasis should be on observing the counting procedures of the client's inventory teams to determine whether they understand the inventory instructions and are careful and diligent in carrying them out. Auditors also should test-count some of the items (the number depends on their evaluation of the client's procedures) as an additional test of the effectiveness of the procedures (Figure 16.3). Auditors normally record some, but not all, of their counts for subsequent comparison with the final inventory listing. The

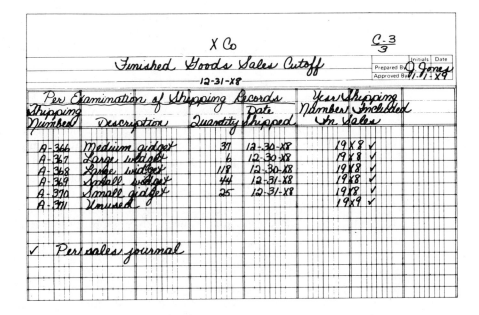

Figure 16.4   Finished goods sales cutoff.

purpose of this step is to detect any changes of the counts after they have been completed, as well as to provide a record of specific items counted by the auditors.

Though the recorded test counts provide evidence that counts of actual items are not changed later, they do not prevent the subsequent inclusion of additional count sheets or tags containing fictitious items. To guard against this deception, auditors should account for the numbers of all inventory sheets or tags as either used or unused. Also, they should record the number of the last line used on several inventory sheets. When the inventory later is compiled, the auditors should determine that it includes only items from inventory sheets they recorded as actually being used and that no items were added to the sheets for which they recorded the last line used.

During the inventory observation, auditors also obtain and test the information necessary to check the client's inventory cutoff; that is, that the physical item and its related cost were treated in a consistent manner (completeness). In the finished goods example, the cutoff must be tested to determine whether items included in inventory are excluded from sales, and vice versa. To test the sales cutoff, auditors prepare a schedule such as the one shown in Figure 16.4. The shipping number, description, quantity, and date shipped are obtained from the shipping department records during the inventory observation. The year in which the shipping number is included in sales is determined at a later date after all accounting transactions have been recorded. The schedule indicates that the sales cutoff was proper and that items shipped prior to the audit date were excluded from inventory and included in sales. Evidence regarding the sale cutoff also is gathered with the confirmation procedures in the accounts receivable section. If an item is recorded as a sale (and account receivable) before the end of the year but is not shipped until after the end of the year, the customer should take exception to a confirmation request that includes the unshipped item in the balance. This is one of many examples of the relation of audit procedures between working paper sections.

A final matter with which auditors must be concerned during the inventory observation is the existence of obsolete, excess, or slow-moving items (valuation). Often the plant personnel involved in taking the physical inventory, such as production and shop supervisors, storekeepers, and others, are very knowledgeable in this area, and some well-directed inquiries may yield pertinent information. The possibility of obsolescence also may be detected by the alert and inquisitive auditor who notes items with unusual amounts of dust or rust or prior-year inventory tags.

Because many of the audit procedures performed at an inventory observation cannot be quantified in working papers in a reasonable manner (such as observations of count teams, inquiries regarding obsolescence, etc.), it is common practice to summarize the work performed in a memorandum such as that shown in Figure 16.5. The memorandum describes, in reasonable detail, the steps taken to give the auditor relative assurance that a correct count was made. The last paragraph of the memorandum is the auditor's opinion concerning the client's inventory count. The writer of the memorandum noted a possible problem of slow-moving and possibly obsolete items. The note at the bottom of the memorandum indicates that a problem did exist and subsequently was solved by recognition of the obsolescence factor in valuing the inventory. All problems raised during an audit, both major and minor, must be resolved. Unresolved problems in an auditor's working papers may be damaging evidence in any subsequent litigation.

Inventories Held by Others If significant amounts of inventories are held by public warehouses or other custodians, the auditor may decide between direct observation and confirmation. We know from Chapter 12 that the general presumption is personal knowledge of the auditor is more competent evidence than knowledge of third parties. There are exceptions, however, such as bulk commodity storage. An auditor would probably receive little assurance that his or her client's inventory of 5,000 bushels of corn existed by observing a grain storage facility containing 100,000 bushels, some or none of which may represent the client's inventory. In this case confirmation with the facility may produce more competent evidence. If confirmation procedures are used to obtain evidence as to the existence of inventories, additional procedures should be performed such as investigating the client's controls over the warehouse activity, reviewing a report on the controls of the warehouse prepared by other CPAs, or observing physical counts at the warehouse. The point is to obtain evidence of the existence of the warehouse and inventory independent of and as a supplement to the confirmation.

Auditors have been victimized by obtaining what appeared to be proper confirmations of what turned out to be nonexistent inventories in nonexistent warehouses.

Tests of Inventory Pricing   The inventory pricing method and the type of cost system used by the client largely determine the audit procedures employed in testing inventory pricing. Because pricing methods and cost systems vary widely, so do the related audit procedures. The calculation of LIFO inventory requires not only the pricing of individual items, but also overall calculations of inventory layers based on price index numbers. Compliance with federal income tax regulations is an important aspect of the audit of LIFO inventory calculations. Finished goods prices based on the FIFO or average cost method can be determined by the use of job-order, process, or standard costs. The audit of a job-order cost system usually involves a review of the categories of cost flowing through the control accounts (material, labor, and overhead) and tests of these costs in the jobs in progress at year end. The auditor of a process cost system concentrates on the flow and accumulation of costs by cost center for the major products. In a standard cost system, the audit emphasis is on testing the standard cost buildups for major inventory items and reviewing variances for an approximation of actual costs.

Cost, however, is only one aspect of inventory pricing. The auditor also must determine that cost does not exceed market. As previously noted, the lower of current replacement cost or net realizable value is the proper accounting principle for inventory pricing. The replacement cost test often is made on an overall basis by reviewing the unit cost of production after the end of the year as well as reviewing the unit cost of major raw material items. A decline in either of these costs may indicate that replacement cost is lower than inventory cost and that a detailed analysis by product should be made. Net realizable value normally is defined as net selling price less estimated cost to sell. Cost to sell often is estimated as a percentage of the net selling price and computed by dividing total selling expense by sales.

An example of a raw materials price test is shown in Figure 16.6, where the prices used to calculate the inventory are compared with the purchase prices of the items (this is a simplified example that assumes a FIFO method; many inventory pricing tests are more complicated). Note that the auditor lists and examines the number of most recent vendor invoices necessary to cover the quantity of each inventory item tested.

Tests of Summarization   The auditor must ascertain whether the inventory has been properly summarized (completeness and valuation). Tests of the client's inventory summary schedules include (1) tracing physical quantities to the client's count records and the auditor's recorded test counts, (2) tracing prices to the client's cost accounting records and the auditor's price test working papers, (3) reviewing the unit of measure for reasonableness in relation to quantity and price (e.g., if paint is counted and recorded in units of gallons but is priced in units of

X CO.

INVENTORY OBSERVATION MEMORANDUM

Prepared by: Dan Sharp

Date: 1-1-X9

Kim McDoniel and I arrived at the Manufacturing Plant at 7:00 a.m. on 1-1-X9 to begin our inventory observation. The first thing we did was to obtain a copy of the inventory instructions and discuss them with the Controller. We took a plant tour and discussed with the Controller the sequence in which he wished to have the inventory observed and cleared since the Company wanted to begin production as soon as possible in every area and wanted to do so in the production cycle sequence.

Kim McDoniel and I began observing the count team procedures and making test counts in the designated areas. Upon completion of one area, we would clear it and production would begin. The client was to work only within that area, i.e., there was no movement from that area into other areas of the plant. Then we would go to the next area that was ready.

Kim called me to the raw materials area where she had been observing procedures and making test counts while I was clearing the area. She indicated that several dozen feet of pipe were not on the inventory at all and other items were recorded at obviously wrong amounts. According to the monthly inventory summaries, it would have been impossible to use the quantities that would have been necessary to get this amount reduced to what the inventory showed at this time. I discussed this with the Controller who assigned a new count team to the area with instructions to recount all items. Subsequent test counts by Kim indicated that the recounts were accurate. In all other cases, the inventory teams appeared to understand their instructions and to be working conscientiously.

We went back to the main plant and continued the inventory in all areas and cleared them as soon as possible. Kim McDoniel and I split up these areas and made selected test counts on Xerox copies of the client's count sheets which we maintained for controls and as a record of our test counts. We inquired of the individuals in charge of the inventory in each area as to obsolete, excess or slow moving goods, and they knew of none except for a small pile of scrap which was excluded from the inventory. We saw no items during our observation that appeared obsolete, excess, or slow moving.

Figure 16.5   Inventory observation memorandum.

Inventory Observation Memorandum
Page 2
Date: 1-1-X9

We accumulated the last five receiving documents before inventory
and the first five after the inventory that had been received on
1-1-19X9. We also had the shipping cut-off accumulated. This
amounts to five shipping documents before inventory and one shipping document for a shipment on 1-1-19X9.

Per the inventory instructions, the client personnel were to place
an X beside each item on their count sheets if it had not been used
at all in the last 6 months. This was done and there are several
throughout the count sheets. These will have to be followed up at
final to see that they are properly valued in the final inventory
listing.

See ① below.

In my opinion, the procedures followed by the client resulted in a
correct and accurate count of all goods on hand at 12-31-19X8, and
all slow moving material was properly identified as such for later
follow up.

Dan Sharp
1-1-X-9

① All items indicated by an X were reduced in value by 25% in the
final inventory listing to recognize their slow moving and possibly obsolete nature. Our review indicates that the 25% is reasonable.

J. Jones
1-21-X9

Figure 16.5   (Continued)

barrels, a substantial inventory error could result), (4) testing the calculations of quantity times price, and (5) adding the dollar amounts of individual inventory items to arrive at the total inventory amount. If the client's inventory is maintained on EDP equipment and the auditor uses a generalized computer audit program as described in Chapter 14, most of these procedures would be applied to all inventory items; otherwise, the procedures would probably be applied on a test basis.

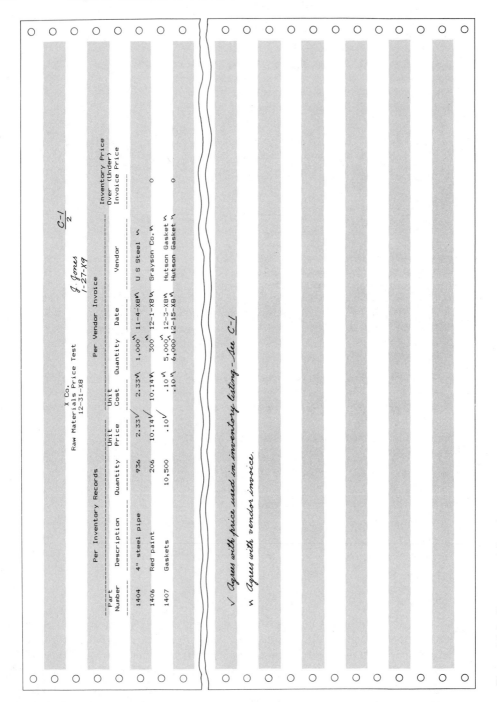

X Co.
Raw Materials Price Test
12-31-X8

J. Jones
1-27-X9

$\frac{C-1}{2}$

Part Number	Description	Per Inventory Records			Per Vendor Invoice				Inventory Price Over (Under) Invoice Price
		Quantity	Unit Price	Unit Cost	Quantity	Date	Vendor	
1404	4" steel pipe	936	2.33 √	2.33 ʌ	1,000	11-4-X8 ʌ	U S Steel ʌ	
1406	Red paint	206	10.14 √	10.14 ʌ	300	12-1-X8 ʌ	Grayson Co. ʌ	0
1407	Gaskets	10,500	.10 √	.10 ʌ	5,000	12-3-X8 ʌ	Hutson Gasket ʌ	
				.10 ʌ	6,000	12-15-X8 ʌ	Hutson Gasket ʌ	0

√ *Agrees with price used in inventory listing - See C-1*

ʌ *Agrees with vendor invoice.*

Figure 16.6 Raw materials price test.

Review for Obsolete, Excess, or Slow-Moving Inventory   The auditor's review for obsolete, excess, or slow-moving inventory must extend beyond the inquiries and observations during the inventory observation to include inquiry of top management and a review of perpetual or other inventory usage records. Though top management may not be as familiar with the usage of individual items as a shop supervisor, they will be more knowledgeable of major policy decisions that could result in large-scale obsolescence, such as plans to discontinue a product line or to make significant changes in a product. For this reason, the subject of obsolete inventory is discussed with top management and often is included in the management representation letter. Perpetual or other inventory usage records usually are examined for major items to determine whether the quantity on hand will be used in a reasonable time on the basis of past usage. The business approach can be useful also if the auditor is aware of industry trends in product changes, supplies of raw materials, and manufacturing processes.

Review for Liens or Pledges of Inventory (Disclosure)   The inventory audit procedures designed to detect liens and pledges of inventories are similar to those for accounts receivable, including the review of minutes and debt instruments, confirmation with financial institutions with which the client does business, and inquiry of management. One unique aspect of inventory subject to lien is that it sometimes is fenced or otherwise segregated from other inventory; financial institutions occasionally place signs in the area stating that the inventory is pledged. Such restrictions on the inventory should be noted during the inventory observation.

Other Inventory Procedures   There is no single approach to the audit of inventories. Certain types of inventories require laboratory analysis (to be sure, for example, that an underground gasoline tank is not filled with water). The ingenuity of the auditor is a key factor in the examination of inventories. The auditor may also ask management to make certain formal representations regarding inventory such as that all excess or obsolete inventory has been reduced to net realizable value and that the client has satisfactory title to all inventory (see page 704 in Chapter 18 for the form of such representations).

SUMMARY OF IMPORTANT PROCEDURES FOR INVENTORY

• Review and evaluate the effect of the internal control structure on the scope of inventory work.

• Perform analytical procedures.

- Observe client counts of inventory quantities and perform test counts.

- Account for and control inventory tags or listings.

- Test inventory shipping and receiving cutoffs.

- Test inventory pricing to determine that lower of cost or market concept is used.

- Test summarization of inventory.

- Review for obsolete, excess, or slow-moving inventory through inquiry, observation, and review of perpetual inventory records.

- Search for liens or pledges of inventory by review of minutes, debt instruments, and confirmations.

Current Liabilities

In examining assets, an auditor places primary emphasis on verifying the amounts recorded as assets (existence). In examining liabilities, however, the auditor should place primary emphasis not on what is recorded, but on what is *not* recorded (completeness). The auditor seldom finds amounts recorded as liabilities that are not liabilities, but unrecorded liabilities are not unusual. In fact, they are inherent in an accounting process with periodic reporting. At some time, a decision must be made to terminate the accounting process and to issue financial statements with the understanding that revisions will be made only if material.

Although controls normally are established to detect unrecorded liabilities in a major area such as the purchase of raw materials, many minor liabilities such as the late reimbursement of an expense account or small utility bills do not become known until after the accounting process has been terminated. In addition, few companies attempt to record the exact amount of every existing liability at each periodic closing of the accounting records (although the amount unrecorded should be immaterial), because some liabilities such as taxes, insurance, and royalties cannot be determined precisely until some later time. For these reasons, the business approach to the audit must be used if the auditor is to make a sufficient investigation of both recorded and unrecorded liabilities.

Current liabilities include both amounts currently due (such as accounts payable) and amounts that have been incurred but are not yet due (such as accrued interest payable). Normally, the amounts not due are expected to be due within one year.

Although accounts payable and accrued liabilities normally are unsecured, in some circumstances assets can be held by others or pledged to secure their payment. Also, officers, stockholders, or other companies may guarantee payment. Short-term notes payable and the current portion of long-term debt often are collateralized. All of these conditions should be disclosed in the financial statements. Any other factors regarding current liabilities that are important in evaluating the financial statements should be disclosed, such as amounts due officers and stockholders or significant amounts of past-due accounts payable.

The accounting records in support of current liabilities usually are much less extensive than those supporting current assets. Many companies merely list and record by journal entry in one year all unpaid invoices applicable to that year that are received by some specified cutoff date (say the 20th of the following month) in the next year. Accrued liabilities usually are recorded by journal entry and supported by worksheet computations.

The internal control structure for accounts payable is related closely to controls over purchasing, receiving, cash disbursements, and inventory, whereas control over accruals normally is exercised by controlling the related expense account.

Audit Objectives

The objectives (assertions) in the audit of current liabilities are as follows:

1. To determine whether all (completeness) current liabilities existing or incurred (existence and obligations) as of the audit date are reflected properly in the financial statements (valuation).

2. To determine whether current liabilities consist of amounts due within one year or the natural operating cycle of the business (presentation).

3. To determine whether disclosures concerning current liabilities are adequate (disclosure).

Audit Procedures and Working Papers

The audit procedures and working papers applicable to accounts payable and accrued liabilities are considered in this section; the current portion of long-term debt and notes payable are considered in the long-term liability section.

Analytical Procedures   For accounts payable and accrued liabilities the auditor may compare (1) current-year balances with current-year budget and prior-year actual, (2) ratio of accounts payable to purchases for current and prior years, (3) overdue accounts payable to total accounts payable for current and prior years, and (4) balances due to related parties for current and prior years. Note that it is not sufficient to establish that there is no change between periods;

the auditor must also consider whether there should be a change that does not appear. If the auditor knows property tax rates increased in the current year, for example, substantially equal accrued property tax balances between years should be investigated.

Accounts Payable   As part of the first step of evaluating the internal control structure for accounts payable, the auditor must consider, on the basis of the procedures and controls used, the potential for the existence of material unrecorded liabilities. The potential for unrecorded liabilities is evaluated in part on the results of control risk assessment tests of controls for the purchasing and cash disbursements functions and in part on dual-purpose tests of procedures for recording liabilities and the resulting account balances. The magnitude of this potential determines the scope of subsequent procedures.

A review of the purchases controls in Chapter 8 shows that the vendor's invoice and the company's receiving report are compared in the accounts payable department. The existence of this procedure should lower the probability that received merchandise is not accounted for and that some accounts payable invoices might be unrecorded. On this basis, the auditor might reduce the tests that search for unrecorded liabilities. Other examples are (1) client review and investigation of prenumbered purchase orders and receiving reports that are unmatched with vendor invoices at month end, (2) client reconciliation of monthly statements received from vendors to recorded accounts payable, and (3) monthly reconciliation of detail accounts payable with the general ledger control account. All of these controls should reduce the likelihood of unrecorded accounts payable and allow the auditor to reduce the number of accounts payable confirmations sent. The existence and completeness of accounts payable generally are tested by confirmation of balances with vendors and a review of disbursements after the audit date.

Confirmation   Confirmation of accounts payable is not designated specifically as a generally accepted auditing procedure in *SAS No. 1,* as is the confirmation of accounts receivable; nevertheless, it is a procedure that most auditors use.[1] One must keep in mind the difference in approaches to auditing assets and liabilities to understand the method of selecting the accounts to which confirmation requests will be sent. Recall that in the audit of liabilities the auditor is more concerned with what is not recorded but should be than with what is recorded. Therefore, confirmation requests generally are sent to a client's principal vendors and suppliers, regardless of their account balance at the audit date. Confirmations thus test completeness as well as existence. The auditor's objective

---

[1] The requirements for the confirmation of accounts receivable (and the physical observation of inventories) arose as a result of the *McKesson Robbins* case, which was discussed in Chapter 4. The fraud was largely perpetuated by the use of fictitious accounts receivable and inventories. Had significant unrecorded liabilities been a major issue, one can speculate that confirmation of accounts payable might also have been made a requirement in *SAS No. 1.*

may be to obtain confirmations from the accounts *most likely* to have large accounts payable balances, not necessarily from the accounts that have large *recorded* balances. For this reason, the auditor often sends confirmation requests to accounts with zero balances. The auditor is not attempting to obtain a high dollar coverage of account balances but is searching for unrecorded liabilities. Consider the following example.

Vendor	Purchases from Vendor During the Year	Payable Balance at End of Year
A Company	$ 35,000	$ 11,000
B Company	1,150,000	110,000
C Company	1,200,000	—
D Company	246,000	30,000

In this case, the auditor may select B and C for confirmation, even though both A and D have larger year-end balances than C. A sample of other accounts may also be confirmed.

Accounts selected for confirmation are listed on a confirmation control schedule such as Figure 16.7. This schedule serves the dual purpose of recording the amount confirmed by the vendor and reconciling it to the amount shown in the client's detailed accounts payable listing. All differences between the client's accounting records and the confirmation from the vendor should be not only reconciled but also audited. In Figure 16.7, the payment in transit from the client to the vendor has been traced to the outstanding checklist in the bank reconciliation (indicated by $\checkmark$; also see Figure 15.3). The auditor must understand the relationships of the various sections of the audit well enough to realize instinctively that if a vendor had not received a payment from the client that was made before or on the audit date, the check could not have cleared the bank by the audit date and, therefore, must be listed as outstanding. In Figure 16.7, the unrecorded liability was traced to the vendor's invoice for a December purchase that was recorded by the client in January (indicated by Ⓐ). Because the amount is immaterial, it has been posted to the summary of entries passed for consideration in the aggregate. If the amount had been material, the auditor would have proposed an adjusting entry.

An illustration of an accounts payable confirmation is shown in Figure 16.8. It is similar to an accounts receivable confirmation in that it requests an outside party to provide information about the client directly to the auditor; however, an important difference is that whereas the accounts receivable confirmation contains the customer's balance according to the client's records, the accounts payable confirmation contains a request for the vendor to state the balance due from the client and attach a statement of the items making up the balance. The differ-

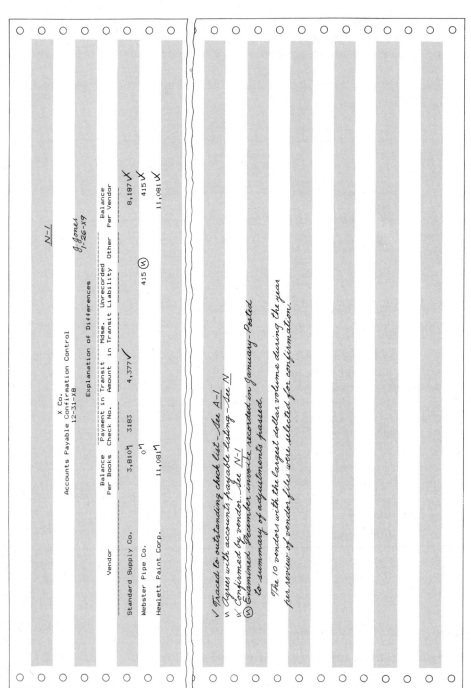

Figure 16.7 Accounts payable confirmation control.

```
                         X CO.
                    122 WEST AVE.
              CENTER CITY, ARKANSAS 70000            N - 1
                                                     ———
                                                      1

                                                January 2, 19X9


Standard Supply Co.
222 Elm Street
Center City, Arkansas 70000

Gentlemen:

      Our auditors, Partner & Co., are now engaged in an examina-
tion of our financial statements.  In connection therewith,
please advise them in the space provided below whether or not
there is a balance due you by this company as of December 31,
19X8.  If there is a balance due, please attach a statement of the
items making up such balance.

      After signing and dating your reply, please mail it directly
to Partner & Co., 999 Verify Street, Center City, AR 70000.  A
stamped, addressed envelope is enclosed for your convenience.



                              Very truly yours,

                              Bruce Lee
                              Bruce Lee
                              Controller



Partner & Co.:                           N-1
                                         8187⁰⁰
Our records indicate that a balance of $_____ was due from X
Co. at December 31, 19X8, as itemized in the attached statement.
Dated: 1-11-X9 _____ Signed: Von Graham, Treas.
```

Figure 16.8 Accounts payable confirmation.

ence is due to the different emphasis in auditing assets and liabilities. With the accounts receivable confirmation, the auditor is attempting to verify the recorded balance; with the accounts payable confirmation, he or she is attempting to learn of all amounts due to a vendor whether recorded or not.

Review of Subsequent Disbursements   The second procedure used in the audit of accounts payable is the review of disbursements subsequent to the audit date (usually performed as part of the review of subsequent events and transactions, discussed in another section). In making this review, which normally covers the period from the audit date to the date of completion of work in the client's office, the auditor examines unpaid invoices and the invoices or other support for disbursements to determine the period to which they are applicable (often a minimum amount is established to avoid examining minor items). If a disbursement is found that is applicable to the period before the audit date, the auditor reviews the accounts payable (and accrued liabilities) listing to determine whether the amount owed is recorded properly as a liability at the audit date. If it is not, it represents an unrecorded liability.

The advantage of this procedure is that it provides much broader account coverage than would be practicable with confirmations; the disadvantage is that any invoice representing an unrecorded liability not paid or received by the client prior to the end of the auditor's work in the client's office would not be detected. Such amounts may be detected by confirmation. Thus, a combination of accounts payable confirmation and a review of subsequent disbursements, together with work performed in other sections such as cash, inventories, and cost of sales, normally provides the audit evidence necessary to satisfy the auditor regarding accounts payable.

SUMMARY OF IMPORTANT AUDIT PROCEDURES FOR ACCOUNTS PAYABLE

- Review and evaluate the effect of the internal control structure on the scope of accounts payable work.

- Perform analytical procedures.

- Send confirmations to selected vendors; send second requests to vendors who fail to respond to first requests.

- Review disbursements subsequent to the audit date and unpaid invoices to determine whether any represent unrecorded liabilities.

Accrued Liabilities   The approaches to auditing accrued liabilities are as varied as the types of accrued liability accounts. Some can be tested by reference to the subsequent payment of the liability (accrued payroll and payroll taxes), whereas others must be estimated or calculated on the basis of transactions in other accounts (accrued interest on the basis of interest-bearing debt outstanding and accrued royalties on the basis of sales). Figure 16.9 illustrates an audit lead schedule for accrued liabilities.

The following are examples of the internal control structure that an auditor would consider in establishing the scope of substantive tests of accrued liabilities: (1) client use of standard monthly journal entries to record recurring accruals such as property taxes, interest, and so forth should reduce the likelihood of omitting the accruals and allow the auditor to make overall tests of reasonableness rather than detail calculations, and (2) client preparation and use of a tax calendar to serve as a reminder of tax return due dates should reduce the likelihood of overlooking the payment of various taxes, which in turn should permit the auditor to spend less time examining tax payments.

In Figure 16.9 accrued payroll has been tested on an overall basis by reference to the total payroll paid in the subsequent period. The auditor has determined the total payroll for the two-week period ended January 3, 19X9, by examination of the payroll register (indicated by x). This amount was multiplied by the fraction representing the payroll period in 19X8 (11 of the 14 days). The computed amount does not agree exactly with the amount recorded on the books because it was computed on an overall basis, whereas the book amount was computed by payroll group or individual employee. The difference, however, is reasonable and, furthermore, should not be considered an error to be posted to the summary of entries passed. Variations such as this are to be expected when overall tests are used, and they do not imply that the client's records are incorrect.

Accrued interest is cross-referenced to R, which is the schedule reference for long-term debt. The audit of accrued interest is discussed in that section.

Accrued property taxes are cross-referenced to a detail audit schedule, *P-1*, which is shown in Figure 16.10. This schedule summarizes the transactions in accrued property taxes for the year. The provision for property tax expense for the current year has been related to the expense section of the working papers and reviewed for reasonableness. This provision is an example of a situation in which an estimate must be made by the client and reviewed by the auditor, because it is assumed that the actual tax for the year will not be known until the tax bills are received at some date after the financial statements are issued. In practice, the period covered by the tax and the date the tax bills are rendered vary by taxing authority within each state. The auditor should be familiar with the practices of the taxing authorities within whose states his or her clients operate. In the example, the auditor was aware that there had been no tax rate increases and, from the audit of property, knew that there had been no significant variations in property balances. Thus, the auditor found that property tax expense in an amount approximately equal to the amount paid for the prior year was reasonable (indicated by ①). Note that merely comparing the provision for the current year with the amount paid for the prior year, without consideration of the factors that could

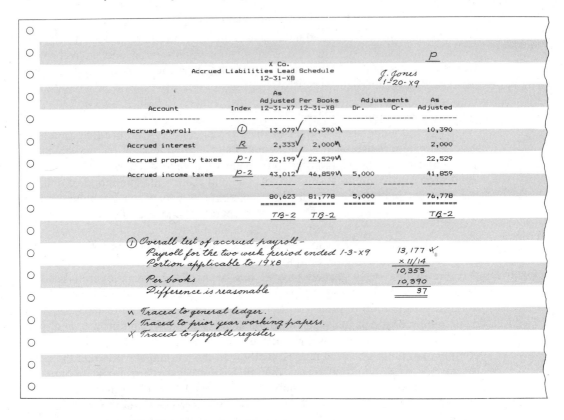

Figure 16.9   Accrued liabilities lead schedule.

make them different, is not effective auditing. The auditor also has examined *receipted* tax bills and canceled checks to substantiate the tax payments (indicated by √).

Because of the significance of income tax expense and the related accrued tax liability, the auditor should have a basic understanding of federal income tax laws and regulations, as well as those of the states and any foreign countries in which his or her clients operate. In addition, the auditor must comprehend the differences between pretax accounting income and taxable income, timing differences and permanent differences, income taxes and deferred taxes, and the myriad of other concepts in FASB pronouncements covering accounting for income taxes. With this knowledge, the auditor is prepared to begin an audit of income taxes. The procedure consists generally of an analysis of the accrual account for the year and the testing of payments during the year by reference to canceled checks and prior-year tax returns. The auditor also should check the calculation of income tax expense for the current year and the amount of any deferred taxes arising from timing differences, in all cases considering the propriety of the

```
                                                          P-1

                          X Co.
                   Accrued Property Taxes          J. Jones
                        12-31-X8                   1-20-X9

     Balance 12-31-X7                                22,199   P

     Accrual for property tax expense          (1) 22,500   20

     Payments during the year—
                   Check No.  Taxing Authority    Amount
                   ---------  ----------------    ------

                     2119     State of Arkansas   12,376 √
                     2280     City of Hypothetical 9,794 √  22,170
                                                  ------------------
     Balance 12-31-X8                                22,529   P
                                                  ==================
```

(1) *Provision for the year is reasonable as it approximates the amount actually paid in the prior year and there have been no tax rate increases or significant property additions.*

√ *Examined receipted tax bill and canceled check.*

Figure 16.10   Accrued property taxes.

amounts used in the calculations. In addition, the auditor should inquire as to the status of all unsettled prior-year returns and any revenue-agent examinations in progress. In many accounting firms, auditors prepare the income tax returns for the clients they audit, unless the client prepares his or her own return. In some cases, particularly in the larger accounting firms, a separate tax department prepares all tax returns.

In auditing accrued liabilities, the auditor must not become so involved with testing calculations and reviewing the reasonableness of estimates that he or she forgets where the emphasis should be placed in the audit of liabilities. The auditor must consider what accrued liabilities should be recorded that are not recorded (completeness). Because accrued liabilities generally are accrued expenses, a good starting point in a search for unrecorded accrued liabilities is the client's expense accounts. It is often necessary to accrue such expenses as payroll, payroll taxes, vacation pay, sick pay, commissions, insurance, income, property and excise taxes, pensions, bonuses, interest, profit-sharing, and royalties. The auditor should consider the necessity of these as well as other accruals in each audit.

SUMMARY OF IMPORTANT AUDIT PROCEDURES
FOR ACCRUED LIABILITIES

• Review and evaluate the effect of the internal control structure on the scope of accrued liabilities work.

• Perform analytical procedures.

• Examine subsequent payments of accrued liabilities made before the field work is completed and compare payment with accrued balance.

• Test computations of accrued balances by reference to such factors as interest rates, commission rates, royalty rates, tax rates, and historical data for accruals such as warranty costs, insurance, and so on.

• Determine that all necessary accrued liabilities have been recorded.

Chapter 16
Glossary of Terms

(listed in order of appearance in the chapter, with accompanying page reference where the term is discussed)

Term	*Page in Chapter*
Inventory cutoff a determination that items received before the inventory date are included in inventory, accounts payable, and purchases and that items shipped before the inventory date are excluded from inventory and included in sales and accounts receivable.	615

Chapter 16
References

American Institute of Certified Public Accountants. *Professional Standards*
AU Section 331—Receivables and Inventories;

AU Section 901—Public Warehouses—Controls and Auditing Procedures for Goods Held.

Johnson, Johnny R., Leitch, Robert A., and Neter, John. "Characteristics of Errors in Accounts Receivable and Inventory Audits," *The Accounting Review* (April 1981), pp. 270–293.

Chapter 16
Review Questions

16-1.   State the objectives in the audit of inventories.

16-2.   Give three examples of controls that may affect the scope of substantive tests of inventories.

16-3.   What analytical procedures may an auditor apply to inventories?

16-4.   Discuss the auditor's responsibility for an accurate physical inventory.

16-5.   What is the purpose of the auditor's review of the client's written physical inventory instructions?

16-6.   Comment on the following statement: "During the physical inventory, the auditor should make and record as many test counts as possible because his or her primary concern is to count as large a percentage of the dollar value of the inventory as possible."

16-7.   How does the auditor guard against inclusion in the final inventory listing of count sheets or tags containing fictitious inventory items?

16-8.   Why does an auditor record some inventory test counts?

16-9.   What is the purpose of the inventory cutoff test?

16-10.   What procedures can the auditor perform during the inventory observation to test for obsolete, excess, or slow-moving items?

16-11.   State the general approaches to auditing job-order, process, and standard cost systems.

16-12. Describe the audit tests made of the client's inventory summary schedules.

16-13. Why is the subject of obsolete inventory discussed with top management and included in the management representation letter?

16-14. Describe the audit procedures designed to detect liens and pledges of inventory.

16-15. How do the auditor's approach and emphasis in auditing assets differ from those in auditing liabilities?

16-16. State the objectives in the audit of current liabilities.

16-17. Describe how analytical procedures may be applied to accounts payable and accrued liabilities.

16-18. The auditor normally uses two approaches to the audit of accounts payable. What are they and why are both used?

16-19. How does the auditor select the accounts to which accounts payable confirmations will be sent? Why is this method of selection used?

16-20. What is the purpose of a confirmation control schedule?

16-21. What are the similarities and differences in the form of accounts receivable and payable confirmation letters?

16-22. How and for what period is the review of subsequent disbursements made?

16-23. Name two approaches to auditing accrued liabilities.

16-24. What background knowledge must an auditor possess to effectively audit income tax liability and expense?

16-25. What is a good starting point in an auditor's search for unrecorded accrued liabilities?

Chapter 16
Objective Questions Taken from CPA Examinations

16-26.   An inventory turnover analysis is useful to the auditor because it may detect
a. Inadequacies in inventory pricing.
b. Methods of avoiding cyclical holding costs.
c. The optimum automatic reorder points.
d. The existence of obsolete merchandise.

16-27.   An auditor would be *most* likely to learn of slow-moving inventory through
a. Inquiry of sales personnel.
b. Inquiry of stores personnel.
c. Physical observation of inventory.
d. Review of perpetual inventory records.

16-28.   An auditor will usually trace the details of the test counts made during the observation of the physical inventory taking to a final inventory schedule. This audit procedure is undertaken to provide evidence that items physically present and observed by the auditor at the time of the physical inventory count are
a. Owned by the client.
b. *Not* obsolete.
c. Physically present at the time of the preparation of the final inventory schedule.
d. Included in the final inventory schedule.

16-29.   If the perpetual inventory records show lower quantities of inventory than the physical count, an explanation of the difference might be unrecorded
a. Sales.
b. Sales discounts.
c. Purchases.
d. Purchase discounts.

16-30.   When perpetual inventory records are maintained in quantities and in dollars, and control over inventory is weak, the auditor would probably
a. Want the client to schedule the physical inventory count at the end of the year.
b. Insist that the client perform physical counts of inventory items several times during the year.
c. Increase the extent of tests for unrecorded liabilities at the end of the year.
d. Have to disclaim an opinion on the income statement for that year.

16-31.   A CPA is engaged in the annual audit of a client for the year ended December 31, 19X9. The client took a complete physical inventory under the CPA's observation on December 15 and adjusted its inventory control account and detail perpetual inventory records to agree with the physical inventory. The client considers a sale to be made in the period that goods are shipped. Listed in the following table are four items taken from the CPA's sales cutoff worksheet. Which item does *not* require an adjusting entry on the client's books?

Date (Month/Day)

	Shipped	Recorded as a Sale	Credited to Inventory Control
a.	12/31	1/2	12/31
b.	1/2	12/31	12/31
c.	12/10	12/19	12/12
d.	12/14	12/16	12/16

16-32. Which of the following is *not* one of the independent auditor's objectives regarding the examination of inventories?
a. Verifying that inventory counted is owned by the client.
b. Verifying that the client has used proper inventory pricing.
c. Ascertaining the physical quantities of inventory on hand.
d. Verifying that all inventory owned by the client is on hand at the time of the count.

16-33. In a manufacturing company, which one of the following audit procedures would give the *least* assurance of the valuation of inventory at the audit date?
a. Testing the computations of standard overhead rates.
b. Examining paid vendors' invoices.
c. Reviewing direct labor rates.
d. Obtaining confirmation of inventories pledged under loan agreements.

16-34. Some firms that dispose of only a small part of their total output by consignment shipments fail to make any distinction between consignment shipments and regular sales. Which of the following would suggest that goods have been shipped on consignment?
a. Large debits to accounts receivable and small periodic credits.
b. Large debits to accounts receivable and large periodic credits.
c. Numerous shipments of small quantities.
d. Numerous shipments of large quantities and few returns.

16-35. Purchase cutoff procedures should be designed to test whether or *not* all inventory
a. Purchased and received before the end of the year was paid for.
b. Ordered before the end of the year was received.

    c. Purchased and received before the end of the year was recorded.

    d. Owned by the company is in the possession of the company at the end of the year.

16-36.   Which of the following audit procedures would provide the *least* reliable evidence that the client has legal title to inventories?

    a. Confirmation of inventories at locations outside the client's facilities.

    b. Analytical comparison of inventory balances to purchasing and sales activities.

    c. Observation of physical inventory counts.

    d. Examination of paid vendors' invoices.

16-37.   When auditing a public warehouse, which of the following is the most important audit procedure with respect to disclosing unrecorded liabilities?

    a. Confirmation of negotiable receipts with holders.

    b. Review of outstanding receipts.

    c. Inspection of receiving and issuing procedures.

    d. Observation of inventory.

16-38.   An examination of the balance in the accounts payable account is ordinarily *not* designed to

    a. Detect accounts payable that are substantially past due.

    b. Verify that accounts payable were properly authorized.

    c. Ascertain the reasonableness of recorded liabilities.

    d. Determine that all existing liabilities at the balance sheet date have been recorded.

16-39.   In order to efficiently establish the correctness of the accounts payable cutoff, an auditor will be most likely to

    a. Compare cutoff reports with purchase orders.

    b. Compare vendors' invoices with vendors' statements.

    c. Coordinate mailing of confirmations with cutoff tests.

    d. Coordinate cutoff tests with physical inventory observation.

16-40.   Which of the following audit procedures is *least* likely to detect an unrecorded liability?

    a. Analysis and recomputation of interest expense.

    b. Analysis and recomputation of depreciation expense.

    c. Mailing of standard bank confirmation form.

    d. Reading of the minutes of meetings of the board of directors.

16-41.   Only one of the following four statements, which compare confirmation of accounts payable with suppliers and confirmation of accounts receivable with debtors, is true. The true statement is that

a. It is less likely that the confirmation request sent to the supplier will show the amount owed him or her than that the request sent to the debtor will show the amount due from him or her.

b. Confirmation of accounts payable with suppliers is a more widely accepted auditing procedure than is confirmation of accounts receivable with debtors.

c. Statistical sampling techniques are more widely accepted in the confirmation of accounts payable than in the confirmation of accounts receivable.

d. Compared to the confirmation of accounts payable, the confirmation of accounts receivable will tend to emphasize accounts with zero balances at the balance sheet date.

16-42.   Which of the following *best* explains why accounts payable confirmation procedures are *not* always used?

a. Accounts payable are generally insignificant and can be audited by utilizing analytical procedures.

b. The auditor may feel certain that the creditors will press for payment.

c. Reliable externally generated evidence supporting a client's payable balances is generally available for audit inspection on the client's premises.

d. Creditors seldom respond to confirmation requests so results are of questionable use.

16-43.   Which of the following procedures relating to the examination of accounts payable could the auditor delegate entirely to the client's employees?

a. Test footings in the accounts payable ledger.

b. Reconcile unpaid invoices to vendors' statements.

c. Prepare a schedule of accounts payable.

d. Mail confirmation for selected account balances.

16-44.   The audit procedures used to verify accrued liabilities differ from those employed for the verification of accounts payable because

a. Accrued liabilities usually pertain to services of a continuing nature, whereas accounts payable are the result of completed transactions.

b. Accrued liabilities balances are less material than accounts payable balances.

c. Evidence supporting accrued liabilities is nonexistent, whereas evidence supporting accounts payable is readily available.

d. Accrued liabilities at year end will become accounts payable during the following year.

16-45.   The auditor is *most* likely to audit accrued commissions payable in conjunction with the

a. Sales cutoff review.

b. Verification of contingent liabilities.

c. Review of post balance sheet date disbursements.

d. Examination of trade accounts payable.

Chapter 16
Discussion/Case Questions and Problems

16-46.   Audit procedures should be designed to accomplish specific audit objectives. Review the following inventory audit procedures and indicate which audit objectives are being accomplished and how.

a. Observe the taking of the client's physical inventory.

b. Account for the sequence of inventory tags and trace each tag to the physical inventory listing.

c. Compare the unit prices on the client's final inventory listing with vendor invoices.

d. Inquire of management as to obsolete goods.

e. Test the receiving cutoff to determine that only goods on hand are included in the final inventory listing.

f. Confirm inventory held by a public warehouse.

16-47.   Assume that a CPA's client proposes to have an independent firm that specializes in inventory taking count the merchandise rather than use their own employees. Under these conditions, would it be acceptable for the CPA to forego the inventory observation? Support your answer.

16-48.   Your audit client, Household Appliances, Inc., operates a retail store in the center of town. Because of lack of storage space, Household keeps inventory that is not on display in a public warehouse outside of town. The warehouse supervisor receives inventory from suppliers and, on request from your client by a shipping advice or telephone call, delivers merchandise to customers or to the retail outlet.

The accounts are maintained at the retail store by a bookkeeper. Each month the warehouse supervisor sends to the bookkeeper a quantity report indicating opening balance, receipts, deliveries, and ending balance. The bookkeeper compares book quantities on hand at month-end with the warehouse supervisor's report and adjusts his books to agree with the report. No physical counts of the merchandise at the warehouse were made by your client during the year.

You are now prepared for your examination of the current year's financial statements in this recurring engagement. Last year you rendered an unqualified opinion.

Required:

a. Prepare an audit program for the observation of the physical inventory of Household Appliances, Inc. (1) at the retail outlet and (2) at the warehouse.

b. As part of your examination, would you verify inventory quantities at the warehouse by means of (1) a warehouse confirmation (Why?) or (2) test counts of inventory at the warehouse (Why?)?

c. Since the bookkeeper adjusts the books to quantities shown on the warehouse supervisor's report each month, what significance would you attach to the year-end adjustments if they were substantial? Discuss.

(AICPA adapted)

16-49.   To audit a company's handling of the sales and purchases cutoffs at the close of the fiscal year ended December 31, 19X1, you have compiled the data listed on the following schedule. All sales and purchases of significant amount from December 26, 19X1, to January 4, 19X2, inclusive, are included. Refer to page 641.

The company realized a gross profit of 30 percent on each sale, and all sales and purchases were recorded as of the invoice dates. Items marked "B" were FOB destination; all other items were FOB shipping point.

The physical inventory taken by the company included only those items actually on hand as of the close of business December 31, 19X1. All items on hand were included except a special machine (see "A"). This special machine was made to order by the company's supplier for one of the company's customers and was in the shipping room ready for shipment. It was excluded from the physical inventory.

The company maintains a perpetual inventory system. The inventory account and the subsidiary records have been adjusted to the physical inventory.

Complete the schedule on page 641 by showing for each item the required adjustment, if any.

(Used with permission of Ernst & Whinney)

16-50.   Late in December 19X9, your CPA firm accepted an audit engagement at Fine Jewelers, Inc., a corporation that deals largely in diamonds. The corporation has retail jewelry stores in several Eastern cities and a diamond wholesale store in New York City. The wholesale store also sets the diamonds in rings and in other quality jewelry.

The retail stores place orders for diamond jewelry with the wholesale store in New York City. A buyer employed by the wholesale store purchases diamonds in the New York diamond market, and the wholesale store then fills the orders from the retail stores and from independent customers and maintains a substantial inventory of diamonds. The corporation values its inventory by the specific identification cost method.

INVENTORY CUTOFF TEST
ACS COMPANY
12-31-X1

Prepared _____ Initials _____ Date _____
Approved _____

Description	Selling Price	Invoice Data	Shipping Data	Receiving Data	Accounts Receivable Dr.(Cr.)	Adjustments			
						Sales Dr.(Cr.)	Inventory Dr.(Cr.)	Cost of Sales Dr.(Cr.)	Accounts Payable Dr.(Cr.)
Sales:									
a	6000 -	12-28-X1	12-27-X1						
b	8000 -	12-28-X1	12-29-X1						
c	5000-B	12-29-X1	1-3-X2						
d	6000 -	12-31-X1	1-3-X2						
e	7000 -	12-31-X1	1-2-X2						
f	9000-B	12-31-X1	12-31-X1						
g	4000 -	1-3-X2	1-4-X2						
h	5000 -	1-5-X2	12-31-X1						
i	6000 -	1-4-X2	1-5-X2						
Purchases:									
a	5000-B	12-27-X1	12-27-X1	12-31-X1					
b	7000-B	12-28-X1	12-31-X1	1-3-X2					
c	8000 -	12-31-X1	12-31-X1	1-3-X2					
d	7000 -	12-31-X1	1-3-X2	1-4-X2					
e	6000 -	1-3-X2	12-31-X1	1-2-X2					
f	9000 -	1-3-X2	12-31-X1	1-3-X2					
g	7000-B	1-4-X2	12-31-X1	1-3-X2					
h	4000 -	1-4-X2	1-5-X2	1-6-X2					

Required:

Assume that at the inventory date you are satisfied that Fine Jewelers, Inc., has no items left by customers for repair or sale on consignment and that no inventory owned by the corporation is in the possession of outsiders.

a. Discuss the problems the auditor should anticipate in planning for the observation of the physical inventory on this engagement because of the

    (1) Different locations of inventories.

    (2) Nature of the inventory.

b. (1) Explain how your audit program for this inventory would be different from that used for most other inventories.

    (2) Prepare an audit program for the verification of the corporation's diamond and diamond jewelry inventories, identifying any steps that would apply only to the retail stores or the wholesale store.

c. Assume that a shipment of diamond rings was in transit by corporation messenger from the wholesale store to a retail store on the inventory date. What additional audit steps would you take to satisfy yourself as to the gems that were in transit from the wholesale store on the inventory date?

(AICPA adapted)

16-51.   Decker, CPA, is performing an audit of the financial statements of Allright Wholesale Sales, Inc., for the year ended December 31, 19X0. Allright has been in business for many years and has never had its financial statements audited. Decker is satisfied with the ending inventory and is considering alternative audit procedures to gain satisfaction with respect to management's representations concerning the beginning inventory, which was not observed.

    Allright sells only one product (bottled brand X beer), and maintains perpetual inventory records. In addition, Allright takes physical inventory counts monthly. Decker has already confirmed purchases with the manufacturer and has decided to concentrate on evaluating the reliability of perpetual inventory records and performing analytical procedures to the extent that prior years' unaudited records will enable such procedures to be performed.

Required:

What audit tests, including analytical procedures, should Decker apply to evaluate the reliability of perpetual inventory records and gain satisfaction regarding the January 1, 19X0, inventory?

(AICPA adapted)

16-52.   You have been assigned to the audit of Hogeye Manufacturing Co. as of December 31, 19X8. Hogeye maintains its raw material inventory on a FIFO basis. The balance at December 31, 19X8 was $216,385. In performing the raw material inventory price test, you prepared an audit working paper that included the following items to which you wish to give further attention.

	Per Books		Per Vendor Invoices		
Item	Price	Quantity	Price	Quantity	Date Received
Springs	$1.15	1,037	$1.11	5,000	11-3-X8
Clips	.52	3,816	.52	4,000	1-6-X9
			.40	4,000	10-14-X8
Bars	2.50	11,509	2.50	5,000	11-18-X8
			2.05	7,000	10-31-X8
Paint	5.05	619	5.05	750	1-13-X7
Tin	3.13	7,616	3.15	10,000	8-20-X8

Other raw material items included in your sample and price tested with no exception total $53,118.

Required:

1. Determine the amount of pricing error in the sample.

2. Project the sample results to the population.

3. Discuss any of the preceding items you would investigate further and describe what revisions you would suggest to the format of the preceding audit schedule.

16-53. Mincin, CPA, is the auditor of the Raleigh Corporation. Mincin is considering the audit work to be performed in the accounts payable area for the current year's engagement.

 The prior year's working papers show that confirmation requests were mailed to 100 of Raleigh's 1,000 suppliers. The selected suppliers were based on Mincin's sample, which was designed to select accounts with large dollar balances. Raleigh and Mincin spent a substantial number of hours resolving relatively minor differences between the confirmation replies and Raleigh's accounting records. Alternative audit procedures were used for those suppliers who did not respond to the confirmation requests.

Required:

a. Identify the accounts payable audit objectives that Mincin must consider in determining the audit procedures to be followed.

b. Identify situations in which Mincin should use accounts payable confirmations and discuss whether Mincin is required to use them.

c. Discuss why the use of large dollar balances as the basis for selecting accounts payable for confirmation might not be the most efficient approach and indicate what more efficient procedures could be followed when selecting accounts payable for confirmation.

(AICPA adapted)

16-54. The following are situations or questions pertaining to the audit of accounts payable:

a. With regard to statements requested from vendors, the auditor's memo states,

"We requested statements from all vendors with balances over $2,000 as shown by the trial balance. "Do you feel this procedure is satisfactory? Give reasons for your answer.

b. Why should an auditor be particularly careful to investigate past due accounts payable?

c. Discuss some of the sources from which the auditor can prepare a list of vendors from whom statements should be requested.

d. All vendors' statements on hand and received by the auditor have been reconciled by the company at the auditor's request. How much checking of the recon-cilements should be done?

e. In connection with the year-end audit of trade accounts payable, the following are noted; describe briefly what each could indicate and what audit procedures you would follow in the circumstances:

  (1) Several long-standing credit balances.

  (2) A number of debit balances included in accounts payable.

  (3) A substantial dollar amount of purchase commitments in a situation of declining market prices.

(Used with permission of Ernst & Whinney)

16-55. Your firm has been engaged to examine the financial statements of Brown Appliances, Inc., for the year ended December 31. The company manufactures major appliances sold to the general public through dealers and distributors. Significant financial information of the company, as of December 31, is as follows:

Trade receivables	$12,000,000
Inventories	14,000,000
Property—net	6,000,000
Other assets	3,000,000
	$35,000,000
Trade accounts payable	$ 4,000,000
Other liabilities	6,000,000
Stockholders' equity	25,000,000
	$35,000,000
Net sales for the year	$74,000,000
Net income for the year	$ 3,000,000

You are to audit the trade accounts payable of a division of Brown Appliances, Inc. The trade accounts payable aggregate $2,500,000. Excerpts from a memorandum on control risk follows:

  Invoices from suppliers are received in the purchasing department, where they are matched with receiving reports and checked to the applicable purchase order for quantities and pricing. Invoices and receiving reports are then forwarded to the accounting department for clerical checking and final approval for payment.

On the payment date, invoices with attached receiving reports are separated into two groups: one group of invoices with prior-month distribution charges, the other group with current-month distribution charges. The check register is then prepared, with each group having a separate total and check number sequence. The accounts payable for monthly financial statement purposes is the total of the check register for invoices with prior month distribution charges. A voucher register is not maintained.

The purchasing department holds unmatched receiving reports and unmatched invoices.

Cutoff procedures as established by the company appear adequate; however, the company makes a practice of not recording inventory in transit.

Vendors' statements received by the company are forwarded to a clerk in the accounting department. He does not check all charges appearing on the vendors' statements, but does reconcile all old outstanding charges appearing thereon.

An accounts payable listing has been prepared by the company for the auditors. As explained above, this listing was prepared from the check register of December charges paid in January, and shows vendor, check number, invoice date, date paid, and amount. A quick review of the listing reveals the following:

> January-dated invoices amounting to $200,000 appear on the listing payable to Talley and Parks Advertising Agency, for advertising to appear in *Better Homes and Gardens* magazine in February and March. This was included in the year-end accounts payable listing at the request of the vice-president of advertising because she wanted to more closely match advertising department budgeted expense with actual expenditures for the year. The distribution was made to advertising expense.

> Amounts appear on the listing as payments for payrolls, payroll taxes, other taxes, profit-sharing plans, etc.

> No amounts appear on the listing for legal or accounting services.

Required:
Discuss the problems and procedures involved in auditing this company's accounts payable. Specifically discuss the auditing procedures you recommend be used in your examination and the adjustments you recommend be made to the accounts payable listing.

(Used with permission of Ernst & Whinney)

CHAPTER 17

Auditing the Capital Asset and Financing Base Cell

Learning Objectives   *After reading and studying the material in this chapter, the student should*

Know the characteristics of the accounts comprising the capital asset and financing base cell.

Understand how important features of the internal control structure associated with each account in the capital asset and financing base cell affect the scope of that account.

Know the audit objectives of each account in the capital asset and financing base cell.

Be able to determine and apply the audit procedures necessary to accomplish the audit objectives for each account in the capital asset and financing base cell.

Understand the preparation of audit working papers to document the audit procedures for each account in the capital asset and financing base cell.

The approaches to capital asset and financing base accounts are similar in that the beginning balance is established first (normally from the prior-year audit), and then the current-year transactions are audited. The audit of these accounts differs from the audit of working capital accounts, in which the auditor anticipates an almost complete turnover of the amounts included in the balance at the end of the year compared with those at the beginning of the year. Items such as property and equipment, long-term debt, and equity tend to have long lives, and once they have been established as properly recorded amounts, the auditor's concern is with the accounting for the ultimate realization or disposition of these items. Thus, if the auditor is satisfied with the beginning balance and current transactions, he or she generally is satisfied with the ending balance.

Property and Equipment and Accumulated Depreciation

The property and equipment accounts represent the cost of a company's productive facilities, which may be depreciable (costs of buildings and machinery), depletable (costs of natural resources such as oil and gas), amortizable (cost of leasehold improvements), or fixed (such as land). Leased property and equipment also are included in the balance sheet if they are capitalizable under generally accepted accounting principles. In certain limited situations, such as in a quasi-reorganization or in personal financial statements, property and equipment are stated on a basis other than cost. Section D40.102 of FASB *Accounting Standards* states, however, that "property, plant, and equipment shall not be written up by an enterprise to reflect appraisal, market or current values which are above cost to the enterprise." In recent years there has been an increased tendency to write down property and equipment where restructurings or other circumstances indicate that cost will not be recovered.

Cost is represented by cash or the value of other consideration given in the event of purchase. The determination of purchase cost can be complicated if stock or other securities with no ready market are used. Cost also may be represented by the sum of the direct costs of labor, material, and interest in the event of construction (an allocation of overhead may be applicable in some cases).

Even after a unit of property is acquired by purchase or construction, a continuing determination of its cost is necessary, because of the need to distinguish subsequent expenditures that represent its maintenance or repair. Additions, betterments, and improvements to a unit of property that are capitalized should result in either an extension of its original life (the conversion of a furnace to coal when gas becomes unavailable) or new or improved operations (the regearing of an electric motor to allow it to operate at high speeds), and often result in the retirement (removal from the account) of the converted or replaced part. Maintenance and repairs should be charged to expense as incurred, and include the costs of painting, cleaning, and overhauling, as well as the costs of repairing breakdowns. Although painting and cleaning prolong the life of an asset, such costs usually are taken into consideration in the establishment of its original life and, therefore, should not be capitalized.

Depreciation may be computed by any method that is "systematic and rational." The straight-line, declining-balance, sum-of-the-years'-digits, and unit-of-production methods are commonly used.

Because of the low volume of activity and the long-term nature of the assets, a company's detail accounting records for property and equipment often are not as elaborate or as carefully maintained as those for other accounts such as cash, accounts receivable, or inventories. Property and equipment records normally should include a detail property ledger and, if construction activity is significant, a construction work order system. These records are important to the company's determination and the auditor's examination of the cost of retired or abandoned assets. Formal policies regarding approval of capital expenditures, distinction between capital and maintenance expenditures, and the reporting and recording of asset retirements are significant aspects of the internal control structure in the property section.

Audit Objectives

The objectives (assertions) in the audit of property and equipment and related accumulated depreciation are as follows:

1. To determine whether the amount shown as property and equipment in the financial statements represents all (completeness) physical facilities (existence) owned by the company (rights) and associated with the productive process (presentation), and all retired or abandoned property is removed properly from the accounts.

2. To determine whether property and equipment are stated at cost that is properly capitalizable and whether depreciation expense is adequate and is computed in accordance with generally accepted accounting principles (valuation and allocation).

3. To determine whether the accumulated depreciation is reasonable in relation to the expected useful life of the property (allocation).

4. To determine whether the disclosures concerning property are adequate and in accordance with generally accepted accounting principles (disclosure).

Audit Procedures and Working Papers

The procedures necessary to satisfy the auditor depend on his or her evaluation of the client's internal control structure applicable to the property section, as well as in related areas such as purchasing and cash disbursements (illustrated in Chapter 8). For example, if supporting documents are examined at the time accounts payable vouchers are prepared, the auditors might adjust the tests of property purchases. Tests of procedures for distinguishing between capital and expense transactions and computing depreciation are dual-purpose tests; they will be explained later in this section.

Some other examples of the effect of the internal control structure on the scope of substantive tests of property and equipment are as follows: (1) a formal budgeting system with investigation of variances may detect payments that are misclassified between maintenance and property and allow the auditor to reduce the scope of his or her work on property additions and repairs and maintenance, (2) failure of the client to tag and periodically account for property and equipment may cause the auditor to increase the scope of his or her search for unrecorded retirements, or (3) review and approval of the monthly depreciation entry by a supervisor who did not actively participate in its preparation may allow the auditor to reduce the scope of his or her tests of depreciation expense.

The lead schedule for property and equipment and accumulated depreciation normally summarizes the activity in the major accounts for the year and relates the accumulated depreciation to the applicable asset account (Figure 17.1).

Analytical Procedures   The auditor should compare (1) the property and equipment account balances for the current year with the current-year budget and prior-year actual balances, (2) property and equipment additions to the capital budget, (3) depreciation expense for the current year with the prior year, and (4) ratios of accumulated and current-year depreciation expense to property and equipment balances of the current and prior years. Significant unexpected variations, or lack thereof, should be investigated for misclassified additions (presentation), unrecorded retirements (existence), or erroneous depreciation calculations (allocation).

Audit of Property Additions   The audit procedures for property additions are designed to determine whether the additions represent physical facilities owned by the company (existence and rights), are stated at cost (valuation), and are properly capitalizable (presentation). The auditor analyzes additions in greater detail than shown on the lead schedule. An example of such an analysis, often referred to as a vouching schedule, is shown in Figure 17.2. In this example, the auditor has chosen to examine all additions to equipment in excess of $2,000, although sampling plans also could be used. The audit procedure indicated by √ includes (1) examination of vendor invoice and canceled check, indicating that the item was owned by the company and recorded at cost, (2) examination of receiving report, indicating that a physical item was received, and (3) review of the capitalization decision based on the description of the item. Major additions should be traced to Board of Director approval in the minutes. Additional evidence of the physical existence of the item is gained from inspecting it during the inventory observation. The auditor also has noted by ① and ② whether each addition was a new or replacement item. This information is useful in auditing property retirements.

As a test for property units that may have been charged to expense (completeness), an analysis similar to that described above is made of the maintenance and rent expense accounts, and the work indicated by √ is performed. Because the review of the capitalization/expense decision is a significant aspect of this work, it often is performed simultaneously with the work on property additions.

Audit of Property Retirements   In the audit of property retirements, the auditor wants to determine whether recorded retirements are shown properly and, more important, whether there are significant unrecorded property retirements.

E

J. Jones
1-24-X9

X Co.
Property and Equipment and Allowance for Depreciation Lead Schedule
Dec. 31, 19X8

Depr. Rate	Description	Property and Equipment				Allowance for Depreciation			
		Balance 12-31-X7	Additions	Retirements	Balance 12-31-X8	Balance 12-31-X7	Additions	Retirements	Balance 12-31-X8
—	Land	55,041	0	0	55,041	0	0	0	0
5%	Buildings	287,869	19,013	10,854	296,028	21,751	13,037	10,379	24,409
10%	Equipment	226,526	24,757	9,678	241,605	61,702	21,065	8,374	74,393
33%	Automobiles	12,314	0	0	12,314	5,813	4,101	0	9,914
		581,750	43,770	20,532	604,988	89,266	38,203	18,753	108,716
		TB-1	F-3	F-3	TB-1	TB-1	20	F-3	TB-1

F-1
F-2

Figure 17.1 Property and equipment and accumulated depreciation lead schedule.

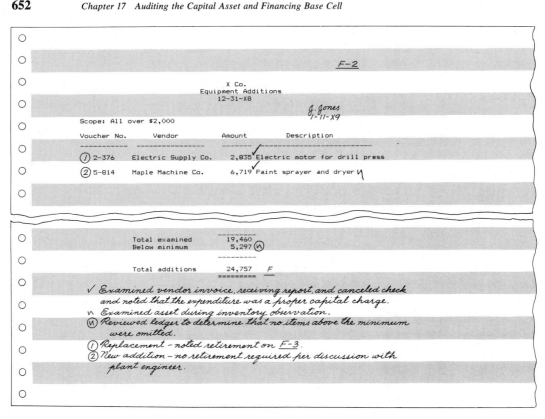

Figure 17.2   Equipment additions.

Figure 17.3 illustrates some audit procedures that might be applied to property retirements.

The recorded retirements are tested by tracing the original cost of the item, together with the dates acquired and retired, to the detail property ledger (indicated by √). Accumulated depreciation, if not recorded separately for each item, must be recomputed on the basis of the depreciation rate applicable to such assets and the periods they were held (indicated by ∧). Salvage proceeds can be traced to the cash receipts book or deposit slip (indicated by ✗). With this information, the resulting net gain or loss from property retirements can be recomputed and related to an income or expense account (see the reference to the *40* schedule). The remaining data relate to the federal income tax effect of the transactions and are used by the auditor in auditing the income tax liability and expense accounts.

The effectiveness of the auditor's search for unrecorded property retirements depends on his or her business knowledge and vigilance. As noted in the prepayment section, a reduction of property insurance coverage may be a result of property retirements. The auditor should investigate any significant reduction in coverage to determine whether it was due to property retirements and, if so,

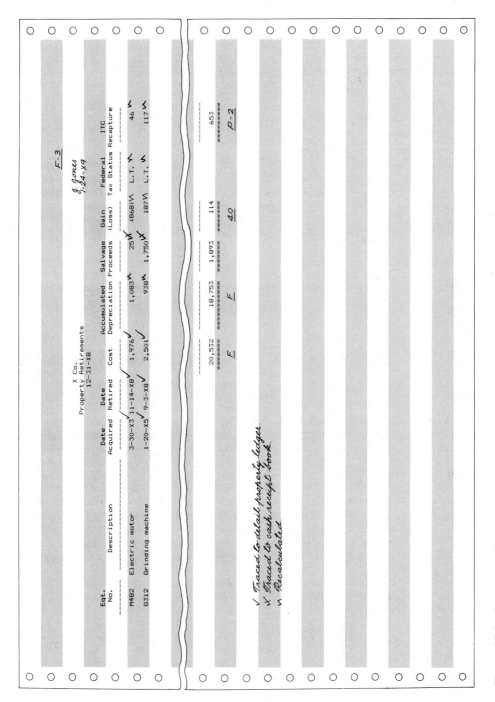

Figure 17.3 Property retirements.

whether the retirements were recorded properly. This example shows that an auditor must be aware of the impact of transactions in one section of the audit on balances and transactions in other sections. Also, in the work on property additions, the auditor noted whether major additions represented new or replacement items (see ① and ② in Figure 17.2). Because a replacement implies that an old asset was retired when the new asset was placed in service, the auditor can use this information to determine whether the retirement was recorded in the accounting records.

Other procedures used in the search for unrecorded retirements include a review of the miscellaneous or other income account for salvage credits and scrap sales, inquiry of operating and management personnel, and a properly planned plant tour. Proceeds from the sale of scrap or used equipment may indicate unrecorded retirements and should be investigated if material. In this connection, the auditor should consider the controls over the accumulation and sale of scrap. Lack of controls in this area (which is not unusual) can result not only in unrecorded property retirements, but also in misappropriation of proceeds from the sale of scrap and salvaged items.

Inquiry of operating and management personnel should include discussion not only of actual retirements made during the year but also of assets on hand that are no longer being used. For example, a decision to discontinue a product line may result in the disposal of many pieces of equipment used to produce that line. Because the equipment is still on hand, it should not be recorded as a retirement in the accounting records, but it should be reduced in value (after considering the related accumulated depreciation) to the estimated amount to be realized on its disposition. It also may be appropriate to reclassify the equipment to other assets if it will no longer be used in production.

The plant tour normally should be made early in the audit, because it provides the auditor with a knowledge of the production process that will be important in other sections of the audit, as well as in the search for unrecorded retirements. It sometimes is coordinated with the physical inventory observation. To be an effective procedure in the search for unrecorded retirements, the plant tour must be planned properly. To stroll through a plant inspecting certain items of equipment provides no evidence about unrecorded retirements (although it may be useful in verifying the physical existence of additions). During the search for unrecorded retirements, the auditor is interested in the pieces of equipment that are *not* in the plant but are still recorded in the accounting records. To make the test effective, the auditor must select certain items of equipment from the accounting records and then locate and identify them during the plant tour. Any items that cannot be located would represent unrecorded retirements and should be removed from the accounting records. Because of the nature of the audit work performed in the search for unrecorded property retirements, the auditor normally documents it in a memorandum.

Audit of Depreciation   Auditors can become so involved in the detail calculations of depreciation expense that they lose overall perspective of the account. They should remember that depreciation expense results from the allocation of the cost of assets over an *estimated* time period by an *arbitrary* method and that it may be unrealistic to expect to calculate and verify this allocation to the nearest dollar. Usually, groups of assets with similar lives and the same depreciation method, such as buildings and equipment, can be tested on an overall basis. For example, if equipment is depreciable on a straight-line basis over ten years with a 10 percent salvage value, the auditor could average the beginning and ending balances of the asset account, reduce it by 10 percent, and multiply the remaining balance by 10 percent. This figure is seldom exactly equal to the client's depreciation expense because of the uneven rate of additions and retirements during the year, fully depreciated assets, and other factors, but it gives the auditor an idea of the reasonableness of the calculation. If the overall calculation is materially different from the client's amount, detail tests of individual items may be necessary.

Auditors also must be satisfied that all depreciation calculations are made on a basis consistent with the calculation of the prior year. They must review not only the obvious factors, such as the depreciation rates and methods, but also other factors, such as estimated salvage values and methods of considering current-year property additions and retirements. For example, a change in computing depreciation on current-year additions from a standard half-year to the actual number of months in service might not be immediately obvious but could have a material effect on depreciation expense if large additions were made near the beginning or end of a year.

In addition to testing depreciation expense for the year, the auditor must evaluate the adequacy of the balance of accumulated depreciation. The auditor is not an appraiser, but depreciation is not a valuation process. It is a process of allocation, and the auditor can use his or her business judgment to determine the reasonableness of the allocation of the remaining cost of an asset over its remaining useful life. In considering the reasonableness of the remaining useful life of an asset, the auditor must take into account not only its physical condition, but technological innovations and other factors as well. For example, a remaining estimated life of 15 years for a black-and-white TV camera owned by a TV station would be unreasonable if the station had switched to full color. Also, an estimated life of 30 years for a natural gas pipeline might be unreasonable if the natural gas reserves amounted to only a 10-year supply (consideration would be given to possible future discoveries). Such examples show the importance of the business approach in the audit.

Property Disclosures Disclosures of depreciation amounts and methods of calculation are required by generally accepted accounting principles. In addition, disclosure should be made of any mortgages or liens. Many, although not all, mortgages arise in the initial acquisition of an item of property. In the audit of property additions, the auditor must be alert for mortgages associated with any non-cash acquisitions of property. Mortgages and liens also may be detected by review of notes, bonds, and loan agreements, confirmation with financial institutions, review of minutes, and inquiry of management, all of which have been discussed in other sections.

SUMMARY OF IMPORTANT AUDIT PROCEDURES
FOR PROPERTY AND EQUIPMENT

- Review and evaluate the effect of the internal control structure on the scope of property and equipment work.

- Perform analytical procedures.

- Analyze property and equipment additions and examine supporting vendor invoices, canceled checks, receiving reports, and capitalization decisions.

- Analyze repair and maintenance expense and examine supporting vendor invoices, canceled checks, receiving reports, and expense decisions.

- Test recorded property and equipment retirements by tracing cost and accumulated depreciation to the detail property ledger.

- Search for unrecorded property and equipment retirements by inquiry of management and operating personnel, tour of plant to identify selected items, and investigation of major additions that represent replacements, reduction of insurance coverage or property tax base, and salvage credits and scrap sales.

- Test depreciation expenses by reference to the asset base, expected useful life, and depreciation method.

- Evaluate the adequacy of the accumulated depreciation.

- Review property additions, loan agreements, minutes, and confirmations and inquire of management regarding disclosure of liens and mortgages.

Long-Term Investments and Intangibles

Long-term investments can take many forms. They may be debt or equity, marketable or nonmarketable, affiliated or nonaffiliated, and so on. Auditors depend on their knowledge of generally accepted accounting principles to determine the appropriate valuations and disclosures in each case. Long-term investments may not be significant for a manufacturing company but may constitute the most significant asset of an investment company.

The physical evidence of long-term investments usually takes the form of stock or bond certificates (other forms include joint venture agreements, real estate deeds, and mineral leases) with evidence of ownership indicated either on the certificate (registered form) or by possession (bearer form). Certificates may be held by the company that owns them or by a bank or other financial institution as custodian for the company. If held by the company, the certificates should be stored in a bank safe deposit box or similar location. Control risk is reduced if dual access (the requirement that two individuals be present for access) is required for entry to the box.

Long-term investments may be valued on the basis of cost, underlying equity, lower of cost or market, or market value. General disclosures relating to long-term investments include the type of investment and basis of valuation; additional disclosures apply in many cases.

Intangibles include goodwill, franchises, patents, and organizational costs. The existence and ownership of goodwill subsequent to the transaction in which it is established are subjective and difficult to evaluate. However, other intangibles are represented by legal documents, such as franchise agreements, patents, or corporate articles of incorporation. Acquisition cost, less amortization, is generally the valuation basis for intangibles. Costs of developing, maintaining, or restoring intangible assets that are not specifically identifiable, have indeterminate lives, or are inherent in a continuing business and related to an enterprise as a whole—such as goodwill—should be deducted from income when incurred. Amortization is usually computed on the straight-line method over the periods estimated to be benefited but not to exceed 40 years.

Audit Objectives

The objectives (assertions) in the audit of long-term investments and intangibles are as follows:

1. To determine whether all (completeness) long-term investments are represented by certificates of ownership owned by and held by or for the company, and that intangibles are represented by contractual rights, privileges, or earning power (goodwill) owned by the company (existence and rights).

2. To determine whether long-term investments are properly stated on the basis of accounting principles applicable in the circumstances, and whether intangibles are stated at cost less amortization (valuation and presentation).

3. To determine whether disclosures concerning long-term investments and intangibles are adequate and in accordance with generally accepted accounting principles (disclosure).

Audit Procedures and Working Papers

The auditor must consider the internal control structure for the physical security or evidence of ownership of long-term investments, cash disbursements for long-term investments and intangibles, and amortization policies for intangibles.

The following are some of the possible effects of the internal control structure on the scope of substantive tests: (1) maintaining investment securities in a bank safe deposit box, as opposed to an office safe, may allow the auditor to perform the security count at a time other than year end, (2) board of director authorization and approval of acquisition of investments, patents, and so forth may allow the auditor to reduce the scope of work on additions to these accounts, and (3) standard monthly journal entries to amortize the balances of intangibles should reduce the chance of omitting amortization and allow the auditor to reduce the extent of tests of amortization.

Analytical Procedures   The auditor may make the following comparisons in performing analytical procedures for these accounts: (1) current-year balance with current-year budget and prior-year actual, (2) ratio of investment income (dividends and interest) to balance in investment accounts for the current and prior year, (3) amortization costs for the current and prior year, and (4) ratio of amortization costs to unamortized balances for the current and prior year. Such comparisons may identify improperly recorded purchases and sales of investments and intangible assets and erroneous recording of investment income or amortization of intangible assets.

Security Count   One means of determining that long-term investments exist and are owned by the company is physical inspection of the certificates, often referred to as a security count.

Security counts must be made as of the audit date, unless provisions can be made to verify that there has been no access to the certificates between the audit date and the date they are inspected. This verification can often be provided by examination of banks' records of access to safe deposit boxes (usually confirmed to the auditor by the bank in writing) or the use of seals by the auditor. This precaution is necessary to prevent the removal and sale or pledge of the investments as of the audit date to cover a shortage, and their subsequent replacement without the auditor's knowledge.

A security count of any size requires careful planning because, once the count is underway, it is very difficult to modify the procedures to any great extent. Among the more essential matters that should be considered are (1) obtaining a list of the locations of all securities, and the type and volume of securities at each place, (2) providing for the simultaneous control or count of all securities and cash, (3) arranging for the continuous presence of representatives of the client during the count, and (4) preparing lists of securities to be counted.

The working paper schedule evidencing the security count should include such details as company name, certificate number, number of shares, par value, face value, interest rate, due date, and issue date. An example of such a working paper is shown in Figure 17.4. Note that there is evidence on the working paper that the auditor inspected each certificate, that the inspection was performed in

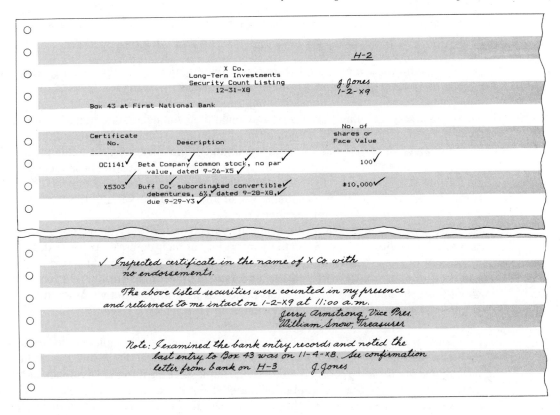

Figure 17.4 Long-term investments—security count.

the presence of company officers, and that the certificates were returned intact to the company officers. The security count sheet is later compared with the description of the investments in the accounting records.

Although the auditor cannot be expected to recognize or uncover forged securities, tests of apparent authenticity should be made during the count by noting the signatures of the trustee, registrar, transfer agent, and corporate officers, the presence of a corporate seal, and so forth.

Confirmation Certificates evidencing long-term investments may be held for the company by financial institutions or others. If certificates are held by a reputable bank or other financial institution, the auditor will normally confirm their existence with the holder. If, however, the certificates are held by an institution that is unknown to the auditor, he or she should not accept a confirmation without some inquiry into the nature of the institution. In addition, in the case of bonds, debentures, loans, and other debt obligations, the amount due should be confirmed directly with the debtor.

Valuation   Once the auditor has established the proper valuation basis for an investment under generally accepted accounting principles, he or she should apply audit procedures to that basis. If cost is the valuation basis, the auditor should examine documentation (broker's advice, canceled check, etc.) for the acquisition of the investment. If underlying equity is the valuation basis, audited financial statements of the investee constitute sufficient evidential matter as to the equity in the underlying net assets, but unaudited financial statements do not. Therefore, if an investment accounted for by the equity method is material, the scope of an auditor's examination may be limited if the financial statements of the investee company are not audited. Finally, if market is the valuation basis, market quotations from such sources as *The Wall Street Journal* or *Barron's* may be used if the prices are based on a reasonable broad and active market and there are no restrictions on the transfer of the investment.

Because intangible assets are generally valued on the basis of cost less amortization, the auditor should evaluate the propriety of their deferral, examine documentation of their acquisition cost (franchise and merger agreements, invoices, canceled checks, etc.), and test the accuracy of the amortization. He or she should also evaluate the amortization period to determine whether any current events or circumstances warrant revision.

Investment-Related Income   It is often convenient and efficient to audit dividend and interest income at the time investments are audited, and the audit procedures are usually recorded on the same audit working papers. Dividends can be tested by multiplying the number of shares (from the security count schedule if there were no changes during the year) by the dividend rate (per *Standard & Poor's Dividend Record,* audited financial statements of the investee, etc.). Interest income can be recomputed on the basis of face amount, interest rate, and period held (from the security count schedule or confirmation).

SUMMARY OF IMPORTANT AUDIT PROCEDURES
FOR LONG-TERM INVESTMENTS AND INTANGIBLES

• Review and evaluate the effect of the internal control structure on the scope of long-term investments and intangibles work.

• Perform analytical procedures.

• Perform security count or obtain confirmation to establish existence and rights of ownership.

• Test valuation by reference to broker's advice, canceled check, audited financial statements of investee, market values from financial publications, and franchise and merger agreements.

• Test investment-related income by reference to published dividend and interest sources.

• Test amortization of intangibles for accuracy and consistency.

• Review agreements and minutes for necessary disclosures.

Long-Term Liabilities

Long-term liabilities include loans, bonds, and notes payable that generally are due after one year from the balance sheet date, although certain amounts due within one year may be classified as long-term if both the intention and ability to refinance on a long-term basis are demonstrated.

Long-term liabilities, such as loans, bonds, and notes, have several characteristics that require particular attention from the auditor. First, they are often collateralized or secured by certain of the company's assets. The result is restriction of the free transferability of such assets and, in some cases, restriction of the manner in which they may be used.

Second, the debt instrument may be subject to the provisions of a separate but related debt agreement that also may place restraints on the company's operations. Provisions commonly found in debt agreements include requirements that the company maintain specified working capital and debt-to-equity ratios, as well as restrictions on payment of dividends, purchase of treasury stock, and merger or sale of the company or a significant portion of its assets. Violation of any of these provisions generally constitutes an event of default, which allows the debtholder to require immediate payment. If a provision is violated inadvertently and the debtholder has no reason to believe the loan is in danger, he or she will usually, on request from the company, waive the right to immediate payment. If a waiver is obtained, the financial statements should disclose that a violation occurred and was waived by the debtholder. If a waiver is refused, the debt should be classified as a current liability because payment can be demanded at any time by the debtholder. Obviously, such an event could have a catastrophic effect on a company.

Readers of financial statements normally are interested in many aspects of long-term debt. For example, the impending maturity of a large debt can create cash flow problems for a company, or the replacement at maturity of low-interest-rate with high-interest-rate debt can have an adverse effect on earnings. Therefore, disclosures concerning long-term debt should include a complete description of the terms of the debt, as well as the collateral and any restrictions imposed by a debt agreement.

In addition to the controls over cash receipts and disbursements, other control features specifically applicable to long-term debt include the requirements that all borrowings be approved by the board of directors and that a checklist of requirements and restrictions in debt agreements be maintained to prevent inadvertent noncompliance.

Audit Objectives

The objectives (assertions) in the audit of long-term liabilities are as follows:

1. To determine whether all (completeness) long-term liabilities existing or incurred (existence and obligations) as of the audit date are reflected properly in the financial statements (valuation).

2. To determine whether long-term liabilities consist of amounts due after one year from the audit date (or operating cycle), or short-term obligations for which the intention and ability to refinance on a long-term basis have been demonstrated (presentation).

3. To determine whether disclosures regarding long-term liabilities are adequate (disclosure).

Audit Procedures and Working Papers

The first step is to review and test the internal control structure applicable to long-term debt. Tests of controls over cash receipts are included in Chapter 8. Dual-purpose tests discussed in this section are used to test other controls.

Specific examples of the effect of the internal control structure on substantive tests for long-term liabilities are as follows: (1) the requirement that the board of directors authorize all borrowings reduces the probabilities of unrecorded borrowings and may allow the auditor to limit the search for unrecorded borrowings by confirmation and other means, (2) the utilization of a bond trustee would allow the auditor to limit confirmation work to one confirmation with the trustee, and (3) a calendar of principal and interest payments helps to prevent overlooking a payment and lets the auditor reduce the time spent in determining that all required principal and interest payments have been made. After reviewing and testing the controls, the auditor should prepare an audit lead schedule similar to the one in Figure 17.5.

Analytical Procedures   In performing analytical procedures on long-term liabilities, the auditor may compare (1) balances of the current and prior year, (2) recorded borrowings and repayments to cash flow budgets, and (3) computed average interest rate (calculated by dividing interest expense by the average of the beginning and ending debt balances) with the stated interest rate. The auditor

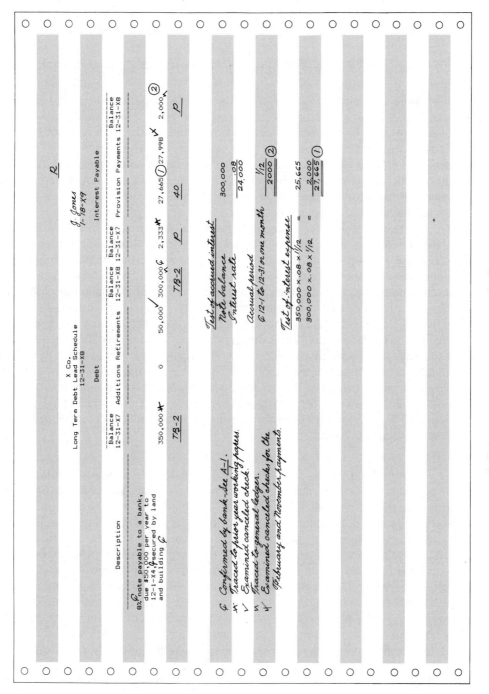

Figure 17.5   Long-term debt lead schedule.

should investigate significant variations to determine whether borrowings and repayments are properly recorded and interest expense is properly calculated.

Tests of Borrowings, Repayments, and Accrued Interest   Because long-term debt transactions often are material, the auditor usually examines all transactions in the account for the year, although samples may be used if the volume of transactions is large and the size of individual transactions is small. The auditor normally traces the proceeds from any borrowings to the cash receipts records, deposit slips, and bank statement, and audits payments by examining canceled checks (indicated by √ in Figure 17.5) and canceled notes, if paid in full. The authorization of all significant borrowings and any repayments not made in accordance with the terms of the debt instrument should be traced to minutes of meetings of the board of directors.

Interest payable is tested on the same schedule as long-term debt so it can be related visually to the long-term debt balance. The simple example with only one note presents no problem, but if 30 or 40 notes were outstanding, this format would allow the auditor to determine quickly whether interest had been computed for each note. The fact that interest has been computed for each note, however, does not guarantee that it is computed correctly. The auditor tested interest expense at ① in Figure 17.5 by multiplying the outstanding balance by the interest rate and the fraction of the year it was outstanding. The accrued balance at the end of the year was tested in a similar manner at ② with the further step of relating the date to which interest was paid (the beginning of the accrual period) to the bank confirmation filed in the cash section (Figure 15.4). In addition, canceled checks were examined for two months' interest payments (indicated by ✗) in Figure 17.5), and the provision for interest expense was cross-referenced to the related expense account.

Confirmation   The approach to confirming long-term debt is similar to that for accounts payable because the objectives are similar. The confirmation letter ordinarily should not indicate the balance or other details of the debt but should request that the debtholder furnish that information directly to the auditor. By using this procedure, the auditor anticipates that the debtholder will furnish the details of all notes held, whether or not they are recorded by the client. If the debtholder is a bank, the standard bank confirmation form (Figure 15.4) should be used; otherwise, a separate letter requesting similar information must be prepared. Note that in Figure 17.5 the pertinent data have been indicated as confirmed by the bank and cross-referenced to the bank confirmation (see ¢). Confirmations normally are sent to all financial institutions with which the client has had dealings during the year, regardless of whether or not there is a balance at the end of the year. Although auditors anticipate that they will not receive replies to all of their requests for confirmation of accounts receivable and accounts payable, they usually require confirmation from all significant debtholders before releasing their opinion on the financial statements. Thus, personal follow-up by the auditor and the client may be needed in addition to second requests.

Review of Debt Agreements   The importance of debt agreements has been stressed. The auditor's review of these agreements must be performed carefully and thoroughly. If the meaning or intent of a provision in an agreement is unclear, the auditor should ask the client to request an interpretation from the debtholder. All violations of a debt agreement, no matter how minor, should be referred to the client so that waivers can be requested. In this area materiality is inherent; if a debtholder believes a provision is significant enough to include in a debt agreement, the auditor must assume that a violation of that provision is material.

The review of debt agreements often is documented with the use of a checklist of the debt agreement provisions in the permanent audit file. This checklist must be reviewed each year and an indication made by each provision as to whether or not it was complied with. Because this procedure requires a knowledge of all aspects of the audit, it generally is performed by the audit senior and is reviewed closely by the audit manager and partner.

Debtholders occasionally require a letter from the auditors stating whether they became aware of any violations of the loan agreement while performing the audit. An example of such a letter is shown in Chapter 21.

Classification and Disclosure   Although the stated maturity date of a note often determines its classification as either a long- or short-term liability, other factors, such as the intent and ability to refinance or an unwaived violation of a debt agreement, may change that classification. In this phase of the examination, as in others, the auditor must not accept anything at face value, but must consider the possibility that unusual facts or circumstances may result in a different interpretation.

The information about long-term liabilities that is to be disclosed in the financial statements should be requested in the confirmation from the debtholder. Occasionally, the auditor receives a reply from a debtholder that is complete except for a description of any liens or collateral, and the auditor is unable to tell whether there are none or they were omitted by oversight. The only recourse is to return the confirmation (or preferably a copy of it) to the debtholder with a request that the omitted information be supplied or, if there are no liens or collateral, that this be indicated. It would be imprudent to accept an oral addition or correction to a written confirmation.

SUMMARY OF IMPORTANT AUDIT PROCEDURES
FOR LONG-TERM LIABILITIES

- Review and evaluate the effect of the internal control structure on the scope of long-term liabilities work.

- Perform analytical procedures.

- Trace new borrowings to authorizations in minutes and cash receipts records, deposit slips, and bank statements.

- Trace repayments to canceled checks and canceled notes.

- Recompute interest expense for the period and accrued interest at end of period.

- Obtain confirmation of amount and terms of long-term debt.

- Review the provisions of debt agreements to determine compliance.

- Evaluate the propriety of classification and disclosure of long-term liabilities.

Equity Accounts

Equity accounts include common and preferred stock, additional paid-in capital, retained earnings, valuation accounts for marketable securities and foreign currency translation, and treasury stock (partnership and proprietorship capital also would be included, but are not discussed in this text). Transactions in these accounts are relatively infrequent, but can be important.

The articles of incorporation of a company state the classes of stock it is authorized to issue, as well as the rights and preferences of each class, the number of shares of each class that is authorized, the par value, if any, of such stock, and any restrictions that may attach to it. The articles of incorporation of some companies provide for the restriction of dividends on common stock in the event that all preferred dividends are not paid; those of other companies, particularly companies that are closely held, require stock to be offered to the company at a certain price (such as book value) before it can be sold to another party. Thus, the articles of incorporation are the source of many financial statement disclosures.

The corporate secretary is normally responsible for the records relating to the number of shares of issued and outstanding stock. The procedures used by a company to account for and control the number of shares of stock issued and outstanding are determined largely by the number of its stockholders. If the number of stockholders is small, a company usually maintains a stock certificate book or stockbook. This book is similar to a checkbook in that it consists of a detachable stock certificate attached to a permanently bound stub on which can be entered the number of shares, date the certificate was issued, and name of the stockholder. When stock is sold or transferred, the stock certificate of the original stockholder is surrendered to the company so that it can be marked "canceled" and reattached to the stub from which it was issued. A new certificate is issued to the new stockholder. The number of shares issued at any time is determined by adding the numbers of shares shown on all stock certificate stubs that do not have canceled certificates attached to them. This procedure is adequate if the number of stockholders and stock transfers is small but obviously would be impractical if hundreds or thousands of shares were transferred daily.

Public companies whose stock is traded actively usually employ banks or other financial institutions to act as transfer agents and registrars. As transfer agents, these institutions receive and issue certificates and maintain lists of stockholders for use in mailing stockholder reports, paying dividends, and so forth. As registrars, they maintain records of the number of shares issued and canceled to check on the transactions of the transfer agent and to guard against mistakes that could result in an overissue of stock.

Treasury stock should be recorded at cost, and it is generally shown as a deduction from other equity items in the balance sheet. Neither dividends attributable to treasury stock nor gains or losses on its disposition should be recorded as income. Treasury stock certificates should be stored in a safe deposit box and safeguarded in the same manner as investment securities.

The retained earnings account should contain few transactions other than net income or loss and dividend distributions. *FASB Statement No. 16* requires, with certain exceptions, that all items of profit and loss recognized during a period, including accruals of estimated losses from loss contingencies, be included in earnings for that period. Only two items may be treated as prior period adjustments—corrections of errors in the financial statements of a prior period and tax adjustments resulting from realization of income tax benefits of preacquisition operating loss carry-forwards of purchased subsidiaries.

Many companies have stock option plans for officers and key employees. If these plans are used, records must be maintained of the number of options authorized, granted, exercised, and expired, as well as option prices and periods covered.

Audit Objectives

The objectives (assertions) in the audit of the equity accounts are as follows:

1. To determine whether the equity accounts and all (completeness) of the transactions therein as shown in the financial statements (existence) are presented in accordance with generally accepted accounting principles (valuation).

2. To determine whether adequate disclosure is made of all restrictions, rights, options, and other matters important to an understanding of the financial statements (presentation and disclosure).

Audit Procedures and Working Papers

In examining equity accounts, an auditor must keep in mind that the audit is being made of the company and *not* of its stockholders. Transfers of shares between stockholders and the number of shares owned by individual stockholders are theoretically of no concern to the auditor, because they have no effect on the financial statements being audited. The auditor is concerned only with the total authorized, issued, and outstanding stock and not with its ownership, although knowledge of ownership may aid the auditor in identifying related parties. Auditors normally do not confirm stock ownership with individual stockholders and, in fact, this would be impractical to do if stock is held by nominees or sold from one individual to another without being sent to the company for transfer. (Such a sale would not affect the ownership of the buyer but would be imprudent, because dividends and other distributions would continue to be sent to the seller.)

The auditor may review and test the internal control structure applicable to the equity accounts, including tests of controls over cash receipts and cash disbursements; however, because of the limited number of transactions and their importance, the auditor often examines all transactions in the accounts. The cost of reviewing and testing the internal control structure applicable to this account may exceed the benefits from reduction of substantive tests. However, certain controls may affect the extent of substantive tests. Some examples are (1) the use of independent transfer agents and registrars allows the auditor to gather evidence of the number of shares issued and outstanding with a confirmation rather than through an examination of the stockbook and (2) the use of an imprest bank account may allow the auditor to reduce the scope of examination of individual dividend payments.

The audit of the equity accounts follows an approach similar to that used for property and equipment in that a beginning balance is established (usually in the prior-year audit), and then current-year transactions are audited. In addition, certain procedures are applied to the year-end balance.

All equity accounts should be analyzed (often on a schedule maintained in the permanent audit file), and transactions during the year should be audited by examination of supporting documents and authorizations. For example, if additional stock is sold during the year, the proceeds should be traced to the cash receipts book and bank statement and the authorization of the sale should be traced to minutes of stockholder or directors' meetings. Particular attention should be paid to the valuation attributed to stock issued for noncash consideration, the treatment of gains or losses from sale or retirement of treasury stock, the propriety of entries to retained earnings other than net income or loss and dividends, and the accounting treatment of stock dividends and splits.

Analytical Procedures   For the equity section of the balance sheet the auditor will compare (1) the current balance with the budgeted and prior-year amounts and (2) dividend payments with cash-flow budgets. All significant changes should be investigated.

Tests of Dividends   Total dividends declared during a year can be tested on an overall basis by multiplying the number of shares outstanding at the dividend record date by the dividend rate per share. This procedure provides evidence that the proper amount was calculated, but the auditor also should obtain evidence that it was paid to the stockholders.

Some companies engage a bank or trust company as a dividend-paying agent, often the same one that acts as transfer agent. In these cases, the company pays the total dividend to its dividend-paying agent, which makes the dividend distributions to the individual stockholders. The auditor examines the canceled check for the total dividend and the notice of receipt from the agent. The agreement between the company and the dividend-paying agent usually places the responsibility for the proper distribution of the dividend, and liability for incorrect dividend payments, on the agent. If this is the case, the auditor normally does not examine the agent's records of dividend payments to individual stockholders.

If a company pays its own dividends, the auditor should test the propriety of the payments to the individual stockholders. An example of such a test, which may be done on a sample basis, is shown in Figure 17.6. The auditor obtained the stockholder's name and number of shares owned of record as of the dividend record date from the stockbook (indicated by √). He or she also totaled the number of shares owned by all stockholders and related it to the total outstanding

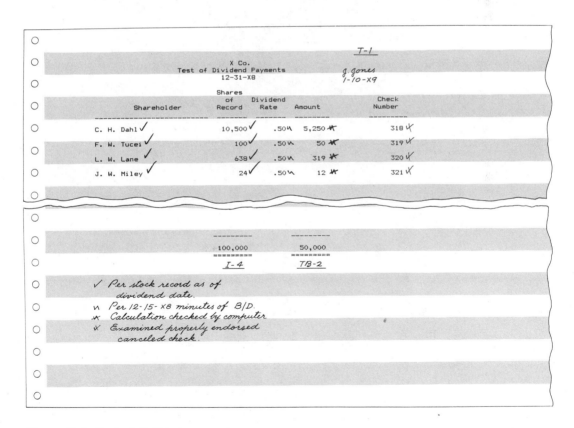

Figure 17.6   Test of dividend payments.

as shown in the account analysis in the permanent audit file (*I-4* is an illustration of a method of indexing the permanent audit file). The auditor then compared the dividend rate with that shown in the minutes of the specific meeting at which the dividend was declared and checked the calculation of the individual dividend payments. Finally, he or she examined the canceled check in payment of the dividend, noting particularly that it was endorsed properly by the stockholder.

Examination of Stockbook and Treasury Stock   If a company maintains its own stock records, the auditor should examine the stockbook to determine whether the proper amount is shown as being issued in the financial statements. Because many of the same stockbook stubs and canceled certificates are examined each year, the auditor commonly maintains a permanent audit file schedule that can be used to document the examination for several years. An illustration of such a schedule is shown in Figure 17.7. The auditor must account for all certificate numbers by examining the stockbook stubs for outstanding shares (indicated by ∧), canceled certificates for retired shares (indicated by √), and unissued certificates for the balance. The total of the shares outstanding has been

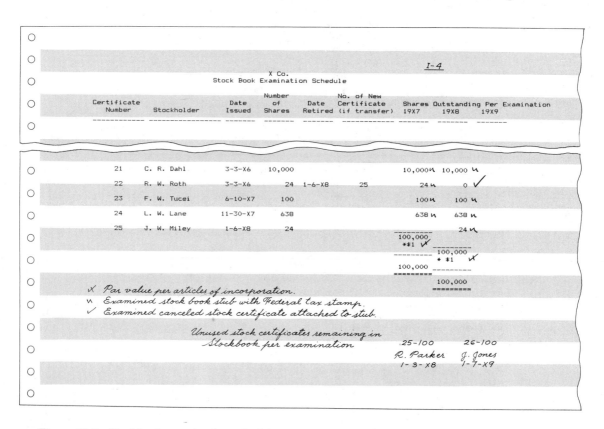

Figure 17.7   Stockbook examination schedule.

multiplied by the par value to produce the dollar amount of capital stock shown in the financial statements. A step not indicated in Figure 17.7, but used by some auditors because of the importance of the stockbook, is to ask the client to acknowledge its return in writing after it has been examined.

If the client possesses treasury stock, it should be inspected. The schedule evidencing this inspection should include the certificate number, date, and number of shares. All treasury stock certificates should be in the name of the company. The inspection should be made in a manner similar to that of a security count, described earlier in this chapter.

Confirmation   If the client employs a transfer agent and registrar, there will be no stock certificate book to examine. Instead, the number of shares issued and outstanding should be confirmed in writing directly from the transfer agent and registrar to the auditor.

Matters Requiring Disclosure

The general disclosures required of all companies under generally accepted accounting principles, such as capital changes, stock options, liquidation value of preferred stock, and limitations on stock transfers, usually can be related to corporate documents such as the articles of incorporation or minutes of meetings of stockholders or directors. Normally, they present no special problems.

Disclosures of restrictions such as limitations or prohibitions on payment of cash dividends and purchase of treasury stock are more difficult to detect. Most restrictions of this nature are due to provisions in debt and lease agreements and should be found by use of the procedures discussed in the long-term debt section, such as review of debt (and lease) agreements and minutes, and confirmations with debtholders. Other restrictions may arise from the laws of the state in which a company is incorporated. For example, several states have laws prohibiting the payment of dividends to the extent of the cost of treasury stock, thereby necessitating the disclosure of a restriction of retained earnings if treasury stock is held. To discover these disclosures the auditor must be familiar with the corporate codes of the states in which clients operate.

SUMMARY OF IMPORTANT AUDIT PROCEDURES FOR EQUITY ACCOUNTS

• Review and evaluate the effect of the internal control structure on the scope of equity accounts work.

• Perform analytical procedures.

- Analyze changes in equity accounts for the period and examine support for changes, such as minutes of board of directors meetings, deposit slips, and bank statements for issuance of capital stock.

- Test dividends by reference to board of director meeting minutes for dividend rate and capital stock records for number of shares.

- Examine stockbook and treasury stock or confirm with the transfer agent and registrar to determine the number of shares issued and outstanding.

- Trace description of stock, par value, and number of shares authorized to articles of incorporation.

- Review minutes, debt agreements, and other sources for restrictions on dividends and capital stock transactions that require disclosure in the financial statements.

Chapter 17
Glossary of Terms

(listed in order of appearance in the chapter, with accompanying page reference where the term is discussed)

Term	*Page in Chapter*
Vouching schedule an analysis of individual additions to a specific account that is used by the auditor to indicate the evidence examined for such additions.	650
Unrecorded property retirements the sale, scrap, or other disposition of a physical property item that has not been recorded in the accounting records.	652
Security count the physical inspection of investment and other securities.	658
Debt or loan agreement a legal document that places restrictions on a debtor for as long as the related debt is outstanding.	661

**Chapter 17
References**

American Institute of Certified Public Accountants. *Professional Standards*
AU Section 332—Long-Term Investments.

**Chapter 17
Review Questions**

17-1.   State the objectives in the audit of property and equipment and related accumulated depreciation.

17-2.   What analytical procedures may be applied to property and equipment?

17-3.   State the audit procedures applied to property and equipment to determine whether additions are
a. Recorded at cost.
b. Represented by actual physical items.
c. Properly capitalizable.

17-4.   What test does the auditor make to determine if property additions are complete?

17-5.   List five procedures the auditor could use to detect unrecorded property retirements.

17-6.   Explain how and why an auditor usually tests depreciation expense on an overall basis.

17-7.   What factors should an auditor consider in evaluating the adequacy of accumulated depreciation?

17-8.   What procedures does the auditor use in his or her search for mortgages and liens on property and equipment?

17-9.   State the objectives in the audit of long-term investments and intangibles.

17-10. Describe four analytical procedures that may be applied to long-term investments and intangibles.

17-11. Why are security counts often made on the audit date? Under what circumstances may they be made at other dates?

17-12. What evidence would an auditor examine for investments valued at cost? Underlying equity? Market value?

17-13. How does the CPA audit dividend and interest income?

17-14. What is the significance of the violation of a provision of a debt agreement?

17-15. State the objectives in the audit of long-term liabilities.

17-16. Give three analytical procedures an auditor may apply to long-term liabilities.

17-17. What audit procedures does an auditor apply to borrowings and repayments of long-term debt?

17-18. How is the audit of accrued interest payable related to an audit working paper in the cash section?

17-19. Why does the concept of materiality not apply to violations of a debt agreement?

17-20. Name two factors that can determine the financial statement classification of long-term debt, other than its maturity date.

17-21. Describe the two methods that may be used to control the number of shares of stock issued and outstanding.

17-22. State the objectives in the audit of the equity accounts.

17-23.   Describe two analytical procedures that may be applied to the equity accounts.

17-24.   Explain how and why the audit approach to testing dividend payments would differ for companies paying their own dividends and those employing dividend-paying agents.

17-25.   Why does the auditor examine the client's stockbook?

Chapter 17
Objective Questions Taken from CPA Examinations

17-26.   In violation of company policy, Lowell Company erroneously capitalized the cost of painting its warehouse. The auditor examining Lowell's financial statements would most likely detect this when
a. Observing, during the physical inventory observation, that the warehouse had been painted.
b. Examining the construction work orders supporting items capitalized during the year.
c. Discussing capitalization policies with Lowell's controller.
d. Examining maintenance expense accounts.

17-27.   The auditor may conclude that depreciation charges are insufficient by noting
a. Large amounts of fully depreciated assets.
b. Continuous trade-ins of relatively new assets.
c. Excessive recurring losses on assets retired.
d. Insured values greatly in excess of book values.

17-28.   Which of the following accounts would most likely be reviewed by the auditor to gain reasonable assurance that additions to the equipment account are *not* understated?
a. Repairs and maintenance expense.
b. Depreciation expense.
c. Gain on disposal of equipment.
d. Accounts payable.

17-29.   Which of the following audit procedures would be *least* likely to lead the auditor to find unrecorded fixed asset disposals?
a. Examination of insurance policies.
b. Review of repairs and maintenance expense.

  c. Review of property tax files.

  d. Scanning of invoices for fixed-asset additions.

17-30. Once the initial audit of a newly constructed industrial plant has been performed, with respect to consistency, which of the following is of *least* concern to the continuing auditor in the following year?

  a. Prior years' capitalization policy.

  b. Prior years' capitalized costs.

  c. Prior years' depreciation methods.

  d. Prior years' depreciable life.

17-31. Which of the following would provide the best form of evidential matter pertaining to the annual valuation of a long-term investment in which the independent auditor's client owns a 30-percent voting interest?

  a. Market quotations of the investee company's stock.

  b. Current fair value of the investee company's assets.

  c. Historical cost of the investee company's assets.

  d. Audited financial statements of the investee company.

17-32. When an auditor is unable to inspect and count a client's investment securities until after the balance-sheet date, the bank where the securities are held in a safe deposit box should be asked to

  a. Verify any differences between the contents of the box and the balances in the client's subsidiary ledger.

  b. Provide a list of securities added and removed from the box between the balance-sheet date and the security-count date.

  c. Confirm that there has been *no* access to the box between the balance-sheet date and the security-count date.

  d. Count the securities in the box so the auditor will have an independent direct verification.

17-33. In verifying the amount of goodwill recorded by a client, an auditor can obtain the most convincing evidence by comparing the recorded value of assets acquired with the

  a. Assessed value as evidenced by tax bills.

  b. Seller's book value as evidenced by financial statements.

  c. Insured value as evidenced by insurance policies.

  d. Appraised value as evidenced by independent appraisals.

17-34. The auditor should insist that a representative of the client be present during the physical examination of securities in order to

  a. Lend authority to the auditor's directives.

b. Detect forged securities.

c. Coordinate the return of all securities to proper locations.

d. Acknowledge the receipt of securities returned.

17-35. When negotiable securities are of considerable volume, planning by the auditor is necessary to guard against

a. Unauthorized negotiation of the securities before they are counted.

b. Unrecorded sales of securities after they are counted.

c. Substitution of securities already counted for other securities that should be on hand but are *not*.

d. Substitution of authentic securities with counterfeit securities.

17-36. Two months before year end the bookkeeper erroneously recorded the receipt of a long-term bank loan by a debit to cash and a credit to sales. Which of the following is the most effective procedure for detecting this type of error?

a. Analyze the notes payable journal.

b. Analyze bank confirmation information.

c. Prepare a year-end bank reconciliation.

d. Prepare a year-end bank transfer schedule.

17-37. The auditor can best verify a client's bond sinking fund transactions and year-end balance by

a. Confirmation with individual holders of retired bonds.

b. Confirmation with the bond trustee.

c. Recomputation of interest expense, interest payable, and amortization of bond discount or premium.

d. Examination and count of the bonds retired during the year.

17-38. Of the following, which is the most efficient audit procedure for verification of interest earned on bond investments?

a. Tracing interest declarations to an independent record book.

b. Recomputing interest earned.

c. Confirming interest rate with the issuer of the bonds.

d. Vouching the receipt and deposit of interest checks.

17-39. During an examination of a publicly held company, the auditor should obtain written confirmation regarding debenture transactions from the

a. Debenture holders.

b. Client's attorney.

c. Internal auditors.

d. Trustee.

17-40. During its fiscal year, a company issued a substantial amount of first-mortgage bonds at a discount. When performing audit work in connection with the bond issue, the independent auditor should
a. Confirm the existence of the bondholders.
b. Review the minutes for authorization.
c. Trace the net cash received from the issuance to the bond payable account.
d. Inspect the records maintained by the bond trustee.

17-41. To ascertain the exact name of the corporate client, the auditor relies primarily on
a. Corporate minutes.
b. Bylaws.
c. Articles of incorporation.
d. Tax returns.

17-42. When a company has treasury stock certificates on hand, a year-end count of the certificates by the auditor is
a. Required when the company classifies treasury stock with other assets.
b. Not required if treasury stock is a deduction from stockholders' equity.
c. Required if the company had treasury stock transactions during the year.
d. Always required.

17-43. Which of the following is the *most* important consideration of an auditor when examining the stockholders' equity section of a client's balance sheet?
a. Changes in the capital stock account are verified by an independent stock transfer agent.
b. Stock dividends and/or stock splits during the year under audit are approved by the stockholders.
c. Stock dividends are capitalized at par or stated value on the dividend declaration date.
d. Entries in the capital stock account can be traced to a resolution in the minutes of the board of directors' meetings.

17-44. An audit program for the examination of the retained earnings account should include a step that requires verification of the
a. Market value used to charge retained earnings to account for a two-for-one stock split.
b. Approval of the adjustment to the beginning balance as a result of a write-down of an account receivable.
c. Authorization for both cash and stock dividends.
d. Gain or loss resulting from disposition of treasury shares.

17-45.   If a company employs a capital stock registrar and/or transfer agent, the registrar or agent, or both, should be requested to confirm directly to the auditor the number of shares of each class of stock

a. Surrendered and canceled during the year.

b. Authorized at the balance sheet date.

c. Issued and outstanding at the balance sheet date.

d. Authorized, issued, and outstanding during the year.

Chapter 17
Discussion/Case Questions and Problems

17-46.   A staff assistant who was performing work in the property section of the Theta Industries audit prepared the vouching schedule for property additions shown below. Review this schedule and make notes of any deficiencies in the schedule or audit matters that require further attention.

Theta Industries
Property Additions
12-31-Z8

Vo. No.	Vendor	Amount	Description
1-403	Midway Ford	3,500√	Down payment on truck
3-112	Computerland	3,618√	Personal computer
5-016	Dover Construction	2,947	Pave driveway
7-358	Termite-Tex	731√	Annual termite inspection
9-274	Bean Furniture	9,822√	Desk
9-501	Dover Construction	1,713√	Paint offices
9-088	Dover Construction	1,713√	Paint offices
	Total	24,080	

√ Examined canceled check.

17-47.   In connection with a recurring examination of the financial statements of the Louis Manufacturing Company for the year ended December 31, 19X9, you have been assigned the audit of the manufacturing equipment, manufacturing equipment–accumulated depreciation, and repairs to manufacturing equipment accounts. Your review of Louis's policies and procedures has disclosed the following pertinent information:

1. The manufacturing equipment account includes the net invoice price plus related freight and installation costs for all of the equipment in Louis's manufacturing plant.

2. The manufacturing equipment and accumulated depreciation accounts are supported by a subsidiary ledger that shows the cost and accumulated depreciation for each piece of equipment.

3. An annual budget for capital expenditures of $1,000 or more is prepared by the budget committee and approved by the board of directors. Capital expenditures over $1,000 that are not included in this budget must be approved by the board of directors, and variations of 20 percent or more must be explained to the board. Approval by the supervisor of production is required for capital expenditures under $1,000.

4. Company employees handle installation, removal, repair, and rebuilding of the machinery. Work orders are prepared for these activities and are subject to the same budgetary control as other expenditures. Work orders are not required for external expenditures.

Required:
a. Cite the major objectives of your audit of the manufacturing equipment, manufacturing equipment–accumulated depreciation, and repairs of manufacturing equipment accounts. Do not include in this listing the auditing procedures designed to accomplish these objectives.
b. Prepare the portion of your audit program applicable to the audit of 19X9 additions to the manufacturing equipment account.
(*AICPA adapted*)

17-48.   In connection with the annual examination of Johnson Corp., a manufacturer of janitorial supplies, you have been assigned to audit the fixed assets. Johnson Corp. maintains a detailed property ledger for all fixed assets. You prepared an audit program for the balances of property and equipment but have yet to prepare one for accumulated depreciation and depreciation expense.

Required:
Prepare a separate comprehensive audit program for the accumulated depreciation and depreciation expense accounts.
(*AICPA adapted*)

17-49.   One procedure for determining the existence of property and equipment is physical observation, although other methods may be as effective in some cases. Discuss means of gathering evidence as to the physical existence of the following property and equipment items, other than direct observation.

a. A producing oil well.

b. An apartment building.

c. An automobile.

d. A mineral lease.

17-50. During your audit of property and equipment, you review the following construction work order listing:

Work Order No.	Description	Amount Authorized	Amount Expended
3103	Construct branch sales office	$38,000	$40,500
3104	Replace fence around plant	7,600	6,950
3106	Resurface parking lot	5,900	6,030
3107	Install additional boiler	18,000	38,100
3108	Construct addition to president's residence	16,000	26,500
3109	Install drapes and carpets in treasurer's office	2,700	2,800

List the items you would select for additional audit follow-up and give your reasons for listing them.

17-51. Your new assistant auditor informed you that he has completed the audit of depreciation expense, and on review of his work you find that it consisted of checking the clerical accuracy of the multiplication of the depreciation rate times the asset balance. What additional factors should he have considered in the audit of depreciation expense?

17-52. You have been engaged to examine the financial statements of the Elliott Company for the year ended December 31, 19X9. You performed a similar examination as of December 31, 19X8.

Following is the trial balance for the company as of December 31, 19X9:

	Dr. (Cr.)
Cash	$128,000
Interest receivable	47,450
Dividends receivable	1,750
6½% secured note receivable	730,000
Investments at cost:	
Bowen common stock	322,000
Investments at equity:	
Woods common stock	284,000

Land	185,000
Accounts payable	(31,000)
Interest payable	(6,500)
8% secured note payable to bank	(275,000)
Common stock	(480,000)
Paid-in capital	(800,000)
Retained earnings	(100,500)
Dividend revenue	(3,750)
Interest revenue	(47,450)
Equity in earnings of investment carried at equity	(40,000)
Interest expense	26,000
General and administrative expense	60,000

You have obtained the following data concerning certain accounts:

The 6½ percent note receivable is due from Tysinger Corporation and is secured by a first mortgage on land sold to Tysinger by Elliott on December 21, 19X8. The note was to have been paid in 20 equal quarterly payments beginning March 31, 19X9, plus interest. Tysinger, however, is in very poor financial condition and has not made any principal or interest payments to date.

The Bowen common stock was purchased on September 21, 19X8, for cash in the market where it is actively traded. It is used as security for the note payable and held by the bank. Elliott's investment in Bowen represents approximately one percent of the total outstanding shares of Bowen.

Elliott's investment in Woods represents 40 percent of the outstanding common stock that is actively traded. Woods is audited by another CPA and has a December 31 year end.

Elliott neither purchased nor sold any stock investments during the year other than those noted above.

Required:

For the following account balances, discuss (1) the types of evidential matter you should obtain and (2) the audit procedures you should perform during your examination.

a. 6½ percent secured note receivable.

b. Bowen common stock.

c. Woods common stock.

d. Dividend revenue.

(*AICPA adapted*)

17-53.   The schedule on page 683 was prepared by the controller of World Manufacturing Inc., for use by the independent auditors during their examination of World's year-end financial statements. All procedures performed by the audit assistant were noted at the bottom "Legend" section, and it was properly initialed, dated and indexed, and then submitted to a senior member of the audit staff for review. Control risk was evaluated and is considered to be low.

World Manufacturing, Inc.
Marketable Securities
Year Ended December 31, 19X1

										Dividend & Interest		
			Face	*Gen.*	*Purch.*	*Sold*		*Gen.*				
Description		*Serial*	*Value*	*Ledger*	*in*	*in*		*Ledger*	*12/31*	*Pay*	*Amt.*	*Accruals*
of Security		*No.*	*of Bonds*	*1/1*	*19X1*	*19X1*	*Cost*	*12/31*	*Market*	*Date(s)*	*Rec.*	*12/31*
Corp.	*Yr.*											
Bonds % *Due*												
										1/15	300[b,d]	
A	6 Y1	21-7	10000	9400[a]				9400	9100	7/15	300[b,d]	275
D	4 X3	73-0	30000	27500[a]				27500	26220	12/1	1200[b,d]	100
G	9 Y8	16-4	5000	4000[a]				4000	5080	8/1	450[b,d]	188
Rc	5 X5	08-2	70000	66000[a]		57000[b]	66000					
Sc	10 Y9	07-4	100000	____	100000[e]	____	____	100000	101250	7/1	5000[b,d]	5000
				106900	100000	57000	66000	140900	141650		7250	5563
				a,f	f	f	f	f,g	f		f	f

Stocks

										3/1	750[b,d]	
P 1,000 shs.		1044		7500[a]				7500	7600	6/1	750[b,d]	
Common										9/1	750[b,d]	
										12/1	750[b,d]	250
U 50 shs.		8530		9700[a]				9700	9800	2/1	800[b,d]	
Common										8/1	800[b,d]	667
				17200				17200	17400		4600	917
				a,f				f,g	f		f	f

Legends and comments relative to above:
a = Beginning balances agreed to 19X0 working papers.
b = Traced to cash receipts.
c = Minutes examined (purchase and sales approved by the board of directors).
d = Agreed to 1099.
e = Confirmed by tracing to broker's advice.
f = Totals footed.
g = Agreed to general ledger.

Required:

a. What information that is essential to the audit of marketable securities is missing from this schedule?

b. What are the essential audit procedures that were not noted as having been performed by the audit assistant?

(*AICPA adapted*)

17-54. A company issued bonds for cash during the year under audit. To ascertain that this transaction was properly recorded, the auditor might perform some or all of the following procedures.

a. Request a statement from the bond trustee as to the amount of the bonds issued and outstanding.

b. Confirm the results of the issuance with the underwriter or investment banker.

c. Trace the cash received from the issuance to the accounting records.

d. Verify that the net cash received is credited to an account entitled "Bonds Payable."

Discuss the audit objectives accomplished by each of these procedures. Select the procedure you consider the "best," and state why you selected it.

(*AICPA adapted*)

17-55. Johnson, CPA, has been engaged to examine the financial statements of Broadwall Corporation for the year ended December 31, 19X1. During the year, Broadwall obtained a long-term loan from a local bank pursuant to a financing agreement, which provided that the

1. Loan was to be secured by the company's inventory and accounts receivable.

2. Company was to maintain a debt to equity ratio not to exceed two to one.

3. Company was not to pay dividends without permission from the bank.

4. Monthly installment payments were to commence July 1, 19X1.

In addition, during the year the company borrowed, on a short-term basis, from the president of the company, substantial amounts just prior to the year end.

Required:

a. For purposes of Johnson's audit of the financial statements of Broadwall Corporation, what procedures should Johnson employ in examining the described loans? *Do not discuss the internal control structure.*

b. What financial statement disclosures should Johnson expect to find with respect to the loans from the president?

(*AICPA adapted*)

17-56. During the audit of notes payable of Mohamed Tractor Co., a CPA was reviewing the terms of a related loan agreement. She noted that the note matured within 12 months of the audit date but the loan agreement provided that the term of the note could be extended an additional 12 months at the option of the company, provided there had been "no adverse changes in its financial or operating conditions."

How can the CPA audit the classification of notes payable as a long-term liability in this case?

17-57. Discuss the audit procedures that a CPA might use in gathering evidence of the following transactions and balances.

a. The refinancing (cancellation of old note and issuance of a new note) of a note payable to a bank.
b. Acquisition of treasury stock.
c. Year-end balance in additional paid-in capital account (assume that no transactions are shown for the current year).
d. Issuance of common stock to acquire another company.
e. Exercise of employee stock options.
f. Issuance of employee stock options.
g. Sale of treasury stock.

17-58. Companies that have stock option plans normally include a footnote in their financial statements that describes the plan and states the number of options for shares authorized, granted, exercised, and expired, the option prices, and the market prices of the stock on the grant and exercise dates.

As this information is not normally considered to be a part of the accounting records, what is the auditor's responsibility for it? If you feel audit procedures should be employed, list those that you think should be applied.

17-59. Kalinki Supply Company is a small, privately held corporation that manufactures and sells Christmas tree ornaments. The capital stockbook is maintained by the corporate secretary. Treasury stock is kept in a bank safe deposit box. The equity section of the corporation's balance sheet as of December 31, 19X6, the audit date, is shown in the following statement.

Common stock, $10 par value,		
100,000 shares authorized and issued		$1,000,000
Paid-in capital		1,000,000
Retained earnings—		
Beginning of year	$5,324,816	
Add—Net income	419,605	
Less—Dividends, $10 per share	(99,000)	
End of year		5,645,421
		$7,645,421
Less—Treasury stock, 1,000 shares, at cost		87,000
		$7,558,421

There were no capital stock transactions during the year. State the objectives for auditing the equity section. Develop an audit program to audit the equity section of Kalinki Supply Company.

17-60.   Jones, CPA, the continuing auditor of Sussex, Inc., is beginning the audit of the common stock and treasury stock accounts. Jones has decided to design substantive tests with minimum reliance on the internal control structure.

Sussex has no par, no stated value common stock, and acts as its own registrar and transfer agent. During the past year Sussex both issued and reacquired shares of its own common stock, some of which the company still owned at year end. Additional common stock transactions occurred among the shareholders during the year.

Common stock transactions can be traced to individual shareholders' accounts in a subsidiary ledger and to a stock certificate book. The company has not paid any cash or stock dividends. There are no other classes of stock, stock rights, warrants, or option plans.

Required:

What substantive audit procedures should Jones apply in examining the common stock and treasury stock accounts?

(*AICPA adapted*)

Auditing the Operations, Contingencies, and Subsequent Events Cell

---

Learning Objectives   *After reading and studying the material in this chapter, the student should*

Know the characteristics of the accounts comprising the operations, contingencies, and subsequent events cell.

Understand how important features of the internal control structure associated with operations, contingencies, and subsequent events affect the scope of substantive tests in those areas.

Know the audit objectives in the operations, contingencies, and subsequent events areas.

Be able to determine and apply the audit procedures necessary to accomplish the audit objectives in the operations, contingencies, and subsequent event cells.

Understand the preparation of audit working papers to document the audit procedures in the operations, contingencies, and subsequent event cells.

This chapter will include examples of the audit objectives, procedures, and working papers involved in the audit of revenue, expense, contingencies, and subsequent events. Important relationships exist among these elements, particularly revenue and expense; therefore, they should be examined together.

Revenue and Expense

Investors and other users of financial statements of business enterprises rely on the statement of income as an indication of a company's performance for a given period. They often use information from this statement as a guide in projecting expected future performance. In determining the objectives for the audit of revenue and expense, the auditor should keep in mind the use made of the statement of income.

An important concept in the determination of net income is that all items of expense needed to generate a certain amount of revenue be recognized in the same period as the revenue. The concept appears in the professional literature in numerous places, including Section 178.104 of FASB *Accounting Standards,* which states, "The major objective in accounting . . . is the matching of appropriate costs against revenue in order that there may be a proper determination of the realized income."

If net income is to be an effective criterion for gauging the performance of the company and estimating its future performance, unusual and infrequent items that are not the result of normal operations and may not recur should be segregated. Otherwise, the reader of the financial statements may be misled into anticipating the continuation of performance that was actually the result of such nonrecurring items.

Except for the requirement to segregate extraordinary items, companies have considerable leeway in the classification of revenues and expenses within the income statement, provided that the classification is consistent between periods. Most companies that sell a physical product subtract the cost of the product from revenue to arrive at an amount designated as gross profit. Because the profitability of many companies depends on maintaining or increasing the gross profit ratio (the ratio of gross profit to revenue), this ratio is watched closely by many investors. Other companies, particularly those selling services, do not compute gross profit, but subtract all costs and expenses except income taxes from revenue to arrive at net income before income taxes; income tax expense is then subtracted from this amount to arrive at net income. Several disclosures concerning revenues and expenses are required by generally accepted accounting principles (the amount of research and development expenditures, the segregation of current and deferred income taxes, etc.).

Revenue and expense accounts are subject to many of the same internal control structures as are the related asset and liability accounts. In particular, they are often subject to budgetary controls. These controls can be very effective if variations between the actual and budgeted amounts are investigated carefully by management

Audit Objectives

The objectives (assertions) in the audit of revenue and expense are as follows:

1. To determine whether all (completeness) revenues and expenses (rights and obligations) applicable to the audit period (occurrence) have been recognized and are matched properly (allocation) in accordance with generally accepted accounting principles.

2. To determine whether all material unusual and infrequent items are segregated properly in the income statement (presentation).

3. To determine whether revenues and expenses are classified properly and consistently (presentation).

4. To determine whether disclosures concerning revenue and expense are adequate and in accordance with generally accepted accounting principles (disclosure).

Audit Procedures and Working Papers

Although some detail auditing is performed, the auditor relies heavily on the internal control structure and overall tests in the revenue and expense area. Tests of controls, including controls applicable to shipping, billing, cash receipts, and accounts receivable, are discussed in Chapters 7 and 8. The same controls would apply to revenue. For example, the requirement that billings not be recorded until supported by a shipping notice reduces the probability of recording both invalid accounts receivable *and* invalid sales. If this control does not exist, the auditor may increase the number of accounts receivable confirmations mailed *and* trace a sample of sales transactions to the related shipping notices to compensate for higher control risk. In addition, similar tests of controls would be made in the areas of (1) receiving, cash disbursements, and accounts payable, and (2) payroll. These controls would apply to expenses. For example, if cash disbursements are classified in accordance with a formal chart of accounts and the classification is reviewed by a supervisor, the probability of misclassification may be small. However, if these controls do not exist, the auditor may analyze the major expense accounts and review the propriety of any large charges included therein. The auditor may also perform other tests of procedures and controls such as tests of material issues and of the cost accounting system.

As described in the three previous chapters, many revenue and expense accounts are audited in connection with related asset and liability accounts (e.g., depreciation expense with property and equipment, interest expense with notes payable, allowance for doubtful accounts with accounts receivable). The tests of controls plus the audit work performed on the related asset and liability accounts provide the auditor with evidence regarding the revenue and expense accounts. The auditor supplements this evidence with the procedures described in the following sections.

Analytical Procedures   The auditor places heavy emphasis on analytical procedures in the revenue and expense area. Chronologically, these procedures are usually done early in the audit. Some of the more important procedures are discussed in the following sections.

Review of operations   In its simplest form, the review of operations consists of comparing amounts in the income statement for the year being audited with expected amounts (e.g., the budget for the year and the actual amounts for the prior year if no changes are anticipated) and determining the underlying reasons for significant variations or the lack thereof. Determining the variations may be simply a clerical function, but obtaining explanations of the variations and evaluating their reasonableness require an ability to work with people, as well as persistence and judgment.

Explanations for significant variations are often obtained from client personnel. The auditor should discuss a variation with the individual who is most knowledgeable in the particular area. For example, the sales manager might be the best person to explain an increase in sales, whereas the plant or maintenance supervisor should be asked to explain a material variation in maintenance expense. As discussed in Chapter 12, the explanation should come from someone outside of the accounting department, if possible.

Although auditors prefer information from outside of the accounting department, they must be prepared for the inevitable misunderstandings that arise in discussions with individuals who lack a financial background. Auditors can limit such misunderstandings by evaluating carefully the reasonableness of the explanations in light of the auditors' overall knowledge of the company's operations.

After explanations have been obtained from client personnel, they should be corroborated. Although client explanations may save the auditor considerable time in searching for the reasons for variations, they should not be accepted as audit evidence without corroboration. The client is, after all, the subject of the audit. As an illustration, if the auditor were informed that selling expense declined because three market researchers were terminated, this explanation could be verified by an examination of the payroll records.

The review of operations should be performed at an early stage of the audit, in which case it serves two purposes in addition to providing evidence of the application of analytical procedures to the income and expense accounts. First, it is an excellent means of familiarizing the auditor with the client's business operations. This knowledge is needed if the auditor is to determine whether the financial statements properly reflect the client's operations. Second, it is a means of spotting, at an early point in the audit, areas that may present problems or require special attention. For example, a decline in maintenance expense when the maintenance supervisor says that there has been no reduction in maintenance work may indicate a change in the accounting capitalization policy and may necessitate more detail audit work in the maintenance and property areas; or a decline in interest expense when outstanding debt has increased and interest rates have not changed may indicate that interest expense was charged to an incorrect account or was underaccrued. Thus, the review of operations is an important audit procedure and should be performed by an experienced staff member.

A partial example of one form of a review of operations is shown in Figure 18.1. In this example, sales were analyzed by market area (they could also be analyzed by product, type of service, etc.) and compared with the budgeted and prior-year amounts. Variations were computed (percentage as well as amount variations may also be helpful), and significant variations were explained. Although the explanations were obtained from the president, the auditor examined evidence to support the explanations.

A review of this type would be important in complying with *SAS No. 21* on segment information, which requires an analysis and inquiry regarding the bases for determining segment information and accounting for intersegment transfers and allocation of common assets and expenses. The auditor should also perform analytical procedures on the segment information and determine whether it is presented consistently from period to period.

Ratio tests   The ratio tests that can be applied in each audit vary by industry and by individual company. Many of these ratios have been discussed, such as the gross profit ratio, the ratio of bad debt write-offs to revenues, and the ratio of selling expense to revenue. Another ratio usually computed in audits of corporations is income taxes as a percentage of net income before income taxes. An investigation should be made of any significant difference between this ratio and the combined federal and state corporate rates. The auditor should recognize important relationships between financial statement amounts and should review them to see whether any appear out of line or inconsistent.

Test of reasonableness   Though detail audit procedures are important, the auditor should not become so engrossed with the details that he or she ignores obvious indications of problems with the financial statements. There are many overall tests of reasonableness (sometimes called predictive auditing) that an auditor can and should apply. For example, a quick overall test of revenue for a particular product may be made by calculating an average price of the product (from a review of several sales invoices throughout the year) and multiplying it by the number of units of the product sold (from sales statistics or inventory reports; also, compare sales with plant capacity). The resulting answer seldom exactly equals the recorded revenue for that product, but it should approximate it. Many companies maintain elaborate sales statistics in the sales department, which can be used to determine the reasonableness of the sales amount. In addition, budget reports can be helpful in reviewing the reasonableness of most items of expense. If any overall tests yield unreasonable results, the auditor will expand the detail tests.

Regression analysis, discussed in Chapter 12, is another method of determining predicted values for comparison with current-year actual values. It is

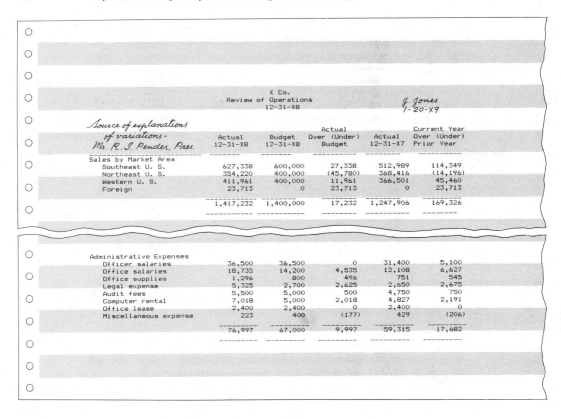

Figure 18.1   Review of operations.

particularly useful in predicting revenue and expense amounts. Deloitte Haskins & Sells have developed a microcomputer program referred to as STAR (Statistical Techniques for Analytical Review) that uses regression analysis to predict such values. The predicted values are then compared with the recorded amounts and differences are calculated. The program also contains an audit interface section that is designed to answer the question of how much difference should be considered unusual. Based on a calculation of the standard error of the regression estimate and on the statistical assurance (tolerable error and risk of incorrect acceptance) desired by the auditor, the STAR program determines the portion, if any, of the recorded amounts that should be considered as unusual differences and prints such amounts as an excess to be investigated.

As an example, if an auditor were examining the financial statements of a carwash, he or she may believe that there should be a relationship between the cost of water used and the amount of revenue earned. The STAR program could be used to predict monthly revenue for the year under audit based on a regression

Sales

Sales increased by approximately 14% during the current year. Approximately 10% of this increase was due to a price increase of widgets as of the beginning of the year with the balance due to an increase in volume (see tests of invoice prices on 10-4 and review of production records on 20-5). A review of sales by market area shows the Northeast U.S. under budget and prior year while all other market areas were over budget and the prior year. The sales manager of the Northeast U.S. market resigned early in the year and there was a delay in finding a replacement (verified by review of payroll records). As a result, the marketing effort in the Northeast was behind schedule most of the year. A branch office was opened in Mexico City this year, accounting for the small initial foreign sales...

Administrative expenses

Administrative expenses for the current year were 15% over budget and 30% over the prior year. An additional employee was hired in the accounting department and considerable overtime was worked (verified by review of payroll records) in converting from a manual to a computerized inventory system and in accounting for the new foreign operations. Also, an increase in officer salaries was approved by the Board of Directors (see 1-14-X8 Board of Directors minutes at XX). Finally, legal expense increased over prior year and budget due to the filing of an antitrust action against the company. (see 40-1).

Figure 18.1   (Continued)

model constructed from the monthly observations of the previous three years for revenue and water expense. The output of the STAR program is shown in Figure 18.2. It indicates that month 38 (February) has an overstatement that should be investigated. Data for a PPS sample for that month are also generated.

Auditors who do not have access to such sophisticated programs as STAR may still use the regression programs in commercial microcomputer software such as Lotus 1-2-3 and many hand-held calculators to predict amounts such as current-year monthly revenue and expense amounts based on audited monthly amounts for prior years. Relationships between different accounts also may be developed and used as predictors provided they are plausible and relevant to the audit.

Account Analysis   The auditor usually analyzes certain expense accounts because of large unexplained variations from budgeted or prior-year amounts or to gain information about the expenditures that are included in them, as well as to document the authenticity of the expenses. Legal expense is an example of such

STAR -- Statistical Techniques for Analytical Review

REPORT PRINTED ON JANUARY 20, 1989 AT 08:32

JOB   :CARWASH
CLIENT   :UNIVERSAL CAR WASH, INC
YEAR END :12/31/88

APPLICATION NUMBER # 2 (REVENUE) REPORT TYPE 1

REPORT REVIEWED BY : *J. Jones*   DATE : *1-20-X9*

SPECIFICATIONS FOR MODEL

NAME OF VARIABLE	SOURCE/DESCRIPTION OF VARIABLE	UNITS	BYPASS
Y REVENUE	CO1	1	NONE
X1 WATER EXPENSE	CO2	1	NONE

NUMBER OF OBSERVATIONS :
USED TO GENERATE MODEL   36
USED FOR PROJECTIONS   12
                                ____
  TOTAL   48
                                ====

NO OBSERVATIONS HAVE BEEN BYPASSED

THE DATA PROFILE IS CROSS-SECTIONAL

STEPWISE MULTIPLE REGRESSION MODEL

	INPUT DATA		REGRESSION FUNCTION ETC.	
DESCRIPTION	MEAN	STANDARD ERROR	CONSTANT OR COEFFICIENT	STANDARD ERROR
CONSTANT			-4466.6758	
INDEPENDENT VARIABLES				
X1 WATER EXPENSE	725.5278	48.4208	15.3043	0.7156
DEPENDENT VARIABLE				
Y REVENUE	6637.0278	768.0952		
Y' REGRESSION ESTIMATE			6637.0278	204.9895
COEFFICIENT OF :				
CORRELATION			0.9648	
REGRESSION IMPROVEMENT			0.7331	
RESIDUAL VARIATION			0.0309	

Figure 18.2   The output of the STAR program.

694

REGRESSION ESTIMATE [Y'(t)] OF REVENUE FOR OBSERVATION t :
Y'(t) = -4466.676 + 15.3043*X1(t)

AUDIT OF PROJECTION DATA

MONETARY PRECISION = 1500 (SAME UNITS AS DEPENDENT VARIABLE)
RELIABILITY FACTOR = 3
DIRECTION OF TEST IS OVERSTATEMENT

------------------------------ REGRESSION PROJECTIONS ------------------------------

| | | | | | OPTIONAL SAMPLE DATA | | |
OBS NO	RECORDED AMOUNT	REGRESSION ESTIMATE	RESIDUAL	EXCESS TO BE INVESTIGATED	SELECTION INTERVAL	RANDOM START	MAXIMUM ITEMS
37	7350	7364	-14				
38	7203	6246	957	670	500	121	15
39	7086	6859	227				
40	7290	7165	125				
41	7540	7777	-237				
42	7667	7930	-263				
43	7842	8159	-317				
44	7975	8389	-414				
45	8152	8542	-390				
46	7988	8465	-477				
47	7897	8389	-492				
48	7679	8083	-404				
	91669	93368	-1699	670			15

END OF REPORT ON APPLICATION 2

Figure 18.2   (continued)

an account that could contain significant information concerning contingent liabilities. Figure 18.3 illustrates a working paper analysis of legal expense. Note that the auditor has examined the vouchers in payment of the legal expense as well as the invoices from the attorney and the canceled check (indicated by √). The first voucher was for a legal retainer that was of little interest to the auditor. The second voucher, however, was for legal representation in an antitrust complaint. The antitrust complaint, which could result in damages being assessed against the

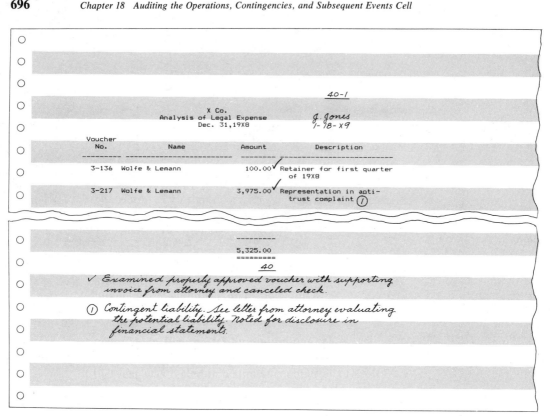

Figure 18.3 Analysis of legal expense.

company, represents a contingent liability, which (per ①) has been evaluated by the attorney in a letter obtained in connection with the subsequent review and has been noted for disclosure in the financial statements.

Other expense accounts that usually are analyzed include repairs and maintenance (for capital items charged to expense), rents (for identification of lease liabilities), and miscellaneous expense (because it is often the repository of unusual or misclassified charges and expenses).

Classification and Disclosure   A number of revenue and expense transactions require special classification or disclosure, and the auditor must be alert to such transactions during the work on revenue and expense. Examples are the classification of extraordinary items and losses from discontinued operations and disclosure of certain gains and losses. The auditor also should be satisfied with the level of summarization of the revenue and expense accounts in the income statement—for example, that all significant accounts are shown separately and all insignificant accounts are aggregated.

SUMMARY OF IMPORTANT AUDIT PROCEDURES
FOR REVENUE AND EXPENSE

- Review and evaluate the effect of the internal control structure on the scope of revenue and expense work.

- Perform analytical procedures, including review of operations, ratio tests, and tests of reasonableness.

- Analyze selected accounts and examine supporting documentation to explain unusual variations, gain information about the accounts, and document the authenticity of the accounts.

- Review the classification and disclosure of revenue and expense transactions.

Minutes

Although minutes may contain information that is relevant to all sections of the audit, they are particularly important to the operations, contingencies, and subsequent events cell.

As part of each examination, the auditor should extract or obtain copies of the minutes of all meetings of stockholders (or partners in the case of a partnership), board of directors, and subcommittees of the board of directors (the executive committee, compensation committee, finance committee, etc.). The extracts or copies must be made from or compared with the original signed minutes to ensure their authenticity, and a notation should be made on them to this effect.

Because almost all important actions of a company are approved in these minutes, they should be subjected to a careful review. Matters of auditing significance that might be found in a review of the minutes include the following:

1. Authorization for new bond or stock issues.

2. Authorization of dividend payments.

3. Plans for plant expansion (which might involve significant purchase commitments) or the acquisition of other companies.

4. Threatened or pending litigation against the client.

5. Adoption of pension, profit-sharing, or stock option plans.

6. Approval of important contracts and agreements (including employment agreements).

7. Approval of the purchase or sale of significant assets.

The auditor should next ascertain that important actions noted in the minutes have been properly reflected or disclosed in the financial statements. Important actions also are cross-referenced to the sections of the working papers in which they are recorded or audited. For example, a resolution of the board of directors declaring a dividend of $0.50 a share would be cross-referenced to the retained earnings section of the working papers where a calculation such as the following might be found.

Number of shares of common stock outstanding, per examination of stockbook	100,000
Dividend per share, per board of directors' authorization	$ 0.50
Total dividend paid per *TB-2*	$ 50,000

Minutes of prior years also should be reviewed during an auditor's first examination of a particular company. In this review, the auditor is primarily interested in actions having a continuing effect on the company and its financial statements.

Commitments and Contingencies

Although commitments and contingencies are not recorded in the financial statements, generally accepted accounting principles require their disclosure, usually in footnotes. Because these disclosures are a basic part of the financial statements, they should be subjected to audit procedures just as though they were a recorded amount.

Commitments are important to readers of financial statements because they represent future cash flow requirements. Some common commitments are those related to leases, pension plans, and construction expenditures.

Statement of Financial Accounting Standards No. 13 specifies the accounting required for leases. From the lessee's standpoint, leases are classified as either capital or operating leases. Capital leases are reported as assets and liabilities in the balance sheet, whereas operating leases are disclosed as commitments. Operating lease disclosures include minimum rental commitments in the aggregate and for each of the next five years, total rental expense, and a general description of the leasing arrangements.

Pension plan disclosures are set forth in *SFAS No. 87* and include details regarding the description of the plan, the net periodic pension cost amount, a reconciliation of balance sheet amounts with the funded status of the plan, various rates used in the calculation of pension amounts, and other information.

Disclosure of the amount of construction expenditures anticipated in the succeeding year assists the reader of the financial statements in projecting future cash flow requirements and usually is included in a footnote.

Statement of Financial Accounting Standards No. 5   provides guidance as to whether an estimated loss from a contingency should be recorded or disclosed. Examples of contingencies commonly disclosed in financial statements are pending or threatened litigation, guarantees of indebtedness, threat of expropriation of assets, and proposed assessment of additional taxes. Certain contingencies, such as those of the environmental and product liability type, relate to matters that may normally not be shown in the accounting records of the entity, but may be so pervasive as to affect the viability and survival of the business (declaration of bankruptcy by asbestos companies is an example).

Audit Objectives

The objectives (assertions) in the audit of commitments and contingencies are as follows:

1. To determine whether all (completeness) significant commitments and contingencies (existence and obligations) as of the balance sheet date are shown properly (valuation and presentation) in the financial statements.

2. To determine whether the disclosures of commitments and contingencies are made in accordance with generally accepted accounting principles (disclosure).

Audit Procedures and Working Papers

The auditor often finds that clients with strong internal control structures in the conventional areas, such as cash receipts and disbursements and inventories, have surprisingly weak procedures and controls in the areas of commitments and contingencies. This is an area in which the auditor may have difficulty in distinguishing between accumulating and auditing the information.

Some controls that the auditor may consider include (1) formal client procedures to review each lease to determine its capital or operating characteristics, allowing the auditor to limit tests in this area, (2) board of director approval of the construction budget, reducing the auditor's time spent in evaluating this commitment, and (3) in-house legal counsel review and evaluation of pending litigation, lessening the time spent by the auditor in assessing this contingency.

Analytical Procedures   Because of the nature of commitments and contingencies, analytical procedures have limited application. However, commitments and contingencies that exist at the end of one year are often relevant at the end of the next year. For example, (1) large construction projects often extend over several years so that related commitments would have to be disclosed at the end of each year, (2) litigation often extends for several years, so that disclosure should be made at the end of each year it is pending, and (3) such items as pension plans and leases normally cover many years, thereby requiring continuous disclosure. Therefore, the auditor should compare the commitments and contingencies existing at the end of the prior year with those expected for the current year and account for any differences.

Pensions   Pension plan disclosure data are audited by examining the terms of the contract between the client and the insurance company (a copy should be maintained in the permanent audit file and updated annually) and by confirming these terms with the insurance company. Using the information in the confirmation, the auditor recomputes pension expense and reviews the pension footnote to see whether the required disclosures are made.

Leases   The accumulation of information for the disclosure of lease commitments can be very time-consuming if adequate records are not maintained by the client. Figure 18.4 is an example of a schedule on which lease disclosure information is accumulated and audited. The pertinent lease information has been traced to an *executed* lease agreement (indicated by $\sqrt{}$) and the spreading of the lease payments into time periods has been recomputed (indicated by $\wedge$). The classification of the leases as operating leases under *FASB No. 13* has also been checked. Total rental expense for the year has been cross-referenced to an expense account. The auditor should also review the applicable footnote for proper disclosure.

Other Procedures   Auditors must be alert in every section of their work for contingent liabilities. Some of the procedures specifically designed to detect contingent liabilities include the following:

1. Review of questions about the existence of contingent liabilities on confirmations from bank and other financial institutions.

2. Review of minutes of meetings of directors and stockholders for actions indicating the existence of contingent liabilities (hiring of special legal counsel, discussion of possible asset expropriation, approval of the guarantee of third-party obligations, etc.).

3. Analysis of the legal expense account for information about litigation and claims for which legal counsel has been engaged.

4. Confirmation directly with legal counsel of the details of litigation and claims being handled for the client. This procedure is discussed further in the subsequent events section.

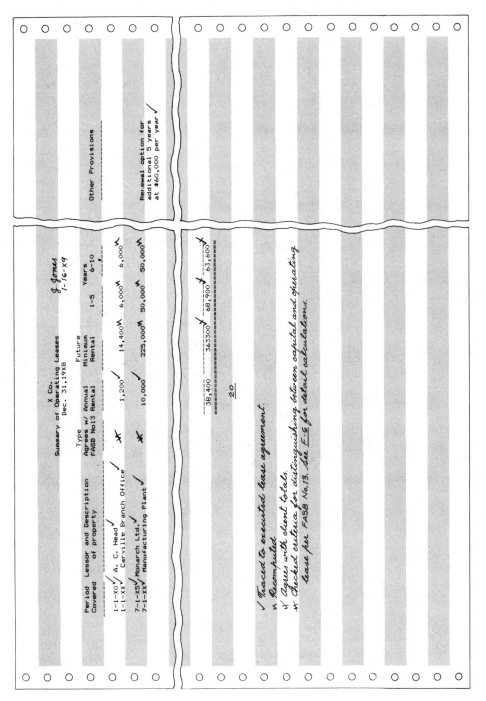

Figure 18.4   Summary of operating leases.

5. Inquiry of management. The existence of contingent liabilities is a matter that normally is included in the representation letter obtained from management.

Subsequent Events

Generally, an auditor's examination is not completed and the financial statements are not issued until after the audit date, that is, the date as of which the audit is performed. The period between the audit date and the date the financial statements are issued usually can be divided into three segments: (1) time required for the client to complete, total, and balance the accounting records and otherwise prepare them for audit, (2) time required for the auditor to perform the examination in the client's office (referred to as field work), and (3) time after leaving the client's office required for the auditor to perform quality-control reviews and reproduce and deliver the report. "Subsequent events" may occur anytime during this period (segments one, two, and three), and consist of events or transactions that have a material effect on the financial statements and therefore require adjustments or disclosure in the statements. The "subsequent period" extends through segment two. See Chapter 19 for the auditor's responsibility for segment three.

Because the auditor is in the client's office and has access to the accounting records and management during the subsequent period, he or she has a responsibility to search for material events through that date that might require adjustment of, or disclosure in, the financial statements (the auditor's report also is dated as of the end of field work). Such events can be classified into two types:

1. Events that provide additional information about conditions that existed as of the audit date and affect estimates inherent in the preparation of financial statements.

2. Events that provide information about conditions arising after the audit date.

Information provided by the first type of event should be used to evaluate further the accounting estimates reflected in the financial statements, and the financial statements should be adjusted if changes in the estimates are necessary as a result of the additional information. An example would be the final settlement before the end of the field work of a major lawsuit that arose before the audit date. The settlement would provide additional evidence on the amount of the liability as of the audit date.

Information provided by the second type of event should not result in adjustment of the financial statements (except that stock dividends and splits may be reflected retroactively) but may require disclosure. An example of this type of event is an occurrence after the audit date that results in the filing of a major lawsuit against the client. Neither the event nor the lawsuit would affect the amounts shown in the financial statements as of the audit date, and, therefore, the financial statements should not be adjusted. The event should be disclosed, however, because it could have a material future effect on the client's financial statements.

Detection and evaluation of the foregoing types of events concern the auditor in the audit of subsequent events.

Audit Objectives

The objectives (assertions) in the audit of subsequent events are as follows:

1. To determine whether the financial statements are adjusted (presentation) when necessary for all (completeness) subsequent events (occurrence) that provide additional information about accounting estimates (valuation).

2. To determine whether adequate disclosure (disclosure) is made when necessary of all (completeness) subsequent events (occurrence) reflecting new conditions that may have a material future effect on the company.

Audit Procedures and Working Papers

The audit procedures applied to the period subsequent to the audit date can be divided into four general groups, discussed in the following sections.

Review of Subsequent Financial Records   To the extent that transactions subsequent to the audit date have been summarized in interim financial statements, these statements should be read and compared with the financial statements being audited. Any unusual or unexpected variations or trends (a loss when operations previously had been profitable, significant decreases in assets or increases in liabilities, etc.) should be investigated. For the period from the date of the latest interim financial statements to the last day of field work, the auditor should review the basic accounting records for unusual and significant transactions that may affect the financial statements being audited. Such records include the general ledger, general journal, cash receipts and disbursements records (the review of the cash disbursement records should be coordinated with the review of subsequent transactions as part of the accounts payable work), and sales and expense journals. The review of minutes should also be updated through the last day of field work.

Inquiries of Management   Discussions should be held on the last day of field work with the chief executive and financial officers as well as other company officials who may be knowledgeable about the subjects in question. Among the matters discussed would be the following.

1. The existence of any material commitments or contingencies as of the audit date or the last day of field work.

2. Material changes in the equity accounts, long-term debt, or working capital subsequent to the audit date.

3. Unusual adjustments made after the audit date or subsequent changes in accounting estimates made as of the audit date.

4. Changes in trends of sales, expenses, and profit after the audit date.

5. Changes in raw material prices after the audit date and their effect on replacement cost of inventories.

6. Cancellation of sales orders or losses of important customers after the audit date.

7. Catastrophes after the audit date (expropriations, fires, explosions, etc.).

8. New contracts or agreements or renegotiation of old ones subsequent to the audit date when sales of products, wages, leases, and so on are affected.

9. Cash flow requirements for the coming year and sources of financing.

10. Effect of development of substitute products, model changes, and so forth.

11. Related party transactions.

The listing is not all-inclusive, but gives examples of the types of matters that should be covered. The inquiries should be tailored to the operations of each client. The discussions also serve as bases for management's written representations.

Management Representations   During an audit made in accordance with generally accepted auditing standards, an auditor is required by AU Section 333 (*SAS No. 19*) to obtain certain representations from management. These representations may take the form of letters from management to the auditor or preprinted certificates that the auditor furnishes management for signature. Management representations serve the dual purpose of (1) emphasizing to the client company's management their responsibility for complete and accurate financial statements (the representations may clarify any management misunderstandings as to required disclosures), and (2) providing audit evidence, particularly in areas not susceptible to normal audit procedures. They should not be used, however, as a substitute for customary audit procedures, and they do not relieve the auditor of the responsibility for performing the examination in accordance with generally accepted auditing standards. An example of a management representation letter is shown in Figure 18.5.

Some common representations obtained from management together with the reasons for obtaining them are shown below.

1. A representation that the financial statements being examined by the auditor are the final statements for the year, and management is responsible for determining that they are presented fairly in accordance with generally accepted accounting principles. This representation emphasizes management's responsibility for the fairness of the financial statements and, if an error is discovered after the financial statements are issued, it prevents management from maintaining that they knew of and disclosed the error to the auditor.

2. A representation that there are no material unrecorded assets or liabilities and no contingent assets or liabilities that are not disclosed properly in the financial statements. Examples are unrecorded claims receivable or payable and liabilities from lawsuits or as guarantor of third-party obligations. Because transactions of this nature are difficult to detect with normal audit procedures, additional assurance is sought from management as the party most likely to be aware of such transactions.

3. A representation that all agreements relating to capital stock are disclosed properly in the financial statements. This representation concerns the disclosure of such items as stock repurchase agreements and stock option plans. Although items of this nature usually are approved by the board of directors or the stockholders and included in the minutes of their meetings, such approval is not a legal requirement in all states. Therefore, a representation covering these matters is requested from management.

4. A representation that transactions with other entities were based on arm's-length dealings. This representation is one of several audit procedures for determining the existence of related parties. Disclosure of transactions with related parties is usually necessary for a fair presentation of the financial statements.

5. A representation that there have been no events or transactions subsequent to the audit date that would have a material effect on the financial statements that have not been disclosed therein. The auditor's responsibility extends beyond the audit date for material transactions that affect the financial statements; a representation is obtained to remind management

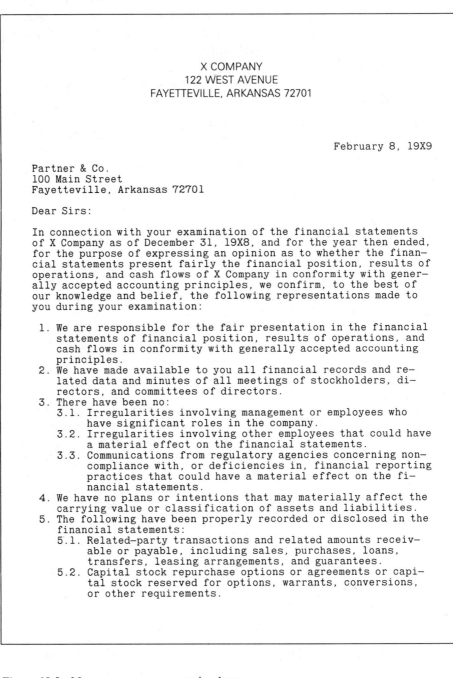

X COMPANY
122 WEST AVENUE
FAYETTEVILLE, ARKANSAS 72701

February 8, 19X9

Partner & Co.
100 Main Street
Fayetteville, Arkansas 72701

Dear Sirs:

In connection with your examination of the financial statements
of X Company as of December 31, 19X8, and for the year then ended,
for the purpose of expressing an opinion as to whether the financial statements present fairly the financial position, results of
operations, and cash flows of X Company in conformity with generally accepted accounting principles, we confirm, to the best of
our knowledge and belief, the following representations made to
you during your examination:

1. We are responsible for the fair presentation in the financial
   statements of financial position, results of operations, and
   cash flows in conformity with generally accepted accounting
   principles.
2. We have made available to you all financial records and related data and minutes of all meetings of stockholders, directors, and committees of directors.
3. There have been no:
   3.1. Irregularities involving management or employees who
        have significant roles in the company.
   3.2. Irregularities involving other employees that could have
        a material effect on the financial statements.
   3.3. Communications from regulatory agencies concerning non-
        compliance with, or deficiencies in, financial reporting
        practices that could have a material effect on the fi-
        nancial statements.
4. We have no plans or intentions that may materially affect the
   carrying value or classification of assets and liabilities.
5. The following have been properly recorded or disclosed in the
   financial statements:
   5.1. Related-party transactions and related amounts receiv-
        able or payable, including sales, purchases, loans,
        transfers, leasing arrangements, and guarantees.
   5.2. Capital stock repurchase options or agreements or capi-
        tal stock reserved for options, warrants, conversions,
        or other requirements.

Figure 18.5   Management representation letter.

    5.3. Arrangements with financial institutions involving re-
strictions on cash balances and line–of–credit or similar arrangements.

    5.4. Agreements to repurchase assets previously sold.

6. There are no:

    6.1. Violations or possible violations of laws or regulations
whose effects should be considered for disclosure in the
financial statements or as a basis for recording a loss
contingency.

    6.2. Other material liabilities or gain or loss contingencies
that are required to be accrued or disclosed by Statement
of Financial Accounting Standards No. 5.

7. There are no unasserted claims or assessments that our lawyer
has advised us are probable of assertion and must be disclosed in accordance with Statement of Financial Accounting
Standards No. 5.

8. The accounting records underlying the financial statements
accurately and fairly reflect, in reasonable detail, the
transactions of the company.

9. Provision, when material, has been made to reduce excess or
obsolete inventories to their estimated net realizable value.

10. The company has satisfactory title to all owned assets, and
there are no liens or encumbrances on such assets nor has any
asset been pledged.

11. Provision has been made for any material loss to be sustained
in the fulfillment of, or from inability to fulfill, any
sales commitments.

12. Provision has been made for any material loss to be sustained
as a result of purchase commitments for inventory quantities
in excess of normal requirements or at prices in excess of
the prevailing market prices.

13. We have complied with all aspects of contractual agreements
that would have a material effect on the financial statements
in the event of noncompliance.

14. No events have occurred subsequent to the balance sheet date
that would require adjustment to, or disclosure in, the financial statements.

Blair Mills
_____
Blair Mills, President

Bruce Lee
_____
Bruce Lee, Controller

Figure 18.5   (continued)

that their responsibility also extends beyond the audit date and to supplement the limited procedures performed by the auditor during this period.

6. A representation that all financial and accounting records were furnished to the auditor and none was withheld. This representation is primarily a reminder to management of their obligation to the auditor.

7. A representation that minutes of all meetings of stockholders and directors (and any subcommittees) held during the period from the beginning of the year being audited to the date the audit is completed have been furnished the auditor. This representation, usually signed by the corporate secretary, constitutes evidence for the auditor that all minutes have been accounted for and that none has been overlooked or withheld.

8. A representation that there are no agreements to repurchase assets previously sold. This representation is intended to detect significant contingencies that may not be evident in the accounting records.

9. A representation that there have been no violations of laws or regulations, the effects of which should be considered for disclosure in the financial statements or as a basis for recording a loss contingency. This representation is intended to bring to the auditor's attention violations of environmental, product safety, or similar laws and regulations that are difficult to detect from the accounting records.

An example of a management representation letter is shown in Figure 18.5.

The representations usually are signed by the chief executive officer (chairman of the board of directors or president) and the chief financial officer (financial vice-president, treasurer, or controller), because these individuals should be the most knowledgeable about the subjects of the representation. Auditors should not accept the representations of lower-level officers in place of those of the chief executive and financial officers. The dates of the representations should coincide with the last day of audit work in the client's office, which would make them effective through the date to which the auditor's responsibility extends.

Letters from Legal Counsel   The auditor should ask management to request the company's legal counsel (usually identified from an analysis of legal expense—see Figure 18.3) to confirm directly to the auditor a description and evaluation of pending or threatened litigation, claims, or other contingent liabilities as of the audit date and the end of field work for which legal counsel has been engaged. For many years, attorneys routinely replied to these requests in various forms, generally without reservation. In the mid-1970s, however, after the SEC charged two prominent law firms with violations of the Securities Exchange Act, auditors began to have difficulty in obtaining adequate responses to such requests.

Although the entire matter was complex and involved numerous issues, the principal area of disagreement was unasserted claims. The auditors maintained that unasserted claims should be included in the attorney's response, and attorneys maintained that they could not be responsible for unasserted claims. Furthermore, the attorneys argued that such matters are usually unimportant unless disclosed to the auditor and published in the financial statements, in which case the appropriate party would be likely to assert the claims.

After two years of discussion between committees of the AICPA and the American Bar Association and considerable internal dissent within each group, *SAS No. 12* was issued. In this statement the attorney is asked to comment only on unasserted claims listed by management and to acknowledge professional responsibility to advise management with regard to the possible disclosure of unasserted claims.[1]

The following information is requested of legal counsel: (1) regarding pending or threatened litigation—(a) evaluation *and* (b) completeness of management's information; and (2) regarding unasserted claims—(a) evaluation *but not* completeness of management's information and (b) confirmation of legal counsel's responsibility to consult with the client concerning disclosure of unasserted claims. Thus, attorneys may advise clients regarding disclosure requirements for unasserted claims under *FASB Statement No. 5,* whereas the auditor who expresses an opinion on the financial statements may be unaware of the advice given. This is the point that bothers many auditors. The American Bar Association has indicated that attorneys may be required to resign their engagement if their advice concerning disclosures is disregarded by the client.

Figure 18.6 illustrates an audit inquiry of legal counsel with one pending lawsuit and no unasserted claims.

In determining whether the financial statements are affected by a material uncertainty due to litigation, claims, and assessments, the language used by lawyers in their responses must be considered carefully. Unequivocal statements of opinion to the effect that actions against the client have "little or no merit," that the client "will be able to successfully defend the action," or that the ultimate liability to the client "will not be material" can usually be accepted as evidence that no material uncertainties exist regarding those matters. On the other hand, vague opinions that the client has "a good chance of prevailing" or "meritorious defenses" suggest the existence of an uncertainty. It is important that the auditor not make an evaluation of the outcome of a legal matter when legal counsel is unwilling or unable to do so.

The auditor's reporting problems resulting from limitations on a lawyer's response are discussed in Chapter 20.

---

[1] Some auditors consider this accommodation to be unsatisfactory, and have suggested that their responsibilities in the area of unasserted claims be modified unless attorneys become more responsive. See Benjamin Benson, "Lawyers' Responses to Audit Inquiries—A Continuing Controversy," *Journal of Accountancy* (July 1977), pp. 72–78.

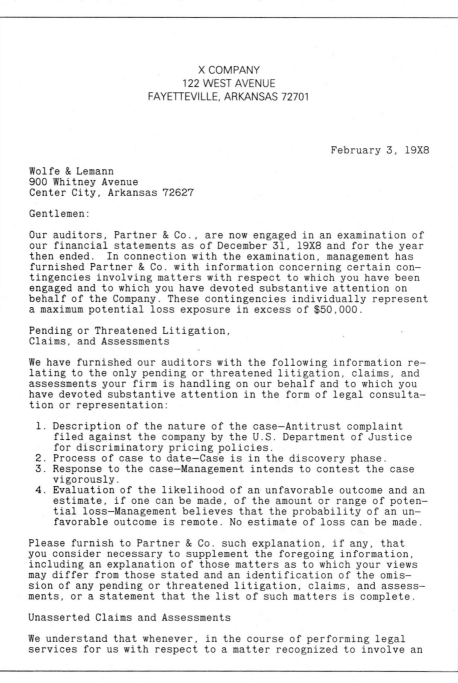

X COMPANY
122 WEST AVENUE
FAYETTEVILLE, ARKANSAS 72701

February 3, 19X8

Wolfe & Lemann
900 Whitney Avenue
Center City, Arkansas 72627

Gentlemen:

Our auditors, Partner & Co., are now engaged in an examination of
our financial statements as of December 31, 19X8 and for the year
then ended. In connection with the examination, management has
furnished Partner & Co. with information concerning certain contingencies involving matters with respect to which you have been
engaged and to which you have devoted substantive attention on
behalf of the Company. These contingencies individually represent
a maximum potential loss exposure in excess of $50,000.

Pending or Threatened Litigation,
Claims, and Assessments

We have furnished our auditors with the following information relating to the only pending or threatened litigation, claims, and
assessments your firm is handling on our behalf and to which you
have devoted substantive attention in the form of legal consultation or representation:

  1. Description of the nature of the case—Antitrust complaint
     filed against the company by the U.S. Department of Justice
     for discriminatory pricing policies.
  2. Process of case to date—Case is in the discovery phase.
  3. Response to the case—Management intends to contest the case
     vigorously.
  4. Evaluation of the likelihood of an unfavorable outcome and an
     estimate, if one can be made, of the amount or range of poten-
     tial loss—Management believes that the probability of an un-
     favorable outcome is remote. No estimate of loss can be made.

Please furnish to Partner & Co. such explanation, if any, that
you consider necessary to supplement the foregoing information,
including an explanation of those matters as to which your views
may differ from those stated and an identification of the omission of any pending or threatened litigation, claims, and assessments, or a statement that the list of such matters is complete.

Unasserted Claims and Assessments

We understand that whenever, in the course of performing legal
services for us with respect to a matter recognized to involve an

unasserted possible claim or assessment that may call for financial statement disclosure, if you have formed a professional conclusion that we must disclose or consider disclosure concerning
such possible claim or assessment, as a matter of professional
responsibility to us, you will so advise us and will consult with
us concerning the question of such disclosure and the applicable
requirements of <u>Statement of Financial Accounting Standards No.
5.</u> Please specifically confirm to Partner & Co. that our understanding is correct.

   We will be representing to Partner & Co. that there are no
unasserted possible claims or assessments that you have advised
are probable of assertion and must be disclosed in accordance
with <u>Statement of Financial Accounting Standards No. 5</u> in the financial statements currently under examination.

Other Matters

Your response should include matters that existed at December 31,
19X8 and for the period from that date to the date of your response. Please specifically identify the nature of and reasons
for any limitation on your response.

   Also, please furnish Partner & Co. with the amount of any
unpaid fees due you as of December 31, 19X8 for services rendered
through that date.

   Please mail your reply directly to Partner & Co., 100 Main
Street, Fayetteville, Arkansas 72701. A stamped, addressed envelope is enclosed for your convenience. Also, please furnish us
a copy of your reply.

                              Very truly yours,
                              X Company

                              By *Blair Mills*
                              Blair Mills, President

Figure 18.6   Inquiry of Client's lawyer.

SUMMARY OF IMPORTANT AUDIT PROCEDURES
FOR SUBSEQUENT EVENTS

- Review subsequent transactions as shown in interim financial statements, general ledger, journal entries, cash receipts and disbursements journals, minutes, and so on.

- Inquire of management regarding subsequent events and transactions.

- Obtain representation letters.

- Obtain letters from legal counsel.

Chapter 18
Glossary of Terms

(listed in order of appearance in the chapter, with accompanying page reference where the term is discussed)

Term	*Page in Chapter*
Review of operations the application of analytical procedures to the income statement to identify and investigate unusual amounts and variations.	690
Subsequent events events that provide additional information about conditions that existed as of the audit date and affect estimates in the financial statements or that provide information about conditions arising after the audit date.	702
Management representations written statements from management to the auditor confirming their responsibility for the financial statements and for representations made to the auditor.	704
Unasserted claim a potential claim against the client that has not yet been asserted by the claimant in the form of litigation or otherwise.	709

Chapter 18
References

American Institute of Certified Public Accountants. *Professional Standards*

AU Section 333—Client Representations;

AU Section 337—Inquiry of a Client's Lawyer Concerning Litigation, Claims, and Assessments;

AU Section 560—Subsequent Events.

Benis, Martin. "The Small Client and Representation Letters," *Journal of Accountancy* (September 1978), pp. 78–84.

Hall, Thomas W., and Butler, A. A. "Assuring Adequate Attorneys' Replies to Audit Inquiries," *Journal of Accountancy* (September 1981), pp. 83–91.

Jiambalvo, James, and Wilner, Neil." Auditor Evaluation of Contingent Claims," *Auditing: A Journal of Practice and Theory* (Fall 1985), pp. 1–11.

Roberts, Ray, "Client Representation Letters and the Discovery of Irregularities," *California CPA Quarterly* (June 1980), pp. 19–23.

Chapter 18
Review Questions

18-1.   Explain the importance to investors and others of the statement of income.

18-2.   State the objectives of the audit of revenue and expense.

18-3.   On what procedures does the auditor place heavy reliance in the audit of revenue and expense?

18-4.   What are the purposes of the review of operations?

18-5.   Name four ratio tests that may be applied in the audit of revenue and expense.

18-6.   Describe an overall test of revenue for reasonableness.

18-7.   Discuss how regression analysis may be used in the audit of revenue and expense.

18-8.   Give two reasons for analyzing an expense account.

18-9.   List four expense accounts that would usually be analyzed and indicate the reasons.

18-10.   Name three types of transactions an auditor must be alert to for proper classification and disclosure.

18-11.   List seven examples of matters of interest to an auditor that may be found in a review of minutes of stockholders and board of directors.

18-12.   Why should the auditor be concerned with commitments and contingencies, since no amounts are shown for them in the financial statements?

18-13.   State the objectives of the audit of commitments and contingencies.

18-14.   What analytical procedures may be applied to commitments and contingencies?

18-15.   List five audit procedures that are specifically designed to detect contingencies.

18-16.   What are the two types of subsequent events that may require adjustment to, or disclosure in, the financial statements? Give an example of each.

18-17.   State the objectives of the audit of subsequent events.

18-18.   List the four general groups of audit procedures applied to subsequent events.

18-19.   Name eight documents or records that would be examined in the review of subsequent events. For what period would the review be conducted?

18-20.   List eleven matters that would be discussed with management in connection with the audit of subsequent events.

18-21.   What are the purposes of management representations?

18-22.   List and explain nine types of representations that may be obtained from management.

18-23.   Which client personnel normally make the representations to the auditor?

18-24.   What information is a company's legal counsel requested to confirm to the auditor?

18-25.   Why are some auditors not satisfied with letters received from legal counsel?

Chapter 18
Objective Questions Taken from CPA Examinations

18-26.   An auditor compares 19X5 revenues and expenses with those of the prior year and investigates all changes exceeding 10 percent. By this procedure the auditor would be most likely to learn that

    a. Fourth quarter payroll taxes were *not* paid.

    b. The client changed its capitalization policy for small tools in 19X5.

    c. An increase in property tax rates has *not* been recognized in the client's accrual.

    d. The 19X5 provision for uncollectible accounts is inadequate because of worsening economic conditions.

18-27. Auditors sometimes use comparisons of ratios as audit evidence. For example, an unexplained decrease in the ratio of gross profit to sales may suggest which of the following possibilities?

    a. Merchandise purchases being charged to selling and general expense.

    b. Fictitious sales.

    c. Unrecorded purchases.

    d. Unrecorded sales.

18-28. Before expressing an opinion concerning the results of operations, the auditor would *best* proceed with the examination of the income statement by

    a. Applying a rigid measurement standard designed to test for understatement of net income.

    b. Analyzing the beginning and ending balance sheet inventory amounts.

    c. Making net income comparisons to published industry trends and ratios.

    d. Examining income statement accounts concurrently with the related balance sheet accounts.

18-29. As a result of analytical procedures, the independent auditor determines that the gross profit percentage has declined from 30 percent in the preceding year to 20 percent in the current year. The auditor should

    a. Require footnote disclosure.

    b. Consider the possibility of an error in the financial statements.

    c. Express an opinion that is qualified due to inability of the client company to continue as a going concern.

    d. Evaluate management's performance in causing this decline.

18-30. Which of the following procedures would ordinarily be expected to best reveal unrecorded sales at the balance sheet date?

    a. Compare shipping documents with sales records.

    b. Apply gross profit rates to inventory disposed of during the period.

    c. Trace payments received subsequent to the balance sheet date.

    d. Send accounts receivable confirmation requests.

18-31. An auditor would most likely identify a contingent liability by obtaining a(an)

    a. Related party transaction confirmation.

    b. Accounts payable confirmation.

    c. Transfer agent confirmation.

    d. Confirmation of open letters of credit from a bank.

18-32.   With respect to contingent liabilities, the auditor may request confirmation from a bank regarding notes receivable
  a. Held by the bank in a custodial account.
  b. Held by the bank for collection.
  c. Collected by the bank.
  d. Discounted by the bank.

18-33.   Beta, Inc., is an affiliate of the audit client and is audited by another firm of auditors. Which of the following is *most* likely to be used by the auditor to obtain assurance that all guarantees of the affiliate's indebtedness have been detected?
  a. Examine supporting documents for all entries in intercompany accounts.
  b. Obtain written confirmation of indebtedness from the auditor of the affiliate.
  c. Send a bank confirmation request to all of the client's lender banks.
  d. Review client minutes and obtain a representation letter.

18-34.   When auditing contingent liabilities, which of the following procedures would be *least* effective?
  a. Reading the minutes of the board of directors.
  b. Reviewing the bank confirmation letter.
  c. Examining customer confirmation replies.
  d. Examining invoices for professional services.

18-35.   An auditor is concerned with completing various phases of the examination after the balance-sheet date. This "subsequent period" extends to the date of the
  a. Auditor's report.
  b. Final review of the audit working papers.
  c. Public issuance of the financial statements.
  d. Delivery of the auditor's report to the client.

18-36.   Which of the following subsequent events will be *least* likely to result in an adjustment to the financial statements?
  a. Culmination of events affecting the realization of accounts receivable owned as of the balance sheet date.
  b. Culmination of events affecting the realization of inventories owned as of the balance sheet date.
  c. Material changes in the settlement of liabilities which were estimated as of the balance sheet date.
  d. Material changes in the quoted market prices of listed investment securities since the balance sheet date.

18-37.   In connection with the annual audit, which of the following is not a "subsequent events" procedure?

    a. Review available interim financial statements.

    b. Read available minutes of meetings of stockholders and directors and, for meetings for which minutes are not available, inquire about matters dealt with at such meetings.

    c. Make inquiries with respect to the financial statements covered at the auditor's previously issued report if new information has become available during the current examination that might affect that report.

    d. Discuss with officers the current status of items in the financial statements that were accounted for on the basis of tentative, preliminary, or inconclusive data.

18-38. A major customer of an audit client suffers a fire just prior to completion of year-end field work. The audit client believes that this event could have a significant direct effect on the financial statements. The auditor should

    a. Advise management to disclose the event in notes to the financial statements.

    b. Disclose the event in the auditor's report.

    c. Withhold submission of the auditor's report until the extent of the direct effect on the financial statements is known.

    d. Advise management to adjust the financial statements.

18-39. A written representation from a client's management which, among other matters, acknowledges responsibility for the fair presentation of financial statements, should normally be signed by the

    a. Chief executive officer and the chief financial officer.

    b. Chief financial officer and the chairman of the board of directors.

    c. Chairman of the audit committee of the board of directors.

    d. Chief executive officer, the chairman of the board of directors, and the client's lawyer.

18-40. Which of the following expressions is *least* likely to be included in a client's representation letter?

    a. No events have occurred subsequent to the balance sheet date that require adjustments to, or disclosure in, the financial statements.

    b. The company has complied with all aspects of contractual agreements that would have a material effect on the financial statements in the event of non-compliance.

    c. Management acknowledges responsibility for illegal actions committed by employees.

    d. Management has made available all financial statements and related data.

18-41. Brown accepted an engagement to audit the 19X5 financial statements of XYZ Company. XYZ completed the preparation of the 19X5 financial statements on February 13, 19X6, and Brown began the field work on February 17, 19X6. Brown completed the field work on March 24, 19X6, and completed the report on March 28, 19X6. The client's representation letter normally would be dated

    a. February 13, 19X6.
    b. February 17, 19X6.
    c. March 24, 19X6.
    d. March 28, 19X6.

18-42.   The auditor's primary means of obtaining corroboration of management's information concerning litigation is a
    a. Letter of audit inquiry to the client's lawyer.
    b. Letter of corroboration from the auditor's lawyer upon review of the legal documentation.
    c. Confirmation of claims and assessments from the other parties to the litigation.
    d. Confirmation of claims and assessments from an officer of the court presiding over the litigation.

18-43.   Which of the following is *not* an audit procedure which the independent auditor would perform with respect to litigation, claims, and assessments?
    a. Inquire of and discuss with management the policies and procedures adopted for identifying, evaluating, and accounting for litigation, claims, and assessments.
    b. Obtain from management a description and evaluation of litigation, claims, and assessments that existed at the balance sheet date.
    c. Obtain assurance from management that it has disclosed all unasserted claims that the lawyer has advised are probable of assertion and must be disclosed.
    d. Confirm directly with the client's lawyer that all claims have been recorded in the financial statements.

18-44.   If a lawyer refuses to furnish corroborating information regarding litigation, claims, and assessments, the auditor should
    a. Honor the confidentiality of the client-lawyer relationship.
    b. Consider the refusal to be tantamount to a scope limitation.
    c. Seek to obtain the corroborating information from management.
    d. Disclose this fact in a footnote to the financial statements.

18-45.   An attorney is responding to an independent auditor as a result of the audit client's letter of inquiry. The attorney may appropriately limit the response to
    a. Asserted claims and litigation.
    b. Matters to which the attorney has given substantive attention in the form of legal consultation or representation.
    c. Asserted, overtly threatened, or pending claims and litigation.
    d. Items that have an extremely high probability of being resolved to the client's detriment.

Chapter 18
Discussion/Case Questions and Problems

18-46. During your audit of Fraudulent Fabrics, you note that the company's gross profit ratio increased to 25 percent this year from 20 percent last year. List the possible causes of this increase and the audit procedures you would employ or expand to investigate each possible cause.

18-47. In your audit of June Company, you are investigating an increase in sales during the current year and have made inquiry of the sales manager, who tells you the increase is due to a sales price increase during the year. When you ask to see a current price list to verify the increase, the sales manager becomes angry and asks if you do not trust him. How would you reply?

18-48. As auditor of Royal Radio Broadcasting Company, you have learned from past audit experience, familiarity with broadcasting industry practice, and a review of Royal's contracts and agreements the following information regarding Royal's operations.

a. Local advertising accounts for about 80 percent and national advertising about 20 percent of Royal's revenue.

b. Salespersons receive a 12-percent commission on sales.

c. Music license fees average 10 percent of sales.

d. Fixed expenses consist of salaries of about $850,000 and depreciation of $100,000 per year.

e. Variable operating expenses such as power and supplies approximate 10 percent of sales.

If, on beginning the audit of Royal for the current year, you learn that total revenue is $4,000,000, what would you expect net income to be under normal operations? Explain your answer.

18-49. During the planning phase of an audit engagement, it was decided that special attention should be paid to the time spent testing some of the income statement accounts. The auditors believed that some accounts required considerable attention and others required very little work. To gain more insight into this matter, the auditors decided to test an account that had taken a considerable number of hours to analyze in the prior-year audit. The account selected was maintenance expense. In previous years, support for all charges to this account in excess of $1,000 had been examined to determine whether the account contained a material amount that belonged in fixed-asset additions. The balance in the account last year was $50,000, and the net income before taxes for the same year was $250,000.

The auditors decided to ascertain whether they had put too much effort into the analysis of this account last year. To do so, they decided to use regression analysis and predict last year's maintenance expense on the basis of the number of machine-hours spent the same year. This predicted figure will be compared with the $50,000 amount on last year's income statement to determine whether there was a difference significant enough to justify the audit effort they devoted to this account.

The auditors collected the number of machine-hours and maintenance expense amounts by month for the 24-month period prior to the current fiscal year. A regression analysis revealed that maintenance expense is fully variable and is expected to change $0.50 for each machine-hour spent. In the prior year, 80,000 machine-hours were spent.

Required:

a. In prior years, were the auditors justified in auditing maintenance expense in the described manner? Why or why not?

b. What is your answer if we assume that 60,000 machine-hours were spent? 20,000 hours?

c. What additional factors should be considered in deciding on the scope of the maintenance expense examination for this year?

d. Why might regression analysis provide misleading data in making this decision?

18-50.   You have decided to use regression analysis in your analytical audit of sales commission expense. Using the monthly balances of the prior three years' amounts of sales (independent variable) and sales commission expense (dependent variable), you computed a regression equation of $\hat{Y}_i = 6.43 + .07\,X_i$ and an r^2 of .85. With this information, predict sales commission expense for each month of the current year based on the following current-year data. Indicate the months, if any, that you would investigate further and what procedures you would apply.

Month	Sales	Sales Commissions
Jan.	$1,842,000	$127,000
Feb.	1,825,000	121,000
Mar.	1,939,000	138,000
Apr.	2,142,000	154,000
May	1,842,000	141,000
June	1,960,000	150,000
July	2,149,000	152,000
Aug.	2,415,000	180,000
Sept.	2,561,000	161,000
Oct.	2,352,000	176,000
Nov.	2,423,000	185,000
Dec.	1,796,000	156,000

18-51.   When examining documentation supporting costs and expenses, an auditor must consider its availability and its adequacy. Discuss the availability and adequacy of documentation you would expect for the following expenses.
a. Purchase of stationery and supplies.
b. Officer travel expenses.
c. Rental expense on office space.
d. Cost of taxi to send sick employee home.
e. Purchase of hams for Christmas gifts to customers.
f. Contribution (purchase of tickets to Policemen's Ball).
g. Payment of income taxes.
h. Payment of directors' fees ($500 per meeting).
i. Employee salary expense.
j. Payment of FICA taxes withheld from employees.
k. Payment of electric bill.

18-52.   Commitments and contingencies can take many forms, including the following:
a. Guarantee of the debt of an affiliated company.
b. Contract with a builder to construct a plant.
c. Maintenance of an unrecorded bank account for illegal political contributions.
d. Discriminatory hiring practices.
e. Violation of antitrust laws.
f. Infringement on patent rights.
g. Disputes with taxing authorities.
      State the audit procedures that could reasonably be employed to detect each of these commitments and contingencies.

18-53.   In general, a lease will be considered a capital lease if it meets any one of the following criteria.
a. The lease transfers ownership of the property to the lessee by the end of the lease term.
b. The lease contains an option to purchase the property at a bargain price.
c. The lease term is equal to 75 percent or more of the estimated economic life of the property.
d. The present value of the rentals and other minimum lease payments is equal to 90 percent or more of the fair value of the leased property.
      Explain how you would audit a lease classification as capital or operating on the basis of these criteria. Indicate the specific documentation you would examine and how you would satisfy yourself as to fair value of rentals, estimated economic life, and so forth.

18-54.   During the examination of the annual financial statements of Amis Manufacturing, Inc., the company's president, R. Alderman, and Luddy, the auditor, reviewed matters that were supposed to be included in a written representation letter. On receipt of the following client representation letter, Luddy contacted Alderman to state that it was incomplete.

To E. K. Luddy, CPA

In connection with your examination of the balance sheet of Amis Manufacturing, Inc. as of December 31, 19X2, and the related statements of income, retained earnings, and cash flows for the year then ended, for the purpose of expressing an opinion as to whether the financial statements present fairly the financial position, results of operations, and cash flows of Amis Manufacturing, Inc. in conformity with generally accepted accounting principles, we confirm, to the best of our knowledge and belief, the following representations made to you during your examination. There were no

- Plans or intentions that may materially affect the carrying value or classification of assets and liabilities.

- Communications from regulatory agencies concerning noncompliance with, or deficiencies in, financial reporting practices.

- Agreements to repurchase assets previously sold.

- Violations or possible violations of laws or regulations whose effects should be considered for disclosure in the financial statements or as a basis for recording a loss contingency.

- Unasserted claims or assessments that our lawyer has advised are probable of assertion and must be disclosed in accordance with *Statement of Financial Accounting Standards No. 5*.

- Capital stock repurchase options or agreements or capital stock reserved for options, warrants, conversions, or other requirements.

- Compensating balance or other arrangements involving restrictions on cash balances.

R. Alderman, President
Amis Manufacturing, Inc.

March 14, 19X3

Required:
Identify the other matters that Alderman's representation letter should specifically confirm.
(AICPA adapted)

18-55.   The field work for the December 31, 19X8 audit of Bypass Manufacturing Company was completed on February 20, 19X9, and the audit report was delivered to the client on March 1, 19X9. The following material transactions and events came to the auditor's attention subsequent to December 31, 19X8. Indicate whether each transaction or event should result in (1) adjustment of, (2) disclosure in, or (3) no effect on, the December 31, 19X8 financial statements.

a. On January 10, 19X9, the company announced the sale of a product line accounting for 20 percent of its 19X8 revenues.

b. On January 18, 19X9, the company filed an antitrust suit against a major competitor.

c. On January 28, 19X9, in a surprise announcement, a major customer with a large uncollected year-end balance declared bankruptcy.

d. On February 10, 19X9, the company declared a two for one split of its common stock.

e. On February 24, 19X9, a serious explosion injuring dozens of workers at one of the client's plants was reported in the news media.

f. On March 4, 19X9, a lawsuit against the company that was disclosed in a footnote to the financial statements was settled for an amount substantially in excess of the estimated amount shown in the footnote.

18-56.   In connection with her examination of Flowmeter, Inc., for the year ended December 31, 19X8, Hirsch, CPA, is aware that certain events and transactions that took place after December 31, 19X8, but before she issues her report dated February 28, 19X9, may affect the company's financial statements.

The following material events or transactions have come to her attention.

1. On January 3, 19X9, Flowmeter, Inc., received a shipment of raw materials from Canada. The materials had been ordered in October 19X8 and shipped FOB shipping point in November 19X8.

2. On January 15, 19X9, the company settled and paid a personal injury claim of a former employee as the result of an accident that occurred in March 19X8. The company had not previously recorded a liability for the claim.

3. On January 25, 19X9, the company agreed to purchase for cash the outstanding stock of Porter Electrical Co. The acquisition is likely to double the sales volume of Flowmeter, Inc.

4. On February 1, 19X9, a plant owned by Flowmeter, Inc., was damaged by a flood and an uninsured loss of inventory resulted.

5. On February 5, 19X9, Flowmeter, Inc., issued and sold to the general public $2,000,000 in convertible bonds.

Required:

For each of the events or transactions above, indicate the audit procedures that should have brought the item to the attention of the auditor and the form of adjustment or disclosure in the financial statements, including the reasons. Arrange your answer in the following format:

Item No.	Audit Procedures	Adjustment or Disclosure and Reasons

(AICPA adapted)

18-57.   Barge Construction Company constructs large oil barges, each requiring from six to nine months to build. The company follows the percentage-of-completion method of recording construction revenue for financial statement purposes. At the audit date, two barges were under construction (one estimated as 96 percent complete and one as 41 percent complete), and there was a backlog of one barge under firm contract (although informal understandings had been reached to construct five other barges, for which materials had been ordered).

All the barges were built under fixed price contracts, including one constructed for the U.S. government during the current year. Warranty costs are recorded as incurred, and have not been significant. The completed-contract method of recording revenue is used for federal income tax purposes; the company's federal income tax returns have never been examined by the Internal Revenue Service.

The CPA performing the audit of the Barge Construction Company is preparing to discuss subsequent events with management. He has a standard checklist of inquiries, but he is wondering if there are not some specific additional questions he should ask in this case. What specific inquiries would you make on the basis of the preceding information?

18-58.   During his review of subsequent events in connection with the audit of Jordon Match Co., Ron Gray, CPA, was informed by the corporate secretary that although there had been two meetings of the board of directors subsequent to the audit date, no minutes had been prepared. The corporate secretary stated that he had been too busy to prepare the minutes but that the meetings had been routine and no significant matters had been discussed that would require disclosure in the financial statements. He offered to give Gray a letter to this effect.

Discuss each of the following courses of action open to Gray.

a. Accept the letter from the corporate secretary (who will be the one who subsequently prepares and signs the minutes) and issue the audit opinion.

b. Refuse to accept the letter of the corporate secretary and refuse to issue the audit opinion.

c. Attend the next board of directors' meeting and obtain oral confirmation that no significant matters had been discussed that would require disclosure in the financial statements.

What action should Gray take?

18-59.   During an audit of Miller Carpet Company, Kelley, CPA, learned that the company had been charged with discriminatory hiring policies and that lawsuits totaling $10 million had been brought against it because of this alleged practice. Kelley discussed the matter with the company's legal counsel, who pointed out that the company had a very strong defense and that few successful cases had been brought under the particular statutes involved. She was optimistic that the company would incur no liability.

When Kelley received the legal counsel's letter replying to the request for a description and evaluation of pending or threatened litigation, it contained the same optimistic evaluation of the discrimination suit but concluded by stating that no opinion could be expressed regarding the potential outcome of the suit. When Kelley contacted the legal counsel by phone to discuss the letter, he was told that the law firm had a policy against giving opinions on the outcome of future litigation but that the auditor could read between the lines and see that she considered the possibility of an adverse outcome to be very remote.

Discuss the quality of evidence represented by the letter from legal counsel and any other actions or options open to Kelley.

18-60.   Windek, a CPA, is nearing the completion of an examination of the financial statements of Jubilee, Inc., for the year ended December 31, 19X0. Windek is currently concerned with ascertaining the occurrence of subsequent events that may require adjustment or disclosure essential to a fair presentation in conformity with generally accepted accounting principles.

Required:
a. Briefly explain what is meant by the phrase *subsequent event*.
b. How do those subsequent events that require financial statement adjustment differ from those that require financial statement disclosure?
c. What procedures should be performed in order to ascertain the occurrence of subsequent events?
(*AICPA adapted*)

CHAPTER 19

The Standard Audit Report

Learning Objectives   *After reading and studying the material in this chapter, the student should*

Know the four standards of reporting.

Be able to relate the standards of reporting to the standard audit report.

Understand the significance of each key phrase in the standard audit report.

Understand auditors' reporting obligations as they relate to prior-year financial statements and other information.

In the first chapters of this text, the organizational structures under which auditors operate and the legal and ethical framework in which the audit function is performed were discussed, and an overview of the audit process was provided. In the next chapters, we explored some of the methods that auditors use in their study and assessment of inherent and control risks and the gathering of evidence with substantive tests to provide a basis for the auditor's opinion on the fairness of the financial statements.

The remainder of this text covers the reporting methods that auditors use to communicate their opinions to the users of their clients' financial statements. It is the purpose of this chapter to lay a general framework for reporting, with particular emphasis on the standard audit report.

The Standards of Reporting

The guidelines used to write the audit report are the standards of reporting established by the AICPA. Of the ten generally accepted auditing standards, four relate to reporting.

These four standards of reporting are as follows:

1. The report shall state whether the financial statements are presented in accordance with generally accepted accounting principles.

2. The report shall identify those circumstances in which such principles have not been consistently observed in the current period in relation to the preceding period.

3. Informative disclosures in the financial statements are to be regarded as reasonably adequate unless otherwise stated in the report.

4. The report shall either contain an expression of opinion regarding the financial statements, taken as a whole, or an assertion to the effect that an opinion cannot be expressed. When an overall opinion cannot be expressed, the reasons therefor should be stated. In all cases where an auditor's name is associated with financial statements, the report should contain a clear-cut indication of the character of the audit, if any, and the degree of responsibility he is taking.

The Standard Audit Report

Before 1934, the opinion paragraph of the standard audit report began with the phrase "we certify that in our opinion," which led to the reports being referred to as "auditor's certificates." The term *certificate* has been replaced with the title "independent auditor's report" to emphasize the fundamental aspect of independence of the audit function.

Addressing the Report

A survey of auditor's reports included in annual reports of public companies would find some addressed to the stockholders, some addressed to the board of directors, and some addressed to both. The audit report may be addressed to the company whose financial statements are being audited or to its board of directors or stockholders, except where the company whose financial statements the auditor is engaged to audit is not the client; in those cases, it is customary to address the report to the auditor's client. In the increasing number of cases in which the auditor is elected or ratified by the stockholders, the auditor may acknowledge this by addressing the report to them.

An Examination of the Report

The standard audit report consists of (1) an opening paragraph (a description of the financial statements and a statement that they are the representations of management), (2) a scope paragraph (descriptions of the auditor's responsibility to detect errors and irregularities and the general nature of audit procedures and a statement as to the adequacy of the procedures), and (3) an opinion paragraph (the auditor's opinion regarding the fair presentation of the financial statements). The report form is as follows:

Independent Auditor's Report

(Opening Paragraph)

We have audited the accompanying balance sheet of X Company as of December 31, 19XX, and the related statements of income, retained earnings, and cash flows for the year then ended. These financial statements are the responsibility of the Company's management. Our responsibility is to express an opinion on these financial statements based on our audit.

(Scope Paragraph)

We conducted our audit in accordance with generally accepted auditing standards. Those standards require that we plan and perform the audit to obtain reasonable assurance about whether the financial statements are free of material misstatement. An audit includes examining, on a test basis, evidence supporting the amounts and disclosures in the financial statements. An audit also includes assessing the accounting principles used and significant estimates made by management, as well as evaluating the overall financial statement presentation. We believe that our audit provides a reasonable basis for our opinion.

(Opinion Paragraph)

In our opinion, the financial statements referred to above present fairly, in all material respects, the financial position of X Company as of December 31, 19XX, and the results of its operations and its cash flows for the year then ended in conformity with generally accepted accounting principles.

(Date)

Modifications to this standard report form are discussed in the next chapter.

Audit of Financial Statements

The first phrase in the report is that the auditors have audited the various financial statements (which are specifically named). Although the distinction between the audit of accounting records and financial statements may appear academic to some report readers, it is an important difference to the auditors. Reference to financial statements has a broad connotation in that it implies the gathering of evidence beyond that produced by the client's accounting records.

For instance, Chapter 18 explains that auditors request the client's legal counsel to confirm to them in writing the status of any pending litigation. A possible result of these attorneys' letters is footnote disclosure of a contingent liability in the financial statements or an adjusting entry recording a liability. An audit of the accounting records alone might not disclose this situation.

The confirmation of accounts payable is another example of the audit of financial statements rather than accounting records. Auditors often send letters to some of the client's creditors for which no balance is shown, asking for the detail of the amounts owed by the client at the balance sheet date. If an accounts payable is omitted on the client's records, the creditor's independently derived figure should disclose the omission.

Since the scope of the audit generally includes other procedures similar to the illustrations in the two preceding paragraphs, auditors consider it proper to report that they have audited the *financial statements* (which include footnotes) rather than the *accounting records*. In addition, if the audit is related to the accounting records, some limiting phrase would be required in recognition of the fact that the sampling and testing procedures employed would probably result in not all records being audited.

Representations of Management

The opening paragraph includes a statement that the financial statements are the representations of management. The purpose of this statement is to prevent confusion as to who is responsible for the presentations in the financial statements. Auditors often assist their clients in preparing financial statements; nevertheless, the responsibility for those statements lies with management, not the auditors.

Generally Accepted Auditing Standards

The next important phrase is reference to generally accepted auditing standards in the scope paragraph. During the course of an audit, dozens, perhaps hundreds, of procedures are used to acquire the evidence on which the opinion is based. Reference to each of these procedures would be ponderous and repetitious, particularly since they are acts performed under the general guidelines of generally accepted auditing standards. Therefore, the report merely contains a statement that generally accepted auditing standards were followed.[1] Furthermore, there is some belief that modification of the scope paragraph might be misunderstood by the readers. As an example, an auditor who uses the work of a specialist (such as an actuary, appraiser, attorney, or engineer) in performing an audit generally does not refer to the specialist in the audit report (AU Section 336), because such reference might be considered (1) a qualification of the report, (2) a division of responsibility, or (3) an indication that a more thorough audit had been made than would appear if no such reference had been made.

Although the three general standards are discussed throughout the text, one, in particular, warrants special attention—the standard on independence. It would

---

[1]Note that the auditors need not perform all *customary* audit procedures. If, for example, the auditors did not confirm accounts receivable or observe inventories because it was impracticable or impossible to do so, but satisfied themselves by means of alternative auditing procedures, they need not describe the circumstances or alternative procedures employed. What is required is that they perform all audit procedures *necessary* for them to form an opinion regarding the financial statements.

be improper for the auditors to issue a standard audit report if they did not adhere to the ethical rule on independence. A special type of disclaimer, shown in Chapter 21, is applicable to the situation in which independence is impaired.

The second standard of field work is another example of a required auditing standard for the issuance of a standard audit report. Although there is no mention of the assessment of control risk in the scope paragraph of the standard report, it is assumed that such an assessment was made and that the second standard of field work was followed if the audit was made in accordance with generally accepted auditing standards.

Materially Misstated

The scope paragraph explains that generally accepted auditing standards require that an audit be designed to evaluate whether financial statements are *materially misstated*. (Materiality is discussed in Chapter 5.) This is an attempt to explain to users the extent of the auditor's responsibility for the detection of errors and irregularities. This phrase also emphasizes that an auditor does not attempt to determine whether financial statements are precise or accurate. The objective is to determine whether the financial statements are materially misstated.

Reasonable Assurance

The scope paragraph also describes the general nature of the procedures an auditor employs to obtain *reasonable assurance* that the financial statements are free of material misstatement. These procedures are described as (1) examination of evidence, on a test basis, that supports the amounts and disclosures included in the financial statements; (2) assessment of the appropriateness of the accounting principles used and significant estimates made by management; and (3) assessment of the appropriateness of the overall financial statement presentation.

This description emphasizes several points regarding the impreciseness of evidence gathering techniques and financial statement presentation. First, the readers of the report are told that evidence is gathered and examined on a test basis. This implies that an item not selected for testing could be in error and not be detected. However, the audit has been planned and performed so that any such undetected error should not result in a material misstatement. Additionally, the assessment of inherent and control risks is subjective. Therefore, the audit provides reasonable, but not complete, assurance. Second, the reference to appropriateness of accounting principles and estimates suggests rather subtly that a number of subjective judgments (e.g., a choice between LIFO and FIFO inventory methods and an estimate of the allowance for doubtful accounts) are involved in the presentation of financial statements. Conclusive evidence regarding some of these judgments may not be available. This is further support for providing reasonable, but not complete, assurance. Finally, reference to overall presentation indicates that the auditor's concern is with the financial statements taken as a whole and not individual elements thereof.

Appropriateness of Auditing Procedures

The scope paragraph concludes with a statement that the auditor believes that the auditing procedures applied were appropriate to support the opinion that follows in the opinion paragraph. The auditor is stating that, notwithstanding the limitations previously discussed in this paragraph, a positive conclusion has been formed that the scope of the audit procedures is adequate.

The Auditor's Opinion

The opinion paragraph of the standard audit report begins with the words *in our opinion*. This phrase is an expression of the fact that, although auditors have a special expertise in accounting and auditing, no guarantee or factual statement regarding accuracy or even fairness can be made to readers of the report for the reasons discussed in the preceding paragraph.

Nevertheless, the readers and users of financial statements have a right to expect that the phrase *in our opinion* represents the sound judgment of professional experts, and this is the message that auditors intend to convey. Such an expression of opinion is required to meet the last standard of reporting.

A complete set of general-purpose financial statements normally consists of a balance sheet (also referred to as a statement of financial position or condition), a statement of income (or of earnings), a statement of retained earnings (sometimes combined with the statement of income), and a statement of cash flows; although other statements may be needed in certain circumstances. The auditor must understand which phrase in the audit report applies to each financial statement.

The phrase *financial position* in the opinion paragraph refers to the balance sheet. Accordingly, if an auditor were expressing an opinion on a balance sheet only, an example of the opinion paragraph would be:

> In our opinion, the *balance sheet* of X Company presents fairly, in all material respects, its *financial position* as of December 31, 19X2, in conformity with . . .

Note that this example makes no reference to results of operations or cash flows. To do so would be inappropriate, because the balance sheet does not purport to present either of these.

A statement of income and a statement of retained earnings (or a combined statement of income and retained earnings) are ordinarily considered essential for a fair presentation of "results of operations." Therefore, an audit report covering these two statements would include the following wording in the opinion paragraph:

> In our opinion, the *statements of income and retained earnings* of X Company present fairly, in all material respects, its *results of operations* for the year ended December 31, 19X2, in conformity with . . .

No reference is made to financial position or cash flows in this example, because the financial statements needed to express an opinion as to those attributes of a company (the balance sheet and statement of cash flows) have not been presented.

The importance of an understanding of the relationship between the financial statements and the opinion being expressed will become apparent when qualifications (sometimes applying to only one of several financial statements) of the audit report are discussed in the next chapter.

Fair Presentation

The opinion paragraph of the standard audit report contains the phrase "present fairly, in all material respects, the financial position of X Company as of December 31, 19XX, and the results of its operations and its cash flows for the year then ended in conformity with generally accepted accounting principles."

The current report style, which includes the preceding phrase, evolved from earlier versions that contained no reference to fairness or to generally accepted accounting principles and used such words as *true* and *correct*. Gradually, these terms gave way to *fairly,* a word the accounting profession felt better expressed the subjective nature of financial statements. The phrase *in all material respects* was also added to provide further emphasis that the auditor's report does not attest to the absolute accuracy of the financial statements.

However, there is no clear agreement within the accounting profession as to the proper relationship between the word *fairly* and the phrase *generally accepted accounting principles*. Some believe that there is a general presumption that financial statements are fair *if* they are presented in accordance with generally accepted accounting principles, whereas others believe that two separate opinions are needed: one that the financial statements are fairly presented and the other that they are presented in accordance with generally accepted accounting principles.

Influential groups outside of the accounting profession have been unwilling to accept the former definition. One of the first real evidences of this reluctance appeared in the *Continental Vending* case, summarized in Chapter 4. A statement was made by the court to the effect that adherence to generally accepted accounting principles was only *one* determinant of fairness and was not a complete defense for the auditors.

Since then, the question of the relationship between fairness and accounting principles has gained increasing attention, especially in the auditing literature. As a result of this attention, *SAS No. 5*, entitled *The Meaning of "Present Fairly in Conformity with Generally Accepted Accounting Principles" in the Independent Auditor's Report,* was issued. The following is one conclusion of the statement:

> The independent auditor's judgment concerning the "fairness" of the overall presentation of financial statements should be applied within the framework of generally accepted accounting principles. Without that framework the auditor would have no

uniform standard for judging the presentation of financial position, results of operations, and cash flows in financial statements.

Coupled with the preceding statement are further comments and discussions that seem to indicate that the concepts of fairness and accounting principles are broadening somewhat. For example, AU Section 411 (*SAS No. 5*) contains these additional comments:

> Generally accepted accounting principles recognize the importance of recording transactions in accordance with their substance. The auditor should consider whether the substance of transactions differs materially from their form.

AU Section 411 (*SAS No. 5*) goes on to specify that the auditor must form a judgment as to whether

> . . . the information presented in the financial statements is classified and summarized in a reasonable manner . . . [and] the financial statements reflect the underlying events and transactions in a manner that presents the financial position, results of operations, and cash flows stated within a range of acceptable limits, that is, limits that are reasonable and practicable to attain in financial statements.

In view of this statement, there may be a presumption that when auditors use the term *present fairly,* they are implying a broader responsibility to financial statement users than was previously thought to be the case. Auditors are now rendering their opinion that financial statements are informative of matters that may affect their use, understanding, and interpretation, and that, in their opinion, the statements are not materially misstated.

Some within the profession have taken the position that fairness is not a property that can be objectively measured by the auditor and recommended that the word *fairly* be deleted from the auditor's report. This recommendation has not been followed.

Generally Accepted Accounting Principles

The term *generally accepted accounting principles,* as it is understood by auditors, is set forth in AU Section 411 (*SAS No. 5*) as follows:

> The phrase "generally accepted accounting principles" is a technical accounting term which encompasses the conventions, rules, and procedures necessary to define accepted accounting practice at a particular time. It includes not only broad guidelines of general application, but also detailed practices and procedures. . . .

The reader may remember from Chapter 3 that Rule 203 of the AICPA *Code of Professional Ethics* prohibits a member of the AICPA from expressing an opinion that financial statements are presented in accordance with generally accepted accounting principles if they contain a departure from an accounting principle established by a body designated to issue such principles (at present the Financial Accounting Standards Board and the Governmental Accounting Standards Board), unless it can be demonstrated that owing to unusual circumstances, the principle would cause the financial statements to be misleading. AU Section 411 acknowledges this primary source of accounting principles and goes on to suggest other sources, generally in order of their authority, including pronouncements of bodies composed of expert accountants that follow a due process procedure (AICPA Industry Audit Guides and AICPA Statements of Position), practices or pronouncements that are widely recognized as representing prevalent practice (FASB Technical Bulletins and AICPA Accounting Interpretations), and other accounting literature (APB Statements, AICPA Issue Papers, FASB Statements of Financial Accounting Concepts, pronouncements of other professional associations or regulatory agencies, and accounting textbooks and articles).

AU Section 411 concludes with the following paragraph:

> Specifying the circumstances in which one accounting principle should be selected from among alternative principles is the function of bodies having authority to establish accounting principles. When criteria for selection among alternative accounting principles have not been established to relate accounting methods to circumstances, the auditor may conclude that more than one accounting principle is appropriate in the circumstances. The auditor should recognize, however, that there may be unusual circumstances in which the selection and application of specific accounting principles from among alternative principles may make the financial statements taken as a whole misleading.

Thus, where two or more accounting principles are applicable in a particular circumstance, and all of them are generally accepted, the management of the company being audited, as well as the auditor, may have to determine the *most appropriate* principle to be used. As noted in Chapter 4, this was the essence of the court's position in the *Barchris Construction Company* case (in which the court decided that a gain on a sale/lease-back should have been deferred and amortized over the life of the related lease rather than being recognized as income in one year, although both practices were in existence at the time), and the *Continental Vending* case (in which the court ruled that compliance with generally accepted accounting principles was not a complete defense if the financial statements were not fairly presented).

Although it is included as a separate standard of reporting, adequate disclosure in financial statements is often considered to be encompassed within generally accepted accounting principles. Whether adequate disclosure is considered as a separate requirement or as part of generally accepted accounting principles, there is no question but that it is essential to the fair presentation of financial statements. Examples of such disclosures include important subsequent events, restrictions on payment of dividends, guarantees of debt, commitments and contingencies, related party transactions, and depreciation and inventory methods.

Consistent Application of Accounting Principles

Until recently the opinion paragraph of the auditor's report included a phrase attesting to the consistent application of accounting principles between periods. The Auditing Standards Board, although agreeing with the desirability of informing users of financial statements of changes in accounting principles, maintained that this disclosure, like other financial statement disclosures, was the responsibility of management. They observed that the auditor's proper function was to consider the propriety of the change in accounting principle and the adequacy of the disclosure of the change. Thus, the ASB decided that auditors should not refer to consistency in their report unless an inconsistency in the application of accounting principles was not properly recorded or disclosed; in that case the financial statements would not be presented in accordance with generally accepted accounting principles.

However, the SEC objected to the elimination of the consistency reference from the auditor's report. In a compromise between the ASB and the SEC, it was decided that no reference would be made to consistency in the auditor's standard report if the accounting principles were consistently applied; however, instances of inconsistent application of accounting principles would be noted in an explanatory paragraph of the auditor's report. Examples of this modification of the standard audit report are presented in the next chapter.

Report Date

The date of an auditor's report has a significance not always fully understood by the general public. This is the date to which the auditor assumes responsibility for detection of subsequent events that might have a material effect on the audited financial statements. This is normally the date on which the auditor completes his or her work in the client's office (often referred to as the end of field work).

Consider the following facts. An audit is being performed as of December 31, 19X6. The auditors must allow the company time to close and balance its financial records before work on the audit can begin, so it is January 17, 19X7, before the audit work commences in the client's office. By February 3, 19X7, the audit staff has substantially completed its work, and the audit partner arrives at the client's office to review the audit work and clear any problems with the client. This review is completed on February 4, 19X7, and that evening the audit staff returns to their office to have a quality-control review made of the audit report and audit working papers and to have the audit report typed and duplicated. Because February is a very busy time of year, the quality-control reviews and report duplication are not completed until February 8, 19X7. The completed and signed report is delivered to the client on February 9, 19X7. What should be the date of the auditor's report?

The audit report should be dated as of the last day of field work, which in this case would be February 4, 19X7. The audit staff is in the client's office through this date and has access to financial records and management personnel necessary to perform a review of transactions and events subsequent to the audit date that might affect the audited financial statements. After the audit team leaves the client's office, this information is no longer readily available, and the auditor has no responsibility to make any inquiry or to perform any auditing procedure subsequent to this date (except with respect to filings under the Securities Act of 1933— see Chapter 4).

Although the auditor has no responsibility to search for subsequent events affecting the financial statements after the date of the report, any event coming to his or her attention between that date and the date the financial statements are issued should be reflected in the financial statements, or the auditor should qualify the report. In either event, the dating of the auditor's report will be affected. The auditor would have the option of dual dating the report, that is, using the original date for the overall report and a subsequent date for the subsequent event or transaction (e.g., February 4, 19X7, except for Note 8, as to which the date is February 7, 19X7), or using only the later date. In the latter case, it would be necessary for the auditor to return to the client's office and perform a subsequent review from the original date to the later date.

Report Coverage of Prior-Year Financial Statements

The example of the audit report shown on page 729 of this chapter is applicable to financial statements covering only one year. It has become common (and is required in many SEC filings) for companies to present financial statements for two or more years. In such cases, the language of the standard audit report must be modified. The auditor should update the report (reexpress a previous opinion or, depending on the circumstances, express a different opinion from that previously expressed) on the prior-year financial statements if he or she has audited them. The updating is performed by referring to both the current and prior-year(s) financial statements in the report.

The updated report is dated as of the end of field work of the most recent audit. Reports with differing opinions and the modification of previously issued reports are discussed in Chapter 20. If the prior-year financial statements are unaudited or audited by other auditors, this fact must be disclosed in the current auditor's report, as indicated in the following sections.

Prior-Year Financial Statements Not Audited

Where the prior-year financial statements have not been audited, notations to this effect should be placed above the appropriate column headings in the financial statements, and the auditor should either reissue his or her prior-period report containing a disclaimer of opinion or include a separate paragraph in the current-period report, which might be worded as follows:

> The accompanying balance sheet of X Company as of December 31, 19X1, and the related statements of income, retained earnings, and cash flows for the year then ended were not audited by us and, accordingly, we do not express an opinion on them.

AU Section 504 (*SAS No. 26*) provides that the disclaimer of opinion may be omitted in certain SEC filings (although the applicable financial statements must still be labeled ''unaudited''). There is no justification for this exception in *SAS No. 26,* and the authors believe it is unwarranted.

Prior-Year Financial Statements Audited by Predecessor Auditor

If prior-year financial statements are presented that were examined by predecessor auditors, the predecessor auditors may reissue their report. However, before doing so they should consider whether their original opinion is still applicable. Accordingly, they should (1) read the financial statements of the current period, (2) compare the prior-period financial statements that they reported on with the financial statements to be presented for comparative purposes, and (3) obtain a letter of representation from the successor auditors regarding matters that might have a material effect on, or require disclosure in, the financial statements reported on by the predecessor auditors. The date of a reissued report should be the same date as that used in the original report to avoid the impression that the predecessor auditors' examination extended beyond the original date.[2] If the predecessor auditors' report or the applicable financial statements require revision as a result of the procedures set forth above, dual dating should be used.

If prior-year financial statements are presented, and they were audited by predecessor auditors whose report is not presented, this fact should be disclosed in the successor auditor's report. The following sentence to be added to the opening paragraph is an example of such disclosure:

> The financial statements of X Co. for 19X8 (the prior year) were audited by other auditors whose report dated March 1, 19X9, expressed an unqualified opinion on those statements.

If prior-year financial statements are presented and the predecessor auditors' report on those statements was modified, this fact should also be disclosed in the successor auditors' report.

Reports on Consolidated Statements

To this point we have assumed that the financial statements being reported on were those of a single entity. In practice, the auditor often reports on consolidated (or combined) financial statements, as well as consolidating financial statements.

No particular problem is encountered when the standard audit report is applied to consolidated financial statements. The words *consolidated* and *sub-*

---

[2] Note that the consideration of the effect on prior-year financial statements of information that the auditor obtains during his or her audit of the current-year financial statements distinguishes an updated report (current report date) from a reissued report (original report date).

sidiaries are inserted at the appropriate places to produce the following partial example:

> We have audited the accompanying *consolidated* balance sheet of X Company *and subsidiaries* as of December 31, 19XX, and the related *consolidated* statements of income, retained earnings, and cash flows for the year then ended. . . .

A more complex situation arises when consolidating financial statements are presented in columnar form, and the auditor is expressing a modified opinion regarding one or more of the consolidating companies, the effects of which may or may not carry through to the consolidated financial statements. It is important that the auditor recognize that the scope of the work necessary to express an opinion on the individual companies in a consolidating financial statement may be significantly greater than that necessary to express an overall opinion on the consolidated financial statements.

Annual Reports and Other Documents Containing Audited Financial Statements

Annual reports to stockholders, reports to regulatory agencies, and other documents often include (1) financial statements, together with the related auditor's report, (2) information that is supplementary to the financial statements but required by the FASB or the GASB, and (3) other information, such as a letter to stockholders or management's discussion and analysis of operations. The auditor has certain limited responsibilities for both the supplemental and other information.

The Auditing Standards Board has decided to deal with supplemental information required by the FASB and the GASB by providing general guidance in AU Section 553 (*SAS No. 27*), and specific procedures for particular FASB or GASB requirements in subsequent statements. If supplementary information is required by the FASB or GASB, the auditor would ordinarily do the following:

1. Make inquiries about the method of preparing the information (written client representations are optional).

2. Compare the information for consistency with responses to inquiries of management and knowledge gained in auditing the financial statements.

3. Apply any specific procedures prescribed for the particular FASB or GASB requirement.

Auditors report on supplementary information by exception; that is, auditors do not refer to supplementary information in the report unless (1) the required information is omitted, (2) the required information departs materially from FASB or GASB requirements, (3) they are unable to perform the prescribed procedures, or (4) they are unable to resolve doubts as to adherence of the information to FASB or GASB requirements.

The auditor also should read the other information in documents containing audited financial statements to determine whether it is *materially inconsistent* with the information contained in the financial statements. For example, if a company's normal operations for a year produced a net loss, but an extraordinary gain more than offset the loss and resulted in net income, the text of an annual report that discussed net income for the year without stating that it resulted from an extraordinary gain could be materially inconsistent with the financial statements.

AU Section 550 (*SAS No. 8*) provides that in the event of such a material inconsistency, the auditor should consider an explanatory paragraph in the report, the withholding of the report, or withdrawal from the engagement. In the event of a *material misstatement* in the text, as opposed to a material inconsistency between the text and the financial statements, AU Section 550 (*SAS No. 8*) contains a suggestion that legal counsel be consulted.

Where audited financial statements are included in a registration statement filed pursuant to the Securities Act of 1933, the auditor may write a letter to underwriters whereby he or she takes additional responsibility for certain information contained in the text of the registration statement. These letters are discussed in Chapter 21.

The Effect of Events Subsequent to Issuance of the Audit Report

Occasionally events occur or are discovered after an audit report has been issued that may materially affect the financial statements being reported on. If an event occurs after the audit report has been issued, generally no action is required of the auditor. For example, a major lawsuit may be settled or the client may sell or acquire a significant subsidiary. Such events occurring before the issuance of the auditor's report may have affected amounts or disclosures in the financial statements or the form of the auditor's report. However, if they occur after issuance of the auditor's report, the events will be included in the financial statements of the subsequent year.

If events are discovered after issuance of the auditor's report that existed at that date but were unknown to the auditor, then the auditor may be responsible for taking some action. Here we are generally referring to material errors or irregularities in the financial statements that the auditor failed to detect. If an auditor becomes aware of information that indicates the possible existence of undisclosed material errors or irregularities in financial statements on which he or she has issued a report, the first step is to discuss the information with the client to determine whether (1) the information is reliable, (2) the information would have affected the audit report, and (3) there are likely to be persons currently relying on the financial statements. If the answers are affirmative, the auditor should ask the client to issue corrected financial statements with related auditor's report. Should the client refuse, the auditor should notify (1) the client, (2) appropriate regulatory agencies (for example, the Securities and Exchange Commission for public companies), and (3) any other person known to be relying on the financial statements that the audit report should not be relied on. As might be suspected, the auditor is often in deep legal difficulty at this point.

Revisions to the Auditor's Report

Numerous revisions have been proposed to the auditor's report since it was standardized in the 1930s. None were successful until 1988 when the present form was adopted. Prior to then the report consisted of two paragraphs (the opening and scope paragraphs were combined). No reference was made to the financial statements being the representations of management, reasonable assurance, or material misstatements. The prior report did not attempt to explain the scope of an audit, but it did state whether the accounting principles had been consistently applied.

The revised auditor's report was one of the AICPA's several responses to criticisms of the accounting profession by Congressional committees.

Chapter 19
Glossary of Terms

(listed in order of appearance in the chapter, with accompanying page reference where the term is discussed)

Term	*Page in Chapter*
Specialist a person possessing special skill or knowledge in a particular field other than accounting or auditing whose work is used in an audit of financial statements.	730
Report date the date of the auditor's report, which generally coincides with the last day of field work.	736
Supplementary information information required by a pronouncement of the FASB or GASB, but presented outside of the basic financial statements.	739
Other information information in annual reports prepared by management and distributed to stockholders and others in addition to audited financial statements and the independent auditor's report thereon, such as the president's message, a description of operations, and so on.	739

Chapter 19
References

American Institute of Certified Public Accountants. *Professional Standards*

AU Section 410—Adherence to Generally Accepted Accounting Principles.

AU Section 411—The Meaning of "Present Fairly in Conformity with Generally Accepted Accounting Principles" in the Independent Auditor's Report.

AU Section 431—Adequacy of Disclosure in Financial Statements.

AU Section 530—Dating of the Independent Auditor's Report.

AU Section 550—Other Information in Documents Containing Audited Financial Statements.

AU Section 553—Supplementary Information Required by the Financial Accounting Standards Board.

AU Section 561—Subsequent Discovery of Facts Existing at the Date of the Auditor's Report.

Elliott, Robert K. and Jacobson, Peter D. "The Auditor's Standard Report: The Last Word or in Need of Change," *Journal of Accountancy* (February 1987), pp. 72–78.

Flesher, Tonya K., and Flesher, Dale L. "The Development of the Auditor's Standard Report in the U.S.," *Journal of Accountancy* (December 1980), pp. 60–70.

Landsittel, David L. "The Auditor's Standard Report: The Last Word or in Need of Change," *Journal of Accountancy* (February 1987), pp. 80–84.

Weirich, Thomas R., and Grant, Edward B. "Broadening Financial Reporting: The Auditor's Involvement," *Journal of Accountancy* (November 1981), pp. 104–118.

Chapter 19
Review Questions

19-1.   List the important concepts of the four standards of reporting.

19-2.   The standard audit report consists of three paragraphs. State what each paragraph is called and the information each conveys.

19-3.   To whom should the audit report normally be addressed?

19-4.   Since much of an auditor's work involves an audit of various client financial records, why does the auditor's report state that he or she has audited the financial statements rather than the financial records?

19-5.   Why does the audit report contain a statement that the financial statements are representations of management?

19-6.   How does the auditor explain in the audit report his or her responsibility for the detection of errors and irregularities?

19-7.   What is the significance of the phrase *in our opinion* in the audit report?

19-8.   Define the word *fairly* as used within the context of the auditor's report.

19-9.   Can financial statements not be fair and yet be in accordance with generally accepted accounting principles? Explain.

19-10.   List the conditions specified in AU Section 411 (*SAS No. 5*) for financial statements to "present fairly."

19-11.   What are the rule-making bodies whose pronouncements have been designated as generally accepted accounting principles by the AICPA?

19-12.   Name five sources of generally accepted accounting principles other than the pronouncements of the rule-making bodies referred to in Question 19-11.

19-13.   List the individual financial statements normally included in a complete set and indicate which phrase of the opinion paragraph applies to each statement.

19-14.   What is the significance of the date of the auditor's report?

19-15.   How does the auditor determine the date of the audit report?

19-16.   What is the auditor's responsibility for events during the period between the date of the report and the date the report is issued?

19-17. What is meant by the phrase *dual dating of a report* and when would an auditor use this practice?

19-18. What reporting responsibility does an auditor have for prior-year financial statements presented with current-year audited statements if (1) he or she audited the prior year, (2) the prior year was unaudited, and (3) the prior year was audited by another auditor?

19-19. Distinguish between a reissued and an updated audit report.

19-20. How is the standard audit report adapted to apply to consolidated financial statements?

19-21. What is the auditor's responsibility for information that is supplementary to the financial statements but required by the FASB or GASB? How does the auditor report on such information?

19-22. What is the auditor's responsibility for other information in the text portion of annual reports and other documents containing audited financial statements?

19-23. What actions should an auditor consider if he or she notes a material inconsistency between other information in the text of an annual report and the audited financial statements?

19-24. What action should an auditor take if a major lawsuit is settled for an amount materially different from what was estimated in the financial statements after delivery of his or her report?

19-25. What actions should an auditor take if a material error is found in the financial statements after delivery of his or her audit report?

Chapter 19
Objective Questions Taken from CPA Examinations

19-26. The last reporting standard requires the auditor's report to contain either an expression of opinion regarding the financial statements taken as a whole, or an assertion to the effect that an opinion cannot be expressed. The objective of this standard is to prevent

a. An auditor from reporting on one basic financial statement and *not* the others.

b. An auditor from expressing different opinions on each of the basic financial statements.

c. Management from reducing its final responsibility for the basic financial statements.

d. Misinterpretations regarding the degree of responsibility the auditor is assuming.

*19-27. The standard audit report includes all of the following except a (an)

a. Opening paragraph.

b. Scope paragraph.

c. Explanatory paragraph.

d. Opinion paragraph.

*19-28. The auditor's report may be addressed to any of the following except the client's

a. Chief executive officer.

b. Stockholders.

c. Board of directors.

d. Partners.

*19-29. The standard audit report explicitly states that the financial statements are the representations of the

a. Client.

b. Board of directors.

c. Management.

d. Auditor.

*19-30. The standard audit report explicitly states that the auditor *believes* that

a. "The financial statements are fairly presented."

b. "Our audit provides a reasonable basis for our opinion."

c. "We conducted our audit in accordance with generally accepted auditing standards."

d. "The accounting principles have been consistently applied."

*19-31. The standard audit report explains that an audit includes all of the following except

a. Examining, on a test basis, evidence supporting the amounts and disclosures in the financial statements.

b. Evaluating the internal control structure.

*Not a CPA examination question.

     c. Assessing the accounting principles used and significant estimates made by management.

     d. Evaluating the overall financial statement presentation.

19-32.   Which of the following would *not* be required for the statements to be "presented fairly" in conformity with generally accepted accounting principles?

     a. That generally accepted accounting principles be followed in presenting all material items in the statements.

     b. That the generally accepted accounting principles selected from alternatives be appropriate for the circumstances of the particular company.

     c. That generally accepted accounting principles be applied on a basis consistent with those followed in the prior year.

     d. That the generally accepted accounting principles selected from alternatives reflect transactions in accordance with their substance.

*19-33.   The auditor's standard report should be titled, and the title should include the word

     a. Standard.

     b. Independent.

     c. Opinion.

     d. Audit.

19-34.   The auditor's report should be dated as of the date on which the

     a. Report is delivered to the client.

     b. Field work is completed.

     c. Fiscal period under audit ends.

     d. Review of the working papers is completed.

19-35.   Comparative financial statements include the financial statements of a prior period which were examined by a predecessor auditor whose report is *not* presented. If the predecessor auditor's report was qualified, the successor auditor must

     a. Obtain written approval from the predecessor auditor to include the prior year's financial statements.

     b. Issue a standard comparative audit report indicating the division of responsibility.

     c. Express an opinion on the current year statements alone and make *no* reference to the prior year statements.

     d. Disclose the reasons for any qualification in the predecessor auditor's opinion.

19-36.   If a publicly held entity declines to include in its financial report supplementary information required by the FASB, the auditor should issue

    *Not a CPA examination question.

    a. An unqualified opinion with a separate explanatory paragraph.

    b. Either a disclaimer of opinion or an adverse opinion.

    c. Either an "except for" qualified opinion or a disclaimer of opinion.

    d. Either an adverse opinion or an "except for" qualified opinion.

19-37.   Which of the following best describes the auditor's responsibility for "other information" included in the annual report to stockholders which contains financial statements and the auditor's report?

    a. The auditor has *no* obligation to read the "other information."

    b. The auditor has *no* obligation to corroborate the "other information," but should read the "other information" to determine whether it is materially inconsistent with the financial statements.

    c. The auditor should extend the audit to the extent necessary to verify the "other information."

    d. The auditor must modify the auditor's report to state that the "other information is unaudited" or "*not* covered by the auditor's report."

19-38.   Subsequent to the issuance of the auditor's report, an auditor became aware of facts existing at the report date that would have affected the report had the auditor then been aware of such facts. After determining that the information is reliable, the auditor should next

    a. Notify the board of directors that the auditor's report must *no* longer be associated with the financial statements.

    b. Determine whether there are persons relying or likely to rely on the financial statements who would attach importance to the information.

    c. Request that management disclose the effects of the newly discovered information by adding a footnote to subsequently issued financial statements.

    d. Issue revised pro forma financial statements taking into consideration the newly discovered information.

19-39.   An auditor has been asked to report on the balance sheet of Kane Company but not on the other basic financial statements. The auditor will have access to all information underlying the basic financial statements. Under these circumstances, the auditor

    a. May accept the engagement because such engagements merely involve limited reporting objectives.

    b. May accept the engagement but should disclaim an opinion because of an inability to apply the procedures considered necessary.

    c. Should refuse the engagement because there is a client-imposed scope limitation.

    d. Should refuse the engagement because of a departure from generally accepted auditing standards.

19-40.   When the audited financial statements of the prior year are presented together with those of the current year, the continuing auditor's report should cover
a. Both years.
b. Only the current year.
c. Only the current year, but the prior year's report should be presented.
d. Only the current year, but the prior year's report should be referred to.

19-41.   After issuance of the auditor's report, the auditor has *no* obligation to make any further inquiries with respect to audited financial statements covered by that report unless
a. A final resolution of a contingency that had resulted in a modification of the auditor's report is made.
b. A development occurs that may affect the client's ability to continue as a going concern.
c. An investigation of the auditor's practice by a peer review committee ensues.
d. New information is discovered concerning undisclosed related party transactions of the previously audited period.

19-42.   The auditor concludes that there is a material inconsistency in the other information in an annual report to shareholders containing audited financial statements. If the client refuses to revise or eliminate the material inconsistency, the auditor should
a. Revise the auditor's report to include a separate explanatory paragraph describing the material inconsistency.
b. Consult with a party whose advice might influence the client, such as the client's legal counsel.
c. Issue a qualified opinion after discussing the matter with the client's board of directors.
d. Consider the matter closed since the other information is *not* in the audited financial statements.

*19-43.   If a document containing the auditor's report includes a statement by management taking responsibility for the financial statements, the auditor's report
a. Should omit reference to management's responsibility for the financial statements.
b. Should refer to management's statement of its responsibility for the financial statements.
c. Should state that management is responsible for the financial statements.
d. Should state that management is responsible for the financial statements and refer to management's statement.

*Not a CPA examination question.

*19-44. The auditor's standard report states that the financial statements are presented fairly
   a. With reasonable assurance.
   b. In all material respects.
   c. Without significant error.
   d. On a consistent basis.

*19-45. In the opening paragraph of the standard audit report, auditors acknowledge their responsibility to
   a. Express an opinion based on their audit.
   b. Conduct their audit in accordance with generally accepted auditing standards.
   c. Evaluate the overall financial statement presentation.
   d. Plan and perform the audit to obtain reasonable assurance about whether the financial statements are free of material misstatement.

Chapter 19
Discussion/Case Questions

19-46. You recently hired an accounting major, a graduate of a local university, to assist you in your CPA practice. She has been assisting you in the audit of the balance sheet of a small client. When you were called out of town for a day near the end of the audit, you asked her to draft the audit report for your review when you returned. On your return you found the following:

> I have audited the books and accounts of March Company as of October 31, 19X9.

> I certify that, in my opinion, the Balance Sheet correctly reflects the financial condition of March Company as of that date.

List and discuss the departures from generally accepted auditing standards of reporting that you would call to your assistant's attention.

19-47. You were recently appointed to a committee formed by the local CPA society to investigate possible substandard reporting practices. The following report was submitted to the committee and, as the newest member of the committee, you were asked to make the initial review of the report and to give the committee your recommendations.

> We have examined the balance sheet and related statements of income and expense and surplus of Holly Corporation as of March 31, 19X9. These

*Not a CPA examination question.

financial statements are the responsibility of the Company's management. Our responsibility is to express an opinion based on our audit.

We conducted our audit in accordance with generally accepted accounting principles. These principles require that we perform the audit to obtain reasonable assurance about whether the financial statements are free of misstatement. An audit includes examining, on a test basis, evidence supporting the amounts and disclosures in the financial statements. An audit also includes assessing the accounting principles used and significant estimates made by management, as well as evaluating the overall financial statement presentation. We believe that our audit provides a reasonable basis for our opinion.

In our opinion, the accompanying balance sheet and related statements of income and expense and surplus present fairly the financial position of Holly Corp., as at March 31, 19X9, in conformity with generally accepted accounting principles.

State whether or not you would recommend to the committee that the audit report be found to be in violation of generally accepted auditing standards of reporting, and if so, why.

19-48.   A number of years ago a large public accounting firm used a form of the opinion paragraph shown below.

In our opinion, the financial statements referred to above present fairly the financial position of X Company as of December 31, 19X2, and the results of its operations and its cash flows for the year then ended, and were prepared in conformity with generally accepted accounting principles.

How does this opinion differ from the one included in the present report?
What additional responsibility, if any, is the auditor assuming in the preceding opinion paragraph?
How does the concept of fairness in the above opinion compare with the concept in *SAS No. 5*?

19-49.   On completion of all field work on September 23, 19X5, the following standard report was rendered by Timothy Ross to the directors of The Rancho Corporation.

To the Directors of
The Rancho Corporation:

We have audited the balance sheet and the related statement of income and retained earnings of The Rancho Corporation as of July 31, 19X5. In accordance with your instructions, a complete audit was conducted.

We conducted our audit in accordance with generally accepted auditing standards. These standards require that we plan and perform the audit to obtain adequate assurance about whether the financial statements are free of errors and irregularities. An audit includes examining, on a test basis, evidence supporting the amounts in the financial statements. An audit also includes assessing the accounting principles used and significant estimates made by management, as well as evaluating the overall financial statement presentation. We believe that our audit provides a reasonable basis for our opinion.

In many respects, this was an unusual year for The Rancho Corporation. The weakening of the economy in the early part of the year and the strike of plant employees in the summer of 19X5 led to a decline in sales and net income. After making several tests of sales records, nothing came to our attention that would indicate that sales have not been properly recorded.

In our opinion, with the explanation given above, and with the exception of some minor errors that are considered immaterial, the aforementioned financial statements present fairly the financial position of The Rancho Corporation at July 31, 19X5, and the results of its operations for the year then ended, in conformity with pronouncements of the Financial Accounting Standards Board.

Timothy Ross, CPA
September 23, 19X5

Required:
List and explain deficiencies and omissions in the auditor's report. The type of opinion (unqualified, qualified, adverse, or disclaimer) is of no consequence and need not be discussed.

Organize your answer sheet by paragraph (opening, scope, explanatory, and opinion) of the auditor's report.

(*AICPA adapted*)

19-50. Richard Adkerson, CPA, was reviewing with the president of Central Pond Shipping Company the standard audit report he intended to issue to this new client. The president had the following comments about phrases in the report that he did not understand.

a. How could Adkerson have audited the financial statements when they were not prepared until the audit was almost complete? The president suggested changing the wording to "audited the accounting records."

b. The president knew Adkerson spent considerable time examining canceled checks and suggested that this fact be included in the scope paragraph.

c. The president asked for a slightly stronger statement than "in my opinion" and suggested "in my informed opinion."

d. The president requested that some wording be included stating that the accounting records were correct, because he questioned the competency of his bookkeeper.

e. The president did not completely trust his brother, who was also associated with the company. He asked Adkerson to include in his report a statement that he had not detected any material fraud.

f. The president asked why Adkerson did not comment on consistency because there had been numerous management changes during the year.

How should Adkerson reply to each of these comments?

19-51.   You have been engaged to audit the financial statements of Gridley Corporation for the year ended December 31, 19X7. You completed the work in the client's office on February 22, 19X8 and returned to your office to process the audit report that you drafted. On February 24, 19X8 you read in a newspaper that a major fire had occurred at the client's plant. The final audit report is to be delivered to the client that afternoon.

What date should have appeared on the original draft of the audit report? Why?

What action should you take after reading of the fire at the client's plant?

How would the final audit report be dated?

19-52.   The management of Onbeach Supply Co. desires to include four years' financial statements in this year's annual report. R. Vaughn, CPA, has audited the financial statements of the current and immediately preceding year; however, another CPA audited the financial statements for the preceding year, and the earliest year was unaudited.

Discuss or draft the audit report that Vaughn should issue, assuming that unqualified opinions were given in all of the audited years.

19-53.   In the current year the operating revenue of State Mountain Gas Company declined to $1,700,000 from $2,200,000 in the prior year. Owing to an extraordinary item, however, net income increased by $500,000 in the current year.

The audited financial statements in the annual report were properly prepared to report the effect of the extraordinary item as a separate item before net income. The president's letter, however, discussed only the increase in net income.

What responsibility does the auditor of the financial statements have for the president's letter? What action, if any, should be taken in this case?

19-54.   Before the present form of the standard audit report was adopted, the following form was used:

We have examined the balance sheet of X Company as of December 31, 19X7, and the related statements of income, retained earnings, and changes in financial position for the year then ended. Our examination was made in accordance with generally accepted auditing standards and, accordingly, included such tests of the accounting records and such other auditing procedures as we considered necessary in the circumstances.

In our opinion, the financial statements referred to above present fairly the financial position of X Company as of December 31, 19X7, and the results of its operations and the changes in its financial position for the year then ended, in conformity with generally accepted accounting principles applied on a basis consistent with that of the preceding year.

a. Discuss the substantive differences between the present and prior reports.
b. Which form of report best communicates the auditor's responsibility and is least likely to be misunderstood by the public? Why?

19-55. The Commission on Auditors' Responsibilities recommended the following form of audit report:

Report of Independent Auditors

Financial Statements

The accompanying consolidated balance sheet of XYZ Company as of December 31, 19X6, and the related statements of consolidated income, retained earnings, and changes in consolidated financial position for the year then ended, including the notes, are the representations of XYZ Company's management, as explained in the report by management.

In our opinion, those financial statements in all material respects present the financial position of XYZ Company at December 31, 19X6, and the results of its operations and changes in its financial position for the year then ended in conformity with generally accepted accounting principles appropriate in the circumstances.

We audited the financial statements and the accounting records supporting them in accordance with generally accepted auditing standards. Our audit included a study and evaluation of the company's accounting system and the related controls, tests of details of selected balances and transactions, and an analytical review of the information presented in the statements. We believe our auditing procedures were adequate in the circumstances to support our opinion.

Other Financial Information

We reviewed the information appearing in the annual report [or other document] in addition to the financial statements, and found nothing inconsistent in such other information with the statements or the knowledge obtained in the course of our audits. [Any other information reviewed, such as replacement cost data, would be identified.]

We reviewed the interim information released during the year. Our reviews were conducted each quarter [or times as explained] and consisted primarily of making appropriate inquiries to obtain knowledge of the internal accounting control system, the process followed in preparing such information and of financial and operating developments during the periods, and determining that the information appeared reasonable in the light of the knowledge we obtained from our inquiries during the current year, from any procedures completed to the interim date in connection with our audit for such year, and from our audits for preceding years. Any adjustments or additional disclosures we recommended have been reflected in the information.

Internal Accounting Controls

Based on our study and evaluation of the accounting system and related controls, we concur with the description of the system and controls in the report by management [or, Based on our study and evaluation of the accounting system and controls over it, we believe the system and controls have the following uncorrected material weaknesses not described in the report by management . . .] [or other disagreements with the description of the system and controls in the report by management] [or a description of uncorrected material weaknesses found if there is no report by management]. Nevertheless, in the performance of most control procedures, errors can result from personal factors, and also, control procedures can be circumvented by collusion or overridden. Projection of any evaluation of internal accounting control to future periods is subject to the risk that changes in conditions may cause procedures to become inadequate and the degree of compliance with them to deteriorate.

Other Matters

We reviewed the company's policy statement on employee conduct, described in the report by management, and reviewed and tested the related controls and internal audit procedures. While no controls or procedures can prevent or detect all individual misconduct, we believe the controls and internal audit procedures have been appropriately designed and applied during the year.

We met with the audit committee [or the board of directors] of XYZ Company as often as we thought necessary to inform it of the scope of our audit and to discuss any significant accounting or auditing problems encountered and any other services provided to the company [or indication of failure to meet or insufficient meetings or failure to discuss pertinent problems].

Test Check & Co.
Certified Public Accountants

Required:

a. Discuss the substantive differences between the present audit report and the preceding one.

b. Identify the representations made in the form of report recommended by the Commission on Auditors' Responsibilities that are (1) implied and (2) not implied in the present audit report.

c. State the advantages and disadvantages of the form of report recommended by the Commission on Auditors' Responsibilities.

CHAPTER 20

Modifications of the Standard Audit Report

Learning Objectives   *After reading and studying the material in this chapter, the student should*

Be able to relate the standards of reporting to the various types of audit reports.

Know the circumstances that require a modification of the standard audit report.

Be able to paraphrase a report from the various types of modifications of the standard audit report.

Although many audit reports are of the standard form discussed in Chapter 19, circumstances may arise that make it necessary for the auditor to modify this standard form. The following circumstances can result in a modification of the standard audit report.

1. The auditor's opinion is based in part on the report of another auditor.

2. The auditor wishes to emphasize a matter included in the financial statements.

3. The financial statements are affected by a departure from an authoritative accounting principle promulgated by a body designated by the AICPA Council to establish such principles.

4. Accounting principles have not been consistently applied.

5. The financial statements are affected by uncertainties concerning future events, the outcome of which cannot be estimated at the date of the auditor's report.

6. The scope of the auditor's audit is limited with respect to one or more audit procedures considered necessary in the circumstances.

7. The financial statements are affected by a departure from a generally accepted accounting principle.

The first five circumstances listed result in an unqualified opinion even though the report is a modification of the standard audit report, except that uncertainties may result in a disclaimer of opinion in some cases.

Modifications Other than Qualifications, Disclaimers, or Adverse Opinions

Reference to Other Auditors' Participation in an Audit

Occasionally, more than one auditor may be involved in an audit of a company's financial statements, particularly when numerous subsidiaries, divisions, or investments are involved. In this case, the principal or lead auditor (normally the one examining the parent company and at least one half of the total enterprise in terms of revenues and total assets) must determine whether he or she has performed sufficient substantive work to serve as the principal auditor. In addition to the materiality and importance of the portion of the entity audited to the total entity, the extent of his or her knowledge of the overall financial statements also should be considered. On determining that he or she can serve as principal auditor, a decision must be made as to how to use the reports of the other auditors. The decision may be either to assume responsibility for the other auditors' work, in which case no reference will be made to them in the report, or not to assume responsibility for their work and state the division of responsibility in the audit report. AU Section 543 (*SAS No. 1*) includes a discussion of factors to consider in making the decision whether or not to make reference to other auditors and inquiries to make about their professional reputation and independence. A flowchart of this process is shown in Figure 20.1.

(Opening Paragraph)

. . . Our responsibility is to express an opinion on these financial statements based on our audit. We did not audit the financial statements of B Company, a wholly owned subsidiary, which statements reflect total assets of $3,500,000 as of December 31, 19X7, and total revenues of $9,750,000 for the year then ended. These statements were audited by other auditors whose report has been furnished to us, and our opinion, insofar as it relates to the amounts included for B Company, is based solely on the report of the other auditors.

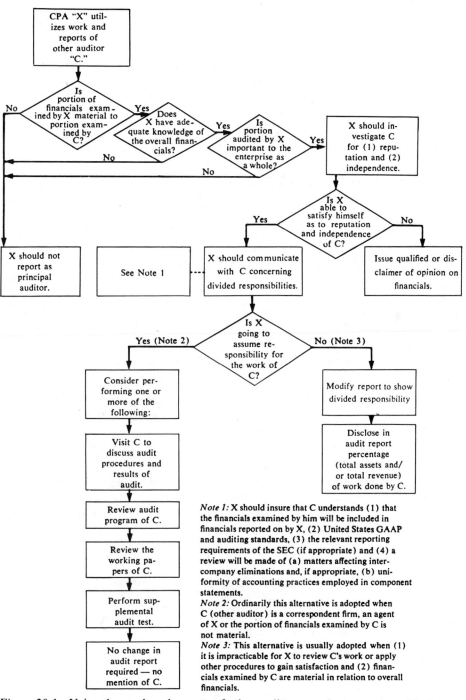

Figure 20.1 Using the work and reports of other auditors—an interpretation of SAP No. 45 (Section 543 of *SAS No. 1*). [*Source:* Dan M. Guy, "SAP Flowcharts—Practitioners Forum," *Journal of Accountancy* (March 1974), p. 84.]

(Scope Paragraph)

. . . as well as evaluating the overall financial statement presentation. We believe that our audit and the report of other auditors provide a reasonable basis for our opinion.

(Opinion Paragraph)

In our opinion, based on our audit and the report of other auditors, the financial statements. . . .

The purpose of referring to another auditor is to set forth clearly the division of responsibility for the performance of the audit. Such reference is not considered a qualification of the audit report. However, if the report of the other auditor is modified, the principal auditor must determine whether the effect of the modification on the financial statements he or she is reporting on is material; if so, he or she should modify the report. If the effect of the other auditor's modification is judged not to be material, then the principal auditor need make no reference in the report to the modification. The other auditors are normally not named but may be, provided they consent and their report is included with the report of the principal auditor.

Emphasis of a Matter Included in the Financial Statements

Sometimes an auditor may wish to emphasize a matter included in the financial statements by using an explanatory paragraph in the audit report. Some auditors are reluctant to use this device, because they are required to select the disclosures to be emphasized and there are few guidelines for such selection. Other auditors have found the explanatory paragraph useful to emphasize related party transactions, changes in accounting estimates, and changes in operating conditions. However, emphasis of a matter in an explanatory paragraph should not be used in place of a qualification.

The following example is an explanatory paragraph used to emphasize a change in an accounting estimate.

(Explanatory Paragraph)

Effective January 1, 19XX, the Company revised its estimates of the residual values of its equipment and the obsolescence rates of inventories of material and supplies, as discussed in Note 1. This revision reflects primarily a change in conditions and not a change in accounting principles or practices. As a result of this revision, with which we concur, net income for the year ended December 31, 19X2, was increased by $500,000.

Because the use of an explanatory paragraph under these circumstances is for the purpose of emphasis rather than disclosure, there is no intention to qualify the auditor's report; accordingly, no reference should be made to the explanatory paragraph in the opinion paragraph. The use of a phrase such as ''with the foregoing explanation'' in the opinion paragraph is not appropriate, because it suggests that a qualification may be intended.

Departure from an Authoritative Accounting Principle

Chapter 3 includes a discussion of Rule 203 in the AICPA *Code of Professional Ethics*. This rule severely restricts the conditions under which an auditor may issue an unqualified audit report on financial statements containing a departure from an accounting principle published by a body designated by the AICPA Council to establish such principles. The rule requires the auditor to demonstrate that, because of unusual circumstances, the financial statements would be misleading if the pronouncement of a designated body were followed. Professional standards require the use of an explanatory paragraph to set forth the information needed to comply with Rule 203. Circumstances involving this aspect of reporting are relatively rare. The following illustration demonstrates one such situation. Only the explanatory paragraph is shown.

> In October, 19X3, the Company extinguished a substantial amount of debt through a direct exchange of new equity securities. Application of *Opinion No. 26* of the Accounting Principles Board to this exchange requires that the excess of the debt extinguished over the present value of the new securities should be recognized as a gain in the period in which the extinguishment occurred. While it is not practicable to determine the present value of the new securities issued, such value is at least $2,000,000 less than the face amount of the debt extinguished. It is the opinion of the Company's management, an opinion with which we agree, that no realization of a gain occurred in this exchange (Note 1), and therefore, no recognition of the excess of the debt extinguished over the present value of the new securities has been made in these financial statements.[1]

Note 1 states that the terms and conditions of the new equity securities are substantially similar to those of the debt securities extinguished, both on the basis of the company's continuing operations and in the event of liquidation, and that, in the opinion of management, no gain was realized as a result of the exchange.

If departures from the prescribed principles can be justified as in the foregoing case, it is appropriate for the auditor to express an unqualified opinion on the financial statements.

Inconsistent Application of Accounting Principles

Although auditors no longer refer to the consistent application of accounting principles in the opinion paragraph of their report, they do modify their audit report to discuss any inconsistent application of accounting principles in an ex-

---

[1]Hortense Goodman and Leonard Lorensen, *Illustrations of Departures from the Auditor's Standard Report, Financial Report Survey 7* (New York: American Institute of Certified Public Accountants), p. 97.

planatory paragraph if the effect on the financial statements is material. By pointing out inconsistent applications of accounting principles in their report, auditors can alert readers to changes in financial statements between periods that are the result of changes in accounting methods rather than changes in economic conditions.

Because the continuous activity of the FASB often results in changes in existing accounting principles, modification of the auditor's report due to inconsistent application of accounting principles is not uncommon.

An example of an explanatory paragraph describing an inconsistent application of accounting principles follows:

> As discussed in Note 3, the company changed its method of computing depreciation from straight-line to declining-balance in 19X8.

Not all factors that affect comparability of financial statements between years result in a modification to the auditor's report due to consistency. AU Section 420 lists the following factors that affect consistency:

1. A change in accounting principle (for example, a change from the straight-line method to the declining balance method of depreciation).

2. A change in the reporting entity (for example, changing specific subsidiaries comprising the group of companies for which consolidated financial statements are presented).

3. A correction of an error in principle (for example, a change from an accounting principle that is not generally accepted to one that is generally accepted).

4. A change in principle inseparable from a change in an estimate (for example, a change from amortizing certain costs to direct charge-off based on a new estimate that the costs no longer have value).

AU Section 420 also lists the following factors that affect comparability of financial statements, but would normally not result in a modification of the standard auditor's report:

1. A change in accounting estimate (for example, a change in the estimated lives of depreciable assets).

2. An error correction not involving an accounting principle (for example, the correction of mathematical mistakes).

3. A change in classification or reclassification (for example, a reclassification made in previously issued financial statements to enhance comparability with current financial statements).

4. A substantially different transaction or event (for example, a change in the type of business conducted by a company).

5. A change expected to have a material future effect (for example, a change having no material effect in the current year, but expected to have a material future effect).

Although the last five factors do not require a modification of the auditor's report, they should be adequately disclosed in the financial statements.

However, it should be pointed out that the task of the auditors is not to apprise report readers of all the reasons that company operations differ from one year to another. Auditors do not serve the function of financial analysts; rather, they give financial statement users an opinion relating to generally accepted accounting principles.

Uncertainties

The term *uncertainties*, as used here, refers to matters that depend on some future events or occurrences or on decisions of parties other than client management for proper accounting determination and that are not susceptible to reasonable estimation. Examples include outcomes of Internal Revenue Service examinations, proceedings of regulatory commissions, and lawsuits, as well as estimates of recoverability of asset values, losses on discontinued operations, and the ability of a company to continue as a going concern.

An entity is considered to be a going concern when it has the ability to continue in operation, recover the recorded amounts of its assets, and meet its obligations. The auditor has a responsibility to evaluate whether there is substantial doubt about an entity's ability to continue as a going concern for a period of up to a year from the date of the audited financial statements. The conditions and events considered and the audit procedures employed to make this evaluation are discussed in Chapter 12.

Auditors generally look to FASB Statement No. 5, "Accounting for Contingencies," for guidance in evaluating uncertainties. This statement provides for the classification of contingencies as remote, reasonably possible, and probable. If the auditor believes that the probability of a material loss is *remote*, no modification of the audit report is necessary. If the auditor believes that the probability of a material loss is *reasonably possible*, but the amount cannot be estimated, the auditor *might* modify the audit report. If the auditor believes that the probability of a material loss is *probable*, but the amount of the loss cannot be estimated, the auditor *should* modify the audit report.

Normally the auditor will modify the audit report for an uncertainty by adding an explanatory paragraph following the opinion paragraph that describes the uncertainty and indicates that its outcome (and therefore the proper accounting determination) depends on future events. In some cases the auditor may issue a disclaimer of opinion for uncertainties, as discussed on page 771.

A summary of the auditor's consideration of uncertainties is shown below.

Probability of Material Loss	Probable Auditor Conclusion	Type of Audit Report Modification
Remote	No modification of audit report	None
Reasonably possible	Might modify audit report (after considering magnitude of reasonably possible loss and likelihood of occurrence)	Explanatory paragraph following opinion paragraph
Probable	Should modify audit report	Explanatory paragraph following opinion paragraph *or* Disclaimer of opinion

A careful distinction must be made between an uncertainty and a departure from generally accepted accounting principles. If the value of an asset is indeterminable, as may be the case for a long-term investment security that is not traded publicly and for which no market value can be ascertained, then an uncertainty exists. However, although the amount to be realized ultimately from a marketable security may not be determinable, an excess of carrying value over market value could represent a departure from generally accepted accounting principles.

An example of an explanatory paragraph for an uncertainty regarding the outcome of a tax examination follows.

> As discussed in Note 5, the Internal Revenue Service has reviewed the Company's federal income tax returns for the years 19X0 to 19X1 and has proposed the assessment of additional income taxes totaling $1,000,000. The principal item being disputed is the taxability of earnings of certain foreign operations. The proposed assessment is being protested by the Company. The ultimate outcome of this matter cannot presently be determined. Accordingly, no provision has been made for any additional federal income taxes which may arise.

The preceding explanatory paragraph would follow an unqualified opinion paragraph.

Modifications Resulting in Qualifications, Disclaimers, or Adverse Opinions

The last three modifications listed at the beginning of this chapter may require qualifications, disclaimers, or adverse opinions if, in the auditor's judgment, the effects are material. These circumstances can be summarized as follows:

1. Uncertainties.

2. Scope limitations

3. Departures from generally accepted accounting principles, which include inadequate disclosures.

Modified reports due to scope limitations and departures from generally accepted accounting principles are not common occurrences because they result from factors that are often within the control of the client to correct. Also uncertainties of such magnitude that they require a disclaimer are not encountered frequently.

Before these circumstances are discussed, the forms of qualifications, disclaimers, and adverse opinions are covered to provide an understanding of the conclusions auditors reach and convey to the readers of their report in each of the circumstances.

When auditors express a qualified opinion, disclaimer of opinion, or adverse opinion, they must disclose in an explanatory paragraph in their report all substantive reasons for such an opinion, as well as the effect of the matter on the financial statements, if reasonably determinable. If the effect is not determinable, this fact should be stated. It is very important that auditors clearly state in this paragraph any reservations they have about the financial statements, including differences of opinion with their client regarding accounting principles, and the possible adverse effects of significant uncertainties. They must avoid any temptation to use vague wording that might lessen the impact of the report modification for their client. Though it is permissible and often desirable to refer to a footnote to the financial statements for additional details and explanations of the circumstances involved (except for scope limitations), reference to a footnote explanation in lieu of an explanatory paragraph is not adequate.

Qualified Reports

The phrase "except for" is used to indicate a qualification of an auditor's opinion and means what the words imply—exception, objection, demurral. The auditor takes exception to, or objects to, some aspects of the financial statements or his or her examination of them. This qualifying phrase may be used if the financial statements contain a departure from generally accepted accounting principles because the auditor would take exception to such departure. It may also be used if the scope of an auditor's work has been limited in some manner; the auditor would be objecting to or taking exception to the lack of evidential matter or to restrictions imposed on the amount of evidential matter he or she has gathered.

The auditor would issue a qualified report only if, in his or her judgment, the subject of the qualification does or could have a material effect on the financial statements, and if the subject of the qualification does not require a disclaimer or an adverse opinion. Thus, the qualifying phrases can be summarized as follows:

	Condition		
Effect	*Scope Limitation*	*Departure From GAAP*	*Uncertainty*
Material	Except for	Except for	Unqualified

Apply the foregoing discussion to the following example. An auditor learns that the Internal Revenue Service recently examined the income tax returns of a client and has proposed a deficiency of $200,000 for additional income taxes. Management of the client states that they intend to protest the proposed deficiency and that, though they are willing to make appropriate footnote disclosure of the matter, they are unwilling to record a liability for the proposed deficiency at the present time. The auditor considers the $200,000 to be material in relation to the financial statements. After reviewing the report of the Internal Revenue agent and management's protest to the deficiency, the auditor concludes that the Internal Revenue Service is correct, and that the proposed deficiency will be upheld. What type of qualification, if any, should be included in the auditor's report?

In this case, sufficient information has been obtained to conclude that an additional liability for income taxes exists and that, without the recording of this liability, the financial statements are not presented fairly in conformity with generally accepted accounting principles. Therefore, an "except for" qualification would be required. Note that footnote disclosure of the matter is not adequate if the financial statements require adjustment.

Assume in the foregoing example that review of the Internal Revenue agent's report and management's proposed protest to the deficiency leaves uncertainty as to the final outcome of the matter. In this case, the auditor is faced with an uncertainty that is not susceptible to reasonable estimation. No modification of the auditor's report is necessary if the auditor considers the probability of loss to be remote. An explanatory paragraph may be added to the auditor's report to disclose the uncertainty if the auditor considers the probability of loss to be reasonably possible or probable.

Assume further that the review of the Internal Revenue agent's report and management's proposed protest of the deficiency convinces the auditor that the client would incur little, if any, additional income tax as a result of the examination. This conclusion may be difficult to reach in practice, but if it could be reached, the auditor could issue an unmodified report without footnote disclosure of the matter because his or her opinion would be that the financial statements are presented fairly in accordance with generally accepted accounting principles.

The Location of the Qualifying Phrase   The location of the qualifying phrase depends on which financial statement or statements are affected by the qualification. In many cases a qualification will affect all of the basic financial statements, but in other situations only individual statements are affected.

If there has been a departure from generally accepted accounting principles that affects all of the basic financial statements (for example, the failure to record an adequate provision for income taxes in the current year), the qualifying phrase "except for" should be placed at the beginning of the opinion paragraph, immediately after the phrase "In our opinion." In this location, it qualifies the fair presentation in accordance with generally accepted accounting principles of (1) financial position (the balance sheet), (2) results of operations (statements of income and retained earnings), and (3) cash flows (statement of cash flows).

Assume that the client has improperly charged to retained earnings a loss on sale of securities that did not meet the criteria for a prior-period adjustment set forth in *FASB No. 16*. Obviously, net income for the year is overstated by the amount of the loss, and the financial statements presenting net income (statements of income, retained earnings, and cash flows) contain a departure from generally accepted accounting principles. But what is the effect on the balance sheet? The amount shown in the balance sheet as retained earnings is the same whether the loss is charged directly to retained earnings or indirectly through the income statement. If the auditor decides that an "except for" qualification is appropriate (rather than an adverse opinion), he or she must place the qualifying phrase in the opinion paragraph so that it applies only to results of operations and cash flows. An example of such wording follows.

> In our opinion, the balance sheet referred to above presents fairly, in all material respects, the financial position of X Company as of December 31, 19X2, and except for the effect of not recording a loss on sale of securities as a reduction of net income as discussed in the preceding paragraph, the statements of income, retained earnings, and cash flows present fairly, in all material respects, the results of its operations and its cash flows for the year ended December 31, 19X2, in conformity with generally accepted accounting principles.

Disclaimers of Opinion

A disclaimer of opinion states that the auditor does not express an opinion on the financial statements. The auditor may use disclaimers if (1) there have been limitations on the scope of his or her examination, or (2) there are significant uncertainties regarding the financial statements. Disclaimers also are used in connection with unaudited financial statements (covered in the next chapter).

Disclaimer Due to Scope Limitations   In the previous section it was stated that the auditor would use a qualified opinion ("except for") in the event of a scope limitation that did not require a disclaimer of opinion. How does the auditor determine whether a disclaimer of opinion or a qualification is appropriate when he or she encounters a scope limitation? One reason relates to the source of the limitation. Auditors view client imposed scope limitations more seriously than scope limitations that result from the timing of the audit work. Another reason relates to the materiality of the scope limitation and the potential effect on the financial statements. This is another area in which the auditor must apply judgment. Few guidelines are given in the professional standards as to how material an item must be to require a disclaimer rather than a qualification. Probably the best guidance can be provided by an illustration of the two possibilities—one situation requiring a qualification and one requiring a disclaimer. Between these two situations are less clear cases in which the auditor must rely on judgment, intuition, and experience.

Suppose an auditor is engaged to perform an audit of a company after the end of its fiscal year and therefore was not on hand to observe the taking of the year-end physical inventory. Also, the inventory records are not adequate to allow a retroactive verification of the year-end quantities. If the amount of inventories shown in the balance sheet is $100,000 compared with total current assets of $500,000, total assets of $900,000, total equity of $600,000, and net income before income taxes for the year of $400,000 (ignore for this purpose the problem of auditing beginning inventories), the maximum potential misstatement (overstatement) is 20 percent of current assets, 11 percent of total assets, 17 percent of total equity, and 25 percent of net income before income taxes for the year. Although the auditor would consider many other factors in evaluating materiality, such as the trend in earnings, the effect on the current ratio, and the possibility of understatement, solely on the basis of the percentages shown he or she might conclude that the effect would be material enough to require qualification but not so material to the overall financial statements as to require a disclaimer of opinion. In contrast, if the amount of inventories shown in the balance sheet is $450,000 instead of $100,000, the maximum potential effect for misstatement (overstatement) is 90 percent of current assets, 50 percent of total assets, 75 percent of total equity, and 112 percent of net income before income taxes for the year. On the basis of these percentages, the auditor might conclude that the potential for misstatement pervades all of the financial statements to the extent that he or she is unable to express an opinion. Thus, it would be appropriate to issue a disclaimer of opinion in this case.[2]

Disclaimer Due to Uncertainties   Although financial statement disclosure or modification of the audit report to include a separate paragraph are often adequate to alert readers to the potential effects of uncertainties, an auditor may decide that the potential effect of a significant uncertainty pervades the financial statements to the extent that they may not be meaningful. In that case, a disclaimer of opinion should be issued (see page 771).

The reason auditors would issue a disclaimer of opinion for an uncertainty, as in the case of scope limitations, relates to materiality. Some uncertainties are more material than others in that their final resolutions are likely to have a greater impact on the financial statements. For example, an event that threatens to impair

---

[2]The percentages used in these illustrations are for teaching purposes only and should not be considered applicable in all circumstances in the determination of materiality.

a firm's entire asset base is more serious than a possible loss on disposition of an investment that constitutes a relatively small portion of the assets. Although there are no definite guidelines on when a disclaimer of opinion should be issued, it is unlikely that some auditors would issue a disclaimer of opinion unless the future existence of the audited entity was in such jeopardy that the going-concern basis for the presentation of financial statements was questionable.

Such an event might occur if a law was passed rescinding or greatly modifying the manner in which a company is allowed to operate. Legislation forbidding racetrack betting certainly would hamper a firm operating such a business. Also, a company's survival prospects might be extremely poor if the market for its products appeared to be disappearing. Auditors might have very substantial doubts as to whether a going-concern assumption is valid for clients in this type of financial condition.

Form of a Disclaimer   The opinion paragraph of a report containing a disclaimer may take the following general format:

> Because of the significance of the [scope limitation or uncertainty] discussed in the preceding paragraph, we are unable to express, and we do not express, an opinion on the financial statements.

Every report containing a disclaimer of opinion should include an explanatory paragraph describing clearly and precisely all significant conditions that gave rise to the disclaimer. The auditor also must disclose any reservations or exceptions with regard to fairness of presentation. In other words, an auditor may not hide behind a disclaimer of opinion if he or she is aware of some deficiency in the financial statements resulting from improper application of accounting principles.

In some cases it may be appropriate to disclaim an opinion on one or more financial statements and to express an unqualified or qualified opinion on others where scope limitations are involved. This approach would usually be inappropriate, however, in the case of an uncertainty, because the basis for such a disclaimer is that some future effect may be so pervasive as to prevent an expression of opinion on the financial statements taken as a whole.

A form of report referred to as a "piecemeal opinion" (expression of opinion on specific financial statement items such as cash, accounts receivable, or accounts payable following a disclaimer of opinion on the financial statements taken as a whole or an adverse opinion) was permissible in certain circumstances at one time. Because a piecemeal opinion tends to offset or contradict the effect of a disclaimer or adverse opinion, its use is now prohibited.

Adverse Opinions

An adverse opinion is an opinion that the financial statements do not present fairly an entity's financial position, results of operations, or cash flows in conformity with generally accepted accounting principles. The adverse opinion is used if the financial statements being reported on contain a departure from generally accepted accounting principles so pervasive that it permeates the financial statements taken as a whole. Thus, the auditor's decision of whether an adverse opinion or "except for" qualification is appropriate in the case of a departure from a generally accepted accounting principle rests on the materiality of the amounts involved. This decision is similar to the choice between a disclaimer of opinion and an "except for" qualification in the case of a scope limitation (discussed on page 768).

Every adverse opinion requires an explanatory paragraph that clearly sets forth the subject of or reason for the adverse opinion and the amounts involved or estimated effect on the financial statements, if reasonably determinable.

The opinion paragraph of a report containing an adverse opinion may take the following form.

> In our opinion, because of the effects of [the departure from generally accepted accounting principles] discussed in the preceding paragraph, the financial statements referred to above do not present fairly, in conformity with generally accepted accounting principles, the financial position of X Company as of December 31, 19XX, or the results of its operations or its cash flows for the year then ended.

It is obvious from reading the paragraph that an adverse opinion is likely to have a very negative effect on the readers of the opinion and the related financial statements; therefore, such opinions are issued only after all attempts to persuade the client to adjust the financial statements have failed. The only other option available to the auditor in this situation is withdrawal from the engagement. If an auditor's relationship with a client is such that he or she is unable to persuade the client not to issue financial statements that contain a departure from generally accepted accounting principles so significant that an adverse opinion is required, then a severance of the auditor-client relationship should be considered.

Summary of the Forms of Qualifications, Disclaimers, and Adverse Opinions

The summary on page 766 of the types of qualifications required for material scope limitations, departures from generally accepted accounting principles, and uncertainties now can be expanded to include circumstances so material as to require a disclaimer or adverse opinion. Although such circumstances have no specific designation in official pronouncements, they are referred to as *pervasive* for teaching purposes in this text.

	Condition		
Effect	*Scope Limitation*	*Departure from GAAP*	*Uncertainty*
Material	Except for Qualification	Except for Qualification	Unqualified
Pervasive	Disclaimer	Adverse	Disclaimer

Uncertainties

Uncertainties are discussed on page 763 together with the use of an explanatory paragraph in the auditor's report to describe the potential effect of the uncertainties. If an uncertainty is so significant that an auditor believes the financial statements may not be meaningful, a disclaimer of opinion may be expressed.

If a disclaimer of opinion is given, the following wording could be used.

> . . . provides a reasonable basis for our disclaimer of opinion.
>
> The company incurred a loss of $1,000,000 for the year ended June 30, 19X2, and it discontinued operations of plants that accounted for $5,000,000 of the total sales of $10,000,000 during the year. Management has indicated that there is a serious question concerning the ability of the company to continue operations unless substantial relief can be obtained through deferred payment agreements with creditors. If the company were required to liquidate its assets, it may be unable to realize its investments in inventories, property and equipment, and deferred charges.
>
> Because of the significance of the possible losses on realization of the investments in the assets noted in the preceding paragraph, we were unable to express, and we do not express, an opinion on the financial statements of X Company.

This example illustrates the uncertainty of the ability of a company to recover the cost of its assets if it is not operating at least on a break-even basis or if it may be forced into liquidation.

Scope Limitations

Auditors should perform all of the auditing procedures they consider necessary to express an unqualified opinion on the financial statements being audited, unless it is impracticable to perform certain procedures or they are instructed specifically by the client to omit or limit certain procedures. Any limitation on the scope of auditors' work, whether client imposed or otherwise, constitutes a scope limitation unless the auditors are able to satisfy themselves by other means. If, for example, auditors are engaged by a client after the end of the client's fiscal year and do not observe the year-end physical inventory, they may be able to observe the inventory at a later date and reconcile to the audit date if there are reliable perpetual inventory records and a strong internal control structure. If the auditors are able to satisfy themselves by this means that the inventory as of the end of the year is stated properly, they need not consider the scope of their work to be limited.

In an earlier section it was stated that a scope limitation would require either an "except for" qualification or a disclaimer of opinion, depending on the materiality of the potential misstatement. Obviously, a scope limitation also involves a modification of the scope paragraph to qualify the phrase "We conducted our audit in accordance with generally accepted auditing standards." If there has been a limitation on the scope of the auditors' work, clearly they have not conducted their audit in accordance with generally accepted auditing standards. Therefore, an exception should be indicated in both the scope and opinion paragraphs for a scope limitation. Following is an example of a modification of the scope paragraph:

> Except as discussed in the following paragraph, we conducted our audit in accordance with generally accepted auditing standards. Those standards require that we plan and perform . . .

A scope limitation should not be discussed in a footnote to the financial statements because the limitation applies to the work of the auditor, and the footnotes to the financial statements constitute the representations of management.

A scope limitation may result from the specific request of a client. An example of an audit report covering this circumstance follows (assume that the potential misstatement is pervasive).

> We were engaged to audit the balance sheet of X Company as of December 31, 19X7, and the related statements of income, retained earnings, and cash flows for the year then ended. These financial statements are the responsibility of the company's management.

> As instructed, we did not request confirmation of accounts receivable balances directly from the company's customers as of December 31, 19XX, and we were unable to satisfy ourselves as to the balances by means of other auditing procedures.

> Because of the significance of the matter discussed in the preceding paragraph, the scope of our work was not sufficient to enable us to express, and we do not express, an opinion on these financial statements.

In the example, the words *As instructed* in the explanatory paragraph make clear that the limitation was imposed by the client and was not of the auditor's choosing. Needless to say, an auditor should consider carefully whether he or she should perform an audit if significant scope limitations have been imposed by a client.

Note that when a scope limitation is so pervasive as to require a disclaimer, the opening paragraph is modified ("We were engaged to audit . . ." rather than "We have audited . . ." and responsibility for expressing an opinion is omitted), the scope paragraph is omitted entirely (there was no audit to describe in the scope paragraph), an explanatory paragraph is added to describe the scope limitation, and the opinion paragraph disclaims an opinion.

Inadequate accounting records also may give rise to a scope limitation. The following example illustrates a report qualified (assume that a disclaimer is unnecessary) because of inadequate accounting records.

> Except as explained in the following paragraph, we conducted our audit in accordance with generally accepted auditing standards. Those standards require . . .

> Because of the inadequacy of prior-year records, we were unable to obtain sufficient evidence to form an opinion as to whether at December 31, 19XX, manufacturing equipment ($500,000) is stated at cost and as to the adequacy of the related accumulated depreciation ($150,000) and depreciation expense for the year ($40,000).

> In our opinion, except for the effect of such adjustments, if any, as might have been determined to be necessary had we been able to examine evidence regarding manufacturing equipment and the related accumulated depreciation and depreciation expense, the financial statements referred to above present fairly, in all material . . .

Note that the qualification is placed so that it applies to the statement of income as well as the balance sheet and statement of cash flows. A misstatement of manufacturing equipment also results in a misstatement of depreciation expense for the year, so the income statement should be, and is, properly covered by the qualification.

A scope limitation also may arise in initial audits. In some cases, auditors who are engaged during a year will be unable to satisfy themselves with regard to the quantities or consistent determination of beginning inventory because they were not present to observe it. If they are unable to satisfy themselves by other means, and if the potential effect is material, they will be unable to audit the statements of income, retained earnings, and cash flows because of the effect of beginning inventory on the determination of cost of sales and net income for the year. An example of report wording where only the balance sheet can be audited follows:

Introductory and Scope Paragraphs Refer Only to the Balance Sheet

Because we were not engaged to audit the related statements of income, retained earnings, and cash flows, we did not extend our auditing procedures to enable us to express, and accordingly we do not express, an opinion on those financial statements.

In our opinion, the balance sheet referred to above presents fairly, in all material respects, the financial position of X Company as of December 31, 19X7, in conformity with generally accepted accounting principles.

Although the preceding example is consistent with the professional literature, disclosure of the reason the auditor was not engaged to audit the complete set of financial statements (scope limitation because of failure to observe beginning inventory) seems desirable.

As brought out in Chapter 18, letters from the client's legal counsel can be a valuable source of evidence in determining the status of contingent liabilities affecting the financial statements. If the auditors are successful in obtaining an appropriate response from the client's legal counsel, and if all necessary disclosures and adjustments have been made in the financial statements, an unqualified opinion can be issued. Unfortunately, the appropriate replies regarding contingent liabilities are not always forthcoming. The legal counsel may not furnish the desired reply about potential liabilities arising from claims or lawsuits, because (1) they do not believe it is proper to divulge information on claims or litigation, or (2) the outcome of the claim or litigation is so uncertain that the legal counsel cannot make an accurate evaluation.

Refusal by an attorney to furnish the information requested from him or her (see page 710 for an example of an audit inquiry letter to legal counsel) normally would constitute a limitation on the scope of an audit and would preclude issuance of an unqualified report. A scope limitation has occurred, because the requested information is available but is being withheld by the attorney. In contrast, the inability of an attorney to respond because the outcome of claims or litigation is uncertain and not subject to reasonable estimation is not a scope limitation, because the information requested (for example, the outcome of a lawsuit) is not available. The latter case is an example of uncertainty and, if pervasive may result in a disclaimer of opinion.

Departures from Generally Accepted Accounting Principles

Departures from generally accepted accounting principles require a qualified ("except for") opinion if the effect is material, and an adverse opinion if the effect is pervasive. Inadequate disclosure is considered a departure from generally accepted accounting principles. The meaning of the term *generally accepted accounting principles* within the context of the auditor's report is discussed in Chapter 19. The reader should refer to that discussion and AU Section 411 if the meaning of the term is not understood.

An audit report on financial statements involving a departure from generally accepted accounting principles (assume that an adverse opinion is not required) might be worded as follows:

. . . provides a reasonable basis for our opinion.

As explained in Note 3, the provision for pension expense for the year ($200,000) was less than the amount required by generally accepted accounting principles. Had the required provision been made, pension expense would have been increased by approximately $150,000 and net income would have been decreased by approximately $100,000 ($.16 per share).

In our opinion, except for the effect of the underprovision for pension expense as described in the preceding paragraph, the financial statements referred to above present fairly, in all material respects, the . . .

In the example, it must be assumed that the effect of the unrecorded pension liability is material in relation to the balance sheet, because the qualification applies to it as well as to the statements of income and cash flows.

An illustration of an auditor's report containing an adverse opinion as a result of a departure from generally accepted accounting principles is shown below.

. . . provides a reasonable basis for our opinion.

As set forth in Note 2, land owned by the company is stated in the accompanying balance sheet at appraised value, which is $700,000 in excess of cost. Had this land been stated at cost, in accordance with generally accepted accounting principles, property and equipment and stockholders' equity would be reduced by this amount as of December 31, 19X2. The recording of appraised value has no effect on the statements of income and cash flows.

In our opinion, because of the significant effect of recording appraised value as discussed in the preceding paragraph, the balance sheet referred to above does not present fairly the financial position of X Company as of December 31, 19X2, in conformity with generally accepted accounting principles. However, in our opinion, the statements of income and retained earnings and cash flows present fairly the results of operations and cash flows for the year ended December 31, 19X2, in conformity with generally accepted accounting principles.

This example illustrates how a departure from generally accepted accounting principles can affect one rather than all of the basic financial statements.

The requirement for adequate disclosure is stated specifically in the standards of reporting; however, the auditor must not confuse long and rambling footnotes with adequate disclosure (they actually may make understanding more difficult for the reader). The auditor must also understand that disclosure is not and cannot be used as a substitute for proper accounting. For example, the failure to record a significant and known liability cannot be remedied by disclosure of the unrecorded liability in a footnote; the financial statements can be corrected only by recording the proper liability.

The topic of auditors' liability included a discussion in Chapter 4 of the *Continental Vending Machine Corporation (Continental) case.* One of the most important aspects of this case involved the adequacy of the disclosure of balances and transactions between Continental, its president, and an affiliated company. A comparison of the footnote to the financial statements describing these balances and transactions with the statement the prosecution successfully contended should have been made illustrates the necessity for clear and adequate disclosure. Following is the footnote as it appeared in the financial statements.

> The amount receivable from Valley Commercial Corporation (an affiliated company of which Mr. Harold Roth is an officer, director and stockholder) bears interest at 12% a year. Such amount, less the balance of the notes payable to that company, is secured by the assignment to the Company of Valley's equity in certain marketable securities. As of February 15, 1963, the amount of such equity at current market quotations exceeded the net amount receivable.[3]

The government contended that the footnote should have read as follows.

> The amount receivable from Valley Commercial Corporation (an affiliated company of which Mr. Harold Roth is an officer, director and stockholder), which bears interest at 12% a year, was uncollectible at September 30, 1962, since Valley had loaned approximately the same amount to Mr. Roth, who was unable to pay. Since that date, Mr. Roth and others have pledged as security for the repayment of his obligation to Valley and its obligation to Continental (now $3,900.000, against which Continental's liability to Valley cannot be offset) securities which, as of February 15, 1963, had a market value of $2,978,000. Approximately 80% of such securities are stock and convertible debentures of the Company.[4]

An auditor must avoid any inclination to accept less than a necessarily harsh disclosure to pacify a client.

Adequate disclosure relates to the form, arrangement, and content of the financial statements, including related notes. If disclosures required by generally accepted accounting principles are omitted, the auditor should provide the information in the report if practicable (practicable in this context means that the information is reasonably obtainable and does not require the auditor to prepare

---

[3]Denzil Y. Causey, Jr., *Duties and Liabilities of the CPA* (Austin, Texas: Bureau of Business Research, The University of Texas at Austin, 1973), p. 239.

[4]Ibid., p. 240.

basic financial information such as a statement of cash flows or segment information), unless the omission from the report is permitted by generally accepted auditing standards. A qualified or adverse opinion should also be expressed. Such a report might be worded in the following manner:

> . . . provides a reasonable basis for our opinion.
>
> The Company's financial statements do not disclose that subsequent to the end of the year the company issued $10,000,000 of 8% debentures that are due in 19Y0. The debenture agreement restricts the payment of future cash dividends to earnings after December 31, 19X3.
>
> In our opinion, except for the omission of the information in the preceding paragraph, the financial statements referred to above present . . . .

In practice, qualifications and adverse opinions necessitated by inadequate disclosure are rare. Because the auditor must disclose the omitted information in an explanatory paragraph of the report, the client normally prefers to make the disclosure in the financial statements to avoid receiving an audit report that contains the omitted disclosure and takes exception to the fair presentation of the financial statements.

See Figure 20.2 for a summary of the discussion to this point in the chapter.

Different Reports on Different Years

If an auditor is reporting on financial statements covering two or more years, he or she may modify the report (explanatory paragraph, qualification, adverse, or disclaimer of opinion) for one or more years while issuing a standard report for others. For example, if a material departure from generally accepted accounting principles occurs in the latest year being reported on, the auditor would qualify the report for the latest year and issue an unqualified report on the previous year.

An example of the reporting format for such a report is shown below.

> The company has excluded from property and debt in the accompanying 19X7 balance sheet certain lease obligations that were entered into in 19X7 that, in our opinion, should be capitalized in order to conform with generally accepted accounting principles. If these lease obligations were capitalized, property would be increased by $600,000, long-term debt by $550,000, and retained earnings of $50,000 as of December 31, 19X7, and net income and earnings per share would be increased by $50,000 and $.50, respectively, for the year then ended.
>
> In our opinion, except for the effects on the 19X7 financial statements of not capitalizing certain lease obligations as described in the preceding paragraph, the financial statements referred to above present fairly, in all material respects, the

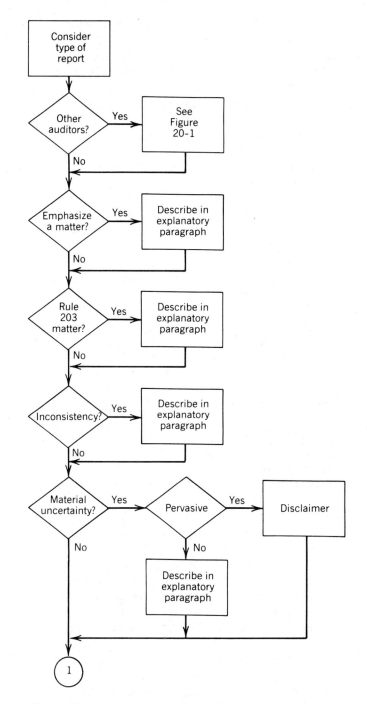

Figure 20.2   Summary flowchart of modified audit reports.

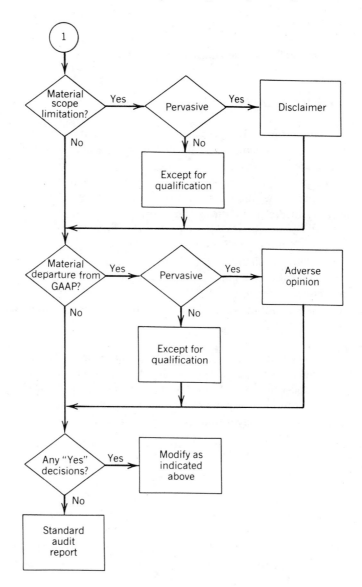

Figure 20.2   (Continued)

financial position of X Company as of December 31, 19X7 and 19X6, and the results of its operations and its cash flows for the years then ended in conformity with generally accepted accounting principles.

Changes in Updated Reports

The requirement for updating previously issued reports on prior-year comparative financial statements was discussed in Chapter 19. Circumstances such as the subsequent resolution of an uncertainty, discovery of an uncertainty in a subsequent period, and the subsequent restatement of prior-year financial statements may cause the auditor to issue an updated report that differs from the original report. In these situations the auditor should prepare an appropriate report and include an explanatory paragraph disclosing (1) the date of the auditor's previous report, (2) the type of report previously issued, (3) the circumstances that caused the auditor to change the report, and (4) that the auditor's updated report on the financial statements of the prior period is different from his or her previous report on those statements.

An example of an explanatory paragraph describing a change in an updated report follows:

In our report dated March 1, 19X2, our report on the 19X1 financial statements was modified for the effects on the 19X1 financial statements of certain litigation. As explained in Note X, the litigation was settled as of November 1, 19X2, at no material cost to the Company. Accordingly, our present report on the 19X1 financial statements is different from our previous report.

Commentary

The significant effect on a company of receiving an audit report containing a qualification, disclaimer, or adverse opinion can be illustrated by reference to the practices of the Securities and Exchange Commission. Generally, the SEC will not accept for filing under the Securities Act of 1933 or the Securities Exchange Act of 1934 financial statements for which the related auditor's report is modified because of a scope limitation or a departure from a generally accepted accounting principle.

The failure of the management of a company to make the required filings under the securities acts may result in the suspension of trading in the company's stock and possible civil and criminal penalties. Thus, the SEC views qualifications, disclaimers, and adverse opinions as serious matters, and it has provided auditors of companies subject to SEC jurisdiction with a powerful tool to prevent limitations on the scope of their work and departures from generally accepted accounting principles. Most other users of financial statements such as bankers, other credit grantors, and stockholders share the SEC's view as to the serious nature of modifications of the auditor's report.

Chapter 20
Glossary of Terms

(listed in order of appearance in the chapter, with accompanying page reference where the term is discussed)

	Page in
Term	*Chapter*

Scope limitation   restrictions on the scope of an auditor's work, whether im-   771
posed by the client or by circumstances such as the timing of the work,
the inability to obtain sufficient competent evidence, or an inadequacy in
the accounting records that require a qualification or disclaimer of
opinion.

Departures from generally accepted accounting principles   the use of unaccept-   774
able accounting principles, the misapplication of acceptable accounting
principles, or inadequate disclosure that requires a qualification or adverse opinion.

Chapter 20
References

American Institute of Certified Public Accountants. *Professional Standards*

AU Section 500—The Fourth Standard of Reporting (substantially all individual
statements in Section 500 are applicable to this chapter).

Firth, Michael. "Qualified Audit Reports: Their Impact on Investment Decisions," *The
Accounting Review* (July 1978), pp. 642–650.

Mutchier, Jane F. "Empirical Evidence Regarding the Auditor's Going-Concern Opinion
Decision," *Auditing: A Journal of Practice and Theory* (Fall 1986), pp. 148–
163.

Chapter 20
Review Questions

20-1.   List the modifications of the standard audit report that normally do not result in a
qualification, disclaimer, or adverse opinion.

20-2.   When more than one auditor is involved in an audit of a company's financial
statements, what two important decisions about reporting must the principal auditor make?

20-3. What disclosure is made in the principal auditors' report if they decide to assume responsibility for other auditors' work? If they decide not to assume responsibility for other auditors' work?

20-4. Give three examples of matters that might be emphasized in an explanatory paragraph of the audit report.

20-5. Under what conditions should the phrase "with the foregoing explanation" be used in the opinion paragraph to refer to a matter emphasized in an explanatory paragraph?

20-6. Under what condition may an auditor issue an unqualified opinion on financial statements containing a departure from an accounting principle published by a body designated by the AICPA Council to establish accounting principles? If this condition is met, what form will the auditor's report take?

20-7. What modification is made to an auditor's report if accounting principles are not applied consistently?

20-8. List the factors that affect comparability of financial statements between years and result in a modification of the auditor's report due to consistency.

20-9. List the factors that affect comparability of financial statements, but would normally not result in a modification of the standard auditor's report.

20-10. What are examples of uncertainties that might affect the auditor's report?

20-11. Describe how auditors may use FASB Statement No. 5 as guidance in determining whether and how to modify the audit report.

20-12. List three circumstances that may result in a qualification, disclaimer, or adverse opinion.

20-13. Explain the meaning and use of the "except for" qualification.

20-14. Where should a qualifying phrase be placed if it is the auditor's intention to qualify all of the basic financial statements?

20-15. What is the purpose of a disclaimer of opinion and when is it used?

20-16.   Under what conditions would an auditor issue a disclaimer of opinion rather than an "except for" qualification?

20-17.   What is a piecemeal opinion and under what conditions is it appropriate for the auditor to use it?

20-18.   What does an adverse opinion state and when is it used?

20-19.   How does an auditor decide whether to use an "except for" qualification or an adverse opinion?

20-20.   List three conditions or reasons for limitations on the scope of an auditor's work.

20-21.   Discuss the forms an auditor's report may take as the result of a scope limitation.

20-22.   How is the scope paragraph of an auditor's report modified if the auditor's scope has been limited so that a qualification is required? A disclaimer is required?

20-23.   Why would it be improper to discuss the scope limitation in a footnote?

20-24.   What forms of audit report are required to describe departures from generally accepted accounting principles and when is each used?

20-25.   Why are qualifications and adverse opinions because of inadequate disclosure rare in actual practice.

Chapter 20
Objective Questions Taken from CPA Examinations

20-26.   The principal auditor is satisfied with the independence and professional reputation of the other auditor who has audited a subsidiary but wants to indicate the division of responsibility. The principal auditor should modify
a. Only the scope paragraph of the report.
b. Only the opinion paragraph of the report.
c. All three paragraphs of the report.
d. The report to include an explanatory paragraph.

20-27. If the principal auditor decides to make reference to the other auditor's examination, the opening paragraph must specifically indicate the
   a. Magnitude of the portion of the financial statements examined by the other auditor.
   b. Name of the other auditor.
   c. Name of the consolidated subsidiary examined by the other auditor.
   d. Type of opinion expressed by the other auditor.

20-28. An auditor includes an explanatory paragraph in an otherwise unmodified report to emphasize that the entity being reported upon had significant transactions with related parties. The inclusion of this explanatory paragraph
   a. Violates generally accepted auditing standards if this information is already disclosed in footnotes to the financial statements.
   b. Necessitates a revision of the opinion paragraph to include the phrase "with the foregoing explanation."
   c. Is appropriate and would *not* negate the unqualified opinion.
   d. Is considered an "except for" qualification of the report.

20-29. Management of Blue Company has decided not to account for a material transaction in accordance with the provisions of an FASB Standard. In setting forth its reasons in a note to the financial statements, management has clearly demonstrated that due to unusual circumstances the financial statements presented in accordance with the FASB Standard would be misleading. The auditor's report should include an explanatory paragraph and contain a(an)
   a. Adverse opinion.
   b. Unqualified opinion.
   c. "Except for" qualified opinion.
   d. Disclaimer of opinion.

*20-30. If there were *no* changes during the reporting period in the application of accounting principles, this fact should
   a. Be disclosed in the opinion paragraph of the auditor's report.
   b. Be disclosed in a footnote to the financial statements.
   c. Not be disclosed in the auditor's report.
   d. Be disclosed in an explanatory paragraph of the auditor's report.

20-31. Which of the following requires modification of the auditor's report to include an explanatory paragraph regarding consistency?
   a. The correction of an error in the prior year's financial statements resulting from a mathematical mistake in capitalizing interest.

*Not a CPA examination question.

    b. The change from the cost method to the equity method of accounting for investments in common stock.

    c. A change in the estimate of provisions for warranty costs.

    d. A change in depreciation method that has *no* effect on current year's financial statements but is certain to affect future years.

*20-32. If an auditor believes there is a remote probability that resolution of an uncertainty will have a material effect on the financial statements, the auditor should issue a(an)

    a. Unmodified report.

    b. Disclaimer of opinion.

    c. "Except for" qualified opinion.

    d. Modified report that includes an explanatory paragraph describing the uncertainty.

20-33. When the financial statements are prepared on the going concern basis but the auditor concludes there is substantial doubt whether the client can continue in existence and also believes there are uncertainties about the recoverability of recorded asset amounts on the financial statements, the auditor may issue a(an)

    a. Adverse opinion.

    b. "Except for" qualified opinion.

    c. Disclaimer of opinion.

    d. Unmodified report.

*20-34. When an auditor issues an "except for" qualification because of a scope limitation, which paragraphs of the standard audit report should be modified?

    a. Scope and opinion paragraphs.

    b. Opening and opinion paragraphs.

    c. Opening and scope paragraphs.

    d. All three paragraphs.

20-35. When the auditor is unable to determine the amounts associated with the illegal acts of client personnel because of an inability to obtain adequate evidence, the auditor should issue a(an)

    a. "Except for" qualified opinion.

    b. Unqualified opinion.

    c. Adverse opinion.

    d. Unqualified opinion with an explanatory paragraph.

*Not a CPA examination question.

20-36. A limitation on the scope of the audit sufficient to preclude an unqualified opinion will always result when management
a. Asks the auditor to report on the balance sheet and *not* on the other basic financial statements.
b. Refuses to permit its lawyer to respond to the letter of audit inquiry.
c. Discloses material related party transactions in the footnotes to the financial statements.
d. Knows that confirmation of accounts receivable is *not* feasible.

20-37. Restrictions imposed by a client prohibit the confirmation of accounts receivable by direct communication with debtors. These receivables account for 30 percent of all assets and alternative audit procedures can *not* be applied, although the independent auditor was able to examine satisfactory evidence for all other items in the financial statements. The independent auditor should issue a(an)
a. Disclaimer of opinion.
b. Adverse opinion.
c. Unqualified opinion.
d. "Except for" qualified opinion.

20-38. When a client will *not* make essential corporate minutes available to the auditor, the audit report will probably contain a(an)
a. Unqualified opinion.
b. Adverse opinion.
c. Qualified opinion.
d. Disclaimer of opinion.

20-39. An auditor would issue an adverse opinion if
a. The audit was begun by other independent auditors who withdrew from the engagement.
b. A qualified opinion can *not* be given because the auditor lacks independence.
c. The restriction on the scope of the audit was significant.
d. The statements taken as a whole do not fairly present the financial condition, results of operations, and cash flows of the company.

20-40. The management of a client company believes that the statement of cash flows is not a useful document and refuses to include one in the annual report to stockholders. As a result of this circumstance, the auditor's opinion should be
a. Qualified due to inadequate disclosure.
b. Qualified due to a scope limitation.
c. Adverse.
d. Unqualified.

20-41. When financial statements are presented that are *not* in conformity with generally accepted accounting principles, an auditor may issue a(an)

	"Except for" opinion	*Disclaimer of opinion*
a.	Yes	No
b.	Yes	Yes
c.	No	Yes
d.	No	No

20-42. An auditor's report includes a statement that "the financial statements do not present fairly the financial position, results of operations or cash flows in conformity with generally accepted accounting principles." This auditor's report was probably issued in connection with financial statements that were
   a. Prepared on a comprehensive basis of accounting other than generally accepted accounting principles.
   b. Restricted for use by management.
   c. Misleading.
   d. Condensed.

20-43. In which of the following circumstances would an auditor be most likely to express an adverse opinion?
   a. The statements are *not* in conformity with the FASB Statements regarding the capitalization of leases.
   b. Information comes to the auditor's attention that raises substantial doubt about the entity's ability to continue as a going concern.
   c. The chief executive officer refuses the auditor access to minutes of board of directors' meetings.
   d. Tests of controls show that the entity's internal control structure is so weak that it can *not* be relied upon.

20-44. When the financial statements contain a departure from generally accepted accounting principles, the effect of which is material, the auditor should
   a. Qualify the opinion and explain the effect of the departure from generally accepted accounting principles in an explanatory paragraph.
   b. Qualify the opinion and describe the departure from generally accepted accounting principles within the opinion paragraph.
   c. Disclaim an opinion and explain the effect of the departure from generally accepted accounting principles in an explanatory paragraph.
   d. Disclaim an opinion and describe the departure from generally accepted accounting principles within the opinion paragraph.

20-45. When reporting on comparative financial statements, which of the following circumstances ordinarily should cause the auditor to change the previously issued report on the prior year's financial statements?

    a. A change in accounting principle caused a modification of the current year's auditor's report.

    b. The prior year opinion was unqualified and the current year opinion was qualified due to a scope limitation.

    c. A major uncertainty that caused a modified report on the prior year's financial statements was resolved during the current year.

    d. The financial statements of the prior year are restated following a pooling of interests in the current year.

Chapter 20
Discussion/Case Questions

20-46. Brown & Brown, CPAs, was engaged by the board of directors of Cook Industries, Inc. to audit Cook's calendar year 19X5 financial statements. The following report was drafted by an audit assistant at the completion of the audit. It was submitted to Brown, the partner with client responsibility for review on March 7, 19X6, the date of the completion of field work. Brown has reviewed matters thoroughly and properly concluded that an adverse opinion was appropriate.

    Brown also became aware of a March 14, 19X6 subsequent event which the client has properly disclosed in the notes to the financial statements. Brown wants responsibility for subsequent events to be limited to the specific event referred to in the applicable note to the client's financial statements.

    The financial statements of Cook Industries, Inc., for the calendar year 19X4 were examined by predecessor auditors who also expressed an adverse opinion and have not reissued their report. The financial statements for 19X4 and 19X5 are presented in comparative form.

Accountants Report

To the President of Cook Industries, Inc.

    We have audited the financial statements of Cook Industries, Inc. for the year ended December 31, 19X5. These financial statements are the responsibility of the Company's management. Our responsibility is to express an opinion on these financial statements based on our audit.

    We conducted our audit in accordance with generally accepted auditing standards. Those standards require that we plan and perform the audit to obtain reasonable assurance about whether the financial statements are free of material misstatement. An audit includes examining, on a test basis, evidence supporting the amounts and disclosures in the financial statements. An audit also includes assessing the accounting principles used and significant estimates made by management, as well as evaluating the overall financial presentation. We believe that our audit provides a reasonable basis for our opinion. As discussed in Note K to the financial statements, the Company has properly disclosed a subsequent event dated March 14, 19X6.

As discussed in Note G to the financial statements, the Company carries its property and equipment at appraisal values, and provides depreciation on the basis of such values. Further, the company does not provide for income taxes with respect to differences between financial income and taxable income arising because of the use, for income tax purposes, of the installment method of reporting gross profit from certain types of sales.

In our opinion, the financial statements referred to above do not present fairly the financial position of Cook Industries, Inc. as of December 31, 19X5, or the results of its operations for the year then ended.

Brown & Brown, CPAs

March 7, 19X6

Required:
Identify the deficiencies in the draft of the proposed report. Do *not* redraft the report or discuss corrections.

(AICPA adapted)

20-47.   You are the auditor of X Company and during your audit for the year ended September 30, 19X7, you note that approximately 76 percent of the company's sales were to one customer. In the prior year, no single customer accounted for more than 28 percent. You believe disclosure of this fact is significant because the loss of this customer could seriously affect future operations of X Company. Management of X Company refuses to include this information in the financial statements, maintaining that this type of information is not often found in financial statements and that it could have a negative effect on the negotiation of the renewal of a bank loan now in progress.
a. How would you reply to X Company management with regard to this disclosure?
b. Assume that you are unable to persuade X Company management to make the disclosure that you consider appropriate, and draft the audit report that you would issue.

20-48. Y Company has never been audited and is to be acquired by one of your present clients and combined on a pooling-of-interest basis. Your client includes ten years of financial statements in its annual report and has instructed you to audit Y Company for the previous ten years so that ten years of restated financial statements can be included in the annual report again this year. During this audit, you note that Y Company had substantial gains from sales of long-term investment securities in 19X7 and 19X8. However, the gains in 19X7 were presented as extraordinary items, whereas the 19X8 gains were reported as part of ordinary operations. You find that the different reporting was caused by a change in the criteria for extraordinary items contained in the professional literature that became effective in late 19X7. Thus, both transactions were reported properly in conformity with the accounting principles in effect during the respective years, and the inconsistency arose from action taken by a standard setting body, not Y Company.

a. Will you modify your audit report for lack of consistency? Explain your reasoning.

b. Draft the audit report you will issue, assuming that you have no other reservations regarding the financial statements.

20-49. In connection with your audit of Z Company for the year ended December 31, 19XX, you find that as a result of an improper cutoff of inventory shipments at the end of the year, approximately $6,000 of sales applicable to the subsequent year were recorded in the current year. During the current year, sales totaled $5,000,000, and net income was $850,000. Management of Z Company refuses to adjust the financial statements for the $6,000 error.

a. What position would you take with the management of Z Company regarding the correction of this error? How would you explain your position?

b. Draft the audit report you will issue, assuming that you are satisfied with the financial statements otherwise.

20-50. You have been engaged to audit W Company, a new company formed to explore for oil and gas. During the year, W Company acquired several large undeveloped lease holdings for $1,000,000 and drilled several exploratory wells, all of which were dry. At December 31, 19XX, the financial statements showed total assets of $1,100,000 (including the cost of the undeveloped leases) and net worth of $400,000. In your discussion with the management of W Company regarding the recoverability of the cost of the leases, they maintain that, despite the unsuccessful efforts to date, the cost of the leases could be recovered, because the geologic features underlying certain of the leases are favorable for the formation of hydrocarbons and a productive oil well recently had been drilled near their leases. They are able to supply you with an opinion of an outside geologist and other documentary support for their position.

a. What type of audit report would you issue to W Company? Explain your reasons fully.

b. Draft the audit report you will issue, assuming that you are otherwise satisfied with the financial statements.

c. Assume that management believes that the leases probably will not be productive of oil or gas but insists that they be shown in the financial statements at cost, as this presentation would be in accordance with generally accepted accounting principles. Would this change the type of audit report you would issue? Explain why or why not.

d. Draft the audit report you would issue on the basis of the assumption in c, if it would differ from the report you drafted in b.

20-51.   During the current year, your client, U Company, acquired B Company in a business combination accounted for as a pooling-of-interest. B Company previously had reported on a fiscal year ending on June 30, whereas U Company used a year ending December 31. Considerable time and cost would be involved in restating and auditing the prior-year financial statements of B Company on a December 31 year-end for combination with U Company on a pooling-of-interest basis. The management of U Company decides to combine B Company for the current year, which they believe is most important to readers of the financial statements, but not for prior years, because they do not consider the extra cost justified. You think the financial statements of B Company are significant in relation to those of U Company in the current and prior years, and that failure to combine them for the prior year would make the financial statements of that year misleading when taken as a whole. Current and one-year-prior financial statements are to be included in the annual report.

a. Discuss the propriety of management's position regarding the restatement of current and prior-year financial statements.

b. Explain the reporting problems, if any, in the case.

c. Draft an appropriate audit report.

20-52.   As a normal procedure in all of your audits, you request management of your clients to furnish you a management representation letter including, among other things, representations that the financial statements are presented fairly in all material respects, that there are no material unrecorded liabilities, and so on. One of your clients, T Company, has had a recent change in management soon after the end of the company's fiscal year, December 31. As you are concluding your audit for the year, you ask the new management to sign the normal management representation letter. They respond that they are unwilling to do so because they do not have full knowledge of the company's affairs for the year being audited.

a. Discuss the reasonableness of the new management's position.

b. Under these particular circumstances, would failure to obtain a management representation letter be considered a scope limitation?

c. Draft the audit report you would issue.

20-53.   Your client, S Company is a major manufacturer of widgets. Your audit report for the previous year was unqualified. During the current year, several class-action suits were filed against the company claiming significant damages as a result of alleged price fixing within the widget industry during the previous three years. The company is contesting the suits, and in connection with the current-year audit, legal counsel for S Company has furnished you a letter stating that they are optimistic, but still uncertain, as to the final outcome of these suits. You conclude that it is reasonably possible that the outcome of the suit will be adverse to S Company.

a. Discuss the reporting problem involved in the case.

b. Draft an audit report covering two years based on the information provided.

20-54.   During 19X7, R Company, your client, changed its method, effective January 1, 19X7, of computing inventory cost from the average cost method to the last-in, first-out method. This change had the effect of reducing net income for the year ended December 31, 19X7 by $300,000 ($.26 per share), a material amount.

a. How can the company justify the change in inventory pricing as required by *APB Opinion No. 20?*

b. Draft an audit report covering two years that you will issue, assuming that you are otherwise satisfied with the financial statements.

20-55.   Q Company is a gas distribution company that is regulated by the state public service commission. The commission must approve all rate changes made by Q Company, but Q Company is allowed to collect higher rates subject to refund in the event they are disapproved subsequently by the commission. During the year ended September 30, 19X5, Q Company increased its rates to its customers and collected an additional $2,000,000, a material amount. You have completed your audit of Q Company in November, and the state public service commission has not yet approved or disapproved the rate increase.

a. Explain the reporting problem involved in the case.

b. Draft an audit report that you will issue covering two years.

20-56.   You recently were engaged to audit the financial statements of P Company, a company that previously has not been audited. During your work, you learn that three years ago a serious fire destroyed most of the company's accounting records, including those substantiating the cost of its property and equipment. You physically observe the major items of property and equipment included in the financial statements, but you are unable to determine when and at what price most of it had been acquired. Property and equipment is a material item in the balance sheet.

a. Describe the reporting problem involved in the case.

b. Draft an audit report covering the matter, assuming that you have no other reservations about the financial statements.

c. If your report is qualified, how long do you anticipate the same qualification will continue?

20-57.   On September 30, 19X5, White & Co., CPAs, was engaged to audit the consolidated financial statements of National Motors, Inc. for the year ended December 31, 19X5. The consolidated financial statements of National had not been audited the prior year. National's inadequate inventory records precluded White from forming an opinion as to the proper application of generally accepted accounting principles to inventory balances on January 1, 19X5. Therefore, White decided not to express an opinion on the results of operations for the year ended December 31, 19X5. National elected not to present comparative financial statements.

Rapid Parts Company, a consolidated subsidiary of National, was audited for the year ended December 31, 19X5, by Green & Co., CPAs. Green completed its field work on February 28, 19X6, and submitted an unmodified report on Rapid's financial statements on March 7, 19X6. Rapid's statements reflect total assets and revenues constituting 22 percent and 25 percent, respectively, of the consolidated totals of National. White decided not to assume responsibility for the work of Green. Green's report on Rapid does not accompany National's consolidated statements.

White completed its field work on March 28, 19X6, and submitted its auditor's report to National on April 4, 19X6.

Required:
Prepare the White & Co. audit report on the consolidated financial statements of National Motors, Inc.

(AICPA adapted)

20-58.   Devon Incorporated engaged Smith to audit its financial statements for the year ended December 31, 19X3. The financial statements of Devon Incorporated for the year ended December 31, 19X2, were audited by Jones whose March 31, 19X3, auditor's report expressed an unmodified opinion. This report of Jones is not presented with the 19X3–19X2 comparative financial statements.

Smith's working papers contain the following information that does not appear in footnotes to the 19X3 financial statements as prepared by Devon Incorporated:

- One director appointed in 19X3 was formerly a partner in Jones' accounting firm. Jones' firm provided financial consulting services to Devon during 19W9 and 19W8, for which Devon paid approximately $1,600 and $9,000, respectively.

- The company refused to capitalize certain lease obligations for equipment acquired in 19X3. Capitalization of the leases in conformity with generally accepted accounting principles would have increased assets and liabilities by $312,000 and $387,000 respectively, and decreased retained earnings as of December 31, 19X3, by $75,000, and would have decreased net income and earnings per share by $75,000 and $.75 respectively for the year then ended. Smith has concluded that the leases should have been capitalized and that the effect is material.

- During the year, Devon changed its method of valuing inventory from the first-in, first-out method to the last-in, first-out method. This change was made because management believes LIFO more clearly reflects net income by providing a closer matching of current costs and current revenues. The change had the effect of reducing inventory at December 31, 19X3 by $65,000 and net income and earnings per share by $38,000 and $.38 respectively for the year then ended. Although the effect of the change on the current year is material, the effect of the change on prior years was immaterial; accordingly, there was no cumulative effect of the change. Smith firmly supports the company's position.

After completion of the field work on February 29, 19X4, Smith concludes that the expression of an adverse opinion is not warranted.

Required:
Prepare the body of Smith's report dated February 29, 19X4, and addressed to the Board of Directors to accompany the 19X3–19X2 comparative financial statements.

(AICPA adapted)

20-59. During your audit work as of December 31, 19X7, you discovered a lawsuit against your client, Alpha Corporation, asserting a material claim for negligence in producing defective toys. The management of Alpha has refused to disclose the lawsuit on the grounds that the probability of an unfavorable outcome is remote. Legal counsel has opined that there is at least a reasonable possibility of an unfavorable outcome and that the effect of the suit could be material to the financial statements.
a. Discuss the reporting problem involved in the case.
b. Draft the audit report you would issue.

20-60. The field work on Triple Steel Corporation has been completed. You were responsible for preparing the preliminary draft of the financial statements and auditors' report; however, a staff accountant assisted you. You had the draft statements and report typed for presentation to the supervisor, Joan Fisher. You have worked for Joan before and know she demands the very best work.

You are now reviewing the draft to make sure it is final in all respects.

Required:

a. Review the following financial statements and auditors' report. Note any changes that will have to be made to them before you submit them to the supervisor. Changes may be required because of omissions (e.g., inadequate disclosure) or carelessness in drafting the report (e.g., different amounts appearing for the same item in different places). It will not be necessary to check the clerical accuracy of the statements.

b. List any matters that you want to be sure have been investigated and discussed with management.

(Adapted and used with permission of Ernst & Whinney)

AUDITORS' REPORT

Board of Directors
Triple Steel Corporation
Detroit, Michigan

We have audited the accompanying financial statements of Triple Steel Corporation for the year ended June 30, 19X2. These financial statements are the responsibility of management. Our responsibility is to express an opinion on these financial statements based on our audit.

We conducted our audit in accordance with generally accepted auditing standards. Those standards require that we plan and perform the audit to obtain reasonable assurance about whether the financial statements are free of material misstatement. An audit includes examining, on a test basis, evidence supporting the amounts and disclosures in the financial statements. An audit also includes assessing the accounting principles used and significant estimates made by management, as well as evaluating the overall financial statement presentation. We believe that our audit provides a reasonable basis for our opinion. We previously made a similar audit of the financial statements for the preceding year.

In our opinion, the accompanying balance sheet and statements of operations and retained earnings present fairly the financial position of Triple Steel Corporation at June 30, 19X2, and the results of its operations for the year then ended in conformity with generally accepted accounting principles.

Detroit, Michigan
August 10, 19X2

Balance Sheet
Triple Steel Corporation

	June 30	
	19X2	*19X1*
ASSETS		
Current assets		
Cash and certificates of deposit	$ 3,548,583	$ 3,447,058
Trade receivables, less allowance of $30,000	1,465,410	2,326,510
Inventories—Notes A and C:		
Finished products	1,671,230	1,146,555
Work in process	1,068,312	1,038,238
Materials and supplies	914,173	879,668
	3,653,715	3,064,461
Prepaid taxes and insurance	340,290	420,086
Total current assets	9,007,998	9,258,115
Other assets		
Cash value of life insurance	136,298	127,618
Miscellaneous deposits and accounts	203,342	133,060
	339,640	260,678
Properties—on the basis of cost—Note B		
Land	815,130	721,161
Buildings	3,886,339	3,802,183
Machinery and equipment	20,965,042	19,710,505
	25,666,511	24,233,849
Less accumulated depreciation and amortization	12,595,431	11,645,132
	13,071,080	12,588,717
	$22,418,718	$22,107,510

Balance Sheet
Triple Steel Corporation

	June 30	
	19X2	*19X1*
LIABILITIES AND STOCKHOLDERS' EQUITY		
Current liabilities		
Accounts payable	$ 1,278,981	$ 1,103,641
Payrolls and amounts withheld therefrom	229,594	256,010
Taxes, other than income taxes	342,333	241,339
Pension plan contributions and other current liabilities	210,939	222,635
Federal income taxes	130,488	185,050
Current portion of long-term debt	400,000	400,000
Total current liabilities	2,592,335	2,408,675
Long-term debt		
5½% First mortgage sinking fund bonds—Note C	4,000,000	4,400,000
Deferred federal income taxes	32,000	—0—
Stockholders' equity—Notes D, E, and F		
Common stock, $2.50 par value:		
Authorized 500,000 shares		
Issued and outstanding 357,419 shares		
(19X1—357,024)	893,548	892,560
Additional paid-in capital	2,842,772	2,835,016
Retained earnings	12,058,063	11,571,259
	15,794,383	15,298,835
	$22,418,718	$22,107,510

See notes to financial statements.

Statement of Operations and Retained Earnings
Triple Steel Corporation

	Year Ended June 30	
	19X2	*19X1*
Net sales	$21,643,276	$24,019,044
Interest and other income	151,213	203,998
	21,794,489	24,223,042
Costs and expenses:		
Cost of products sold, exclusive of depreciation	17,467,856	18,324,089
Provision for depreciation of properties	1,397,773	1,274,509
Selling, administrative, and general expenses	777,850	763,246
Interest on long-term debt	264,000	286,000
Federal income taxes	900,000	1,780,000
	20,807,479	22,427,844
Net income for the year	987,010	1,795,198
Retained earnings at July 1	11,571,260	10,275,441
	12,558,270	12,070,639
Cash dividend paid—$1.40 a share	500,206	499,380
Retained earnings at end of year	$12,058,064	$11,571,259

Statement of Cash Flows
Triple Steel Company
June 30, 19X2

Source of funds	
From operations:	
Net income	$ 987,010
Provision for depreciation	1,397,773
Increase in deferred income taxes	32,000
Total from operations	2,416,783
Proceeds from sale of common stock	8,744
Decrease in net current assets	433,777
Total	$2,859,304
Application of funds	
Additions to property, plant, and equipment	$1,880,136
Increase in other assets	78,962
Cash dividend	500,206
Reduction in long-term debt	400,000
Total	$2,859,304
See notes to financial statements	

Notes to Financial Statements
Triple Steel Corporation
June 30, 19X2

Note A—Inventory. Inventories have been stated at the lower of cost or market prices. Cost as to raw material content of certain inventories, in the amount of $2,568,882 at June 30, 19X2, has been determined by the last-in, first-out method and, as to the remainder of the inventories, has been determined by methods that are substantially equivalent to the first-in, first-out method.

Note B—Pensions. The company has pension plans covering substantially all employees. The total pension expense for 19X2 and 19X1 was $110,000 and $115,000, respectively, including amortization of prior service cost over a period of 40 years. The company's policy is to fund pension cost accrued. Unfunded prior service cost under the plans was approximately $350,000 at June 30, 19X2.

Note C—First Mortgage Bonds. The corporation is required to pay $400,000 annually on the first mortgage bonds until retirement on June 30, 19X3.

All properties (with minor exceptions), life insurance policies, and certain inventories ($2,687,320) are pledged in connection with the bonds.

Note D—Common Stock Optioned to Officers and Employees. Certain officers and key employees have been granted options entitling them to purchase shares of common stock at $19.50 and $29.875 per share, which represented the fair market value on the dates of grant. At July 1, 19X1, options were outstanding for 941 shares. During 19X2, options for 393 shares were exercised for an aggregate option price of $8,744. At June 30, 19X2, options for 546 shares were outstanding and exercisable for an aggregate option price of $13,639. No shares were available for additional options at the beginning or end of the year.

The excess of proceeds over par value of the common stock sold during 19X2, amounting to $7,755, has been credited to additional capital and comprised the only change in that account.

Note F—Restrictions on Dividends. The indenture relating to the first mortgage bonds requires the company to maintain net current assets, as defined, of not less than $3,000,000 and otherwise restricts the declaration of dividends, other than stock dividends. At June 30, 19X2, retained earnings of $1,549,391 were free of such restrictions.

Other Types of Reports

Learning Objectives   *After reading and studying the material in this chapter, the student should*

Understand the three levels of assurance that a CPA may provide on financial statements.

Know the general nature of the procedures and the form of report for each of the three levels of assurance.

Be knowledgeable of the types of reports that qualify as special reports.

Understand the purposes and major sections of letters for underwriters and reports on prospective financial statements and accompanying information in auditor-submitted documents.

In the two preceding chapters the form of audit report applicable to general-purpose financial statements was discussed. This form, generally recognized by readers of published annual reports, applies to all financial statements that purport to show financial position, results of operations, and cash flows in conformity with generally accepted accounting principles. CPAs issue other types of reports, however, that are less familiar to the general public. This chapter contains discussions of some of these types of reports, including reports on unaudited, compiled, and reviewed financial statements, special reports, letters for underwriters, and reports on prospective financial statements and accompanying information in auditor-submitted documents.

   When auditors issue a standard audit report, they express the type of opinion that constitutes positive assurance on the related financial statements. In contrast, some of the reports discussed in this chapter express a form of negative (limited) assurance. An example of negative assurance is "*nothing* came to our attention to indicate that the financial statements are *not* fairly presented." To appreciate the implications of negative assurance, one must remember that the less work CPAs perform, the stronger negative assurance (that they know of nothing wrong with the financial statements) they could give. In other words, the more ignorant they are of the financial statements, the surer they are that they know of no reason why the statements are not fairly presented. Because many within the accounting profession believe that negative assurance reports might result in a decline in the quality of work performed by CPAs, their use was restricted for many years to reports that were not publicly distributed, such as letters for underwriters and certain special reports. More recently, however, due to pressures to expand its responsibilities, the accounting profession has authorized the use of negative assurance in reports on reviews of general-purpose financial statements.

The concept of differential reporting for public and nonpublic companies is also introduced in this chapter. The Accounting and Review Services Committee (with standing equal to that of the Auditing Standards Board) is designated to issue pronouncements in connection with unaudited financial statements of nonpublic entities.[1] Its pronouncements take the form of Statements on Standards for Accounting and Review Services (SSARS), and it has established the concept of compilation and review that are discussed later in this chapter. A summary of certain services CPAs may provide, classified by type of company, is provided in Figure 21.1.

Public Company	*Nonpublic Company*
Audits, including special reports[a]	Audits, including special reports[a]
Reviews of interim financial information[a]	Reviews of financial statements[b]
Preparation of unaudited financial statements[a]	Compilations[b]

[a] Standards are established by the Auditing Standards Board through Statements on Auditing Standards.

[b] Standards are established by the Accounting and Review Services Committee through Statements on Standards for Accounting and Review Services.

Figure 21.1   Certain CPA services classified by type of company.

The three general levels of assurance that a CPA may provide on financial information, together with examples of each, are shown in Figure 21.2. The descriptions of the levels of assurance may be subject to question. For example, even though a CPA provides no assurance in reports on unaudited or compiled financial statements, surely one would expect him or her to detect obvious errors

---

[1] *SSARS No. 2* defines a nonpublic entity as any other than (a) one whose securities are publicly traded either nationally, regionally, or locally, (b) one that files with a regulatory agency in preparation of the sale of securities in a public market, or (c) a subsidiary, joint venture, or other entity controlled by an entity covered by (a) or (b).

Levels of Assurance	Example	Type of Assurance
Maximum	Standard audit report	Positive
	Special reports on:	
	Audited financial statements that are prepared in accordance with a comprehensive basis of accounting other than generally accepted accounting principles	Positive
	Specified audited elements, accounts, or items of a financial statement	Positive
	Report on condensed financial statements	Positive
	Examination of financial forecasts and projections	Positive
Limited	Review of financial statements of a nonpublic company	Negative
	Review of interim financial information of a public company	Negative
	Letter for underwriter covering unaudited financial statements and certain subsequent changes therein	Negative
Minimum	Compiled financial statements of a nonpublic company	None
	Compiled financial forecasts and projections	None
	Unaudited financial statements of a public company	None

Figure 21.2   Levels of assurance that a CPA may provide on financial information.

and omissions, such as failure to record depreciation or income taxes. A more uncertain question is the level of limited assurance provided by a review. Is it slightly below an audit, slightly above unaudited, halfway between audited and unaudited, or at some other level? These questions are still to be addressed by the accounting profession.

Reports Providing Maximum Levels of Assurance

The standard audit report is covered in the two preceding chapters, so this section will be devoted to a discussion of other types of reports that provide a maximum level of assurance.

AU Section 621 defines *special reports* or *special purpose reports* as those issued in connection with (1) financial statements that are prepared in accordance with a comprehensive basis of accounting other than generally accepted accounting principles, (2) specified elements, accounts, or items of a financial statement, (3) compliance with aspects of contractual agreements or regulatory requirements related to audited financial statements, and (4) financial statements presented in prescribed form, or schedules that require a prescribed form of auditor's report.

Reports on Financial Statements Prepared in Accordance with a Comprehensive Basis of Accounting Other than Generally Accepted Accounting Principles

A comprehensive basis of accounting other than generally accepted accounting principles is defined in AU Section 621 (*SAS No. 14*) as one with at least one of the following characteristics:

1. A basis of accounting required to comply with the regulations of a government regulatory agency having jurisdiction over an entity.

2. A basis of accounting used for income tax reporting purposes.

3. The cash basis of accounting.

4. A basis of accounting having "substantial support" [the term *substantial support* is not defined] that is applied to all material items, such as the price-level basis of accounting.

If the financial statements being reported on have at least one of these characteristics, a separate paragraph should be added to the report to describe, or refer to a note to the financial statements that describes, the basis of accounting employed and how it differs from generally accepted accounting principles (the monetary effect need not be stated). Furthermore, a statement must be made that the financial statements are not intended to be presented in conformity with generally accepted accounting principles. The opinion paragraph should state the auditor's opinion as to whether or not the financial statements are presented fairly in conformity with the basis of accounting described in the separate paragraph or footnote.

The cash basis of accounting will be considered as an example. These statements are prepared on the basis of cash receipts and disbursements without adjustment for uncollected assets (e.g., accounts receivable) or unpaid liabilities (e.g., accounts payable). If the omitted assets or liabilities are material, financial statements prepared on a cash basis would not be in conformity with generally accepted accounting principles. In certain situations, however, cash-basis financial statements are necessary, such as when a company uses the cash basis for income tax purposes or when a partnership is required by its articles of partnership to compute and distribute income to its partners on a cash basis.

Cash basis financial statements should be referred to as statements of assets and liabilities arising from cash transactions (rather than balance sheets) and statements of cash receipts and disbursements (rather than statements of income). Disclosure should be made of the basis on which the financial statements were prepared and the nature of omitted assets and liabilities. A report on such statements might be worded as follows:

We have audited the accompanying statement of assets, liabilities and capital arising from cash transactions of A Company as of December 31, 19XX, and the related statements of cash revenues received and expenses paid and changes in partners' capital accounts for the year then ended. These financial statements are the responsibility of the Company's management. Our responsibility is to express an opinion on these financial statements based on our audit.

We conducted our audit in accordance with generally accepted auditing standards. Those standards require that we plan and perform the audit to obtain reasonable assurance about whether the financial statements are free of material misstatement. An audit includes examining, on a test basis, evidence supporting the amounts and disclosures in the financial statements. An audit also includes assessing the accounting principles used and significant estimates made by management, as well as evaluating the overall financial statement presentation. We believe that our audit provides a reasonable basis for our opinion.

As further described in Note 1 and as provided in the partnership agreement, revenue and expenses are recognized only when cash is received or paid, and receivables and payables are not included in the accompanying financial statements. Accordingly, these statements do not purport to present financial position, results of operations, and cash flows in conformity with generally accepted accounting principles.

In our opinion, the financial statements referred to above present fairly, in all material respects, the assets, liabilities, and capital arising from cash transactions of A Company as of December 31, 19XX, and the cash revenues received and expenses paid and changes in the partners' capital accounts for the year then ended on the basis of accounting described above.

The general standards and standards of field work are applicable to audits of cash-basis financial statements.

Reports on Specified Elements, Accounts, or Items of a Financial Statement

The need for an audit report on specific elements of a financial statement could arise from provisions of franchise, lease, and royalty agreements (where payments are based on sales, production, etc.), or provisions of agreements for business combinations (where the value of the acquired company may be based in part on its net current assets).

Auditors must approach such engagements with care, because materiality must be considered within the context of the individual element or account being reported on and not the financial statements as a whole. If the engagement is not performed in connection with an audit of the financial statements, the auditors should also be aware that it may be necessary to examine several or even most of the accounts in order to express an opinion on only one. For example, a report on inventories might require the auditors to examine cash, cost of sales, accounts payable, and perhaps other accounts because of their potential effect on inventories. They must also be certain that they are not placed in the position of interpreting rather than reporting compliance with legal agreements or contracts (e.g., a royalty agreement may not specify whether sales are to be adjusted for returns and allowances, bad debts, other income, etc.). An opinion of legal counsel should be requested for any ambiguous provisions.

A report for this type of engagement should identify the account that was audited, state that the audit was made in accordance with generally accepted auditing standards, identify the basis on which the information is presented, and express an opinion as to whether the account is fairly presented on the basis indicated.

Also, *SAS No. 35* permits an accountant to perform an engagement, such as a purchase investigation in connection with a proposed acquisition, in which the scope is limited to applying agreed-upon procedures that are not sufficient for expressing an opinion on one or more specified elements, accounts, or items of a financial statement, provided (1) the parties involved have a clear understanding of the procedures to be performed and (2) distribution of the report is restricted to the parties involved. In this case a form of negative assurance is used.

Reports on Condensed Financial Statements

Public companies may be required to present condensed financial statements that are derived from previously audited financial statements. Because these condensed financial statements omit many disclosures required by generally accepted accounting principles, the standard audit report is not appropriate. If the auditors are satisfied with the condensed financial statements and have issued an unqualified opinion on the financial statements from which they were derived, the auditors may provide assurance similar to the following:

> We have audited, in accordance with generally accepted auditing standards, the balance sheet of X Company as of December 31, 19X5, and the related statements of income, retained earnings, and cash flows for the year then ended (not presented herein); and in our report dated February 15, 19X6, we expressed an unqualified opinion on those financial statements. In our opinion, the information set forth in the accompanying condensed financial statements, which is the responsibility of management, is fairly stated, in all material respects, in relation to the financial statements from which it was derived.

If the auditors' report on the audited financial statements was modified, they should consider whether a similar modification is applicable to their report on the condensed financial statements.

Examination of Financial Forecasts and Projections

Financial Forecasts   The preparation and issuance of financial forecasts have received increased attention from the accounting profession. To provide guidance to the CPA who is associated with such forecasts, the AICPA has issued *Statement on Standards for Accountants' Services on Prospective Financial Information* which describes the applicable examination procedures and reporting format. The statement defines a financial forecast as a set of prospective financial statements that presents to the best of the responsible party's[2] knowledge and belief, an entity's expected financial position, results of operations, and cash flows. Financial forecasts may be for "general" or "limited" use, that is, for use by the public or restricted to use by the responsible party and others with whom direct negotiations are being held.

The CPA's purpose in examining a financial forecast is to determine whether (1) the underlying assumptions are reasonable as a basis for management's forecast and (2) the forecast is properly prepared based on the stated assumptions and the presentation conforms with the recommendations in AICPA *Guide for Prospective Financial Statements*. This will require the CPA to evaluate the client's procedures for preparing the forecast. The CPA should also identify and evaluate the important assumptions by analyzing prior periods' financial results and forecasts of similar businesses, reviewing contracts, agreements, and minutes, and using business knowledge to identify market trends, competitive conditions, pending laws and regulations, macroeconomic and political conditions, technological influences, and dependence on major customers and suppliers. The CPA must then determine that the computations made to translate the assumptions into the forecasted amounts are mathematically accurate, the accounting principles used in the forecast are consistent with generally accepted accounting principles, the assumptions are identified in the forecast and are internally consistent, and the presentation follows the guidelines in *Guide for Prospective Financial Statements*.

The CPA's standard report on a financial forecast describes the forecasted statements, describes the CPA's examination, and expresses positive assurances as to the presentation of the forecast in conformity with AICPA guidelines and the reasonableness of the underlying assumptions. The following is an illustration of the form of such a report:

> We have examined the accompanying forecasted balance sheet, statements of income, retained earnings, and cash flows of XYZ Company as of December 31, 19X8, and for the year then ending. Our examination was made in accordance with standards for an examination of a forecast established by the American Institute of Certified Public Accountants and, accordingly, included such procedures as we con-

---

[2]The responsible party is the person responsible for the assumptions underlying the prospective financial statements, usually management, but could be someone such as a party considering acquiring the entity.

sidered necessary to evaluate both the assumptions used by management and the preparation and presentation of the forecast.

In our opinion, the accompanying forecast is presented in conformity with guidelines for presentation of a forecast established by the American Institute of Certified Public Accountants, and the underlying assumptions provide a reasonable basis for management's forecast. However, there will usually be differences between the forecasted and actual results, because events and circumstances frequently do not occur as expected, and those differences may be material. We have no responsibility to update this report for events and circumstances occurring after the date of this report.

CPAs should issue an "except for" qualification or an adverse opinion if they believe the forecast departs from AICPA presentation guidelines. An adverse opinion should be issued if one or more significant assumptions are not disclosed or are not reasonable. A significant scope limitation should result in a disclaimer of opinion. The report may also be modified for reference to other accountants, inclusion of comparative historical information, emphasis of a matter, or to describe a larger engagement. When CPAs are not independent, as defined by the applicable code of professional ethics, they may compile, but not examine a financial forecast. A flowchart for reporting on an examination of a financial forecast is shown in Figure 21.3.

Financial Projections Projections differ from forecasts in that, rather than presenting *expected* results, they present results given one or more hypothetical assumptions. This allows the reader to evaluate the effect on the statements of the occurrence of the assumptions. For example, projected financial statements may be prepared to show the effect of the construction of a new manufacturing plant. The projections may be based on assumptions about one or more production or interest rates. A reader could then evaluate the effect of the rates on his or her decision to construct the plant.

The guidelines for preparation, presentation, and examination of financial forecasts are generally applicable to financial projections, except that the CPA need not obtain evidence to support the hypothetical assumptions. A form of report for the examination of a financial projection is as follows:

We have examined the accompanying projected balance sheet and statements of income, retained earnings, and cash flows of X Company as of December 31, 19X8, and for the year then ending. Our examination was made in accordance with standards for an examination of a projection established by the American Institute of Certified Public Accountants and, accordingly, included such procedures as we considered necessary to evaluate both the assumptions used by management and the preparation and presentation of the projection.

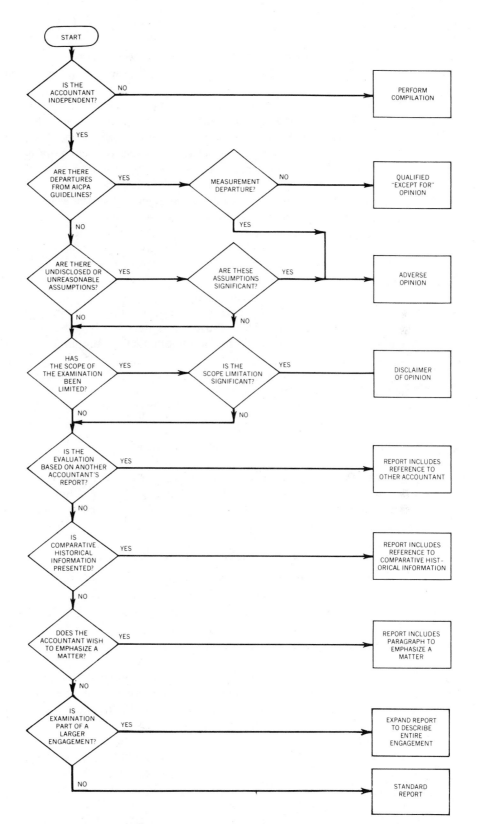

Figure 21.3 Flowchart for reporting on the examination of prospective statements.

The accompanying projection and this report were prepared for the D Bank for the purpose of negotiating a loan to expand X Company's plant, and should not be used for any other purpose.

In our opinion, the accompanying projection is presented in conformity with guidelines for the presentation of a projection established by the American Institute of Certified Public Accountants, and the underlying assumptions provide a reasonable basis for management's projection assuming the granting of the requested loan for the purpose of expanding X Company's plant as described in the summary of significant assumptions. However, even if the loan is granted and the plant is expanded, there will usually be differences between the projected and the actual results, because events and circumstances frequently do not occur as expected, and those differences may be material. We have no responsibility to update this report for events and circumstances occurring after the date of this report.

Financial projections should be for "limited" use only, that is, only the responsible party and others with whom negotiations are being held (D Bank in the foregoing example). This restriction is imposed because the general public cannot discuss or inquire about the hypothetical assumptions as can parties directly involved in the negotiations.

The report modifications previously discussed for a financial forecast also apply to a financial projection.

Reports Providing Limited Levels of Assurance

Limited levels of assurance are provided after the CPA performs a review of the related statements. The term *review* has a precise meaning to CPAs, and the minimum review procedures to be performed are described in the applicable professional standards.

Review of Financial Statements of a Nonpublic Company

AR Section 100 (*SSARS No. 1*) defines a review as "performing inquiry and analytical procedures that provide the accountant with a reasonable basis for expressing limited assurance that there are no material modifications that should be made to the statements in order for them to be in conformity with generally accepted accounting principles or, if applicable, with another comprehensive basis of accounting." To perform a review, a CPA must understand (1) the accounting principles and practices of the industry in which the client operates, and (2) the client's organization, operating characteristics, and the nature of its assets, liabilities, revenues, and expenses. The CPA should make *inquiries* of management regarding the accounting principles and practices in use, the procedures used for recording transactions, and the procedures for accumulating financial statement information. Additional inquiries should cover actions taken at meetings of stockholders and boards of directors, changes in accounting principles, and subsequent events. The *analytical procedures* are similar to the analytical procedures performed in an audit and include comparisons of current financial results with prior years' and budgeted results and evaluation of the relationships of the elements of the financial statements that would be expected to conform to a predictable pattern. There is no requirement for the CPA to gather any evidence to corroborate the inquiries and analytical procedures unless he or she becomes aware that the information may be incorrect, incomplete, or otherwise unsatisfactory. Each page of the financial statements should include a reference such as "See Accountant's Review Report."

A report on a review consists of three paragraphs (assuming no exceptions) that describe the scope of the review, disclaim an opinion on the financial statements, and provide negative assurance as to conformity with generally accepted accounting principles. An illustration follows:

> We have reviewed the accompanying balance sheet of Guy Company as of December 31, 19X3, and the related statements of income, retained earnings, and cash flows for the year then ended, in accordance with standards established by the American Institute of Certified Public Accountants. All information included in these financial statements is the representation of the management of Guy Company.
>
> A review consists principally of inquiries of company personnel and analytical procedures applied to financial data. It is substantially less in scope than an audit performed in accordance with generally accepted auditing standards, the objective of which is the expression of an opinion regarding the financial statements taken as a whole. Accordingly, we do not express such an opinion.
>
> Based on our review, we are not aware of any material modifications that should be made to the accompanying financial statements in order for them to be in conformity with generally accepted accounting principles.

The CPA should describe in a separate paragraph of the report any departures from generally accepted accounting principles, including omission of any required disclosures, that come to his or her attention as a result of performing the review. The reporting of uncertainties and inconsistencies in the application of generally accepted accounting principles is optional. CPAs may not issue a review report on financial statements of an entity of which they are not independent. A flowchart of *SSARS No. 1* is presented in the appendix to this chapter.

If a CPA is engaged to perform an audit of a nonpublic entity and the client subsequently requests that the engagement be changed to a review (or a compilation), the CPA should consider the reason for the request and the additional effort and cost to complete the audit. If the audit is substantially complete and the reason for the request is to prohibit the CPA from performing audit procedures such as corresponding with legal counsel or obtaining a management representation letter, the CPA should not consent to a change in the engagement.

Review of Interim Financial Information of a Public Company

CPAs may also perform limited reviews of interim (but not annual) financial information of public companies. The SEC requires disclosure in a note to the annual financial statements of unaudited quarterly data, and a review of these data by an independent public accountant. The SEC encourages, but does not require, companies to have their unaudited interim statements reviewed quarterly by their auditor rather than at the end of the year.

AU Section 722 (*SAS No. 36*) applies to reviews of interim financial information (1) that is presented alone by a public entity and purports to conform with the provisions of *APB Opinion No. 28* (Interim Financial Reporting) and (2) that accompanies or is included in a note to audited financial statements of a public or nonpublic entity.[3] The statement implies that the CPA will normally have audited the company's financial statements for one or more annual periods, and that such audits will provide a practical basis for the review procedures. The procedures would consist primarily of inquiries and analytical procedures. Examples would include (1) inquiries concerning (a) the accounting system, (b) significant changes in the internal control structure, and (c) subsequent events; (2) analytical procedures consisting of comparison of the financial information with prior interim periods and anticipated results, and evaluation of the relationships of the elements of the financial information that would be expected to conform to a predictable pattern; (3) reading of minutes and the interim financial information; and (4) obtaining representations from management. All pages of the financial information should be clearly marked as "unaudited."

For interim financial information presented alone, the form of report consists of three paragraphs (assuming no departures from generally accepted accounting principles are noted in the review; no reporting is required of uncertainties or lack of consistency in the application of accounting principles) describing the scope of the review, disclaiming an opinion on the financial statements taken as a whole, and expressing negative assurance that the CPA is not aware of any departures from generally accepted accounting principles. An example of such a report follows:

> We have made a review of the interim financial information of Granger Company as of March 31, 19X4, and for the three-month period then ended, in accordance with standards established by the American Institute of Certified Public Accountants.
>
> A review of interim financial information consists principally of obtaining an understanding of the system for the preparation of interim financial information, applying analytical procedures to financial data, and making inquiries of persons responsible for financial and accounting matters. It is substantially less in scope than an audit performed in accordance with generally accepted auditing standards, the objective of

---

[3]The SEC requires footnote disclosure in audited financial statements of certain larger companies of selected interim financial information. This section would have very limited applicability to nonpublic entities, as few would have reason to make such disclosures.

which is the expression of an opinion regarding the financial statements taken as a whole. Accordingly, we do not express such an opinion.

Based on our review, we are not aware of any material modifications that should be made to the accompanying financial information for it to be in conformity with generally accepted accounting principles.

Departures from generally accepted accounting principles, including inadequate disclosure (but note that disclosure requirements under *APB Opinion No. 28* are considerably less extensive than those necessary for annual general purpose financial statements), should be described in an additional paragraph.

When the interim financial information accompanies or is included in a note to audited financial statements, the review procedures set forth above should be performed. If the results of the review are satisfactory and if the information is designated as unaudited, CPAs ordinarily need not modify their report on the audited financial statements to make reference to their review or the interim financial information.

Letter for Underwriter Covering Unaudited Financial Statements and Certain Subsequent Changes Therein

Before considering the form of letters for underwriters (also commonly referred to as "comfort letters"), one must understand their purpose. They are *not* required by any of the federal securities acts, and copies are *not* filed with the SEC. They may be, and usually are, requested by underwriters (normally, investment bankers assisting a company in the sale of securities either by purchase for subsequent resale or on a commission basis) as one means of meeting their responsibilities under the Securities Act of 1933, which was discussed in Chapter 4. In general, this act provides that certain persons (including underwriters) may limit or avoid liability under the act if, *after reasonable investigation,* they had *reasonable grounds to believe* and did believe that the registration statement (a document filed with the SEC containing a detailed description of a company and its operations, including financial statements) was true and no material facts were omitted. A comfort letter is considered one element of a reasonable investigation by the underwriters.

Comfort letters have been a source of conflict between auditors and underwriters and their attorneys for many years. For their own protection, underwriters would like to expand the data covered in comfort letters, whereas auditors have tried to restrict the data covered by such letters. *SAP No. 48* (later codified into *SAS No. 1*) was issued in an attempt to resolve the conflicts. One of its important provisions is a clear statement that the underwriters are responsible for the sufficiency of any procedures performed by the auditor to give negative assurance in the comfort letter.

A comfort letter may cover all or some of the following topics:

1. Independence of the auditor.

2. Compliance of the audited financial statements included in the registration statement with SEC accounting requirements.

3. Negative assurance regarding unaudited financial statements and interim financial information included in the registration statement.

4. Negative assurance regarding decreases in certain financial statement items subsequent to the date of the latest financial statements included in the registration statement.

5. Negative assurance regarding financial data included in the text section (as opposed to the financial statement section) of the registration statement.

The topic of independence is not controversial. The auditor must be able to state that he or she is independent in order to have audited the necessary financial statements for inclusion in the registration statement. The representation concerning independence is a statement of fact rather than of opinion.

In contrast, the representation regarding compliance with SEC accounting requirements is the auditor's opinion and is presented as such. The SEC accounting requirements include those within the 1933 act, the form on which the registration statement is being prepared, Regulation S-X, and the *Financial Reporting Releases*.

If the audited financial statements included in the registration statement are not current (the determination of what is current under various conditions is defined by rules of the SEC and policies of underwriters), unaudited financial statements as of a current date must be included. It is on these unaudited financial statements that the auditor may give negative assurance. In most cases, it is impractical, because of time limitations, to perform an audit as of a current date, yet the investing public, through the underwriters as their representatives, needs some assurances about the unaudited statements. The accounting profession concluded that the public interest would be served best if negative assurance on general-purpose financial statements were allowed in this situation. Auditors must include in the letter the specific steps performed as a basis for their negative assurance.

The fourth topic included in comfort letters is negative assurance about decreases in certain financial statement items subsequent to the date of the latest financial statements included in the registration statement. The purpose of this section is to alert the underwriter at the latest practicable time (usually within five days of the effective date of the registration statement) to decreases in important financial statement items (such as declines in sales, net income, net assets, etc.) that the underwriters may consider adverse. Thus the underwriters have an opportunity to cancel the offering or at least delay it until all material adverse conditions are properly disclosed in the registration statement. The auditor searches for decreases in important financial statement items by reviewing minutes and any financial statements prepared after those included in the registration statement, and by inquiring of certain company officials as to significant transactions during the period subsequent to the date of the latest financial statements. As a result of this work, the auditor may give negative assurance that there have been no decreases in important financial statement items. If decreases have occurred, they must be disclosed in the letter.

The final comfort letter topic is negative assurance about financial data included in the text section of the registration statement. This topic has been the source of most of the controversy between auditors and underwriters. The controversy arises because of requests by underwriters that procedures be performed that auditors consider (1) beyond their competence (such as procedures related to nonfinancial or subjective data), or (2) lacking in substance (such as comparison of amounts in the registration statement with amounts shown on a client-prepared worksheet). AU Section 631 (*SAS No. 38*) recommends that auditors limit their procedures and comments to information that is expressed in dollars and has been obtained from accounting records subject to the internal control structure or has been computed from such records. The data to which the procedures were applied, the procedures themselves, and the auditors' findings must be enumerated clearly.

Because of the negative assurances contained in comfort letters, each letter must contain a statement restricting its use to the underwriter. Comfort letters are never distributed beyond the client and the underwriter, and the general public generally is unaware that they exist.

AU Section 631 contains examples of comfort letters that may be appropriate in various situations. As in the case of the standard audit report, auditors should use the standard wording of a comfort letter when it is appropriate, but they must consider carefully whether the letter accurately communicates the work they have done and their findings for each engagement.

Reports Providing a Minimum Level of Assurance

Many small nonpublic companies are unable to employ a high level of accounting talent and need outside assistance in the preparation of both historical and prospective financial statements. CPAs provide a useful service by rendering such assistance. They may also be associated[4] with unaudited financial statements of public companies. This section covers the CPA's responsibilities in these instances.

Compiled Financial Statements of a Nonpublic Company

AR Section 100 (*SSARS No. 1*) defines a compilation as "presenting in the form of financial statements information that is the representation of management

---

[4]CPAs are associated with financial statements that they prepare or assist in preparing or when they consent to the use of their name in a report or document (excluding tax returns) containing the financial statements.

(owners) without undertaking to express any assurance on the statements.'' To compile financial statements, CPAs should understand the industry and nature of the business in which the client is engaged, including the form of its accounting records, the qualifications of its accounting personnel, the accounting basis on which the financial statements are to be presented, and the form and content of the financial statements. However, CPAs are not required to make inquiries or to perform any procedures to validate the information provided to them unless it appears to be incomplete or incorrect. Each page of the financial statements should contain a reference such as ''See Accountant's Compilation Report.''

A report on a compilation of financial statements containing all disclosures required by generally accepted accounting principles is shown in the following:

> I have compiled the accompanying balance sheet of Clay Company as of December 31, 19X4, and the related statements of income, retained earnings, and cash flows for the year then ended in accordance with standards established by the American Institute of Certified Public Accountants.
>
> A compilation is limited to presenting in the form of financial statements information that is the representation of management. I have not audited or reviewed the accompanying financial statements and, accordingly, do not express an opinion or any other form of assurance on them.

CPAs may also compile financial statements that omit substantially all disclosures required by generally accepted accounting principles if this fact is clearly stated in the report and is not, to their knowledge, done to mislead the users of the statements. In such case, a third paragraph in the following form would be added to the report.

> Management has elected to omit substantially all of the disclosures required by generally accepted accounting principles. If the omitted disclosures were included in the financial statements, they might influence the user's conclusions about the company's financial position, results of operations, and cash flows. Accordingly, these financial statements are not designed for those who are not informed about such matters.

A third paragraph should also be added if the financial statements are compiled on the prescribed form of a bank, trade association, government agency, and so forth, and the form contains departures from generally accepted accounting principles, including inadequate disclosure. As the form is presumed to meet the needs of the body requesting it, a paragraph in the following form is added:

> These financial statements (including related disclosures) are presented in accordance with the requirements of (name of body), which differ from generally accepted

accounting principles. Accordingly, these financial statements are not designed for those who are not informed about such differences.

If CPAs become aware of a departure from generally accepted accounting principles other than under the aforementioned circumstances, they should modify their report and include a separate paragraph that discusses the departure. As in the case of a review, disclosures of uncertainties and inconsistencies in the application of accounting principles are optional if adequately disclosed in the financial statements. CPAs may issue a compilation on financial statements even though they are not independent provided the lack of independence is disclosed in the report (but not the reason therefor). A flowchart of *SSARS No. 1* is presented in the appendix to this chapter.

Compilation of Financial Forecasts and Projections

CPAs may compile financial forecasts and projections. A compilation consists of (1) assembling the forecast or projection based on the client's assumptions, (2) considering whether the underlying assumptions appear to be obviously inappropriate, and (3) reading the forecast or projection for presentation in conformity with AICPA guidelines. A form of report for the compilation of a financial forecast is as follows:

> We have compiled the accompanying forecasted balance sheet and statements of income, retained earnings, and cash flows of XYZ Company as of December 31, 19XX, and for the year then ending, in accordance with standards established by the American Institute of Certified Public Accountants.
>
> A compilation is limited to presenting in the form of a forecast information that is the representation of management and does not include evaluation of the support for the assumptions underlying the forecast. We have not examined the forecast and, accordingly, do not express an opinion or any other form of assurance on the accompanying statements or assumptions. Furthermore, there will usually be differences between the forecasted and actual results, because events and circumstances frequently do not occur as expected, and those differences may be material. We have no responsibility to update this report for events and circumstances occurring after the date of this report.

A report on the compilation of a financial projection would contain two paragraphs similar to those shown above plus an additional paragraph limiting the use of the report to its intended purpose.

Similar modifications may be made to reports based on compiled financial forecasts and projections as are made to reports based on compiled historical financial statements (e.g., an additional paragraph may be added to describe lack of independence).

Unaudited Financial Statements of a Public Company

When CPAs are associated with financial statements of a public company that have not been audited or reviewed, they must disclaim an opinion on the statements. An example of the form of report is as follows:[5]

> The accompanying balance sheet of Wilson Company as of December 31, 19X4, and the related statements of income, retained earnings, and cash flows for the year then ended were not audited by us and, accordingly, we do not express an opinion on them.

In addition to attaching a disclaimer to the financial statements, the CPA should make sure that each page of the financial statements is marked clearly as unaudited.

CPAs have no responsibility to apply any procedures beyond reading the financial statements for obvious material errors. In some cases, for their own satisfaction, CPAs may wish to perform certain steps in connection with the preparation of unaudited financial statements that might be considered auditing procedures. For example, they may wish to review bank reconciliations, tax returns, and other documents supporting amounts shown in the financial statements. However, they should make no reference to these steps in the report. To describe any procedures performed might cause the reader to believe that an audit was performed.

CPAs may detect errors in the data used to prepare financial statements even though they do not perform an audit. For example, they may note that incorrect prices were used to compute inventory or that certain necessary accrued liabilities for such items as payroll or income taxes have been omitted. In this situation, they should suggest that the accounting records and financial statements be corrected. If the client refuses to make the necessary corrections, the CPAs must either state their reservations regarding the financial statements in their disclaimer or withdraw from the engagement. An example of the wording that might be added to a disclaimer follows:

> The accompanying financial statements do not include $25,000 of income tax expense and liability in the statement of income and balance sheet, respectively, as required by generally accepted accounting principles.

It would not be appropriate to issue a qualified or adverse opinion, because no audit has been performed and without an audit, no opinion—unqualified, qualified, or adverse—can be expressed.

Closely related to the situation presented by unaudited financial statements is the situation in which CPAs are not independent. CPAs are not prohibited from

---

[5]Note that the wording of this type of disclaimer is different from that used in the case of a scope limitation on an audit. See Chapter 20.

being an officer, director, or stockholder of a company, although many accounting firms place restrictions on such relationships. As pointed out in Chapter 3, however, any of these relationships, plus several others, result in a loss of independence, and without independence there can be no audit. No matter how extensive the procedures a CPA performs, the engagement cannot be in accordance with generally accepted auditing standards if the CPA lacks independence. Accordingly, if CPAs who are not independent are associated with financial statements, they must issue a disclaimer and specifically state that they are not independent (although reasons for lack of independence are not to be given). The form recommended by AU Section 504 (*SAS No. 26*) follows:

> We are not independent with respect to XYZ Company, and the accompanying balance sheet as of December 31, 19XX, and the related statements of income, retained earnings, and cash flows for the year then ended were not audited by us and, accordingly, we do not express an opinion on them.

When a CPA lacks independence, the requirements to omit a description of any work performed and to mark all pages as unaudited are the same as those discussed for unaudited financial statements.

Engagement letters specifying the services to be performed are indispensable if the preparation of unaudited financial statements is to be undertaken. The lack of such a letter was one of several issues involved in the *1136 Tenants' Corp.* case discussed in Chapter 4. Another issue that had serious implications for CPAs preparing unaudited financial statements was the holding by the court that the CPAs had a duty to investigate "suspicious" circumstances noted during their work, even though an audit was not being performed. This holding conflicts directly with the statement in AU Section 504 that a CPA has no responsibility to perform any procedures on unaudited financial statements beyond reading them for obvious errors. There are few, if any, engagements in which a CPA does not encounter circumstances that could be considered, at least by hindsight, unusual, questionable, or suspicious. Therefore, a significant expansion of the CPA's work may be necessary to meet the guidelines of the court. For this and other reasons (low fees, desire of the staff for more challenging work, etc.), some accounting firms discourage clients seeking preparation of unaudited financial statements. Others have found this service to be an important element in the development of their professional practice.

When the preparation of unaudited financial statements is undertaken, CPAs are well advised to develop a reasonable understanding of the business operations of their client. This knowledge will allow them to make overall evaluations as to the reasonableness of the financial data they prepare. Such evaluations cannot ensure that the financial statements are presented fairly, but they are more desirable than merely copying numbers from a general ledger to a financial statement without an understanding of what they mean and what relationships should reasonably be expected. There is no requirement for gaining such an understanding when a CPA is associated with unaudited financial statements of a public company, although the requirement does exist when a CPA compiles financial statements of a nonpublic company. This inconsistency led some members of the Auditing Standards Board to dissent to the issuance of *SAS No. 26* because they believed it allowed a lower level of service to be performed for a public company than a nonpublic company.

Reports on Accompanying Information in Auditor-Submitted Documents

Reports on accompanying information in auditor-submitted documents (formerly referred to as long-form reports) may provide either limited or minimum assurance. Accompanying information (as opposed to "other information" and "supplemental information" discussed in Chapter 20) is any information submitted by the CPA to his or her client in a document containing the basic financial statements. It is presented outside of the basic financial statements and is not considered necessary for their presentation in accordance with generally accepted accounting principles. Accompanying information includes details or explanations of amounts shown in the basic financial statements, consolidating information, historical summaries of the basic financial statements, statistical data derived from the basic financial statements, as well as nonaccounting information. For example, such a report might contain a section for accounts receivable including analyses of receivables by type, age, and major customers compared by amount and percentage with those of the prior year, and analyses of the allowance for doubtful accounts for the year including ratios of total amount written off to total revenues, total amount over 90 days old to the balance in the allowance account, and so forth. Similar comments and analyses could be included for all significant balance sheet and income statement accounts. A description of significant audit procedures performed may also be included as a separate section of the report.

The inclusion of such details opens the possibility that a reader will misunderstand the responsibility the auditors are assuming for the accompanying data in the report. Remember that the auditors' opinion relates to the financial statements taken as a whole and not to individual accounts. Therefore, in commenting on individual accounts, auditors must be careful that the wording does not convey more assurance than they are prepared to give. It is also important to remember that although auditors may assist in preparing the accompanying information, it consists basically of representations of management.

The report normally begins with the standard audit report to establish the auditor's responsibility for the basic financial statements. To comply with the fourth standard of reporting, the report should include another paragraph indicating the degree of responsibility taken for the accompanying information. This paragraph might be worded as follows:

> Our audit was made for the purpose of forming an opinion on the basic financial statements taken as a whole. The accompanying information is presented for pur-

poses of additional analysis and is not a required part of the basic financial statements. Such information has been subjected to the auditing procedures applied in the audit of the basic financial statements and, in our opinion, is fairly stated in all material respects in relation to the basic financial statements taken as a whole.[6]

Reports on accompanying information are not as common today as they were several years ago. At one time, the annual auditor's report, including accompanying information, was the only reliable financial information available to many managers and stockholders, because internal financial statements were not prepared. Today, however, few companies attempt to operate without periodic, timely, and reliable financial information. For such companies, the report on accompanying information would be a needless duplication of effort. Also, because of the continually rising cost of professional auditing services, a report on accompanying information would be much more expensive to prepare today than it was several years ago. The combination of reduced need and increased expense has diminished the use of reports on accompanying information significantly.

[6]The last sentence could be "Such information has not been subjected to the auditing procedures applied in the audit of the basic financial statements, and, accordingly, we express no opinion on it."

Appendix to Chapter 21

Flowchart of Statement on Standards for Accounting and Review Services No. 1, Compilation and Review of Financial Statements

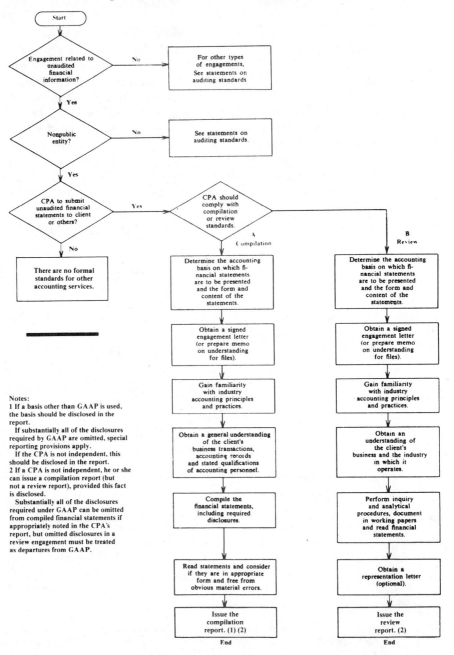

Notes:
1 If a basis other than GAAP is used, the basis should be disclosed in the report.
    If substantially all of the disclosures required by GAAP are omitted, special reporting provisions apply.
    If the CPA is not independent, this should be disclosed in the report.
2 If a CPA is not independent, he or she can issue a compilation report (but not a review report), provided this fact is disclosed.
    Substantially all of the disclosures required under GAAP can be omitted from compiled financial statements if appropriately noted in the CPA's report, but omitted disclosures in a review engagement must be treated as departures from GAAP.

Source: T. R. Weirich and G. M. Pintar, "Interpretation and Flowchart of SSARS No. 1," *Journal of Accountancy* (November 1979) p. 61.

Chapter 21
Glossary of Terms

(listed in order of appearance in the chapter, with accompanying page reference where the term is discussed)

Term	*Page in Chapter*
Negative (limited) assurance a type of assurance provided by a CPA that he or she is not aware of misstatements (but not that the information is fairly presented).	801
Accounting and Review Services Committee a senior technical committee of the AICPA with authority to issue pronouncements (Statements on Standards of Accounting and Review Services) dealing with unaudited financial statements of nonpublic companies.	802
Special reports audit reports on financial statements (and portions thereof) that do not purport to present financial position, results of operations, or cash flows in conformity with generally accepted accounting principles.	803
Examination of prospective financial statements evaluation of the (1) preparation of the statements, (2) support underlying the assumptions, and (3) presentation of the statements for conformity with AICPA guidelines.	807
Financial forecast prospective financial statements that present to the best of the responsible party's knowledge and belief, an entity's expected financial position, results of operations, and cash flows.	807
Financial projection prospective financial statements that present, to the best of the responsible party's knowledge and belief, given one or more hypothetical assumptions, an entity's expected financial position, results of operations, and cash flows.	808
Review (nonpublic company) performance of inquiry and analytical procedures that provide the accountant with a reasonable basis for expressing negative (limited) assurance that there are no material modifications that should be made to accompanying financial statements for them to conform with generally accepted accounting principles or, if applicable, with another comprehensive basis of accounting.	810
Review (interim financial information of a public company) application of knowledge of financial reporting practices to significant accounting matters of which the accountant becomes aware through inquiries and analyt-	812

**Chapter 21
References**

American Institute of Certified Public Accountants, *Professional Standards*

AU Section 504—Association with Financial Statements.

AU Section 551—Reporting on Information Accompanying the Basic Financial Statements in Auditor-Submitted Documents.

AU Section 621—Special Reports.

AU Section 622—Special Reports—Applying Agreed-Upon Procedures to Specified Elements, Accounts, or Items of a Financial Statement.

AU Section 634—Letters for Underwriters.

AU Section 722—Review of Interim Financial Information.

AU Section 2100—Financial Forecasts and Projections

AR Section 100—Compilation and Review of Financial Statements.

AR Section 200—Reporting on Comparative Financial Statements.

AR Section 300—Compilation Reports on Financial Statements Included in Certain Prescribed Forms.

Clay, John R., and Holton, Stephen D. "Prescribed Form Engagements: Some Practical Guidance," *Journal of Accountancy* (May 1982), pp. 66–78.

Clay, Raymond J., and Santora, John R. "Computer-Prepared Statements: Search for a Solution," *Journal of Accountancy* (March 1983), pp. 92–96.

Derstine, Robert P., and Bremser, Wayne G. "SSARS Review: What Are CPAs Doing?" *Journal of Accountancy* (April 1983), pp. 28–36.

Jones, Wm. Jarell, and Ward, Catherine C. "Forecasts and Projections for Third Party Use," *Journal of Accountancy* (April 1986), pp. 100–102.

Pallais, Don, and Guy, Dan M. "Prospective Financial Statements," *Journal of Accountancy* (April 1986), pp. 90–99.

Rosenberg, Rita F. J. "SSARS in Action," *The CPA Journal* (February 1985), pp. 10–18.

Stilwell, Martin C. "Prospective Reporting and Small Business Clients," *Journal of Accountancy* (May 1986), pp. 68–84.

Chapter 21
Review Questions

21-1.   What is negative assurance within the context of an auditor's report? How does it differ from positive assurance?

21-2.   What body establishes standards for all audits and for reviews of interim financial information and preparation of unaudited financial statements of public companies?

21-3.   What body establishes standards for reviews and compilations of financial statements of nonpublic companies?

21-4.   Define a special report according to AU Section 621.

21-5.   What is the general reporting format on financial statements prepared in accordance with a comprehensive basis of accounting other than generally accepted accounting principles?

21-6.   Describe the reporting format of a report on specific elements, accounts, or items of a financial statement. What type of assurance is provided?

21-7.   Discuss the format of a report on condensed financial statements. What type of assurance is provided?

21-8.   Define a financial forecast.

21-9.   How does a financial projection differ from a financial forecast?

21-10.   What is the CPA's purpose in examining a financial forecast or projection?

21-11.   Describe the reporting format for reports on examinations of financial forecasts and projections. What type of assurance is given?

21-12.   When reporting on an examination of prospective financial statements, what is the CPA's responsibility should he or she determine that
a. The forecast departs from AICPA guidelines?
b. One or more significant assumptions are not reasonable?
c. There is a significant scope limitation?
d. Other accountants performed part of the examination?
e. Historical financial information is included?
f. He or she wants to emphasize a matter?
g. He or she is not independent?

21-13.   Define a review of the financial statements of a nonpublic company.

21-14.   Describe the background information that a CPA should have to perform a review of a nonpublic client.

21-15.   Describe the reporting format for a review of the financial statements of a nonpublic entity. What type of assurance is expressed?

21-16.   When performing a review of the financial statements of a nonpublic entity, what is the CPA's reporting obligation if he or she determines that the statements are materially affected by (a) a departure from generally accepted accounting principles, (b) an uncertainty, and (c) an inconsistency in the application of generally accepted accounting principles?

21-17.   What procedures would a CPA perform in a review of interim financial information of a public company?

21-18.   Describe the reporting format for a report on a review of interim financial information of a public company. What type of assurance is given?

21-19.   Discuss the CPA's responsibility if disclosures in interim financial statements are not adequate. What basis does the CPA use in evaluating the adequacy of disclosures in interim financial statements?

21-20.   List the five topics that may be covered in a letter for underwriters.

21-21.   When is a CPA associated with financial statements?

21-22.   Define a compilation of financial statements.

21-23.   What understanding of a client's affairs must a CPA have to compile financial statements?

21-24.   Describe the reporting format for a report on a compilation. What type of assurance is given?

21-25.   Under what conditions may a CPA compile financial statements that omit substantially all disclosures required by generally accepted accounting principles? How would this affect the form of his or her report?

21-26.   How do the following matters affect a CPA's reporting responsibilities in performing a compilation?
   a. A departure from generally accepted accounting principles.
   b. Uncertainties.
   c. Inconsistent application of accounting principles.
   d. Lack of independence.

21-27.   Describe the compilation of a financial forecast or projection and the form of report that may be issued.

21-28.   What is a CPA's reporting responsibility when associated with unaudited financial statements of a public company?

21-29.   What type of report should CPAs issue on financial statements if they have performed all necessary audit procedures but they are not independent?

21-30.   Define *accompanying information* in an auditing context and give an example. What is a CPA's responsibility for this information?

Chapter 21
Objective Questions Taken from CPA Examinations

21-31.   In which of the following reports should an accountant *not* express negative or limited assurance?
a. A standard review report on financial statements of a nonpublic entity.
b. A standard compilation report on financial statements of a nonpublic entity.
c. A standard comfort letter on financial information included in a registration statement of a public entity.
d. A standard review report on interim financial statements of a public entity.

21-32.   If the auditor believes that financial statements prepared on the entity's income tax basis are *not* suitably titled, the auditor should
a. Issue a disclaimer of opinion.
b. Explain in the notes to the financial statements the terminology used.
c. Issue a compilation report.
d. Modify the auditor's report to disclose any reservations.

21-33.   An auditor's report on financial statements prepared in accordance with a comprehensive basis of accounting other than generally accepted accounting principles should include all of the following *except*
a. Reference to the note to the financial statements that describes how the basis of preparation differs from generally accepted accounting principles.
b. Disclosure of the fact that the financial statements are *not* intended to be presented in conformity with generally accepted accounting principles.
c. An opinion as to whether the basis of accounting used is appropriate under the circumstances.

    d. An opinion as to whether the financial staements are presented fairly in conformity with the basis of accounting described.

21-34.   When reporting on financial statements prepared on a comprehensive basis of accounting other than generally accepted accounting principles, the independent auditor should include in the report a paragraph that
    a. States that the financial statements are *not* intended to be in conformity with generally accepted accounting principles.
    b. States that the financial statements are *not* intended to have been examined in accordance with generally accepted auditing standards.
    c. Refers to the authoritative pronouncements that explain the comprehensive basis of accounting being used.
    d. Justifies the comprehensive basis of accounting being used.

21-35.   Which of the following is a prospective financial statement for general use upon which an accountant may appropriately report?
    a. Financial projection.
    b. Partial presentation.
    c. Pro forma financial statement.
    d. Financial forecast.

21-36.   The party responsible for assumptions identified in the preparation of prospective financial statements is usually
    a. A third-party lending institution.
    b. The client's management.
    c. The reporting accountant.
    d. The client's independent auditor.

21-37.   An accountant associated with prospective financial statements may *not*
    a. Perform a review.
    b. Perform a compilation.
    c. Perform an examination.
    d. Apply agreed-upon procedures.

21-38.   Which of the following would the accountant most likely investigate during the review of financial statements of a nonpublic entity if accounts receivable did *not* conform to a predictable pattern during the year?
    a. Sales returns and allowances.
    b. Credit sales.
    c. Sales of consigned goods.
    d. Cash sales.

21-39.   During a review of the financial statements of a nonpublic entity, the CPA finds that the financial statements contain a material departure from generally accepted accounting principles. If management refuses to correct the financial statement presentations, the CPA should
a. Attach a footnote explaining the effects of the departure.
b. Disclose the departure in a separate paragraph of the report.
c. Issue a compilation report.
d. Issue an adverse opinion.

21-40.   The objective of a review of interim financial information is to provide the CPA with a basis for
a. Expressing a limited opinion that the financial information is presented in conformity with generally accepted accounting principles.
b. Expressing a compilation opinion on the financial information.
c. Reporting whether material modifications should be made to such information to make it conform with generally accepted accounting principles.
d. Reporting limited assurance to the board of directors only.

21-41.   When an independent accountant issues a comfort letter to an underwriter containing comments on data that have *not* been audited, the underwriter most likely will receive
a. A disclaimer on prospective financial statements.
b. A limited opinion on "pro forma" financial statements.
c. Positive assurance on supplementary disclosures.
d. Negative assurance on capsule information.

21-42.   Comfort letters are ordinarily signed by the
a. Independent auditor.
b. Client.
c. Client's lawyer.
d. Internal auditor.

21-43.   Financial statements compiled without audit or review by an accountant should be accompanied by a report stating that
a. The financial statements have *not* been audited or reviewed and, accordingly, the accountant expresses only limited assurance on them.
b. A compilation is limited to presenting in the form of financial statements information that is the representation of management.
c. The accountant is *not* aware of any material modifications that should be made to the financial statements for them to conform with generally accepted accounting principles.
d. A compilation is less in scope than a review, and substantially less in scope than an examination in accordance with generally accepted auditing standards.

21-44.   A CPA should *not* submit unaudited financial statements of a nonpublic company to a client or others unless, as a minimum, the CPA complies with the provisions applicable to
a. Compilation engagements.
b. Review engagements.
c. Statements on auditing standards.
d. Attestation standards.

21-45.   When an accountant is *not* independent of a client and is requested to perform a compilation of its financial statements, the accountant
a. Is precluded from accepting the engagement.
b. May accept the engagement and need *not* disclose the lack of independence.
c. May accept the engagement and should disclose the lack of independence, but *not* the reason for the lack of independence.
d. May accept the engagement and should disclose both the lack of independence and the reason for the lack of independence.

21-46.   When compiling a financial forecast a CPA should
a. Consider whether the underlying assumptions are appropriate.
b. Be independent of the responsible party.
c. Read the forecast for presentation in conformity with AICPA guidelines.
d. Apply analytical procedures and make inquiries.

21-47.   If an accountant concludes that unaudited financial statements on which the accountant is disclaiming an opinion also lack adequate disclosure, the accountant should suggest appropriate revision. If the client does *not* accept the accountant's suggestion, the accountant should
a. Issue an adverse opinion and describe the appropriate revision in the report.
b. Make a reference to the appropriate revision and issue a modified report expressing limited assurance.
c. Describe the appropriate revision to the financial statements in the accountant's disclaimer of opinion.
d. Accept the client's inaction because the statements are unaudited and the accountant has disclaimed an opinion.

21-48.   Which of the following best describes the auditor's reporting responsibility concerning information accompanying the basic financial statements in an auditor-submitted document?
a. The auditor should report on all the information included in the document.
b. The auditor should report on the basic financial statements but may *not* issue a report covering the accompanying information.
c. The auditor should report on the information accompanying the basic financial

statements only if the auditor participated in the preparation of the accompanying information.

d. The auditor should report on the information accompanying the basic financial statements only if the document is being distributed to public shareholders.

21-49. If information accompanying the basic financial statements in an auditor-submitted document has been subjected to auditing procedures, the auditor may express an opinion which states that the accompanying information is fairly stated in

a. Conformity with generally accepted accounting principles.

b. Terms of negative assurance.

c. All material respects in relation to the basic financial statements taken as a whole.

d. Conformity with principles for presenting accompanying information.

21-50. When an accountant is not independent, the accountant is precluded from issuing a

a. Compilation report.

b. Review report.

c. Management advisory report.

d. Tax planning report.

Chapter 21
Discussion/Case Questions

21-51. You have been engaged by the trustees of Roger Trust to audit the trust as of December 31, 19XX. The audit is for the purpose of assuring the trustees and beneficiaries that trust assets, distributions, and income and expenses have been properly handled and accounted for in accordance with the terms of the trust instrument. The trust instrument provides that accounting records are to be maintained on the cash basis.

a. State the type of audit report you consider most appropriate in this circumstance and explain why.

b. Draft the report you would issue if, after your examination, you had no reservations about the financial statements.

21-52. Steam Clean, Inc., produces unique washing machines under a license agreement with Tom Nessinger, who invented the unique process. Nessinger has engaged you to audit the sales of Steam Clean, Inc., which are the basis for royalty payments to him (he is to be paid $10 for each washing machine sold).

During your audit, you find that the sales amount on which Nessinger was paid excludes (1) 15 units for which the sales prices were never collected (written off as bad debts), (2) 17 units that were returned because of defects, (3) 21 units sold at a reduced price as demonstrators, (4) 106 units manufactured and sold by a foreign subsidiary, and (5) 57 units that were modified slightly from the original design. Nessinger disputes the exclusion of all of these units from sales on which royalty payments were made.

Discuss and draft the form of audit report you would issue in this case.

21-53. On March 12, 19X5, Brown & Brown, CPAs, completed the audit of the financial statements of Modern Museum, Inc., for the year ended December 31, 19X4. Modern Museum presents comparative financial statements on a modified cash basis. Assets, liabilities, fund balances, support, revenues, and expenses are recognized when cash is received or disbursed, except that Modern includes a provision for depreciation of buildings and equipment. Brown & Brown believes that Modern's three financial statements, prepared in accordance with a comprehensive basis of accounting other than generally accepted accounting principles, are adequate for Modern's needs and wishes to issue an auditor's special report on the financial statements. Brown & Brown has gathered sufficient competent evidential matter in order to be satisfied that the financial statements are fairly presented according to the modified cash basis. Brown & Brown audited Modern's 19X3 financial statements and issued the auditor's special report expressing an unqualified opinion.

Required:
Draft the auditors' report to accompany Modern's comparative financial statements.

(*AICPA adapted*)

21-54. Sam Sheppard, CPA, has been asked by the management of his client, Indian Togs, Inc., to examine the financial forecast of the company for the coming year.
a. What is a financial forecast, and how does it differ from a financial projection?
b. What is the objective of Sheppard's examination of the company's financial forecast?
c. What procedures might Sheppard use to evaluate (1) the assumptions and (2) the preparation and presentation of the forecast?
d. Assuming that Sheppard's examination is satisfactory, draft a report on the examination of the financial forecast.

21-55. Your client, Byrd and Byrd, Inc., a regional trucking company, has prepared a financial forecast for the coming year and has asked you to examine it and issue a report to accompany it. Management's assumptions, on which the forecast is based, are as follows.

Summary of Forecast Assumptions

---

1. Inflation will average 2 percent next year.

2. There will be no change in accounting principles or tax rates.

3. The company will acquire a new route between Tulsa and Kansas City.

4. Motor fuel will be in adequate supply, although at a slightly higher cost.

5. There will be no net expansion of the company's truck fleet; a few new trucks will be purchased to replace older models.

6. Real GNP growth will moderate in the coming year to a real rate of 2 percent.

7. Industrywide, truck shipment miles will increase 5 percent.

8. The union agreement with the Teamsters will be renegotiated without a strike and for no pay increase.

Evaluate these assumptions for reasonableness and consistency. Also, state the procedures you would use to determine whether the assumptions are suitably supported.

21-56.   John Wilguess, CPA, has been engaged to review the financial statements of Lucky Oil Company, a nonpublic company, for the year ended June 30, 19X4. The previous year's financial statements of Lucky Oil Company were compiled by another CPA. Wilguess has had no experience with this company or the oil industry.
a. Discuss the knowledge Wilguess should acquire to perform a review of Lucky Oil Company. What sources could Wilguess consult to obtain this knowledge?
b. Describe the procedures Wilguess would ordinarily perform in a review of the financial statements of Lucky Oil Company. Be specific as to procedures for Lucky Oil Company, not just procedures in general.
c. The owner of Lucky Oil Company has requested that the financial statements of both the current and prior year be presented. Assuming that Wilguess is satisfied with the current year and that the predecessor's compilation report is not presented, draft the report that Wilguess may issue.
d. If the predecessor's compilation report is reissued, discuss the factors the predecessor should consider to determine whether his report is still appropriate and the procedures he should perform.

21-57.   In connection with a review of the December 31, 19X5, financial statements of Quick Profits Real Estate, a nonpublic company, Hilton and Hilton, CPAs, noted that certain parcels of land were recorded at appraised value that exceeded cost. Management of the company refused to change the financial statements to show the land at cost.

a. What courses of action should Hilton and Hilton consider?

b. If it is concluded that modification of their standard review report is appropriate for the land recorded at appraised value and the review is otherwise satisfactory, draft the report that Hilton and Hilton should issue.

c. If the company, in addition to recording land at appraised value, also changed the method of computing depreciation on its buildings from the double-declining balance method to the straight-line method, how would the review report of Hilton and Hilton be affected?

21-58. The following report was drafted by a staff assistant at the completion of the calendar year 19X6 review engagement of RLG Company, a continuing client. The 19X5 financial statements were compiled. On March 6, 19X7, the date of the completion of the review, the report was submitted to the partner with client responsibility. The financial statements for 19X5 and 19X6 are presented in comparative form.

To the Board of Directors of RLG Company

We have reviewed the accompanying financial statements of RLG Company for the year ended December 31, 19X6, in accordance with standards established by Statements on Standards for Auditing and Review Services.

A review consists principally of analytical procedures applied to financial data. It is substantially more in scope than a compilation, but less in scope than an audit in accordance with generally accepted auditing standards, the objective of which is the expression of an opinion regarding the financial statements taken as a whole.

Based on our compilation and review, we are not aware of any material modifications that should be made to the 19X5 and 19X6 financial statements in order for them to be consistent with the prior year's financial statements.

The accompanying 19X5 financial statements of RLG Company were compiled by us and, accordingly, we do not express an opinion on them.

March 6, 19X7

Required

Identify the deficiencies in the draft of the proposed report. Group the deficiencies by paragraph. Do *not* redraft the report.

(*AICPA adapted*)

21-59.   John Alvis, CPA, has completed his review of the interim financial information of Wilson and Love, a public company, for the six months ended June 30, 19X5.
a. Discuss the form of report that Alvis may issue.
b. What should be the date of the report and to whom should it be addressed?
c. Discuss the form of the modification, if any, that should be made to Alvis's report as the result of (1) departures from generally accepted accounting principles, (2) inadequate disclosures, (3) uncertainties, and (4) lack of consistency in the application of accounting principles.
d. If the management of Wilson and Love state in an interim report to stockholders that Alvis has reviewed the financial information but will not agree to include his report, what action should Alvis take?

21-60.   As a condition for a public offering of securities by your largest and most important audit client, the underwriter requires a comfort letter containing the following items.

1. An unequivocal statement that you are independent with respect to your client within the meaning of the Securities Act of 1933.

2. Negative assurance regarding the audited financial statements included in the registration statement.

3. Negative assurance about decreases in certain financial statement items during a period subsequent to the date of the latest financial statements in the registration statement.

4. Negative assurance about certain financial information in the text section of the registration statement, including the percentage of capacity at which the client's plant operated during the year.

A meeting is to be held for the underwriter, your client, and you to review the procedures for the public offering. Before the meeting gets underway, the underwriter shows you a copy of a comfort letter issued by another office of your firm in connection with a previous public offering that exactly conforms with the underwriter's requirements, and the client states that the comfort letter is so standard that it is not worth discussing at this meeting. What matters, if any, would you wish to discuss concerning the comfort letter?

21-61.   Becky Maupin, CPA, has been asked to compile the financial statements of George's Diner, a nonpublic company, for the year ended April 30, 19X5.
a. What understanding should Maupin establish with George before accepting the engagement? Must this understanding be in writing?
b. Under what conditions could Maupin accept the engagement if she is not familiar with the diner industry?

c. What procedures must Maupin perform before issuing her compilation report? Discuss the form of report Maupin may issue.

21-62. Steve White, CPA, has completed the compilation of the financial statements of the Elbow Macaroni Factory, a nonpublic entity, and is now considering the form of report that he should issue.

a. Discuss the general form of a compilation report.

b. If White performed additional procedures such as a review of the bank reconciliations and tax returns and a test of inventory pricing, how would the general form of the compilation report be modified? Why?

c. What factors should White consider before issuing his compilation report if the owner of the Elbow Macaroni Factory requests that substantially all disclosures required by generally accepted accounting principles be omitted? ·

d. How would White's compilation report be affected if he has not yet been paid for compiling the prior year financial statements of the Elbow Macaroni Factory?

e. How would White's compilation report be affected if he determines that the macaroni tax credit was not considered in computing the company's tax liability and that the effect on the financial statements is material?

f. What action should White take if he believes that modification of his report is not adequate to indicate the deficiencies in the financial statements taken as a whole?

21-63. Walter Kunitake, CPA, has been asked by the management of Russell Company, a nonpublic real estate agency, to compile a set of financial statements as of the company's year end, November 30, 19X4.

a. What is the purpose of a compilation?

b. If requested by the management of Russell Company, may Kunitake merely type or reproduce the financial statements without performing a compilation?

c. What effect would Kunitake's lack of knowledge of the real estate agency business have on the engagement?

d. What knowledge of Russell Company should Kunitake acquire to compile the financial statements?

e. Draft the report Kunitake would issue if he was satisfied with the compiled financial statements.

21-64. Slow Burn Candle, Inc., a public company, asked its CPA, Parker Granger, to assist it in preparing footnotes for unaudited financial statements as of June 30, 19X5. Granger has previously audited the company's annual financial statements as of December 31, 19X4.

a. If Granger assisted in drafting footnotes for the unaudited financial statements, but did not append his name to them, would he be deemed to be associated with them? Why or why not?

b. If Granger did *no* work on the unaudited financial statements and only consented to a statement in a transmittal letter that he was the company's auditor, would he be deemed to be associated with them? Explain.

c. If Granger is deemed to be associated with the unaudited financial statements, what is his reporting responsibility?

d. What is Granger's reporting responsibility if the unaudited financial statements are presented in comparative form with audited financial statements?

21-65.   May Co. is a small refinery owned by several individuals who are not active in its management. To supply them with reliable information about the company's operations for the year, you are requested to prepare a report on accompanying information in connection with this year's audit. You are asked specifically to include the following items in your report.

a. An aged trial balance of accounts receivable as of the end of the year.

b. An analysis of the allowance for doubtful accounts for the year and your conclusion as to its adequacy.

c. An analysis of insurance coverage at the end of the year and your recommendation for any changes.

d. An analysis of the major additions to property and equipment for the year and a description of the procedures you used to audit the additions.

e. An analysis of accrued liabilities at the end of the year and a comment regarding the income tax returns subject to review by the IRS.

f. A schedule showing the percentage of the total outstanding common stock owned by each stockholder of record as shown in the stockbook.

g. Your comments as to why revenues increased during the year.

Discuss the appropriateness of including each of these matters in your report on accompanying information.

Index